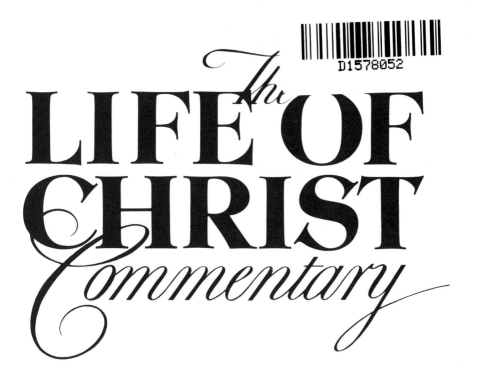

The LIFE OF CHRIST Commentary

John F. Walvoord
Roy B. Zuck
Editors

Harvest Hills Alliance Church
199 Harvest Wood Dr. N.E.
Calgary, AB. T3K 3T7
Ph.226-0990 Fax.226-2019

VICTOR BOOKS ®
A DIVISION OF SCRIPTURE PRESS PUBLICATIONS INC.
USA CANADA ENGLAND

D1578052

The Bible translation used in this commentary is taken from the
non-anglicised text of the *Holy Bible, New International Version,* © 1973,
1978, 1984, International Bible Society. Used by permission of
Zondervan Bible Publishers.

Recommended Dewey Decimal Classification: 220.7
Suggested Subject Headings: BIBLE COMMENTARY

Library of Congress Catalog Card Number: 88-62847
ISBN: 0-89693-626-0

VICTOR BOOKS
A division of Scripture Press
Wheaton, Illinois 60187

CONTENTS

MAPS

CHARTS AND DIAGRAMS

PREFACE

The Life of Christ Commentary is an exposition of the four Gospels—Matthew, Mark, Luke, and John—written and edited by the Dallas Theological Seminary faculty members. It is designed for pastors, laypersons, Bible teachers, serious Bible students, and others who want a comprehensive but brief and reliable commentary on the Gospels. This material was first published as part of the New Testament volume of *The Bible Knowledge Commentary.*

The Gospels present the life of Christ from four perspectives. Matthew presents Jesus Christ as the Messiah of Israel and explains God's kingdom program. Mark shows Christ as the action-oriented Son of God and Son of Man who called His followers to a life of discipleship. Luke is addressed to Gentiles and stresses the universal message of the Gospel. John portrays much of Jesus' ministry not found in the other three Gospels (called the Synoptic Gospels). John stressed the fact that Jesus is God manifest in the flesh so that people would come to believe in Him.

This four-way composite portrait of Jesus Christ is more than four biographies. Instead, these books present carefully selected material from Jesus' life, each with a different theological emphasis. Taken together, the overall purpose of the Gospels is to show who Jesus Christ is—God's Son, Israel's Messiah, and the world's Saviour—so that people will come to Him in faith and receive eternal life.

Each writer of the commentary material discusses how the purpose of the Bible book unfolds, how each part fits with the whole and with what precedes and follows it. Problem passages, puzzling Bible-time customs, difficult sayings of Jesus, and alleged contradictions are carefully considered and discussed. Occasionally Greek words are explained. They are transliterated for the benefit of readers not proficient in the biblical languages. A number of maps, charts, and diagrams are included.

The material on each Gospel includes an *Introduction* (discussion of items such as authorship, date, purpose, style, unique features), *Outline, Commentary,* and *Bibliography.* In the *Commentary* section, summaries of entire sections of the text are given, followed by the detailed comments on the passage verse by verse and often phrase by phrase. All words quoted from the *New International Version* appear in boldface type, as do the verse numbers at the beginning of paragraphs. The *Bibliography* entries, suggested for further study, are not all endorsed in their entirety by the authors and the editors. The writers and editors have listed both works they have consulted and others that would be useful to readers.

The New Testament Consulting Editor, Dr. Stanley D. Toussaint, has added to the quality of this commentary by reading the manuscripts and offering helpful suggestions. His work is greatly appreciated. We also express thanks to Lloyd Cory, former Victor Books Reference Editor; to Barbara Williams, whose careful editing enhanced the material appreciably; to hardworking Production Coordinator Myrna Jean Hasse; and to the many manuscript typists at Scripture Press and Dallas Theological Seminary for their diligence.

May this commentary on the four Gospels give you a new appreciation of Jesus Christ—of His ministry and mission; His life, death, and resurrection; and His person and purpose.

John F. Walvoord

Roy B. Zuck

EDITORS

John F. Walvoord, A.B., M.A., Th.M., Th.D., D.D.
Chancellor and Minister-at-Large
Dallas Theological Seminary
(Formerly President, 1952–86, and Professor of Systematic
Theology 1936–86)
Dallas Theological Seminary

Roy B. Zuck, A.B., Th.M., Th.D.
Vice President for Academic Affairs and Academic Dean
Professor of Bible Exposition
Dallas Theological Seminary
Editor, *Bibliotheca Sacra*

CONSULTING EDITOR

Stanley D. Toussaint, A.B., Th.M., Th.D.
Chairman and Professor of Bible Exposition
Dallas Theological Seminary

CONTRIBUTING AUTHORS

Louis A. Barbieri, Jr., A.B., Th.M., Th.D.
Pastor, Des Plaines Bible Church, Des Plaines, Illinois
(Formerly Dean of Students, 1980–87, and Assistant Professor
of Bible Exposition, 1977–87)
Dallas Theological Seminary
Matthew

Edwin A. Blum, B.S., Th.M., Th.D., D.Theol.
Vice President for Personnel
Pacific Construction Co., Ltd., Honolulu, Hawaii
(Formerly Associate Professor of Historical Theology, 1969–87)
Dallas Theological Seminary
John

John D. Grassmick, A.B., Th.M., Ph.D. cand.
Associate Professor of New Testament Literature and Exegesis
Dallas Theological Seminary
Mark

John A. Martin, A.B., Th.M., Th.D.
Dean of Faculty
Associate Professor of Bible Exposition
Dallas Theological Seminary
Luke

ABBREVIATIONS

A. *General*

act.	active	n., nn.	note(s)
Akk.	Akkadian	n.d.	no date
Apoc.	Apocrypha	neut.	neuter
Aram.	Aramaic	n.p.	no publisher, no place of
ca.	*circa*, about		publication
cf.	*confer*, compare	no.	number
chap., chaps.	chapter(s)	NT	New Testament
comp.	compiled, compilation,	OT	Old Testament
	compiler	p., pp.	page(s)
ed.	edited, edition, editor	par., pars.	paragraph(s)
eds.	editors	part.	participle
e.g.	*exempli gratia*, for example	pass.	passive
Eng.	English	perf.	perfect
et al.	*et alii*, and others	pl.	plural
fem.	feminine	pres.	present
Gr.	Greek	q.v.	*quod vide*, which see
Heb.	Hebrew	Sem.	Semitic
ibid.	*ibidem*, in the same place	sing.	singular
i.e.	*id est*, that is	s.v.	*sub verbo*, under the word
imper.	imperative	trans.	translation, translator,
imperf.	imperfect		translated
lit.	literal, literally	viz.	*videlicet*, namely
LXX	Septuagint	vol., vols.	volume(s)
marg.	margin, marginal reading	v., vv.	verse(s)
masc.	masculine	vs.	versus
ms., mss.	manuscript(s)	Vul.	Vulgate
MT	Masoretic text		

B. *Abbreviations of Books of the Bible*

Gen.	Ruth	Job	Lam.	Jonah
Ex.	1, 2 Sam.	Ps., Pss. (pl.)	Ezek.	Micah
Lev.	1, 2 Kings	Prov.	Dan.	Nahum
Num.	1, 2 Chron.	Ecc.	Hosea	Hab.
Deut.	Ezra	Song	Joel	Zeph.
Josh.	Neh.	Isa.	Amos	Hag.
Jud.	Es.	Jer.	Obad.	Zech.
				Mal.

Matt.	Acts	Eph.	1, 2 Tim.	James
Mark	Rom.	Phil.	Titus	1, 2 Peter
Luke	1, 2 Cor.	Col.	Phile.	1, 2, 3 John
John	Gal.	1, 2 Thes.	Heb.	Jude
				Rev.

C. *Abbreviations of Bible Versions, Translations, and Paraphrases*

ASV	American Standard Version	NKJV	New King James Version
JB	Jerusalem Bible	Ph.	New Testament in Modern English (J.B. Phillips)
KJV	King James Version	RSV	Revised Standard Version
NASB	New American Standard Bible	Sco.	New Scofield Reference Bible
NEB	New English Bible	Wms.	The New Testament (Charles B. Williams)
NIV	New International Version		

TRANSLITERATIONS

Hebrew

Consonants

א — '	ד — $\underline{d}$	י — y	ס — s	ר — r
ב — b	ה — h	כ — k	ע — '	שׂ — ś
ב — $\underline{b}$	ו — w	ך — $\underline{k}$	פ — p	שׁ — š
ג — g	ז — z	ל — l	ף — p	ת — t
ג — $\underline{g}$	ח — ḥ	מ — m	צ — ṣ	ת — $\underline{t}$
ד — d	ט — ṭ	נ — n	ק — q	

Daghesh forte is represented by doubling the letter.

Vocalization

בָּה — bâh	בָ — bā	בֹּ — bo[1]	בְּ — bĕ
בּוֹ — bô	בֹ — bō	בֻּ — bu[1]	בְּ — bᵉ
בּוּ — bû	בֻ — bū	בֶּ — be	בָּה — bāh
בֵּ — bê	בֶּ — bē	בִּ — bi[1]	בָּא — bā'
בֶּ — bè	בִ — bī	בַּ — bă	בָּה — bēh
בִּ — bî	בַ — ba	בָּ — bŏ	בָּה — beh

[1] In closed syllables

Greek

α, ᾳ — a		ξ — x		γγ — ng	
β — b		ο — o		γκ — nk	
γ — g		π — p		γξ — nx	
δ — d		ρ — r		γχ — nch	
ε — e		σ, ς — s		αἰ — ai	
ζ — z		τ — t		αὐ — au	
η, ῃ — ē		υ — y		εἰ — ei	
θ — th		φ — ph		εὐ — eu	
ι — i		χ — ch		ηὐ — ēu	
κ — k		ψ — ps		οἰ — oi	
λ — l		ω, ῳ — ō		οὐ — ou	
μ — m		ῥ — rh		υἱ — hui	
ν — n		ʽ — h			

MATTHEW

Louis A. Barbieri, Jr.

INTRODUCTION

It is fitting that the New Testament begins with four accounts of the life of Jesus Christ. These accounts present the "good news" concerning the Son of God, telling of His life on earth and His death on the cross for the sin of mankind. The first three Gospels take a similar view of the facts surrounding this Person, while the Fourth Gospel is unique in its presentation. Because of this common view of Jesus Christ the first three New Testament books are called the Synoptic Gospels.

The Synoptic Problem

1. The problem stated. "Synoptic" comes from the Greek adjective *synoptikos,* which is from two words *syn* and *opses-thai,* "to see with or together." While Matthew, Mark, and Luke have distinctive purposes, they nevertheless view the life of Jesus Christ in a common way. However, some differences in the Gospel narratives must also be accounted for. These similarities and differences raise the question of the sources of the Gospels, thus positing a "Synoptic problem."

Most conservative scholars acknowledge that the Gospel writers made use of various sources. For example, the genealogical records of both Matthew and Luke may have come from temple records or oral tradition. Luke stated at the beginning of his Gospel (Luke 1:1) that many had written down the facts concerning the Lord Jesus. This implies that Luke could have drawn on a number of written accounts. That the individual writers may have used different sources for their material is a valid conclusion. However, this is not what critical scholars mean when they talk about sources. Most critical scholars view the "sources" as extensive writings which were joined together by skilled editors to produce

their own accounts. This conclusion has led to several explanations of these sources.

a. The Urevangelium theory. Some scholars conclude that an original Gospel (known in German as the *Urevangelium*) now lost, was the source for the biblical editors as they compiled their accounts. The major objection to this view is that no trace of such a writing has ever been discovered. No scholar can point to a document as the possible *Urevangelium.* Also, while such an explanation would account for the similarities, it in no way explains the differences in the Gospel stories of the same events.

b. The oral tradition theory. Some have concluded that the basic sources for the Gospels came from oral tradition, an oral testimony that developed around Jesus Christ. Normally such a testimony involved four steps: (1) The event occurred. (2) The event was told and repeated often enough so that it became widely known. (3) The event became fixed so that it was then told exactly the same way. (4) The event was written down in an account. An objection to this view is similar to the *Urevangelium* theory: this view accounts for similarities in the stories but it fails to account for the differences. Furthermore, why would an eyewitness of the events limit himself to stories from oral tradition?

c. The document theory. A popular view today is that the biblical editors made use of various written sources to compile their accounts. This viewpoint usually posits the following: (1) The first written account was the Gospel of Mark. A major reason for this position is that only 7 percent of the Gospel of Mark is unique, as 93 percent of Mark can be found in Matthew and Luke. (2) In addition to

Mark a second written document existed which basically contained discourse material. This document is known as "Q", an abbreviated form of the German word for source, *Quelle*. The approximately 200 verses common to Matthew and Luke which are not found in Mark must have come from "Q". (3) The editors used at least two other sources. One source reflects verses in Matthew not found in either Mark or Luke, and the other source reflects verses in Luke not found in either Matthew or Mark. This theory with its lines of dependence could be charted in this way:

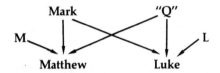

This theory has several problems. First, it has difficulty with tradition. Conservative scholars have generally held that Matthew was the first of the written Gospels. While not all conservatives agree, this tradition does have some weight behind it and should not be shrugged off as "mere tradition" as sometimes tradition is correct. Second, this theory cannot account for the fact that occasionally Mark made a comment that neither Matthew nor Luke included. Mark wrote that the rooster crowed a second time (Mark 14:72), but neither Matthew nor Luke included that fact. Third, if Mark were the first Gospel, written after Peter's death around A.D. 67–68, then Matthew and Luke would probably have been written later after the destruction of Jerusalem in A.D. 70. One would then expect that destruction to have been mentioned as a fitting climax to the Lord's words in Matthew 24–25 or Luke's statement in 21:20-24; however, neither mentioned the event. Fourth, the greatest problem is the whole speculation about the existence of "Q". If such a document existed and were thought of so highly by Matthew and Luke that they quoted extensively from it, why did not the church also regard it highly and preserve it?

d. The form critical theory. This widely held view assumes the document theory, but takes it a step further. When the Gospel accounts were compiled, a multiplicity of documents existed, not simply four documents (Matthew, Mark, Luke, and "Q"). Interpreters today seek to discover and classify these documents, called "forms," and also to get behind the forms and discover exactly what the first-century church was seeking to communicate through them. The literal facts communicated in the forms are not sufficient in themselves; the truth is discovered by going behind the literal story. The facts in the stories are considered "myths" which the church built up around Jesus Christ. By scraping away the myths or "demythologizing," kernels of truth concerning Jesus are discovered.

While this theory is widely held, it has some serious problems. It is virtually impossible to classify the "forms" into exact categories. It is doubtful if any two interpreters would agree on the classifications. Furthermore, this view says that the first-century church caused these stories to be told the way they were, but the view never adequately explains what caused the church. In other words, this view has purposefully overlooked the living witness of Jesus Christ and the true impact His life and death made on first-century believers.

2. A proposed solution. The similarities and differences in the Gospel accounts can be solved through a composite viewpoint. First, the Gospel writers of the first century had extensive personal knowledge of much of the material they recorded. Matthew and John were disciples of Jesus Christ who spent a considerable amount of time with the Lord. Mark's account may be the reflections of Simon Peter near the end of his life, and Luke could have learned many facts through his relationship with Paul and others. These facts would have been used in writing the four accounts.

Second, oral tradition was involved. For example, Acts 20:35 refers to a saying of Christ not recorded in the Gospels. Paul in 1 Corinthians 7:10 gave a quotation from the Lord; when Paul wrote this, possibly none of the Gospels had yet been written. Third, written documents told some of the stories about Jesus Christ. Luke acknowledged this fact as he began his Gospel (Luke 1:1-4). None of these facts, however, gives the dynamic needed to record an inspired account of Jesus Christ's life that is free from all error. Fourth, another element must be included to help solve the Synoptic problem, namely, the dynamic of the Holy Spirit's ministry of inspiration as the Gospel writers recorded the accounts. The Lord promised the disciples that the Holy Spirit would teach them all things and remind them of all Jesus had told them (John 14:26). This dynamic guarantees accuracy, whether the author was making use of his memory, passed-down oral traditions, or written accounts available to him. Whatever the source, the direction of the Holy Spirit assured an accurate text. The better one understands the various stories about the Lord, the clearer the "difficulties" become, for there was a divine superintendence over the authors regardless of the sources they used.

The Authorship of the First Gospel. When one deals with the question of who wrote a particular Bible book, the evidence is normally twofold: evidence outside the book ("external evidence") and evidence within the book itself ("internal evidence"). External evidence strongly supports the view that the Apostle Matthew wrote the Gospel that bears his name. Many early church fathers cited Matthew as its author, including Pseudo Barnabas, Clement of Rome, Polycarp, Justin Martyr, Clement of Alexandria, Tertullian, and Origen. (For further attestation see Norman L. Geisler and William E. Nix, *A General Introduction to the Bible.* Chicago: Moody Press, 1968, p. 193.) Matthew was certainly not one of the more prominent apostles. One might think the First Gospel would have been written by Peter, James, or John. But the extensive tradition that Matthew wrote it strongly commends him as its author.

Internal evidence also supports the fact that Matthew was the author of the First Gospel. This book has more references to coins than any of the other three Gospels. In fact this Gospel includes three terms for coins that are found nowhere else in the New Testament: "The two-drachma tax" (Matt. 17:24); "a four-drachma coin" (17:27), and "talents" (18:24). Since Matthew's occupation was tax collecting, he had an interest in coins

and noted the cost of certain items. The profession of tax collector would necessitate an ability to write and keep records. Matthew obviously had the ability, humanly speaking, to write a book such as the First Gospel.

His Christian humility comes through as well, for Matthew alone continually refers to himself throughout his Gospel as "Matthew the tax collector." But Mark and Luke do not continually use that term of contempt when speaking of Matthew. Also, when Matthew began to follow Jesus, he invited his friends to a "dinner" (Matt. 9:9-10). Luke, however, called the dinner "a great banquet" (Luke 5:29). The omissions from the First Gospel are significant too, for Matthew omitted the Parable of the Pharisee and the Tax Collector (Luke 18:9-14) and the story of Zacchaeus, a tax collector who restored fourfold what he had stolen (Luke 19:1-10). The internal evidence concerning the authorship of the First Gospel points to Matthew as its most likely author.

The Original Language of the First Gospel. While all the extant manuscripts of the First Gospel are in Greek, some suggest that Matthew wrote his Gospel in Aramaic, similar to Hebrew. Five individuals stated, in effect, that Matthew wrote in Aramaic and that translations followed in Greek: Papias (A.D. 80–155), Irenaeus (A.D. 130–202), Origen (A.D. 185–254), Eusebius (fourth century A.D.), and Jerome (sixth century A.D.). However, they may have been referring to a writing by Matthew other than his Gospel account. Papias, for example, said Matthew compiled the sayings (*logia*) of Jesus. Those "sayings" might have been a second, shorter account of the Lord's words, written in Aramaic and sent to a group of Jews for whom it would have been most meaningful. That writing was later lost, for no such version exists today. The First Gospel, however, was probably penned by Matthew in Greek and has survived until today. Matthew's *logia* did not survive, but his Gospel did. This was because the latter, part of the biblical canon and thus God's Word, was inspired and preserved by the Spirit of God.

The Date of the First Gospel. Pinpointing the writing of the First Gospel to a specific year is impossible. Various dates for the book have been suggested by conservative scholars. C.I. Scofield in the original *Scofield Reference Bible* gave A.D. 37 as a possible date. Few scholars give a date after A.D. 70, since Matthew made no reference to the destruction of Jerusalem. Furthermore, Matthew's references to Jerusalem as the "Holy City" (Matt. 4:5; 27:53) imply that it was still in existence.

But some time seems to have elapsed after the events of the Crucifixion and the Resurrection. Matthew 27:7-8 refers to a certain custom continuing "to this day," and 28:15 refers to a story being circulated "to this very day." These phrases imply the passing of time, and yet not so much time that the Jewish customs had ceased. Since church tradition has strongly advocated that the Gospel of Matthew was the first Gospel account written, perhaps a date somewhere around A.D. 50 would satisfy all the demands mentioned. It would also be early enough to permit Matthew to be the first Gospel account. (For further discussion and an alternate view [that Mark was the first of the four Gospels] see "Sources" under the *Introduction* to Mark.)

The Occasion for Writing the First Gospel. Though the precise occasion for the writing of this account is not known, it appears Matthew had at least two reasons for writing. First, he wanted to show unbelieving Jews that Jesus is the Messiah. Matthew had found the Messiah, and he wanted others to come into that same relationship. Second, Matthew wrote to encourage Jewish believers. If indeed Jesus is the Messiah, a horrible thing had occurred. The Jews had crucified their Messiah and King. What would now become of them? Was God through with them? At this point Matthew had a word of encouragement, for though their act of disobedience would bring judgment on that generation of Israelites, God was not through with His people. His promised kingdom would yet be instituted with His people at a future time. In the meantime, however, believers are responsible to communicate a different message of faith in this Messiah as they go into all the world to make disciples among all nations.

Some Outstanding Characteristics of the First Gospel

1. The Book of Matthew places great emphasis on the teaching ministry of Jesus Christ. Of the Gospel accounts Matthew has the largest blocks of discourse material. No other Gospel contains so much of Jesus' teachings. Matthew 5–7 is commonly referred to as the Sermon on the Mount; chapter 10 includes Jesus' instructions to His disciples as they were sent out to minister; chapter 13 presents the parables of the kingdom; in chapter 23 is Jesus' "hot" denunciation of the religious leaders of Israel; and chapters 24–25 are the Olivet Discourse, a detailed explanation of future events relating to Jerusalem and the nation.

2. Some of the material in Matthew is arranged logically rather than chronologically. As examples, the genealogical tables are broken into three equal groups, a large number of miracles are given together, and the opposition to Jesus is given in one section. Matthew's purpose is obviously more thematic than chronological.

3. The First Gospel is filled with Old Testament quotations. Matthew includes approximately 50 direct citations from the Old Testament. In addition about 75 allusions are made to Old Testament events. This is undoubtedly because of the audience for whom the book was intended. Matthew primarily had Jews in mind as he wrote, and they would have been impressed by the many references to Old Testament facts and events. In addition, if this Gospel was written around A.D. 50, not many New Testament books were available for Matthew to have cited. Those books may not have been known to his readers or even to Matthew himself.

4. The First Gospel shows that Jesus Christ is the Messiah of Israel and explains God's kingdom program (Stanley D. Toussaint, *Behold the King: A Study of Matthew*, pp. 18–20). "If indeed Jesus is Messiah," a Jew would ask, "what has happened to the promised kingdom?" The Old Testament clearly taught that the Messiah would bring in a glorious utopian reign on the earth in which the nation Israel would have a prominent

position. Since the nation rejected its true King, what happened to the kingdom? The Book of Matthew includes some "mysteries" about the kingdom, which had not been revealed in the Old Testament. These "mysteries" show that the kingdom has taken a different form in the present Age, but that the promised Davidic kingdom will be instituted at a future time when Jesus Christ returns to earth to establish His rule.

5. The First Gospel has a summary statement in its first verse: "A record of the genealogy of Jesus Christ the Son of David, the Son of Abraham." Why does David's name appear before Abraham's? Would not Abraham, the father of the nation, be more significant to a Jewish mind? Perhaps Matthew listed the name of David first because the King who would rule over the nation was to come through David (2 Sam. 7:12-17). Jesus Christ came with a message for His own nation. But in the plan of God, His message was rejected. Therefore a universal message reaches out to the entire world. The promise of blessings for all the nations of the world came through Abraham and the covenant God made with him (Gen. 12:3). It is significant that Matthew did include Gentiles, such as the Magi from the East (Matt. 2:1-12), the centurion with his great faith (8:5-13), and the Canaanite woman who had greater faith than Christ had seen in all Israel (15:22-28). Also the book concludes with the Great Commission to "go and make disciples of all nations" (28:19).

OUTLINE

COMMENTARY

I. Introduction of the King (1:1–4:11)

A. Presentation by ancestry (1:1-17) (Luke 3:23-38)

1:1. From the very first words of his Gospel, Matthew recorded his central theme and character. **Jesus Christ** is the main character in Matthew's presentation, and the opening verse connected Him back to two great covenants in Jewish history: the Davidic (2 Sam. 7) and the Abrahamic (Gen. 12; 15). If Jesus of Nazareth is the fulfillment of these two great covenants, is He related to the rightful line? This is a question the Jews would have asked, so Matthew traced Jesus' lineage in detail.

1:2-17. Matthew gave Jesus' lineage through His legal father, **Joseph** (v. 16). Thus this genealogy traced Jesus' right to the throne of **David**, which must come through **Solomon** and his descendants (v. 6). Of particular interest is the inclusion of **Jeconiah** (v. 11) of whom Jeremiah said, "Record this man as if childless" (Jer. 22:30). Jeremiah's prophecy related to the actual occupation of the throne and the reception of blessing while on the throne. Though Jeconiah's sons never occupied the throne, the line of rulership did pass through them. If Jesus had been a *physical* descendant of Jeconiah, He would not have been able to occupy David's throne. Luke's genealogy made it clear that Jesus was a physical descendant of David through another son named Nathan (Luke 3:31). But Joseph, a descendant of Solomon, was Jesus' *legal* father, so Jesus' right to the throne was traced through Joseph.

Matthew traced Joseph's line from Jeconiah through the latter's son **Shealtiel** and grandson **Zerubbabel** (Matt. 1:12). Luke (3:27) also refers to Shealtiel, the father of Zerubbabel, in Mary's line. Does Luke's account, then, mean that Jesus was a physical descendant of Jeconiah, after all? No, because Luke's Shealtiel and Zerubbabel were probably different persons from those two in Matthew. In Luke Shealtiel was the son of Neri, but Matthew's Shealtiel was the son of Jeconiah.

Another interesting fact about Matthew's genealogy is the inclusion of four Old Testament women: **Tamar** (Matt. 1:3), **Rahab** (v. 5), **Ruth** (v. 5), and Solomon's **mother** (v. 6), Bathsheba. All of these women (as well as most of the men) were questionable in some way. Tamar and Rahab were prostitutes (Gen. 38:24; Josh. 2:1), Ruth was a foreigner, a Moabitess (Ruth 1:4), and Bathsheba committed adultery (2 Sam. 11:2-5). Matthew may have included these women in order to emphasize that God's choices in dealing with people are all of His grace. Perhaps also he included these women in order to put Jewish pride in its place.

When the fifth woman, **Mary** (Matt. 1:16), was mentioned in the genealogy, an important change occurred. The genealogy consistently repeated, **the father of,** until it came to Mary. At that point Matthew changed and said **of whom was born Jesus.** The "of whom" is a feminine relative pronoun (*ex hēs*), clearly indicating that Jesus was the physical Child of Mary but that Joseph was not His physical father. This miraculous conception and birth are explained in 1:18-25.

Matthew obviously did not list every individual in the genealogy between **Abraham** and **David** (vv. 2-6), between **David** and **the Exile** (vv. 6-11), and between **the Exile** and Jesus (vv. 12-16). Instead he listed only **14 generations** in each of these time periods (v. 17). Jewish reckoning did not require every name in order to satisfy a genealogy. But why did Matthew select 14 names in each period? Perhaps the best solution is that the name "David" in Hebrew numerology added up to 14. It should be noted that in the period from the Exile to the birth of Jesus (vv. 12-16) 13 new names appeared. Many scholars feel that Jeconiah (v. 12), though repeated from verse 11, provides the 14th name in this final period.

Matthew's genealogy answered the important question a Jew would rightfully ask about anyone who claimed to be King of the Jews. Is He a descendant of David through the rightful line of succession? Matthew answered yes!

B. Presentation by advent (1:18–2:23) (Luke 2:1-7)

1. HIS ORIGIN (1:18-23)

1:18-23. The fact that Jesus was born "of Mary" only, as indicated in the genealogical record (v. 16), demanded

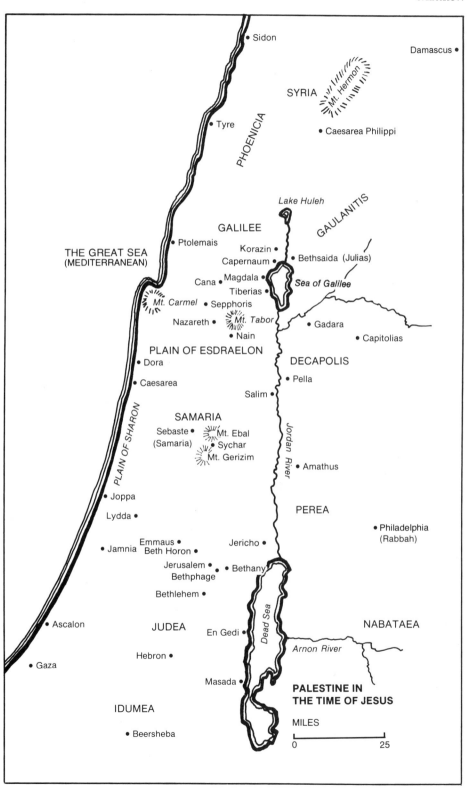

Sidon

Damascus •

SYRIA

Mt. Hermon

Tyre •

PHOENICIA

• Caesarea Philippi

Lake Huleh

GALILEE

GAULANITIS

THE GREAT SEA
(MEDITERRANEAN)

• Ptolemais

Korazin •

Capernaum •

• Bethsaida (Julias)

Cana •

Magdala •

Sea of Galilee

Tiberias •

Mt. Carmel

• Sepphoris

Nazareth •

Mt. Tabor

• Gadara

• Nain

• Capitolias

PLAIN OF ESDRAELON

• Dora

DECAPOLIS

• Caesarea

• Pella

Salim •

PLAIN OF SHARON

SAMARIA

Sebaste •
(Samaria)

Mt. Ebal

• Sychar

Mt. Gerizim

Jordan River

• Amathus

• Joppa

Lydda •

PEREA

• Philadelphia
(Rabbah)

Emmaus •

Jericho •

• Jamnia

Beth Horon •

Jerusalem •

Bethphage

• Bethany

Bethlehem •

Dead Sea

JUDEA

En Gedi •

NABATAEA

• Ascalon

Hebron •

Arnon River

• Gaza

Masada •

PALESTINE IN
THE TIME OF JESUS

IDUMEA

MILES

• Beersheba

0   25

19

further explanation. Matthew's explanation can best be understood in the light of Hebrew marriage customs. Marriages were arranged for individuals by parents, and contracts were negotiated. After this was accomplished, the individuals were considered married and were called husband and wife. They did not, however, begin to live together. Instead, the woman continued to live with her parents and the man with his for one year. The waiting period was to demonstrate the faithfulness of the pledge of purity given concerning the bride. If she was found to be with child in this period, she obviously was not pure, but had been involved in an unfaithful sexual relationship. Therefore the marriage could be annulled. If, however, the one-year waiting period demonstrated the purity of the bride, the husband would then go to the house of the bride's parents and in a grand processional march lead his bride back to his home. There they would begin to live together as husband and wife and consummate their marriage physically. Matthew's story should be read with this background in mind.

Mary and Joseph were in the one-year waiting period when Mary **was found to be with child.** They had never had sexual intercourse and Mary herself had been faithful (vv. 20, 23). While little is said about Joseph, one can imagine how his heart must have broken. He genuinely loved Mary, and yet the word came that she was pregnant. His love for her was demonstrated by his actions. He chose not to create a public scandal by exposing her condition to the judges at the city gate. Such an act could have resulted in Mary's death by stoning (Deut. 22:23-24). Instead he decided **to divorce her quietly.**

Then **in a dream** (cf. Matt. 2:13, 19, 22), **an angel** told **Joseph** that Mary's condition was not caused by a man, but through **the Holy Spirit** (1:20; cf. v. 18). The Child Mary carried in her womb was a unique Child, for He would be **a Son** whom Joseph should **name Jesus for He** would **save His people from their sins.** These words must have brought to Joseph's mind the promises of God to provide salvation through the New Covenant (Jer. 31:31-37). The unnamed angel also told Joseph that this was in keeping with God's eternal plan, for **the**

Prophet Isaiah had declared 700 years before that **the virgin will be with Child** (Matt. 1:23; Isa. 7:14). While Old Testament scholars dispute whether the Hebrew *'almâh* should be rendered "young woman" or "virgin," God clearly intended it here to mean virgin (as implied by the Gr. word *parthenos*). Mary's miraculous conception fulfilled Isaiah's prophecy, and her **Son** would truly be **Immanuel . . . God with us.** In light of this declaration **Joseph** was not to **be afraid** to take **Mary** into his **home** (Matt. 1:20). There would be misunderstanding in the community and much gossip at the well, but Joseph knew the true story of Mary's pregnancy and God's will for his life.

2. HIS BIRTH (1:24-25)

1:24-25. As soon as **Joseph** awakened from this dream, he obeyed. He violated all custom by immediately taking **Mary** into his **home** rather than waiting till the one-year time period of betrothal had passed. Joseph was probably thinking of what would be best for Mary in her condition. He brought her home and began to care and provide for her. But there was **no** sexual relationship between them **until** after the **birth** of this Child, Jesus. Matthew simply noted the birth of the Child and the fact that He was named **Jesus,** whereas Luke, the physician (Col. 4:14), recorded several details surrounding the birth (Luke 2:1-7).

3. HIS INFANCY (CHAP. 2)

a. *In Bethlehem (2:1-12)*

2:1-2. Though not all scholars agree on the timing of the arrival of the **Magi from the East,** they apparently came some time **after** the birth of **Jesus.** Jesus and Mary and Joseph, though still in Bethlehem, were now in a house (v. 11), and Jesus was called a Child (*paidion,* vv. 9, 11) rather than a newborn Infant (*brephos,* Luke 2:12).

The exact identity of the Magi is impossible to determine, though several ideas have been suggested. They have been given traditional names and identified as representatives of the three groups of peoples that descended from Noah's sons, Shem, Ham, and Japheth. More likely they were Gentiles of high position from a country, perhaps Parthia, northeast of Babylon, who were given a special

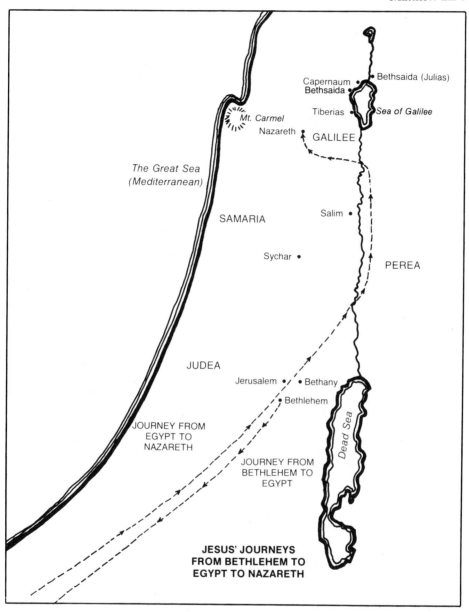

Capernaum •
Bethsaida •
Tiberias •
Nazareth •
Mt. Carmel
Bethsaida (Julias)
Sea of Galilee
GALILEE

The Great Sea
(Mediterranean)

SAMARIA

Salim •

Sychar •

PEREA

JUDEA
Jerusalem •/ • Bethany
• Bethlehem

JOURNEY FROM
EGYPT TO
NAZARETH

JOURNEY FROM
BETHLEHEM TO
EGYPT

Dead Sea

**JESUS' JOURNEYS
FROM BETHLEHEM TO
EGYPT TO NAZARETH**

revelation by God of the birth of the **King of the Jews.** This special revelation may simply have been in the sky, as might be indicated by their title "Magi" (specialists in astronomy) and by the fact they referred to a **star** which they **saw.** Or this revelation could have come through some contact with Jewish scholars who had migrated to the East with copies of Old Testament manuscripts. Many feel the Magi's comments reflected a knowledge of Balaam's prophecy concerning the "star" that would "come out of Jacob" (Num. 24:17). Whatever the source, they came to Jerusalem **to worship** the newborn King of the Jews. (According to tradition three Magi traveled to Bethlehem. But the Bible does not say how many there were.)

2:3-8. It is no surprise that **King Herod . . . was disturbed** when the Magi came to **Jerusalem** looking for the One who had been "born King" (v. 2). Herod was not the rightful king from the line of

David. In fact he was not even a descendant of Jacob, but was descended from Esau and thus was an Edomite. (He reigned over Palestine from 37 B.C. to 4 B.C. See the chart on the Herods at Luke 1:5.) This fact caused most of the Jews to hate him and never truly to accept him as king, even though he did much for the country. If someone had been rightfully born king, then Herod's job was in jeopardy. He therefore **called** the Jewish scholars **together** and inquired **where the Christ was to be born** (Matt. 2:4). Interestingly Herod connected the One "born king of the Jews" (v. 2) with "the Christ," the Messiah. Obviously Israel had a messianic hope and believed that the Messiah would be born.

The answer to Herod's question was simple, because Micah **the prophet** had given the precise location centuries before: the Messiah would be born in **Bethlehem** (Micah 5:2). This answer from **the people's chief priests and teachers of the Law** (scribes, KJV) was apparently carried back to **the Magi by Herod** himself. Then Herod asked them when they had first seen their **star** (Matt. 2:7). This became critical later in the account (v. 16); it showed that Herod was already contemplating a plan to get rid of this young King. He also instructed the Magi to return and tell him the location of this King so that he might come **and worship Him.** That was not, however, what he had in mind.

2:9-12. The journey of the Magi from Jerusalem wrought a further miracle. **The star they had seen in the East** now reappeared and led them to a specific **house** in Bethlehem where they found **the Child** Jesus. Bethlehem is about five miles south of Jerusalem. "Stars" (i.e., planets) naturally travel from east to west across the heavens, not from north to south. Could it be that "the star" which the Magi saw and which led them to a specific house was the Shekinah glory of God? That same glory had led the children of Israel through the wilderness for 40 years as a pillar of fire and cloud. Perhaps this was what they saw in the East, and for want of a better term they called it a "star." All other efforts to explain this star are inadequate (such as a conjunction of Jupiter, Saturn, and Mars; a supernova; a comet; etc.).

Nevertheless they were led to the Child and going in, they **worshiped Him.** Their worship was heightened by the giving of **gifts . . . gold . . . incense and . . . myrrh.** These were gifts worthy of a king and this act by Gentile leaders pictures the wealth of the nations which will someday be completely given to the Messiah (Isa. 60:5, 11; 61:6; 66:20; Zeph. 3:10; Hag. 2:7-8).

Some believe the gifts had further significance by reflecting on the character of this Child's life. Gold might represent His deity or purity, incense the fragrance of His life, and myrrh His sacrifice and death (myrrh was used for embalming). These gifts were obviously the means by which Joseph took his family to Egypt and sustained them there until Herod died. The wise men were **warned** by God **not to** return and report **to Herod, so they returned to their** homes **by another route.**

b. In Egypt (2:13-18)

2:13-15. After the visit of the Magi, **Joseph** was warned by **an angel of the Lord** to take Mary and Jesus and flee **to Egypt.** This warning was given **in a dream** (the second of Joseph's four dreams: 1:20; 2:13, 19, 22). The reason was **Herod** would be searching **for the Child to kill Him.** Under cover of darkness, Joseph obeyed, and his family **left** Bethlehem (see map) and journeyed into **Egypt.** Why Egypt? The Messiah was sent to and returned from Egypt so that the prophet's words, **Out of Egypt I called My Son,** might be **fulfilled.** This is a reference to Hosea 11:1, which does not seem to be a prophecy in the sense of a prediction. Hosea was writing of God's calling Israel out of Egypt into the Exodus. Matthew, however, gave new understanding to these words. Matthew viewed this experience as Messiah being identified with the nation. There were similarities between the nation and the Son. Israel was God's chosen "son" by adoption (Ex. 4:22), and Jesus is the Messiah, God's Son. In both cases the descent into Egypt was to escape danger, and the return was important to the nation's providential history. While Hosea's statement was a historical reference to Israel's deliverance, Matthew related it more fully to the call of the Son, the Messiah, from Egypt. In that sense, as

Matthew "heightened" Hosea's words to a more significant event—the Messiah's return from Egypt—they were "fulfilled."

2:16-18. As soon as **Herod** learned that **the Magi** had not complied with his orders to give him the exact location of the newborn King, he put into action a plan **to kill all the** male children **in Bethlehem.** The age of **two . . . and under** was selected in compliance **with the time . . . the Magi** saw "the star" in the East. Perhaps this time reference also indicated that when the Magi visited Jesus, He was under two years of age.

This slaughter of the male children is mentioned only here in the biblical record. Even the Jewish historian Josephus (A.D. 37–?100) did not mention this dastardly deed of putting to death innocent babies and young children. But it is not surprising that he and other secular historians overlooked the death of a few Hebrew children in an insignificant village, for Herod's infamous crimes were many. He put to death several of his own children and some of his wives whom he thought were plotting against him. Emperor Augustus reportedly said it was better to be Herod's sow than his son, for his sow had a better chance of surviving in a Jewish community. In the Greek language, as in English, there is only one letter difference between the words "sow" (*huos*) and "son" (*huios*).

This event too was said to be the fulfillment of a prophecy by **Jeremiah.** This statement (Jer. 31:15) referred initially to the **weeping** of the nation as a result of the death of **children** at the time of the Babylonian Captivity (586 B.C.). But the parallel to the situation at this time was obvious, for again children were being slaughtered at the hands of non-Jews. Also, **Rachel's** tomb was near Bethlehem and **Rachel** was considered by many to be the mother of the nation. That is why she was seen weeping over these children's deaths.

c. In Nazareth (2:19-23)

2:19-23. After Herod died . . . Joseph was again instructed by **an angel of the Lord.** This was the third of four times an angel appeared to him **in a dream** (cf. 1:20; 2:13, 19, 22). He was made aware of Herod's death and told to return **to the land** (v. 20). Joseph obediently followed the Lord's instruction and

was planning to return **to the land of Israel,** perhaps to Bethlehem. However, a son of Herod, **Archelaus, was** ruling over the territories of **Judea,** Samaria, and Idumea. Archelaus, noted for tyranny, murder, and instability, was probably insane as a result of close family intermarriages. (He ruled from 4 B.C. to A.D. 6. See the chart on the Herods at Luke 1:5). God's warning to Joseph (again **in a dream,** Matt. 2:22; cf. 1:20; 2:13, 19) was not to return to Bethlehem, but instead to move back to the northern **district of Galilee** to the **town** of Nazareth. The ruler of this region was Antipas, another son of Herod (cf. 14:1; Luke 23:7-12), but he was a capable ruler.

The fact that the family moved to Nazareth was once again said to be in fulfillment of prophecy (Matt. 2:23). However, the words **He will be called a Nazarene,** were not directly spoken by any Old Testament prophet, though several prophecies come close to this expression. Isaiah said the Messiah would be "from [Jesse's] roots" like "a Branch" (Isa. 11:1). "Branch" is the Hebrew word *nēṣer,* which has consonants like those in the word "Nazarene" and which carry the idea of having an insignificant beginning.

Since Matthew used the plural **prophets,** perhaps his idea was not based on a specific prophecy but on the idea that appeared in a number of prophecies concerning Messiah's despised character. Nazareth was the town which housed the Roman garrison for the northern regions of Galilee. Therefore most Jews would not have any associations with that city. In fact those who lived in Nazareth were thought of as compromisers who consorted with the enemy, the Romans. Therefore to call one "a Nazarene" was to use a term of contempt. So because Joseph and his family settled in Nazareth, the Messiah was later despised and considered contemptible in the eyes of many in Israel. This was Nathanael's reaction when he heard Jesus was from Nazareth (John 1:46): "Can anything good come from there?" This concept fit several Old Testament prophecies that speak of the lowly character of the Messiah (e.g., Isa. 42:1-4). Also the term "Nazarene" would have reminded Jewish readers of the similar-sounding word "Nazirite" (Num. 6:1-21). Jesus was more devoted to God than the Nazirites.

23

C. Presentation by an ambassador (3:1-12)

(Mark 1:1-8; Luke 3:1-9, 15-18; John 1:19-28)

3:1-2. In Matthew's story of the Messiah-King, he skipped the next 30 years or so of Jesus' life. Matthew picked up the story with the introductory ministry of **John the Baptist,** the "ambassador" of the King. In the Scriptures several men were named John, but only one had the distinguishing name John the Baptist, that is, the Baptizer. While self-imposed proselyte baptism was known to the Jews, John's baptism was unusual for he was the first person who came baptizing others.

John's ministry was conducted **in the Desert of Judea,** barren and rugged land west of the Dead Sea. His message was forthright and had two parts: (1) a soteriological aspect, **repent,** and (2) an eschatological aspect, **for the kingdom of heaven is near.** The concept of a coming kingdom was well known in Old Testament Scriptures. But the idea that repentance was necessary in order to enter this kingdom was something new and became a stumbling block to many Jews. They thought that as children of Abraham they would automatically be granted entrance into Messiah's kingdom. John's message, however, was that a change of mind and heart (*metanoeite,* "repent") was necessary before they could qualify for the kingdom. They did not realize how far they had drifted from God's Law and the requirements laid down by the prophets (e.g., Mal. 3:7-12).

The eschatological aspect of John's message has caused modern-day commentators greater problems. Not all scholars agree on John's meaning; in fact even conservative scholars are divided. What was John preaching? He announced a coming kingdom, which simply means "a coming rule." This rule was to be heaven's rule: "the kingdom of heaven." Does that mean God would then begin to rule in heavenly spheres? Obviously not, for God has always ruled over heavenly spheres since Creation. John must mean that God's heavenly rule was about to be extended directly to earthly spheres. God's rule over the earth had drawn near and was about to be instituted through the person of the Messiah for whom John

was preparing the way. No one hearing John preach asked him what he was talking about, for the concept of Messiah's rule over the kingdom of earth was a common thread in Old Testament prophecy. The requirement for that institution, however, was that the nation repent.

3:3-10. John's message was a fulfillment of the prophecy in Isaiah 40:3 with reflections of Malachi 3:1. All four Gospels relate John the Baptist to Isaiah's words (Mark 1:2-3; Luke 3:4-6; John 1:23). **Isaiah 40:3,** however, refers to "highway construction workers" who were called on to clear the way in the desert for the return of the Lord as His people, the exiles, returned to Judah from the Babylonian Captivity in 537 B.C. In similar fashion, John the Baptist was in the desert preparing the way for the Lord and His kingdom by calling on people to return to Him.

John was thus **a voice of one calling in the desert** to **prepare** a remnant to receive the Messiah. His preaching "in the Desert of Judea" (Matt. 3:1) suggests that he came to separate people from the religious systems of the day. He dressed similarly to Elijah (**clothes . . . of camel's hair and . . . a leather belt;** cf. 2 Kings 1:8; Zech. 13:4). And he ate **locusts and wild honey.** Locusts were eaten by the poor (Lev. 11:21). Like Elijah he was a rough outdoorsman with a forthright message.

Large numbers of **people . . . from Jerusalem and all Judea** went to hear John the Baptist. Some accepted his message and confessed **their sins,** submitting to water baptism, the identifying sign of John's ministry. John's baptism was not the same as Christian baptism, for it was a religious rite signifying confession of sin and commitment to a holy life in anticipation of the coming Messiah.

However, not all believed. **The Pharisees and Sadducees,** who came to see what he was doing, rejected his appeal. Their feelings were summed up in John's words to them (Matt. 3:7-10). They believed that they, as physical sons of **Abraham,** were automatically qualified for Messiah's kingdom. John completely repudiated Pharisaic Judaism and said that **God,** if necessary, could **raise up . . . stones** to become His **children.** God could take outsiders, Gentiles, if necessary to find individuals to follow Him. Judaism was in danger of being removed. Unless there was productive **fruit in keeping with repentance** (v. 8), God would remove the **tree**.

3:11-12. The relationship of John the Baptist to the coming Messiah was clearly seen. John believed he was not even worthy **to carry** (or untie) the **sandals** of the Coming One. John was simply an introducer who was preparing a remnant for the Messiah, and who was baptizing in **water** those who responded. The Coming One would **baptize** them **with the Holy Spirit and with fire.** Those hearing John's words would have been reminded of two Old Testament prophecies: Joel 2:28-29 and Malachi 3:2-5. Joel had given the promise of the outpouring of the Holy Spirit on Israel. An actual outpouring of the Spirit did occur in Acts 2 on the day of Pentecost, but experientially Israel did not enter into the benefits of that event. She will yet experience the benefits of this accomplished work when she turns in repentance at the Lord's Second Advent. The baptism "with fire" referred to the judging and cleansing of those who would enter the kingdom, as prophesied in Malachi 3. This symbolism was carried through by John who spoke of the separation that occurs when a **winnowing fork** tosses up grain, **wheat** is then gathered **into the barn**, and **chaff** is burned **up.** John was saying that the Messiah, when He came, would prepare a remnant (wheat) for the kingdom by empowering and cleansing the people. Those who reject Him (chaff) would be judged and cast into eternal **unquenchable fire** (cf. Mal. 4:1).

D. *Presentation through approval (3:13-4:11)*

1. BY BAPTISM (3:13-17)

(MARK 1:9-11; LUKE 3:21-22)

3:13-14. After years of silence in Nazareth, **Jesus** appeared among those listening to John's preaching and presented Himself as a candidate for baptism. Only Matthew recorded John's opposition to this act: **I need to be baptized by You, and do You come to me?** John recognized Jesus did not fit the requirements for his baptism, since his baptism was for repentance from sin. Of what did Jesus have to repent? He had never sinned (2 Cor. 5:21; Heb. 4:15; 7:26;

1 John 3:5), so He could not be officially entering into John's baptism even though He was seeking **to be baptized by John.** Some feel Jesus was confessing the sins of the nation as Moses, Ezra, and Daniel had done on previous occasions. However, another possibility is suggested in Matthew 3:15.

3:15. Jesus' response to John was that it was fitting for Him to take part in John's baptism at this time in order **to fulfill all righteousness.** What did Jesus mean? The Law included no requirements about baptism, so Jesus could not have had in view anything pertaining to Levitical righteousness. But John's message was a message of repentance, and those experiencing it were looking forward to a coming Messiah who would be righteous and who would bring in righteousness. If Messiah were to provide righteousness for sinners, He must be identified with sinners. It was therefore in the will of God for Him to be baptized by **John** in order to be identified (the real meaning of the word "baptized") with sinners.

3:16-17. The significant thing about the baptism of **Jesus** was the authentication from **heaven.** As Jesus came up **out of the water . . . the Spirit of God** came down on Him in the form of **a dove.** As One **went up,** the Other came down. **A voice from heaven**—the voice of God the Father—**said, This is My Son, whom I love; with Him I am well pleased** (cf. Eph. 1:6; Col. 1:13). God repeated these words about Christ on the Mount of Transfiguration (Matt. 17:5). All three Persons of the Godhead were present at this event: the Father who spoke of His Son, the Son who was being baptized, and the Spirit who descended on the Son as a dove. This verified for John that Jesus is the Son of God (John 1:32-34). It was also in keeping with Isaiah's prophecy that the Spirit would rest on the Messiah (Isa. 11:2). The descent of the Holy Spirit empowered the Son, the Messiah, for His ministry among people.

2. BY TEMPTATION (4:1-11)

(MARK 1:12-13; LUKE 4:1-13)

4:1-2. After being baptized, **Jesus was led** immediately **by the Spirit** of God **into the desert** (traditionally near Jericho; see map) for a period of testing. This period of time was a necessary period

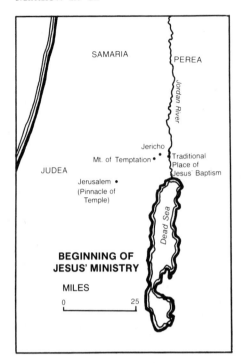

SAMARIA

PEREA

Jordan River

JUDEA

Jericho

Mt. of Temptation •

Jerusalem •
(Pinnacle of
Temple)

• • Traditional
Place of
Jesus' Baptism

Dead Sea

**BEGINNING OF
JESUS' MINISTRY**

MILES

0   25

4:5-7. The second test by Satan appealed to personal display or popularity. This test built on the first, for if He is **the Son of God** and the Messiah, nothing could harm Him. Satan **took Him to . . . the highest point of the temple.** Whether this was actual or simply a vision cannot be determined dogmatically. Here Satan made a subtle suggestion to Jesus as the Messiah. In effect he was reminding Jesus of Malachi's prophecy (Mal. 3:1), which had led to a common belief among the Jews that Messiah would suddenly appear in the sky, coming down to His temple. Satan was saying, in essence, "Why don't You do what the people are expecting and make some marvelous display? After all, the Scripture says **His angels** will protect You and You won't even hurt a **foot** as You come down." Satan may have thought if Jesus could quote Scripture to him, he could quote it too. However, he purposely did not quote Psalm 91:11-12 accurately. He left out an important phrase, "in all Your ways." According to the psalmist, a person is protected only when he is following the Lord's will. For Jesus to cast Himself **down** from the pinnacle of the temple in some dramatic display to accommodate Himself to the people's thinking would not have been God's will. Jesus responded, again from Deuteronomy (6:16), that it would not be proper to **test . . . God** and expect Him to do something when one is out of His will.

4:8-11. Satan's final test related to God's plan for Jesus. It was and is God's design that Jesus Christ rule the world. Satan **showed** Jesus **the kingdoms of the world** with all **their splendor.** These kingdoms presently are Satan's, as he is "the god of this Age" (2 Cor. 4:4) and "the prince of this world" (John 12:31; cf. Eph. 2:2). He had the power to **give** all these kingdoms to Jesus at that time—**if** only Jesus would **bow down and worship** him. Satan was saying, "I can accomplish the will of God for You and You can have the kingdoms of this world right now." This of course would have meant Jesus would never have gone to the cross. He supposedly could have been the King of kings without the cross. However, this would have thwarted God's plan for salvation and would have meant Jesus was worshiping an inferior. His response, once again from Deuteronomy (6:13 and 10:20), was that **God** alone should be

under God's direction—a time in which the Son obeyed (Heb. 5:8). **After fasting 40 days,** when the Lord **was hungry,** the tests began. From God's standpoint the tests demonstrated the quality of the Lord. It was impossible for the divine Son to sin, and that fact actually heightened the tests. He could not give in to the tests and sin, but He had to endure until the tests were completed.

4:3-4. The first test pertained to the matter of sonship. Satan assumed that if He were the Son, perhaps He could be persuaded to act independently of the Father. Satan's test was subtle for since He is **the Son of God,** He has the power to turn the **stones** all around Him into **bread.** But that was not the will of His Father for Him. The Father's will was for Him to be hungry in the desert with no food. To submit to Satan's suggestion and satisfy His hunger would have been contrary to God's will. Jesus therefore quoted Deuteronomy 8:3, which affirms that **man does not live on bread alone, but** by God's **Word.** It is better to obey God's Word than to satisfy human desires. The fact that Jesus quoted from Deuteronomy showed that He recognized the inerrant authority of that book, one often criticized by scholars.

Satan's Temptations of Eve and of Jesus

Temptation	Genesis 3	Matthew 4
Appeal to physical appetite	You may eat of any tree (3:1).	You may eat by changing stones to bread (4:3).
Appeal to personal gain	You will not die (3:4).	You will not hurt Your foot (4:6).
Appeal to power or glory	You will be like God (3:5).	You will have all the world's kingdoms (4:8-9).

worshiped and served. Jesus resisted this temptation also.

Interestingly Satan's temptations of Eve in the Garden of Eden correspond to those of Jesus in the desert. Satan appealed to the physical appetite (Gen. 3:1-3; Matt. 4:3), the desire for personal gain (Gen. 3:4-5; Matt. 4:6), and an easy path to power or glory (Gen. 3:5-6; Matt. 4:8-9). And in each case Satan altered God's Word (Gen. 3:4; Matt. 4:6). Satan's temptations of people today often fall into the same three categories (cf. 1 John 2:16). The One who had identified Himself with sinners by baptism and who would provide righteousness proved He is righteous, and revealed His approval by the Father. Satan then **left** Jesus. At that moment God sent **angels** to minister to His needs.

II. Communications from the King (4:12–7:29)

A. Beginning proclamations (4:12-25)

1. BY WORD (4:12-22)

(MARK 1:14-20; LUKE 4:14-15)

a. His sermon (4:12-17)

4:12-16. Matthew presented an important time factor in his account when he noted **Jesus** did not officially begin His public ministry until **John** the Baptist **had been put in prison.** The reason for John's imprisonment was not presented here, but it was stated later (14:3). When Jesus learned of John's imprisonment, He went from **Nazareth** and settled **in Capernaum** (Luke 4:16-30 explains why He left Nazareth). This region was the area settled by the tribes **of Zebulun and Naphtali** after the conquest of Joshua's

time. **Isaiah** had prophesied (Isa. 9:1-2) that **light** would come to this region, and Matthew saw this movement of Jesus as fulfillment of this prophecy. One of Messiah's works was to bring **light** into **darkness,** for He would be a light to both Jews and Gentiles (cf. John 1:9; 12:46).

4:17. When John was imprisoned, **Jesus began to preach.** His words had a familiar ring: **Repent, for the kingdom of heaven is near** (cf. 3:2). The twofold message of John was now proclaimed by the Messiah. The work of God was rapidly moving toward the establishing of the glorious kingdom of God on earth. If one wanted to be a part of the kingdom, he must repent. Repentance was mandatory if fellowship with God was to be enjoyed.

b. His summons (4:18-22)

(Mark 1:16-20; Luke 5:1-11)

4:18-22. Since Jesus is the promised Messiah, He had the right to call men from their normal pursuits of life to **follow** Him. This was not the first time these men had met Jesus, for the Fourth Gospel relates Jesus' first meeting with some of the disciples (John 1:35-42). Jesus now **called** these **fishermen** to leave their profession behind and to begin following Him permanently. He would take them from fishing for fish and **make** them **fishers of men.** The message of the coming kingdom needed to be proclaimed widely so that many could hear and could become, by repentance, subjects of His kingdom. The calling carried with it a cost, for it involved leaving not only one's profession but also one's family responsibilities. Matthew noted that **James** and **John** . . . **left** not only

27

their fishing, but also **their father** to begin following Jesus.

2. BY DEEDS (4:23-25)
(LUKE 6:17-19)

4:23. The work of the Lord was not limited to preaching. His deeds were as important as His words, for a great question in the minds of the Jews would be, "Can this One claiming to be Messiah perform the works of Messiah?" Matthew 4:23 is an important summary statement crucial to Matthew's theme (cf. 9:35, almost identical to 4:23). Several important elements are included in this verse. (1) **Jesus went throughout Galilee, teaching in their synagogues.** The ministry of this One who claimed to be King of the Jews was conducted among the Jews. He ministered in synagogues, places of Jewish gatherings for worship. (2) This One was involved in "teaching" and **preaching.** He thus was involved in a prophetic ministry for He is "the Prophet" announced in Deuteronomy 18:15-19. (3) He was proclaiming **the good news of the kingdom.** His message was that God was moving to fulfill His covenantal program with Israel and to establish His kingdom on the earth. (4) He was **healing every disease and sickness among the people** (cf. "teaching," "preaching," and "healing" in Matt. 9:35). This authenticated that He is indeed the Prophet, for His words were backed up by authenticating signs. All these actions should have convinced the Jewish people that God was moving in history to accomplish His purposes. They were responsible to get ready by repenting from their sins and acknowledging Jesus as the Messiah.

4:24-25. The ministry of Jesus—and probably also the ministry of the four men he called (vv. 18-22)—was dramatic for multitudes of people heard of Jesus and began to flock to Him. The **news about Him spread all over Syria,** the area north of Galilee. As people came, they brought many who were afflicted with a variety of illnesses and Jesus **healed them** all. No wonder **large crowds** began to follow Jesus **from Galilee,** from **the Decapolis** (lit., "10 cities"; an area east and south of the Sea of Galilee), from **Jerusalem** and **Judea, and the region across** (west of) **the Jordan** River (see map, p. 19).

B. Continuing pronouncements (chaps. 5–7)

1. THE SUBJECTS OF HIS KINGDOM (5:1-16)

a. Their character (5:1-12)
(Luke 6:17-23)

5:1-12. As the multitudes continued to flock to Jesus (cf. 4:25), **He went up on a mountainside and sat down.** It was the custom of Rabbis to sit as they taught. **His disciples came to Him and He began to teach them.** Matthew 5–7 is commonly called "the Sermon on the Mount" because Jesus delivered it on a mountain. Though the mountain's exact location is unknown, it was undoubtedly in Galilee (4:23) and was apparently near Capernaum on a place which was "level" (Luke 6:17). "Disciples" refers not to the Twelve, as some suggest, but to **the crowds** following Him (cf. Matt. 7:28, "the crowds were amazed at His teaching").

Jesus instructed them in view of His announcement of the coming kingdom (4:17). Natural questions on the heart of every Jew would have been, "Am I eligible to enter Messiah's kingdom? Am I righteous enough to qualify for entrance?" The only standard of righteousness the people knew was that laid down by the current religious leaders, the scribes and Pharisees. Would one who followed that standard be acceptable in Messiah's kingdom? Jesus' sermon therefore must be understood in the context of His offer of the kingdom to Israel and the need for repentance to enter that kingdom. The sermon did not give a "Constitution" for the kingdom nor did it present the way of salvation. *The sermon showed how a person who is in right relationship with God should conduct his life.* While the passage must be understood in the light of the offer of the messianic kingdom, the sermon applies to Jesus' followers today for it demonstrates the standard of righteousness God demands of His people. Some of the standards are general (e.g., "You cannot serve both God and money" [6:24]); some are specific (e.g., "If someone forces you to go one mile, go with him two miles" [5:41]); and some pertain to the future (e.g., "many will say to Me on that day, 'Lord, Lord, did we not prophesy in Your name?' " [7:22]).

Jesus began His sermon with "the Beatitudes," statements beginning with

Blessed are. "Blessed" means "happy" or "fortunate" (cf. Ps. 1:1). The qualities Jesus mentioned in this list, "the poor in spirit," "those who mourn," "the meek," etc., obviously could not be products of Pharisaic righteousness. The Pharisees were concerned primarily with external qualities, but the qualities Jesus mentioned are internal. These come only when one is properly related to God through faith, when one places his complete trust in God.

The poor in spirit (Matt. 5:3) are those who consciously depend on God, not on themselves; they are "poor" inwardly, having no ability in themselves to please God (cf. Rom. 3:9-12). **Those who mourn** (Matt. 5:4) recognize their needs and present them to the One who is able to assist. Those who are **meek** (v. 5) are truly humble and gentle and have a proper appreciation of their position. (*Praeis*, the Gr. word rendered "meek," is translated "gentle" in its three other usages in the NT: 11:29; 21:5; 1 Peter 3:4.) **Those who hunger and thirst for righteousness** (Matt. 5:6) have a spiritual appetite, a continuing desire for personal righteousness. **The merciful** (v. 7) extend mercy to others, thus demonstrating God's mercy which has been extended to them. **The pure in heart** (v. 8) are those who are inwardly clean from sin through faith in God's provision and a continual acknowledging of their sinful condition. **The peacemakers** (v. 9) show others how to have inward peace with God and how to be instruments of peace in the world. They desire and possess God's **righteousness** even though it brings them persecution (v. 10).

These qualities contrast sharply with Pharisaic "righteousness." The Pharisees were not "poor in spirit"; did not "mourn" in recognition of their needs; were proud and harsh, not humble and gentle; they felt they had attained righteousness and therefore did not have a continual appetite or desire for it; they were more concerned with "legalities" of God's and their own laws than with showing mercy; were pure ceremonially but not inwardly; created a rift, not peace in Judaism; and certainly did not possess true righteousness. Jesus' followers who possess these qualities become heirs of **the kingdom** (vv. 3, 10) on **earth** (v. 5), receive spiritual comfort (v. 4) and

satisfaction (v. 6), receive **mercy** from God and others (v. 7), **will see God** (v. 8), that is, Jesus Christ, who is God "in a body" (1 Tim. 3:16; cf. John 1:18; 14:7-9). His followers were known as God's **sons** (Matt. 5:9; cf. Gal 3:26) for they partook of His righteousness (Matt. 5:10).

People possessing these qualities would naturally stand out in the crowd and would not be understood by others. Thus they would be **persecuted**; others would speak **evil** of them (v. 11). However, Jesus' words encouraged His followers, for they would be walking in the train of **the prophets**, who also were misunderstood and **persecuted** (v. 12; cf. 1 Kings 19:1-4; 22:8; Jer. 26:8-11; 37:11-16; 38:1-6; Dan. 3; 6; Amos 7:10-13).

b. Their circle of influence (5:13-16)
(Mark 9:50; Luke 14:34-35)

5:13-16. To demonstrate the impact these people would make on their **world**, Jesus used two common illustrations: **salt** and **light.** Jesus' followers would be like salt in that they would create a thirst for greater information. When one sees a unique person who possesses superior qualities in specific areas, he desires to discover why that person is different. It is also possible that salt means these people serve as a preservative against the evils of society. Whichever view one takes, the important quality to note is that salt ought to maintain its basic character. If it fails to be **salty,** it has lost its purpose for existence and should be discarded.

A **light** is meant to **shine** and give direction. Individuals Jesus described in verses 3-10 would obviously radiate and point others to the proper path. Their influence would be evident, like **a city on a hill** or **a lamp . . . on its stand.** A concealed lamp, placed **under a bowl** (a clay container for measuring grain) would be useless. Light-radiating people live so that others **see** their **good deeds** and give praise not to them but to their **Father in heaven.** (V. 16 includes the first of 15 references by Jesus in the Sermon on the Mount to God as "your [or 'our' or 'My'] Father in heaven," "your heavenly Father," "your Father." Also see vv. 45, 48; 6:1, 4, 6, 8-9, 14-15, 18, 26, 32; 7:11, 21. One who stands in God's righteousness by faith in Him has an intimate spiritual relationship to Him, like that of a child to his loving father.)

2. THE SUBSTANCE OF HIS MESSAGE (5:17-20)

5:17-20. This section presents the heart of Jesus' message, for it demonstrates His relationship to the Law of God. Jesus was not presenting a rival system to the Law of Moses and the words of the Prophets, but a true fulfillment of **the Law** and **the Prophets**—in contrast with the Pharisees' traditions. "The Law and the Prophets" refer to the entire Old Testament (cf. 7:12; 11:13; 22:40; Luke 16:16; Acts 13:15; 24:14; 28:23; Rom. 3:21). **I tell you the truth** is literally, "Surely (or Verily, KJV) I say to you." "Surely" renders the word "Amen" (Gr. *amēn*, transliterated from the Heb. *'āman*, "to be firm, true"). This expression, "I tell you the truth," points to a solemn declaration that the hearers should note. It occurs 31 times in Matthew alone. (In the Gospel of John this Gr. word always occurs twice: "Amen, Amen." Cf. comments on John 1:51.)

Jesus' fulfillment would extend to the **smallest** Hebrew **letter**, the "jot" (lit., *yôd*), and even to the smallest **stroke** of a Hebrew letter, the "tittle." In English a jot would correspond to the dot above the letter "i" (and look like an apostrophe), and a tittle would be seen in the difference between a "P" and an "R". The small angled line that completes the "R" is like a tittle. These things are important because letters make up words and even a slight change in a letter might change the meaning of a word. Jesus said He would **fulfill** the **Law** by obeying it perfectly and would fulfill the prophets' predictions of the Messiah and His kingdom. But the responsibility of the people was made clear. The **righteousness** they were currently seeking—**that of the Pharisees and the teachers of the Law**—was insufficient for entrance into **the kingdom** Jesus was offering. The righteousness He demanded was not merely external; it was a true inner righteousness based on faith in God's Word (Rom. 3:21-22). This is clear from what follows.

3. THE SUBSTANTIATION OF HIS MESSAGE (5:21-7:6)

a. Rejection of Pharisaic traditions (5:21-48)

Jesus rejected the traditions of the Pharisees (vv. 21-48) and their practices (6:1-7:6). Six times Jesus said, "You have heard that it was said. . . . But I tell you" (5:21-22, 27-28, 31-32, 33-34, 38-39, 43-44). These words make it clear that Jesus was presenting (a) what the Pharisees and teachers of the Law were saying to the people and, by contrast, (b) what God's true intent of the Law was. This spelled out His statement (v. 20) that Pharisaic righteousness is not enough to gain entrance into the coming kingdom.

5:21-26. Jesus' first illustration pertained to an important commandment, **Do not murder** (Ex. 20:13). The Pharisees taught that murder consists of taking someone's life. But the Lord said the commandment extended not only to the act itself but also to the internal attitude behind the act. Of course, murder is wrong, but the anger prompting the act is also as wrong as plunging in a knife. Furthermore, becoming **angry** and assuming a position of superiority over another by calling him a derogatory name (such as the Aram. **Raca** or **You fool!**) demonstrates sinfulness of the heart. A person with such a sinful heart obviously is a sinner and therefore is headed for **the fire of hell** ("hell" is lit., "Gehenna"; cf. Matt. 5:29-30; 10:28; 18:9; 23:15, 33; 7 of the 11 references to Gehenna are in Matt.). "Gehenna" means valley of Hinnom, the valley south of Jerusalem where a continually burning fire consumed the city refuse. This became an apt name for the eternal punishment of the wicked.

Such wrongful attitudes should be dealt with and made right. Reconciliation between brothers must be accomplished whether the "innocent" (5:23-24) or the "offending" (vv. 25-26) brother takes the first step. Without such reconciliation, gifts presented **at the altar** mean nothing: Even **on the way** to a **court** trial a defendant should seek to clear up any such problem. Otherwise the Sanhedrin, the Jewish court of 70 members, would send him to **prison** and he would be penniless.

5:27-30. A second practical illustration dealt with the problem of **adultery** (Ex. 20:14). Once again the Pharisees' teaching was concerned only with the outward act. They said the only way one could commit adultery was through an act of sexual union. They correctly quoted the commandment, but they missed its point. **Adultery** begins within one's heart (looking **lustfully**) and follows in the act. The lustful desire, **in the heart,** as wrong as the act, indicates that one is not rightly related to God.

Jesus' words recorded in Matthew 5:29-30 have often been misunderstood. Obviously Jesus was not teaching physical mutilation, for a blind man could have as much of a problem with lust as a sighted person, and a man with only one **hand** might use it also **to sin.** Jesus was advocating the removal of the inward cause of offense. Since a lustful heart would ultimately lead to adultery, one's heart must be changed. Only by such a change of heart can one escape **hell** ("Gehenna"; cf. v. 22).

5:31-32 (Matt. 19:3-9; Mark 10:11-12; Luke 16:18). Among the Jewish leaders were two schools of thought regarding the matter **of divorce** (Deut. 24:1). Those who followed Hillel said it was permissible for a husband to divorce **his wife** for any reason at all, but the other group (those following Shammai) said divorce was permissible only for a major offense. In His response, the Lord strongly taught that marriage is viewed by God as an indissoluble unit and that marriages should not be terminated by divorce. The "exception clause," **except for marital unfaithfulness** (*porneias*), is understood in several ways by Bible scholars. Four of these ways are: (a) a single act of adultery, (b) unfaithfulness during the period of betrothal (Matt. 1:19), (c) marriage between near relatives (Lev. 18:6-18), or (d) continued promiscuity. (See comments on Matt. 19:3-9.)

5:33-37. The matter of making **oaths** (Lev. 19:12; Deut. 23:21) was next addressed by the Lord. The Pharisees were notorious for their oaths, which were made on the least provocation. Yet they made allowances for mental reservations within their oaths. If they wanted to be relieved of oaths they had made **by heaven . . . by the earth . . . by Jerusalem,** or **by** one's own **head,** they could argue that since God Himself had not been involved their oaths were not binding.

But Jesus said oaths should not even be necessary: **Do not swear at all.** The fact that oaths were used at all emphasized the wickedness of man's heart. Furthermore, swearing "by heaven," "by the earth," or "by Jerusalem" *is* binding, since they are **God's throne . . . footstool,**

and **city,** respectively. Even the color of the hair on their heads was determined by God (Matt. 5:36). However, Jesus later in His life responded to an oath (26:63-64), as did Paul (2 Cor. 1:23). The Lord was saying one's life should be sufficient to back up one's words. A **yes** always ought to mean **yes,** and a **no** should mean **no.** James seems to have picked up these words of the Lord in his epistle (James 5:12).

5:38-42 (Luke 6:29-30). The words **Eye for eye, and tooth for tooth** come from several Old Testament passages (Ex. 21:24; Lev. 24:20; Deut. 19:21); they are called the *lex talionis,* the law of retaliation. This law was given to protect the innocent and to make sure retaliation did not occur beyond the offense. Jesus pointed out, however, that while the rights of the innocent were protected by the Law, the righteous need not necessarily claim their rights. A righteous man would be characterized by humility and selflessness. Instead he might go "the extra mile" to maintain peace. When wronged by being struck on a **cheek,** or sued for his **tunic** (undergarment; a **cloak** was the outer garment), or forced to travel with **someone a mile,** he would not strike back, demand repayment, or refuse to comply. Instead of retaliating he would do the opposite, and would also commit his case to the Lord who will one day set all things in order (cf. Rom. 12:17-21). This was seen to its greatest extent in the life of the Lord Jesus Himself, as Peter explained (1 Peter 2:23).

5:43-48 (Luke 6:27-28, 32-36). The Pharisees taught that one should **love** those near and dear to him (Lev. 19:18), but that Israel's enemies should be hated. The Pharisees thus implied that their hatred was God's means of judging their **enemies.** But Jesus stated that Israel should demonstrate God's love even to her enemies—a practice not even commanded in the Old Testament! God loves them; **He causes His sun to rise on** them and He **sends rain** to produce their crops. Since His love extends to everyone, Israel too should be a channel of His love by loving all. Such love demonstrates that they are God's **sons** (cf. Matt. 5:16). Loving only **those who love you** and greeting **only your brothers** is no more than **the tax collectors** and **pagans** do—a cutting remark for Pharisees!

31

Jesus concluded this section by saying, **Be perfect therefore, as your heavenly Father is perfect.** His message demonstrated God's righteous standard, for God Himself truly is the "standard" of righteousness. If these individuals are to be righteous, they must be as God is, "perfect," that is, mature (*teleioi*) or holy. Murder, lust, hate, deception, and retaliation obviously do not characterize God. He did not lower His standard to accommodate humans; instead He set forth His absolute holiness as the standard. Though this standard can never be perfectly met by man himself, a person who by faith trusts in God enjoys His righteousness being reproduced in his life.

b. Rejection of Pharisaic practices (6:1–7:6)

The Lord then turned from the Pharisees' teachings to examine their hypocritical deeds.

6:1-4. Jesus first spoke of the Pharisees' almsgiving. **Righteousness** is not primarily a matter between a person and others, but between a person and God. So one's **acts** should not be demonstrated **before** others for then his **reward** should come from them (vv. 1-2). The Pharisees made a great show of their giving **to the needy . . . in the synagogues and on the streets,** thinking they were thus proving how righteous they were. But the Lord said that in giving one should **not** even **let** his **left hand know what** his **right hand is doing,** that is, it should be so **secret** that the giver readily forgets what he gave. In this way he demonstrates true righteousness before God and not before people, so God in turn **will reward** him. One cannot be rewarded, as the Pharisees expected, by *both* man and God.

6:5-15 (Luke 11:2-4). Jesus then spoke about the practice of prayer, which the Pharisees loved to perform publicly. Rather than making prayer a matter between an individual and God, the Pharisees had turned it into an act **to be seen by men**—again, to demonstrate their supposed righteousness. Their prayers were directed not to God but to other men, and consisted of long, repetitive phrases (Matt. 6:7).

Jesus condemned such practices. Prayer should be addressed **to your Father, who is unseen** (cf. John 1:18; 1 Tim. 1:17) and who **knows what you**

need (Matt. 6:8); it is not "to be seen by men." But Jesus also presented a model prayer for His disciples to follow. This prayer is commonly called "the Lord's Prayer," but it is actually "the disciples' prayer." This prayer, which is repeated by many Christians, contains elements that are important for all praying: (1) Prayer is to begin with worship. God is addressed as **Our Father in heaven.** Worship is the essence of all prayer. (In vv. 1-18 Jesus used the word "Father" 10 times! Only those who have true inner righteousness can address God in that way in worship.) (2) Reverence is a second element of prayer, for God's **name** is to be **hallowed,** that is, revered (*hagiasthētō*). (3) The desire for God's kingdom—**Your kingdom come**—is based on the assurance that God will fulfill all His covenant promises to His people. (4) Prayer is to include the request that His **will be** accomplished today **on earth as it is** being accomplished **in heaven,** that is, fully and willingly. (5) Petition for personal needs such as **daily** food is also to be a part of prayer. "Daily" (*epiousion,* used only here in the NT) means "sufficient for today." (6) Requests regarding spiritual needs, such as forgiveness, are included too. This implies that the petitioner has already forgiven those who had offended him. Sins (cf. Luke 11:4), as moral **debts,** reveal one's shortcomings before God. (7) Believers recognize their spiritual weakness as they pray for deliverance from **temptation** to **evil** (cf. James 1:13-14).

Jesus' words in Matthew 6:14-15 explain His statement about forgiveness in verse 12. Though God's forgiveness of **sin** is not based on one's forgiving others, a Christian's forgiveness *is* based on realizing he has been forgiven (cf. Eph. 4:32). Personal fellowship with God is in view in these verses (not salvation from sin). One cannot walk in fellowship with God if he refuses to **forgive** others.

6:16-18. **Fasting** was a third example of Pharisaic "righteousness." The Pharisees loved to **fast** so that others would see them and think them spiritual. **Fasting** emphasized the denial of the flesh, but the Pharisees were glorifying their flesh by drawing attention to themselves. The Lord's words emphasized once again that such actions should be done **in secret** before God. Nor was one to follow the

Pharisees' custom of withholding olive **oil** from his **head** during fasting. As a result, God alone would know and would **reward** accordingly.

In all three examples of Pharisaic "righteousness"—almsgiving (vv. 1-4), praying (vv. 5-15), and fasting (vv. 16-18)—Jesus spoke of **hypocrites** (vv. 2, 5, 16), public ostentation (vv. 1-2, 5, 16), receiving **their reward in full** when their actions are done before men (vv. 2, 5, 16), acting **in secret** (vv. 4, 6, 18), and being rewarded by the **Father, who sees** or "knows," when one's actions are done secretly (vv. 4, 6, 8, 18).

6:19-24 (Luke 12:33-34; 11:34-36; 16:13). One's attitude toward wealth is another barometer of righteousness. The Pharisees believed the Lord materially blessed all He loved. They were intent on building great **treasures on earth.** But treasures built here are subject to decay (**moth** destroys cloth and **rust** destroys metal; cf. James 5:2-3) or theft, whereas **treasures** deposited **in heaven** can never be lost.

The Pharisees had this problem because their spiritual **eyes** were diseased (Matt. 6:22). With their **eyes** they were coveting money and wealth. Thus they were in spiritual **darkness.** They were slaves to the master of greed, and their desire for money was so great they were failing in their service to their true Master, **God. Money** is the translation of the Aramaic word for "wealth or property," *mamōna* ("mammon," kjv).

6:25-34 (Luke 12:22-34). If a person is occupied with the things of God, the true Master, how will he care for his ordinary needs in life, such as food, clothing, and shelter? The Pharisees in their pursuit of material things had never learned to live by faith. Jesus told them and us **not** to **worry about** these things, for **life** is **more important than** physical things. He cited several illustrations to prove His point. **The birds of the air** are fed by the **heavenly Father, and the lilies of the field** grow in such a way that their **splendor** is greater than **even** Solomon's. Jesus was saying God has built into His Creation the means by which all things are cared for. The birds are fed because they diligently work to maintain their lives. They do not **store** up great amounts of food, but continually work. And believers are far **more valuable** to God

than birds! The lilies grow daily through a natural process. Therefore an individual need not be anxious about his existence (Matt. 6:31), for **by worrying he can** never **add** any amount of time, not even **a single hour, to his life.** Rather than being like **the pagans** who are concerned about physical needs, the Lord's disciples should be concerned about the things of God, **His kingdom and His righteousness.** Then **all these needs will be** supplied in God's timing. This is the life of daily faith. It does no good to worry— **do not worry** occurs three times (vv. 25, 31, 34; cf. vv. 27-28)—or be concerned **about tomorrow for** there are sufficient matters to attend to **each day.** Worrying shows that one has "little faith" in what God can do (v. 30; cf. **you of little faith** in 8:26; 14:31; 16:8). As a disciple cares each day for the things God has trusted to him, God, his **heavenly Father** (6:26, 32), cares for his daily needs.

7:1-6 (Luke 6:41-42). A final illustration of Pharisaic practices pertains to judging. The Pharisees were then judging Christ and finding Him to be inadequate. He was not offering the kind of kingdom they anticipated or asking for the kind of righteousness they were exhibiting. So they rejected Him. Jesus therefore warned them against hypocritical judging.

This passage does not teach that judgments should never be made; Matthew 7:5 *does* speak of removing **the speck from your brother's eye.** The Lord's point was that a person should not be habitually critical or condemnatory of a **speck of sawdust** in someone else's **eye** when he has **a plank**—a strong hyperbole for effect—**in his own eye.** Such action is hypocritical (**You hypocrite, v. 5; cf.** "hypocrites" in 6:2, 5, 16). Though judgment is sometimes needed, those making the distinctions (*krinō,* **judge,** means "to distinguish" and thus "to decide") must first be certain of their own lives.

Furthermore when seeking to help another, one must exercise care to do what would be appreciated and beneficial. One should never entrust holy things (**what is sacred**) to unholy people (**dogs;** cf. "dogs" in Phil. 3:2) or **throw . . . pearls to pigs.** Dogs and pigs were despised in those days.

33

4. THE SUMMONS TO THE LISTENERS (7:7-29)

7:7-11 (Luke 11:9-13). Earlier in this sermon Jesus had given the disciples a model prayer (Matt. 6:9-13). Now He assured them that God welcomes prayer, and urged them to come to Him continuously and persistently. This is emphasized by the present tenses in the verbs: "keep on asking"; "keep on seeking"; "keep on knocking" (7:7). Why? Because **your Father in heaven** (v. 11) delights in giving **good gifts** (cf. James 1:17) to those who persist in prayer. (Luke substitutes "the Holy Spirit" for "good gifts," Luke 11:13.) No decent father would give **his son . . . a stone** instead of a round loaf of **bread** (which looked like a stone), or **a snake** instead of a similar-appearing **fish.** If an earthly father, with his sinful **(evil)** nature, delights to do right materially for his **children,** it makes sense that the righteous, heavenly **Father** will **much more** reward His children spiritually for their persistence.

7:12. This verse is commonly referred to as "the Golden Rule." The principle is that what people ordinarily want **others** to **do** for them should be what they practice toward those others. This principle summarizes the essential teachings of **the Law and the Prophets.** But such a principle cannot be consistently practiced by a natural person. Only a righteous person is able to practice this rule and thereby demonstrate the spiritual change that has come about in his life. An individual who is able to live this kind of life obviously possesses the righteousness Jesus demanded (5:20). Such a person's righteous acts do not save him, but because he has been delivered he is able to demonstrate true righteousness toward others.

7:13-14 (Luke 13:24). Elaborating on the Golden Rule, Jesus presented the clear way of access into righteousness. The righteousness He demanded (Matt. 5:20) does not come through the **wide . . . gate** and the **broad . . . road.** Rather it comes **through** the **small . . . gate** and the **narrow . . . road.** In light of the whole sermon, it was obvious Jesus was comparing the wide gate and the broad road to the outward righteousness of the Pharisees. If those listening to Jesus followed the Pharisees' teachings, their path would lead **to destruction** (*apōleian,* "ruin"). The **narrow gate** and road referred to Jesus' teaching, which emphasized not external requirements but internal transformation. Even the Lord Jesus acknowledged that **few would find** the true way, the way **that leads to life** (i.e., to heaven, in contrast with ruin in hell).

7:15-23 (Luke 6:43-44; 13:25-27). After presenting the true way of access into His anticipated kingdom, Jesus gave a warning about **false prophets.** He referred to these advocates of the broad way as **ferocious wolves** who appear harmless as sheep. How can one determine the character of false teachers? He need only look at the **fruit** they produce. **Grapes** and **figs** do not grow on **thornbushes** or **thistles.** Good **fruit** trees produce **good fruit,** but **bad** fruit trees produce **bad fruit.** In Jesus' evaluation, the Pharisees were obviously producing **bad fruit;** the only thing to do with **bad** trees is to **cut** them **down** and destroy them. If they do not fulfill their purpose for existence, they should be removed.

Those hearing this sermon must have wondered about the religious leaders, who seemed to be good men, teaching spiritual truths about Messiah and His kingdom. Jesus made it clear they were not good for they were leading others astray. Even if they were doing supernatural deeds—prophesying in His **name,** driving **out demons,** and performing **many miracles,** they were not obedient to the **Father,** continually doing His **will** (Matt. 7:21). They would be refused admission to **the kingdom** because Jesus had no personal relationship with them (vv. 21, 23).

7:24-27 (Luke 6:47-49). In conclusion Jesus presented the two options open to His listeners. They were now responsible for what they had heard and must make a choice. They could build on one of two foundations. One **foundation** was likened to a big **rock** and the other to **sand.** The foundation determines the ability of a structure to withstand the elements (**rain** and **winds**). The **rock** foundation represented the Lord Himself and the truths He had been presenting, especially the truth concerning inner transformation. The sand spoke of Pharisaic righteousness which the people knew and on which many were basing their hopes. In storms the first would give stability; the second would result in

The Parables of Jesus

1.	The Two Houses	Matthew 7:24-27 (Luke 6:47-49)
2.	The New Cloth and New Wineskins	Matthew 9:16-17
3.	The Sower	Matthew 13:5-8 (Mark 4:3-8; Luke 8:5-8)
4.	The Weeds	Matthew 13:24-30
5.	The Mustard Seed	Matthew 13:31-32 (Mark 4:30-32; Luke 13:18-19)
6.	The Yeast	Matthew 13:33 (Luke 13:20-21)
7.	The Hidden Treasure	Matthew 13:44
8.	The Pearl of Great Price	Matthew 13:45-46
9.	The Fishing Net	Matthew 13:47-50
10.	The Unforgiving Servant	Matthew 18:23-35
11.	The Workers in the Vineyard	Matthew 20:1-16
12.	The Two Sons	Matthew 21:28-32
13.	The Wicked Vinegrowers	Matthew 21:33-46 (Mark 12:1-12; Luke 20:9-19)
14.	The Marriage of the King's Son	Matthew 22:1-14
15.	The Two Servants	Matthew 24:45-51 (Luke 12:42-48)
16.	The 10 Virgins	Matthew 25:1-13
17.	The Talents	Matthew 25:14-30
18.	The Seed Growing Secretly	Mark 4:26-29
19.	The Doorkeeper	Mark 13:34-37
20.	The Rude Children	Luke 7:31-35
21.	The Two Debtors	Luke 7:41-43
22.	The Good Samaritan	Luke 10:25-37
23.	The Friend at Midnight	Luke 11:5-8
24.	The Rich Fool	Luke 12:16-21
25.	The Barren Fig Tree	Luke 13:6-9
26.	The Great Supper	Luke 14:15-24
27.	The Unfinished Tower and the King's Rash War	Luke 14:28-33
28.	The Lost Sheep	Matthew 18:12-14 (Luke 15:4-7)
29.	The Lost Coin	Luke 15:8-10
30.	The Prodigal Son	Luke 15:11-32
31.	The Shrewd Manager	Luke 16:1-9
32.	The Servant's Reward	Luke 17:7-10
33.	The Unjust Judge	Luke 18:1-8
34.	The Pharisee and the Taxgatherer	Luke 18:9-14
35.	The Pounds	Luke 19:1-27

Jesus' "Proverbs"

Statements

"A city on a hill cannot be hidden" (Matt. 5:14).
"Only in his hometown and in his own house is a prophet without honor" (Matt. 13:57).
"If a blind man leads a blind man, both will fall into a pit" (Matt. 15:14).
"A student is not above his teacher" (Luke 6:40).
"The worker deserves his wages" (Luke 10:7).
"Wherever there is a carcass, there the vultures will gather" (Matt. 24:28).

Questions

"You are the salt of the earth. But if the salt loses its saltiness, how can it be made salty again?" (Matt. 5:13)
"Do you bring in a lamp to put it under a bowl or a bed?" (Mark 4:21)
"Do people pick grapes from thornbushes, or figs from thistles?" (Matt. 7:16)

Command

"Physician, heal yourself!" (Luke 4:23)

---

destruction. Thus hearing and heeding Jesus' words is **wise**; one who does not is **foolish**. Only two courses of action are possible—two kinds of roads and gates (Matt. 7:13-14), two kinds of trees and fruit (vv. 15-20), two kinds of foundations and builders (vv. 24-27).

7:28-29. After recording Jesus' "Sermon on the Mount," Matthew wrote, **When Jesus had finished saying these things.** Five times Matthew wrote such a statement (identical or similar words), each time following a collection of Jesus' sayings: v. 28; 11:1; 13:53; 19:1; 26:1. These serve as turning points or shifts in the book's structure.

As a result of this sermon, **the crowds** of people following Jesus **were amazed at His teaching.** "Amazed" (*exeplēssonto*, lit., "struck out") means "overwhelmed." It suggests a strong, sudden sense of being astounded, and is stronger than *thaumazō* ("to wonder or be amazed"). Matthew used *exeplēssonto* four times (7:28; 13:54; 19:25; 22:33). Jesus had just demonstrated the inadequacies of the Pharisees' religious system. The righteousness they knew was not sufficient for entering His kingdom. The **authority** of Jesus is what amazed them, for He taught as a Spokesman from God—**not as the teachers** of His time who were simply reflecting the authority **of the Law.** The contrast between Jesus and the religious leaders was most pronounced.

III. Credentials of the King (8:1–11:1)

By word and deed Jesus Christ had authenticated Himself as the Messiah (chaps. 3–4). In a long sermon He announced the standards for entrance into His kingdom and clearly presented the way of access to it (chaps. 5–7). But the Jews still had questions on their minds. Could this One be the Messiah? If so, could He bring about the changes necessary to institute the kingdom? Did He have the power to bring about change? Matthew therefore presented a number of miracles to authenticate the King to Israel and to prove that He is able to perform His Word. These miracles demonstrated various realms in which Christ has authority.

A. His power over disease (8:1-15)

1. LEPROSY (8:1-4)

   (MARK 1:40-45; LUKE 5:12-16)

8:1-4. Significantly the first healing Matthew recorded was that of **a man with leprosy.** But Jesus had performed several miracles before that (see the list of Jesus' miracles at John 2:1-11). He **came** to Jesus, acknowledging His authority as **Lord** (cf. 7:21; 8:6). **Jesus** healed him—He **touched** the leper! (v. 3)—and then told him to **go . . . to the priest and offer the** proper sacrifice for cleansing from leprosy, as **Moses** prescribed (Lev. 14; two birds, wood, yarn, and hyssop on the first day [Lev. 14:4-8]; and on the eighth day two male lambs, a ewe lamb, flour, and oil [Lev. 14:10]). Jesus told him not to **tell anyone** before he went to the priest. Apparently Jesus wanted the priest to be the first to examine him.

Jesus said this would be **a testimony to the priests**. And so it was, for in the entire history of the nation there was no record of any Israelite being healed from leprosy other than Miriam (Num. 12:10-15). One can imagine the dramatic impact when this man suddenly appeared at the temple and announced to the priests he had been cured of leprosy! This event should have led to an examination of the circumstances surrounding the healing. Jesus in effect was presenting His "calling card" to the priests, for they would have to investigate His claims. (The healed man, however, disobeyed Jesus' orders to tell no one, for he "began to talk freely" [Mark 1:45]. Presumably, however, the man eventually made his way to the temple.)

2. PARALYSIS (8:5-13)

(LUKE 7:1-10)

8:5-13. The second miracle dealing with disease also reflected on Jesus' authority. As He **entered Capernaum, a** Roman **centurion came . . . asking for help** (see Luke 7:2 for comments on centurions). This Gentile approached Jesus as **Lord** (as did the leper, Matt. 8:2) and requested healing for a **servant** of his. Luke has *doulos* ("slave"), whereas Matthew has *pais* ("boy"), which may suggest the slave was young. He was **paralyzed** and **suffering** intensely, and he was near death (Luke 7:2).

When **Jesus** said He would **go and heal him, the centurion replied** that would not be necessary. As **a man** who was used to giving orders, he understood the principle of **authority**. One with authority does not need to be present to accomplish a task. Orders may be carried out by others even at a distance. Jesus marveled at the centurion's **great faith** (cf. Matt. 15:28), for this was the kind of faith He was vainly looking for **in Israel.** Faith such as this made entrance into His **kingdom** possible, regardless of national, racial, or geographical residence (**the East and the West**). (Eating at a banquet often pictured being in the kingdom; cf. Isa. 25:6; Matt. 22:1-14; Luke 14:15-24.) But

those who thought they would automatically gain entrance because of their religious backgrounds (they considered themselves **subjects** [lit., "sons"] **of the kingdom**) would not find entrance (Matt. 8:12). Instead they would be cast into judgment (**thrown outside, into the darkness;** cf. 22:13). Regarding **weeping and gnashing of teeth,** see comments on 13:42. In light of this centurion's faith, Jesus **healed** his servant **at that very hour.**

3. FEVER (8:14-15)

(MARK 1:29-31; LUKE 4:38-39)

8:14-15. As **Jesus** entered **Peter's house** in Capernaum, **He saw Peter's mother-in-law lying in bed with a fever.** Jesus' touch brought healing from **the fever,** but a further miracle was also evident. The woman was also given strength to get **up** from her bed and immediately be involved in work, waiting (*diēkonei*, "serving") **on** the Lord and the many disciples who were still actively following Him. Usually when a fever leaves, one's body is weak for some time, but that was not true here.

B. *His power over demonic forces (8:16-17, 28-34)*

Jesus was capable not only of bringing healing from physical sickness, but also of exercising power over demonic forces.

8:16-17 (Mark 1:32-34; Luke 4:40-41). As Jesus stayed in Peter's home, **many . . . demon-possessed** people **were brought to Him.** Matthew simply recorded that Jesus **healed** them **all,** in fulfillment of words **spoken through . . . Isaiah** (Isa. 53:4). His taking **our infirmities** (*astheneias*) and carrying **our diseases** (*nosous*) was finally accomplished on the cross in His death. But in anticipation of that event, Jesus performed many definite acts of healing in His ministry. By casting out demons, Jesus demonstrated His power over Satan, ruler of the demon world (cf. Matt. 9:34; 12:24).

8:18-27. These verses are discussed later, after verse 34.

8:28-34 (Mark 5:1-20; Luke 8:26-39). A more detailed account of Jesus' authority in the demonic realm is seen in these verses. Jesus **arrived . . . in the region of the Gadarenes.** The name "Gadarenes" comes from the town of Gadara, the capital of the region about eight miles southeast of the southern tip of the Sea of Galilee. Mark and Luke wrote that the place was "the region of the Gerasenes" (Mark 5:1; Luke 8:26). For an explanation of this difference, see comments on those two verses. There Jesus **met . . . two demon-possessed men.** Mark and Luke wrote of one demon-possessed man, but they did not say *only* one. Presumably one of the two was more violent than the other.

The influence of the demons on these men was obvious for they were wild, **violent** men, forced out of the city and living in a graveyard **(tombs).** The demons' two questions implied they knew who Jesus is—the **Son of God**—and also that His coming would ultimately mean their doom (Matt. 8:29). Rather than being forced to become disembodied spirits, **the demons** requested permission to enter a nearby **large herd of pigs.** Mark stated that this herd numbered "about 2,000" (Mark 5:13).

As soon as the demons entered them, **the whole herd rushed down the steep bank into the lake,** the Sea of Galilee, and drowned. Obviously, **those** keeping **the** herd were frightened and **went into the** nearby **town** to report this incredible event. The people of the **town went out,** and because of fear (Luke 8:37), **pleaded** with **Jesus . . . to leave their region.**

C. His power over men (8:18-22; 9:9)

In this section Matthew gave three illustrations to demonstrate the right of the King to ask servants to follow Him and to deny requests from those who were motivated improperly.

8:18-20 (Luke 9:57-58). A **teacher of the Law** (a scribe) **came to** Jesus and, seemingly without thinking, blurted out, **Teacher, I will follow You wherever You go.** Though Jesus desired disciples who would follow Him and work in His harvest fields, He wanted only those who were properly motivated. Jesus' reply to this scribe demonstrated His lowly character for He, in contrast with animals such as **foxes** and **birds,** did not even have a **place** where He could **lay His head** at night. He had no permanent home. The Lord obviously knew the heart of this person and saw that he desired fame in following a prominent Teacher. Such was not Jesus' character. This is the

first of numerous times Jesus referred to Himself or was called by others **the Son of Man** (29 times in Matt., 14 in Mark, 24 in Luke, 13 in John). It points to Jesus as the Messiah (cf. Dan. 7:13-14).

8:21-22 (Luke 9:59-60). A second **man,** already a disciple of Jesus, requested that he be permitted to return home **and bury** his **father.** This man's father was not dead or even at the point of death. This disciple was simply saying he wanted to return home and wait until his father died. Then he would return and follow Jesus. His request demonstrated he felt discipleship was something he could pick up or lay down at will. He put material concerns ahead of Jesus, for he apparently wanted to receive the estate when his father died.

Jesus' response, **Let the dead bury their own dead,** showed that following Him carried with it the highest priority. Jesus said that the physically dead could be cared for by those who are spiritually dead.

8:23–9:8. These verses are discussed after 9:9.

9:9 (Mark 2:13-14; Luke 5:27-28). While it is not clear from either of the two preceding illustrations whether those men did follow **Jesus,** the third illustration is perfectly clear. The Lord met **a man named Matthew sitting** in a **tax collector's booth.** He collected taxes on customs paid at ports, in this case, Capernaum. To him Jesus issued the command, **Follow Me.** Immediately **Matthew got up and** began following Jesus. As King, Jesus had the right to select His disciples. Matthew was no doubt profoundly impressed with Jesus' person, teaching, and authority.

D. His power over nature (8:23-27) (Mark 4:35-41; Luke 8:22-25)

8:23-27. Another realm over which Jesus has authority is nature. This was proved as Jesus and **His disciples** started across the Sea of Galilee, a sea notorious for sudden storms that swept across it. However, in the midst of **a furious storm** (lit., "great earthquake," i.e., great turbulence), **Jesus was** asleep. **The disciples,** fearful of imminent death, awakened Jesus. First He rebuked them: **You of little faith** (cf. 6:30), **why are you so afraid? Then He . . . rebuked the winds and the waves and** there was absolute **calm.** His disciples who were seasoned fishermen had been through storms on this sea that had suddenly ceased. But after the wind would pass, the waves would continue to chop for a while. No wonder Matthew recorded their amazement as they wondered **what kind of Man He is.** They **were amazed** (*ethaumasan;* cf. 9:33) at the supernatural character of the One whose rebuke was sufficient to bring nature into perfect peace. This the Messiah will do when He institutes His kingdom, as He did when He revealed Himself to His disciples.

8:28-34. See comments on these verses under "B. His power over demonic forces (8:16-17, 28-34)."

E. His power to forgive (9:1-8) (Mark 2:1-12; Luke 5:17-26)

9:1-8. Returning from the eastern side of the Sea of Galilee, **Jesus** went **to His own town,** Capernaum. There the faith of **some men** was evident when a **paralytic, lying on a mat** was brought to Jesus. Mark explained that four men lowered him through the roof (Mark 2:3-4). Several religious leaders were present and heard **Jesus** tell this man, **Take heart, son; your sins are forgiven.** (The words "Take heart" are from the Gr. word *tharseō,* used here for the first of seven times in the NT [Matt. 9:2, 22; 14:27; Mark 6:50; 10:49; John 16:33; Acts 23:11]. It means "to take courage or cheer up.") Apparently the illness had resulted from his sin. Jesus was claiming divine authority, for only God can forgive sins (Mark 2:7; Luke 5:21). The leaders stumbled over this and **said to themselves,** Jesus **is blaspheming!** This was the first opposition of the religious leaders to Jesus. **Knowing their thoughts,** Jesus asked them whether it **is easier to say** one's **sins are forgiven, or to** tell him to arise and walk. While either statement could be *spoken* with ease, the first would be "easier" in that it could not be disproved by onlookers. If, however, Jesus had first said, **Get up and walk,** and the man remained paralyzed on his mat, it would be clear Jesus was not who He claimed to be. Jesus therefore spoke not only the easier words, but He also spoke of healing, thereby proving He has power to perform both acts, healing and forgiving sin. As a result **the crowd** was **filled with awe** (this word *ephobēthēsan* differs

from the word for "amazed" [*ethaumasan,* from *thaumazō*], the disciples' reaction after the storm [Matt. 8:27]). They recognized the **authority** behind such actions, and **they praised God.**

9:9. See comments on this verse under "C. His power over men (8:18-22; 9:9)."

F. His power over traditions (9:10-17)

9:10-13 (Mark 2:15-17; Luke 5:29-32). After Matthew began to follow the Lord (Matt. 9:9), he held a **dinner at his house.** Since he had invited many of his associates to this dinner, **many tax collectors and "sinners"** were present. Perhaps this was to introduce them to the Savior. The Jews hated tax collectors, for they collected money to support the Romans, and tax collectors often took in more than necessary and pocketed the difference. Thus **the Pharisees,** who would never eat with such people, **asked** Jesus' **disciples why He** was eating with them. The Lord's response demonstrated that His ministry is directed toward those who realize they have a need: Only **sick** people **need a doctor.** The Pharisees did not think they were **sinners** (sick) so they would never have sought out the Lord (the Physician). The Pharisees always brought the proper sacrifices, but they were totally lacking in compassion toward sinners. When **mercy** is lacking, then religious formalities are meaningless (cf. Hosea 6:6).

9:14-17 (Mark 2:18-22; Luke 5:33-39). Not only did **the Pharisees** question Jesus' participation in this feast with tax collectors and "sinners," but **disciples** of John the Baptist also **came and asked** Jesus a question about taking part in such feasts. It was right for John and his disciples to **fast,** for they were calling people to repentance and to the coming kingdom. But John's disciples asked why Jesus' men were not fasting too.

Jesus answered that the kingdom is like a great feast (cf. Matt. 22:2; Isa. 25:6), in this case a wedding banquet. Since the King was now present, it was inappropriate for Him or His disciples to fast. At a wedding, people are happy and are eating, not mourning or fasting. Jesus did, however, anticipate His rejection for He added that a **time** would **come when the bridegroom** would **be taken** away.

Then He pictured the relationship between His ministry and that of John the Baptist. John was a reformer seeking to bring about repentance among those steeped in the traditions of Judaism. Jesus, however, was not out to **patch** up an old system, like sewing a new **unshrunk cloth on an old garment,** which would then **tear,** or pouring **new wine into old wineskins,** which would then **burst.** His purpose was to bring in something **new.** He had come to lead a group out of Judaism into the kingdom based on Him and His righteousness. True righteousness is not built on the Law or on Pharisaic traditions.

G. His power over death (9:18-26) (Mark 5:21-43; Luke 8:40-56)

9:18-26. In this section two miracles are described. **A ruler** (of the synagogue [Mark 5:22] probably at Capernaum), called Jairus in Mark and Luke, came to Jesus and requested healing for his **daughter** who, Luke added, was 12 years old (Luke 8:42). She had **just died,** Jairus said, but he believed Jesus could give her life. In the parallel Gospel accounts the father said she was "dying," not is "dead" (Mark 5:23; Luke 8:42). This apparent discrepancy is explained by the fact that while Jesus was speaking to Jairus, someone came from his house to tell him the girl had died. Matthew did not mention that detail, and therefore included the report of the girl's death in Jairus' request.

As **Jesus . . . went** on the way to deal with Jairus' daughter, He was interrupted by **a woman who** was **healed** as she in **faith** reached out and touched Jesus' **cloak.** Interestingly the duration of her hemorrhaging was the same as Jairus' daughter's age—**12 years.** The woman was ceremonially unclean (Lev. 15:19-30). Jesus stopped and called her **Daughter** (*thygatēr,* an affectionate term; cf. "the girl" [Matt. 9:24], *korasion,* possibly also an affectionate word like the Eng. "maiden"). Jesus said her faith was the reason she was **healed.** Undoubtedly Jairus' heart must have been encouraged by this act, for he too had faith in Jesus. On the words "take heart" (from *tharseō*) see comments on verse 2.

When the party arrived at Jairus' home, **the flute players and the noisy**

crowd (of mourners, Luke 8:52) had already assembled to weep for the family. They believed the child was **dead,** for when **Jesus** said **the girl** was merely **asleep . . . they laughed.** Jesus was not denying that she was actually dead. He was simply comparing her dead condition to sleep. Like sleep, her death was temporary, and she would rise from it. **After the crowd** was dismissed, Jesus restored the girl to life. Such power truly belongs only to God, and **news of the** event spread throughout the land (cf. Matt. 9:31).

H. His power over darkness (9:27-31)

9:27-31. As **Jesus** traveled **on,** He was **followed** by **two blind men** who appealed to Him on the basis of the fact that He is the **Son of David** (cf. 12:23; 15:22; 20:30-31). This title clearly related Jesus to the messianic line (cf. 1:1). The persistence of **the blind men** was seen as they followed Jesus into a house where He miraculously **restored** their **sight.** Their faith was genuine for they truly believed He was **able to** heal them (9:28). They affirmed His deity when they acknowledged Him as **Lord.** Their sight was restored in keeping with their **faith.** In spite of Jesus' warning to tell no one **about this** event, His fame continued to **spread** throughout the **region** (cf. v. 26; 12:16). His warning was probably given to keep multitudes from thronging to Him merely for the purpose of physical healing. While Jesus did heal many from physical diseases, His miracles were for the purpose of authenticating His claims. Jesus came primarily for spiritual healing, not physical healing.

I. His power over dumbness (9:32-34)

9:32-34. As the two former blind men were leaving the house, a **demon-possessed** man **was brought to Jesus.** The demon had prevented the man from speaking. Jesus immediately healed him. When the **dumb** man **spoke, the crowd** marveled (*ethaumasan;* cf. 8:27) **and said, Nothing like this has ever been seen in Israel.** However, the religious leaders did not draw the same conclusion. They believed that Jesus was performing His miracles by the power of Satan, **the prince of demons** (cf. 10:25; 12:22-37).

J. His power to delegate authority (9:35–11:1)

1. THE WORK OBSERVED (9:35-38)

9:35-38. In verse 35 Matthew summarized Jesus' threefold ministry (see comments on 4:23, with its almost identical wording). **Jesus had been going through all the towns and villages of** Israel, **teaching** and **preaching** about **the kingdom.** His **healing** ministry was for the purpose of authenticating His Person. The spectacular nature of Jesus' ministry attracted large **crowds.**

As Jesus observed the crowds, **He had compassion** toward them. The verb "to have compassion" (*splanchnizomai*) is used in the New Testament only by the Synoptic Gospel writers: five times in Matthew (9:36; 14:14; 15:32; 18:27; 20:34), four in Mark (1:41; 6:34; 8:2; 9:22), and three in Luke (7:13; 10:33; 15:20; see comments on Luke 7:13). Suggesting strong emotion, it means "to feel deep sympathy." The related noun *splanchna* ("sympathy, affection, or inward feelings") is used once by Luke (1:78), eight times by Paul, and once by John (1 John 3:17).

Jesus saw that the people **were harassed and helpless, like sheep without a shepherd.** Like sheep bothered by wolves, lying down and unable to help themselves, and having no shepherd to guide and protect them, the people were maligned by the religious leaders, helpless before them, and wandering about with no spiritual guidance. The religious leaders, who should have been their shepherds, were keeping the sheep from following the true Shepherd. In response to the people's "helpless" condition, Jesus encouraged **His disciples** to beseech the **Lord of the harvest,** namely, God the Father, **to send out** additional **workers** (cf. Luke 10:2). **The harvest** was ready; for the kingdom was at hand (Matt. 4:17). But additional laborers were necessary to complete the harvest.

2. THE WORKERS NOTED (10:1-4) (MARK 3:13-19; LUKE 6:12-16)

10:1-4. It is not surprising that a listing of laborers follows Jesus' injunction in 9:38 to ask the Father for laborers. **Twelve** of the **disciples** (10:1) who were following Jesus (a "disciple," *mathētēs,* was a learner; cf. 11:29) were designated as "apostles." These Twelve were specifi-

cally sent forth ("apostle" means "one sent forth to represent an official") by Jesus and given His **authority to** cast **out** demons **and** heal **every kind of disease and sickness.** The **12 Apostles** were here named in pairs and probably were sent out in that fashion ("He sent them out two by two" [Mark 6:7]).

Each time the 12 Apostles are listed, Peter is mentioned first (because of his prominence) and Judas, last. Jesus had changed Simon's name to **Peter** (John 1:42). Soon after the brothers Peter and **Andrew** followed Jesus, another set of brothers—**James** and **John**—did the same (Matt. 4:18-22). **Philip,** like Andrew and Peter, was from Bethsaida by the Sea of Galilee (John 1:44). Nothing is known about **Bartholomew,** except that he was possibly known as Nathanael (John 1:45-51). **Thomas** was called "Didymus" (twin) in John 11:16; he was one who questioned Jesus' resurrection (John 20:24-27). **Matthew** referred to himself by his former dubious occupation of **tax** collecting (whereas Mark and Luke simply listed him as Matthew). **James son of Alphaeus** is mentioned only in the lists of apostles; **Thaddaeus** may be the same as Judas, son of James (Luke 6:16; Acts 1:13). **Simon the Zealot** had been a member of the revolutionary Jewish Zealots, a political party that sought to overthrow the Roman Empire. And **Judas Iscariot,** of course, later betrayed the Lord (Matt. 26:47-50). "Iscariot" may mean "from Kerioth," a Judean town.

3. THE WORKERS INSTRUCTED (10:5-23)

a. *The appropriate message (10:5-15)* *(Mark 6:7-13; Luke 9:1-6)*

10:5-15. The message the 12 Apostles were to give concerning **the kingdom** (v. 7) was identical to John the Baptist's message (3:1) and Jesus' message (4:17). In addition Jesus told them to limit their proclamation to the nation Israel. In fact He specifically told them **not** to **go** to **the Gentiles or** to **the Samaritans.** The latter were half-breeds, part Jewish and part Gentile, whose origin began soon after 722 B.C. when Assyria conquered the Northern Kingdom and moved conquered peoples of northern Mesopotamia into Israel where they intermarried. The apostles were to **go** only **to the lost sheep of Israel** (cf. 15:24) because the kingdom **message** was for God's covenant people.

She needed to accept her King, who had arrived. If she did the nations would then be blessed through her (Gen. 12:3; Isa. 60:3).

The apostles' message, like their Lord's, would be authenticated by miracles (Matt. 10:8; cf. 9:35). They were not to make elaborate provisions for their travel, thus avoiding the impression they were engaged in a business enterprise. Included in the list of items they were **not** to **take** was **a staff** (cf. Luke 9:3). Mark, however, recorded that the apostles *could* take a staff (Mark 6:8). This problem is solved by observing that Matthew said they were not to "procure" (*ktēsēsthe*) extra items (Matt. 10:9), but Mark wrote that they could "take" (*airōsen*) any staffs they already had.

As the apostles ministered, they in turn were to be ministered to by their recipients. In every **town or village** they were to find a **worthy person . . . and stay** with that individual. Such "worthiness" would obviously be determined by a favorable response to the message preached. Those who rejected the message and failed to **welcome** the apostles were to be passed by. Shaking **the dust off** their **feet** as they left an inhospitable place symbolized their rejection of the Jewish city as if it were a despised Gentile city, whose very dust was unwanted. The Lord said that judgment on such people would be greater than that on **Sodom and Gomorrah** (Gen. 19) when the final **day of judgment** comes. (**I tell you the truth** occurs in Matt. 10:15, 23, 42; cf. comments on 5:18.)

b. The anticipated response (10:16-23)
(Mark 13:9-13; Luke 21:12-17)

10:16-23. The Lord's words to the apostles concerning the response to their ministry were not encouraging. Their task would be difficult for they would be **like sheep among wolves** (cf. 7:15, where false prophets are spoken of as "ferocious wolves"). It would be essential for them to **be as shrewd as snakes and as innocent as doves,** that is, wise in avoiding danger but harmless in not forcibly opposing the enemy. "Innocent" translates *akeraioi* (lit., "unmixed, pure"). It is used only twice elsewhere in the New Testament: Romans 16:19 and Philippians 2:15. In carrying out their ministries the apostles would be taken before their own

Jewish leaders and flogged (cf. Acts 5:40) and **be brought before** Roman **governors and** Herodian **kings.** But the messengers need **not worry,** for the Holy Spirit, called here **the Spirit of your Father,** would give them words to say that would free them from **arrest.**

Even if the persecutions went to the point of betrayal of family members (Matt. 10:21) and extreme hatred (v. 22), Jesus promised them ultimate deliverance. The apostles were to continue their ministries, moving from **place** to place. But even though they moved out for the Lord, they would not be able to reach all **the cities of Israel before the Son of Man** would come.

These words of the Lord probably had an application beyond His own lifetime. What was proclaimed here was more fully demonstrated in the apostles' lives after the day of Pentecost (Acts 2) in the spread of the gospel in the church (e.g., Acts 4:1-13; 5:17-18, 40; 7:54-60). But these words will find their fullest manifestation in the days of the Tribulation when the gospel will be carried throughout the entire world before Jesus Christ returns in power and glory to establish His kingdom on the earth (Matt. 24:14).

4. THE WORKERS COMFORTED (10:24-33)
(LUKE 12:2-9)

10:24-33. Jesus reminded the apostles He was not asking something of them He Himself had not already experienced. In reaction to His casting out a demon, the religious leaders had claimed He was working by the prince of the demons (cf. 9:34). If they accused Jesus (**the Head of the house**) of demonic power, surely they would say the same thing of His servants (**the members of His household**). Beelzebub (the Gr. has *Beezeboul*) was a name for Satan, the prince of the demons, perhaps derived from Baal-Zebub, god of the Philistine city of Ekron (2 Kings 1:2). "Beelzebub" means "lord of the flies," and "Beezeboul" or "Beelzeboul" means "lord of the high place."

However, the apostles need not fear the religious leaders who could destroy only **the** physical **body** (Matt. 10:28). The leaders' true motives will be revealed in the judgment (v. 26). Obedience to God, who ultimately is in charge of physical as well as spiritual life, is far more crucial.

The message they had received from the Lord privately (in the dark . . . whispered), they were to proclaim publicly without fear (speak in the daylight . . . proclaim from the [flat] housetops), for their Father was truly concerned for them and aware of their circumstances. He is aware of the death of a sparrow which is worth so little. Two sparrows were sold for a mere penny (assarion, a Gr. copper coin worth about 1/16 of a Roman denarius, a day's wages). God the Father also knows the number of hairs on a person's head (v. 30). The apostles were instructed not to fear for they, being far more valuable to God than sparrows, were seen and known by Him. Instead they were faithfully to confess (acknowledge, homologēsei) Jesus before men (v. 32). This would result in the Lord's acknowledging His servants before His Father; but failure to confess Him would result in His denial of them. Of the original 12 Apostles, only one, Judas Iscariot, fell into the latter category.

5. THE WORKERS ADMONISHED (10:34-39)
(LUKE 12:51-53; 14:26-27)

10:34-39. Jesus said He had come at this time not . . . to bring peace to the earth . . . but a sword which divides and severs. As a result of His visit to earth, some children would be set against parents and a man's enemies might be those within his own household. This is because some who follow Christ are hated by their family members. This may be part of the cost of discipleship, for love of family should not be greater than love for the Lord (v. 37; cf. comments on Luke 14:26). A true disciple must take his cross and follow Jesus (cf. Matt. 16:24). He must be willing to face not only family hatred, but also death, like a criminal carrying his cross to his own execution. In addition, in those days a criminal carrying his cross was tacitly admitting that the Roman Empire was correct in executing its death sentence on him. Similarly Jesus' followers were admitting His right over their lives. In so doing one would find his life in return for having given it up to Jesus Christ (cf. comments on 16:25).

6. THE WORKERS REWARDED (10:40–11:1)
(MARK 9:41)

10:40-11:1. Those who faithfully served the Lord and who faithfully received these workers were promised rewards. To receive a prophet and his message was tantamount to receiving Jesus Christ. (Here the apostles were called prophets for they were recipients and communicators of God's message; cf. 10:27.) Therefore even a cup of cold water given to one of these little ones, these insignificant disciples of Jesus, would be detected by the One who keeps accounts. The reward is in keeping with the act performed. With these words of instruction, Jesus departed to teach and preach in . . . Galilee (11:1). With the Twelve having received delegated authority from the Lord, it may be assumed that they departed and carried out Jesus' instructions. The words, After Jesus had finished instructing, indicate another turning point in the book (cf. 7:28; 13:53; 19:1; 26:1).

IV. Challenge to the King's Authority (11:2–16:12)

A. Seen in the rejection of John the Baptist (11:2-19)
(Luke 7:18-35)

1. JOHN'S INQUIRY (11:2-3)

11:2-3. Matthew had recorded (4:12) that John the Baptist had been put in prison. The cause for his imprisonment was stated by Matthew later (14:3-4). When John heard of all Jesus was doing, he sent some of his disciples to ask Jesus, Are You the One who was to come, or should we expect someone else? The words "the One who was to come" are a messianic title based on Psalms 40:7 and 118:26 (cf. Mark 11:9; Luke 13:35). John must have thought, If I am Messiah's forerunner and Jesus is the Messiah, why am I in prison? John needed reassurance and clarification, for he had expected the Messiah to overcome wickedness, judge sin, and bring in His kingdom.

2. JESUS' ANSWER (11:4-6)

11:4-6. Jesus did not answer John with a direct yes or no. Instead, He told John's disciples, Go back and report to John what they heard and saw taking place. Among the notable events occurring were the blind being given sight . . . lame people walking, lepers being cured, the deaf hearing, the dead being given life, and the good news being preached to the poor. These works would, of course, indicate that Jesus indeed is the Messiah (Isa. 35:5-6; 61:1). Those who did not miss the true character of the Lord would be truly **blessed.** Though He will ultimately bring judgment to this world by judging sin when He brings in His kingdom, the timing then was not appropriate. Israel's rejection of Him was causing a postponement in establishing the physical kingdom. But all, including John, who truly perceived the person and work of Christ would be blessed.

3. JESUS' DISCOURSE (11:7-19)

11:7-15. John's question prompted **Jesus** to give a discourse **to the crowd.** Perhaps some began to wonder **about** John's commitment to the Messiah in light of his question. So Jesus explained that **John** was not weak and vacillating. He was not a papyrus **reed** that could be shaken by every breeze that blew. Nor was he **a man dressed in fine clothes,** the kind worn **in kings' palaces.** In fact John the Baptist wore the opposite (3:4). John was a true **prophet** who proclaimed the message that God demanded repentance. In fact he was even **more than a prophet,** for he, in fulfillment of Malachi 3:1, was Jesus' own **messenger** or forerunner. Mark in his Gospel (Mark 1:2-3) combined this prophecy from Malachi 3:1 with Isaiah's prophecy (Isa. 40:3) concerning the one who would **prepare** Jesus' **way.** Jesus added that of all men who had lived on earth, none was **greater than John the Baptist.** And **yet** one **who is least in the kingdom** will be **greater than** John. The privileges of Jesus' disciples sharing in the kingdom will be far greater than anything anyone could experience on earth.

But **the kingdom** had been subject to violence and evil men were trying to take it by force (Matt. 11:12). The religious leaders of Jesus' day **(forceful men)** were resisting the movement introduced by John, Jesus, and the apostles. **Forcefully advancing** (*biazetai*) could be rendered in the passive, "is violently treated." (The verb **lay hold of** [*harpazousin*] means "to grasp" in the sense of resisting or laying claim to it on their own). Those leaders wanted a kingdom, but not the kind Jesus was offering. So they were resisting the message and attempting to establish their own rule. But John's message was true, and **if** the nation would **accept it,** and

consequently accept Jesus, John would fulfill the prophecies of Elijah. Only if they accepted the message would John the Baptist be **the Elijah who was to come** (cf. Mal. 4:5). Because the nation rejected the Messiah, Elijah's coming is still future (cf. Mal. 4:6 with Acts 3:21).

11:16-19. Jesus compared that **generation** to a group of little **children sitting in the marketplaces** who could not be pleased by anything. Like children rejecting the suggestions to "play" wedding **(flute . . . dance)** or funeral **(dirge . . . mourn)** music, the people rejected both **John** and Jesus. They were not satisfied with John the Baptist because he did not eat or drink, or with Jesus who did eat and drink with sinners. **They** said John had **a demon,** and they rejected Jesus as **a glutton and a drunkard and a friend of tax collectors and "sinners."** Though that generation was not happy with anything, the **wisdom** of the approach of both John and Jesus would be **proved right** by the results, namely, that many people would be brought into the kingdom.

B. *Seen in the condemnation of the cities (11:20-30)*
(Luke 10:13-15, 21-22)

11:20-24. Though it was not Jesus' primary thrust in His First Advent to pronounce judgment, He did **denounce** sin. Here He specifically pronounced condemnation against **the cities in which** some of His **most** significant **miracles had** occurred—**Korazin . . . Bethsaida,** and **Capernaum,** all three near the Sea of Galilee's northwest shore. By contrast, three terribly wicked Gentile cities—**Tyre and Sidon** (v. 22), cities on the Phoenician coast 35 and 60 miles, respectively, from the Sea of Galilee (cf. 15:21), and **Sodom** (11:23), more than 100 miles south— **would have repented if** they had seen Jesus' **miracles.** Their judgment, though terrible, is less than that on the Jewish cities. All three Galilean cities, in spite of their greater "light," rejected the Messiah, and are today in ruins. Though Jesus lived in Capernaum for some time, it would not **be lifted up to the skies,** or exalted. Instead its inhabitants would **go down to the depths,** literally, to hades, the place of the dead.

11:25-30. In contrast with His condemnation on the three Galilean cities

(vv. 20-24), Jesus issued a great call to those who in faith would turn to Him. Jesus had previously condemned that generation for their childish reactions (vv. 16-19). Here He declared that true discipleship can be enjoyed only by those who come to Him in childlike faith. God in His **good pleasure** (cf. Eph. 1:5) had **hidden** the great mysteries of His wise dealings **from the wise and learned** (the leaders of that day) but had **revealed them to little children.** This was possible because God the **Son** and God the **Father** know each other perfectly in the intimacy of the Trinity (Matt. 11:27). ("Father" occurs five times in vv. 25-27.) Hence the only ones who can know **the Father** and the things He has revealed are those **whom the Son chooses** (cf. John 6:37).

Therefore Jesus issued a call to **all . . . who are weary** (*hoi kopiōntes,* "those tired from hard toil") **and burdened** (*pephortismenoi,* "those loaded down"; cf. *phortion,* "load," in Matt. 11:30) to **come to** Him. People's weariness comes from enduring their burdens, probably the burdens of sin and its consequences. Rather, they should come and yoke themselves with Jesus. By placing themselves under His **yoke** and learning **from** Him, they may **find rest for** their **souls** from sins' burdens. By yoking, they become true disciples of Jesus and join Him in His proclamation of divine wisdom. To **learn** (*mathete*) from Him is to be His disciple (*mathētēs*). People can trade their heavy, tiring burdens for His **yoke** and **burden** (*phortion,* "load"), which by contrast are **easy** and **light.** To serve Him is no burden, for He, in contrast with those who reject Him, is **gentle** (*praus;* cf. 5:5) **and humble.**

C. *Seen in the controversies over His authority (chap. 12)*

1. SABBATH CONTROVERSIES (12:1-21)

a. *Working on the Sabbath (12:1-8)*
   (Mark 2:23-28; Luke 6:1-5)

12:1-8. As **Jesus** and **His disciples were going through the grainfields on the Sabbath,** His disciples **began to pick the wheat and eat the grain.** The **Pharisees** immediately jumped on this "violation" of the Law (Ex. 20:8-11) and accused the **disciples** of working **on the Sabbath.** According to the Pharisees, plucking wheat from its stem is reaping, rubbing the wheat heads between one's palms is threshing, and blowing away the chaff is winnowing!

Jesus, however, disputed the Pharisees' claim, using three illustrations. First, he cited an event in the life of **David** (Matt. 12:3-4). As he fled from Saul, David was given **the consecrated bread which** had been removed from the tabernacle (1 Sam. 21:1-6), and was normally reserved **for the priests** alone (Lev. 24:9). David believed that preserving his life was more important than observing a technicality. Second, **the priests in the temple** were involved in work on the Sabbath (Matt. 12:5; cf. Num. 28:9-10, 18-19), **yet** they were considered blameless. Third, Jesus argued that He Himself was **greater than the temple** (Matt. 12:6; cf. "One greater" in vv. 41-42), for He **is Lord of the Sabbath,** that is, He controls what can be done on it, and He did not condemn the disciples (**the innocent**) for their action. The Pharisees were splitting hairs with their technicalities about reaping, threshing, and winnowing. They failed to understand compassion for people's basic needs (in this case, the disciples' hunger; cf. Deut. 23:24-25), but were intense in their concern for the sacrifices. Jesus reminded them of the words in Hosea 6:6, **I desire mercy, not sacrifice,** that is, inner spiritual vitality, not mere external formality.

b. *Healing on the Sabbath (12:9-14)*
   (Mark 3:1-6; Luke 6:6-11)

12:9-14. The first controversy (vv. 1-8) was barely over when Jesus arrived in the **synagogue.** Since it was **the Sabbath** Day, one would expect Jesus to be in the synagogue. **A man with a shriveled hand was there.** Since the **Pharisees** were continually **looking for** some way **to accuse Jesus, they** undoubtedly planted this man in the synagogue to create an incident. The Pharisees raised the question, **Is it lawful to heal on the Sabbath?** Jesus answered their question, as He often did, with another question. **If** one's **sheep** would fall **into a pit on the Sabbath,** would he not . . . **lift** the sheep **out** of the pit, even though this might be construed as work? An act of mercy toward an animal was perfectly in order. Since people are **much more valuable** than animals, mercy should be extended toward them even on Sabbath Days. Jesus thus removed any possible objection to what He was going to do, for Scripture did not forbid it and His logic was flawless. His healing **the man,** however, did not prompt faith in the Pharisees for they **went out and plotted how they might kill Jesus.**

c. Jesus' reaction (12:15-21)

12:15-21. Jesus knew what the Pharisees were trying to do through these Sabbath controversies. As **many** people continued to follow **Him . . . He healed all their sick** but warned **them not to tell who He** is (cf. 9:30). To publicize that He is the Messiah would only invite more opposition. **This was to fulfill** the prophecy in **Isaiah** (42:1-4), obviously a messianic passage. "It suits Matthew's argument well. First, it shows how the withdrawal of the King fits the work of the Messiah. He shall not wrangle or cry out in the streets. It is also a fitting picture of His compassion, for he will not break a battered reed or put out a smoldering wick. . . . A second argument presented by the prophecy is the divine approval of the Messiah. Though He does not cry out or engage in open conflicts, He is still God's Servant who shall carry out God's program" (Toussaint, *Behold the King,* p. 161).

The Trinity appears in Matthew 12:18 (quoting from Isa. 42:1). God the Father spoke of Christ as **My Servant,** and His **Spirit** was **on** the Messiah, who proclaimed **justice.** In Christ **the nations . . . hope** (Matt. 12:21).

2. SATANIC CONDEMNATION (12:22-37)
(MARK 3:20-30; LUKE 11:14-23; 12:10)

12:22-24. Though the text does not state who **brought** this **demon-possessed man to Jesus . . . they** (v. 22) may refer to **the Pharisees** (cf. v. 14). Probably the Pharisees discovered this man and realized the difficult nature of his case. He **was** both **blind and mute,** so communication with him was almost impossible. The man could not see what someone might want him to do, and while he could hear instructions, he would not be able to respond. Jesus immediately **healed him** by removing the demon, and the man **both** spoke and saw. **The people** (lit., "all the crowds") **were astonished** (*existanto,* "were beside themselves"; cf. comments

on 7:28 on other words for amazement) and asked, **Could this be the Son of David?** In other words, "Is not this the promised Messiah, David's Descendant (cf. 2 Sam. 7:14-16) who has come to rule over us and bring healing to our nation?" While the people were asking this question, the Pharisees were concluding that Jesus' power must be attributed to **Beelzebub, the prince of demons** (cf. Matt. 9:34; on the meaning of "Beelzebub" see comments on 10:25; Mark 3:22).

12:25-29. Knowing what the Pharisees were thinking, **Jesus** defended His authority. This was one of the few times He did so, but the issue was clear. Jesus gave three arguments to answer the claim that He was working by Satan's power. First, He said if He were casting out a demon by Satan's power, then **Satan** would be working **against himself** (vv. 25-26). Why would **Satan** let Jesus cast out a demon and free a man who was already under his control? To do so would divide Satan's **kingdom** and bring it to destruction.

Second, Jesus asked them about contemporary Jewish exorcists, those who were able to cast **out demons** by the power of God (v. 27). The apostles had been given that authority (10:1) and others were thought to possess such power. Jesus was saying in essence, "If you believe exorcists work by the power of God in casting out demons, why do you not think I have that same divine power?"

Third, by driving **out demons,** He was proving He was greater than Satan. He was able to go into Satan's realm (the **strong man's house**), the demonic world, and come away with the spoils of victory (12:29). Since He could do this, He was able to institute **the kingdom of God** among them (v. 28). If He were driving out demons by Satan's power, He certainly could not be offering the people God's kingdom. That would be contradictory. The fact that He was coming to establish the kingdom clearly showed that He worked by the power of **the Spirit of God,** not by Satan's power.

12:30-37. Jesus then invited the people to make a clear decision. They must either be **with** Him or **against** Him. He gave a strong warning to those moving away from Him. Understandably some would not comprehend who Jesus is. A divine Person living among men would naturally not be appreciated fully. That was why allowances for such actions were made: **Anyone who speaks a word against the Son of Man will be forgiven.** But while the person of Jesus was not fully comprehended, the power evidenced through Him should never have been misunderstood, especially by religious leaders.

The nation, because of its leaders, was on the brink of making a decision that would bring irreversible consequences. They were about to attribute incorrectly to Satan the power of **the Holy Spirit** exercised through Jesus and thus to commit **the blasphemy against the Spirit.** This specific sin cannot be reproduced today, for it required Jesus' presence on earth with His performing miracles through the Spirit's power. If, however, the leaders, acting on behalf of the nation, concluded that Jesus was empowered by Satan, they would commit a sin that would never find national or individual forgiveness (**in this Age or in the Age to come**). The consequences would bring about God's judgment on the nation and on any individual who persisted in that view.

The contrasts Jesus made between the **good** tree **and its fruit** and the **bad** tree **and its fruit** demonstrated the choices (cf. 7:16-20). Jesus condemned the Pharisees as a **brood of vipers** who could never **say anything good** because their hearts were **evil.** People are responsible for all their actions and **words,** which will acquit or condemn them **on the day of judgment.**

3. SIGN-SEEKERS (12:38-50)

12:38-42 (Luke 11:29-32). Though Jesus had just performed a significant sign-miracle, the religious leaders asked for **a miraculous sign** (cf. Matt. 16:1). Their statement implied that they rejected the many signs given so far. In effect they were saying, "We would just like to see *one* good sign from You." The Lord suggested that signs should not be necessary for faith, even though He had given them many signs. Only **a wicked and adulterous generation** asked for signs (cf. 16:4). ("Adulterous" [*moichalis*] suggests that Israel was spiritually unfaithful to God by its religious formality and its rejection of the Messiah.)

But no more signs would **be given** to that generation **except the sign of the Prophet Jonah** (cf. 16:4). **As Jonah was . . . in the belly of a huge fish** for **three days and three nights . . . the Son of Man** would be **in the heart of the earth** for **three days and three nights.** (Since the Jews reckoned part of a day as a full day, the "three days and three nights" could permit a Friday crucifixion.) Of course, by giving this sign Jesus was demonstrating that they had already decided to reject Him. For Him to fulfill this sign, He would have to be rejected, die, and be buried. By the time this sign would be accomplished, it would be too late for them to accept His right to rule over the nation as King.

The generation He addressed had an unusual privilege, afforded to no previous generation. **The men of Nineveh . . . repented at the preaching of** a mere man, **Jonah. The Queen of the South** (i.e., the Queen of Sheba; 1 Kings 10:1-13) **came . . . to listen to** the **wisdom** of a man, **Solomon.** The response of the Ninevites and of the Queen was commendable. But **One greater than** Jonah and Solomon (cf. Matt. 12:6) was with this generation, and instead of accepting Him, they were rejecting Him. (The words **One greater than** should be trans. "something greater than," referring to the kingdom, for the word *pleion* ["greater than"] is neuter, not masc.) Their judgment will be certain when they stand before the Judge in the final day. Again pagan peoples were more responsive than the Jewish nation itself (cf. 11:20-24).

12:43-45 (Luke 11:24-26). This generation of sign-seekers stood condemned in the final judgment. To show what their condition on earth would be if they persisted in unbelief, Jesus compared them to **a man** who had found deliverance from a demon (**an evil spirit**), perhaps through a Jewish exorcist (cf. Matt. 12:27). After the man was delivered, he tried by every natural means to **clean** up his life and set things **in order.** But mere "religion" is never effective so the man lacked a supernatural conversion. Consequently he was subject to possession again with more serious ramifications. Instead of one demon possessing him, he became possessed by **seven other spirits.** His latter **condition** was **worse than** his former. The Pharisees

---

New Testament "Mysteries" (previously unknown, but now-revealed truths)

Matthew 13:11—"the secrets [mysteries] of the kingdom of heaven"

Luke 8:10—"the secrets [mysteries] of the kingdom of God"

Romans 11:25—"this mystery . . . Israel has experienced a hardening in part"

Romans 16:25-26—"the mystery hidden for long ages past, but now revealed"

1 Corinthians 4:1—"servants of Christ . . . entrusted with the secret things [mysteries] of God"

Ephesians 1:9—"the mystery of His will"

Ephesians 3:2-3—"the administration of God's grace . . . the mystery made known to me by revelation"

Ephesians 3:4—"the mystery of Christ"

Ephesians 3:9—"this mystery, which for ages past was kept hidden in God"

Ephesians 5:32—"a profound mystery . . . Christ and the church"

Colossians 1:26—"the mystery . . . kept hidden for ages and generations, but . . . now disclosed"

Colossians 1:27—"this mystery, which is Christ in you"

Colossians 2:2—"the mystery of God, namely, Christ"

Colossians 4:3—"the mystery of Christ"

2 Thessalonians 2:7—"the secret power [mystery] of lawlessness is already at work"

1 Timothy 3:9—"keep hold of the deep truths [mysteries] of the faith"

1 Timothy 3:16—"the mystery of godliness is great"

Revelation 1:20—"the mystery of the seven stars . . . is this: [they] are the angels"

Revelation 10:7—"the mystery of God will be accomplished"

Revelation 17:5—"Mystery, Babylon the Great"

---

and other religious leaders were in danger of that happening to them for their attempts at reformation, without the power of God, were sterile. They clearly did not understand God's power, for they had just confused the power of the Spirit with the power of Satan (vv. 24-28). Thus they were wide-open targets for Satan.

12:46-50 (Mark 3:31-35; Luke 8:19-21). As Jesus concluded His statements, **His mother and brothers** desired to communicate with **Him.** The Apostle John made it clear that His brothers (actually half brothers, born to Mary after Jesus was born) did not believe in Him before His resurrection (John 7:5). Perhaps here they were trying to attach themselves to Jesus and receive special favors through family ties. Jesus stated that true discipleship comes not through physical relationships but only through obedience to **the will of** the **Father.** Mere religion (Matt. 12:43-45) and family relationships (vv. 46-50) cannot obtain merit before God. Following God's will makes one a disciple (cf. 7:21).

D. *Seen in the change in the kingdom program (13:1-52)*

The previous chapter (12) is probably the major turning point in the book. The King had authenticated His power by various miracles. But growing opposition to the King climaxed when Israel's leaders concluded that Jesus worked not by divine power but by satanic power (9:34; 12:22-37). While their full rejection of Him did not occur until later, the die was cast. Therefore Jesus turned to His disciples and began to instruct them along different lines. This is one of several major discourses in the Gospel of Matthew (others are in chaps. 5–7; 10; 23–25).

1. THE PARABLE OF THE SOWER (13:1-23)

13:1-9 (Mark 4:1-9; Luke 8:4-8). As **Jesus** continued to minister to **crowds** of people, He did something He had not done before. For the first time in Matthew's Gospel, Jesus told **parables.** The word "parable" comes from two Greek words (*para* and *ballō*), which together mean "to throw alongside." A parable, like an illustration, makes a comparison between a known truth and an unknown truth; it throws them alongside each other. In the first of seven parables in this chapter Jesus told about **a farmer** who sowed **seed** in his field. The emphasis in the story is on the results of the sowing, for the seed **fell** on four kinds of soil: **along the path** (Matt. 13:4), **on rocky places** (v. 5), **among thorns** (v. 7), **and on good soil** (v. 8). So the farmer had four kinds of results.

13:10-17 (Mark 4:10-12; Luke 8:9-10). The disciples immediately noticed a change in Jesus' method of teaching. They **came** and **asked** Him directly **why** He was speaking **in parables.** The Lord gave three reasons. First, He was communicating through parables in order to continue to reveal truth to His disciples (Matt. 13:11-12a). The Lord said He was making known to them **the secrets of the kingdom of heaven.** The word "secrets" is translated "mysteries" in other Bible versions and in most of its other NIV occurrences. This term in the New Testament referred to truths not revealed in the Old Testament but which now were made known to those instructed.

Why did Matthew frequently use the term "kingdom of heaven" whereas Mark, Luke, and John used only "kingdom of God" and never "kingdom of heaven"? Some scholars answer that "heaven" was a softened reference to God by Jews who, out of reverence, avoided saying the word "God." However, Matthew did occasionally write "kingdom of God" (12:28; 19:24; 21:31, 43). And he used the word "God" almost 50 times. A distinction seems intended: The "kingdom of God" never includes unsaved people, but the "kingdom of heaven" includes both saved people and also others who profess to be Christians but are not. This is seen in the Parable of the Wheat and Weeds (see comments on 13:24-30, 36-43), the Parable of the Mustard Seed (see comments on vv. 31-35), and the Parable of the Net (see comments on vv. 47-52).

Significantly Jesus did not speak of any "mysteries" concerning the kingdom of heaven until the nation had made its decision concerning Him. That decision was made by the leaders when they attributed His divine power to Satan (9:34; 12:22-37). Now Jesus unveiled certain additional facts not given in the Old Testament about His reign on earth. Many Old Testament prophets had predicted that the Messiah would deliver the nation Israel and establish His kingdom on the earth. Jesus came and offered the kingdom (4:17), but the nation rejected Him (12:24). In view of that rejection what would happen to God's kingdom? The "secrets" of the kingdom now reveal that an entire Age would intervene between Israel's rejection of the King and her later acceptance of Him.

Second, Jesus spoke in parables to hide the truth from unbelievers. The secrets of the kingdom would be given to the disciples, but would be hidden from the religious leaders who rejected Him (13:11b, **but not to them).** In fact, even what they had previously known would no longer be clear to them (v. 12). Jesus' parabolic instruction thus carried with it a judgmental aspect. By using parables in public, Jesus could preach to as many individuals as before, but He could then draw the disciples aside and explain to them fully the meaning of His words.

Third, He spoke in parables in order to fulfill Isaiah 6:9-10. As **Isaiah** began his ministry, God told him that people would not comprehend his message. Jesus experienced the same kind of response. He preached the Word of God and many people saw but they did not truly perceive; they heard but did **not . . . understand** (Matt. 13:13-15).

By contrast, the disciples were **blessed** because they were privileged to **see** (understand) and **hear** these truths (v. 16), truths that people in Old Testament times **longed to** know (v. 17; cf. 1 Peter 1:10-11). Jesus' disciples heard the same truths as the national leaders, but their response was entirely different. The disciples saw and believed; the leaders saw and rejected. Since the leaders turned from the light they had been **given,** God gave them no additional light.

13:18-23 (Mark 4:13-20; Luke 8:11-15). In Jesus' interpretation of **the Parable of the Sower,** He compared the four results of sowing to four responses to the **kingdom** message. This was **the message** preached by John, Jesus, and the apostles. First, when one **hears** the message but **does not understand it, the** devil **(evil one;** cf. Matt. 13:38-39; 1 John

5:19) **snatches away** the Word that **was sown. This is seed sown** on **the path.** The next two results—represented by seed **on rocky places** that had **no root,** and by seed **among the thorns (worries** and **wealth)** that **choke it** out—speak of hearers' *initial* interest, but with no genuine heartfelt response. The seed on rocky soil speaks of a person who hears the Word but **falls away** (lit., "is offended," *skandalizetai*; cf. Matt. 13:57; 15:12) when he faces **trouble** for having expressed interest in the Word. Only the seed that fell **on good soil** had an abiding result and the production of **a crop** that increased **100, 60, or 30 times what** had been **sown.** The one who believes Jesus' word **(the man who hears the Word and understands it)** will then receive and understand even more (cf. 13:12).

The difference in these results was not in the seed but in the soil on which the seed fell. As the gospel of the kingdom was presented, the good news was the same. The difference was in the individuals who heard that Word. The Lord was not saying that an exact 25 percent of those who heard the message would believe. But He was saying that a majority would not respond positively to the good news. In this parable Jesus demonstrated why the Pharisees and religious leaders rejected His message. They were not "prepared soil" for the Word. The "mystery" concerning the kingdom Jesus presented here was the truth that the good news was rejected by the majority. This had not been revealed in the Old Testament.

2. THE PARABLE OF THE WHEAT AND THE WEEDS (13:24-30, 36-43)

13:24-30. In the second **parable,** Jesus again used the figure of the sower, but with a different twist. After a farmer **sowed** his wheat **seed,** an **enemy came** at night and **sowed weeds** on the same soil. As a result, **the wheat** and **the weeds** grew together and would continue to do so till the time of **harvest,** for removing **the weeds** early would result in destroying **the wheat** (vv. 28-29). Therefore they must **grow together until the harvest** when **the weeds** would **first** be gathered out and destroyed. **Then . . . the wheat** would be gathered **into the barn.**

13:31-35. These verses are discussed later, after verse 43.

13:36-43. As Jesus and **His disciples** came **into** a **house** away from **the crowd** they asked for an explanation of this "wheat and weeds" **parable.** First, He said, the sower of **the good seed is the Son of Man,** the Lord Himself. This fact is an important starting point for understanding parables. The parables cover the time beginning with the Lord Himself on earth ministering and proclaiming the good news.

Second, **the field is the world** into which the good news is spread.

Third, **the good seed** represents **the sons of the kingdom.** The good seed in this parable corresponds to the seed in the first parable that produced a fruitful crop. **The weeds are the sons of the evil one** (cf. v. 19) that had been sown among the wheat by **the enemy . . . the devil.** This condition of the kingdom was never revealed in the Old Testament, which spoke of a kingdom of righteousness in which evil would be overcome.

Fourth, **the harvest is the end of the Age, and the harvesters are angels** (cf. v. 49). This fact gives the ending of the time period suggested by these parables. "The end of the Age" represents the conclusion of the present Age before Christ establishes the messianic kingdom. Thus the parables in Matthew 13 cover the period of time from Christ's work on earth to the time of the judgment at His return. At His second coming, the **angels** will gather the wicked and **throw them into** judgment (vv. 40-42; cf. vv. 49-50; 2 Thes. 1:7-10; Rev. 19:15).

At that time **there will be weeping and gnashing of teeth.** Matthew frequently mentioned this reaction to judgment (Matt. 8:12; 13:42, 50; 22:13; 24:51; 25:30), and Luke mentioned it once (Luke 13:28). Each time it is used, it refers to judgment on sinners before the Millennium is established. "Weeping" suggests sorrow and grief (emotional agony of the lost in hell), and grinding of one's teeth speaks of pain (physical agony in hell). These are some of the many references in Matthew to judgment. **Then the righteous will shine like the sun in the kingdom of their Father** (Matt. 13:43; cf. Dan. 12:3).

In this period between Jesus' rejection and His future return He the King is absent but His kingdom continues, though in a newly revealed form. This

Age is broader than but includes the Church Age. The church did not begin until the day of Pentecost, and it will conclude at the Rapture, at least seven years before the end of this Age. This "mystery period" is characterized by profession of faith but also by a counter-profession that cannot be separated until the final judgment. This mystery period does not involve a universal triumph of the gospel, as postmillennialists affirm, nor does it include Christ's earthly reign. It simply is the time between His two Advents, before He returns to institute the kingdom promised to David through his greater Son.

3. THE PARABLE OF THE MUSTARD SEED (13:31-32)
(MARK 4:30-32; LUKE 13:18-19)

13:31-32. Another parable Jesus presented to the crowd likened **the kingdom of heaven** to a **mustard seed.** This seed was in fact the smallest of the garden seeds known. (Orchard seeds, though smaller, were unknown in that part of the world.) Also "small as a mustard seed" was a proverb by which people then referred to something unusually small (e.g., "faith as small as a mustard seed," 17:20).

Though its seed is so small, a mustard plant grows to a great height (12-15 feet!) in one season, and is a nesting place for **the birds of the air.** Jesus did not directly interpret this parable. However, its meaning may be that the sphere of professing followers, sometimes called Christendom, which Jesus mentioned in the second parable, would have a small beginning but would grow rapidly into a large entity. This group could include both believers and unbelievers, as indicated by the birds lodging in the branches of the tree. Other interpreters feel, however, that the presence of the birds is not an indication of evil but simply an expression of prosperity and bounty.

4. THE PARABLE OF THE YEAST (13:33-35)
(MARK 4:33-34; LUKE 13:20)

13:33-35. In this fourth **parable** Jesus compared **the kingdom of heaven** to **yeast** (leaven) which, when **mixed into a large amount of flour,** continues to work till all **the dough** is permeated. Many expositors teach that the yeast here

represents evil present in the interval of time between the Advents of the King. In the Bible yeast often represents evil (e.g., Ex. 12:15; Lev. 2:11; 6:17; 10:12; Matt. 16:6, 11-12; Mark 8:15; Luke 12:1; 1 Cor. 5:7-8; Gal. 5:8-9). However, if the yeast in this parable represents evil, the idea would be redundant for evil was already represented by the weeds in the second parable. Therefore some feel that Jesus had in mind here the dynamic character of yeast. The nature of yeast is such that once the process of leavening begins, it is impossible to stop. Perhaps Jesus was implying that those who profess to belong to the kingdom would grow in numbers and nothing would be able to stop their advance. This idea fits with the nature of yeast and makes sense in the flow of these parables.

Matthew added (Matt. 13:34-35) that is in keeping with Jesus' earlier statements (cf. vv. 11-12). By speaking **in parables** Jesus was fulfilling Scripture (Ps. 78:2) and at the same time was teaching truths not previously revealed.

13:36-43. See comments on these verses under "2. The Parable of the Wheat and the Weeds (13:24-30, 36-43)."

5. THE PARABLE OF THE HIDDEN TREASURE (13:44)

13:44. In a fifth parable Jesus compared **the kingdom of heaven** to **treasure hidden in a field. A man** having discovered the treasure, then **bought that field** in order to have the treasure for himself. Since the Lord did not interpret this parable, a variety of interpretive views are held. In the flow of this chapter, it seems best to understand this to be a reference to Israel, God's "treasured possession" (Ex. 19:5; Ps. 135:4). One reason Jesus came into the world was to redeem Israel, so that He could be viewed as the One who sold all He had (viz., the glories of heaven; cf. John 17:5; 2 Cor. 8:9; Phil. 2:5-8) in order to purchase the treasure.

6. THE PARABLE OF THE PEARL (13:45-46)

13:45-46. This parable, also not interpreted by the Lord, may be linked with the previous one. The pearl **of great value** may represent the church, the bride of Jesus Christ. **Pearls** are uniquely formed. "Its formation occurs because of an irritation in the tender side of an

Parables of the Kingdom in Matthew 13

Parables	References	Meanings
1. The Sower	13:1–23	The good news of the gospel will be rejected by most people.
2. The Wheat and the Weeds	13:24–30, 36–43	People with genuine faith and people with a false profession of faith will exist together between Christ's two Advents.
3. The Mustard Seed	13:31–32	Christendom, including believers and unbelievers, will grow rapidly from a small beginning.
4. The Yeast	13:33–35	People who profess to belong to God will grow in numbers without being stopped.
5. The Hidden Treasure	13:44	Christ came to purchase (redeem) Israel, God's treasured possession.
6. The Pearl	13:45–46	Christ gave His life to provide redemption for the church.
7. The Net	13:47–52	Angels will separate the wicked from the righteous when Christ comes.

oyster. There is a sense in which the church was formed out of the wounds of Christ and has been made possible by His death and sacrifice" (John F. Walvoord, *Matthew: Thy Kingdom Come*, p. 105). The **merchant** who **sold everything he had** in order to buy the highly valued pearl represents Jesus Christ who through His death provided redemption for those who would believe. These two parables in close proximity—the treasure and the pearl—teach that within the period of time when the King is absent, Israel would continue to exist and the church would be growing.

7. THE PARABLE OF THE NET (13:47-52)

13:47-50. Jesus' seventh parable compares **the kingdom of heaven** to a **net that was let down into the lake** so that a great catch **of fish** was hauled in. **The fishermen pulled** the full net to **shore** and sorted out the **fish,** collecting **the good** ones **in baskets** and throwing **the bad** ones **away.** Jesus said this sorting represents the angelic separation of **the wicked from the righteous** at **the end of the Age** (v. 49; cf. vv. 37-43). This separation will occur when Jesus Christ returns to establish His kingdom on earth (cf. 25:30).

13:51-52. **Jesus asked** the disciples if

they had **understood all** He told them. Their **yes** answer is surprising, for they could not have known the full implications of these parables. In fact the disciples' subsequent questions and actions proved that they did not really comprehend the parables. Jesus, however, was performing the function of an **owner of a house** who could bring **new** and **old** treasures **out of his storeroom.**

In these seven parables He presented some truths they were well aware of and others that were new to them. They knew about a kingdom over which Messiah would rule and reign, but they did not know it would be rejected at the time it was offered. They knew the kingdom would include righteousness, but they did not know it would also include evil. Jesus pointed up a new truth that the period between His rejection and His second coming would be characterized by professing followers, both good and evil. This era would have a small beginning, but it would grow into a great "kingdom" of professors. Once this process began, it could not be stopped, and within it God is maintaining His people Israel and creating His church. This interadvent period will end with a time of judgment in which God will separate the wicked from the righteous and the righteous will then enter the earthly kingdom to rule and reign with Christ. Through these parables Jesus answered the question, What happened to the kingdom? The answer: God's kingdom will be established on earth at Jesus' second coming; meanwhile good and evil coexist.

E. Seen in various rejections (13:53–16:12)

1. REJECTION IN THE CITY OF NAZARETH (13:53-58)

(MARK 6:1-6)

13:53-58. After instructing His disciples, **Jesus** returned to **His hometown** (Nazareth; Luke 1:26-27; Matt. 2:23; 21:11; John 1:45) and taught **the people in their synagogue.** On a previous visit to Nazareth, the populace had rejected His teaching and attempted to throw Him over a cliff (Luke 4:16-29). This time the people were impressed with His **powers** and teachings, but they rejected Him. They remembered Him as **the carpenter's Son** (Matt. 13:55). They mentioned four (half) **brothers** (not cousins) of Jesus, children born to **Mary** and Joseph after the birth of Jesus Christ. Three of these sons—**James . . . Simon, and Judas**—are not to be confused with three of the Twelve by the same names. The people of Nazareth refused to believe in Jesus Christ and hampered His ministry there. Nazareth's problem was the danger of the familiar for the city's residents could not see beyond the young Man who had grown up among them. Surely One so "ordinary" could not be the promised Messiah. Consequently they rejected the Messiah and **took offense at Him.** Jesus was not surprised, for He cited what has become a common proverb, namely, that **a prophet** is not honored **in his** own **hometown** and family. As a result of **their lack of faith,** Jesus performed few **miracles there.**

2. REJECTION IN THE ACTIONS OF HEROD (CHAP. 14)

a. The execution of John the Baptist (14:1-12)

(Mark 6:14-29; Luke 3:19-20; 9:7-9)

14:1-12. As the news concerning **Jesus** and His mighty works spread, **Herod** heard about Jesus and His miraculous powers. This was Herod Antipas, who ruled over a fourth of Palestine (hence the title **the tetrarch**), including

Galilee and Perea. He ruled from 4 B.C. to A.D. 39. His father Herod the Great had killed the Bethlehem babies (2:16). Herod Antipas judged Jesus when He was on trial (Luke 23:7-12). (See the chart on the Herods at Luke 1:5.)

Herod concluded that Jesus was **John the Baptist . . . risen from the dead** (cf. Luke 9:7). Matthew's last reference to John the Baptist was John's sending messengers to Jesus to inquire about Him (Matt. 11:2-14). The story concerning John was now completed by Matthew. **Herod** Antipas **had arrested John . . . because of Herodias. John** had publicly condemned Herod, who was living with Herodias, his sister-in-law. She was **his brother Philip's wife** so this was an immoral relationship. **Herod** Antipas **wanted to** execute **John but** was fearful, for **the people** loved John and thought **him** to be **a prophet.** Therefore he only removed John from the public by placing him **in prison.** But at a **birthday** celebration Salome, Herodias' **daughter . . . danced.** She so delighted Herod **that he** foolishly **promised** her anything she wanted. Her request, **Give me here on a platter the head of John the Baptist,** was not her idea, for she was **prompted by her mother** Herodias. Though this request greatly **distressed** (*lypētheis* means to be grieved or sad to the point of distress; cf. 18:31; 19:22) Herod, he was caught in a trap for his **oath** was at stake (14:9). So he **granted** the wish and **John** was **beheaded.**

John's disciples gave his **body** a decent burial, and reported to **Jesus** what had happened. Herod's act was another illustration of the rejection of Jesus, for Matthew so connected the ministries of these two men that what happened to one was viewed as having a direct effect on the other. Herod, by rejecting the King's forerunner, was rejecting the King who followed him.

b. The exit of Jesus (14:13-36)

When Jesus learned of John the Baptist's death, He withdrew with His disciples to a remote place. From this time on, the ministry of Jesus was directed primarily toward His disciples. His goal seemed to be to instruct them in light of the fact that He would be leaving them. He said almost nothing more to the nation to convince them He is the Messiah.

14:13-21 (**Mark 6:30-44; Luke 9:10-17; John 6:1-14**). The people anticipated where **Jesus** and His disciples were going. **The crowds,** by walking along the north shore of the Sea of Galilee, joined Jesus. Feeling **compassion** (*esplanchnisthē;* cf. comments on Matt. 9:36), **Jesus . . . healed their sick.** When **evening** came, **the disciples** wanted to **send the crowds away** for there were no supplies in that **remote place** (cf. **a solitary place,** 14:13) to feed so many people. But the Lord said, **They do not need to go away. You give them something to eat.** However, they had **only five loaves of bread and two fish.** With these elements in Jesus' hands, a miracle occurred. The bread and fish continually multiplied so that **all** present **ate and were satisfied.** More than enough was available, for **12 basketfuls of broken pieces . . . were left over.** About **5,000 men** were fed on this occasion, plus many **women and children,** perhaps 15,000 to 20,000 in all.

This miracle took place at Bethsaida (see comments on Luke 9:10) just before the Passover (John 6:4). This is the only miracle of Jesus which is recorded in all four Gospels. The significance of this miracle was intended primarily for the disciples. Jesus was illustrating the kind of ministry they would have after His departure. They would be involved in feeding people, but with spiritual food. The source for their feeding would be the Lord Himself. When their supply ran out, as with the bread and fish, they would need to return to the Lord for more. He would supply them, but the feeding would be done through them. The people Jesus fed sensed that He was the anticipated Prophet (John 6:14-15; Deut. 18:15) and tried to make Him King. Surely One who could heal their physical diseases and provide food so abundantly must be the King. But the timing was not correct, for the nation's leaders had decided against Jesus (Matt. 12:24), and His official rejection would soon come.

14:22-36 (**Mark 6:45-56; John 6:15-21**). **Jesus** sent **the disciples** away in **a boat. After** dismissing **the crowd . . . He went up into the hills** alone **to pray** (cf. John 6:15). Sending the disciples **into the boat** did two things: it got them away from the crowd, and it gave them opportunity to ponder the significance of what had just happened through them.

But soon they were in a storm. Somewhere between 3 and 6 in the morning (**the fourth watch of the night**), **Jesus** joined **them, walking on the lake** to their boat—a distance of "three or three and a half miles" (John 6:19). His power over the elements was obvious, but there was also a lesson in faith for the disciples in this experience. Their **fear** of seeing **a ghost** (Matt. 14:26) was relieved when **Jesus** announced that it was He.

But **Peter** wanted greater assurance that it was really the Lord. He said, **Lord, if it's You . . . tell me to come to You on the water.** The Lord's reply was a simple **Come.** Peter's initial response demonstrated his faith for he stepped **out of the boat and** began walking toward the Lord. (Only Matthew recorded Peter's walk on the water.) In all recorded history only two men ever **walked on . . . water,** Jesus and Peter. **But** Peter's faith was challenged **when he saw the wind,** that is, when he saw its effect on the water. As he sank, he **cried** to the **Lord** for help. **Immediately** the Lord **caught him. Jesus** rebuked Peter for his lack of **faith** (cf. 6:30; 8:26; 16:8), which had caused him to sink.

When they reached **the boat,** the storm calmed and the amazed disciples **worshiped Him.** Their concept of Jesus had been expanded and they acknowledged Him as **the Son of God.** Their view of Jesus was in direct contrast with **the men** of **Gennesaret** (14:34), a fertile plain southwest of Capernaum. When these men learned Jesus had arrived, they **brought all their sick** for healing. Their touching **His cloak** recalls a hemorrhaging woman in that area who had touched His garment (9:20). Though they acknowledged Jesus as a great Healer, they did not fully comprehend who He is. The disciples, however, were growing continually in their comprehension of His true identity.

3. REJECTION IN THE CONTROVERSIES WITH THE RELIGIOUS LEADERS (15:1–16:12)

a. *The first controversy and result (chap. 15)*

15:1-9 (**Mark 7:1-13**). News of Jesus' teaching and His mighty acts had spread throughout the land. The officials in **Jerusalem** were aware of all **Jesus** was doing, for a delegation arrived in Galilee **from** Jerusalem to interrogate Jesus over a matter of Jewish **tradition.** Their attack was directed against Jesus' **disciples,** who were accused of failing to observe the elders' tradition of the ceremonial washing of **hands before** eating. This tradition (Rabbinic, not Mosaic) was an elaborate washing ritual involving not only one's hands but also cups, pitchers, and kettles (Mark 7:3-4).

Jesus immediately took the offensive against the religious leaders and asked why they continued to **break the** direct **command of God.** He cited the fifth commandment concerning honoring one's **father and mother** (Matt. 15:4; Ex. 20:12). The Jews considered honoring of parents so important that anyone who cursed **his** parents was to **be put to death** (Ex. 21:17; Lev. 20:9).

Jesus showed how these religious leaders had in effect nullified this commandment (Matt. 15:6). They could simply affirm that a particular item had been **a gift devoted to God.** Then the item could not be used by an individual but was kept separate. This was simply a clever way of keeping things from passing to one's parents. The person would of course continue to keep those things in his own home where they had been supposedly set aside for God. Such action was condemned by Jesus as being hypocritical (v. 7), for while it appeared to be spiritual, it actually was done to keep one's possessions for himself. Thus this failure to help one's parents deliberately violated the fifth commandment of the Decalogue. Such action had been described by **Isaiah** centuries before (Isa. 29:13). Their religion had become a matter of action and man-made rules. **Their hearts** were **far from** God and consequently their **worship** was **in vain** (*matēn,* "fruitless, futile," an adjective used only here [Matt. 15:9] and in the parallel passage, Mark 7:7; it is a variation of the more common adjective *mataios,* "without results, futile").

15:10-20 (Mark 7:14-23). Jesus then turned and warned **the crowd** against the religious leaders' teachings. He said a man is not defiled by what goes **into** his **mouth,** but rather his defiled condition is evidenced by **what comes out of his mouth.** The Pharisees were wrong in thinking their washings kept them spiritually clean.

The disciples reported to Jesus **that** **the Pharisees were offended** (cf. Matt. 13:21, 57) by what He had just said, sensing that His words were directed against them. Jesus added that since the Pharisees had **not** been **planted** by His **heavenly Father** (another of the many times in Matt. where Jesus referred to God as "Father"), they were headed for uprooting (judgment). Jesus said to **leave them** alone, for they had chosen their path and nothing would deter them. **They** were **blind guides,** trying to lead **blind** people; they would **fall into a pit.**

Peter asked for further clarification about Jesus' teaching (**the parable** refers to Jesus' words in 15:11; cf. Mark 7:15-17). So Jesus enlarged on His previous statement. Defilement of a person does not come from the outside. What comes from the outside is simply passed through the digestive system and is eventually eliminated. **But** what comes **out of the mouth** represents what is actually inside one's **heart,** and these may **make** him (or, show him to be) **unclean** (*koinoi,* "common, ceremonially impure"). Evil (*ponēroi*) **thoughts, murder, adultery** (*moicheiai*), **sexual immorality** (*porneiai*), **theft, false testimony, slander**—such actions and words rise from within one's evil heart. **These** matters— **not** whether one eats food **with unwashed hands**—reveal spiritual uncleanness.

15:21-28 (Mark 7:24-30). To get away from the questionings of the religious leaders, **Jesus withdrew** from Israel and went north into **the region of Tyre and Sidon,** the Gentile coastal region of Phoenicia. Tyre was 35 miles from Galilee and Sidon was 60. There He met **a Canaanite woman.** Centuries earlier that area's inhabitants were called Canaanites (Num. 13:29). She pleaded with Him to **have mercy** on her demon-possessed **daughter.** She addressed Him as **Lord, Son of David** (cf. Matt. 9:27; 20:30-31), a messianic title. But even that appeal could not help her, for the timing was not appropriate. When **Jesus** failed to **answer** her and she persisted with her appeal, **the disciples . . . urged** Jesus to **send her away.** They seemed to be asking, "Lord, why don't You go ahead and help this woman? She isn't going to give up until You do."

Jesus reminded them, **I was sent only to the lost sheep of Israel** (cf. 10:6).

He had come to offer to His own people the kingdom promised through David centuries before. Thus it was inappropriate for Him to bring blessings on Gentiles before blessings fell on Israel. But **the woman** was not easily discouraged. She saw in Jesus the only chance for help for her child. On her knees she pleaded, **Lord, help me!** Jesus' reply caused her to realize her position, for He said **it** would **not** be **right to take the children's bread and toss it to their dogs.** He was picturing a family gathered at mealtime around a table, eating food provided by the head of the household. The Gentile woman saw herself in this picture. She was not a child in the family (of Israel) eligible for the choicest morsels of food. But she saw herself as a household dog (a Gentile; the Jews often called Gentiles "dogs") eligible to receive **crumbs that** might **fall from the master's table.** She was not wanting to deprive Israel of God's blessings. She was simply asking that some of the blessing be extended to her in her need. In light of such **great faith** (cf. 8:10), the kind of faith Jesus was looking for in Israel, He **granted** her **request. Her daughter was healed . . . that very hour.** This Gentile woman's faith contrasted with Israel's leaders who were rejecting Jesus.

15:29-39 (Mark 7:31–8:10). Jesus, returning from Tyre and Sidon, **went near the Sea of Galilee . . . into the hills** (cf. Matt. 14:23) where He **sat down. Great crowds** of people brought a multitude of sick people **to Him.** In view of Mark 7:31-37, the crowds referred to in Matthew 15:30-31 may have been Gentiles (also cf. Mark 8:13 with Matt. 15:39). Jesus **healed** their physical illnesses, and people **praised the God of Israel.** Jesus was thus demonstrating what He will do for Gentiles as well as for Jews when His rightful millennial rule will be established on earth.

This ministry lasted about **three days. Jesus** had **compassion for** them (*splanchnizomai;* cf. comments on 9:36; Luke 7:13). He did **not want to send them** home without food. The **disciples** questioned how **in this remote place** (cf. Matt. 14:15) they could buy **enough** food **to feed** them all. When Jesus asked them about their present resources, they said they had **seven** bread **loaves** and **a few small fish.** The disciples must have anticipated that Jesus was going to use

them again to feed this multitude, as He had done earlier (14:13-21). Jesus **told the crowd to sit down,** gave thanks for **the seven loaves and the fish,** and divided the food among **the disciples,** who distributed it **to the people.** After the crowd—estimated this time at **4,000** men, **besides women and children—ate and were satisfied . . . seven basketfuls of broken pieces** were **picked up.**

This miracle demonstrated that the Lord's blessings through His disciples would fall not only on Israel (14:13-21) but also on Gentiles. This is perhaps most clearly seen in Acts 10–11 when Peter shared the good news of salvation with Cornelius and his Gentile household. **After Jesus had** dismissed **the crowd,** He returned to the western shore of the Sea of Galilee to the city of **Magadan,** a variant spelling of Magdala, just north of Tiberias. Mary Magdalene (Matt. 27:56) was from Magdala, also called Dalmanutha (Mark 8:10).

b. The second controversy and result (16:1-12)

16:1-4 (Mark 8:11-13; Luke 12:54-56). As **Jesus** returned to Israel, He was again confronted by religious leaders, **the Pharisees and Sadducees.** They **tested Him by asking** for **a sign from heaven.** By this they were again saying that they rejected all the signs Jesus had performed before their eyes (cf. Matt. 12:38). They were in effect asking Jesus to give them a sign more spectacular than healings, so they could believe. Jesus' response was again condemnatory for He called them **a wicked and adulterous generation** (16:4; cf. 12:39). They were careful observers of **weather** signs and could fairly well forecast whether the weather would be good or threatening. Yet they had been surrounded by spiritual signs relating to the person of Jesus Christ and had missed them all. Such a wicked generation would not receive any special treatment. Jesus was not a sign-worker simply for the sake of working **signs.** He was not a puppet on strings to perform at their command. The only **sign** they would receive was **the sign of Jonah,** which He had previously given them (12:38-42), but they would not recognize that sign until it was too late.

16:5-12 (Mark 8:14-21). As **Jesus** left the religious leaders, He warned His disciples . . . against the yeast of the Pharisees and Sadducees, to whom He had just spoken. Jesus' mention of yeast caused the disciples to think He referred to their having forgotten to bring along bread. But Jesus explained that He was not referring to their lack of bread. He reminded them of previous occasions when He had multiplied loaves and fish so that food was left over (Matt. 14:13-21; 15:29-38). The amount of food was not the issue, for Jesus could care for such a need if it arose. Because they were not trusting Him for that, they were, He said, of little faith (16:8; three other times in Matt. Jesus spoke of "little faith"; 6:30; 8:26; 14:31). He then simply repeated His warning: Be on your guard against the yeast of the Pharisees and Sadducees (cf. 16:6). Their teaching was like pervasive yeast, penetrating and corrupting the nation.

V. Cultivation of the King's Disciples (16:13–20:34)

A. The revelation in view of rejection (16:13–17:13)

1. THE PERSON OF MESSIAH (16:13-16) (MARK 8:27-30; LUKE 9:18-21)

16:13-16. Jesus and the disciples removed themselves from the region around the Sea of Galilee and went north about 30 miles to Caesarea Philippi, that is, Caesarea in the tetrarchy of Herod Philip, Antipas' brother. There Jesus questioned the disciples about their faith in Him. He asked them what the people were saying about Him. Their replies were all flattering, for people were identifying Jesus with John the Baptist . . . Elijah . . . Jeremiah, or one of the prophets. His teachings were certainly similar to theirs. All these answers, of course, were wrong. He then asked the disciples, But what about you? Who do you say I am?

Speaking for the disciples, Peter spoke his now-famous words, You are the Christ, the Son of the living God. As "the Christ," He is the Messiah. Ho christos is the New Testament equivalent of the Old Testament māšîah, which means "the anointed One." In Him are fulfilled all the promises of God to the nation. And as the Old Testament made clear, the Messiah is more than a human being; He is God (Isa. 9:6; Jer. 23:5-6;

Micah 5:2). Peter thus acknowledged Jesus' deity as the Son of the living God. The disciples had come to this conclusion as they observed the Lord Jesus over a period of time, witnessed His miracles, and heard His words.

2. THE PROGRAM OF MESSIAH (16:17-26)

16:17-20. Peter's words brought a word of commendation from the Lord. Peter was blessed because he had come to a correct conclusion about the person of Christ and because great blessing would be brought into his life. The Lord added, however, this was not a conclusion Peter had determined by his own or others' ability. God, the Father in heaven, had revealed it to him. Peter was living up to his name (it means "rock") for he was demonstrating himself to be a rock. When the Lord and Peter first met, Jesus had said Simon would be named Cephas (Aram. for "rock") or Peter (Gr. for "rock"; John 1:41-42).

But his declaration about Messiah's person led to a declaration of Messiah's program. Peter (Petros, masc.) was strong like a rock, but Jesus added that on this rock (petra, fem.) He would build His church. Because of this change in Greek words, many conservative scholars believe that Jesus is now building His church on Himself. Others hold that the church is built on Peter and the other apostles as the building's foundation stones (Eph. 2:20; Rev. 21:14). Still other scholars say that the church is built on Peter's testimony. It seems best to understand that Jesus was praising Peter for his accurate statement about Him, and was introducing His work of building the church on Himself (1 Cor. 3:11).

Building His church was a yet-future work of Jesus Christ, for He had not yet started the process. He said, I will build (future tense) My church, but His program for the nation Israel had to be concluded before another program could be set in motion. This is probably why Jesus said not even the gates of hades would overcome this program. Jews would understand hades' gates to refer to physical death. Jesus was thus telling the disciples His death would not prevent His work of building the church. Later (Matt. 16:21) He spoke of His imminent death. He was therefore anticipating His death

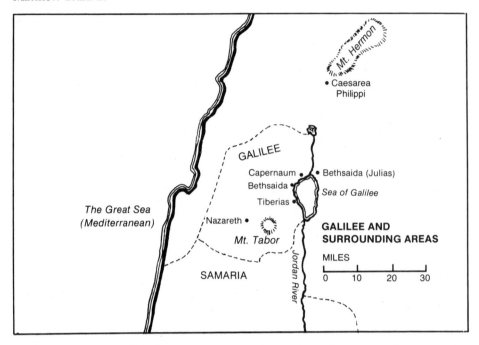

Caesarea
Philippi

Mt. Hermon

GALILEE

Capernaum • • Bethsaida (Julias)
Bethsaida •
Sea of Galilee
Tiberias •

The Great Sea
(Mediterranean)

Nazareth •
Mt. Tabor

GALILEE AND
SURROUNDING AREAS

MILES

SAMARIA

Jordan River

0   10   20   30

and His victory over death through the Resurrection.

His church would *then* begin to be built, starting on the day of Pentecost, and Peter and the other apostles would have important roles in it. He declared that Peter would be given significant authority, **the keys of the kingdom of heaven.** A "key" was a sign of authority, for a trusted steward kept the keys to his master's possessions and dispensed them accordingly (cf. "the keys of death and hades" [Rev. 1:18] and "the key of David" [Rev. 3:7], which Jesus possesses). Peter was told he would possess the keys and be able to **bind** and **loose** people. These were decisions Peter was to implement as he received instruction from **heaven,** for the binding and loosing occurred there first. Peter simply carried out God's directions. This privilege of binding and loosing was seen in Peter's life as he had the privilege on the day of Pentecost to proclaim the gospel and announce to all those who responded in saving faith that their sins had been forgiven (Acts 2). He was able to do the same thing with the household of Cornelius (Acts 10–11; cf. Acts 15:19-20). The same privilege was given all the disciples (John 20:22-23).

After making this great declaration about His future church program, Jesus

told the **disciples not to tell anyone that He** is **the Christ,** the Messiah. The Lord knew it was too late for the nation to respond to His offer, and His rejection was drawing near. There was no reason for His disciples to be trying to convince a nation that had already turned from Him.

16:21-26 (Mark 8:31-38; Luke 9:22-25). Jesus explained **to His disciples that** His death was near. It would be necessary for Him to **go to Jerusalem and** there **suffer many things at the hands of the** religious leaders. Eventually He would **be killed,** but He would rise again from the dead **on the third day.** This is Matthew's first prediction of Jesus' death. Other predictions follow in Matthew 17:22-23 and 20:18-19.

Peter, hearing these words, **took** the Lord **aside and began to rebuke Him.** The disciple who had just been blessed by the Master obviously did not fully comprehend the Master's plan. Peter could not understand how Jesus could be Messiah and yet die at the hands of the religious leaders. Peter probably was so shocked to hear Jesus speak of His death that he failed to hear Him mention His resurrection. Peter's rebuke, however, brought a rebuke from the Lord, for **Peter** was playing the role of **Satan. Jesus** directly addressed Satan, who was seeking to use Peter as his instrument.

Jesus had previously told Satan to get away from Him (4:10); He now repeated that order. Peter was trying to keep the Lord from dying, but that was a primary reason why Jesus came into the world. Trying to thwart the Crucifixion, as Satan had earlier tried to do (4:8-10), resulted from not thinking from God's viewpoint. Though Peter wanted Jesus to follow *his* plan, the Lord showed that discipleship involves a cost. Discipleship does not mean one enjoys glory immediately. A person who **would** follow Jesus **must deny himself** and all his ambitions. He must **take up his cross and follow** Jesus (cf. 10:38). In the Roman Empire a convicted criminal, when taken to be crucified, was forced to carry his own cross. This showed publicly that he was then under and submissive to the rule he had been opposing. Likewise Jesus' disciples must demonstrate their submission to the One against whom they had rebelled. The path Jesus and His followers would travel would be a road of sorrow and suffering. But in so losing one's **life,** one would truly **find** a better **life.** Jesus' similar words (in 10:38-39) were stated in connection with one's attitudes toward his family; here (16:24-25) Jesus spoke in relation to Peter's misunderstanding about His program and the cost of discipleship.

If it were possible for an individual, in preserving his own life, to gain **the whole world,** but in the process lose **his soul,** of what value then would be the possessions of the world? True discipleship involves following Christ and doing His will, wherever that path might lead.

3. THE PICTURE OF MESSIAH'S KINGDOM (16:27–17:13)

16:27-28 (Mark 9:1; Luke 9:26-27). As Jesus continued to instruct His disciples, He spoke prophetically of His second coming when He, **the Son of Man,** would return **in His Father's glory with His angels** (cf. Matt. 24:30-31; 2 Thes. 1:7). As "the Son of . . . God" (Matt. 16:16) He possesses a divine nature, and as "the Son of Man" He possesses a human nature (cf. comments on 8:20). At that time the Lord **will reward** His servants for their faithfulness. Speaking of His return led Him to state that some disciples **standing** there with Him would be permitted to view **His** coming **kingdom** before they experienced **death.** This statement has caused many to misunderstand the kingdom program, for they wonder how the disciples saw the Lord coming in His kingdom. The explanation is found in the following event, the transfiguration (17:1-8).

17:1-8 (Mark 9:2-13; Luke 9:28-36). This chapter division in Matthew is an unfortunate break in the flow of this biblical passage. Jesus had just said that some standing with Him would not die before they saw the Son of Man coming in His kingdom (Matt. 16:28). The continuing story occurred **six days** later when **Jesus took . . . Peter, James, and John** with Him **up a high mountain by themselves.** Luke wrote that this event occurred "about eight days after" (Luke 9:28), which includes the beginning and ending days as well as the six days between. The high mountain may have been Mount Hermon, near Caesarea Philippi (see map), for Jesus was in that region (Matt. 16:13).

There Jesus **was transfigured** (*metemorphōthē,* "changed in form"; cf. Rom. 12:2; 2 Cor. 3:18) **before** this inner circle of disciples (Matt. 17:2). This was a revelation of Jesus' glory. The radiance of His glory was evidenced in **His face** and in His garments that **became as white as the light.** **Moses and Elijah** appeared from heaven in some visible form and talked **with Jesus** (thus demonstrating that conscious existence follows death). Luke wrote that Moses and Elijah talked with Jesus about His coming death (Luke 9:31).

Why were Moses and Elijah, of all Old Testament people, present on this occasion? Perhaps these two men and the disciples suggest all the categories of people who will be in Jesus' coming kingdom. The disciples represent individuals who will be present in physical bodies. Moses represents saved individuals who have died or will die. Elijah represents saved individuals who will not experience death, but will be caught up to heaven alive (1 Thes. 4:17). These three groups will be present when Christ institutes His kingdom on earth. Furthermore the Lord will be in His glory as He was at the transfiguration, and the kingdom will take place on earth, as this obviously did. The disciples were thus enjoying a foretaste of the kingdom the Lord promised (Matt. 16:28).

Peter seemed to sense the significance of the event for he suggested that he erect **three shelters**, for Jesus, **Moses, and . . . Elijah.** He saw in this event the fulfillment of the Jewish Feast of Tabernacles which looked two ways: backward to the wanderings in the wilderness for 40 years, and forward to Israel's full enjoyment of God's blessings when He would gather His people to the land. Peter was correct in his understanding of what was taking place (he saw the kingdom) but he was wrong in his timing.

While Peter **was still speaking,** a more important **voice** spoke from **a bright cloud** that had **enveloped them.** This voice **said, This is My Son, whom I love; with Him I am well-pleased. Listen to Him!** (cf. 3:17) This authentication of the Son of God by the voice of God carried great significance for the disciples. Years later when Peter wrote his second epistle he referred to this event (2 Peter 1:16-18). This authentication of Jesus by the Father caused the terrified **disciples** to fall on their faces. When the Lord Himself told the disciples to **get up . . . they saw no one except Jesus,** for Moses and Elijah had departed.

17:9-13. As this small group returned from **the mountain,** Jesus told the three not to **tell anyone what** they had witnessed **until** after He had risen **from the dead** (cf. 16:20). Some people had already tried to make Jesus King by force, and if news of this event had become commonly known, perhaps others would have attempted to make Jesus King.

This event was a taste of the kingdom, but the disciples were puzzled. Many were teaching that before Messiah could come, **Elijah must** return. Jesus explained that **Elijah** must in fact come and **restore all things** (cf. Mal. 4:5), but **Elijah** had **already come** in the person of **John the Baptist** and his ministry was not recognized. Instead of receiving John the Baptist, the religious leaders had rejected him. As they refused to acknowledge John's ministry and instead rejected him, Jesus too would be rejected. At the first announcement concerning the birth of John, Zechariah his father had been told that he would go before the Lord "in the spirit and power of Elijah" (Luke 1:17). The Lord's earlier words concerning John

(Matt. 11:14) affirmed that he would have been the predicted Elijah *if* the nation had responded in saving faith. Everything necessary to bring in Messiah's kingdom had been performed. The only contingency was the acceptance by the nation of her rightful King.

B. The instruction in view of rejection (17:14–20:34)

1. INSTRUCTION CONCERNING FAITH (17:14-21)

(MARK 9:14-29; LUKE 9:37-43A)

17:14-21. When **Jesus** and the inner circle returned to the other disciples, a **crowd** was gathered because **a man** with **an epileptic** son had sought healing help from the nine **disciples.** They, however, had not been able to drive out **the demon** (v. 18) that possessed **the boy** and caused his epilepsy. The father appealed to Jesus, kneeling **before Him** and addressing Him as **Lord.** The boy's epilepsy had caused him much **suffering** and physical danger; the convulsions even caused him to fall uncontrollably **into the fire** and **into the water.** Mark mentioned the boy's foaming at the mouth (Mark 9:18, 20). **Jesus** asked for **the boy** to be brought to Him, and He rebuked not only the disciples but also the entire crowd for their lack of faith. He immediately drove the demon **out of** the boy and restored him completely **from that moment** (cf. Matt. 15:28).

When **the disciples** inquired why they had not been able to heal the boy, Jesus said their problem was their **little faith** (cf. the "great faith" of the Roman centurion [8:10] and of the Canaanite woman [15:28]). Even a small amount of **faith, as small as a mustard seed** (cf. comments on the mustard seed in 13:31), is adequate to **move** a huge **mountain,** assuming, of course, that the "move" is in God's will. **Nothing** is **impossible** with God (cf. 19:26; Luke 1:37). (Some Gr. mss. add Matt. 17:21, "But this kind does not go out except by prayer and fasting," based on Mark 9:29.) Jesus was instructing the disciples about their future ministries. Their problem often would be lack of faith and failure to seek their Lord's direction. His Word would be sufficient to produce the desired healing but their actions would necessitate great faith and constant contact with the Lord through prayer. When these elements are combined, there is no limit to the works the disciples could accomplish, following His will.

2. INSTRUCTION CONCERNING HIS DEATH (17:22-23)
(MARK 9:30-32; LUKE 9:43B-45)

17:22-23. Again the Lord reminded the disciples that He was **to be betrayed** and wicked **men** would **kill Him.** One could never say that death took Jesus by surprise. He was in control of His life and no one took it from Him (John 10:11, 15, 17-18). He also told the disciples that death would not be the end for Him. Again He said He would rise **on the third day.** Unlike before (Matt. 16:21-23) this announcement of His death was not met by any recorded opposition from **the disciples.** But they **were filled with grief** over the Lord's words. One wonders if they heard the complete message or simply the part about His death.

3. INSTRUCTION CONCERNING RESPONSIBILITY TO GOVERNMENT (17:24-27)

17:24-27. When **Jesus and the disciples arrived** back **in Capernaum,** tax **collectors** were waiting for them. According to custom every Jew 20 years old and above was required to pay a **temple tax** of half a shekel or two drachmas each year to help support the temple (cf. Ex. 30:13-15; Neh. 10:32). Both Peter and Jesus had apparently not yet paid their **tax** (Matt. 17:27b) for that year, so the collectors sought **Peter** out. Their question about the Lord's not paying His **tax** implied that He was not keeping the Law. Peter responded that the Lord would pay the tax in compliance with the Law.

Before **Peter** spoke to the Lord about this matter, **Jesus** asked him if **kings . . . collect duty and taxes from their own sons, or from others.** Peter replied that kings do not collect taxes from family members, for they were **exempt,** but they do collect **from others.** The Lord was demonstrating to Peter that not only should He as King be tax-free, but also His disciples, as **sons** of the kingdom, should be free from such taxes (v. 26). They too had a privileged position, and the King should provide all they needed. However, the Lord did not intend at this time to make an issue (**offend them,** v. 27) over such a small point. The religious leaders were looking for accusations to use against **Jesus.** Peter was told to do something he really enjoyed: the Lord sent him fishing. He was to **throw out** his **line** and a special **catch** would be brought in. This **fish** would have in **its mouth** a specific **four-drachma coin** that would be the exact amount Peter needed to pay the tax for himself and for the Lord.

While Matthew did not record the rest of the story, it may be assumed Peter did as he was commanded, caught the fish, found the money, and paid the tax. The Lord thereby demonstrated His submission to ruling authority.

4. INSTRUCTION CONCERNING HUMILITY (18:1-6)
(MARK 9:33-37, 42; LUKE 9:46-48)

18:1-6. While still in the city of Capernaum, **the disciples** asked **Jesus** a question they had undoubtedly been pondering among themselves: **Who is the greatest in the kingdom of heaven?** The disciples were still anticipating an earthly kingdom and wondering what great positions they would have. In response Jesus took **a little child** (*paidion*), who had no rights according to the Law, and stood him in their midst. He told the disciples a **change** in their thinking was necessary. Greatness **in the kingdom** was not based on great works or words, but on childlike humility of spirit.

Jesus' reply indicated they were asking the wrong question. They should have been concerned about serving the Lord, not asking about positions in the kingdom. Their service needed to be directed toward people, for Jesus spoke about welcoming **a little child . . . in** His **name.** Little thought was directed in those days toward children, but Jesus did not overlook them. In fact, He gave a stern warning concerning any who might place a stumbling block before **one of these little ones who believe in** Him. (Interestingly little children can—and do—believe in Jesus!) **Causes . . . to sin** translates the verb *skandalisē*, "to offend, or cause to fall," a verb Matthew used 13 times. **It would be better for** such an offender **to have a large millstone hung around his neck and to be drowned in the depths of the sea.** A truly humble person does not concern himself with position or power, but is concerned about active service,

61

especially toward those who are most in need.

5. INSTRUCTION CONCERNING OFFENSES
(18:7-14)

18:7-11 (Mark 9:43-48). Jesus continued the previous discussion by talking about those who **cause** offenses. It was obvious such individuals were present in Jesus' time, but the judgment of God (**woe,** twice, Matt. 18:7; **eternal fire,** v. 8; **the fire of hell,** v. 9; cf. 6:22) would fall on them because they were failing to deal with the basic cause of their **sin.** Jesus was not teaching self-mutilation, cutting **off** one's **hand** or **foot** or gouging **out** one's **eye** (cf. 5:29-30). Doing that would not remove the source of offense, which is the heart (cf. 15:18-19). Jesus was saying one must remove whatever offends. To keep from offending, radical changes are often necessary. The disciples were reminded of the value the Lord places on **these little ones** (mikrōn toutōn; cf. 18:6, 14). Children are important to God. It may be God has entrusted the care of little children to a specific group of His angelic beings (**their angels**) who are in constant touch with the heavenly **Father** (cf. Ps. 91:11; Acts 12:15). (Some Gr. mss. add the words of Matt. 18:11, "The Son of Man came to save what was lost," perhaps inserted from Luke 19:10.)

18:12-14 (Luke 15:3-7). In order to demonstrate the importance God attaches to little children, the Lord gave the disciples an illustration. Suppose **a man** who **owns 100 sheep** suddenly discovers only **99** are present. **Will he not leave** them and search **for the one** until he **finds it? In the same way** God (**your Father in heaven;** cf. Matt. 18:10) is concerned about **these little ones** (cf. vv. 6, 10) and does not want to lose **any of** them. Great care must be exercised to avoid all offense.

6. INSTRUCTION CONCERNING DISCIPLINE
(18:15-20)
(LUKE 17:3)

18:15-20. The Lord had just spoken about offenses; now He talked about what should be done when known sin occurs. When a **brother sins against** another, **the two of** them should discuss the matter. If the matter can be settled at that level, there is no need for it to go any further. But if the sinning brother **refuses to listen**

. . . **two or three witnesses** should be taken **along** for a clear **testimony.** This was in keeping with Old Testament precedents, as in Deuteronomy 19:15. If the sinning brother still failed to recognize his error, the situation should be told before **the** entire **church,** or "assembly." The disciples probably would have understood Jesus to mean the matter should be brought before the Jewish assembly. After the establishment of the church, on the day of Pentecost, these words would have had greater meaning for them. One who **refuses** to acknowledge his sin is then to be treated **as** an outsider (**a pagan or a tax collector**).

This corporate action was entrusted to the entire apostolic group. Their actions of binding and loosing were to be directed by **heaven** (Matt. 18:18; cf. comments on 16:19). Clearly all are addressed for the **you** pronouns are plural. Besides their binding and loosing, they were also to engage in corporate prayer. Whenever they came **together in** the **name** of the Lord, He would be **with them.** And if **two or three** would **agree** together **about anything** it would **be done for** them **by the Father in heaven.**

7. INSTRUCTION CONCERNING FORGIVENESS (18:21-35)

18:21-22. **Peter** then asked **Jesus . . . Lord, how many times shall I forgive my brother when he sins against me? Up to seven times?** Peter was being generous here, for the traditional Rabbinic teaching was that an offended person needed to forgive a brother only three times. Jesus' reply was that forgiveness needs to be exercised to a much greater extent. **Not** just **7 times,** but "70 times 7" (NIV marg.), that is, 490 times. Jesus meant that no limits should be set. Then to complete the idea, He told a parable.

18:23-35. Jesus told about **a king who wanted to settle accounts with his servants.** One servant owed a large amount, **10,000 talents.** This probably equaled several million dollars, for a talent was probably a measure of gold, between 58 and 80 pounds. When he could **not . . . pay, the master ordered that** the servant **and his wife . . . children, and** possessions **be sold** so he could **repay** as much of **the debt** as possible. **The servant** pleaded with his master, begging for time to repay his master. The **master took pity on the servant, canceled the debt, and** set him free.

But shortly thereafter this **servant went out** and **found** another servant **who owed him** a much smaller amount, **100 denarii.** A denarius was a Roman silver coin, worth about 16 cents; it represented a laborer's daily wages. The first servant **demanded** payment and refused to show mercy toward his debtor. In fact he had the second servant **thrown into prison until he** paid **the debt. The other servants,** aware of all that **had happened . . .** were **greatly distressed** (*elypēthēsan,* "grieved or sad to the point of distress"; cf. 14:9; 19:22) by this turn of events and **told their master** what had transpired. **The master called** back **the first servant** and jailed him for failing to show mercy to a fellow servant when he had been forgiven a much greater debt.

The Lord was teaching that forgiveness ought to be in direct proportion to the amount forgiven. The first servant had been forgiven all, and he in turn should have forgiven all. A child of God has had all his sins forgiven by faith in Jesus Christ. Therefore when someone sins against him, he ought to be willing to **forgive . . . from** the **heart** no matter how many times the act occurs (cf. 18:21-22; Eph. 4:32).

8. INSTRUCTION CONCERNING DIVORCE
(19:1-12)
(MARK 10:1-12)

19:1-12. Jesus . . . left Galilee for the last time and headed for Jerusalem through **the region of Judea to the** east **side of the Jordan** River. That area was known as Perea. There, as often before, He was **followed** by **large crowds** of needy people, and **He healed them.** But **some Pharisees** sought **to test** Jesus through a question: **Is it lawful for a man to divorce his wife for any and every reason?** The nation was divided over this issue. Followers of Hillel felt a man could divorce his wife for almost any reason, but others, following Shammai, thought one could not divorce his wife unless she were guilty of sexual offense. Without getting involved in the Hillel-Shammai controversy Jesus reminded the religious leaders of God's original purpose in establishing the marriage bond. God made people **male and female** (v. 4; Gen.

1:27). In marriage He joins them **together** in an inseparable bond. This bond is a higher calling than the parent-child relationship, for **a man** is to **leave his father and mother and be** joined **to his wife** in a one-flesh relationship (Gen. 2:24). **Therefore what God has joined together,** men ought **not** separate (*chōrizetō;* in 1 Cor. 7:10 this word means "to divorce").

The Pharisees, realizing that Jesus was speaking of the permanence of the marital relationship, asked why **Moses** made a provision for **divorce** for people in his time (Matt. 19:7). The Lord's answer was that **Moses** granted this permission because people's **hearts were hard** (cf. Deut. 24:1-4). "Because your hearts were hard" is literally, "toward your hardness of heart" (*sklērokardian;* from *sklēros,* "hardness," comes the Eng. "sclerosis," and from *kardian* comes the Eng. "cardiac"). But that was not God's intention for marriage. God intended husbands and wives to live together permanently. Divorce was wrong **except for marital unfaithfulness** (cf. Matt. 5:32).

Bible scholars differ over the meaning of this "exception clause," found only in Matthew's Gospel. The word for "marital unfaithfulness" is *porneia.*

(1) Some feel Jesus used this as a synonym for adultery (*moicheia*). Therefore adultery by either partner in a marriage is the only sufficient grounds for a marriage to end in divorce. Among those holding this view, some believe remarriage is possible but others believe remarriage should never occur.

(2) Others define *porneia* as a sexual offense that could occur only in the betrothal period when a Jewish man and woman were considered married but had not yet consummated their coming marriage with sexual intercourse. If in this period the woman was found pregnant (as was Mary; 1:18-19), a divorce could occur in order to break the contract.

(3) Still others believe the term *porneia* referred to illegitimate marriages within prohibited degrees of kinship, as in Leviticus 18:6-18. If a man discovered that his wife was a near relative, he would actually be involved in an incestuous marriage. Then this would be a justifiable grounds for divorce. Some say this

meaning of *porneia* is found in Acts 15:20, 29 (cf. 1 Cor. 5:1).

(4) Another view is that *porneia* refers to a relentless, persistent, unrepentant lifestyle of sexual unfaithfulness (different from a one-time act of illicit relations). (In the NT *porneia* is broader than *moicheia*). Such a continued practice would thus be the basis for divorce, since such unfaithful and unrelenting conduct would have broken the marriage bond. (On the subject of divorce and remarriage, see comments on 1 Cor. 7:10-16.)

Whatever view one takes on the exception clause, **Jesus** obviously affirmed the permanence of marriage. Those who heard His words understood Him in this way, for they reasoned that if there were no grounds for divorce one would be **better** off never **to marry.** But this was not what Jesus intended, for God has given marriage to people for their betterment (Gen. 2:18). Marriage should be a deterrent to lustful sin and to unfaithfulness (1 Cor. 7:2). But a few either do not have normal sexual desires (they were born **eunuchs** or were castrated), or are able to control those desires for the furtherance of God's program on the earth (Matt. 19:12; cf. 1 Cor. 7:7-8, 26). But **not** all are able to **accept** the single role (Matt. 19:11). Many marry and carry out God's purposes, extending His work in the world.

9. INSTRUCTION CONCERNING CHILDREN
(19:13-15)
(MARK 10:13-16; LUKE 18:15-17)

19:13-15. Many parents were bringing **children . . . to Jesus for Him to place His hands on them and pray for them.** But the **disciples** felt this was a waste of Jesus' time. They began rebuking those bringing their children. Apparently the disciples had already forgotten what Jesus said earlier about the worth of children and the seriousness of causing them to fall (cf. 18:1-14). **Jesus** rebuked the disciples, telling them to **let the little children come** and **not hinder them. The kingdom** of heaven is not limited to adults who might be considered to be worth more than children. Anyone who comes to the Lord in faith is a worthy subject for the kingdom. This implies (19:15) that Jesus had time for all the children, for He did not depart from the region till He had blessed them all.

10. INSTRUCTION CONCERNING RICHES
(19:16-26)
(MARK 10:17-31; LUKE 18:18-30)

19:16-22. A man who was **young** (v. 20), wealthy (v. 22) and a ruler (Luke 18:18; perhaps of the Sanhedrin) **came** and **asked Jesus, Teacher, what good thing must I do to get eternal life?** This ruler was not asking how he could earn salvation. Instead, he wondered how he could be assured of entering Messiah's kingdom. He wanted to know what "good thing" (work) would demonstrate that he was righteous and therefore qualified for the kingdom. **Jesus** replied, **There is only One who is good,** namely, God. Perfection is required (Matt. 5:48; cf. 19:21) therefore one must be as good as God. He must have God's righteousness, which comes through faith in Him (Rom. 4:5). Perhaps Jesus then waited for a response from the ruler to see if he would affirm his belief that Jesus is God, that Jesus, being one with the Father, is good (*agathos*, "intrinsically good").

When the man did not reply, Jesus indicated that **life** (i.e., life in God's kingdom) can be entered only if one gives *evidence* that he is righteous. Since the official standard of righteousness was the Law of Moses, Jesus told the man to **obey the commandments.** The ruler was perceptive for he immediately asked, **Which ones?** Other standards of righteousness were being promoted by the Pharisees, who had added to Moses' commandments far beyond God's intention. The young man was in effect asking Jesus, "Must I keep all the Pharisees' commandments?" **Jesus replied** by repeating several of the commandments from the second table of the Law, the 5th through the 9th commandments forbidding **murder . . . adultery,** stealing, giving **false testimony,** and also the positive command to honor one's parents (Ex. 20:12-16). Jesus did not mention the 10th commandment (Ex. 20:17) concerning coveting, but He did add the summary statement, **Love your neighbor as yourself** (cf. Lev. 19:18; Matt. 22:39; Rom. 13:9; Gal. 5:14; James 2:8).

The young man affirmed he had **kept** all **these** things, but he **still** sensed a **lack** (Matt. 19:20). Whether he had truly kept these commands, only God knows. The young man believed he had and yet he knew something was missing in his life. Jesus put His finger on his problem when He told him to go, sell all his possessions and give to the poor, and he would then have treasure in heaven. Such mercy toward the poor would demonstrate inner righteousness. If he were righteous (based on faith in Jesus as God), he should have given his wealth to the poor and followed Jesus. But instead, the man . . . went away sad (*lypoumenos*, "grieved or sad to the point of distress"; cf. 14:9; 18:31) for he had great wealth. His unwillingness to relinquish his wealth showed he did not love his neighbor as himself. Thus he had not kept all the commandments, and he lacked salvation. Nothing more was written about this young man; probably he never left all and followed Jesus. He loved his money more than God, and thus he violated even the first commandment (Ex. 20:3).

19:23-26. The incident with the young ruler prompted a brief message from Jesus to His disciples. He remarked how difficult it is for a rich man to enter the kingdom of heaven. In fact Jesus said it is easier for a camel to go through the eye of a needle. Since the man was trusting his riches rather than the Lord to save him, he could no more enter the kingdom than a camel (one of the largest animals used by Jews) could go through "the eye of a needle" (*rhaphidos*, a sewing needle; *not* a small gate within another gate as is sometimes suggested). This needle's eye was an extremely small opening. The astonished disciples asked, Who then can be saved? This showed the Pharisees' influence on them, for the Pharisees said God bestows wealth on those He loves. So if a wealthy person cannot make it into the kingdom, seemingly no one can! Jesus answered that salvation is a work of God. What appears to be impossible with men is what God delights to do (cf. 17:20).

11. INSTRUCTION CONCERNING SERVICE AND REWARDS (19:27–20:16)

19:27-30. In the previous incident Jesus told the rich young man to sell all he had and follow Him. This was exactly what the disciples had done, as expressed by Peter. We have left everything to follow You! What then will there be for us? Whereas the young ruler did not leave his possessions (v. 22), Peter and the other disciples had (4:18-22; 9:9; cf. 16:25). Surely then, Peter reasoned, God would bless them for they were not trusting in their wealth! The Lord explained there would be a renewal (*palingenesia*, "rebirth") of all things. Though the nation was then rejecting His offer of the kingdom, the kingdom would come, with its extensive remaking of things spiritual (Isa. 2:3; 4:2-4; 11:9b), political (Isa. 2:4; 11:1-5, 10-11; 32:16-18), and geographical and physical (Isa. 2:2; 4:5-6; 11:6-9; 35:1-2). Christ will then sit on His glorious throne (cf. Matt. 25:31; Rev. 22:1).

The disciples will have a special place in the kingdom, sitting on thrones and judging the 12 tribes of Israel (cf. Rev. 21:12-14). In fact all who leave their homes and relatives for the Lord's sake will receive physical blessings that will more than compensate for their losses (Matt. 19:29). This will be in addition to their eternal life in His kingdom. While it might appear they are giving up everything now and are the last, they will be given everything eternally and will be first. Conversely those, like the rich young ruler, who appear to have everything now (the first) will discover one day they have lost everything (they will be last; cf. 20:16).

20:1-16. Continuing this discussion, Jesus told a parable in which a landowner . . . went out early in the morning and hired men to work in his vineyard for the day, at an agreed price of one denarius, the normal daily pay for a laborer. Later, about the third hour (around 9 A.M.) the landowner encouraged others in the marketplace also to work in the vineyard, not for a stipulated wage but for whatever is right. The landowner employed more laborers about the sixth hour (about noon) and at the ninth hour (3 P.M.), and even some at the eleventh hour (5 P.M.) when only one hour was left for labor.

When it came time (evening, i.e., 6 P.M.) for the landowner to pay the workers, he began with those who had worked the shortest amount of time and paid each of them one denarius. When those who had worked the entire day came for their reckoning, they thought they would receive more than a denarius. They had labored all day and borne the burden of the work and the heat of the

65

day. They had agreed, however, to work for a stipulated amount and that is what they received (v. 13). The landowner argued that he had the right to do what he chose with his money. He reminded them they should not be envious of his generosity toward those who had labored only briefly.

By this illustration, Jesus was teaching that the matter of rewards is under the sovereign control of God, the "Landowner" in the parable. God is the One before whom all accounts will be settled. Many who have prominent places will someday find themselves demoted. And many who often find themselves at the end of the line will find themselves promoted to the head of the line: The last will be first, and the first will be last. (This supports what Jesus had said in 19:28-30.) In the final accounting, the Lord's analysis will carry the greatest and only important weight.

12. INSTRUCTION CONCERNING HIS DEATH (20:17-19)
(MARK 10:32-34; LUKE 18:31-34)

20:17-19. One could never say Jesus did not prepare His disciples for His death. At least three times already He had announced that He was going to die (12:40; 16:21; 17:22-23). He was now on the road to Jerusalem (cf. Jesus' movements geographically: 4:12; 16:13; 17:24; 19:1; 21:1). Once again He told the disciples that death awaited Him in that city. Here He spoke for the first time of His betrayal, mocking, flogging, and crucifixion. But He also reminded them that death was not the end for Him, for He would rise again on the third day (cf. 16:21; 17:23). The disciples gave no response to the Lord's words. Perhaps they could not bring themselves to believe the Lord was indeed going to be treated in that way.

13. INSTRUCTION CONCERNING AMBITION (20:20-28)
(MARK 10:35-45)

20:20-23. Jesus' recent discussion about "the renewal of all things" (19:28) prompted the following incident. The mother of James and John came to Jesus with her two sons and bowed before Him. When Jesus inquired what her request was, she asked that her two sons might be granted places of favor in His kingdom, one seated at His right hand and one at His left. Perhaps she had heard Jesus say His disciples would be seated on thrones (19:28), and she, with typical motherly pride, felt her sons deserved the two best locations.

Jesus did not correct her as to the fact of His coming kingdom. His only question was addressed to the two sons (you is pl.), who apparently had urged their mother to make the request. He asked if they could drink the cup He was about to drink. Jesus was speaking of His coming trials and death as He would be betrayed and die on a cross (26:39, 42). They both replied, We can. Jesus indicated they would indeed share the cup of suffering and death with Him. James suffered death early in the Church Age at the hands of Herod Agrippa I (Acts 12:1-2), and John is thought to have died a martyr's death near the end of the first century.

However, granting positions of honor to His right and left in the kingdom is not His prerogative. Those places will be filled by those . . . whom the Father, the gracious and generous Judge (cf. Matt. 20:1-16), will appoint (v. 23). This account illustrates again that the disciples did not understand Jesus' teaching about humility (cf. 18:1-6). Peter's question (19:27) also demonstrated a desire for position. This the disciples continued to discuss, even to the point of the Lord's death.

20:24-28. When the 10 disciples heard about the request by James and John's mother, they became indignant. They were probably sorry they had not thought of it first! (cf. 18:1) Jesus was of course aware of the friction evident within the group. So He called the Twelve together and reminded them of some important principles. While some people (rulers and high officials) lord it over others, the disciples were not to do so. Greatness in the Lord's kingdom does not come through rulership or authority but through service (20:26-27). Their goal should be serving, not ruling. Those most highly esteemed will be those who serve, those who are humble.

There was no greater example of this principle than the Lord Himself. He did not come into the world to be served, but to serve, and to give His life as a ransom for many. Here was the first clue as to what the death of Christ would accomplish. He had told them on a number of occasions He would die. But He had not indicated the reason for His death. Now it was clear that His death would be to provide a "ransom" (*lytron*, "payment") "for" (*anti*, "in place of") "many" (see the chart, "New Testament Words for Redemption" at Mark 10:45). His death would take the place of many deaths, for only His death could truly atone for sin (John 1:29; Rom. 5:8; 1 Peter 2:24; 3:18). He was the perfect Sacrifice, whose substitutionary death paid the price for sin.

14. INSTRUCTION CONCERNING AUTHORITY (20:29-34)

(MARK 10:46-52; LUKE 18:35-43)

20:29-34. In a final display of His authority before He reached Jerusalem, **Jesus** healed **two blind men** near the city of **Jericho.** The other Synoptic writers (Mark and Luke) repeat this story with a few differences. Matthew wrote of two men; Mark and Luke spoke of one. Mark included the name of the blind man, Bartimaeus. Undoubtedly two men were there and Bartimaeus was the more noticeable of the two. Matthew and Mark said the men were healed when Jesus left Jericho, but Luke said the healing occurred when Jesus approached Jericho. This can be explained by the fact that there were two Jerichos then, an old city and a new one. Jesus was leaving old Jericho (Matt. and Mark) and approaching new Jericho (Luke) when the miracle occurred.

The blind men cried out for help **when they heard . . . Jesus was** passing **by.** Their appeal to Him was based on the fact that He is the **Lord, Son of David.** Earlier two other blind men called Jesus "Son of David" (Matt. 9:27; cf. 15:22). By using this title, they were appealing to Him as Messiah. They persisted in spite of the rebuke from **the crowd** until **Jesus stopped and called them** out. When **He asked** what they wanted, they simply replied they wanted their **sight. Jesus had compassion** (*splanchnistheis;* cf. comments on 9:36) **on them and** exercising His authority as the Messiah, the **Son of David,** He healed them **immediately.** It is interesting that this extended section (17:14-20:34), in which Jesus was teaching the disciples things they would need after His death, ended with a demonstration of

His authority. Truly He is to be believed for He is the Son of David, the Messiah of Israel.

VI. Climax of the King's Offer (chaps. 21-27)

A. The official presentation of the King (21:1-22)

1. THE TRIUMPHAL ENTRY (21:1-11)

(MARK 11:1-11; LUKE 19:28-42; JOHN 12:12-14)

21:1-5. Jesus and the disciples were approaching **Jerusalem** from the east as they came up the road from Jericho. When they reached the town of **Bethphage** on the eastern slopes of **the Mount of Olives,** Jesus **sent two** disciples ahead to **find a donkey** and its **colt.** Though all four Gospel accounts include the Triumphal Entry, only Matthew mentioned a donkey along with the colt. A simple explanation of what some call a contradiction is that when Jesus rode the colt, the mother donkey naturally went along. Perhaps He rode each animal part of the distance (v. 7).

Jesus told the disciples to **bring** the animals **to Him. If anyone** questioned their actions, they were to say **the Lord** needed **them.** As Messiah He had the right to request whatever He needed. Matthew mentioned (vv. 4-5) that this act fulfilled a prophecy, namely, Zechariah 9:9 (cf. Isa. 62:11), which spoke to the nation of the coming of her **King** in a **gentle** manner **riding on . . . a colt, the foal** (lit., **son)** of a donkey. This was not the normal manner in which kings arrived, for they usually came as conquerors riding on horses. A colt was a symbol of peace.

21:6-8. The disciples got the animals, threw **their** garments **on them** to make saddles, and people in the **large crowd spread their cloaks** (cf. 2 Kings 9:13) and tree **branches** on the road. Most of these people were pilgrims from Galilee on their way to Jerusalem to celebrate the Passover. They were familiar with Jesus and the many miracles He had performed in Galilee.

21:9. As the people walked along, some before Jesus and some behind **Him,** they were probably singing some of the pilgrim psalms. Matthew noted that they (including children, v. 15) **shouted** the words of Psalm 118:26, **Blessed is He**

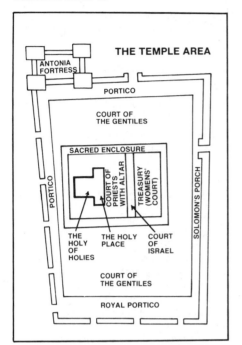

THE TEMPLE AREA

ANTONIA FORTRESS

PORTICO

COURT OF THE GENTILES

SACRED ENCLOSURE

PORTICO

COURT OF PRIESTS WITH ALTAR

TREASURY (WOMENS' COURT)

SOLOMON'S PORCH

THE HOLY OF HOLIES

THE HOLY PLACE

COURT OF ISRAEL

COURT OF THE GENTILES

ROYAL PORTICO

who comes in the name of the Lord. To Him they shouted, **Hosanna to the Son of David.** "Hosanna" is from the Hebrew *hôšî'âh nā'*, "Save (us), we pray," taken from Psalm 118:25. It came to be a note of praise as well as petition.

While the crowd did not fully understand the significance of this event, they seemed to be acknowledging that this One is the promised Seed of David who had come to grant them salvation. Both their actions and words bestowed honor on this One coming into the city, at last presenting Himself publicly as their King.

21:10-11. As **Jesus entered Jerusalem, the** entire **city was** moved **and asked, Who is this?** Since Jesus had usually avoided the city, its inhabitants did not know Him. Those accompanying Jesus from out of town kept answering, **This is Jesus, the Prophet from Nazareth in Galilee** (cf. v. 46). As *the* Prophet, He is the One promised by Moses (Deut. 18:15). Luke recorded that Jesus wept over the city (Luke 19:41) and told the religious leaders that the day was a significant time for the nation: "If you, even you, had only known on this day what would bring you peace—but now it is hidden from your eyes" (Luke 19:42). Jesus may well have had in mind the

significant prophecy of Daniel concerning the time of Messiah's coming and that He had arrived in Jerusalem at the very time predicted by Daniel over 500 years previously (Dan. 9:25-26). This event marked the official presentation of Jesus Christ to the nation of Israel as the rightful Son of David.

2. THE MESSIANIC AUTHORITY (21:12-14)
(MARK 11:15-19; LUKE 19:45-48)

21:12-14. While Matthew's account seems to imply **Jesus entered the temple** immediately after His entry into Jerusalem, the other accounts state that Jesus returned to Bethany after the entry. The cleansing of the temple probably occurred the next morning when Jesus returned to Jerusalem from Bethany (Mark 11:11-16).

As Messiah Jesus entered the temple **area,** His indignation was directed toward those who had changed the character of the temple from a place **of prayer** into a place of corrupt commercialism. Many were making their living from the temple and the sacrifices purchased there. They insisted that in the temple the people could not use money that had been circulating in society, but had to change their money into temple money first, for a fee, and then use the temple money to purchase animals for sacrifice, at inflated prices. Since such extortion was completely contrary to the temple's purposes, the Lord **overturned** their **tables** and **benches** in the outer court of the Gentiles (see sketch) while quoting parts of two Old Testament verses, Isaiah 56:7 and Jeremiah 7:11. (Jesus had previously cleared the temple at the beginning of His ministry [John 2:14-16].)

Jesus further demonstrated His authority by healing **the blind and the lame** who **came to Him at the temple.** (Only Matthew recorded this fact.) Normally such individuals were excluded from the temple, but Jesus' authority brought many changes.

3. THE OFFICIAL INDIGNATION (21:15-17)

21:15-17. As Jesus healed those who came to Him in the temple, **children** ascribed praise to Him, **shouting . . . Hosanna to the Son of David,** clearly a messianic title (cf. comments on v. 9). **The chief priests and the teachers of the Law** were angered by Jesus' works and the children's praises. **Were indignant** comes from a verb meaning "to be stirred up in anger," used only in the Synoptic Gospels (cf. 20:24; 26:8; Mark 10:14, 41; 14:4; Luke 13:14). Their question to Jesus, **Do You hear what these children are saying?** implied a request that Jesus make them stop. Probably many of the "children" **in the temple** were there for the first time, celebrating their becoming men in the society. Such influence on young minds was not thought to be in the best interests of the nation. Jesus replied by quoting from Psalm 8:2, which spoke of **praise** coming **from the lips of children and infants.** By receiving their praise, Jesus was declaring He was worthy of praise as their Messiah. The religious leaders, in rejecting Jesus, did not even have the insights of children, who were receiving Him (cf. Matt. 18:3-4). Consequently Jesus **left** the leaders and departed from the temple. He returned **to the town of Bethany,** about a two-mile walk over the Mount of Olives, **where He spent the night,** probably in the home of Mary, Martha, and Lazarus.

4. THE SYMBOLIC REJECTION (21:18-22) (MARK 11:12-14, 20-25)

21:18-22. As Jesus was making **His way back to the city** of Jerusalem the next morning . . . **He was hungry.** He saw **a fig tree by the road** and noticed it was covered with **leaves.** As He drew closer, He discovered there was no fruit on the tree. Fig trees **bear fruit** first and then the leaves appear, or both appear about the same time. Since the tree was in leaf, figs should have been on it. When Jesus **found** none, He cursed the tree and it **immediately . . . withered.** Mark indicated that the disciples heard Jesus curse the tree, but did not notice the withered condition till they returned to Jerusalem the next morning (Mark 11:13-14, 20). **The disciples** marveled (*ethaumasan*) that the **tree** withered **so quickly.**

Jesus used this event to teach a lesson in **faith,** for if they had genuine faith in God they not only would be able to do miracles such as cursing the **tree,** but they would be able to move mountains (cf. Matt. 17:20). If they truly believed, they would **receive whatever** they prayed **for.** The Lord was teaching the importance of faith rather than doubting or simply marveling. By con-

trast the nation of Israel had failed to exercise faith in Him.

This event may have meaning beyond the lesson in faith, however. Many believe that Jesus saw this fig tree as a symbol of Israel at that time. They too were professing to be fruitful, but a closer examination of the nation revealed they were fruitless. By cursing that generation, Jesus was showing His rejection of them and predicting that no fruit would ever come from them. Within a few days, that generation would reject their King and crucify Him. This ultimately led to judgment on that generation. In A.D. 70 the Romans came, demolished the temple, overran the country of Israel, and ended Israel's political entity (Luke 21:20). Perhaps in cursing the fig tree, Jesus was setting aside that generation. Of course the entire nation was not set aside (cf. Rom. 11:1, 26).

B. The religious confrontation with the King (21:23–22:46)

1. CONFRONTATION WITH THE PRIESTS AND ELDERS (21:23–22:14) (MARK 11:27–12:12; LUKE 20:1-19)

a. The attack (21:23)

21:23. Jesus returned to **the temple courts** He had just recently claimed for His Father. In these courts He confronted various religious groups in the nation. The debate began as **the chief priests and the elders** asked Jesus, **By what authority are You doing these things? And who gave You this authority?** By "these things" they probably meant His Triumphal Entry into the city, His reception of praise from the people, His clearing of the temple, His healing of the blind and the lame (vv. 8-14), and His teaching (v. 23). The leaders understood Jesus was claiming authority as Messiah and wanted to know where He got such authority. He certainly had not received it from them!

b. The response (21:24–22:14)

(1) The baptism of John (21:24-32). **21:24-27 (Mark 11:29-33; Luke 20:3-8).** In response to the religious leaders' question, **Jesus** asked another **question,** promising that if they answered His question, He would answer theirs. He asked, **John's baptism—where did it come from? Was it from heaven, or from**

men? Though this question seemed fairly simple, it prompted a debate among the religious leaders. If they answered that John's baptism was **from heaven,** they knew Jesus would respond, **Then why didn't you believe him?** On the other hand **if** they responded that John's baptism was **from men,** they knew **the people** would be upset with them. John was regarded as **a** great **prophet** by the populace. Jesus thus put them in a position in which *they* had tried to place *Him* on many occasions. **They** finally responded that they did not **know** the answer to Jesus' question. In keeping with His word, **Jesus** therefore refused to answer their question. Instead He gave a parable.

21:28-32. In Jesus' parable **a man** asked his **two sons to go . . . work in the vineyard. The first** son said he would **not** go **but later he changed his mind and went. The other** immediately said he would **go** and work but he never showed up. Jesus then asked, **Which of the two did what his father wanted?** The obvious answer was that **the first** son obeyed. **Jesus** immediately applied this to the religious leaders. While some seemingly accepted the ministry of **John** the Baptist (John 5:35), their actions (Luke 7:29-30) proved they were like the second son. On the other·hand many **tax collectors** and **prostitutes** received the message of John and did the will of the Father. Therefore they would be allowed entrance into **the kingdom of God.** But the religious leaders who **did not repent and believe** would be denied entrance. These religious leaders stood condemned. They must have been stunned by Jesus' words that despised, immoral people such as tax collectors and prostitutes were entering the kingdom and they, the religious leaders, were not!

(2) The Parable of the Landowner (21:33-46; Mark 12:1-12; Luke 20:9-19). **21:33-39.** In **another parable** Jesus continued to demonstrate the response of the nation to His ministry. He told of **a landowner who** went to great expense to make **a vineyard** productive. He **rented** out **the vineyard** to **farmers** who were to care for it. When **harvesttime** came, the landowner **sent his servants . . . to collect** what was rightfully **his.** But the tenant farmers mistreated the **servants,** beating **one,** killing **another,** and stoning **a third.**

Other servants were **sent** with **the same** results. Finally the landowner **sent his son,** thinking they would **respect** him. The farmers, however, reasoned that if they killed the son, the land would be theirs. Therefore they **threw him out of the vineyard and killed him.**

It seems clear that Jesus was speaking of the nation of Israel that had been carefully prepared by God to be His fruitful vineyard (cf. Isa. 5:1-7). The care of the vine had been committed to the nation's religious leaders. But they had failed to acknowledge the Master's right over them and had treated His messengers and prophets badly. They ultimately would even kill His Son, Jesus Christ, outside Jerusalem (cf. Heb. 13:12).

21:40-46. Jesus posed a natural question when He asked His listeners what they thought the landowner would **do to those** unfaithful farmers. Obviously he would not let them continue to operate the vineyard, but he would **bring** judgment on them. The land would be taken away from them and used by **other tenants who** would **give him his** rightful **share of** the **harvest.** This was in keeping with the Scriptures, for Jesus quoted Psalm 118:22-23, which refers to the **rejected** stone which will **become the capstone.**

By way of application Jesus said **the kingdom of God** was being **taken away from** those who heard Him, **and** it would be **given to the people who** would **produce its fruit.** The word for "people" (*ethnei*) is usually translated "nation." (It appears here without an article.) Two interpretations of this verse are often presented. One is that Jesus was saying the kingdom had been taken from the Jewish nation and would be given to Gentile nations who would produce the proper fruit of genuine faith. It is argued that since *ethnei* is singular, not plural, the word refers to the church which is called a nation in Romans 10:19 and 1 Peter 2:9-10. But the kingdom has not been taken completely away from Israel forever (Rom. 11:15, 25). And the church is not now inheriting the kingdom.

A better interpretation is that Jesus was simply saying the kingdom was being taken away from the nation Israel at that time, but it would be given back to the nation in a future day when that nation would demonstrate true repentance and faith. In this view Jesus was using the term "nation" in the sense of generation (cf. Matt. 23:36). Because of their rejection, that generation of Israel would never be able to experience the kingdom of God (cf. comments on 21:18-22). But a future generation in Israel will respond in saving faith to this same Messiah (Rom. 11:26-27), and to that future generation the kingdom will be given. By rejecting Jesus the Stone, these builders (Matt. 21:42) suffered judgment (he on whom it [the Stone] falls will be crushed). The religious leaders (then the chief priests and the Pharisees, v. 45; cf. v. 23) realized Jesus' remarks were directed toward them, and they tried their best to arrest Him. But they were afraid of the . . . people (cf. v. 26), who thought Jesus was a Prophet (cf. v. 11), so they were unable to act.

(3) The Parable of the Wedding Feast (22:1-14; Luke 14:15-24). 22:1-7. In a third parable addressed to the religious leaders (cf. the other two parables in 21:28-32 and 21:33-44) Jesus again referred to God's work in offering the kingdom. The figure of a wedding banquet here portrays the Millennial Age (cf. 9:15; Isa. 25:6; Luke 14:15). The king in this parable had made plans for a wedding banquet for his son. His servants had told those invited that it was time for the banquet, but the invitation was ignored and the guests refused to come. Further effort was put forth to extend the invitation but the same result followed. Since the offer was rejected to the point of mistreating and killing the servants, the king was enraged. He sent his army and destroyed those murderers and burned their city.

Jesus had in mind the effect of the nation's rejection of Him. God had made plans for His Son's millennial reign and the invitation had been extended. But the preaching of John the Baptist, Jesus, and the disciples had largely been ignored. The nation would even kill those extending the offer. Finally in A.D. 70 the Roman army would come, kill most of the Jews living in Jerusalem, and destroy the temple.

22:8-14. The wedding banquet, however, was prepared. Since those who were first invited had rejected the invitation, opportunity to attend was then given to a broader group. Though the invitation was extended to both good and

bad, individual preparation was still necessary. This was evidenced by the fact that one guest at the banquet had not made adequate preparation. He had failed to appropriate what the king provided for he was not wearing the proper wedding clothes. (Apparently the king gave them all wedding clothes as they arrived, for they came off the streets [v. 10]. A person must respond not only outwardly, but also he must be rightly related to God the King by appropriating all the King provides.) Consequently this guest was cast out into a place of separation and suffering. (For comments on weeping and gnashing of teeth, see 13:42.) While the kingdom had now been expanded to include individuals from all races and backgrounds (many are invited), there is an election (few are chosen). And yet individual response is essential.

2. CONFRONTATION WITH THE PHARISEES AND THE HERODIANS (22:15-22) (MARK 12:13-17; LUKE 20:20-26)

22:15-17. This incident illustrates that controversy often makes strange bedfellows. The religious leaders of Israel had one goal: to get rid of Jesus of Nazareth. They would do this through any means possible, even if it meant cooperating with lifelong enemies. The Pharisees were the purists of the nation who opposed Rome and all attempts by Rome to intrude into the Jewish way of life. But the Herodians actively supported the rule of Herod the Great and favored making changes with the times as dictated by Rome. But those issues were less important to them than the pressing issue of getting rid of Jesus. So they sent a delegation to try to trick Jesus.

They began by saying several nice things about Him, but their hypocrisy was obvious for they really did not believe in Him. Their question was, Is it right to pay taxes to Caesar or not? Their cleverly devised question appeared to have no clear-cut answer. They thought they had trapped Jesus. If He answered that it was right to pay taxes to Caesar, He would be siding with the Romans against Israel and most Jews, including the Pharisees, would consider Him a traitor. If, however, He said taxes should not be paid to Rome, He could be accused of being a rebel who opposed the authority of Rome, and the Herodians would be against Him.

22:18-22. Jesus was aware of the hypocrisy in their approach and also of the implications of His answer. He therefore answered their question by demonstrating that government does have a rightful place in everyone's life and that one can be in subjection to government and God at the same time. He asked them to give Him a **coin used** to pay **the tax.** A Roman **denarius,** with its image of Caesar, the Roman emperor, made it obvious they were under Roman authority and taxation. (One coin inscription reads, "Tiberius Caesar Augustus, son of the Divine Augustus.") Therefore the taxes must be paid: **Give to Caesar what is Caesar's.**

But Jesus also reminded them that a sphere of authority belongs to God: **Give to God what is God's.** Individuals are to be subject *also* to His authority. Man has both political *and* spiritual responsibilities. **Amazed** at Jesus' answer, both the Pharisees and the Herodians were silenced.

3. CONFRONTATION WITH THE SADDUCEES (22:23-33)

(MARK 12:18-27; LUKE 20:27-40)

22:23-28. The Sadducees were the next religious group to try to discredit Jesus and His ministry. The Sadducees were the "religious liberals" of their day for they said **there is no resurrection** or angels or spirits (Acts 23:8). Purposely their question centered on the doctrine of resurrection and its implications in a particular case. They cited the story of a woman who **married** a man who later **died.** In accordance with the levirate law (Deut. 25:5-10), her husband's **brother** took her as **his wife** (in order to perpetuate the dead brother's line). But he too died shortly thereafter. This happened with **seven brothers.**

The Sadducees' question therefore was, **At the resurrection, whose wife will she be of the seven, since all of them were married to her?** The Sadducees implied that heaven was simply an extension of things on earth men most enjoy, such as marital relationships. But if this woman had seven husbands, how could her marital relationship be possi-

ble? The Sadducees were trying to make the resurrection appear ridiculous.

22:29-33. The Sadducees' problems arose, Jesus said, because they did **not know the Scriptures or the power of God.** This was a strong denunciation of religious leaders, for of all people certainly they should have known God's Word and His power. God's Word taught the resurrection, and His power can bring people back to life. Jesus then corrected the Sadducees' two false notions: (1) **Heaven,** He said, is not simply an extension of the pleasures people enjoy on earth. In fact in the eternal state **marriage** will be unnecessary. Once individuals have received glorified bodies no longer subject to death, the need for procreation, one of the basic purposes for marriage, will no longer exist. Believers in glorified bodies **will be like the angels in** that regard, for angels do not reproduce themselves. (He did not say people will *become* angels.) Jesus did not answer all the questions about the eternal state and the eternal relationship of those married in this life. But He did answer the immediate question raised by the Sadducees. (2) A more important issue raised by the Sadducees pertained to **the resurrection.** If they had read and understood the Old Testament Scriptures, they would have clearly seen there is a future life and that when a person dies he continues to exist. To the Sadducees the resurrection was ridiculous because they believed death ended man's existence. But Jesus quoted a statement God had made directly to Moses at the burning bush: **I am the God of Abraham, the God of Isaac, and the God of Jacob** (Ex. 3:6). If the Sadducees were correct and Abraham, Isaac, and Jacob had died and were no longer present anywhere, the words "I am" should have been "I was." The use of the present tense, "I am," implied that God is still the God of these patriarchs for they are alive with God and ultimately will share in the resurrection of the righteous. As a result of this encounter, **the crowds . . . were astonished** (*exeplēssonto;* cf. comments on Matt. 7:28; and cf. *ethaumasan* in 22:22) all the more **at His teaching.** Jesus thus successfully answered and defeated these religious experts.

4. CONFRONTATION WITH THE PHARISEES (22:34-46)

(MARK 12:28-37; LUKE 10:25-28)

a. Their interrogation of Jesus (22:34-40)

22:34-40. When **the Pharisees** heard that **Jesus had** answered **the Sadducees,** they quickly sent a representative, a well-versed **expert in the Law,** to Jesus with a **question . . . Which is the greatest commandment in the Law?** This question was being debated among the religious leaders at the time and various commandments were being championed as the greatest. Jesus' quick reply summarized the entire Decalogue. He replied that the **greatest commandment** is to **love the Lord . . . God with all** one's **heart . . . soul, and . . . mind** (cf. Deut. 6:5). He added that **the second** commandment **is** to **love** one's **neighbor as** oneself (cf. Lev. 19:18). The first summarizes the first table of the Law, and the second summarizes the second table. Jesus said, **All the Law and the Prophets hang on these two commandments,** that is, all the Old Testament develops and amplifies these two points: love for God and love for others, who are made in God's image.

Mark reported that the teacher of the Law said Jesus had correctly answered the question, and that love for God and one's neighbor is more important than burnt offerings and sacrifices (Mark 12:32-33). The light was beginning to shine into his heart. He was not far, Jesus said, from the kingdom of God. Mark also added, "From then on no one dared ask Him any more questions" (Mark 12:34). The reason was obvious. Jesus was answering them as no had ever done. In fact in this last incident, the questioner was close to leaving the Pharisees and accepting Jesus. Perhaps they felt they should stop before they would lose any more people to Jesus' cause.

b. Jesus' interrogation of them (22:41-46)

(Mark 12:35-37; Luke 20:41-44)

22:41-46. Since **the Pharisees** refused to ask **Jesus** any further questions, He took the offensive and posed a question to **them.** His question sought to solicit their views concerning Messiah. He asked, **What do you think about the Christ? Whose Son is He?** Their answer came quickly for they knew the Messiah was to come from the line of David. Jesus' reply (vv. 43-45) demonstrated that the

Messiah had to be more than simply a human **son of David,** as many in that time were thinking. If the Messiah were simply an earthly son of David, why did David ascribe deity to Him? Jesus quoted from a messianic psalm (Ps. 110:1), in which David referred to the Messiah as **my Lord.** "Lord" translates the Hebrew *'ăḏōnāy,* used only of God (e.g., Gen. 18:27; Job 28:28). If David called this Son "Lord," He certainly must be more than a human son.

The complexities of this theological discussion were too much for the Pharisees who were not ready to acknowledge the deity of this Son of David. **No one . . . dared** answer His question or debate points of practice or theology with Jesus. All His opponents had been silenced, including the chief priests and elders (Matt. 21:23-27), the Pharisees and Herodians together (22:15-22), the Sadducees (vv. 23-33), and the Pharisees (vv. 34-36).

C. The national rejection of the King (chap. 23)

(Mark 12:38-40; Luke 11:37-52; 20:45-47)

1. HIS WARNING TO THE MULTITUDES (23:1-12)

23:1-12. The hypocrisy and unbelief of the nation's religious leaders, evidenced in chapter 22, prompted a strong message from **Jesus.** He turned **to the crowds and to His disciples,** who were in the temple listening to His debates with the various religious leaders. He warned them about their teachings saying that their *authority* was to be recognized (they **sit in Moses' seat,** i.e., they teach the Law), but their *practices,* being hypocritical, should not be followed. They placed **heavy** burdens **on** people but were not righteous **themselves** (23:4). All their works were performed to be observed by **men. Their phylacteries,** small leather pouches containing strips of parchment with Old Testament verses (Ex. 13:9, 16; Deut. 6:8; 11:18), tied to their left arms and foreheads, were **wide** and thus conspicuous. **And the tassels of their prayer shawls** (Num. 15:38) were **long** and noticeable. **They** loved places **of honor** and to be called **Rabbi,** implying they were scholars. Such was not to be the attitude of Jesus' followers. Titles (such as **Rabbi . . . father . . . teacher)** and position were not to be sought; instead there should be a brotherly relationship among the disciples (Matt. 23:8).

Jesus was not saying there would be no lines of authority among them. But He was emphasizing that service for Him—the one Master (*didaskalos*, lit., "teacher") and one Teacher (*kathēgētēs*, "an authoritative guide," used only here in the NT)—was more important than human positions of honor. Leadership positions should never be a goal in and of themselves, but should always be viewed as opportunities to serve others. The Pharisees, who exalted themselves, would be humbled, and Jesus' followers, by humbling themselves in service, would someday be exalted.

2. HIS WARNINGS TO THE LEADERS (23:13-39)

23:13. In warning the teachers of the Law and the Pharisees of their ultimate destruction if they continued in their present path, Jesus pronounced seven denunciations, each beginning with Woe to you. "Those woes, in contrast to the Beatitudes, denounce false religion as utterly abhorrent to God and worthy of severe condemnation" (Walvoord, *Matthew: Thy Kingdom Come*, p. 171). In six of the seven, Jesus called the leaders you hypocrites.

His first denunciation concerned the fact that the Pharisees were preventing others from entering the kingdom. Their antagonism toward Jesus had caused many to turn away from Him. Many Jews were looking to their leaders for direction. Their failure to accept Jesus as Messiah had placed a stumbling block in the paths of their countrymen. For this they stood condemned.

23:14. The NIV and some Greek manuscripts omit this verse. It may have been added because of Mark 12:40 and Luke 20:47. If it is authentic here, the number of woes is eight. This "woe" demonstrated the inconsistency of the religious leaders for they made long "prayers" to impress people with their spirituality, but also oppressed widows, whom they should have helped.

23:15. This woe addressed the zealous activity of the religious leaders for they actively traveled not only over land but also over the sea to make even a single convert (*prosēlyton*, "proselyte") to Judaism. The problem with this was that

by their actions they were condemning many individuals to eternal damnation. By imposing external restrictions of Rabbinic traditions on their converts, they were preventing these people from seeing the truth. In fact, such a convert became twice as much a son of hell as the Pharisees, that is, he became more pharisaic than the Pharisees themselves! "A son of hell" (lit., "of Gehenna"; cf. v. 33), was one deserving eternal punishment.

23:16-22. In the third woe Jesus pointed out the tricky character of the leaders. (In the first two woes Jesus spoke of the leaders' effects on others; in the other five woes He spoke of the leaders' own characters and actions.) When taking oaths, they made fine lines of distinction that could possibly invalidate their oaths. If one swore by the temple, or by the altar of the temple, it meant nothing to them. While thus appearing to be making a binding oath, they inwardly had no intention of keeping it. But if one swore by the gold of the temple or the gift on the altar, he would be bound by the oath. But Jesus said they were wrong in suggesting that gold was greater than the temple and a gift greater than the altar. Jesus pointed out that any oath based on the temple or things in it was binding for behind the temple was the One who dwelt in it. This was parallel to making an oath by God's throne, for that oath was also binding because of the One who sat on the throne. Such distinctions by the religious leaders were condemned by Jesus, for they were clearly deceptive and dishonest. Jesus denounced those leaders as blind guides (v. 16), blind fools (v. 17), and blind men (v. 19; cf. vv. 24, 26).

23:23-24. The fourth woe related to the pharisaic practice of meticulously tithing all their possessions. They went so far as to carry the practice down to the smallest spices from plants: mint, dill, and cummin. While meticulously following the Law in this area (Lev. 27:30), they failed to manifest the justice, mercy, and faithfulness demanded by the Law. They were majoring on minors, straining out a gnat, while minoring on majors, swallowing a camel. Being so busy with small details, they never dealt with the important matters. Jesus was not saying tithing was unimportant; He was saying they were completely neglecting the one area at the expense of the other. They **should have** been doing both. Since they were not, they were **blind guides.**

23:25-26. The fifth **woe** emphasized the hypocritical nature of the **Pharisees.** They were concerned with external cleanliness, such as **the outside of the cup and dish** from which they would eat. But in their hearts were **greed and self-indulgence.** Their cleansing was primarily for the sake of being seen by men. But they were not above robbery and excesses in their own lives. If cleansing would take place internally, their **outside** would **also be** affected.

23:27-28. In the sixth **woe** Jesus continued the thought of the previous statement about external purification. The fifth woe stressed their actions; the sixth, their appearances. He called the **teachers of the Law and the Pharisees . . . whitewashed tombs.** A custom then was to keep tombs painted white **on the outside** so they would appear **beautiful.** But **inside** the tombs was the decaying flesh of dead people. Similarly, while the Pharisees appeared beautiful **on the outside** because of their religious conformity, they were corrupt and decaying **inside.** They were **full of hypocrisy and wickedness** (*anomias,* "lawlessness").

23:29-32. The final **woe** also emphasized the religious leaders' hypocrisy. They spent time building **tombs** and decorating **the graves of the righteous.** They were quick to **say** that **if they had lived in** the **time of the prophets,** they **would** never have been involved **in shedding the blood** of these righteous men. Jesus knew they were already in the process of planning His death. By that act they would demonstrate they were just like the former generations **who murdered the prophets.** By rejecting the Prophet, they would be following in the footsteps of their forefathers and "filling up" their ancestors' **sin.**

23:33-36. In severe language Jesus condemned the religious leaders, calling them **snakes** and a **brood of vipers,** whose eternal destiny was **hell** (lit., "Gehenna"), the place of eternal punishment (cf. v. 15; cf. comments on Gehenna in 5:22). The evidence that they were deserving of hell would be their continual rejection of the truth. The Lord promised to send them **prophets and wise men and teachers,** but the leaders would reject

their words and even **kill** some and **flog** and **pursue** others. Their response to the proclaimed truth would justify the judgment coming on them. **Abel** was the first **righteous** martyr mentioned in the Hebrew Scriptures (Gen. 4:8) and **Zechariah** was the last martyr (2 Chron. 24:20-22), 2 Chronicles being last in the Hebrew Bible. (In this statement Jesus attested the Old Testament canon.) In 2 Chronicles 24:20, Zechariah is called the "son of Jehoiada," whereas in Matthew he is the **son of Berakiah.** "Son of" can mean descendant; thus Jehoiada, being a priest, could have been Zechariah's grandfather. Or Jesus may have had in mind the Prophet Zechariah who *was* the son of Berakiah (Zech. 1:1). On that **generation** (*genean*) of Jews, who were guilty because they were following their blind (Matt. 23:16-17, 19, 24, 26) leaders, would fall God's judgment for their involvement in shedding innocent **blood.** The Lord was anticipating the nation's continuing rejection of the gospel. Their refusal of the Messiah ultimately led to the destruction of the temple in A.D. 70.

23:37-39 (Luke 13:34-35). In a final lament over the city of **Jerusalem,** Jesus stated His desire for that nation. **Jerusalem,** the capital, represented the entire nation, and people there had killed **the prophets** and stoned **those sent to** them (cf. Matt. 23:34; 21:35). He **longed to gather** the nation **together** much **as a hen gathers her chicks under her wings.** The nation, unlike chicks that naturally run to their mother hen in times of danger, willfully refused (**you were not willing**) to turn to the Lord. They were responsible to make a choice and their choice brought condemnation. The result was their **house** was **left . . . desolate,** or alone. Their "house" could mean their city; this is probably the most commonly accepted view. Or Jesus might have meant the temple or even the Davidic dynasty. Perhaps all these are involved.

But Jesus is not through with the nation and the city of Jerusalem. Though He would soon depart (John 13:33), at a future time He will be seen **again** (Zech. 12:10) and will be accepted, not rejected. In that day the nation will say, **Blessed is He who comes in the name of the Lord,** a quotation of Psalm 118:26. Jesus was speaking of His return to the earth to establish His millennial kingdom. This statement led to the following discussion.

D. The prophetic anticipation of the King (chaps. 24–25)

1. THE INQUIRY TO JESUS (24:1-3)
(MARK 13:1-4; LUKE 21:5-7)

24:1-3. Having completed His discussions and debates with the religious leaders, **Jesus left the temple** to return to Bethany (cf. 26:6) by way of **the Mount of Olives** (24:3). The words Jesus had just uttered were still burning in **His** disciples' ears. He had denounced the nation and said it would be "desolate" (23:38). If Jerusalem and the temple were destroyed, how would there be a nation for Messiah to rule? The **disciples** pointed out the **buildings** of the temple area to Jesus as if to impress Him with their magnificence. What could possibly happen to such impressive buildings, especially to the temple of God? Jesus' response brought them consternation: **Not one stone here will be left on another; every one will be thrown down.** The temple would be destroyed and Jerusalem with it. This, however, prompted **the disciples** to ask when all this would take place. As Jesus reached the Mount of Olives in His walk to Bethany, He sat down and the disciples **came to Him.** Four disciples, Peter, James, John, and Andrew (Mark 13:3), plainly asked Jesus two questions: (1) **When will this happen?** That is, when will the temple be destroyed and not one stone left on another? (2) **What will be the sign of Your coming and of the end of the Age?**

These two questions prompted the following discussion by Jesus, commonly called the Olivet Discourse (Matt. 24–25). The questions related to the destruction of the temple and Jerusalem, and the sign of the Lord's coming and the end of the Age. They have nothing to do with the church, which Jesus said He would build (16:18). The church is not present in any sense in chapters 24 and 25. The disciples' questions related to Jerusalem, Israel, and the Lord's second coming in glory to establish His kingdom. Actually Matthew did not record Jesus' answer to the first question, but Luke did (Luke 21:20). The disciples felt that the destruction of Jerusalem, of which Jesus had spoken, would usher in the kingdom. They were thinking, no doubt, of Zecha-

riah 14:1-2. (The destruction Jesus referred to in Matt. 23:38 occurred in A.D. 70, a destruction separate from the final one in Zech. 14.)

2. THE COMING TIME OF TROUBLE (24:4-26)

24:4-8 (Mark 13:5-8; Luke 21:8-11). Jesus began to describe the events leading up to His return in glory and to indicate signs of that return. In this section (Matt. 24:4-8) He described the first half of the seven-year period preceding His second coming. That period is called the Seventieth Week of Daniel (Dan. 9:27). (However, some premillenarians hold that Christ in Matt. 24:4-8 spoke of general signs in the present Church Age and that the time of trouble begins at v. 9. Others hold that Christ spoke of general signs in vv. 4-14, with the Tribulation beginning at v. 15.) The events described in verses 4-8 correspond somewhat to the seven seals in Revelation 6. (Walvoord, however, holds that all seven of the seal judgments will occur in the second half of the seven-year period; see comments on Rev. 6.)

That period will be characterized by (a) false Christs (Matt. 24:4-5; cf. Rev. 6:1-2; the first seal is Antichrist), (b) **wars and rumors of wars** (Matt. 24:6; cf. Rev. 6:3-4; the second seal is warfare) in which nations **will rise** up **against** each other on a global scale (Matt. 24:7a), and (c) unusual disturbances in nature including **famines** (v. 7b; cf. Rev. 6:5-6; the third seal is famine; the fourth and fifth seals are death and martyrdom [Rev. 6:7-11]) **and earthquakes** (Matt. 24:7b; cf. Rev. 6:12-14; the sixth seal is an earthquake). **These** things, Jesus said, will be **the beginning of birth pains.** As a pregnant woman's birth pains indicate that her child will soon be born, so these universal conflicts and catastrophes will mean the end of this interadvent Age is near.

24:9-14 (Mark 13:9-13; Luke 21:12-19). Jesus began His words (Matt. 24:9) with a time word, **Then.** At the middle point of the seven-year period preceding Christ's second coming, great distress will begin to be experienced by Israel. The Antichrist, who will have risen to power in the world and will have made a protective treaty with Israel, will break his agreement at that time (Dan. 9:27). He will bring great persecution on Israel (Dan. 7:25) and even establish his own center of worship in the temple in Jerusalem (2 Thes. 2:3-4). This will result in the **death** of many Jews (Matt. 24:9) and **many** people departing **from the faith.** Believing Jews **will** be betrayed by nonbelievers (v. 10), and **many** will be deceived by rising **false prophets** (cf. v. 5; Rev. 13:11-15). **Wickedness** will **increase,** causing **the love of most** people (for the Lord) to **grow cold.**

Those who remain faithful to the Lord until **the end** of that period of time **will be saved,** that is, delivered (Matt. 24:13). This does not refer to a personal self-effort at endurance that results in one's eternal salvation, but to physical deliverance of those who trust in the Savior during the Tribulation. They will enter the kingdom in physical bodies.

Also the **gospel of the kingdom will be preached in the whole world** during this period **as a testimony to all nations.** Though this will be a terrible time of persecution, the Lord will have servants who will witness and spread the good news concerning Christ and His soon-coming kingdom. This message will be similar to that preached by John the Baptist, Jesus, and the disciples at the beginning of Matthew's Gospel, but this message will clearly identify Jesus in His true character as the coming Messiah. This is not exactly the same message the church is proclaiming today. The message preached today in the Church Age and the message proclaimed in the Tribulation period calls for turning to the Savior for salvation. However, in the Tribulation the message will stress the coming kingdom, and those who then turn to the Savior for salvation will be allowed entrance into the kingdom. Apparently many will respond to that message (cf. Rev. 7:9-10).

24:15-26 (Mark 13:14-23; Luke 21:20-26). Having given a brief overview of the entire Tribulation period prior to His return, Jesus then spoke of the greatest observable sign within that period, **the abomination that causes desolation.** This abomination was **spoken of** by **Daniel** (Dan. 9:27). It referred to the disruption of the Jewish worship which will be reinstituted in the Tribulation temple (Dan. 12:11) and the establishment of the worship of the world dictator, the Antichrist, in the temple. He will make the temple abominable (and there-

fore desolate) by setting up in the temple an image of himself to be worshiped (2 Thes. 2:4; Rev. 13:14-15). Such an event will be clearly recognizable by everyone.

When that event occurs, **those . . . in Judea** should **flee to the mountains.** They should not be concerned about taking **anything** with them or returning from **the field** for possessions, not even for a **cloak.** The time following this event will be a time of **great distress, unequaled from the beginning of the world . . . and never to be equaled again** (Jer. 30:7). The awful character of the Tribulation period cannot be truly grasped by anyone. This was why Jesus pointed out how difficult the time would be **for pregnant women and nursing mothers** (Matt. 24:19). He encouraged people to **pray that** their escape would **not** have to be in the **winter** when it would be difficult **or on the Sabbath** when travel would be limited.

There was an encouraging note, however, for the Lord declared that **those days** would be **cut short** (v. 22). This meant there will be a termination of this period of time, not that the days will be fewer than 24 hours. If it were to go on indefinitely, **no one would survive. But** the period will come to an end **for the sake of the elect,** those who will be redeemed in the Tribulation and who will enter the kingdom. The elect of this Church Age will have already been raptured before the Tribulation. Much misinformation will be disseminated then **for false Christs** will be all around (vv. 23-24). They all will be preaching messages of salvation and performing **signs and miracles,** seeking **to deceive even the elect.** The Lord warned the disciples **ahead of time** not to be fooled for He would not be on earth working in that way.

3. THE COMING OF THE SON OF MAN (24:27-31)
(MARK 13:24-27; LUKE 21:25-28)

24:27-31. The Lord will not be on the earth bodily at that time, but He will return to earth. And His **coming** will be like **lightning** flashing **from the east . . . to the west;** it will be a splendorous, visible event. **Wherever there is a carcass** (physical corruption), **vultures will** go there to eat it. Similarly, where there is spiritual corruption judgment will follow. The world will have become the domain of Satan's man, the Antichrist, the lawless one (2 Thes. 2:8), and many people will have been corrupted by false prophets (Matt. 24:24). But the Son of Man will come quickly in judgment (v. 27).

Immediately following the distress of that period, the Lord will return. His return will be accompanied by unusual displays in the heavens (v. 29; cf. Isa. 13:10; 34:4; Joel 2:31; 3:15-16) and by the appearing of His "sign" in the sky (Matt. 24:30). The appearance of the sign will cause all the nations to mourn (cf. Rev. 1:7), probably because they will realize the time of their judgment has come.

Exactly what the sign of the Son of Man will be is unknown. The sign of the setting aside of the nation of Israel was the departure of the glory from the temple (Ezek. 10:3, 18; 11:23). Perhaps the sign of the Lord's return will again involve the Shekinah glory. Some believe the sign may involve the heavenly city, New Jerusalem, which may descend at this time and remain as a satellite city suspended over the earthly city Jerusalem throughout the Millennium (Rev. 21:2-3). Or the sign may be the lightning, or perhaps the Lord Himself. Whatever the sign, it will be visible for all to see, for the Lord will return on the clouds . . . with power and great glory (cf. Dan. 7:13). He will then send His angels forth to regather His elect from the four winds, which relates to the earth (cf. Mark 13:27), from one end of the heavens to the other. This involves the gathering of those who will have become believers during the Seventieth Week of Daniel and who will have been scattered into various parts of the world because of persecution (cf. Matt. 24:16). This gathering will probably also involve all Old Testament saints, whose resurrection will occur at this time, so that they may share in Messiah's kingdom (Dan. 12:2-3, 13).

4. THE CONFIRMATION BY PARABLES (24:32-51)

In the previous portion of this sermon (24:4-31) Jesus had spoken directly about His return to earth. Then He gave some practical applications and instructions in light of His return. One should keep in mind that the primary application of this section is directed toward the future generation that will experience the days of the Tribulation and will be looking forward to the immediate coming of the King in glory. A secondary application of this passage, as with much of Scripture, is to believers living today who comprise the body of Christ, the church. The church is not in view in these verses. But just as God's people in a future time are told to be prepared, watchful, and faithful, so too believers today should also be faithful and alert.

a. The fig tree (24:32-44)

24:32-35 (Mark 13:28-31; Luke 21:29-33). Jesus' words, Now learn this lesson, show that He was beginning to apply what He had been teaching. When the twigs of fig trees begin to get tender and put forth leaves, that is a sure sign summer is not far away (cf. Matt. 21:18-20). Just as a fig tree was a harbinger of summer, so these signs (24:4-28) Jesus had been speaking of clearly indicated that His coming would follow shortly. The Lord's emphasis fell on the fact that all these things would be necessary. While various events throughout history have been pointed to as the fulfillment of this prophecy, clearly all these things (pertaining to the Great Tribulation) have never occurred. The completion of all these events is yet future. The generation (genea) of people living in that future day will see the completion of all the events. Jesus was not referring to the generation listening to Him then, for He had already said the kingdom had been taken from that group (21:43). That first-century generation would experience God's judgment. But the generation that will be living at the time these signs begin to take place will live through that period and will see the Lord Jesus coming as the King of glory. This promise is sure, for it would be easier for heaven and earth to pass away than for Christ's words to fail (cf. 5:18).

24:36-41 (Mark 13:32-33; Luke 17:26-37). The precise moment of the Lord's return cannot be calculated by anyone. When the Lord spoke these words, that information was said to be known by only the Father. Christ was obviously speaking from the vantage of His human knowledge (cf. Luke 2:52), not from the standpoint of His divine omniscience. But the period before His coming will be like the time **in the days of Noah. People** then were enjoying the normal pursuits of life, with no awareness of imminent judgment. Life continued normally for the people of Noah's day for they **were eating, drinking, marrying, and giving in marriage.** But **the Flood came and took them all away.** It was sudden and they were unprepared.

As it was in Noah's day, **so it will be** before the glorious **coming of the Lord. Two men will be in the field; one will be taken and the other left. Two women will be grinding with a hand mill; one will be taken and the other left.** Analogous to Noah's day, the individuals who will be "taken" are the wicked whom the Lord will take away in judgment (cf. Luke 17:37). The individuals "left" are believers who will be privileged to be on the earth to populate the kingdom of Jesus Christ in physical bodies. As the wicked were taken away in judgment and Noah was left on the earth, so the wicked will be judged and removed when Christ returns and the righteous will be left behind to become His subjects in the kingdom.

Clearly the church, the body of Christ, cannot be in view in these statements. The Lord was not describing the Rapture, for the removal of the church will not be a judgment on the church. If this were the Rapture, as some commentators affirm, the Rapture would have to be posttribulational, for *this* event occurs immediately before the Lord's return in glory. But that would conflict with a number of Scriptures and present other problems that cannot be elaborated on here (cf., e.g., comments on 1 Thes. 4:13-18 and Rev. 3:10). The Lord's warning emphasized the need to be prepared, for judgment will come at a time when people will least expect it.

24:42-44. The Lord encouraged His disciples to **keep watch** (*grēgoreite,* the word rendered "be alert" in 1 Thes. 5:6), **because** they could **not know on what day the Lord** would **come** (cf. Matt. 25:13). The limits of the Tribulation period are known to God, for the Seventieth Week of Daniel will have a definite starting time and a definite ending time. But the people living then will only know in generalities the limits of the time. Therefore watchfulness is important. If a

person knows the approximate **time** a **thief** may come to break into **his house,** he takes precautions and prepares accordingly. Likewise believers in the Tribulation, who will be looking forward to the coming of the Lord of glory, should be alert. They will know generally, from the signs of the end, when He will return, but they will not know the exact time.

b. The faithful servant (24:45-51)
(Mark 13:34-37; Luke 12:41-48)

24:45-51. The coming of the Lord will be a test of servants. As **the master** in Jesus' story entrusted all his possessions to his **servant,** so God has entrusted the care of all things in this earth to His servants. The responses of the servants are indications of their inward conditions. The Lord wants to find His servants, like the first steward, faithfully carrying out His will (vv. 45-46). Such a **servant** will be rewarded for his faithful service when the Lord returns (v. 47). But a **servant** who fails to carry out his stewardship will be judged severely. Such a servant, concluding that his **master** was not returning for **a long time,** took advantage of others (he beat his fellow servants) and lived wickedly (eating and drinking with drunkards). Like the wicked people of Noah's day (vv. 37-39), he was unaware of the sudden coming judgment (v. 50). But the judgment **will come** and he will be dealt with as one would deal with a hypocrite, which is precisely what an unfaithful servant is. His separation will result in eternal judgment (**weeping and gnashing of teeth;** cf. comments on 13:42) apart from his master. Likewise the judgment of the wicked at the Lord's second coming will separate them eternally from God.

5. THE COMING JUDGMENT ON ISRAEL (25:1-30)

25:1-13. When Christ returns in glory, further separations will occur, as indicated by the Parable of the **10 Virgins.** While various interpretations have been given to this parable, it seems best to understand it as a judgment on living Jews soon after the Lord's return in glory. The context clearly points to that event (24:3, 14, 27, 30, 39, 44, 51). The judgment of the Gentiles (sheep and goats) will occur when the Lord returns (25:31-46). Also at His glorious return,

Israel will be judged as a nation (Ezek. 20:33-44; Zech. 13:1).

Israel therefore is pictured as 10 virgins who are awaiting the return of **the bridegroom.** In wedding customs in Jesus' day, the bridegroom would return from the house of the bride in a procession leading to his own home where a wedding banquet would be enjoyed. In Jesus' parable, He as King will return from heaven with His bride, the church, in order to enter into the Millennium. The Jews in the Tribulation will be some of the invited guests privileged to share in the feast.

But preparation is necessary. In the parable, **five of** the virgins had made adequate preparation for they possessed the necessary **lamps** and extra **oil in jars** (Matt. 25:4). Five others had **lamps but** no extra **oil. At midnight . . . the bridegroom** arrived. The **lamps** of the five virgins without extra oil were **going out.** So they had to go searching for **oil** and missed the arrival of **the bridegroom.** When they returned and found the **wedding** feast in progress, they sought admission but were denied (vv. 10-12).

Israel in the Tribulation will know that Jesus' coming is near, but not all will be spiritually prepared for it. His coming will be sudden, when it is not expected (24:27, 39, 50). Though this passage does not specifically interpret the meaning of the oil, many commentators see it as representing the Holy Spirit and His work in salvation. Salvation is more than mere profession for it involves regeneration by the Holy Spirit. Those who will merely profess to be saved, and do not actually possess the Spirit, will be excluded from the feast, that is, the kingdom. Those who fail to be ready when the King comes, cannot enter His kingdom. Since **the day** and **hour** of His return are unknown, believers in the Tribulation should **keep watch** (*grēgoreite*), that is, be alert and prepared (cf. 24:42).

25:14-30 (Luke 19:11-27). In another parable on faithfulness, Jesus told the story of a master with three **servants.** The master went **on a journey** and **gave** each servant a specific amount of money, **talents.** The talents were of silver (**money** in Matt. 25:18 is *argyrion*, which means silver money). A **talent** weighed between 58 and 80 pounds. Thus the master entrusted his servants with considerable amounts of money. The amounts were in keeping with the men's abilities.

Two of the servants were **faithful** in caring for the master's money (vv. 16-17) and were accordingly rewarded for their faithfulness with additional wealth, additional responsibilities, and sharing of the **master's** joy (vv. 20-23). The third servant, having **received the one talent,** reasoned that his **master** might not be coming back at all. If he did return someday, the servant could simply return the talent to his master without loss from any poor investment (v. 25). But if he failed to return, the servant wanted to be able to keep the talent for himself. He did not want to deposit the talent in a bank where it would be recorded that the talent belonged to the master (v. 27). His reasoning indicated he lacked faith in his master; he proved to be a **worthless servant.** As a result, he lost what he had (v. 29; cf. 13:12), and was cast into judgment. Like the unworthy servant in 24:48-51, he too would be eternally separated from God. On **weeping and gnashing of teeth** see comments on 13:42. The Parable of the 10 Virgins (25:1-13) stressed the need for preparedness for the Messiah's return. This Parable of the Talents stressed the need to serve the King while He is away.

6. THE COMING JUDGMENT ON GENTILES (25:31-46)

When the Lord returns "in His glory," He will judge not only the nation Israel (as in the Parable of the 10 Virgins [vv. 1-13] and the Parable of the Talents [vv. 14-30]) but also the Gentiles. This is not the same as the great white throne judgment, which involves only the wicked and which follows the Millennium (Rev. 20:13-15). The judgment of the Gentiles will occur 1,000 years earlier in order to determine who will and will not enter the kingdom.

25:31-33. The words **the nations** (*ta ethnē*) should be translated "the Gentiles." These are all **people,** other than Jews, who have lived through the Tribulation period (cf. Joel 3:2, 12). They will be judged individually, not as national groups. They are described as a mingling of **sheep** and **goats,** which the Lord will separate.

25:34-40. The King "on His throne" (v. 31) will extend an invitation **to those**

on His right hand, the sheep, to enter the kingdom God had prepared . . . since the Creation of the world. The basis of their entrance is seen in their actions, for they provided food, drink, clothing, and care for the King (vv. 35-36). The King's statement will prompt the sheep to respond that they do not recall ever having ministered directly to the King (vv. 37-39). The King will answer that they performed these services for the least of these brothers of Mine, and by so doing were ministering to the King (v. 40).

The expression "these brothers" must refer to a third group that is neither sheep nor goats. The only possible group would be Jews, physical brothers of the Lord. In view of the distress in the Tribulation period, it is clear that any believing Jew will have a difficult time surviving (cf. 24:15-21). The forces of the world dictator will be doing everything possible to exterminate all Jews (cf. Rev. 12:17). A Gentile going out of his way to assist a Jew in the Tribulation will mean that Gentile has become a believer in Jesus Christ during the Tribulation. By such a stand and action, a believing Gentile will put his life in jeopardy. His works will not save him; but his works will reveal that he is redeemed.

25:41-46. To the goats on His left hand (cf. v. 33) the King will pronounce judgment. They will be told, Depart . . . into the eternal fire prepared not for men but for the devil and his angels (cf. "the kingdom prepared," v. 34). The basis of their judgment will be their failure to extend mercy to the remnant of Jewish believers during the Tribulation. Their lack of righteous works will evidence their unconcern (vv. 42-44; cf. vv. 35-36). Such individuals will sympathize with the world dictator and support his cause. They will be removed from the earth and will be cast into "eternal fire" (v. 41) to undergo eternal punishment (v. 46). With all wickedness removed in the various judgments at the Second Advent, the kingdom will begin on earth with only saved individuals in physical bodies constituting the earthly kingdom as the King's subjects. Glorified saints from Old Testament times and the church, the bride of Christ, will also be present to share in the reign of the King of kings.

In this extended prophetic sermon, Jesus answered His disciples' questions about the sign of His coming and the end of the Age (24:4-31). He also presented practical lessons for those who will be living at that time (24:32-51), encouraging them to faithfulness, watchfulness, and preparedness. By way of application these lessons are relevant to all believers in any Age. He concluded by pointing out the establishment of the kingdom and the judgment of Jews (25:1-30) and of Gentiles (vv. 31-46).

E. The national rejection of the King (chaps. 26–27)

1. THE PRELIMINARY EVENTS (26:1-46)

a. The developing of the plot (26:1-5) (Mark 14:1-2; Luke 22:1-2; John 11:45-53)

26:1-5. The words, When Jesus had finished saying all these things, are the last of five such turning points in the book (cf. 7:28; 11:1; 13:53; 19:1). As soon as Jesus completed the Olivet Discourse, He reminded the disciples that the Passover feast was only two days away and that He would be handed over to be crucified. The events in 26:1-16 occurred on Wednesday. Though there is no record of the disciples' reactions to the Lord's words, Matthew did record the plot that developed among the religious leaders to kill Him. In the palace of the high priest . . . Caiaphas, the plan was begun to arrest Jesus in some sly way but not until the Feast had passed. Their thinking was to wait until the many pilgrims who had converged on Jerusalem for the Passover had gone home. Then they would dispose of Jesus in a quiet way. Their timing was not God's timing, however, and the advancement in the timetable was due in part to the willingness of Judas Iscariot who volunteered to betray the Lord.

b. The anointing by perfume (26:6-13) (Mark 14:3-9; John 12:1-8)

26:6-9. During the final week of His life before the Cross, the Lord spent the nights in Bethany, east of Jerusalem on the south slopes of the Mount of Olives. Matthew recorded an event that took place one evening in the home of . . . Simon the Leper. John described the same event in greater detail (John 12:1-8), giving the names of the individuals. The **woman** who **poured** the oil **on** Jesus' **head** was Mary (John 12:3), and the disciple who first objected to the action was Judas Iscariot (John 12:4). The **perfume** was **very expensive** (Matt. 26:7), worth "a year's wages" (John 12:5; lit., "300 denarii"). Obviously this act of love was costly for Mary.

26:10-13. The Lord was aware of the disciples' comments ("Why this waste?" v. 8) and their heart attitude ("they were indignant," v. 8; cf. 20:24; 21:15) behind their words. Judas Iscariot was not motivated by his concern for **the poor** (John 12:6). He was a thief and was concerned about the money not being put in their common purse which he controlled. Jesus reminded them that because **the poor** would **always** be **with** them they would have many opportunities to show kindness, but He would **not always** be among them.

Mary's **beautiful** act prepared His body **for burial** (Matt. 26:12). Jesus had spoken several times of His coming death (e.g., 16:21; 17:22; 20:18), but the disciples did not seem to believe His words. Mary believed and performed this act as a testimony of her devotion to Him. As a result her sacrificial act is often proclaimed **throughout the world.** Perhaps it was this act and the Lord's approval of it that made Judas willing to betray the Lord. From this scene Judas went to the chief priests and offered to betray Jesus.

c. The plan for betrayal (26:14-16)
(Mark 14:10-11; Luke 22:3-6)

26:14-16. Judas Iscariot must have been viewed by the religious leaders as an answer to their prayers. Judas' offer **to the chief priests** to betray Jesus Christ was more than agreeing to point out Jesus to arresting officers. Judas was offering his services as a witness against Jesus when He would be brought to trial. He would do anything to gain more money (cf. John 12:6). The offer was made in exchange for funds, probably paid out immediately to Judas. **Thirty silver coins** were the redemption price paid for a slave (Ex. 21:32). This same amount was also prophesied as the price for the services of the rejected Shepherd (Zech. 11:12). The exact value of the agreed price cannot be determined because the coinage was not identified; it was simply called "silver"

(*argyria;* cf. Matt. 25:18). But it could have been a substantial amount. The bargain had been struck and **Judas** was now being looked to by the religious leaders as their deliverer from their biggest problem, Jesus of Nazareth. Judas knew he had to follow through, for his word had been given and money had been exchanged.

d. The celebrating of the Passover (26:17-30)

26:17-19 (Mark 14:12-16; Luke 22:7-13). Most Bible students believe that the events recorded in Matthew 26:17-30 took place on Thursday of Passion Week. This was **the first day of the** seven-day **Feast of Unleavened Bread.** On that first day Passover lambs were sacrificed (Mark 14:12). The Feast of Unleavened Bread followed immediately after the Passover; the entire eight-day event was sometimes called the Passover Week (cf. Luke 2:41; 22:1, 7; Acts 12:3-4; see comments on Luke 22:7).

The disciples who were sent to make preparations for **the Passover** meal were Peter and John (Luke 22:8). The place of the Passover celebration is not designated in any of the Gospels, though it took place in **the city** (Matt. 26:18), that is, Jerusalem, probably in the home of someone who acknowledged Jesus as Messiah. That he willingly opened his home indicated he had an awareness of Jesus and His claims. Besides finding the location, the two **disciples . . . prepared the Passover,** that is, they purchased and prepared the food, which probably took them the greater part of the day.

26:20-25 (Mark 14:17-21; Luke 22:14-23; John 13:21-30). When evening came, **Jesus** entered the prepared room, an "upper" (upstairs) room (Luke 22:12), and partook of the Passover supper **with the Twelve.** During the celebration, Jesus said that **one of** those sitting with Him was about to **betray** Him. This revealed Jesus' omniscience (cf. John 2:25; 4:29). Surprisingly no disciple pointed to another with an accusing finger, but each became **very sad and began to** ask if he would be the betrayer. **Jesus** added that **the one** betraying Him had been sharing close fellowship with Him; they had eaten out of **the** same bowl. Jesus said He would **go** (i.e., die) **just as it** had been **written** by prophets (e.g., Isa. 53:4-8; cf. Matt. 26:56). **But woe to the one who**

would betray Him. **It would be better for that one if he had** never **been born.** Jesus was pointing out to Judas the consequences of his betrayal, for while he had already taken the money to betray Jesus the act was not yet accomplished. When **Judas** asked the Lord, **Surely not I, Rabbi? Jesus** clearly pointed him out as the betrayer. Not surprisingly, Judas called Him "Rabbi," not "Lord" as did the other disciples (v. 22; cf. v. 49).

The Lord's words were not understood by the other disciples, as John made clear (John 13:28-29). If they had understood, it is doubtful they would have let Judas leave the room. Since they did not understand, Judas departed (John 13:30).

26:26-30 (Mark 14:22-26; Luke 22:19-20). Jesus then instituted something new in the Passover feast. **While they were eating,** He **took bread** and **gave** it a special meaning. **Then** taking **the cup** of wine, He **gave** it a special meaning too. Jesus said the bread was His **body** (Matt. 26:26) and the wine was His **blood of the** New **Covenant** (v. 28). While Christians disagree on the meanings of these words, it appears Jesus was using these elements as visible reminders of an event about to take place.

The bread and wine represented His body and blood about to be shed, in keeping with the remission of sins promised in the New Covenant (Jer. 31:31-37; 32:37-40; Ezek. 34:25-31; 36:26-28), a covenant that would replace the old Mosaic Covenant. His blood was soon to be shed **for many** (cf. Matt. 20:28) **for the forgiveness of sins.** This portion of the Passover supper has been followed by Christians and called the Lord's Supper or Communion. Jesus committed this ordinance to the church to be followed as a continual reminder of His work in their salvation. It is to be commemorated until He returns (1 Cor. 11:23-26). Jesus told the disciples He would **not** eat this meal again with them **until** the institution of His **Father's kingdom** on earth. After the Passover meal, Jesus and the disciples together sang **a hymn,** left the home, and **went out to the Mount of Olives.**

e. The prayerful vigil (26:31-46)

26:31-35 (Mark 14:27-31; Luke 22:31-38; John 13:36-38). As **Jesus** and the disciples headed for the Mount of Olives, He reminded **them** that soon they would all forsake Him. This would be in keeping with the words of Zechariah who prophesied that **the Shepherd** would be struck down, **and the sheep . . . scattered** (Zech. 13:7). This is one of numerous times Matthew quoted from and alluded to the Book of Zechariah. **But** Jesus promised victory over death, for He said He would rise from the dead and **go ahead of** them **into Galilee** (Matt. 26:32; cf. 28:7). All the disciples were from Galilee and they had ministered with Jews in Galilee.

Whether **Peter** heard the Lord's words concerning Resurrection cannot be known. But he strongly reacted against the idea that he would forsake Jesus. Peter affirmed he would **never** deny the Lord, **even if all** the others did. But **Jesus** predicted that Peter would deny Him **three times** that **very night before** the crowing of **the rooster** in the early morning. **Peter** could not believe he would forsake Jesus; again he affirmed his devotion even if it meant death (26:35). This was the feeling of **all the other disciples** too; they could not believe they would deny the Lord. They would not betray Him (v. 22), so why would they deny Him?

26:36-46 (Mark 14:32-42; Luke 22:39-46; John 18:1). Jesus then went . . . **to a place** known as **Gethsemane,** which means "an oil press." In a field covered with olive trees, oil presses were used to extract oil from the fruit. An olive grove was in that place (John 18:1). There Jesus left **His disciples**—except for **Peter** and **two** of Zebedee's **sons** (James and John, Matt. 4:21) who went **with Him, and He began to** pray. He was experiencing sorrow (*lypeisthai,* "to be grieved or sad to the point of distress"; cf. 14:9; 17:23; 18:31; 19:22) and trouble such as He had never known in His earthly life. He asked the three disciples to **stay** and **keep watch with** Him (26:38). In this hour of His greatest need the Lord wanted those with a sympathetic understanding to be praying with Him.

Separating Himself then from the three, He **prayed** to His **Father,** asking that **if . . . possible . . . this cup be taken away from** Him. The "cup" probably referred to His imminent death. He also may have had in mind His coming separation from the Father (27:46) and

Jesus' Six Trials

Religious Trials

Before Annas	John 18:12-14
Before Caiaphas	Matthew 26:57-68
Before the Sanhedrin	Matthew 27:1-2

Civil Trials

Before Pilate	John 18:28-38
Before Herod	Luke 23:6-12
Before Pilate	John 18:39–19:6

His coming contact with sin as He became sin for mankind (2 Cor. 5:21). A cup, figuratively in the Old Testament, refers to wrath. The significant thing about this prayer, however, was that the Lord submitted His **will** to the **will** of His Father (Matt. 26:39).

When Jesus **returned to** the three, He **found them** asleep. He awakened them and reprimanded **Peter** (not the three) for his inability to bear with Him in prayer. Only a short time before, Peter had twice said he would never forsake the Lord (vv. 33, 35) and yet he could not even pray with Him in His greatest need. Jesus encouraged them (the imperatives and the word **you** are pl.) to keep watching and praying, but He did acknowledge the weakness of the human flesh (v. 41).

As Jesus prayed **a second time,** He recognized that the **cup** (cf. v. 39) could not pass **away unless** He "drank" of **it.** He affirmed a second time that God's **will** must be accomplished whatever the cost (v. 42; cf. v. 39). He returned and **found** the three disciples asleep **again,** but this time He did not wake them.

A **third time** He **prayed** the **same** prayer while the disciples slept on. Their **sleeping and resting** was in stark contrast to His agonizing (v. 37) and praying to the point of exhaustion and perspiration (Luke 22:43-44). He was lonely, for though the disciples were nearby, they were useless in their intercession. And yet He evidenced unswerving obedience— determination to follow the Father's will regardless of the cost. When Jesus **returned to the disciples** the third time, He awakened them with the news His **betrayer** was coming and they must **go** meet him.

2. THE ARREST IN THE GARDEN (26:47-56)
(MARK 14:43-50; LUKE 22:47-53; JOHN 18:2-12)

26:47-56. As Jesus spoke, **Judas . . . arrived** in the garden. He was accompanied by **a large crowd,** including both Roman soldiers (John 18:3) and Jews from the temple guard (Luke 22:52) dispatched **by the chief priests and the elders.** The crowd had **swords and clubs** (Matt. 26:47; Mark 14:43) and torches and lanterns (John 18:3). The large group was considered necessary to make sure Jesus did not get away. Perhaps the leaders felt the pilgrims present for the Passover feast in Jerusalem might somehow try to prevent the arrest.

Judas **had arranged a** sign **with the** officials. **The One** he kissed would be the One to **arrest.** As he approached **Jesus,** he **said, Greetings, Rabbi!** (cf. Matt. 26:25) **and kissed Him.** Jesus' response to Judas indicated that He still loved him, for Jesus addressed him as **Friend** (*hetaire,* "companion" or "associate," used only three times in the NT, each time in Matt. [20:13; 22:12; 26:50]). With this the arresting soldiers probably pushed Judas out of the way and grabbed **Jesus.**

Peter was not to be outdone. (Only John identified him by name [John 18:10].) Having just awakened and perhaps still not fully aware of what was going on, he grabbed **his sword** and attempted to defend Jesus by striking out at one of those in the arresting group. He struck Malchus, **the servant of the high priest** (John 18:10).

The Lord immediately stopped the violence and reprimanded Peter for his efforts. He did not need anyone's defense, for He could have called **on** His **Father** who would have sent **12 legions of angels** to defend Him. A Roman legion numbered about 6,000 soldiers. Such angelic protection (of about 72,000 angels!) could easily have defended Jesus from any opposition. But it was not God's will for Jesus to be rescued. Jesus' arrest occurred because He permitted it. Though Matthew did not mention it Luke, the physician, noted that Jesus healed the man's severed ear (Luke 22:51).

Matthew did record a brief speech by Jesus to His captors. He asked them why they had come out in this manner to arrest Him. He had been in their midst daily, teaching in the temple courts. Arrest had been possible at any time. Obviously these religious leaders feared the people's acknowledgment of Him. But the will of the Father was being fulfilled as well as the writings of the prophets who spoke of His death.

At that point all the disciples deserted Him and fled into the night—though they had vowed they would never do so! (Matt. 26:33, 35) The sheep were scattering (v. 31).

3. THE TRIALS OF THE KING (26:57-27:26)

a. The trial before the Jewish authorities (26:57–27:10)

26:57-58 (Mark 14:53-54; Luke 22:54; John 18:15-16). After Jesus was arrested in Gethsemane, He was led by the soldiers to Caiaphas, the high priest (see the chart on Jesus' six trials). But first there was a brief trial before the former high priest, Annas, who was Caiaphas' father-in-law (cf. comments on John 18:12-13, 19-24; see chart at Acts 4:1). That delaying tactic apparently gave Caiaphas time to assemble the "Sanhedrin" quickly (Matt. 26:59; cf. Acts 4:15 for comments on the Sanhedrin). Peter followed the Lord at a distance and came into the courtyard of the high priest's home to await the outcome.

26:59-68 (Mark 14:55-65; Luke 22:63-65). The purpose of Jesus' trials was to find some legal basis on which to condemn Him to death. Judas' testimony was crucial to the religious leaders' case, but he was nowhere to be found. As a result witnesses were sought against Jesus, a highly unusual court procedure, attempting to find anything that would make Him worthy of death. While many false witnesses volunteered, none of them could agree on anything against Jesus (Matt. 26:60). Finally two witnesses agreed that Jesus had once said, I am able to destroy the temple of God and rebuild it in three days. Jesus had said that approximately three years earlier at the outset of His ministry (John 2:19), referring not to the temple building, but to His body. It is interesting that this statement was here recalled soon before His crucifixion and resurrection. Jesus refused to answer any of the charges brought against Him because He was never officially charged with any crime.

Then the high priest attempted to get Jesus to respond to the accusations brought against Him (Matt. 26:62). Still Jesus remained silent until the high priest placed Him under sacred oath. Once the high priest charged Jesus under an oath by the living God, Jesus had to answer truthfully. Caiaphas insisted that Jesus answer if He was the Christ (the Messiah), the Son of God (v. 63). Jesus answered in the affirmative, adding that in the future He would sit at the right hand of the Mighty One (cf. 25:31) and He would return on the clouds of heaven (cf. 24:30). Here was a clear statement of His deity, clearly understood as such by the high priest, who immediately tore his clothes, which he was forbidden to do by the Law (Lev. 21:10), and declared that Jesus had spoken blasphemy (Matt. 26:65). He said there was no further need of witnesses for the Lord's lips had revealed His guilt.

The people had only two choices. One was to acknowledge that Jesus spoke the truth, and fall down and worship Him as Messiah. The other was to reject Him as a blasphemer and put Him to death. They chose the latter, thus sealing their rejection of the One who came as their Messiah-King.

No further evidence was examined at this point. No one defended Jesus or pointed to the works He had performed among them during the past three years. It appeared that the Sanhedrin had Jesus where they wanted Him. He had just spoken words of blasphemy which all heard. Contrary to all Jewish and Roman law, they took it on themselves to begin to punish the accused. They spit in His face . . . struck Him with their fists, and slapped Him. They asked Him to proph-

85

esy, telling, if He could, **who** had just **hit** Him. These actions they continued doing, seemingly enjoying every moment of it. The Lord remained silent throughout this terrible ordeal, submitting Himself to His Father's will (cf. Isa. 53:7; 1 Peter 2:23).

26:69-75 (Mark 14:66-72; Luke 22:55-62; John 18:17-18, 25-27). While Jesus was undergoing His trial before the Sanhedrin, **Peter** was also undergoing a testing. He had followed the Lord and gained entrance into the house of the high priest (John 18:15-16). As he sat **in the courtyard** (cf. Matt. 26:58) awaiting the outcome of the trial, he had three opportunities to speak up for his Lord. All three times he denied he ever knew the Accused or was in any way ever connected with Him. The first denial occurred when **a servant girl** said in front of the others that he was one of those who had been **with Jesus** (v. 69). **Another girl** at the gate of the courtyard more directly pointed Peter out as one who had indeed been **with Jesus** (v. 71). Finally a number of those present came and accused **Peter** of being **one** who had been with Jesus **for** his Galilean **accent** gave him **away** (v. 73). With the third accusation, Peter **began to call down curses on himself and he swore** (v. 74). The calling of curses on himself was a legal way of seeking to affirm one's innocence; if the calamities did not follow, he would be assumed innocent (cf. Job 31).

As he publicly denied his Lord the third time, **immediately a rooster crowed.** That triggered in his thinking the words of the Lord, **Before the rooster crows, you will disown Me three times** (cf. Matt. 26:34). Peter knew immediately he had failed the Lord. Though he had affirmed that he would never forsake the Lord, he had publicly denied the One he loved. Filled with remorse, he left the courtyard **and wept bitterly.** His tears were tears of true repentance for having forsaken and denied the Lord.

27:1-2 (Mark 15:1). Jesus' first Jewish trials occurred under the cover of darkness. Since Jewish law required trials to be conducted during the day, the chief priests and the elders of the people realized an official trial was necessary. The brief trial recorded in Matthew 27:1 was simply for the court to reaffirm what had taken place earlier. The court decided that **Jesus** must die, but they did not have

the power to put that decision into action (John 18:31). To get a death sentence, they needed to take the case **to Pilate, the governor,** the procurator of Judea and Samaria, A.D. 26–36 (cf. Luke 3:1). Jesus was therefore **bound** and brought by the Jews to Pilate. Pilate's home was in Caesarea, but at this festival time, he was in his Jerusalem palace.

27:3-10. When Judas Iscariot realized the outcome of the deliberations, **he was** filled **with remorse and** went back to the officials. He had not envisioned this as the outcome of his betrayal, but what he had hoped to accomplish is not mentioned in the biblical text. He knew he had **betrayed innocent blood** for he admitted Jesus was not worthy of death. The religious leaders were unsympathetic, pointing out that that was his problem, not theirs. **Judas** decided he had to get rid of **the money** he had received for betraying the Lord. The money was apparently a continual reminder of his action and convicted him of his sin. He went to the temple and **threw the money into the temple** (*naos,* the holy place itself, not the temple precincts). Unlike Peter, however, Judas' remorse did not include repentance, for **he went** from the temple **and hanged himself.** (More details of his action were given by Luke, Acts 1:18-19.)

Judas' act of throwing the betrayal money into the temple caused the religious leaders some problems. They did not feel the money should be **put** into the temple coffers **since it** was **blood money,** money paid to bring about a man's death. Yet they had had no scruples about giving it out in the first place (Matt. 26:15). **They decided to** take **the money** and **buy** a parcel of land (apparently in Judas' name, Acts 1:18) in which to bury **foreigners.** The parcel, which was a **potter's field,** a place where potters dug for clay, became known as **the Field of Blood** (Matt. 27:8), or *Akeldama* in Aramaic (Acts 1:19).

Matthew viewed these events as the fulfillment of a prophecy of **Jeremiah.** But the prophecy Matthew quoted was primarily from Zechariah, not Jeremiah. There is a close resemblance between Matthew 27:9-10 and Zechariah 11:12-13. But there are also similarities between Matthew's words and the ideas in Jeremiah 19:1, 4, 6, 11. Why then did

Matthew refer only to Jeremiah? The solution to this problem is probably that Matthew had both prophets in mind but only mentioned the "major" prophet by name. (A similar situation is found in Mark 1:2-3, where Mark mentioned the Prophet Isaiah but quoted directly from both Isaiah and Malachi.) In addition, another explanation is that Jeremiah, in the Babylonian Talmud (*Baba Bathra* 14b), was placed first among the prophets, and his book represented all the other prophetic books.

b. The trial before the Roman authorities (27:11-26)

27:11-14 (Mark 15:2-5; Luke 23:1-5; John 18:28-38). Compared with the other Gospels, Matthew's record of Jesus' trial before Pilate is rather brief. Luke even mentioned that Pilate sent Jesus to Herod when he learned Jesus was a Galilean (Luke 23:6-12). That gesture brought about a friendship between Pilate and Herod that had not existed before. Matthew mentioned only one trial before Pilate and the one "accusation" that **Jesus** is the King of the Jews. The kingship of Jesus of course was Matthew's main theme. When Pilate asked Jesus, **Are You the King of the Jews?** the answer came in the affirmative. But as John recorded, Jesus' kingdom at that time was not a political kingdom to rival Rome (John 18:33-37). Jesus was no threat to Roman rule. Pilate realized that and sought to release Jesus.

While other accusations were presented **by the chief priests and the elders,** Jesus did not **answer** them, and **Pilate** was greatly surprised (*thaumazein*, "to be amazed"). Jesus need not answer those charges, for He was not being tried for those accusations. Instead He was on trial because they said He claimed to be the King of the Jews, the Messiah (Matt. 26:63-64). Since Pilate had also declared Jesus' innocence (John 18:38), there was no reason for Him to answer the accusations.

27:15-23 (Mark 15:6-14; Luke 23:13-24; John 18:39-40). Pilate had been warned by **his wife** to be careful how he dealt with this prisoner, for He was an **innocent Man** (Matt. 27:19). She had **suffered a great deal** through **a dream** concerning Jesus and shared her experience with her husband. To speculate

beyond the words of the text on the content of her dream would be useless. Since **Pilate** believed Jesus was innocent, he tried to have Him released. It was a **custom** of the governor **to release a prisoner** each year at the Passover in order to gain acceptance with the Jews. His plan to bring about the **release** of **Jesus** involved a notorious prisoner named **Barabbas,** an insurrectionist (John 18:40) and murderer (Mark 15:7). **Pilate** thought that surely the people of the nation loved Jesus, their King, and that only the leaders were envious of Him and of the people's acclaim of Him (Matt. 27:18). He reasoned that if the people had a choice they surely would release **Jesus,** not the notorious **Barabbas.**

However, **Pilate** failed to grasp the determination of the religious leaders to do away with Jesus, for they **persuaded the crowd to ask for Barabbas and to have Jesus executed.** When Pilate asked the crowd **what** he should **do . . . with Jesus who is called Christ . . . they all answered, Crucify Him!** The Greek text shows their cry was one word, "Crucify" (*staurōthētō*). One can almost picture this scene, somewhat like a football stadium in which the crowd shouts "Defense!" Their cheer was "Crucify, crucify!" When Pilate sought further information from the crowd as to Jesus' crimes, the crowd simply **shouted . . . louder, Crucify!**

27:24-26 (Mark 15:15; Luke 23:25; John 19:6-16). Pilate realized **he was getting nowhere** with the crowd, and their threats to report him to Caesar (John 19:12) concerned him. His record with Caesar was not good, and he did not want word of a rival king to reach Caesar's ears, especially if Pilate had released that king. **He** therefore **took water and washed his hands in front of the crowd,** symbolizing his desire to absolve himself from being involved in putting an innocent man to death (Deut. 21:6-9). But his words, **I am innocent of this Man's blood,** did not make him innocent (Acts 4:27). Such an act did not remove Pilate's guilt from this travesty of justice.

When Pilate turned the **responsibility** over to the Jews (Matt. 27:24), however, they readily accepted it. They said, **Let His blood be on us and on our children!** Their words sadly came to pass as the judgment of God came on many of them and their children in A.D. 70 when

HARMONY OF EVENTS AT JESUS' CRUCIFIXION

1. Jesus arrived at Golgotha (Matt. 27:33; Mark 15:22; Luke 23:33; John 19:17).
2. He refused the offer of wine mixed with myrrh (Matt. 27:34; Mark 15:23).
3. He was nailed to the cross between the two thieves (Matt. 27:35-38; Mark 15:24-28; Luke 23:33-38; John 19:18).
4. He gave His first cry from the cross: "Father, forgive them, for they do not know what they are doing" (Luke 23:34).
5. The soldiers took Jesus' garments, leaving Him naked on the cross (Matt. 27:35; Mark 15:24; Luke 23:34; John 19:23).
6. The Jews mocked Jesus (Matt. 27:39-43; Mark 15:29-32; Luke 23:35-37).
7. He conversed with the two thieves (Luke 23:39-43).
8. He gave His second cry from the cross, "I tell you the truth; today you will be with Me in paradise" (Luke 23:43).
9. He spoke the third time, "Woman, here is your son" (John 19:26-27).
10. Darkness came from noon to 3 P.M. (Matt. 27:45; Mark 15:33; Luke 23:44).
11. He gave His fourth cry, "My God, My God, why have You forsaken Me?" (Matt. 27:46-47; Mark 15:34-36)
12. His fifth cry was, "I am thirsty" (John 19:28).
13. He drank "wine vinegar" (John 19:29).
14. His sixth cry was, "It is finished" (John 19:30).
15. He drank wine vinegar from a sponge (Matt. 27:48; Mark 15:36).
16. He cried a seventh time, "Father, into Your hands I commit My spirit" (Luke 23:46).
17. He dismissed His spirit by an act of His own will (Matt. 27:50; Mark 15:37; Luke 23:46; John 19:30).
18. The temple curtain was torn in two (Matt. 27:51; Mark 15:38; Luke 23:45).
19. Roman soldiers admitted, "Surely He was the Son of God" (Matt. 27:54; Mark 15:39).

the Romans destroyed the nation and the temple. In spite of Pilate's four declarations of Jesus' innocence (Luke 23:14, 20, 22; John 19:4), he fulfilled his commitment to the Jews by releasing **Barabbas** and turning **Jesus** over for crucifixion after He had been **flogged.**

4. THE CRUCIFIXION OF THE KING (27:27-56)

27:27-31 (Mark 15:16-20; John 19:1-5). Jesus was brought **into the Praetorium,** the common meeting courtyard crowded with Roman **soldiers.** The Praetorium may have been at Pilate's residence, the Castle of Antonia, though others suggest Herod's palace. The Praetorium was a large area, for 600 soldiers were there ("company of soldiers" is lit., "cohort," one-tenth of a legion).

There **they** removed His clothing and mocked Him by (a) putting **on Him** a **scarlet robe,** clothing for a king, (b) placing **a crown of thorns . . . on His head,** and (c) giving Him **a staff** for a

"scepter." They **knelt** before **Him and mocked Him** by saying, **Hail, King of the Jews!** What a tragic figure Jesus presented at that moment. They degraded Him further by spitting **on Him,** and striking **Him on the head again and again** with the staff. Unknown to them, their actions fulfilled Isaiah's prophecy concerning the Savior's marring (Isa. 52:14). Because of the known cruelty of Roman soldiers, Jesus was probably beaten to the point where few would have recognized Him. Yet He silently bore the unjust treatment, submitting to the will of His Father (cf. 1 Peter 2:23). With their sport completed, the soldiers again dressed Jesus in **His own clothes** and **led Him away to** be crucified.

27:32-38 (Mark 15:21-28; Luke 23:26-34; John 19:17-27). Matthew recorded only a few of the events that occurred when Jesus was taken to the place of crucifixion. **Simon** of **Cyrene,** a city in North Africa populated with many Jews, was **forced . . . to carry the cross**

(actually the crossbeam) when Jesus could no longer carry it Himself, being weak from the beatings. Eventually the procession **came to a place** known as **Golgotha**, which in Aramaic **means the Place of the Skull**. This was not a place of skulls, a cemetery, or place of execution, but a hill that in some way resembled a skull. This was located either at the site of the present Church of the Holy Sepulchre, which was then outside Jerusalem's walls, or at Gordon's Calvary.

Jesus was then **offered . . . wine . . . mixed with gall,** a drink given to dull the senses and make the pain of crucifixion somewhat easier to bear. Jesus **refused to drink** the mixture, for He wanted to be in complete control of His senses even while hanging on the cross. The actual crucifixion was briefly noted by Matthew. He made no reference to the nails being driven into the Lord's hands and feet, but he did record the dividing of **His clothes (by casting lots)** by those crucifying Him. A few Greek manuscripts add to Matthew 27:35 that this action fulfilled Psalm 22:18. Though this probably was not part of Matthew's original account, John pointed out that same prophecy (John 19:24).

Over the **head** of a person being **crucified** was **written** an inscription containing the **charge** that brought him there. Over Jesus' head, was written THIS IS JESUS, THE KING OF THE JEWS, for that truly was the charge for which Jesus was dying. Though each Gospel account presents a slight variation in the wording, the sign probably included a combination of all the accounts. Thus it would have read, "This is Jesus of Nazareth, the King of the Jews." John noted that Pilate had the charge written there in Aramaic, Latin, and Greek (John 19:20). The words "the King of the Jews" offended the chief priests, but Pilate refused to change what he had written (John 19:21-22). Jesus was **crucified** between **two robbers** (Matt. 27:38), whom Luke called "criminals" (Luke 23:33).

27:39-44 (Mark 15:29-32; Luke 23:35-43). While Jesus was hanging on the cross, He was subject to continual verbal abuse by **those** passing **by.** In mockery, they recalled what Jesus had said earlier about destroying **the temple** and raising **it** up **three days** later (John

2:19; cf. Matt. 26:61). Surely He must be a false leader, they thought, because His alleged ability **to destroy** the temple was now gone! If He were **the Son of God,** then He ought to be able to perform a miracle and **come down from the cross.** His inability to do that proved, they reasoned, that His claim was false. He had previously **saved others . . .** but now He could not **save Himself;** in this way too He was disqualified, they alleged. They said that if He came **down . . . from the cross,** they would **believe in Him.** One wonders, however, if even such an act as this would have prompted them to believe. They claimed if He were really **the Son of God . . .** God would **rescue Him.**

Besides the passersby (27:39-40) and the religious leaders (vv. 41-43), **the robbers . . . crucified with Him also** insulted **Him** (v. 44). Luke, however, recorded that a change of heart took place in one of the robbers (Luke 23:39-43). The irony of this scene was that Jesus could have done the things the crowd was shouting for Him to do. He could have come down from the cross and physically saved Himself. He did not lack the power to accomplish His deliverance. But it was not in the Father's will to do that. It was necessary that the Son of God die for others. He therefore patiently bore their insults.

27:45-50 (Mark 15:33-37; Luke 23:44-46; John 19:28-30). Matthew made no reference to the time when the crucifixion began. But Mark indicated that it began at the "third hour" (Mark 15:25), around 9 A.M. Matthew noted specifically that **from the sixth hour,** noon, **until the ninth hour,** 3 P.M., **darkness came over all the land.** In this period of darkness Jesus became the Sin-offering for the world (John 1:29; Rom. 5:8; 2 Cor. 5:21; 1 Peter 2:24; 3:18) and as such was forsaken by the Father. Near the end of this period of time, **Jesus** could bear the separation no longer and **cried out in a loud voice, Eloi, Eloi, lama sabachthani?** These Aramaic words mean, **My God, My God, why have You forsaken Me?** (a quotation of Ps. 22:1) Jesus sensed a separation from the Father He had never known, for in becoming sin the Father had to turn judicially from His Son (Rom. 3:25-26).

Some of those standing near the cross misunderstood Jesus' words. They heard "Eloi," but thought Jesus was trying to call for **Elijah** (Matt. 27:47). In Greek the word "Elijah" sounds more like "Eloi" than it does in English. Thinking His lips and throat had become dry, someone thought a **drink** of **wine vinegar** would moisten His vocal cords so He could speak plainly. Others, however, **said** to **leave** Jesus **alone** and **see if Elijah** would come and deliver **Him.** Their jeers were obviously still being directed against Jesus.

With one last cry **Jesus . . . gave up His spirit,** committing it into the hands of His Father (Luke 23:46). Jesus was in complete control of His life and died at the precise moment He determined by dismissing His spirit. No man took Jesus' life from Him, as He had said (John 10:11, 15, 17-18). He laid His life down in keeping with God's plan and He was involved in taking it back up again in His resurrection.

27:51-53 (Mark 15:38; Luke 23:44-45). At the time of Jesus' death, three momentous events occurred. First, **the curtain of the temple was torn in two from top to bottom.** This curtain separated the holy place from the holy of holies in the temple (Heb. 9:2-3). The fact that this occurred from top to bottom signified that God is the One who ripped the thick curtain. It was not torn from the bottom by men ripping it. God was showing that the way of access into His presence was now available for everyone, not simply the Old Testament high priest (Heb. 4:14-16; 10:19-22).

Second, at Christ's death a strong earthquake occurred, splitting **rocks** (Matt. 27:51). Truly the death of Christ was a powerful, earthshaking event with repercussions affecting even the creation. A third event mentioned was recorded only by Matthew. **The tombs of many holy** (righteous) **people** (v. 52) were opened, probably at a Jerusalem cemetery. The NIV suggests that these saints were resurrected when Jesus died and then went into Jerusalem **after Jesus' resurrection.** A number of commentators agree with this view. Many others, however, say that since Christ is the firstfruits of the dead (1 Cor. 15:23), their resurrection did not occur till He was raised. In this view, the phrase "after

Jesus' resurrection" goes with the words **were raised to life** and **came out of the tombs.** This is possible in the Greek, and is suggested in the KJV and the NASB. The tombs, then, **broke open** at Christ's death, probably by the earthquake, thus heralding Christ's triumph in death over sin, but the bodies were not raised till Christ was raised.

These people returned to Jerusalem, **(the Holy City)** where they were recognized by friends and family. Like Lazarus (John 11:43-44), Jairus' daughter (Luke 8:52-56), and the widow of Nain's son (Luke 7:13-15), they too passed through physical death again. Or some say they may have been raised with glorified bodies like the Lord's. Walvoord suggests this event was "a fulfillment of the Feast of the Firstfruits of harvest mentioned in Leviticus 23:10-14. On that occasion, as a token of the coming harvest, the people would bring a handful of grain to the priest. The resurrection of these saints, occurring after Jesus Himself was raised, is a token of the coming harvest when all the saints will be raised" (Walvoord, *Matthew: Thy Kingdom Come,* p. 236).

27:54-56 (Mark 15:39-41; Luke 23:47-49). A Roman **centurion** (cf. Matt. 8:5; see Luke 7:2 for comments on centurions) and other Roman guards were impressed and **terrified** with the unusual circumstances surrounding the death of this Man, for such accompanying signs had never been observed in previous crucifixions. Their response was, **Surely He was the Son of God!** The momentous events of the day struck fear into the soldiers' hearts.

Also some **women were there,** observing **from a distance** the Lord's death. These women **had followed Jesus from Galilee** and had been caring **for His needs.** Among this group were **Mary Magdalene** (cf. Matt. 28:1; Mark 16:9; John 20:18), **Mary the mother of James and Joseph** (perhaps the same as "Mary the wife of Clopas," John 19:25), **and the mother of Zebedee's sons,** James and John (Matt. 4:21; 10:2). John mentioned that Mary, Jesus' mother, and Mary's sister were also present at the foot of the cross (John 19:25-27). While Matthew made no reference to what the women may have said or how they felt, their hearts must have been broken as they observed the death of their Lord, whom

FORTY DAYS—from Resurrection to Ascension

SUNDAY MORNING

1. An angel rolled away the stone from Jesus' tomb before sunrise (Matt. 28:2-4).
2. Women who followed Jesus visited Jesus' tomb and discovered Him missing (Matt. 28:1; Mark 16:1-4; Luke 24:1-3; John 20:1).
3. Mary Magdalene left to tell Peter and John (John 20:1-2).
4. The other women, remaining at the tomb, saw two angels who told them about the Resurrection (Matt. 28:5-7; Mark 16:5-7; Luke 24:4-8).
5. Peter and John visited Jesus' tomb (Luke 24:12; John 20:3-10).
6. Mary Magdalene returned to the tomb and Jesus appeared to her alone in the garden (Mark 16:9-11; John 20:11-18): *His first appearance.*
7. Jesus appeared to the other women (Mary, mother of James, Salome, and Joanna) (Matt. 28:8-10): *His second appearance.*
8. Those who guarded Jesus' tomb reported to the religious rulers how the angel rolled away the stone. They were then bribed (Matt. 28:11-15).
9. Jesus appeared to Peter (1 Cor. 15:5): *His third appearance.*

SUNDAY AFTERNOON

10. Jesus appeared to two men on the road to Emmaus (Mark 16:12-13; Luke 24:13-32): *His fourth appearance.*

SUNDAY EVENING

11. The two disciples from Emmaus told others they saw Jesus (Luke 24:33-35).
12. Jesus appeared to 10 apostles, with Thomas absent, in the Upper Room (Luke 24:36-43; John 20:19-25): *His fifth appearance.*

THE FOLLOWING SUNDAY

13. Jesus appeared to the 11 Apostles, including Thomas, and Thomas believed (John 20:26-28): *His sixth appearance.*

THE FOLLOWING 32 DAYS

14. Jesus appeared to seven disciples by the Sea of Galilee and performed a miracle of fish (John 21:1-14): *His seventh appearance.*
15. Jesus appeared to 500 (including the Eleven) at a mountain in Galilee (Matt. 28:16-20; Mark 16:15-18; 1 Cor. 15:6): *His eighth appearance.*
16. Jesus appeared to His half-brother James (1 Cor. 15:7): *His ninth appearance.*
17. At Jerusalem Jesus appeared again to His disciples (Luke 24:44-49; Acts 1:3-8): *His 10th appearance.*
18. On the Mount of Olives Jesus ascended into heaven while the disciples watched (Mark 16:19-20; Luke 24:50-53; Acts 1:9-12).

they loved and had served. With the approach of night, they apparently returned to the city and lodged there, for in a few days they were seeking to assist in the preparation of Jesus' body for burial (Matt. 28:1; Mark 16:1-3; Luke 24:1).

5. THE BURIAL OF THE KING (27:57-66)

27:57-61 (Mark 15:42-47; Luke 23:50-56; John 19:38-42). No known preparation had been made for Jesus' burial; normally the body of a crucified criminal would simply have been discarded without ceremony. However, **a rich man from Arimathea** (a town east of Joppa), **named Joseph,** asked **Pilate . . . for Jesus' body.** Joseph, a member of the Sanhedrin, had not agreed with the council's decision to crucify Jesus (Luke 23:51). Instead he was one who had been looking for the kingdom of God and was a believer in Jesus. **Pilate** granted his request, surprised that Jesus was already dead (Mark 15:44-45). Another account reported Joseph was assisted in the burial by Nicodemus (John 19:39; cf. John 3:1-21). These two men **took the body** of Jesus and following burial customs of the time, **wrapped** the body in **linen** with a mixture of myrrh and aloes, spices used in burial (John 19:40; cf. Matt. 2:11). This procedure was done rapidly in order to be completed before the Sabbath began at nightfall. Joseph **placed** the wrapped body **in his own new tomb . . . cut out of the rock** near the place of crucifixion. Why Joseph of Arimathea would own a tomb in Jerusalem cannot be determined. Possibly Jesus had made arrangements ahead of time with him and he had purchased the tomb especially for this occasion. Joseph and Nicodemus **rolled a big stone** across the tomb's **entrance.**

Matthew noted that **Mary Magdalene and the other Mary** sat **across from the tomb** (27:61), no doubt in mourning. Interestingly these women accompanied Jesus' body right up to the minute it was buried, whereas Jesus' disciples had all abandoned Him (26:56).

27:62-66. It is a little surprising that a group of unbelievers would remember Jesus' prediction that He would **rise again** on the third day, while the believing disciples seemingly forgot. **The** very **next day** after His death, that is, on the Sabbath, **the chief priests and the Pharisees went to Pilate** and informed him of Jesus' words. While they did not believe in Jesus (whom they blasphemously called **that deceiver**), they feared **His disciples** might **come . . . steal the body, and** attempt to fabricate a resurrection lie. If this were to happen, the **deception** would **be worse than** anything Jesus had accomplished in His life. The Resurrection was the one thing these leaders feared, so they suggested **the tomb . . . be made secure until the third day.**

Pilate agreed with their suggestion and ordered that **a guard** be sent to **the tomb** to **make** it **as secure as** possible. The Roman guard not only sealed the tomb (presumably with the official Roman **seal** and with a cord and wax, which if tampered with, could be detected) but also continued to keep a **guard** at the scene. Their presence made stealing the body impossible.

VII. Confirmation of the King's Life (chap. 28)

A. The empty tomb (28:1-8)
   (Mark 16:1-8; Luke 24:1-12; John 20:1-20)

1. THE OCCASION (28:1-4)

28:1-4. At dawn on the first day of the week, several women **went** to **the tomb** of Jesus. They knew where the Lord had been laid for they had seen Joseph and Nicodemus roll the stone over the door of the tomb (27:56). The women were returning to the tomb on Sunday morning, now that **the Sabbath** was over, to anoint Jesus' body for burial (Mark 16:1). **There was,** however, **a violent earthquake** associated with **an angel** coming **from heaven and** rolling away **the stone** from the door of **the tomb.** The **appearance** of the angel **was like lightning, and his clothes were white as snow.** The Roman soldiers guarding the tomb **were so** frightened by the angel **that they shook** and apparently fainted. They had been sent there to seal and guard the tomb, but their power was useless before this angelic messenger.

2. THE PROCLAMATION (28:5-8)

28:5-8. Though the soldiers were afraid, **the angel** had a special message for **the women.** To them he announced the fact of the Resurrection, for the One they sought was no longer there, but had **risen just as He said.** He had told them several times He would rise on the third day (16:21; 17:23; 20:19). If He had failed to rise, He would have been a deceiver unworthy of further devotion. One proof He had risen was the empty tomb. The women were encouraged to **come and see the place where** the Lord had been lying. **Then** the angel told them to **go quickly and tell** the **disciples** that **He** had **risen from the dead and** would be **going ahead of** them **into Galilee,** just as He had said (26:32). They would **see Him . . . there,** and indeed they did (28:16-20; John 21:1-23). But these words did not preclude His appearing to them on other occasions, as He did later that day (John 20:19-25). **The women** obeyed the angel's instructions for they **hurried away from the tomb,** intending to find the **disciples** and **tell** them the good news. They were filled with joy over the fact of the Resurrection, but they were fearful for they could not possibly comprehend the full implications of this momentous event.

B. The personal appearance (28:9-10)

28:9-10. As the women were on their way to tell the disciples what had happened, **suddenly Jesus met them.** Hearing His greeting, they recognized Him immediately and they fell at **His feet and worshiped Him.** By His appearance Jesus alleviated their fears and repeated the same message the angel had previously given: **Do not be afraid** (v. 10; cf. v. 5). He told them to **tell** the disciples (**My brothers**) **to go to Galilee** where He would appear before them. The Galilean ministry of Jesus was prominent in Matthew's account and it was natural for Jesus to meet His disciples there. They were all from Galilee and would be returning to Galilee after the Feast. There Jesus would meet them.

C. The "official" explanation (28:11-15)

28:11-15. While the women were running to find the disciples and tell them of the Resurrection, another group was moving rapidly to counteract the truth. Some of those who had been guarding the tomb overcame their fear, **went into the city, and reported to the chief priests** all **that had** transpired. It was imperative that the priests have an explanation to counter the truth. After deliberation **the chief priests** and **elders . . . devised a plan. They gave the soldiers** who had guarded the tomb **a large sum of money** and told **them** what to report to their superiors. The fabricated lie was that the **disciples** of Jesus had come **during the night and** had stolen **away the body of** Jesus **while the soldiers were asleep.** Such a report would not have been well received by the officials for a soldier who fell asleep on guard duty would be put to death (Acts 12:19). The Jewish leaders realized this as well, but promised to make things right with the superiors. When this was brought to the attention of **the governor,** they promised to **satisfy him and keep** the soldiers **out of trouble.** Such satisfaction obviously would involve the payment of another large sum of money. **The soldiers took the money**

offered by the Jewish leaders **and did as they were instructed.**

As a result, **this story** was **widely circulated among the Jews,** and many believed the disciples had really stolen Jesus' body. But the logic of the explanation does not hold up. If the soldiers were asleep, how would they have known what had happened to the body of Jesus? And why would they admit "sleeping on the job"? The disciples' courage during this period was not sufficient to carry out such a plot. They were afraid and had scattered when Jesus was arrested. To execute this kind of plot was beyond their ability. But the truth is often harder for a person to believe than a lie, and many still swallow this lie.

D. The official commissioning (28:16-20) (Luke 24:36-49)

28:16-20. Matthew did not record the meeting of **Jesus** with the 10 disciples later that same day (John 20:19-23) or the appearance 8 days later to **the 11 disciples** (John 20:24-29). But he did record an appearance occurring some time later in **Galilee,** where He promised He would meet them (Matt. 26:32; cf. 28:7, 10) at a **mountain.** Which mountain He specified is unknown. When Jesus appeared **they worshiped Him, but some doubted.** Since Jesus had appeared to them earlier and verified Himself to them, they were not doubting the Resurrection. There was probably simply a brief question among some of them as to whether this was truly Jesus appearing to them. There was no indication that any miraculous element was involved in His being there and since unusual circumstances had occurred with previous visits, perhaps they wondered.

Their doubts were quickly dispelled, for **Jesus** spoke **to them** claiming **all authority in heaven and on earth.** This authority (*exousia,* "official right or power") had been given to Jesus by the Father and now He was instructing the disciples to **go** on the basis of that authority. Their field was to include **all nations,** not just Israel (see comments on 10:5-6). They were to **make disciples** by proclaiming the truth concerning Jesus. Their hearers were to be evangelized and enlisted as Jesus' followers. Those who believed were to be baptized in water **in the name of the Father and of the Son** and of the Holy Spirit. Such an act would associate a believer with the person of Jesus Christ and with the Triune God. The God whom they served is one God and yet is three Persons, Father, Son, and Holy Spirit. Those who respond are also to be taught the truths Jesus had specifically communicated to the Eleven. Not all that Jesus taught the disciples was communicated by them but they did teach specific truths for the new Church Age as they went abroad. Jesus' commission, applicable to all His followers, involved one command, "Make disciples," which is accompanied by three participles in the Greek: "going," baptizing, and teaching.

The final words of the Lord recorded by Matthew were a promise that He would be with them always until the very end of the Age. Though the Lord did not remain physically with the Eleven, His spiritual presence was with them until their tasks on earth were finished. These final words of the Lord were carried out by the apostles as they went everywhere, proclaiming the story of their Messiah, Jesus Christ, the King of the Jews.

BIBLIOGRAPHY

Boice, James Montgomery. *The Sermon on the Mount.* Grand Rapids: Zondervan Publishing House, 1972.

Criswell, W.A. *Expository Notes on the Gospel of Matthew.* Grand Rapids: Zondervan Publishing House, 1961.

Edersheim, Alfred. *The Life and Times of Jesus the Messiah.* Reprint (2 vols. in 1). Grand Rapids: Wm. B. Eerdmans Publishing Co., 1971.

Gaebelein, A.C. *The Gospel of Matthew: An Exposition.* Reprint (2 vols. in 1). Neptune, N.J.: Loizeaux Brothers, 1961.

Hendriksen, William. *Exposition of the Gospel according to Matthew.* New Testament Commentary. Grand Rapids: Baker Book House, 1973.

Ironside, Henry Allen. *Expository Notes on the Gospel of Matthew.* Neptune, N.J.: Loizeaux Brothers, 1948.

Kelly, William. *Lectures in the Gospel of Matthew.* 5th ed. Neptune, N.J.: Loizeaux Brothers, 1943.

Morgan, G. Campbell. *The Gospel according to Matthew.* New York: Fleming H. Revell Co., 1929.

Pentecost, J. Dwight. *The Sermon on the Mount.* Portland, Ore.: Multnomah Press, 1980.

————. *The Words and Works of Jesus Christ.* Grand Rapids: Zondervan Publishing House, 1981.

Plummer, Alfred. *An Exegetical Commentary on the Gospel according to St. Matthew.* 1915. Reprint. Grand Rapids: Baker Book House, 1982.

Scroggie, W. Graham. *A Guide to the Gospels.* London: Pickering & Inglis, 1948.

Tasker, R.V.G. *The Gospel according to Matthew.* The Tyndale New Testament Commentaries. Grand Rapids: Wm. B. Eerdmans Publishing Co., 1961.

Thomas, W.H. Griffith. *Outline Studies in the Gospel of Matthew.* Grand Rapids: Wm. B. Eerdmans Publishing Co., 1961.

Toussaint, Stanley D. *Behold the King: A Study of Matthew.* Portland, Ore.: Multnomah Press, 1980.

Walvoord, John F. *Matthew: Thy Kingdom Come.* Chicago: Moody Press, 1974.

Wiersbe, Warren, W. *Meet Your King.* Wheaton, Ill.: Scripture Press Publications, Victor Books, 1980.

MARK

John D. Grassmick

INTRODUCTION

Mark is the shortest of the four Gospels. From the 4th till the 19th centuries it was largely neglected by scholars because it was commonly regarded as an abridgment of Matthew. But by the end of the 19th century the theory that Mark was the *first* Gospel written gained widespread acceptance. Since then Mark has been the object of intense interest and study.

Authorship. Technically Mark's Gospel is anonymous since it does not name its author. The title "according to Mark" (*Kata Markon*) was added later by a scribe some time before A.D. 125. However, sufficient evidence is available from early church tradition (external evidence) and from information within the Gospel itself (internal evidence) to identify the author.

The unanimous testimony of the early church fathers is that Mark, an associate of the Apostle Peter, was the author. The earliest known statement of this comes from Papias (ca. A.D. 110), who quoted the testimony of John the elder, probably an alternate designation for the Apostle John. Papias' quotation named Mark as author and included the following information about Mark: (1) He was not an eyewitness follower of Jesus. (2) He accompanied the Apostle Peter and heard his preaching. (3) He wrote down accurately all that Peter remembered of Jesus' words and works "but not in order," that is, not always in chronological order. (4) He was Peter's "interpreter," probably meaning he explained Peter's teaching to a wider audience by writing it down rather than translating Peter's Aramaic discourses into Greek or Latin. (5) His account is wholly reliable (cf. Eusebius *Ecclesiastical History* 3. 39. 15).

This early evidence is confirmed by testimony from Justin Martyr (*Dialogue* 106. 3; ca. A.D. 160), the *Anti-Marcionite Prologue* to Mark (ca. A.D. 160–180), Irenaeus (*Against Heresies* 3. 1. 1-2; ca. A.D. 180), Tertullian (*Against Marcion* 4. 5; ca. A.D. 200), and the writings of Clement of Alexandria (ca. A.D. 195) and Origen (ca. A.D. 230), both cited by Eusebius (*Ecclesiastical History* 2. 15. 2; 6. 14. 6; 6. 25. 5). Thus the external evidence for Marcan authorship is early and is derived from various centers of early Christianity: Alexandria, Asia Minor, Rome.

Though not explicitly stated, most interpreters assume that the Mark mentioned by the church fathers is the same person as the "John (Hebrew name), also called Mark" (Latin name) referred to 10 times in the New Testament (Acts 12:12, 25; 13:5, 13; 15:37, 39; Col. 4:10; 2 Tim. 4:11; Phile. 24; 1 Peter 5:13). Objections raised against this identification are not convincing. No evidence exists for "another" Mark who had close connections with Peter nor is it necessary to suggest an "unknown" Mark in light of the New Testament data.

Internal evidence, though not explicit, is compatible with the historical testimony of the early church. It reveals the following information: (1) Mark was familiar with the geography of Palestine, especially Jerusalem (cf. Mark 5:1; 6:53; 8:10; 11:1; 13:3). (2) He apparently knew Aramaic, the common language of Palestine (cf. 5:41; 7:11, 34; 14:36). (3) He understood Jewish institutions and customs (cf. 1:21; 2:14, 16, 18; 7:2-4).

Several features also point to the author's connection with Peter: (a) the vividness and unusual detail of the narratives, that suggest that they were derived from the reminiscences of an "inner-circle" apostolic eyewitness such as Peter (cf 1:16-20, 29-31, 35-38; 5:21-24,

35-43; 6:39, 53-54; 9:14-15; 10:32, 46; 14:32-42); (b) the author's use of Peter's words and deeds (cf. 8:29, 32-33; 9:5-6; 10:28-30; 14:29-31, 66-72); (c) the inclusion of the words "and Peter" in 16:7, which are unique to this Gospel; and (d) the striking similarity between the broad outline of this Gospel and Peter's sermon in Caesarea (cf. Acts 10:34-43).

In light of both external and internal evidence it is reasonable to affirm that the "John/Mark" in Acts and the Epistles authored this Gospel. He was a Jewish Christian who lived in Jerusalem with Mary his mother during the early days of the church. Nothing is known about his father. Their home was an early Christian meeting place (cf. Acts 12:12). Perhaps it was the location of Jesus' last Passover meal (cf. comments on Mark 14:12-16). Mark was probably the "young man" who fled away naked after Jesus' arrest in Gethsemane (cf. comments on 14:51-52). Peter's calling him "my son" (cf. 1 Peter 5:13) may mean Mark became a Christian through Peter's influence.

During the church's early days in Jerusalem (ca. A.D. 33-47) Mark no doubt became familiar with Peter's preaching. Later he went to Antioch and accompanied Paul and Barnabas (Mark's cousin; cf. Col. 4:10), as far as Perga on their first missionary journey (cf. Acts 12:25; 13:5, 13; ca. A.D. 48-49). For an unstated reason he returned home to Jerusalem. Because of his desertion Paul refused to take him on his second journey. Instead Mark served with Barnabas on the island of Cyprus (cf. Acts 15:36-39; ca. A.D. 50-?). Sometime later, perhaps by A.D. 57, he went to Rome. He was a fellow worker with Paul during Paul's first Roman imprisonment (cf. Col. 4:10; Phile. 23-24; ca. A.D. 60-62). After Paul's release Mark apparently remained in Rome and served with Peter on his arrival in "Babylon," Peter's code word for Rome (cf. 1 Peter 5:13; ca. A.D. 63-64). (Some, however, take Babylon to refer to the city on the Euphrates River; cf. comments on 1 Peter 5:13.) Probably because of severe persecution under Emperor Nero and Peter's martyrdom, Mark left Rome for a time. Finally Paul, during his second imprisonment in Rome (ca. A.D. 67-68), requested Timothy who was in Ephesus to pick up Mark who was presumably somewhere in Asia Minor and bring him to Rome because Paul considered him useful in his ministry (cf. 2 Tim. 4:11).

Sources. To say that Mark was the author of this Gospel does not mean he created the material in it. A "Gospel" was a unique literary form in the first century. It was not simply a biography of Jesus' life, a chronicle of His "mighty deeds," or a set of reminiscences by His followers, though it contains elements of all these. Rather it is a theological proclamation to a particular audience of God's "good news" centered in the historical events of Jesus' life, death, and resurrection. In line with his purpose Mark arranged and adapted the historical material he acquired from his sources.

His major source was the preaching and instruction of the Apostle Peter (cf. comments under "Authorship"). Presumably he heard Peter preach many times in Jerusalem in the early days (ca. A.D. 33-47) and may have taken notes. He also probably had personal conversations with him. Mark also had contact with Paul and Barnabas (cf. Acts 13:5-12; 15:39; Col. 4:10-11). Presumably Mark included at least one reminiscence of his own (cf. Mark 14:51-52). Other sources of information include: (a) units of oral tradition that circulated in the early church individually or as a topical (e.g., 2:1-3:6) or temporal/geographical (e.g., chaps. 14-15) series of events forming a continuous narrative; (b) independent traditional sayings of Jesus linked together by "catch words" (e.g., 9:37-50); and (c) oral tradition which Mark summarized (e.g., 1:14-15; 3:7-12; 6:53-56). Under the oversight of the Holy Spirit Mark used these sources to compose a historically accurate and trustworthy Gospel.

There is no certain evidence that Mark used *written* sources, though the Passion narrative (chaps. 14-15) may have come to him at least partially written. This raises the problem of Mark's relationship to Matthew and Luke.

Many scholars believe that Mark was the first Gospel written and that Matthew and Luke used it as a primary source document along with material from other sources. Luke, in fact, stated that he used other documents (Luke

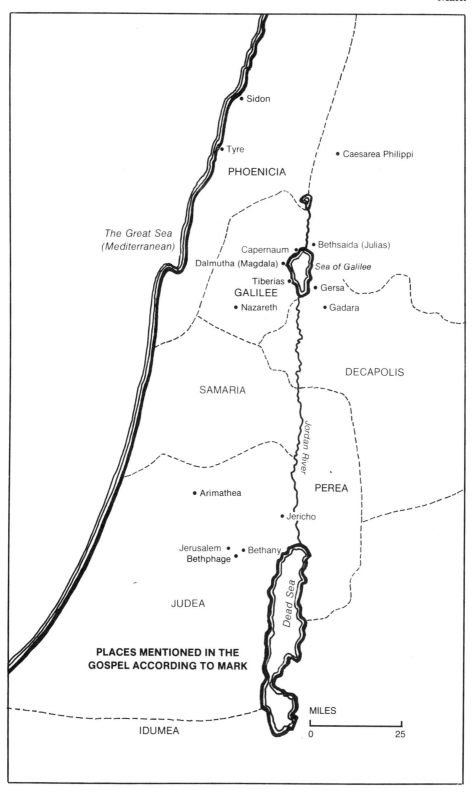

PLACES MENTIONED IN THE GOSPEL ACCORDING TO MARK

1:1-4). Several arguments support the priority of Mark: (1) Matthew incorporates about 90 percent of Mark, and Luke over 40 percent—over 600 of Mark's 661 verses are found in Matthew and Luke combined. (2) Matthew and Luke usually follow Mark's order of events in Jesus' life, and where either of them differs for topical reasons the other always holds to Mark's order. (3) Matthew and Luke hardly ever agree *against* the content of Mark in passages where they all deal with the same subject. (4) Matthew and Luke often repeat Mark's exact words but where they differ in wording, the language of one or the other is simply grammatically or stylistically smoother than Mark's (cf., e.g., Mark 2:7 with Luke 5:21). (5) Matthew and Luke seem to alter Mark's wording in some instances to clarify his meaning (cf. Mark 2:15 with Luke 5:29) or to "tone down" some of his strong statements (cf., e.g., Mark 4:38b with Matt. 8:25; Luke 8:24). (6) Matthew and Luke sometimes omit words and phrases from Mark's "full" descriptions to make room for additional material (cf., e.g., Mark 1:29 with Matt. 8:14; Luke 4:38).

Five major objections have been raised against the theory of Marcan priority: (1) Matthew and Luke agree with each other against the content of Mark in some passages dealing with the same subject. (2) Luke omits all reference to the material in Mark 6:45-8:26 which is unusual if he used Mark. (3) Mark occasionally has bits of information not found in the same incident reported in Matthew or Luke (cf. Mark 14:72). (4) The early church fathers apparently believed in the priority of Matthew instead of Mark. (5) Marcan priority practically requires the view that Matthew and/or Luke were written after the destruction of Jerusalem in A.D. 70.

In response to the first objection, the agreements of Luke and Matthew against Mark involve a very small number of passages (ca. 6%) and are probably due to common sources (i.e., oral tradition) which they used in addition to Mark. The second objection falters on the commonly acknowledged fact that the Gospel writers selected material from their sources in line with their purposes. Luke may have omitted reference to material in Mark 6:45-8:26 in order not to interrupt the

development of his own journey-to-Jerusalem theme (cf. Luke 9:51). This also answers the third objection in addition to the fact that Mark had Peter as an eyewitness source. The fourth objection stems from the arrangement of the Gospels in the New Testament canon. To infer from this that the early fathers believed Matthew was *written* first is not valid. They were concerned about the apostolic authority and apologetic value of the Synoptic Gospels, not their historical interrelationships. Thus Matthew, written by an apostle and beginning with a genealogy that linked it nicely to the Old Testament, was given first place. Furthermore, if Matthew were the first Gospel written and it were used by Mark and Luke, one would expect to find places where Luke follows Matthew's order of events and Mark does not—but this does not occur. It is also more difficult to explain why Mark would shift from Matthew's order than vice versa. Displacement of order favors Marcan priority. In response to the fifth objection, Marcan priority does not necessitate dating Matthew and/or Luke after A.D. 70 (cf. comments on "Date").

Some literary dependence seems to be the only way to explain adequately the close relationship between the Synoptic Gospels. The priority-of-Mark theory, though not without problems, accounts best for the basic outline of events and the detailed similarities between the Synoptic Gospels. The differences are probably due to a combination of oral and written traditions which Matthew and Luke used independently in addition to Mark. (For further discussion and an alternate view on the Synoptic problem [priority of Matt.] see the *Introduction* to Matt.)

Date. Nowhere does the New Testament have any explicit statement regarding the date of Mark. The discourse centered around Jesus' prediction of the destruction of the Jerusalem temple (cf. comments on 13:2, 14-23) suggests that Mark's Gospel was written before A.D. 70, when the temple was destroyed.

Early testimony from the church fathers is divided on whether Mark wrote his Gospel before or after the martyrdom of Peter (ca. A.D. 64-68). On one hand, Irenaeus (*Against Heresies* 3. 1. 1) declared that Mark wrote *after* the "departure" (*exodon*) of Peter *and* Paul (thus after A.D. 67 or 68). By the word *exodon* Irenaeus probably meant "departure in death." The word is used this way in Luke 9:31 and 2 Peter 1:15. This is clearly supported by the *Anti-Marcionite Prologue* to Mark which asserts, "After the death of Peter himself, he [Mark] wrote down this same Gospel. . . ." On the other hand, Clement of Alexandria and Origen (cf. Eusebius *Ecclesiastical History* 2. 15. 2; 6. 14. 6; 6. 25. 5) placed the writing of Mark's Gospel *during* Peter's lifetime stating, in fact, that Peter participated in its production and ratified its use in the church.

Because of conflicting external evidence the question of date remains problematic. Two options are available. One view is that the Gospel can be dated between A.D. 67–69 if one accepts the tradition that it was written after the deaths of Peter *and* Paul. Advocates of this view usually hold either that Matthew and Luke were written after A.D. 70 or that they were written before Mark. A second view is that the Gospel can be dated prior to A.D. 64–68 (when Peter was martyred) if one accepts the tradition that it was written during Peter's lifetime. On this view one can accept the priority of Mark (or Matt.) and still hold that all the Synoptic Gospels were written before A.D. 70.

The second view is preferred for these reasons: (1) Tradition is divided though the more reliable evidence supports this view. (2) The priority of Mark (cf. comments under "Sources"), particularly Mark's relationship to Luke, which antedates Acts (cf. Acts 1:1), points to a date before A.D. 64. The fact that Acts closes with Paul still in prison prior to his first release (ca. A.D. 62) pushes the date for Mark before A.D. 60. (3) It is historically probable that Mark (and perhaps Peter also for a short time) could have been in Rome during the latter part of the 50s (cf. comments under "Authorship" and under "Place of Origin and Destination"). Thus a plausible dating would seem to be A.D. 57–59 during the early part of Emperor Nero's reign (A.D. 54–68).

Place of Origin and Destination. The almost universal testimony of early church fathers (cf. references under "Authorship") is that Mark's Gospel was written in Rome primarily for Gentile Roman Christians.

The following evidence from the Gospel itself supports this: (1) Jewish customs are explained (cf. 7:3-4; 14:12; 15:42). (2) Aramaic expressions are translated into Greek (cf. 3:17; 5:41; 7:11, 34; 9:43; 10:46; 14:36; 15:22, 34) (3) Several Latin terms are used rather than their Greek equivalents (cf. 5:9; 6:27; 12:15, 42; 15:16, 39). (4) The Roman method of reckoning time is used (cf. 6:48; 13:35). (5) Only Mark identified Simon of Cyrene as the father of Alexander and Rufus (cf. 15:21; Rom. 16:13). (6) Few Old Testament quotations or references to fulfilled prophecy are used. (7) Mark portrayed a particular concern for "all the nations" (cf. comments on Mark 5:18-20; 7:24–8:10; 11:17; 13:10; 14:9), and at a climactic point in the Gospel a Gentile Roman centurion unwittingly proclaimed Jesus' deity (cf. 15:39). (8) The tone and message of the Gospel are appropriate to Roman believers who were encountering persecution and expecting more (cf. comments on 9:49; 13:9-13). (9) Mark assumed that his readers were familiar with the main characters and events of his narrative, so he wrote with more of a theological than a biographical interest. (10) Mark addressed his readers as Christians more directly by explaining the meaning for them of particular actions and statements (cf. 2:10, 28; 7:19).

Characteristics. Several features make Mark's Gospel unique among the Gospels. First, it emphasizes Jesus' actions more than His teaching. Mark recorded 18 of Jesus' miracles but only four of His parables (4:2-20, 26-29, 30-32; 12:1-9) and one major discourse (13:3-37). Repeatedly Mark wrote that Jesus taught without recording His teaching (1:21, 39; 2:2, 13; 6:2, 6, 34; 10:1; 12:35). Most of the teaching he did include came out of Jesus' controversies with the Jewish religious leaders (2:8-11, 19-22, 25-28; 3:23-30; 7:6-23; 10:2-12; 12:10-11, 13-40).

Second, Mark's writing style is vivid, forceful, and descriptive, reflecting an eyewitness source such as Peter (cf., e.g., 2:4; 4:37-38; 5:2-5; 6:39; 7:33; 8:23-24; 14:54). His use of Greek is nonliterary, close to the everyday speech of that time with a recognizable Semitic flavoring. His use of Greek tenses, especially the "historical present" tense (used over 150 times), simple sentences linked by "and," frequent use of "immediately" (*euthys*; cf. comments on 1:10), and the use of forceful words (e.g., lit., "impelled," 1:12) lend vividness to his narrative.

Third, Mark portrayed his subjects with unusual candor. He emphasized the responses of Jesus' hearers with various expressions of amazement (cf. comments on 1:22, 27; 2:12; 5:20; 9:15). He related the concern of Jesus' family over His mental health (cf. 3:21, 31-35). He candidly and repeatedly drew attention to the disciples' lack of understanding and failures (cf. 4:13; 6:52; 8:17, 21; 9:10, 32; 10:26). He also highlighted Jesus' emotions such as His compassion (1:41; 6:34; 8:2; 10:16), His anger and displeasure (1:43; 3:5; 8:33; 10:14), and His sighs of distress and sorrow (7:34; 8:12; 14:33-34).

Fourth, Mark's Gospel is dominated by Jesus' movement toward the Cross and the Resurrection. From Mark 8:31 onward Jesus and His disciples were "on the way" (cf. 9:33; 10:32) from Caesarea Philippi in the north through Galilee to Jerusalem in the south. The rest of the narrative (36%) was devoted to events of the Passion Week—the eight days from Jesus' entry into Jerusalem (11:1-11) to His resurrection (16:1-8).

Theological Themes. Mark's portrait of Jesus and its meaning for discipleship stand at the center of his theology. In the opening verse Jesus Christ is identified as "the Son of God" (1:1). This was confirmed by the Father (1:11; 9:7) and affirmed by demons (3:11; 5:7), by Jesus Himself (13:32; 14:36, 61-62), and by a Roman centurion at Jesus' death (15:39). It was also confirmed by His authoritative teaching (1:22, 27) and His sovereign power over disease and disability (1:30-31, 40-42; 2:3-12; 3:1-5; 5:25-34; 7:31-37; 8:22-26; 10:46-52), demons (1:23-27; 5:1-20; 7:24-30; 9:17-27), the domain of nature (4:37-39; 6:35-44, 47-52; 8:1-10), and death (5:21-24, 35-43). All this was convincing proof that "the kingdom of God"—His sovereign rule—had come near to people in Jesus, both in His words and works (cf. comments on 1:15).

Yet paradoxically Mark stressed Jesus' demand that the demons be silent (1:25, 34; 3:12) and that His miracles not be publicized (1:44; 5:43; 7:36; 8:26). He stressed Jesus' use of parables in teaching the crowds (4:33-34) because His kingly rule was then veiled, a mystery, recognized only by people of faith (4:11-12). Mark stressed the disciples' slowness to understand the meaning of Jesus' presence with them despite private instruction (4:13, 40; 6:52; 7:17-19; 8:17-21). He stressed Jesus' demand for silence even from the disciples following Peter's confession of His identity (8:30). Jesus did this because of the Jews' misleading views about the Messiah, which were contrary to the purpose of His earthly ministry. He did not want His identity declared openly till He had made clear to His followers the kind of Messiah He was and the character of His mission.

Mark recorded Peter's confession, "You are the Christ" (8:29), in its simplest, most direct form. Jesus did not accept or reject this title but turned the disciples' attention from the question of His identity to that of His activity (8:31, 38). He used the preferred designation "Son of Man" and taught His disciples that He must suffer, die, and rise again. The title, Son of Man, used 12 times *by Jesus* in Mark versus His one use of the title "Christ" ("the Messiah," 9:41), was especially suited to His total messianic mission—present and future (cf. comments on 8:31, 38; 14:62). He was the suffering Servant of Yahweh (Isa. 52:13-53:12) who gave up His life for others in submission to God's will (Mark 8:31). He was also the Son of Man who will come in glory to render judgment and establish His kingdom on earth (8:38-9:8; 13:26; 14:62). But before the glorious triumph of His messianic reign He must first suffer and die under the curse of God for human sin (14:36; 15:34) as a ransom for many (10:45). This had important implications for all who would follow Him (8:34-38).

It was hard for Jesus' 12 disciples to grasp this. They envisioned a reigning Messiah, not One who would suffer and die. In his special discipleship section (8:31-10:52) Mark portrayed Jesus "on the way" to Jerusalem teaching His disciples what it meant to follow Him. The prospect was not attractive. But in

His transfiguration He gave three of them a reassuring preview of His future coming in power and glory (9:1-8). At the same time the Father confirmed Jesus' sonship and commanded them to obey Him. Throughout this section the disciples "saw" but not as they ought (8:22-26). Again Mark emphasized that they followed Jesus with amazement, misunderstanding, and even fear of what lay ahead (9:32; 10:32). At Jesus' arrest they all deserted Him (14:50). With restraint Mark recorded Jesus' crucifixion and the accompanying phenomena that elucidated its meaning (15:33-39).

But Mark emphasized the empty tomb and the angel's message that Jesus was alive and was going ahead of His disciples into Galilee (14:28; 16:7), the place of their initial ministry (6:6b-13). His abrupt conclusion dramatically declared that Jesus is alive to lead His disciples and care for their needs as He had done previously. Thus their "journey" of discipleship was to go on in light of and determined by Jesus' death and resurrection (9:9-10).

Occasion and Purpose. Mark's Gospel contains no direct statement about this, so that information must be derived from a study of its contents and presumed historical setting. Because such assessments differ, various views have been given.

Some suggested purpose statements: (a) to present a biographical portrait of Jesus as the Servant of the Lord, (b) to win converts to Jesus Christ, (c) to give instruction to new Christians and strengthen their faith in the face of persecution, (d) to provide material for evangelists and teachers to use, and (e) to correct false ideas about Jesus and His messianic mission. These suggestions, though helpful, seem either to exclude portions of the Gospel from consideration or fail to account for Mark's emphases.

Mark's purpose was basically *pastoral*. The Christians in Rome had already heard and believed the good news of God's saving power (Rom. 1:8) but they needed to hear it again with a new emphasis to catch afresh its implications for their lives in a dissolute and often hostile environment. They needed to understand the nature of discipleship— what it meant to follow Jesus—in light of

who Jesus is and what He had done and would keep doing for them.

Like a good pastor, Mark presented "the gospel about Jesus Christ, the Son of God" (1:1) in a way that would meet this need and continue to shape his readers' lives. He achieved this through his portraits of Jesus and the 12 disciples with whom he expected his readers to identify (cf. comments under "Theological Themes"). He showed how Jesus Christ is the Messiah because He is the Son of God, and His death as the suffering Son of Man was God's plan for people's redemption. In light of this he showed how Jesus cared for His disciples and taught them about discipleship in the context of His death and resurrection— the same kind of care and teaching needed by all who follow Jesus.

OUTLINE

character of God's kingdom (4:1-34)

E. Jesus' miracles demonstrating His sovereign power (4:35-5:43)

F. Conclusion: Jesus' rejection at Nazareth (6:1-6a)

V. Jesus' Ministry in and beyond Galilee (6:6b-8:30)

A. Introductory summary: Jesus' teaching tour of Galilee (6:6b)

B. Jesus' sending forth of the Twelve and John the Baptist's death (6:7-31)

C. Jesus' self-disclosure to the Twelve in word and deed (6:32-8:26)

D. Conclusion: Peter's confession that Jesus is the Christ (8:27-30)

VI. Jesus' Journey to Jerusalem (8:31-10:52)

A. The first Passion prediction unit (8:31-9:29)

B. The second Passion prediction unit (9:30-10:31)

C. The third Passion prediction unit (10:32-45)

D. Conclusion: The faith of blind Bartimaeus (10:46-52)

VII. Jesus' Ministry in and around Jerusalem (11:1-13:37)

A. Jesus' entry into Jerusalem (11:1-11)

B. Jesus' prophetic signs of God's judgment on Israel (11:12-26)

C. Jesus' controversy with the Jewish religious leaders in the temple courts (11:27-12:44)

D. Jesus' prophetic Olivet Discourse to His disciples (chap. 13)

VIII. Jesus' Suffering and Death in Jerusalem (chaps. 14-15)

A. Jesus' betrayal, the Passover meal, and His disciples' desertion (14:1-52)

B. Jesus' trials, crucifixion, and burial (14:53-15:47)

IX. Jesus' Resurrection from the Dead near Jerusalem (16:1-8)

A. The women's arrival at the tomb (16:1-5)

B. The angel's announcement (16:6-7)

C. The women's response to the news of Jesus' resurrection (16:8)

X. Disputed Epilogue (16:9-20)

A. Three of Jesus' post-resurrection appearances (16:9-14)

B. Jesus' commission to His followers (16:15-18)

C. Jesus' Ascension and the disciples' ongoing mission (16:19-20)

COMMENTARY

I. The Title (1:1)

1:1. The opening verse (a verbless phrase) stands as the book's title and theme. The word **gospel** (*euangeliou*, "good news") does not refer to Mark's book, known as "the Gospel of Mark." Instead it refers to the good news **about Jesus Christ.**

Those acquainted with the Old Testament knew the importance of the word "gospel" (cf. Isa. 40:9; 41:27; 52:7; 61:1-3). "News" meant that something significant had happened. When Mark used the word, it had become a technical term signifying Christian preaching about Jesus Christ. "The gospel" is the proclamation of God's power through Jesus Christ to save all who believe (Rom. 1:16). It was an important term in the theological shaping of Mark's narrative (Mark 1:14-15; 8:35; 10:29; 13:9-10; 14:9).

For Mark, **the beginning of the** gospel was the historical facts of the life, death, and resurrection of Jesus. Later the apostles proclaimed it, beginning (e.g., Acts 2:36) where Mark ended.

The gospel is "about Jesus Christ," **the Son of God.** "Jesus," His divinely given personal name (cf. Matt. 1:21; Luke 1:31; 2:21), is the Greek equivalent of the Hebrew *y^ehôšûa'* ("Joshua"), "Yahweh is salvation."

"Christ" is the Greek equivalent of the Hebrew title *Māšîah* ("Messiah, Anointed One"). It was used specifically of the Deliverer anticipated in the Jewish world who would be God's Agent in fulfilling Old Testament prophecies (e.g., Gen. 49:10; Pss. 2; 110; Isa. 9:1-7; 11:1-9; Zech. 9:9-10). The anticipated Messiah is Jesus. Though the title "Christ" became part of Jesus' personal name in early Christian usage, Mark intended its full titular force as shown by his usage (cf. Mark 8:29; 12:35; 14:61; 15:32).

The title "Son of God" points to Jesus' unique relationship to God. He is a Man (Jesus)—and God's "Special Agent" (Messiah)—but He is also fully divine. As the Son He depends on and obeys God the Father (cf. Heb. 5:8).

II. Introduction: The Preparation for Jesus' Public Ministry (1:2-13)

Mark's brief introduction presents three preparatory events that are necessary for a proper understanding of Jesus' life-mission: the ministry of John the Baptist (vv. 2-8), Jesus' baptism (vv. 9-11), and Jesus' temptation (vv. 12-13). Two recurring words bind this section together: "the desert" (erēmos; vv. 3-4, 12-13) and "the Spirit" (vv. 8, 10, 12).

A. Jesus' forerunner, John the Baptist (1:2-8)
(Matt. 3:1-12; Luke 3:1-20; John 1:19-37)

1. JOHN'S FULFILLMENT OF OLD TESTAMENT PROPHECY (1:2-3)

1:2-3. Mark began by putting his account in its proper scriptural context. Aside from Old Testament quotations by Jesus this is the only place Mark referred to the Old Testament in his Gospel.

Verse 2 blends Exodus 23:20 (LXX) and Malachi 3:1 (Heb.), and Mark 1:3 is from Isaiah 40:3 (LXX). Mark adopted a traditional understanding of these verses so he could use them without explanation. In addition he emphasized the word "way" (hodos, lit., "road, highway"), an important theme in Mark's explanation of discipleship (Mark 8:27; 9:33; 10:17, 32, 52; 12:14).

Mark prefaced this composite quotation from three Old Testament books with the words: **It is written in Isaiah the prophet.** This illustrates a common practice by New Testament authors in quoting several passages with a unifying theme. The common theme here is the "wilderness" (desert) tradition in Israel's history. Since Mark was introducing the ministry of John the Baptist in the desert, he cited Isaiah as the source because the Isaiah passage refers to "a voice . . . calling" **in the desert.**

Under the Holy Spirit's guidance Mark gave those Old Testament texts a messianic interpretation by altering "the way before Me" (Mal. 3:1) to **Your way,** and "the paths of our God" (Isa. 40:3, LXX) to **paths for Him.** Thus the speaker, **I,** was God who **will send** His **messenger** (John) **ahead of You** (Jesus) **who will prepare** Your (Jesus') way. John was a **voice** urging the nation of Israel to **prepare** (pl. verb) **the way for the Lord** (Jesus) and to **make straight** "paths for Him" (Jesus). The meaning of these metaphors is given in John's ministry (Mark 1:4-5).

2. JOHN'S ACTIVITY AS A PROPHET (1:4-5)

1:4. In fulfillment of the preceding prophecy, **John came** (egeneto, "appeared") on the stage of history as the last Old Testament prophet (cf. Luke 7:24-28; 16:16), signaling a turning point in God's dealings with mankind. John was **baptizing in the desert region** (erēmō, dry, uninhabited country) **and preaching a baptism of repentance.** The word "preaching" (kēryssōn) could be rendered "proclaiming as a herald," appropriate in light of the prediction in Mark 1:2-3.

John's baptism was no innovation since Jews required Gentiles wanting to be admitted into Judaism to be baptized by self-immersion. The startling new element was that John's baptism was designed for God's covenant people, the Jews, and it required their repentance in view of the coming Messiah (cf. Matt. 3:2).

This baptism is described as one relating to or expressive of repentance **for** (eis) **the forgiveness of sins.** The Greek preposition eis could be referential ("with reference to") or purpose ("leading to") but probably not cause ("on account of"). "Repentance" (metanoia) occurs in Mark only here. It means "a turn about, a deliberate change of mind resulting in a change of direction in thought and behavior" (cf. Matt. 3:8; 1 Thes. 1:9).

"Forgiveness" (aphesin) means "the removal or cancellation of an obligation or barrier of guilt." It refers to God's gracious act whereby "sins" as a debt are canceled, based on Christ's sacrificial death (cf. Matt. 26:28). Forgiveness was not conveyed by the outward rite of baptism, but baptism was a visible witness that one had repented and as a result had received God's gracious forgiveness of sins (cf. Luke 3:3).

1:5. Using hyperbole (cf. also vv. 32-33, 37), Mark showed the great impact John made on all areas of Judea and **Jerusalem.** The people **went out** and **were baptized by** John **in the Jordan River** (cf. v. 9) as they confessed **their sins** to God. The imperfect tense of the Greek verbs portrays in motion-picture fashion the continual procession of people who kept going out to hear John's preaching and to be baptized by **him.**

The verb "baptize" (*baptizō,* intensive form of *baptō,* "to dip") means "to immerse, submerge." Being baptized by John in the Jordan marked the "turn" of a Jew to God. It identified him with the repentant people who were preparing for the coming Messiah.

Included in the performance of the baptismal rite was the people's open confession of sins. The verb "confessing" (*exomologoumenoi,* "agree with, acknowledging, admitting"; cf. Acts 19:18; Phil. 2:11), is intensive. They openly agreed with God's verdict on their sins (*hamartias,* "failure to hit the mark," i.e., God's standard). Every Jew familiar with the nation's history knew they had fallen short of God's demands. Their willingness to be baptized by John in the desert was an admission of their disobedience and an expression of their turning to God.

3. JOHN'S LIFESTYLE AS A PROPHET (1:6)

1:6. John's attire and diet marked him as a man of the desert and also depicted his role as God's prophet (cf. Zech. 13:4). In this way he resembled the Prophet Elijah (2 Kings 1:8), who was equated in Malachi 4:5 with the messenger (Mal. 3:1) cited earlier (cf. Mark 1:2; 9:13; Luke 1:17). **Locusts** (dried insects) **and wild honey** were the common diet in desert regions. Locusts are listed in Leviticus 11:22 among the "clean" foods.

4. JOHN'S MESSAGE AS A PROPHET (1:7-8)

1:7. The opening words are literally, "And he was proclaiming as a herald, saying . . ." (cf. v. 4). Mark summarized John's **message** in order to focus on its main theme, the announcement of a greater Person still to come who would baptize people with the Holy Spirit (v. 8).

The words, **After me** (in time) **will come One** echo Malachi 3:1 and 4:5, but the precise identity of the Coming One remained hidden even to John till after

Jesus' baptism (cf. John 1:29-34). No doubt Mark avoided the term "Messiah" because of popular misconceptions associated with it. Mark 1:8 suggests why the Coming One is **more powerful than** John.

John emphasized the importance of the Coming One and showed his own humility (cf. John 3:27-30) by declaring that he was **not worthy to stoop down** (words recorded only by Mark) **and untie** the **thongs** (leather straps) used to fasten His **sandals.** Even a Hebrew slave was not required to do this menial task for his master!

1:8. This verse contrasts I with **He.** John administered the outward sign, **water** baptism; but the Coming One would actually bestow the life-giving Spirit.

When used in connection with water, the word "baptize" normally indicated a literal immersion (cf. vv. 9-10). When used with the words **Holy Spirit** it metaphorically means coming under the Spirit's life-giving power.

I **baptize** is literally "I baptized," probably indicating that John was addressing those he had already baptized. His baptism **with** (or "in") "water" was limited and preparatory. But those who received it pledged to welcome the Coming One who would **baptize** them **with the** Holy Spirit (cf. Acts 1:5; 11:15-16). The bestowal of the Spirit was an expected feature of the Messiah's coming (Isa. 44:3; Ezek. 36:26-27; Joel 2:28-29).

B. *Jesus' baptism by John the Baptist (1:9-11)*
(Matt. 3:13-17; Luke 3:21-22)

1. JESUS' BAPTISM IN THE JORDAN (1:9)

1:9. Mark abruptly introduced the Coming One (v. 7) as **Jesus.** In contrast with "all the people" from Judea and Jerusalem (v. 5), He **came** to **John** in the desert region **from Nazareth in Galilee.** Nazareth was an obscure village never mentioned in the Old Testament, the Talmud, or the writings of Josephus, the well-known first-century Jewish historian. Galilee, about 30 miles wide and 60 miles long, was the populous northernmost region of the three divisions of Palestine: Judea, Samaria, and Galilee.

John **baptized** Jesus **in** (*eis*) **the Jordan** River (cf. v. 5). The Greek prepositions *eis* ("into," v. 9) and *ek* ("out of," v. 10) suggest baptism by immersion. Jesus' baptism probably occurred near Jericho. He was about 30 years old at this time (Luke 3:23).

In contrast with all others, Jesus made no confession of sins (cf. Mark 1:5) since He is without sin (cf. John 8:45-46; 2 Cor. 5:21; Heb. 4:15; 1 John 3:5). Mark did not state why Jesus submitted to John's baptism; however, three reasons may be suggested: (1) It was an act of obedience, showing that Jesus was in full agreement with God's overall plan and the role of John's baptism in it (cf. Matt. 3:15). (2) It was an act of self-identification with the nation of Israel whose heritage and sinful predicament He shared (cf. Isa. 53:12). (3) It was an act of self-dedication to His messianic mission, signifying His official acceptance and entrance into it.

2. THE DIVINE RESPONSE FROM HEAVEN (1:10-11)

1:10. Mark used the Greek adverb *euthys* ("immediately, at once") here for the first of 42 occurrences in his Gospel (the NIV omits it here). Its meaning varies from the sense of immediacy (as here) to that of logical order ("in due course, then"; cf. 1:21 ["when"]; 11:3 ["shortly"]).

Three things set **Jesus** apart from all others who had been baptized. First, **He saw heaven being torn open.** The forceful verb, "being torn open" (*schizomenous*, "split") reflects a metaphor for God's breaking into human experience to deliver His people (cf. Pss. 18:9, 16-19; 144:5-8; Isa. 64:1-5).

Second, He saw **the Spirit descending on Him like a dove,** in a visible dovelike form, not in a dovelike way (cf. Luke 3:22). The dove imagery probably symbolized the Spirit's creative activity (cf. Gen. 1:2). In Old Testament times the Spirit came on certain people to empower them for service (e.g., Ex. 31:3; Jud. 3:10; 11:29; 1 Sam. 19:20, 23). The coming of the Spirit on Jesus empowered Him for His messianic mission (cf. Acts 10:38) and the task of baptizing others with the Spirit, as John predicted (Mark 1:8).

1:11. Third, Jesus heard **a voice . . . from heaven** (cf. 9:7). The Father's words, expressing His unqualified approval of Jesus and His mission, echoed three verses: Genesis 22:2; Psalm 2:7; Isaiah 42:1.

In the first declaration, **You are My Son,** the words "You are" affirm Jesus' unique sonship with the Father. The significance of these words is found in Psalm 2:7 where God addressed the anointed King as His Son. At His baptism Jesus began His official role as God's Anointed One (cf. 2 Sam. 7:12-16; Ps. 89:26; Heb. 1:5).

The second clause, **whom I love,** is literally, "the Beloved One" (*ho agapētos*). This is either a title ("the Beloved") or a descriptive adjective ("beloved" Son). As a title it stresses the intensity of love between God the Father and the Son without losing its descriptive force. As an adjective, it can be understood in the Old Testament sense of an "only" Son (cf. Gen. 22:2, 12, 16; Jer. 6:26; Amos 8:10; Zech. 12:10), equivalent to the Greek adjective *monogenēs* ("only, unique"; cf. John 1:14, 18; Heb. 11:17). This more interpretive rendering points to Jesus' preexistent sonship.

The words **with You I am well pleased** point to the kind of kingly Son Jesus was to be in His earthly mission. The verb *eudokēsa* is in the past tense ("I *was* well pleased"). Timeless in force, it is rendered in English in the present tense to indicate that God is pleased with His Son at all times. God's delight never had a beginning and will never end.

These words come from Isaiah 42:1 in which God addressed His Servant whom He had chosen, the One in whom He delights, and on whom He had put His Spirit. Isaiah 42:1 begins the first of a series of four prophecies about the true Servant-Messiah in contrast with the disobedient servant-nation of Israel (cf. Isa. 42:1-9; 49:1-7; 50:4-9; 52:13–53:12). The true Servant would suffer greatly in fulfilling God's will. He would die as a "guilt offering" (Isa. 53:10), and He Himself would serve as the sacrificial Lamb (cf. Isa. 53:7-8; John 1:29-30). At His baptism Jesus began His role as the Lord's suffering Servant. Mark gives prominence to this feature of Jesus' messianic mission (Mark 8:31; 9:30-31; 10:32-34, 45; 15:33-39).

Jesus' baptism did not change His divine status. He did not *become* the Son of God at His baptism (or at the transfiguration, 9:7). Rather, His baptism showed the far-reaching significance of His acceptance of His messianic vocation as the suffering Servant of the Lord as well as the Davidic Messiah. Because He is the Son of God, the One approved by the Father and empowered by the Spirit, He is the Messiah (not vice versa). All three Persons of the Trinity are involved.

C. Jesus' temptation by Satan (1:12-13) (Matt. 4:1-11; Luke 4:1-13)

1:12. After His baptism Jesus went forward in the power of the Spirit and **at once** (euthys, "immediately") **the Spirit sent Him** farther **out into the desert** region. The word "sent" is from a strong verb (ekballō) meaning "drive out, expel, send away." Mark used it to denote the expulsion of demons (vv. 34, 39; 3:15, 22-23; 6:13; 7:26; 9:18, 28, 38). Here it reflects Mark's forceful style (cf. "led," Matt. 4:1; Luke 4:1). The thought is that of strong moral compulsion by which the Spirit led Jesus to take the offensive against temptation and evil instead of avoiding them. The desert (erēmos; cf. Mark 1:4) region, dry uninhabited places, was viewed traditionally as the haunt of evil powers (cf. Matt. 12:43; Luke 8:29; 9:24). The traditional temptation site is northwest of the Dead Sea immediately west of Jericho.

1:13. Jesus **was in the desert for 40 days.** Despite possible appeal to various Old Testament verses (Ex. 34:28; Deut. 9:9, 18; 1 Kings 19:8), the closest parallel is that of the victory of David over Goliath who had opposed Israel 40 days (1 Sam 17:16).

Jesus was **being tempted by Satan.** "Tempted" is a form of peirazō, which means "put to the test, make trial of" in order to discover the kind of person someone is. It is used either in a good sense (God's testing, e.g., 1 Cor. 10:13; Heb. 11:17) or in a bad sense of enticement to sin by Satan and his cohorts. Both senses are involved here. God put Jesus to the test (the Spirit led Him to it) to show He was qualified for His messianic mission. But also Satan tried to draw Jesus away from His divinely appointed mission (cf. Matt. 4:1-11; Luke 4:1-13). Jesus' sinlessness does not rule out the fact that He was actually tempted; in fact,

it bears witness to His true humanity (cf. Rom. 8:3; Heb. 2:18).

The tempter was Satan, the adversary, the one who opposes. Mark did not use the term "the devil" (slanderer; Matt. 4:1; Luke 4:2). Satan and his forces are in constant, intense opposition against God and His purposes, especially Jesus' mission. Satan tempts people to turn aside from God's will, accuses them before God when they fall, and seeks their ruin. Jesus encountered the prince of evil personally before confronting his forces. He entered on His ministry to defeat him and set his captives free (Heb. 2:14; 1 John 3:8). As the Son of God, He battled Satan in the desert, and the demons confessed Him as such (cf. Mark 1:24; 3:11; 5:7).

The reference to **wild animals** is recorded only by Mark. In Old Testament imagery, "the wilderness" was the place of God's curse—a place of desolation, loneliness, and danger where frightening, ravenous animals lived (cf. Isa. 13:20-22; 34:8-15; Pss. 22:11-21; 91:11-13). The presence of wild animals stresses the hostile character of the desert region as Satan's domain.

In contrast with the dangerous wild animals is God's protecting care through the **angels** who **attended** (lit., "were serving," diēkonoun) Jesus throughout the temptation period (though the verb could be rendered "began to serve Him," i.e., after the temptation). They supplied general aid and the assurance of God's presence. Mark did not mention fasting (cf. Matt. 4:2; Luke 4:2), probably because Jesus' stay in the desert region clearly implied it.

Mark's temptation account is brief (in contrast with Matt. and Luke). He said nothing about the temptation's content, its climactic end, or Jesus' victory over Satan. His concern was that this began an ongoing conflict with Satan who kept attempting through devious means to get Jesus to turn aside from God's will (cf. Mark 8:11, 32-33; 10:2; 12:15). Because of the vocation Jesus accepted in His baptism, He faced a confrontation with Satan and his forces. Mark's Gospel is the record of this great encounter which climaxed at the Cross. At the outset Jesus established His personal authority over Satan. His later exorcisms of demons were based on His victory in this encounter (cf. 3:22-30).

III. Jesus' Early Galilean Ministry (1:14–3:6)

The first major section of Mark's Gospel includes a summary statement of Jesus' message (1:14-15); the calling of the first disciples (1:16-20); Jesus' exorcising and healing ministry in and around Capernaum (1:21–45); five controversies with Jewish religious leaders (2:1–3:5), and a plot by the Pharisees and Herodians to kill Jesus (3:6). Throughout the section Jesus demonstrated His authority over all things both by His words and deeds.

A. Introductory summary: Jesus' message (1:14-15) (Matt. 4:12-17; Luke 4:14-21)

Jesus began His ministry in Galilee (cf. Mark 1:9) after John the Baptist was arrested by Herod Antipas (see chart on the Herods at Luke 1:5) for the reason stated in Mark 6:17-18. Before entering Galilee, Jesus ministered in Judea for about a year (cf. John 1:19–4:45), which Mark did not mention. This shows that Mark's purpose was not to give a complete chronological account of Jesus' life.

1:14. The words **was put in prison** translate to paradothēnai, from paradidomi, "deliver up or hand over." The verb is used of Jesus' betrayal by Judas (3:19), suggesting that Mark set up a parallel between John's and Jesus' experiences (cf. 1:4, 14a). The passive voice without a stated agent implies that God's purpose was being fulfilled in John's arrest (cf. parallel to Jesus, 9:31; 14:18) and that the time for Jesus' ministry in Galilee had now come (cf. comments on 9:11-13).

Jesus came into Galilee proclaiming (kēryssōn; cf. 1:4) **the good news** (euangelion; cf. v. 1) **of** (from) **God.** Possibly the words "of the kingdom" (KJV) should be included before "of God" because of their presence in many Greek manuscripts.

1:15. Jesus' two declarations and two commands summarize His message. The first declaration, **The time has come,** emphasizes the distinctive note of fulfillment in Jesus' proclamation (cf. Luke 4:16-21). God's appointed time of preparation and expectation, the Old Testament era, now stood fulfilled (cf. Gal. 4:4; Heb. 1:2; 9:6-15).

The second declaration, **The king-** **dom of God is near,** presents a key feature of Jesus' message. "Kingdom" (basileia) means "kingship" or "royal rule." Involved in the term is the sovereign authority of a ruler, the activity of ruling, and the realm of rule including its benefits (Theological Dictionary of the New Testament [hereafter TDNT]. Grand Rapids: Wm. B. Eerdmans Publishing Co., s.v. "basileia," 1:579-80). Thus "the kingdom of God" is a dynamic (not static) concept that refers to God's sovereign activity of ruling over His Creation.

This concept was familiar to the Jews of Jesus' day. In light of Old Testament prophecy (cf. 2 Sam. 7:8-17; Isa. 11:1-9; 24:23; Jer. 23:4-6; Micah 4:6-7; Zech. 9:9-10; 14:9) they were expecting a future messianic (Davidic) kingdom to be established on earth (cf. Matt. 20:21; Mark 10:37; 11:10; 12:35-37; 15:43; Luke 1:31-33; 2:25, 38; Acts 1:6). So Jesus' hearers naturally understood His reference to the kingdom of God to be the long-awaited messianic kingdom.

Jesus said God's rule "is near" (ēngiken, "has come near" or "has arrived"; cf. same verb form in Mark 14:42 ["Here comes"]). But it was not near in the form the Jews expected. Rather it had arrived in the sense that Jesus, the Agent of God's rule, was present among them (cf. Luke 17:20–21). This was "the good news from God."

The required response to which Jesus summoned His hearers was a double command: **Repent and believe the good news!** Repentance and faith (belief) are bound together in one piece (not temporally successive acts). To "repent" (metanoeō; cf. Mark 1:4) is to turn away from an existing object of trust (e.g., oneself). To "believe" (pisteuō, here pisteuete en, the only NT appearance of this combination) is to commit oneself wholeheartedly to an object of faith. Thus to believe in the good news meant to believe in Jesus Himself as the Messiah, the Son of God. He is the "content" of the good news (cf. v. 1). Only by this means can one enter into or receive (as a gift) the kingdom of God (cf. 10:15).

As a nation Israel officially rejected these requirements (cf. 3:6; 12:1-12; 14:1-2, 64-65; 15:31-32). Furthermore Jesus taught that His earthly Davidic reign would not come immediately (cf. Luke 19:11). After God completes His present purpose of saving Jews and Gentiles and building His church (cf. Rom. 16:25-27; Eph. 3:2-12), Jesus will return and set up His kingdom on this earth (Matt. 25:31, 34; Acts 15:14-18; Rev. 19:15; 20:4-6). The nation of Israel will be restored and redeemed (Rom. 11:25-29).

So the kingdom of God has two aspects, both centering in Christ (cf. Mark 4:13-31): (1) It is already present, though veiled, as a spiritual realm (Mark's emphasis; cf. 3:23-27; 10:15, 23-27; 12:34). (2) It is still future when God's rule will be openly established on earth (cf. 9:1; 13:24-27).

B. Jesus' call of four fishermen (1:16-20)
(Matt. 4:18-22; Luke 5:1-11)

Jesus' call of four fishermen, to be His followers comes immediately after the summary of His message. So Mark made clear that to repent and believe in the gospel (Mark 1:15) is to break with one's old way of life and to follow Jesus, to make a personal commitment to Him in response to His call. With this call Jesus began His work in Galilee. This anticipated His appointing and sending out the Twelve (3:13-19; 6:7-13, 30).

1:16. The **Sea** (a Semitic label) **of Galilee,** a warm-water lake about 7 miles wide, 13 miles long, and 685 feet *below* sea level, was the scene of a thriving fishing industry. It was geographically central to Jesus' Galilean ministry.

As He was walking along the shore, **Jesus . . . saw Simon** (surnamed Peter) and **Andrew,** his **brother,** each throwing out a circular casting **net** (10-15 feet diameter) **into the lake.** The significant thing about this, Mark explained (*gar,* **for**), is that **they were fishermen** by trade.

1:17-18. The words **Come, follow Me** are literally, "Come after Me," a technical expression that meant "Go behind Me as a disciple." Unlike a Rabbi whose pupils sought him out, **Jesus** took the initiative and called His followers.

The call included Jesus' promise: **and I will make you** to become (*genesthai*) **fishers of men.** He had "caught" them for His kingdom; now He would equip them to share His task, to become (*genesthai* implies preparation) fishers who catch "men" (generic for "people"; cf. 8:27).

The fishing metaphor was probably suggested by the brothers' occupation but

also had an Old Testament background (cf. Jer. 16:16; Ezek. 29:4-5; Hab. 1:14-17). Though the prophets used this figure to express divine judgment, Jesus used it positively as a means to avoid divine judgment. In view of the impending righteous rule of God (cf. Mark 1:15) Jesus summoned these men to the task of gathering people out of the "sea" (OT imagery for sin and death, e.g., Isa. 57:20-21).

At once (*euthys;* cf. Mark 1:10) Simon and Andrew **left their nets** (their old calling) **and followed Him.** In the Gospels the verb "follow" (*akoloutheō*), when referring to *individuals,* expresses the call and response of discipleship. Later events (cf. vv. 29-31) show that their response meant not a repudiation of their homes but rather giving Jesus their full allegiance (cf. 10:28; 1 Cor. 7:17-24).

1:19-20. On the same occasion Jesus saw **James** and **John,** the sons **of Zebedee** (cf. 10:35), **in** their **boat, preparing** (from *katartizō,* "put in order, make ready") **their nets** for another night's fishing. They were partners to Simon (cf. Luke 5:10). **Without delay** (*euthys*) Jesus **called them** to follow Him. **They left** behind their old way of life (fishing boat and nets) and prior claims (**their father Zebedee** and **the hired** helpers) **and followed** (lit., "went away after") **Him** as disciples.

Mark did not mention any previous contact with Jesus by these fishermen (cf. John 1:35-42). Later Jesus gathered the Twelve around Himself in a Teacher-pupil relationship (Mark 3:14-19). Mark abbreviated historical events (1:14-20) to emphasize Jesus' authority over people and the obedience of His followers.

Discipleship is prominent in Mark's Gospel. Jesus' call would pose two questions in the minds of Mark's readers: "Who is this One who calls?" and "What does it mean to follow Him?" Mark gave them an answer in his Gospel. He assumed similarities between the Twelve (cf. comments on 3:13; 13:37) and his readers. Discipleship is the expected norm for all who believe the gospel (cf. 1:15).

C. Jesus' authority over demons and disease (1:21-45)

The authoritative nature (v. 22) and importance (vv. 38-39) of Jesus' word already experienced by the four fishermen was demonstrated further by His powerful deeds. Verses 21-34 describe a single, perhaps typical, Sabbath Day's activities in Capernaum: His power over demons (vv. 21-28), the healing of Peter's mother-in-law (vv. 29-31), and the healing of others after sunset (vv. 32-34). Then verses 35-39 present a brief withdrawal for prayer and a summary of a preaching tour in Galilee. One significant event on that tour was the healing of a leper (vv. 40-45). Jesus' authoritative words and deeds provoked both amazement and alarm and set the stage for controversies (2:1–3:5).

1. THE CURE OF A DEMONIAC (1:21-28)
(LUKE 4:31-37)

1:21-22. The four disciples accompanied Jesus into nearby **Capernaum** (cf. 2:1; 9:33), on the northwestern shore of the Sea of Galilee. It was their hometown and became the hub of Jesus' Galilean ministry (cf. Luke 4:16-31). In due course (*euthys;* cf. Mark 1:10), on **the Sabbath** (Saturday) **Jesus** attended the regular worship service in **the synagogue,** a Jewish place of assembly and worship (cf. vv. 23, 29, 39; 3:1; 6:2; 12:39; 13:9). No doubt by invitation from the ruler of the synagogue, He **began to teach** (cf. Acts 13:13-16). Mark often referred to Jesus' **teaching** ministry (Mark 2:13; 4:1-2; 6:2, 6, 34; 8:31; 10:1; 11:17; 12:35; 14:49), but recorded little of what Jesus taught.

His hearers **were amazed** (*exeplēssonto,* lit., "astounded, struck out of their senses, overwhelmed"; also in 6:2; 7:37; 10:26; 11:18) at the manner and the content (cf. 1:14-15) of Jesus' teaching. **He taught** with direct **authority** from God and had the power to evoke decisions. This contrasted sharply with **the teachers of the Law** (lit., "scribes") who were schooled in the written Law and its oral interpretation. Their knowledge was derived from scribal tradition, so they simply quoted the sayings of their predecessors.

1:23-24. **Just then** (*euthys;* cf. v. 10), the presence of Jesus and His authoritative teaching in the synagogue provoked a strong outburst from **a man** under control of **an evil spirit** (lit., "an unclean spirit," Semitic for "demon"; cf. v. 34).

The demon spoke through the man who **cried out, What do You want with us. . . ?** These words translate a Hebrew

idiom which expresses the incompatibility of opposing forces (cf. 5:7; Josh. 22:24; Jud. 11:12; 2 Sam. 16:10; 19:22).

This question, in the NIV, could be punctuated more forcefully as a declaration: "**You** have **come** (into the world) **to destroy** (ruin, not annihilate) **us.**" The pronoun "us" in both sentences indicates that this demon perceived the significance of Jesus' presence (cf. Mark 1:15) to all the demonic forces. Jesus was the ultimate threat to their power and activity.

The demon, in contrast with most people, recognized Jesus' true character and identity as **the Holy One of God** (cf. 3:11; 5:7), the One empowered by the Holy Spirit. Thus the evil spirit knew the explanation for Jesus' authority.

1:25-26. In a few direct words (no incantations) **Jesus sternly** rebuked (*epetimēsen;* cf. 4:39) the evil spirit and ordered the demon to **come out of** the man. The words **Be quiet** translate the forceful *phimōthēti,* "be muzzled or silenced" (cf. 4:39). Submitting to Jesus' authority, **the evil spirit** convulsed (cf. 9:26) **the** possessed **man,** and **with a loud shriek,** left **him.**

Jesus did not accept the demon's defensive utterance (1:24) because doing so would have undermined His task of confronting and defeating Satan and his forces. His authority over evil spirits was evidence that God's rule had come in Jesus (cf. v. 15). This initial exorcism set the pattern for the sustained conflict Jesus had with demons—an important element in Mark's account. (See the list of Jesus' miracles at John 2:1-11.)

1:27-28. All **the people** were greatly **amazed** (*ethambēthēsan,* "surprised, astonished"; cf. 10:24, 32). Their question, **What is this?** referred both to the nature of Jesus' teaching and His expulsion of a demon with only a word of command. His **teaching** was qualitatively **new** (*kainē*) **and** came **with authority** (cf. 1:22) that extended even to demonic forces who were forced to **obey** (submit to) **Him** (cf. 4:41). In summary, Mark declared that very soon (*euthys;* cf. 1:10) all **Galilee** heard the **news about Him.**

2. THE HEALING OF SIMON'S MOTHER-IN-LAW (1:29-31)
(MATT. 8:14-15; LUKE 4:38-39)

1:29-31. Immediately (*euthys;* cf. v. 10) after leaving **the synagogue** Sabbath service, Jesus and the four disciples **went to the nearby home of Simon** (Peter) **and Andrew.** This house became something of a headquarters for Jesus when He was in Capernaum (cf. 2:1; 3:20; 9:33; 10:10). He was promptly (*euthys*) **told** that **Simon's mother-in-law was** lying **in bed** burning **with a fever.** In compassionate response **Jesus** stood beside her and without a word simply grasped **her hand and** raised **her up. The fever left** completely, and without weakness **she began to** serve (*diēkonei,* imperf.) her guests.

3. THE HEALING OF MANY PEOPLE AT SUNSET (1:32-34)

(MATT. 8:16-17; LUKE 4:40-41)

1:32-34. This summary portrays the excitement in Capernaum generated by the miracles on that Sabbath. The double time reference, **that evening after sunset,** made it clear that **the people** of Capernaum waited until the Sabbath Day was over (sunset) before moving the sick lest they break the Law (cf. Ex. 20:10) or Rabbinic regulations which prohibited burden-bearing on that day (cf. Mark 3:1-5).

The townspeople **brought** (lit., "kept carrying," imperf.) **to Jesus all the** physically **sick and demon-possessed** (not "possessed with devils," KJV, since there is only one devil). Again, a clear distinction is maintained between physical sickness and demon possession (cf. 6:13). It seemed as if **the whole town** (hyperbole; cf. 1:5) had **gathered at the door** of Simon's house. In compassionate response to this human need **Jesus healed many** (a Heb. idiom meaning "all who were brought"; cf. v. 32; 10:45; Matt. 8:16) **who had** a wide variety of **diseases. He also drove out** (*exebalen,* from *ekballō;* cf. Mark 1:12, 39) **many demons, but** as before (vv. 23-26) He repeatedly silenced their cries of recognition, showing that they were powerless before Him.

The miracles accompanying Jesus' preaching increased His popularity. He performed miracles not to impress people with His power but to authenticate His message (cf. v. 15).

4. A WITHDRAWAL FOR PRAYER AND A PREACHING TOUR IN GALILEE (1:35-39)

(LUKE 4:42-44)

1:35. Despite a full day of ministry (vv. 21-34), **Jesus got up** the next morning

very early, before daybreak (about 4 A.M.) **and went** out **to a solitary** (*erēmon,* "uninhabited, remote") **place** (cf. v. 4) **where He** spent time praying. He withdrew from the acclaim of the Capernaum crowds to a wilderness place—the kind of place where He initially confronted Satan and withstood his temptations (cf. vv. 12-13).

Mark selectively portrayed Jesus at prayer on three crucial occasions, each in a setting of darkness and aloneness: near the beginning of his account (v. 35), near the middle (6:46), and near the end (14:32-42). All three were occasions when He was faced with the possibility of achieving His messianic mission in a more attractive, less costly way. But in each case He gained strength through prayer.

1:36-37. The crowds, returning to Simon's door and expecting to find Jesus, discovered He was gone. **Simon and his companions** (cf. v. 29) **went** out **to look for Him** (lit., "to hunt Him down," from *katadiōkō,* occurring only here in the NT). Their exclamation, **Everyone is looking for You!** implied some annoyance because they thought Jesus was failing to capitalize on some excellent opportunities in Capernaum.

1:38-39. Jesus' reply showed that they too did not understand Him or His mission. His plan was to **go** elsewhere— **to the nearby villages,** populous market towns, **so** that He could **preach** (cf. vv. 4, 14) **there also,** in addition to Capernaum. His explanatory statement, **That** ("to preach") **is why I have come,** probably does not refer to leaving Capernaum (He left to pray, v. 35) but rather to His coming from God on a divine mission. His purpose was to proclaim "the good news of God" (v. 14) and confront people with the demand to "repent and believe" it (v. 15). Since the Capernaum crowds sought Him as a Miracle-worker, He deliberately departed to preach elsewhere.

Verse 39 summarizes His tour throughout Galilee (cf. v. 28) which probably lasted several weeks (cf. Matt. 4:23-25). His main activity was **preaching** (cf. Mark 1:14-15) **in** the local **synagogues, and** His **driving out** (*ekballōn;* cf. v. 34) **demons** dramatically confirmed His message.

5. THE CLEANSING OF A LEPER (1:40-45) (MATT. 8:1-4; LUKE 5:12-16)

1:40. On Jesus' Galilean tour, **a man with leprosy came to Him** (a bold move for a leper). "Leprosy" included a variety of serious skin diseases ranging from ringworm to true leprosy (Hanson's bacillus), a progressively disfiguring disease. This man experienced a pitiful existence due not only to the physical ravages of the disease but also to ritual uncleanness (cf. Lev. 13–14) and exclusion from society. Leprosy brought anguish at all levels: physical, mental, social, and religious. It serves as an illustration of sin.

The Rabbis regarded leprosy as humanly incurable. Only twice does the Old Testament record that God cleansed a leper (Num. 12:10-15; 2 Kings 5:1-14). Yet this leper was convinced that Jesus could cleanse him. Without presumption (**If You are willing**) and without doubting Jesus' ability (**You can make me clean**), he humbly **begged** Jesus to heal him.

1:41-42. Moved by **compassion** (*splanchnistheis,* "having deep pity"), **Jesus . . . touched** the untouchable and **cured** the incurable. His touch showed that Jesus was not bound by Rabbinic regulations regarding ritual defilement. Both this symbolic touch (cf. 7:33; 8:22) and Jesus' authoritative pronouncement—**I am willing** (pres. tense), **be clean** (aorist pass., decisive act received)—constituted the cure. It was immediate (*euthys;* cf. 1:10), complete, visible to all who saw him.

1:43-44. The forceful words, **sent him away** (*exebalen;* cf. v. 12), **at once** (*euthys;* cf. v. 10), and **a strong warning** (cf. 14:5) emphasize the need for prompt obedience to the instructions in 1:44.

First, Jesus sternly warned (same verb in 14:5) him: **Don't tell this** (his cure) **to anyone.** This could be a temporary prohibition that was in force till the man had been pronounced clean by **the priest.** However, Jesus often commanded silence and sought to minimize the proclaiming of His true identity and miraculous powers (cf. 1:25, 34; 3:12; 5:43; 7:36; 9:9). Why did Jesus do this? Some contend that Mark and the other Gospel writers inserted these commands for silence as a literary device to explain why the Jews did not recognize Jesus as the Messiah during His earthly ministry.

This view is called "the messianic secret," that is, Jesus' messiahship was kept secret.

A more satisfactory view is that Jesus wanted to avoid misunderstandings that would precipitate a premature and/or erroneous popular response to Him (cf. comments on 11:28). He did not want His identity declared till He had made the character of His mission clear (cf. comments on 8:30; 9:9). Thus there was a progressive withdrawal of the veil from His identity until He openly declared it (14:62; cf. 12:12).

Second, Jesus instructed the former leper to **show** himself **to** the priest, who alone could declare him ritually clean, **and** to **offer the sacrifices** prescribed by **Moses** (cf. Lev. 14:2-31).

This demand is qualified by the phrase **as** (*eis,* "for") **a testimony to them.** This phrase could be understood in a positive sense ("a convincing witness") or negative sense ("an incriminating witness") to either the people in general or the priests in particular. In this context, as in the two other occurrences of this phrase (Mark 6:11; 13:9), the negative sense is preferred. Thus "testimony" means an item of proof which can serve as incriminating evidence (cf. TDNT, s.v. "*martys,*" 4:502-4) and "them" refers to the priests.

The cleansing of the leper was an undeniable messianic sign (cf. Matt. 11:5; Luke 7:22) that God was working in a new way. If the priests declared the leper clean but rejected the One who cleansed him, their unbelief would be incriminating evidence against them.

1:45. **Instead** of obeying Jesus' command to silence, the man **went out and began to talk freely** (lit., "to proclaim [*kēryssein*] it much"), making known the story of his cure far and wide. Mark did not say whether he obeyed Jesus' command to show himself to the priest.

As a result, Jesus' preaching ministry in the synagogues of Galilee (cf. v. 39) was interrupted. He **could not enter a town openly** without encountering large crowds seeking special favors. Even when He withdrew to **lonely** (*erēmois,* "uninhabited, remote"; cf. v. 35) **places . . . the people** kept coming **from** all directions.

The deliverance Jesus brought transcended the Mosaic Law and its regulations. Though the Law provided for the ritual purification of a leper, it was powerless to cleanse a person from the disease or to effect inward spiritual renewal.

D. Jesus' controversies with Jewish religious leaders in Galilee (2:1–3:5)

Mark brought together the five episodes in this section because of the common theme of conflict in Galilee between Jesus and the Jewish religious leaders. Thus they are not in strict chronological order. A similar unit of five controversies in the temple at Jerusalem is recorded in 11:27–12:37.

The conflict here concerned Jesus' authority over sin and the Law. The first incident is introduced by a summary statement (2:1-2) of Jesus' preaching. Mark often used this literary device to summarize Jesus' activity and keep his narrative moving on to events that suited his purpose (cf. 1:14-15, 39; 2:1-2, 13; 3:7-12, 23; 4:1, 33-34; 8:21-26, 31; 9:31; 10:1; 12:1).

1. THE HEALING OF A PARALYTIC MAN AND FORGIVENESS (2:1-12) (MATT. 9:1-8; LUKE 5:17-26)

2:1-2. A few days later when Jesus returned to **Capernaum** (cf. 1:21), it was reported that **He** was at **home** (probably Peter's house; cf. 1:29). In the freedom of Jewish custom **many** uninvited people crowded into the house and around **the door,** thus preventing access. Jesus was speaking (imperf., *elalei*) **the Word** (cf. 1:14-15; 4:14, 33) **to them.**

2:3-4. Four **men** brought **a paralytic** (paralyzed man) **on a mat** (poor man's "bed," KJV), hoping to **get him to Jesus. But they could not . . . because of the crowd.** Like many Palestinian dwellings, this house probably had an outside stairway leading to a flat **roof.** So the men went onto the roof. **After digging through it** (a composite of grass, clay, clay tiles, and laths), **they made an opening . . . above Jesus** and **lowered** the **paralyzed man** before Him (probably using fishing ropes that lay at hand).

2:5. Jesus viewed the determined effort of the four as visible evidence of **their faith** in His power to heal this man. He did not rebuke this interruption to His teaching but unexpectedly told **the**

paralytic, Son (an affectionate term), **your sins are forgiven.**

In the Old Testament disease and death were viewed as the consequences of man's sinful condition, and healing was predicated on God's forgiveness (e.g., 2 Chron. 7:14; Pss. 41:4; 103:3; 147:3; Isa. 19:22; 38:16-17; Jer. 3:22; Hosea 14:4). This does not mean there is a corresponding sin for each occurrence of sickness (cf. Luke 13:1-5; John 9:1-3). Jesus simply showed that this man's physical condition had a basic spiritual cause.

2:6-7. The **teachers of the Law** (lit., "scribes"; cf. 1:22; Luke 5:17) who were present were offended by Jesus' veiled pronouncement. **Only God can forgive sins** (cf. Ex. 34:6-9; Pss. 103:3; 130:4; Isa. 43:25; 44:22; 48:11; Dan. 9:9). In the Old Testament forgiveness of sins was never attributed to the Messiah. The scribes regarded such **talk** by **this fellow** (contemptuous tone) as a pretentious affront to God's power and authority, blasphemy against **God,** a serious offense punishable by death from stoning (Lev. 24:15-16). In fact such a charge became the basis for a formal condemnation later (cf. Mark 14:61-64).

2:8-9. Immediately (*euthys*; cf. 1:10) **Jesus** perceived **in His spirit** (inwardly; cf. 14:38) their hostile thoughts **and He** confronted them directly with pointed counterquestions (a rhetorical device in Rabbinic debate; cf. 3:4; 11:30; 12:37).

The scribes expected a physical healing, but Jesus pronounced the man's **sins . . . forgiven.** They probably thought that a pronouncement of forgiveness was **easier** than one of healing because healing was visible and immediately verifiable.

2:10. This verse presents an interpretive problem due to the awkward change of addressee in the verse's middle. Jesus seemed to be addressing the scribes (v. 10a) but there is an abrupt break in the verse after which He addressed **the paralytic.** Another problem in light of the overall emphasis of Mark is the public use of the title **Son of Man** by Jesus so early in His ministry (cf. 9:9; 10:33). Apart from 2:10 and 28, this title does not occur in Mark's account until after Peter's confession (8:29). After that it occurs 12 times and is crucial to Jesus' self-disclosure *to His disciples* (cf. 8:31, 38; 9:9, 12, 31;

Mark 2:11-18

10:33, 45; 13:26; 14:21 [twice], 41, 62; see comments on 8:31).

In light of these difficulties 2:10a is probably a parenthetical, editorial comment by Mark (cf. similarly, vv. 15c, 28; 7:3-4, 19; 13:14). He inserted it into the narrative to explain the significance of this event for his readers: that Jesus as the risen Son of Man **has authority** (*exousian,* the right and power) **on earth to forgive sins,** something the scribes did not fully recognize. Only here in the Gospels is the forgiveness of sins attributed to the Son of Man.

This view contributes to the literary unity of the passage: forgiveness is declared (2:5), questioned (vv. 6-9), validated (v. 11), and recognized (v. 12). The initial words in verse 10, **But that you may know,** could thus be translated, "Now you (Mark's readers) should know that. . . ." The last clause signals the end of Mark's comment and a return to the incident itself.

2:11-12. Jesus commanded the paralytic to **get up** (a test of his faith), **take his mat, and go home** (demand of obedience). The man was enabled to do this immediately (*euthys;* cf. 1:10) **in full view of them all,** including Jesus' critics. They were forced to recognize that the man had received God's forgiveness. This showed the character of salvation Jesus brought, namely, healing whole persons. **Everyone** (probably including the scribes) was **amazed** (*existasthai,* lit., "out of their minds"; cf. 3:21; 5:42; 6:51) and **praised** (ascribed glory to) **God** because of Jesus' display of supernatural power.

2. THE CALL OF LEVI AND EATING WITH SINNERS (2:13-17)
(MATT. 9:9-13; LUKE 5:27-32)

2:13. **Jesus went out** from Capernaum to **the lake** (Sea of Galilee) **once again** (cf. 1:16). To summarize His activity, Mark stated that Jesus was teaching **a large crowd** which kept on coming **to hear Him.** His withdrawal from populous centers is a recurring pattern in Mark (cf. 1:45; 2:13; 3:7, 13; 4:1; 5:21; etc.) and recalls the "wilderness" theme (cf. 1:4, 12-13, 35, 45).

2:14. Capernaum was a customs post on the caravan route from Damascus to the Mediterranean Sea. **Levi** (surnamed Matthew; cf. 3:18; Matt. 9:9; 10:3) was a Jewish **tax** official in the service of Herod

Antipas, the ruler of Galilee (see the chart on the Herods at Luke 1:5). For such service, often involving fraudulent practices, these officials were despised by the Jews. Yet Jesus extended to Levi a gracious call to **follow** Him and leave his old calling behind (cf. Mark 1:17-18).

2:15-16. Shortly afterward, Levi gave a **dinner** for **Jesus** and **His disciples.** This is the first mention (of 43) in Mark of the "disciples" as a distinct group. Mark added an editorial comment explaining that **there were** many (disciples) **who followed** Jesus, not just the five mentioned so far in Mark's Gospel.

Eating with Jesus were **many tax collectors** (Levi's former associates) **and "sinners,"** a technical term for common people regarded by the Pharisees as untaught in the Law, who did not abide by rigid pharisaic standards. For Jesus and His disciples to share a meal (an expression of trust and fellowship) with them offended **the Law** teachers **who were Pharisees.** The Pharisees, the most influential religious party in Palestine, were deeply devoted to the Mosaic Law. They strictly regulated their lives by the supposedly binding interpretations of it passed down in oral tradition and were meticulous about maintaining ceremonial purity (cf. 7:1-5). They criticized Jesus for not being a separatist, for failing to observe their pious distinction between "the righteous" (they themselves) and "the sinners."

2:17. **Jesus** answered their criticism with a well-known proverb (recognized as valid by His opponents) and a statement of His mission which vindicated His conduct. The words, **the righteous,** are used ironically to refer to those who saw themselves as such, namely, the Pharisees (cf. Luke 16:14-15). They saw no need to repent and believe (cf. Mark 1:15). But Jesus knew that everyone, including "the righteous," are sinful. He came (into the world) to call **sinners,** those who humbly acknowledge their need and receive His gracious forgiveness, to God's kingdom. This was why Jesus ate with sinners (cf. 2:5-11, 19-20).

3. THE DISCUSSION ABOUT FASTING AND THE NEW SITUATION (2:18-22)
(MATT. 9:14-17; LUKE 5:33-39)

2:18. Mark's initial statement explained that **John's disciples** (John the

113

Baptist's remaining followers) **and the Pharisees** (and their disciples or adherents) **were fasting,** presumably while Jesus and His disciples were feasting at Levi's house. The Old Testament prescribed fasting for all Jews only on the annual Day of Atonement, as an act of repentance (Lev. 16:29), but the Pharisees promoted voluntary fasts on every Monday and Thursday (cf. Luke 18:12) as an act of piety. In response to a critical inquiry, **Jesus** showed the incongruity of **fasting** for His disciples (Mark 2:19-22), though He allowed it if practiced properly (cf. Matt. 6:16-18).

2:19-20. Jesus' counterquestion set up a comparison and a veiled analogy to Himself. As it is inappropriate for **guests** (lit., "sons of the bridal chamber," the groom's attendants) to **fast** (an expression of sorrow) in the presence **of the bridegroom,** so it was inappropriate for Jesus' disciples to fast (in sorrow) **while He** was **with them.**

His presence with them constituted a situation as joyous as a wedding festival. **But** this situation would change, for **the time** (lit., "days") would **come when the Bridegroom** (Jesus) would **be taken** (*aparthē*, implying violent removal; cf. Isa. 53:8) **from them and on that day** (His crucifixion) the disciples would **fast** in the metaphorical sense of experiencing sorrow in place of joy. This allusion to His coming death is the first hint of the Cross in Mark's Gospel.

2:21-22. For the first time Mark used two of Jesus' parables, both of which had broader relevance than to fasting. Jesus' presence with His people was a time of newness (fulfillment) and signaled the passing of the old.

An attempt to bind the newness of the gospel to the old religion of Judaism is as futile as trying to **patch an old** (*palaion,* "worn out by use") **garment** with a new, **unshrunk** piece of **cloth.** When **the new** (*kainon,* "qualitatively new") **piece** (*plērōma,* "fullness") becomes wet, it **will** shrink, **pull away from the old,** and make a larger hole.

It is equally disastrous to pour **new** (*neon,* "fresh"), not fully fermented **wine into old** (*palaios,* "worn out by use," with no elasticity, brittle) **wineskins.** Inevitably, as **the** new **wine** ferments (expands), it **will burst the skins and both the wine and the wineskins will be**

ruined. Salvation, available through Jesus, was not to be mixed with the old Judaistic system (cf. John 1:17).

4. THE PICKING AND EATING OF GRAIN ON THE SABBATH (2:23-28)
(MATT. 12:1-8; LUKE 6:1-5)

2:23-24. While walking on a footpath **through** someone's **grainfields** one **Sabbath,** Jesus' **disciples . . . began** picking **some heads of grain** to eat. This was legitimate (Deut. 23:25), but the **Pharisees** viewed it as reaping, an act of work forbidden **on the Sabbath** (cf. Ex. 34:21), so they demanded an explanation from **Jesus.**

2:25-26. In response Jesus appealed to Scripture and a precedent set by **David** and **his companions** when they **were hungry and in need** (1 Sam. 21:1-6). The words "his companions" and "in need" are key elements in this incident. David **entered the** tabernacle court, requested **the consecrated bread** (cf. Lev. 24:5-9) which was restricted by Mosaic legislation to **the priests** (cf. Lev. 24:9) and **gave some to his** men. Jesus used this action which God did not condemn, to show that the Pharisees' narrow interpretation of the Law blurred God's intention. The spirit of the Law in respect to human need took priority over its ceremonial regulations.

Mark stated that David's action occurred **in the days of Abiathar the high priest,** but the high priest was actually Ahimelech, his father (1 Sam. 21:1). A plausible explanation is to render the introductory phrase: "in the passage about Abiathar, the high priest" (cf. parallel phrase in Mark 12:26). This was a customary Jewish way of indicating the section of the Old Testament where a desired incident could be found. Abiathar became high priest shortly after Ahimelech and proved more prominent than he, thus justifying the use of his name here.

2:27-28. With the words, **Then He said to them,** Mark appended two principles: (1) He quoted Jesus' words that **the Sabbath was** instituted (by God) **for** mankind's benefit and refreshment, **not** that people were made to keep burdensome regulations pertaining to it. (2) Mark concluded (**so,** in light of vv. 23-27) with an editorial comment (cf. v. 10) on the meaning of Jesus' statement for his readers. **The Son of Man** (cf. 8:31) **is Lord** (Master) **even of the Sabbath;** He has sovereign authority over its use, as the next incident demonstrates.

5. THE HEALING OF THE MAN WITH A WITHERED HAND ON THE SABBATH (3:1-5) (MATT. 12:9-14; LUKE 6:6-11)

3:1-2. On **another** Sabbath occasion **in the synagogue** (probably Capernaum; cf. 1:21) Jesus saw **a man with a shriveled hand** (his "right" one; cf. Luke 6:6). **Some of them** (Pharisees, cf. Mark 3:6) **were watching Jesus** closely to see what He would do so they might find **a reason to accuse** Him. They permitted healing on the Sabbath only if a life was in danger. This man's problem was not life-threatening and could wait till the next day; so if Jesus healed him, they could accuse Him of being a **Sabbath**-violator, an offense punishable by death (cf. Ex. 31:14-17).

3:3-4. Jesus commanded **the man, Stand up** so the whole gathering could see his **shriveled hand. Then** He **asked** the Pharisees a rhetorical question concerning which of two kinds of action was really consistent with the purpose of **the Sabbath** in the Mosaic Law. The obvious answer is: **to do good** and **to save life** (*psychēn*, "soul"; cf. 8:35-36). Yet failure to use the Sabbath to meet this man's need (cf. 2:27) was **to do evil** (harmful misuse of its purpose) and, as ultimately happened, their malicious plotting on the Sabbath (cf. 3:6) led them **to kill.** The moral (not legal) issue of "doing good" on the Sabbath was at stake, and the Pharisees refused to debate it.

3:5. Jesus **looked around** (from *periblepomai*, an all-inclusive penetrating look; cf. v. 34; 5:32; 10:23; 11:11) at the Pharisees **in anger.** This is the only explicit reference to Jesus' anger in the New Testament. It was nonmalicious indignation coupled with deep sorrow (grief) at their obstinate insensitivity (*pōrōsei*, "hardening"; cf. Rom. 11:25; Eph. 4:18) to God's mercy and human misery.

When the man held out **his hand** at Jesus' command, it was instantly and **completely restored.** Jesus did not use any visible means that might be construed as "work" on the Sabbath. As Lord of the Sabbath (Mark 2:28) Jesus freed it

from legal encumbrances, and in grace delivered this man from his distress.

E. Conclusion: Jesus' rejection by the Pharisees (3:6)

3:6. This verse climaxes the section on Jesus' conflicts in Galilee with the religious establishment (2:1–3:5). It is Mark's first explicit reference to Jesus' death, which now began to cast its shadow over His mission. **The Pharisees** conspired immediately (*euthys;* cf. 1:10) **with the Herodians** (cf. 12:13), influential political supporters of Herod Antipas, in an unprecedented common effort to destroy Jesus (cf. 15:31-32). His authority confronted and overwhelmed their authority, so He must be killed. Their problem was how.

IV. Jesus' Later Galilean Ministry (3:7–6:6a)

The second major section of Mark's Gospel begins and concludes structurally like the first one (cf. 1:14-15 with 3:7-12; 1:16-20 with 3:13-19; 3:6 with 6:1-6a). It shows the development of Jesus' mission in the context of opposition and unbelief.

A. Introductory summary: Jesus' activity around the Sea of Galilee (3:7-12) (Matt. 12:14-21)

3:7-10. This summary passage is similar in context and character to 2:13. An added element is that **Jesus withdrew with His disciples** (emphatic first position in Gr.), who shared in both the hostility and the popular acclaim directed toward Jesus.

Many people **from Galilee followed** (nontechnical sense, "went along with") and, attracted by **all He was doing** (i.e., healing miracles), **many . . . came** from areas outside Galilee—from the south, **Judea, Jerusalem, Idumea;** the east, Transjordan (Perea); and the north, the coastal cities of **Tyre and Sidon** (in Phoenicia). Jesus spent time in all these areas (except Idumea; 5:1; 7:24, 31; 10:1; 11:11). So intense was the impact of Jesus' healing ministry and the desire of **those with diseases** (*mastigas*, "scourges," cf. 5:29 ["suffering"], 34) **to touch Him** that **He told His disciples to have a small boat ready** to escape the rush of the crowds. Only Mark reported this detail, suggesting the memory of an eyewitness such as Peter.

3:11-12. In the crowds were demoniacs, people whose speech and behavior were dominated by **evil spirits.** They recognized Jesus' true status as **the Son of God** and were greatly threatened by His presence. Jesus did not accept their repeated (imperf. verbs) cries of recognition, and ordered (cf. 1:25; 4:39; 8:30, 32-33; 9:25) them **not to tell who He was** (cf. 1:24-25, 34). In silencing their untimely cries Jesus reaffirmed His submission to God's plan for the *progressive* disclosure of His identity and mission.

B. *Jesus' appointment of the Twelve (3:13-19)*

(Matt. 10:1-4; Luke 6:12-16)

3:13. From the lakeside lowlands **Jesus went up into the hills** (of central Galilee; cf. 6:46). Taking the initiative, He summoned to Himself **those He wanted,** namely the Twelve (3:16-19), **and they came** from the crowd **to Him** (cf. Luke 6:13). Mark had already said that Jesus had many other disciples (cf. Mark 2:15).

3:14-15. He appointed (lit., "made") 12 for two reasons: (a) so they could **be with Him** (immediate association for training) and (b) be sent **out** by Him to **preach** (cf. 1:4, 14) **and to have** (delegated) **authority to drive out** (*ekballein;* cf. 1:34, 39) **demons** (their future mission; cf. 6:7-13). Mark devoted attention to their association with Jesus and preparation for their ministries.

Nearly all major ancient Greek manuscripts and most early versions omit the phrase, **designating them apostles.** This seems preferable; its inclusion in a few early manuscripts was probably due to the influence of Luke 6:13 and because Mark used the term "apostles" only in Mark 6:30 where it is appropriate in a nontechnical sense.

The number 12 corresponds to the 12 tribes of Israel, thus expressing Jesus' claim on the whole nation. "The Twelve" became an official designation or title for those appointed by Jesus on this occasion (cf. 4:10; 6:7; 9:35; 10:32; 11:11; 14:10, 17, 20, 43). Though significantly linked with Israel, they are never called a new or spiritual "Israel." Rather they were the nucleus of a coming new community, the church (cf. Matt. 16:16-20; Acts 1:5-8).

3:16-19. These verses give a traditional list of the names of the appointed Twelve. **Simon** (cf. 14:37) heads the list. Jesus surnamed him **Peter** (cf. John 1:42), the Greek equivalent of the Aramaic *Cephas,* which means a "stone or rock." This probably described his leadership role during Jesus' ministry and in the early church (cf. Matt. 16:16-20; Eph. 2:20), and did not refer to his personal character. **James** and **John,** Zebedee's sons, are surnamed **Boanerges,** a Hebrew idiom Mark interpreted as **Sons of Thunder** (cf. Mark 9:38; 10:35-39; Luke 9:54), though a more complimentary meaning (now unknown) may have been intended by Jesus.

Apart from **Andrew** (cf. Mark 1:16; 13:3), **Judas Iscariot** (cf. 14:10, 43), and possibly **James son of Alphaeus** as "James the younger" (cf. 15:40), the remaining names do not occur again in Mark: **Philip** (cf. John 1:43-45), **Bartholomew** (Nathanael; John 1:45-51), **Matthew** (Levi; cf. Mark 2:14), **Thomas** (cf. John 11:16; 14:5; 20:24-28; 21:2), James son of Alphaeus (probably not Levi's brother; cf. Mark 2:14), **Thaddaeus** (Judas son of James; cf. Luke 6:16; Acts 1:13), and **Simon the Zealot** ("Zealot" probably indicated his zeal for God's honor, not an extreme nationalism). In contrast was Judas Iscariot (a "man from Kerioth," the only non-Galilean; cf. John 6:71; 13:26), **who betrayed** Jesus to His enemies (cf. Mark 14:10-11, 43-46).

C. *The Beelzebub accusation and Jesus' identity of His true family (3:20-35)*

This section has a "sandwich" structure in which the account concerning Jesus' family (vv. 20-21, 31-35) is divided by the Beelzebub accusation (vv. 22-30). This deliberate literary device is used several times by Mark (cf. 5:21-43; 6:7-31; 11:12-26; 14:1-11, 27-52) for different reasons. Here Mark pointed out a parallel in the charges made against Jesus (cf. 3:21 and 30) but at the same time made a distinction between general opposition to Jesus and a distortion of the Holy Spirit's work through Him.

1. THE CONCERN OF JESUS' FAMILY FOR HIM (3:20-21)

3:20-21. These verses are unique to Mark. After **Jesus entered a house** (in

Capernaum; cf. 2:1-2), such a large crowd demanded His attention **that He and His disciples** had no time **to eat** (cf. 6:31). **When His family** (lit., "those with Him," a Gr. idiom for kinsmen, not "friends," KJV; cf. 3:31) **heard** that His ceaseless activity prevented proper care for His needs, **they** came (probably from Nazareth) **to take charge of Him** (*kratēsai,* a word used for making an arrest; cf. 6:17; 12:12; 14:1, 44, 46, 51) **for** (*gar;* cf. "for" in 1:16) the people kept saying **He** was **out of His mind,** a mentally unbalanced religious fanatic (cf. Acts 26:24; 2 Cor. 5:13).

2. JESUS' REFUTATION OF THE BEELZEBUB ACCUSATION (3:22-30) (MATT. 12:22-32; LUKE 11:14-23; 12:10)

3:22. Meanwhile a delegation of **Law teachers** (scribes) **came down from Jerusalem** to investigate Jesus. They repeatedly charged (a) that **He** was **possessed by Beelzebub** (demon-possessed; cf. v. 30), and (b) that **He** was **driving out demons** through a power alliance with Satan, **the prince** (ruler) **of demons** (cf. v. 23).

The spelling "Beelzebub" came into English translations from the Latin Vulgate which derived it from the Hebrew "Baalzebub" meaning "Lord of the flies," the name of an ancient Canaanite deity (cf. 2 Kings 1:2). But the spelling "Beelzeboul" (NIV marg.) has better Greek manuscript support. It reflects the later Hebrew "Baalzebul" (not used in the OT) meaning: "Lord of the dwelling place (temple)," that is, of evil spirits in the New Testament contexts (cf. Matt. 10:25; Luke 11:17-22).

3:23-27. Jesus summoned His accusers and refuted their charges **in parables** (short proverbial sayings, not stories). He dealt with the second accusation first (vv. 23-26) by showing the absurdity of their underlying assumption that **Satan** acts against **himself.** He used two illustrations to make the self-evident point that **if a kingdom** or **a house** (household) **is divided against itself** in purpose and goals, it **cannot stand.** The same applies to Satan if it is assumed that **Satan opposes** himself **and his realm is divided.** This would mean that **his end has come,** that is, his power, not his personal existence. Clearly this is false, for Satan remains strong (cf. v. 27; 1 Peter 5:8). So

the charge that Jesus' exorcisms were due to Satan's power was false.

The analogy in Mark 3:27 refuted their first accusation (v. 22) showing **in fact** (lit., "on the contrary") that the opposite was true. Satan is **the strong man.** His **house** is the realm of sin, sickness, demon possession, and death. **His possessions** are people who are enslaved by one or more of these things, and demons are his agents who carry out his diabolical activity. **No one can enter** his realm to **carry off** (*diarpasai,* "plunder") his possessions **unless he first** binds the strong man (shows he is more powerful). **Then he can rob** (*diarpasei,* "plunder") the realm, releasing the enslaved victims. At His temptation (cf. 1:12-13) and through His exorcisms Jesus demonstrated that He is the Stronger One, empowered by the Holy Spirit (cf. 3:29). His mission is to confront and overpower (not cooperate with) Satan and to deliver those enslaved by him.

3:28-30. In light of the preceding charges Jesus issued a strong warning. The words, **I tell you the truth** (lit., "Amen [truly], I say to you"), are a recurring formula of solemn affirmation (13 times in Mark) found only in the Gospels and always spoken by Jesus.

Jesus declared, **All the sins and blasphemies** (derogatory words vs. God) **of men** (generic, "people") are open to God's gracious forgiveness (cf. 1:4) with one exception—blasphemies **against the Holy Spirit.** In light of the context this refers to an attitude (not an isolated act or utterance) of defiant hostility toward God that rejects His saving power toward man, expressed in the Spirit-empowered person and work of Jesus. It is one's preference for darkness even though he has been exposed to light (cf. John 3:19). Such a persistent attitude of willful unbelief can harden into a condition in which repentance and forgiveness, both mediated by God's Spirit, become impossible. This person **is guilty** (*enochos,* "liable to, in the grasp") **of an eternal sin** (sing, the ultimate sin because it remains forever unforgiven; cf. Matt. 12:32). Judas Iscariot (cf. Mark 3:29; 14:43-46) proved the reality of these words.

Mark explained that Jesus **said** all **this because they** (the Law teachers, 3:22) kept **saying He** was demon-possessed (v. 22b). Jesus did not actually say the scribes had committed this unpardonable sin; but they came perilously close by attributing His exorcisms to satanic power when they really were accomplished by the Holy Spirit. They were close to calling the Holy Spirit "Satan."

3. JESUS' TRUE FAMILY (3:31-35)
(MATT. 12:46-50; LUKE 8:19-21; 11:27-28)

3:31-32. The arrival of **Jesus' mother** (Mary; cf. 6:3) **and His brothers** (cf. 6:3) resumes the narrative suspended in 3:21. **Standing outside** the house, **they sent someone** through the **crowd . . . around Him,** requesting a private conversation in an attempt to restrain His activity.

3:33-35. Jesus' rhetorical question (v. 33) was not a repudiation of family relationships (cf. 7:10-13). He was highlighting the far deeper issue of a person's relationship to Him. It is qualitative in force: "**Who are** the sort of people who **are My mother and My brothers?"** Then looking (from *periblepomai;* cf. 3:5) at **those seated in a circle around Him** (His disciples in contrast with those standing outside, v. 31), Jesus asserted that their kinship went beyond natural family ties. Jesus broadened the reference beyond those present by stating that **whoever does God's will is** a member of His family. The words **brother and sister and mother,** all occurring without an article in Greek (thus qualitative), figuratively denote Jesus' spiritual family. Doing God's will (e.g., 1:14-20) characterizes those who are Jesus' spiritual kinfolk.

D. Jesus' parables depicting the character of God's kingdom (4:1-34)

This group of parables constitutes the first of two lengthy units in Mark's Gospel devoted to Jesus' teaching (cf. also 13:3-37). Mark selected these parables (as implied in 4:2, 10, 13, 33) from a larger collection to depict the character of God's kingdom (cf. 4:11 with 1:15).

They were given in a climate of growing hostility and opposition (cf. 2:3-3:6, 22-30), but also enormous popular acclaim (cf. 1:45; 2:2, 13, 15; 3:7-8). Both responses showed people's failure to grasp who Jesus really is. "Parable" is a transliteration of the Greek *parabolē,* "comparison." It can designate a variety of figurative forms of speech (e.g., 2:19-22; 3:23-25; 4:3-9, 26-32; 7:15-17; 13:28). But usually a parable is a short discourse that conveys spiritual truth by making a vivid comparison. The truth to be taught is compared to something in nature or a common-life experience. A parable usually expresses a single important truth, though occasionally a subordinate feature expands its total meaning (cf. 4:3-9, 13-20; 12:1-12). A parable draws its hearers to take part in a situation, evaluate it, and apply its truth to themselves. (See the list of Jesus' 35 recorded parables at Matt. 7:24-27.)

1. INTRODUCTORY SUMMARY (4:1-2)
(MATT. 13:1-2)

4:1-2. Once again (cf. 2:13; 3:7) **Jesus** was teaching a large crowd **by the lake** (Sea of Galilee). **The crowd** was **so large that He** was forced to sit in **a boat . . . out on the lake** and teach those who lined the shore. This time **He taught them many things by parables.**

2. THE PARABLE OF THE SOILS (4:3-20)
a. Jesus' statement of the Soils Parable (4:3-9)
(Matt. 13:3-9; Luke 8:4-8)

Both before and after Jesus told this parable, He urged the crowd to listen carefully (cf. Mark 4:3, 9, 23).

4:3-9. As **a farmer** (lit., "one who sows") scattered **seed** over his unplowed field, **some fell along the** well-trodden foot **path** (cf. 2:23). **Some fell on rocky places** having no depth of **soil** because limestone was close to the surface. **Other seed fell among thorns** (ground containing unearthed thorn plant roots). And **still other** seeds **fell on good soil.**

Not all the seed produced a crop. **Birds . . . ate** the seed that fell on the path (4:4). **The sun . . . scorched** the tender plants that **quickly** (*euthys;* cf. 1:10) sprouted in the **shallow** rocky soil **and they withered** (4:6). Thorns **grew up and choked** other **plants,** making them unproductive (v. 7).

By contrast, the seed on the good soil took root, **grew, and produced** an abundant harvest. It brought yields up to **30, 60,** and **even 100 times** (v. 8) the seed sown, depending on the fertility of the soil. Back then a yield of 10 to 1 was considered a fine crop.

b. Jesus' explanation for teaching in parables (4:10-12)
(Matt. 13:10-17; Luke 8:9-10)

4:10. The change of scene here is significant. Verses 10-20 occurred later (cf. vv. 35-36; Matt. 13:36), but Mark put them here to illustrate the principle stated in Mark 4:11, 33-34, and thereby show the importance of parables. **When Jesus was alone** with **the Twelve and the others around Him** (other true disciples; cf. 3:34), they **asked Him about the parables** in general, and the Parable of the Soils in particular (cf. 4:13).

4:11-12. These verses must be viewed in the context of unbelief and hostility (cf. 3:6, 21-22, 30). To those who believed, **to you** (emphatic first position in Gr.), the disciples, God had **given** the **secret of the kingdom of God** (cf. 1:15). **But to those on the outside** (of the circle of disciples, the unbelieving crowd) **everything,** His whole message and mission, was stated **in parables.** The word "parables" here has the special sense of "enigmatic speech." The crowd did not really understand Jesus.

Both groups were confronted by Jesus and His message (cf. 1:14-15). God enabled the disciples to see in Him the "secret" (*mystērion*) about the kingdom. This refers to the disclosure of God's *present* kingdom plan which is to be an Age of "seed-sowing" (cf. 4:13-20; 13:10). It was previously hidden to the prophets, but now was revealed to people of His choice (cf. Rom. 16:25-26).

The basic "secret," common to all the kingdom parables, is that in Jesus, God's rule (kingdom) has come into human experience in a new spiritual form. The disciples had believed in Jesus. God had already given (*dedotai,* perf. pass.) them this "secret," though so far they understood little of its full impact.

On the other hand those blinded by unbelief saw in Jesus nothing but a threat to their existence. They rejected Him and did not come to know the "secret" of God's kingdom. Jesus' parables served to conceal its truths from them.

They were like the Israelites in Isaiah's day (Isa. 6:9-10). Isaiah said that this spiritual blindness and deafness that comes to people is God's judgment. He particularly referred to Israel as a nation (cf. Mark 6:9, "this people") for rejecting God's revelation, especially as expressed in Jesus. They would see or hear the imagery of a parable but they would not understand its spiritual meaning. Other-wise (*mēpote,* "lest perhaps") **they might turn** to God (repent) **and be forgiven** by Him.

Jesus' audiences were not denied the opportunity to believe in Him. But after they persistently closed their minds to His message (cf. 1:15), they were excluded from further understanding of it by His use of parables. Yet even the parables, which veiled the truth, were meant to provoke thought, enlighten, and ultimately reveal it (cf. 12:12). They uniquely preserved people's freedom to believe, while demonstrating that such a decision is effected by God's enabling (cf. 4:11a).

c. Jesus' interpretation of the Soils Parable (4:13-20)
(Matt. 13:18-23; Luke 8:11-15)

4:13. The two questions here emphasize the importance of the Soils Parable. If Jesus' disciples did not **understand** (*oidate,* "intuitively comprehend") its meaning, then they would not **understand** (*gnōsesthe,* "comprehend by experience") **any** of the kingdom parables.

4:14-20. **The farmer** (sower) is not identified, but the context indicates he probably represents Jesus and all who sow (proclaim) **the Word** (message) of God, which is the **seed** (cf. 1:15, 45; 2:2; 6:12). In 4:15-20 a change occurs: the kinds of soil represent various types of hearers in whom the **seed** is sown.

Many **people** give one of three negative responses to Jesus' message. **Some . . .** hear the **Word** with hard-hearted indifference. **Satan** (like the birds) **comes** immediately (*euthys;* cf. 1:10) **and takes** it **away.** In effect, there was no response.

Others . . . hear the **Word** with a hasty (*euthys*), enthusiastic, but shallow profession of acceptance. However, **they last only a short time** because the Word takes **no root** in them. **When trouble** (lit., "hardships") **or persecution comes** (like a hot sun) on account **of the Word, they** quickly (*euthys*) **fall away** (*skandalizontai,* "are repelled"; cf. comments on 14:27). Their profession proves not to be genuine.

Still others . . . **hear the Word** but are preoccupied with the cares and riches of this life. Three competing concerns—distracting **worries of this life** (lit., "the present Age"); **the deceitfulness** (deceptive lure) **of wealth;** and **desires for** all sorts of **other things** in place of the Word—enter into their lives (like thriving thorn plants). These things **choke the Word, making it** (the Word, *not* the hearer) **unfruitful** (cf. 10:22), indicating they are not true believers.

By contrast, **others . . . hear the Word, accept it** (*paradechontai*, "welcome it for themselves"), **and produce a crop,** or bear spiritual fruit. These are genuine disciples. In the future harvest they will have fruitful yields of varying amounts: **30, 60,** or . . . **100** (cf. 4:24-25 with Matt. 25:14-30; Luke 19:11-27).

Giving out the news of God's kingdom is like sowing seed on various kinds of soil. At Jesus' first coming and in the present Age the kingdom is largely veiled in the face of satanic opposition and human unbelief. But despite this, God's rule takes hold in those who accept Jesus' message and His rule manifests itself in spiritual fruitfulness. But God's kingdom will be openly established on earth at Jesus' second coming with a glory yet undisclosed (cf. Mark 13:24-27). Then there will be an abundant harvest. Thus the parable displayed God's kingdom as both *present but veiled* and *future but openly glorious* (cf. 1:14-15).

3. THE PARABLE OF THE LAMP AND THE MEASURE (4:21-25)

(LUKE 8:16-18; MATT. 5:15 AND LUKE 11:33; MATT. 7:2 AND LUKE 6:38; MATT. 10:26 AND LUKE 12:2; MATT. 13:12; 25:29 AND LUKE 19:26)

Jesus used the parabolic sayings of these verses on various occasions (cf. above references). Mark put them here because their message reinforced the message of Jesus' kingdom parables and demonstrated the need for a proper response to them. Mark 4:23-24a recalls verses 3 and 9, indicating that Mark understood these words to be part of Jesus' parabolic teaching to all (cf. vv. 26, 30) rather than the continuation of Jesus' private address to His disciples.

4:21-23. In this parable Jesus pointed out the self-evident fact that **a lamp,** a lighted wick in a shallow clay bowl full of oil, was not meant to be lit and then hidden **under a** measuring **bowl** (as was done at bedtime) **or a bed** (lit., "dining couch"). Rather, **it** was to be placed **on its stand** where it would give light. Then Jesus explained (*gar,* **for) whatever** was **hidden** or **concealed** (during the night) was **meant to be brought out into the open** (for use in the day). This story from everyday life conveyed a spiritual truth for **anyone** willing to learn from it.

4:24-25. If a person accepts His proclamation (cf. 1:15), God will give him a share in His kingdom now **and even more** will be added in its future manifestation (cf. 4:21-23). But if one rejects His Word, that one suffers absolute loss because even the opportunity he has for a share in the kingdom now **will** someday **be taken** away **from him.**

4. THE PARABLE OF THE EARTH BEARING FRUIT BY ITSELF (4:26-29)

This is Mark's only unique parable. Like the Soils Parable, it presents a comprehensive picture of the coming of God's kingdom: sowing (v. 26), growing (vv. 27-28), and harvesting (v. 29), with emphasis on the growing phase. Only one person, the sower (not identified), appears in all three phases.

4:26. The initial words in this parable could be rendered: "**The kingdom of God** is as follows: it **is like.** . . ." In phase one, the sower **scatters seed on the ground.**

4:27-28. In phase two the sower appears but is not active. After planting **the seed,** he leaves it and goes about his duties **night and day** without anxious thought for the seed. Meanwhile it germinates, **sprouts, and grows** in a way he did **not know** and cannot explain.

The **soil** (lit., "the earth") **produces grain** which develops to maturity in successive stages. The soil does this **all by itself** (*automatē*; cf. the Eng. "automatic"). This key Greek word (emphatic by position) could be translated "without visible cause" implying "without human agency," and thus refers to work done by God (cf. similar situations in Josh. 6:5; Job 24:24; Acts 12:10). God works in the life-bearing seed which, when planted in good soil, grows stage by stage and produces grain without human intervention.

4:29. The sower's ultimate interest is phase three, the harvest. Whenever (future) **the grain is ripe, he** immediately (*euthys;* cf. 1:10) **puts the sickle to it** (lit., "sends forth the sickle," a figure of speech for "sending forth the reapers"; cf. Joel 3:13) **because the harvest has come** (*parestēken,* "stands ready"). Some interpreters view this parable as a picture of evangelism. Some take it as depicting spiritual growth in a believer. Others see it as a picture of the coming of God's kingdom by the mysterious, sovereign work of God. Its emphasis is on growth under God's initiative in the interim phase between the proclamation by Jesus (the lowly Sower) and His disciples and the ultimate manifestation of the kingdom by Jesus (the mighty Harvester). The third view is preferred in light of Mark 4:26a and the overall context of the kingdom parables.

5. THE PARABLE OF THE MUSTARD SEED (4:30-32)

(MATT. 13:31-32; LUKE 13:18-19)

4:30-32. This parable has an elaborate double-question introduction which states in essence that the emergence of God's **kingdom** is similar to what happens to **a mustard seed** (the common black mustard, *sinapis nigra*) after it is sown on **the ground.** In Jewish thinking, its small size was proverbial since it was **the smallest** of all the seeds sown in the field. It took 725-760 mustard seeds to weigh a gram (28 grams equal one ounce). The mustard shrub is an annual plant which, growing from seed, **becomes the largest of all garden plants** (*ta lachana,* "large, fast-growing annual shrubs") in Palestine, reaching a height of 12-15 feet in a few weeks. **Birds of the air** (undomesticated fowl) are attracted by its seed and the **shade** of its large **branches** (cf. TDNT, s.v. "*sinapi,*" 7:287-91). This parable emphasizes the contrast between the smallest of the seeds growing into the tallest of the shrubs. It contrasts the insignificant, even enigmatic beginning of God's kingdom, embodied in the presence of Jesus, with the greatness of the end result to be established at His Second Advent when it will surpass all the earth's kingdoms in power and glory.

The reference to the birds may simply indicate the surprising size of the end result. Or perhaps they represent evil

forces (cf. v. 4), but this would indicate an abnormal development of God's kingdom. Probably they represent the incorporation of the Gentiles into God's kingdom program (cf. Ezek. 17:22-24; 31:6). What God had promised to do (Ezek. 17), He began to do in Jesus' mission. (The kingdom, however, is not to be identified with the church; cf. comments on Mark 1:15.)

6. CONCLUDING SUMMARY (4:33-34)

4:33-34. These verses summarize the purpose and approach of Jesus' parabolic teaching (cf. vv. 11-12). His practice was to speak **the Word** (cf. 1:15) **to them,** the crowds plus the disciples, through parables which He adapted to their levels of understanding.

Because of misconceptions about God's kingdom, **Jesus . . . did not** teach about it **without using a parable** (in figurative speech). **But to His own disciples** privately (*kat'idian;* cf. 6:31-32; 7:33; 9:2, 28; 13:3) **He explained** (lit., "kept on explaining") **everything** about His mission as it related to God's kingdom. This dual approach, illustrated here in chapter 4, is assumed throughout the rest of the Gospel.

E. *Jesus' miracles demonstrating His sovereign power (4:35–5:43)*

Mark's selection of parables is followed by a series of miracles, indicating that what Jesus *did* (His works) authenticated what He *said* (His words). Both relate to the presence of God's sovereign rule (kingdom) in Jesus.

With only three exceptions Mark put all the miracles he recorded before 8:27. (Cf. the list "The Miracles of Jesus" at John 2:1-11.) This was to highlight the fact that Jesus would not tell His disciples about His coming death and resurrection until they openly acknowledged Him as God's Messiah.

This section contains four miracles that clearly show Jesus' sovereign authority over various hostile powers: a storm at sea (4:35-41); demon possession (5:1-20); incurable physical illness (5:25-34); and death (5:21-24, 35-43).

1. THE CALMING OF THE STORM ON THE LAKE (4:35-41)

(MATT. 8:23-27; LUKE 8:22-25)

4:35-37. The vivid details indicate

that Mark recorded an eyewitness report, probably from Peter. On the **evening of that day** of teaching by the lake (cf. v. 1), Jesus took the initiative and decided to cross **over to the other** (east) **side** of the Sea of Galilee with **His 12 disciples.** Though not stated, He probably desired relief from the crowds and rest. Perhaps also He sought a new sphere of ministry (cf. 1:38). Even so, **other boats,** carrying those who wanted to remain with Jesus, tagged along.

His disciples, several of them experienced fishermen, took charge of the voyage. The words, **just as He was,** refer back to 4:1 and link Jesus' teaching in a boat with His miracle-work in a boat (cf. the disciples' address, "Teacher," v. 38).

The journey was interrupted by **a** sudden **furious squall,** common on this lake, surrounded by high hills and narrow valleys that functioned as wind tunnels. A storm in the evening was especially dangerous, and on this occasion the boisterous **waves broke over** (lit., "kept spilling over into") **the boat so that it was nearly swamped.**

4:38-39. Exhausted from a full day of teaching, **Jesus** was **sleeping . . . in the stern,** on a sailor's leather rowing **cushion. The** panic-stricken **disciples woke Him** with a cry of reproach (cf. 5:31; 6:37; 8:4, 32) at His apparent indifference to their situation. Though they called Him **Teacher** (Gr. for the Heb. *Rabbi*), they did not yet understand His teaching.

Jesus **rebuked** (lit., "ordered"; cf. 1:25) **the wind and said to the waves,** "Be silent! Be muzzled and remain so!" (the force of the Gr. perf. tense, *pephimōso*) This verb, "be muzzled," was somewhat of a technical term for dispossessing a demon of his power (cf. 1:25) and may suggest that Jesus recognized demonic powers behind the ferocious storm. But at His command **the wind** stopped and **the lake** became **completely calm.**

4:40-41. Jesus rebuked **His disciples** for being **afraid** (*deiloi*, "cowardly fear") in a crisis. Despite Jesus' tutoring (vv. 11, 34) it still had not dawned on them that God's authority and power were present *in Jesus*. This is what He meant by His second question, **Do you still have no faith?** (cf. 7:18; 8:17-21, 33; 9:19)

In stilling the storm Jesus assumed the authority exercised only by God in the Old Testament (cf. Pss. 89:8-9; 104:5-9; 106:8-9; 107:23-32). That is why the disciples **were terrified** (lit., "feared a great fear") when they saw that **even the** forces of nature did **obey Him.** The verb "terrified" (from *phobeomai*, "have awe;" cf. *deilos*, "cowardly fear," in Mark 4:40) refers to a reverence that overtakes people in the presence of supernatural power (cf. 16:8). However, their question to one another, **Who is this?** indicated that they did not fully comprehend the significance of it all.

2. THE CURE OF THE GERASENE DEMONIAC (5:1-20)

(MATT. 8:28-34; LUKE 8:26-39)

a. A description of the demoniac (5:1-5)

5:1. Jesus and His disciples **went to** the east side of **the lake** (Sea of Galilee) into **the region of the Gerasenes.** Greek manuscripts are divided on the precise location involved, citing three names: Gadarenes (Matt. 8:28), Gergesenes (from Origen), and Gerasenes. (See comments on Luke 8:26). Reliable evidence favors the name Gerasenes which probably referred to the small town Gersa (modern Khersa) located on the lake's eastern shore. Most of its inhabitants were Gentiles (cf. Mark 5:11, 19).

5:2-5. The vivid details of this whole account reflect both an eyewitness report and the report of townspeople who had long been familiar with this demoniac. As soon as (*euthys;* cf. 1:10) **Jesus got out of the boat,** He encountered **a man with an evil spirit** (cf. 5:8, 13 with 1:23) **from** (*ek,* "out of") **the tombs.** These were probably cavelike rooms cut into the rocks of nearby hills which served as tombs and sometimes as haunts for demented people. Matthew mentioned demoniacs, whereas Mark and Luke focused attention on one, probably the worst case.

Mark 5:3-5 elaborately describes his pathetic condition. He **lived in the tombs** (an outcast); he was uncontrollable for **no one could . . . subdue** (from *damazō,* "to tame a wild animal") **him,** not even with fetters for his feet or **a chain** for his hands. He went about **night and day** shrieking wildly and cutting **himself with** sharp **stones,** perhaps in a demonic form of worship.

Such behavior shows that demon possession is not mere sickness or insanity but a desperate satanic attempt to distort and destroy God's image in man (cf. TDNT, s.v. "*daimōn*," 2:18-19).

b. The command to the demon (5:6-10)

5:6-7. The brief statement of Jesus' encounter with the demoniac (v. 2) is now related in more detail. Three things indicate that the demon possessing the man was fully aware of Jesus' divine origin and superior power: he knelt before **Him** (in homage, not worship); he used Jesus' divine name in an attempt to gain control over Him (cf. 1:24); and he brazenly appealed to **Jesus** not to punish him. The words, **Most High God,** were used in the Old Testament, often by Gentiles, to refer to the superiority of the true God of Israel over all man-made gods (cf. Gen. 14:18-24; Num. 24:16; Isa. 14:14; Dan. 3:26; 4:2; cf. comments on Mark 1:23-24).

The plea, **Swear to God,** was used in exorcisms and should be rendered, "I implore you by (I appeal to) God." The demon did not want Jesus to **torture** him by sending him to his final punishment then (cf. 1:24; Matt. 8:29; Luke 8:31).

5:8. This verse is a brief explanatory (*gar,* for) comment by Mark (cf. 6:52). **Jesus was** commanding **him,** the demon, to leave the **man.** Throughout this section there is fluctuation between the personality of the man and the demon who possessed him.

5:9-10. These verses resume the conversation of verse 7. The demon said through the man, **My name is Legion for we are many.** Many evil powers controlled this man and subjected him to intense oppression. They tormented him as one combined force under the leadership of one demon, their spokesman. This accounts for the alternating singular ("my") and plural ("we") pronouns. Repeatedly the leading demon **begged Jesus** earnestly **not to send them out of the area** (lit., "region"; cf. v. 1) into a lonely exile where they could not torment people.

The Latin word "Legion," commonly known in Palestine, denoted a Roman army regiment of about 6,000 soldiers, though it probably also meant a very large number (cf. v. 15). To people under Roman domination the word no doubt suggested great strength and oppression.

c. The loss of the herd of pigs (5:11-13)

5:11. The Jews considered **pigs** "unclean" animals (cf. Lev. 11:7). But the farmers on the east side of the Sea of Galilee with its predominantly Gentile population raised pigs for the meat markets in the Decapolis, "the 10 cities" of that region (cf. Mark 5:20).

5:12-13. The demons (cf. v. 9) specifically **begged Jesus** to **send** them **among** (*eis* here suggests movement toward) **the pigs** so that they might **go into them** as their new hosts. They knew they were subject to Jesus' command, and in a desperate attempt to avoid being consigned to a disembodied state until final judgment, they made this appeal.

Jesus **gave them permission** to do so. When the demons left the man and entered **the pigs, the** whole **herd, about 2,000 in number,** stampeded **down the steep bank into the lake and were drowned** (lit., "one after another they drowned themselves"). The "sea" perhaps symbolized the satanic realm.

d. The plea of the townspeople (5:14-17)

5:14-15. The herdsmen **tending the pigs** fled in fear **and reported this** startling event **in the town** (probably Gersa; cf. v. 1) **and** the surrounding **countryside.** The report was so unbelievable that many **people went** to investigate the incident for themselves. **They saw the** former demoniac **sitting there, dressed** (cf. Luke 8:27) **and in his right mind,** rational and self-controlled (contrast Mark 5:3-5). So complete was the transformation that the townspeople **were afraid** (awed; cf. 4:41).

5:16-17. The herdsmen (and perhaps the disciples) rehearsed what had happened to the . . . man—and to the pigs, a detail Mark emphasized to show that this economic loss (not the man) was the people's major concern. As a result the townspeople began urging Jesus to leave. Apparently they feared further losses if He stayed. There is no record that He ever returned to that area.

e. The request of the restored man (5:18-20)

5:18-20. In contrast with the local inhabitants (cf. v. 17), **the man who had been demon-possessed** was begging (*parekalei,* the same word used by the demon, v. 10) **to go with Jesus.** Jesus' miracles repelled some (vv. 15-17) and attracted others (vv. 18-20).

The words, "to go with Him" (lit., "in order that he might be with Him"), recall a similar clause in 3:14 that describes one of the purposes for which Jesus called the Twelve. It is in this sense that Jesus refused the man's request.

Jesus told **him** to go to his **home** (immediate family) and **family** (lit., "to yours," your own people) from whom he had been estranged **and** report to **them** all that **the Lord,** the Most High God (cf. 5:7; Luke 8:39) had **done for** him **and how He** had shown **mercy on** him. **The man** obeyed **and began to** proclaim (cf. Mark 1:4, 14) **in the Decapolis** (a league of 10 Gr. cities all but one east of the Jordan) the wonderful things **Jesus** (cf. "Lord," 5:19) **had done for him.** Those who heard him **were amazed** (*ethaumazon*, cf. "astonished"; 6:6a; 12:17; 15:5, 44).

Since this man was a Gentile and his preaching activity was confined to a Gentile area where Jesus was not welcome, Jesus did not give His usual injunction to silence (cf. 1:44; 5:43; 7:36).

3. THE HEMORRHAGING WOMAN AND JAIRUS' DAUGHTER (5:21-43)
(MATT. 9:18-26; LUKE 8:40-56)

This section, like Mark 3:20-35, has a "sandwich" structure. The account of the raising of Jairus' daughter from the dead (5:21-24, 35-43) is divided by the incident of the woman with a hemorrhage (5:25-34). What appeared to be a disastrous delay in the healing of the woman actually assured the restoration of Jairus' daughter. It was providentially ordered to test and strengthen Jairus' faith.

a. *Jairus' earnest request (5:21-24)*
(Matt. 9:18-19; Luke 8:40-42)

5:21-24. Jesus and His disciples returned **to the other** (west) **side of the** Sea of Galilee, probably to Capernaum. As before in this area, **a large crowd gathered around** Jesus **while He was** still **by the lake.**

On this occasion, **Jairus came** to Him. As **one of the synagogue rulers,** he was a lay official responsible for the physical management of the synagogue building and the worship services. He was a respected leader in the community.

Not all the religious leaders were hostile to Jesus.

Jairus' **little daughter** (an only daughter, Luke 8:42) was **dying** (lit., "was at the point of death"). Matthew's abbreviated treatment of this event (135 words whereas Mark used 374) accounts for his statement that the girl had already died (Matt. 9:18). In humility, Jairus **pleaded earnestly** (lit., "begged much"; cf. Mark 5:10) **with** Jesus to **come and put** His **hands on her so that she** might **be healed** (lit., "saved," delivered from physical death) **and live.** The practice of "laying on of hands" in healing symbolized the transfer of vitality to a needy recipient; it was popularly associated with Jesus' healings (cf. 6:5; 7:32; 8:23, 25). Jairus probably knew about Jesus' power from previous associations (cf. 1:21-28) and was confident that He could save his daughter's life.

As **Jesus went with** Jairus, **a great crowd followed** them **and pressed** ("kept thronging," from *synthlibō*; cf. v. 31) **around Him.**

b. *The healing of the woman with a hemorrhage (5:25-34)*
(Matt. 9:20-22; Luke 8:43-48)

5:25-27. An unnamed **woman** with an incurable condition joined the crowd. **She had suffered** (lit., "was in") **bleeding for 12 years** (cf. v. 42). This may have been a chronic menstrual disorder or a uterine hemorrhage. Her condition made her ritually unclean (cf. Lev. 15:25-27), excluding her from normal social relations since any who came in contact with her would become "unclean."

She had suffered greatly from various treatments by **many doctors.** She **had spent all she** owned in a desperate attempt to get well. Nothing helped; in fact her condition **grew worse.**

But because **she** had **heard about** Jesus' healing power (which aroused her faith), **she came up behind Him in the crowd and touched His cloak** (outer garment). She did this despite her "uncleanness" and with a desire to avoid an embarrassing public disclosure of her malady.

5:28. She kept telling herself that **if** she could **just touch His clothes,** she would **be healed** and then she could slip away unobserved. Perhaps her faith was mixed with a popular notion that a healer had power in his clothing, or she may have known someone who had been healed in this way (cf. 3:10; 6:56).

5:29. When the woman touched Jesus' garment, **immediately** (*euthys*; cf. 1:10) **her bleeding stopped. She felt** (lit., "knew," from *ginōskō*, "know experientially"; cf. 5:30) **by a physical sensation in her body that she was freed** (lit., "had been healed") **from her suffering.** The healing occurred without overt participation by Jesus.

5:30. Yet **Jesus** immediately (*euthys*) **realized** in Himself (from *epiginōskō*, "know fully"; cf. v. 29) **that power had gone out from Him** or, more literally, "power from Him (on account of who He is) had gone out."

This unusual expression has been understood in two ways. One view maintains that God the Father healed the woman and Jesus was not aware of it till afterward. The other view is that Jesus Himself, wishing to honor the woman's faith, willingly extended His healing power to her. The latter view is more consistent with Jesus' healing ministry. Power did not leave Him without His knowledge and will. However, He exercised it only at the Father's bidding (cf. 13:32). The touch of the garment had no magical effect.

Aware of *how* the miracle took place, Jesus **turned around . . . and asked, Who touched My clothes?** He wanted to establish a personal relationship with the healed person, untainted with quasi-magical notions.

5:31-32. Jesus' question seemed absurd to **His disciples** (the Twelve; cf. Luke 8:45) because the crowd was pressing (from *synthlibō*; cf. Mark 5:24) in and many **people** were touching Him. This emphasized Jesus' ability to distinguish the touch of one who in faith expected deliverance from the inadvertent touch of those **crowding against** Him. There was, and still is, a great difference between the two. So **Jesus kept looking around** (*perieblepeto*; "was looking penetratingly"; cf. 3:5, 34) at the people surrounding Him in order **to see who had** touched Him in this way.

5:33-34. Then the woman, the only one who understood Jesus' question, **came** in humility, and **trembling with fear** (from *phobeomai*, "to have awe, reverence"; cf. 4:41) because she knew

what had happened to her, in courage and gratitude told Him everything. The affectionate title, **Daughter** (its only recorded use by Jesus) signified her new relationship with Him (cf. 3:33-35). Jesus attributed her cure to her **faith** rather than the touch of His clothing. Her faith **healed** her (lit., "has saved or delivered you"; cf. 5:28; 10:52) in that it caused her to seek healing *from Jesus.* Faith, confident trust, derives its value not from the one who expresses it, but from the object in which it rests (cf. 10:52; 11:22).

Jesus said, **Go in peace and be freed** (lit., "be healthy") **from your suffering** (cf. 5:29). This assured her that her healing was complete and permanent. In her extremity of need—incurable illness and socio-religious isolation—she was a living "dead" person for 12 years. Her restoration to wholeness of life anticipated the dramatic raising of Jairus' daughter who died after living for 12 years.

c. The raising of Jairus' daughter to life (5:35-43)

(Matt. 9:23-26; Luke 8:49-56)

5:35-36. The delay (cf. vv. 22-24) caused by the woman's healing (vv. 25-34) was a severe test of Jairus' faith. His fears that his little **daughter** would die before **Jesus** got there were confirmed by the report of **some men** (unidentified friends and relatives) **from his house** that she had died. They concluded that her death ended any hope that **Jesus** could help so they suggested that it was futile to **bother** (lit., "trouble") **the Teacher** (cf. 4:38) any further.

Jesus overheard the message but refused to accept its implications. This is the force of the verb translated **ignoring** (*parakousas*), which means "refuse to listen" (cf. Matt. 18:17). The present imperatives in Jesus' reassuring words to **Jairus** could be rendered: "Stop fearing (i.e., in unbelief); just keep on believing." He had already exercised faith in coming to Jesus, he had seen the relationship between faith and Jesus' power (Mark 5:25-34); now he was exhorted to **believe** that Jesus could restore his lifeless daughter.

5:37-40a. Including Jairus, Jesus let only three disciples—**Peter, James, and John**—accompany Him **to the** house as witnesses (cf. Deut. 17:6). These three disciples served as legal witnesses here in anticipation of Jesus' resurrection, then at His transfiguration (Mark 9:2), and in Gethsemane (14:33).

At the house the elaborate ritual of Jewish mourning had already begun. The **commotion** (*thorybon*, "an uproar") included the activity of hired mourners (cf. Jer. 9:17; Amos 5:16), weeping, and antiphonal **wailing.**

Jesus entered the house and rebuked the mourners because, **He** told **them . . . the child** was **not dead but asleep.** Did Jesus mean she was just in a coma? Friends and relatives (cf. Mark 5:35) as well as the professional mourners who **laughed** scornfully at His words, knew she was dead (cf. Luke 8:53). Was Jesus simply describing death as sleep, implying a state of "sleep" between death and resurrection? This is not supported elsewhere in the New Testament (cf. Luke 23:42-43; 2 Cor. 5:6-8; Phil. 1:23-24). Probably He was saying that in this case death was *like* sleep. From a mourner's point of view, the girl's death would turn out to be like "a sleep" from which she was awakened. Her condition was not final and irrevocable (cf. Luke 8:55; John 11:11-14).

5:40b-42. After **He put . . . out** all the mourners, Jesus **took the** girl's parents **and the** three **disciples** (cf. v. 37) **with Him** into her room. Then **He took her . . . hand and** spoke the Aramaic words, *Talitha koum!* This was a command, not a magical formula. Mark translated it for his Greek-speaking readers, **Little girl . . . get up,** adding the clause **I say to you** to emphasize Jesus' authority over death. Since Galileans were bilingual, Jesus spoke both Aramaic, His mother tongue—a Semitic language related to Hebrew—and Greek, the *lingua franca* of the Greco-Roman world. He likely also spoke Hebrew.

At Jesus' command, **immediately** (*euthys;* cf. 1:10) **the girl** got **up and** began walking around for (*gar*), Mark explained, **she was 12 years old.** The parents and three disciples **were completely astonished** (from *existēmi,* lit., "out of their minds with great amazement"; cf. 2:12; 6:51).

5:43. Jesus then gave two **orders.** The first was a **strict** injunction to silence. Jesus did not want the miracle to attract

people to Him for the wrong reasons (cf. comments on 1:43-45).

The second command, that the girl be given food, displayed His compassion and also confirmed that she was restored to good health. Her body had been resuscitated, returned to natural life, but was still subject to death, and needed to be sustained by food. This contrasts with a *resurrected* body (cf. 1 Cor. 15:35-57).

F. Conclusion: Jesus' rejection at Nazareth (6:1-6a) (Matt. 13:53-58)

6:1. From Capernaum **Jesus** went about 20 miles southwest **to His hometown,** Nazareth (cf. 1:9, 24), where He had lived and ministered previously (cf. Luke 4:16-30). He was **accompanied by His disciples,** returning as a Teacher (Rabbi) surrounded by His students. This was a public mission, and He was preparing His disciples by example for their own missions (cf. Mark 6:7-13).

6:2-3. On **the Sabbath . . . He** taught **in the synagogue** (cf. 1:21), probably expounding on the Law and the Prophets. **Many . . . were amazed** (*exeplēssonto,* "astounded, struck out, overwhelmed"; cf. 1:22; 7:37; 10:26; 11:18) at His teaching.

But some asked disparaging questions about the origin of (a) **these things,** His teaching, (b) the **wisdom . . . given Him** (lit., "to this One"), and (c) His power to do **miracles** elsewhere (cf. 6:5). Only two answers were possible: His source was God, or Satan (cf. 3:22).

Despite His impressive words and deeds, He was too ordinary for them. The derogatory question, **Isn't this the carpenter?** implied, "He is a common laborer like the rest of us." All His immediate family—mother, brothers, and sisters—were known to the townspeople, and they were ordinary people. The phrase **Mary's Son** was also derogatory since a man was not described as his mother's son in Jewish usage even if she was a widow, except by insult (cf. Jud. 11:1-2; John 8:41; 9:29). Their words, calculated insults, also suggested they knew there was something unusual about Jesus' birth.

His brothers and **sisters** (cf. Mark 3:31-35) were most likely children of Joseph and Mary born after Jesus' birth rather than Joseph's children by a previous marriage or Jesus' cousins. **James** became a leader in the early church at Jerusalem (cf. Acts 15:13-21), and authored the Epistle of James (James 1:1). **Judas** was probably Jude, author of the Epistle of Jude (Jude 1). Nothing more is known of **Joses** and **Simon** or His sisters. Perhaps Joseph was not mentioned because he was already dead.

Thus since the townspeople could not explain Jesus, **they took offense** (from *skandalizomai*, "to be caused to stumble, to be repelled"; cf. comments on Mark 14:27) **at Him,** finding no reason to believe He was God's Anointed One.

6:4. Jesus responded to their rejection with the proverb that a prophet is not appreciated at **home.** He was like an Old Testament **prophet** (cf. v. 15; 8:28) whose words were often rejected and who was dishonored most by those who knew Him best (cf. 6:17-29).

6:5-6a. Because of such persistent unbelief Jesus **could not do any miracles there except** to lay His hands on (cf. 5:23) **a few sick people and heal them.** There was no limitation on His power, but His purpose was to perform miracles in the presence of faith. Only a few here had faith to come to Him for healing.

Even Jesus **was amazed** (*ethaumasen,* "astonished"; cf. 5:20; 12:17; 15:5, 44) **at their** unbelief, their unwillingness to believe that His wisdom and power were from God. So far as is known, He never returned to Nazareth.

The people of Nazareth represent Israel's blindness. Their refusal to believe in Jesus pictured what the disciples would soon experience (cf. 6:7-13) and what Mark's readers (then and now) would experience in the advance of the gospel.

V. Jesus' Ministry in and beyond Galilee (6:6b–8:30)

The third major section of Mark's Gospel begins structurally like the first two sections (cf. 6:6b with 1:14-15 and 3:7-12; 6:7-34 with 1:16-20 and 3:13-19), but concludes with Peter's confession of Jesus as Messiah (8:27-30) instead of a statement of rejection (cf. 3:6; 6:1-6a). During this phase of His ministry Jesus directed more attention to His disciples. In the face of opposition, He revealed to them by both words and deeds who He really is. Much of this time was spent outside of Galilee.

A. Introductory summary: Jesus' teaching tour of Galilee (6:6b) (Matt. 9:35-38)

6:6b. This statement summarizes Jesus' third tour of Galilee (for the first, cf. 1:35-39; Mark did not mention the second, cf. Luke 8:1-3). Despite His rejection at Nazareth, **Jesus** was going **around** the neighboring villages **teaching** (cf. Mark 1:21). This set the stage for the Twelve's mission.

B. Jesus' sending forth of the Twelve and John the Baptist's death (6:7-31)

This section has a "sandwich" structure (cf. 3:20-35; 5:21-43). The narrative of the mission of the Twelve (6:7-13, 30-31) is divided by the account of John the Baptist's death (6:14-29). This indicates that the death of John the messenger did not silence his message. The forerunner's death prefigured Jesus' death. And Jesus' message would still be proclaimed by His followers.

1. THE MISSION OF THE TWELVE (6:7-13) (MATT. 10:1, 5-15; LUKE 9:1-6)

6:7. In order to extend His ministry on this Galilean tour, Jesus **sent** (from *apostellō;* cf. 3:14; 6:30) **the Twelve out two by two,** a common practice in that day for practical and legal reasons (cf. 11:1; 14:13; John 8:17; Deut. 17:6; 19:15).

The Twelve were His authorized representatives in keeping with the Jewish concept of *šelûḥîm,* that is, a man's representative (*šālîaḥ*) was considered as the man himself (cf. Matt. 10:40 and TDNT, s.v. "*apostolos,*" 1:413-27). They were to fulfill a *special* commission and bring back a report (cf. Mark 6:30; so Jesus' unusual instructions (vv. 8-11) pertained only to that particular mission.

He **gave them authority** (*exousian;* the "right" and the "power"; cf. 2:10; 3:15) **over evil spirits.** This power to exorcise demons (cf. 1:26) would authenticate their preaching (cf. 6:13; 1:15).

6:8-9. The urgency of their mission required that they travel lightly. They were to **take** a **staff** (*rhabdon,* "walking stick") and to **wear sandals** (ordinary footwear). **But** they were **not** to take **bread** (food), a **bag** (probably a traveler's bag for provisions, not a beggar's bag), **money** (small copper coins easily tucked in their cloth **belts**), or **an extra tunic,**

additional inner garment used as a covering at night. They were to depend on God to provide food and shelter through the hospitality of Jewish households.

The two concessions of a staff and sandals are unique to Mark. Both are forbidden in Matthew 10:9-10, and the staff is forbidden in Luke 9:3. Matthew used *ktaomai* ("to procure, acquire"), instead of *airō* ("to take"); so the disciples were not to acquire *additional* staffs or sandals—but to use the ones they already had. Mark and Luke both use *airō*, "to take or carry along." But Luke says, "Take nothing for the journey—no staff (*rhabdon*)," presumably no additional staff; while Mark says, "Take nothing for the journey *except* (cf. Mark 6:5) a staff (*rhabdon*)," presumably the one already in use. Each writer stressed a different aspect of Jesus' instructions.

6:10-11. **Whenever** the disciples entered **a house** as invited guests, they were to **stay there** making it their base of operations **until** they left the **town.** They were not to impose on the hospitality of many people or accept more attractive offers once they were settled.

They should also expect rejection. If **any place** (a household, synagogue, village) would **not** offer hospitality **or listen to** their message, they were to **leave** there and to **shake the dust off** their **feet.** Devout Jews did this when they left Gentile (alien) territory to show that they were dissociating themselves from it. This would tell Jewish hearers they were acting like pagans in rejecting the disciples' message.

This was to be done **as a testimony** (cf. 1:44; 13:9) **against** the citizens. It warned them that the disciples' responsibility to them had been fulfilled and those who rejected the message would have to answer to God for themselves (cf. Acts 13:51; 18:6). No doubt it provoked serious thought and perhaps repentance by some. The KJV statement regarding Sodom and Gomorrah is not in the earliest Greek manuscripts of Mark's text (cf. Matt. 10:15).

6:12-13. In obedience the Twelve **preached** repentance (cf. 1:4, 14-15), **drove out many demons** (cf. 1:32-34, 39), and healed **many sick people** (cf. 3:10). As Jesus' representatives (cf. 6:7; 9:37) they learned that His power extended beyond His personal presence. Their mission showed the coming of God's kingdom (cf. 1:15).

Anointing the sick **with oil** is unique to Mark. This use of olive oil was both because of its medicinal properties (cf. Luke 10:34; James 5:14) and its symbolic value indicating that the disciples acted by Jesus' authority and power, not their own.

2. THE BEHEADING OF JOHN THE BAPTIST (6:14-29)
(MATT. 14:1-12; LUKE 3:19-20; 9:7-9)

a. Popular explanations of Jesus' identity (6:14-16)

6:14-16. The miraculous activity of Jesus and the Twelve throughout Galilee caught the attention of **Herod** Antipas, son of Herod the Great (see the chart on the Herods at Luke 1:5). Herod Antipas was *tetrarch* (ruler of a fourth part of his father's kingdom) of Galilee and Perea under the aegis of Rome from 4 B.C. to A.D. 39 (cf. Matt. 14:1; Luke 3:19; 9:7). Officially he was not a **king** but Mark's use of the title probably reflected local custom in view of Herod's covetous ambitions.

Mark 6:14b-15 presents three opinions which attempt to account for Jesus' **miraculous powers;** He was (a) **John the Baptist** (cf. 1:4-9) risen **from the dead,** (b) **Elijah** (cf. Mal. 3:1; 4:5-6), or (c) a **prophet,** resuming the suspended line of Israel's **prophets.**

Despite other opinions **Herod,** troubled by a guilty conscience, remained convinced that Jesus was **the man** he had **beheaded.** Herod believed **John** the Baptist was risen **from the dead** and was using miraculous powers. Mark 6:17-29 explains verse 16 in a "flashback."

b. Flashback: the execution of John the Baptist (6:17-29)

Mark included this section not only to supplement 1:14 and further clarify 6:16, but also to provide a "passion narrative" of Jesus' forerunner that foreshadowed and paralleled Jesus' own suffering and death. Mark focused on what Herod and Herodias did to John. Perhaps he included so many details to draw a parallel to the Elijah-Jezebel conflict since Jesus later identified John as Elijah (9:11-13).

6:17-18. Mark explained (*gar*, **for**) that **Herod himself had** ordered **John** to be **put in prison.** According to Josephus, this prison was at the fortress-palace of Machaerus near the northeastern shore of the Dead Sea (*The Antiquities of the Jews* 18. 5. 2). Herod **did this because of Herodias,** an ambitious woman who was his second **wife.** Herod had first married a daughter of the Arabian king, Aretas IV. Then he became enamored with his half-niece Herodias (daughter of his half-brother, Aristobulus) who was married to Herod's half-brother (**brother** means half-brother) Philip (her half-uncle; cf. Josephus *The Antiquities of the Jews* 18. 5. 1-2). They had a daughter, Salome. **Herod** divorced his wife in order to marry Herodias who had divorced Philip (not the Philip of Luke 3:1). John had repeatedly denounced this marriage as unlawful (cf. Lev. 18:16; 20:21).

6:19-20. John's bold rebuke infuriated **Herodias** who **nursed a grudge against** him (lit., "had it in for him"). Not satisfied with John's imprisonment, she **wanted to kill him, but** her plans were thwarted **because Herod feared John** (had a superstitious dread of him), whom he knew was **a righteous and holy man.** So he **protected** John from Herodias' murderous intentions by keeping him in prison—a shrewd compromise.

In spite of his immoral lifestyle, **Herod** was fascinated by John. He had a certain attraction for John's preaching, but it left him **greatly puzzled.** The words "greatly puzzled" (*polla ēporei*) have good manuscript support and are preferred on contextual grounds to the reading "he did many things" (*polla epoiei*; NIV marg.; KJV), a reading that may reflect an error of hearing by scribes who copied the text as it was read to them. Herod's conflict between his passion for Herodias and his respect for John showed his vacillating moral weakness.

6:21-23. **Finally** (cf. v. 19) Herodias found an opportunity to carry out a murderous scheme. The occasion was Herod's **birthday . . . banquet,** a luxurious celebration he gave **for his high officials** (in civil government), **military commanders, and the leading men** (prominent citizens) **of Galilee.** Herodias deliberately sent (implied by vv. 24-25) her **daughter,** Salome, into the banquet room to dance in a way that would win Herod's approval.

Salome was a young woman of marriageable age (*korasion,* "girl"; cf. Es. 2:2, 9; Mark 5:41-42), probably in her middle teens. Her skillful and provocative dance **pleased Herod and his . . . guests,** and led him to make her an ostentatious, rash offer as a reward. **He** arrogantly **promised her** anything she wanted and sealed it **with an oath** (cf. Es. 5:6) which included the words **up to half my kingdom** (cf. Es. 7:2). Actually Herod had no "kingdom" (realm) to give (cf. comments on Mark 6:14). He used a proverbial saying for generosity which Salome knew was not to be taken literally (cf. 1 Kings 13:8).

6:24-25. When Salome asked **her mother** what she should **ask for,** Herodias replied with premeditated promptness, **The head of John the Baptist.** She wanted proof that he was dead. **At once** (*euthys*; cf. 1:10) Salome **hurried** back **to the king** with her macabre **request.** She demanded that the deed be done **right now** (*exautēs,* "at once") before Herod could find a way to avoid it. She added the words **on a platter,** suggested perhaps by the festive occasion.

6:26-28. Salome's request deeply grieved (cf. 14:34) Herod. **But because of his oaths** (considered irrevocable) and to save face before **his dinner guests** (cf. 6:21) **he did not** have the courage to reject it. **So he immediately** (*euthys*) ordered the request to be fulfilled.

An executioner (*spekoulatora,* a Latin loanword, probably a bodyguard) **beheaded John in the prison** of the fortress, **brought . . . his head on a platter** to Salome in the banquet hall. **She** in turn **gave it to** Herodias (cf. 9:12-13). John had been silenced, but his message to Herod still stood.

6:29. When **John's disciples** (cf. Matt. 11:2-6) heard about his death, they **came . . . took his body, and** put **it in a tomb.**

3. THE RETURN OF THE TWELVE (6:30-31) (LUKE 9:10A)

6:30-31. The apostles (*apostoloi,* "delegates, messengers") returned to **Jesus,** probably at Capernaum by prearrangement, **and reported to Him all they had done** (they mentioned their "works" first) and taught ("words") in fulfilling their commission (cf. vv. 7-13). The designation "apostles" for the Twelve occurs only twice in Mark (cf. 3:14). It is used in a nontechnical sense to describe their function as "missionaries" (cf. 6:7-9; Acts 14:14) rather than to denote an official title (cf. Eph. 2:19-20).

Jesus directed them to come with Him for a brief, well-earned rest. This was necessary because so many people were coming and going that they had no time to eat (cf. Mark 3:20). They were to come by themselves (kat' idian; cf. 4:34) to a quiet (erēmon, "remote"; cf. 1:35, 45) place (cf. 6:32).

C. Jesus' self-disclosure to the Twelve in word and deed (6:32–8:26)

This section highlights a period in Jesus' ministry when He made several withdrawals from Galilee to minister elsewhere (cf. 6:31; 7:24, 31; 8:22). During this time He showed the Twelve and Mark's readers how He cares for His own.

1. THE FEEDING OF THE 5,000 (6:32-44) (MATT. 14:13-21; LUKE 9:10B-17; JOHN 6:1-14)

6:32-34. These verses are a transition from the successful mission of the Twelve to the resultant presence of a large crowd in a remote place. Two phrases in the fulfillment of Jesus' directive provide the connecting links: by themselves (kat' idian, Gr. idiom meaning "privately"), a phrase Mark used for Jesus' private instruction of individuals (cf. 4:34a; 6:31-32; 7:33; 9:2, 28; 13:3); and to a solitary (erēmon, "remote") place (cf. 1:3-4, 12-13, 35, 45; 6:31-32, 35). The place where they sailed, though unnamed by Mark, was near Bethsaida Julias, a city across the Jordan River on the northeast side of the Sea of Galilee (cf. Luke 9:10).

Many people anticipated their destination and arrived there on foot . . . ahead of them. Their planned rest was interrupted by people in need.

When Jesus . . . saw the large crowd, He felt compassion (not annoyance) toward them. This inner emotion moved Him to help them (cf., e.g., Mark 6:39-44). He viewed them as sheep without a shepherd, lost and helpless, without guidance, nourishment, or protection. In several Old Testament passages (Num. 27:17; 1 Kings 22:17; Ezek. 34:5, 23-25) the sheep/shepherd image is associated with the "wilderness" (erēmos; cf. Mark 6:31-32). This crowd, representing the nation of Israel, received compassion, extensive teaching concerning God's kingdom (cf. Luke 9:11), and the provision of their needs (Mark 6:35-44) from Jesus, the true Shepherd (cf. John 10:1-21).

6:35-38. These verses present a significant dialogue between Jesus and the Twelve after He had taught the crowd all day. Since it was late (after 3 P.M. Jewish time) and they were in a remote (erēmos; cf. vv. 31-32) place, the disciples asked Jesus to dismiss the people . . . so they could buy food in the surrounding . . . villages before sunset.

Unexpectedly, Jesus told them to feed the crowd. He emphasized the word you (hymeis). The disciples' caustic reply showed the inadequacy of their resources and the impossibility of meeting His demand. According to their calculations, to feed such a crowd would take, literally, 200 denarii (NIV marg.). The denarius, the basic Roman silver coin used in Palestine, was the average daily wage for a farm laborer. Consequently 200 denarii was roughly equivalent to eight months of a man's wages, a sum beyond the disciples' means.

Jesus insisted they find out what bread was available, probably back at the boat and also in the crowd. The disciples returned with the answer: a mere five loaves of bread and two fish (salted and dried or roasted).

6:39-44. Mark's vivid description of the miracle indicates an eyewitness report, perhaps Peter's.

To insure orderly distribution, Jesus commanded the disciples to have everyone sit down in groups on the green grass (suggesting springtime). The words "in groups" in verse 39 could be rendered "table company by table company" (symposia symposia, lit., "drinking or eating parties"). But the words "in groups" in verse 40 are literally, "garden plot by garden plot" (prasiai prasiai); they are used figuratively, picturing well-arranged plots of people, perhaps colorfully dressed, seated on the grass in groups of 100s and 50s. The command was a challenge to faith for both the disciples and the crowd.

Jesus, serving as Host, spoke the customary Jewish blessing over the **five loaves** (round wheat or barley cakes) and **two fish** (cf. Lev. 19:24; Deut. 8:10). The words **gave thanks** are from *eulogeō* (lit., "to praise, extol" [God], or "to bless"; cf. Mark 14:22). The object of the blessing in such a prayer was not the food, but God who gave it. Jesus looked **up to heaven,** regarded as where God is (cf. Matt. 23:22), in dependence on the Father for a miraculous provision of food.

Then He **broke the loaves** into pieces, **divided the fish** into portions, and **gave** (lit., "kept giving") **them to His disciples to set before the people.** How the miracle itself took place is not stated, but the imperfect tense of the verb "gave" indicates the bread multiplied in Jesus' hands (cf. Mark 8:6).

The provision was miraculous and abundant. Mark emphasized that **all ate and were** fully **satisfied.** This was confirmed by the fact that **the disciples** collected **12 basketfuls** (*kophinoi,* small wicker baskets; contrast 8:8, 20) of leftovers, probably a basket for each disciple. The count of 5,000 men (*andres,* "males"), a very large crowd by local standards, did not include women and children (cf. Matt. 14:21), who were probably grouped separately for the meal according to Jewish custom.

The usual theme of astonishment at the close of a miracle story is not included here. This, plus subsequent comments in Mark 6:52 and 8:14-21 on this event, indicate that Mark regarded it as an important disclosure to Jesus' disciples of who He is. But they failed to understand its meaning (cf. 6:52).

2. JESUS' WALKING ON THE WATER (6:45-52)
(MATT. 14:22-33; JOHN 6:15-21)

6:45-46. Immediately (*euthys;* cf. 1:10) after feeding the 5,000, **Jesus made** (lit., "compelled") **His disciples** return to their **boat and** set sail (lit., "go before [Him] to the other side") to **Bethsaida** ("house of fishing"). The verb "made" implies an unexplained urgency; but John 6:14-15 states that the people recognized Jesus as the promised future Prophet (cf. Mark 6:14-15) and were determined to make Him King, by force if necessary. Jesus sensed the potential danger of this "messianic enthusiasm" and its effect on the disciples, so He compelled them to embark **while He dismissed the crowd.**

There is a geographical difficulty about the location of "Bethsaida" (cf. 6:32; Luke 9:10; John 12:21). The simplest solution seems to be that Bethsaida Julias (east of the Jordan) spread across to the western side of the Jordan and was called "Bethsaida in Galilee" (cf. John 12:21; 1:44; Mark 1:21, 29), a fishing suburb of Capernaum (cf. John 6:17). The disciples sailed for this town from the northeastern shore of the Sea of Galilee but were blown off course southward, eventually landing at Gennesaret on the western shore (cf. Mark 6:53).

After dismissing the excited crowd, Jesus **went** up on a nearby hillside **to pray** (cf. comments on 1:35).

6:47. At **evening** (sunset till darkness) **the** disciples' **boat was** well out in **the . . . lake** (not the geographical middle) **and** Jesus **was alone on land.** When He was absent (or appeared to be), the disciples often experienced distress and demonstrated a lack of faith (cf. 4:35-41; 9:14-32).

6:48. Jesus continued praying well past midnight. Meanwhile **the disciples** had made little headway out on the lake **because** a strong north **wind** blew **against them.** In the dim light of early dawn, **the fourth watch of the night** (by Roman reckoning, 3 to 6 A.M.; cf. 13:35), Jesus **saw** them **straining at the oars** and **went out to them, walking on the** choppy water's surface. The words **He was about to pass by them** do not mean He was going "to bypass" them. He intended "to pass beside" them in the sense of an Old Testament theophany (cf. Ex. 33:19, 22; 1 Kings 19:11; Mark 6:50b) to reassure them.

6:49-50a. The disciples **cried out** (cf. 1:23) with terror at Jesus' appearance on the water. **They thought He was a ghost** (*phantasma,* a water phantom). Mark explained that they responded this way **because they all saw Him** (not a hallucination by a few) **and were terrified.**

6:50b-52. Immediately (*euthys;* cf. 1:10) Jesus calmed their fears and spoke words of reassurance. **Take courage!** (*tharseite*) **Don't be afraid** (lit., "stop fearing") are familiar Old Testament words to people in distress (cf. the LXX of Isa. 41:10, 13-14; 43:1; 44:2). The first command occurs seven times in the New Testament, always on the lips of Jesus except for Mark 10:49 (cf. Matt. 9:2, 22; 14:27; Mark 6:50; John 16:33; Acts 23:11). The words **It is I** (lit., "I am," *egō eimi*) may simply convey self-identification ("It is I, Jesus"), but they are probably intended here to echo the Old Testament formula of God's self-revelation: "I am who I am" (cf. Ex. 3:14; Isa. 41:4; 43:10; 51:12; 52:6).

When Jesus joined the disciples **in the boat . . . the wind died down** (*ekopasen,* "stopped, rested"; cf. Mark 4:39), an additional demonstration of His mastery over nature (cf. 4:35-41).

The disciples **were completely amazed** (*existanto,* lit., "out of their minds"; cf. 2:12; 5:42) among themselves at this revelation of Jesus' presence and power. Mark alone explained (*gar,* **for**) **they had not** caught on to the meaning of **the loaves** miracle (cf. 6:35-44) as a pointer to His true identity. So they did not recognize Him when He walked on the water; they were spiritually imperceptive (cf. 3:5).

3. SUMMARY STATEMENT: JESUS' HEALING
MINISTRY AT GENNESARET (6:53-56)
(MATT. 14:34-36)

This summary statement marks the climax of Jesus' Galilean ministry just before His departure for the coastal region around Tyre and Sidon (cf. Mark 7:24).

6:53. Jesus and His disciples **had crossed over** the Sea of Galilee from the northeast to the west (cf. v. 45) **and anchored** (moored) **at Gennesaret,** a fertile, populous plain (two miles wide and four miles long), south of Capernaum on the northwestern shore of the lake. Rabbis called this plain "the Garden of God" and "a paradise." A small town there was also called Gennesaret.

6:54-56. Immediately (*euthys;* cf. 1:10) **people recognized Jesus.** As He moved through the **region,** they **carried the sick on mats** to Him for healing. **Everywhere He went . . . the sick** were **placed** in **marketplaces** (open spaces). Several medicinal mineral springs in this area made it a resort for invalids.

They kept begging again and again (*parekaloun;* cf. 5:10, 23) to **touch even the edge of His cloak** as He passed by. The "edge" or "fringe" was a border of blue tassels worn by a loyal Jew on his

outer cloak (cf. Num. 15:37-41; Deut. 22:12).

All who touched Him were healed (lit., "were being saved"; cf. Mark 5:28). These words iterate Mark's earlier reference to a personal faith relationship between Jesus and a sick person (cf. 3:7-10; 5:25-34). Healing was not effected by a touch but by the gracious action of Jesus who honored this means of expressing their faith in Him.

4. THE CONTROVERSY WITH THE RELIGIOUS
LEADERS CONCERNING DEFILEMENT
(7:1-23)
(MATT. 15:1-20)

This passage returns to the theme of conflict between Jesus and the religious leaders (cf. Mark 2:1–3:6). It emphasizes the rejection Jesus encountered in Israel (cf. 3:6, 19-30; 6:1-6a) despite His public popularity (cf. 6:53-56). It serves as a fitting prelude for His ministry to Gentiles (7:24–8:10). The words "unclean" (7:2, 5, 15, 18, 20, 23) and "tradition" (vv. 3, 5, 8, 9, 13) bind the section together.

a. *The charge by the religious leaders*
(7:1-5)
(Matt. 15:1-2)

7:1-2. The **Pharisees** (cf. 2:16; 3:6) **and some** Law **teachers** (cf. 1:22) **from Jerusalem** (cf. 3:22-30) came to investigate **Jesus** and His followers again, presumably at Capernaum (cf. 7:17).

They critically observed **some of** Jesus' **disciples eating food with "unclean" . . . hands.** "Unclean" (*koinais,* "common"), as Mark explained for his Gentile readers, meant **ceremonially unwashed.** It was a technical term among Jews denoting whatever was contaminated according to their religious rituals and thus was unfit to be called holy or devoted to God.

7:3-4. These verses constitute an extended parenthesis in which Mark explained (*gar;* cf. 1:16), **for** the benefit of his Gentile readers who lived outside Palestine, the common Jewish practice of **ceremonial washing.**

The ritual washing regulations were observed by **the Pharisees and all the Jews** (a generalization depicting their custom) as part of **the tradition of the elders** which they followed scrupulously. These interpretations, designed to regulate every aspect of Jewish life, were considered as binding as the written Law and were passed on to each generation by faithful Law teachers (scribes). Later, in the third century A.D., the oral tradition was collected and codified in the Mishnah which, in turn, provided the foundation for and structure of the Talmud.

The most common ritual cleansing was the washing of one's hands with a handful of water, a formal practice required before eating food (cf. TDNT, s.v. "katharos," 3:418-24). This was especially important after a trip to the marketplace where a Jew would likely come in contact with an "unclean" Gentile or such things as money or utensils.

The comment that the Jews observed many other traditions, some of which Mark named, indicates that the issue under discussion involved the whole detailed question of ritual cleansing. For a loyal Jew, to disregard these regulations was a sin; to follow them was the essence of goodness and service to God.

7:5. The religious leaders directed their critical inquiry to **Jesus** who, as the disciples' Teacher, was held responsible for their conduct (cf. 2:18, 24). The Jewish leaders thought that the disciples' failure to observe ritual washing was a symptom of a deeper problem. Their concern was that the **disciples,** and Jesus, did not **live according to the tradition of the elders** (cf. 7:3).

b. Jesus' response and countercharge to His critics (7:6-13) (Matt. 15:3-9)

In reply Jesus made no reference to His disciples' conduct. Rather He addressed two issues underlying the inquiry: (a) the true source of religious authority—tradition or Scripture (Mark 7:6-13), and (b) the true nature of defilement—ceremonial and moral (vv. 14-23).

7:6-8. Jesus quoted Isaiah 29:13 (almost verbatim from the LXX) and applied Isaiah's description of his contemporaries to His questioners whom He called **hypocrites** (occurring only here in Mark).

They were "hypocrites" because they made an outward profession of worshiping God but gave Him no genuine **worship** from **their hearts,** the hidden centers of their thoughts and decisive choices (cf. Mark 7:21; 12:30). Their

worship (a pious act) of God was **in vain** (*matēn,* "futile") because like the Jews of Isaiah's day they were teaching the **rules of men** as authoritative (divine) teachings.

Consequently Jesus charged them with abandoning **the commands of God,** His Law, and instead adhering **to the traditions of men.** He redefined their oral tradition (cf. 7:3, 5), emphasizing its human origin (cf. vv. 9, 13), and He straightforwardly rejected its authority.

7:9. Jesus restated His charge that the religious leaders were clever at sidestepping God's Law **in order to observe** their **own traditions** (cf. v. 8). He supported this verdict by citing a striking illustration (vv. 10-12) which exposed their sin.

7:10. Moses clearly set forth the divine command (cf. v. 13) regarding a person's duty toward his parents. He stated it positively (Ex. 20:12, LXX, the fifth commandment; cf. Deut. 5:16) and negatively (Ex. 21:17, LXX; cf. Lev. 20:9). Such responsibility included adequate financial support and practical care for their needs in their old age (cf. 1 Tim. 5:4, 8). A person who treated his parents with contempt would face the **death** penalty.

7:11-12. Jesus quoted a scribal tradition that sidestepped the divine command. The words, **But you say,** are emphatic, showing the contrast with Moses' words (v. 10). In their "tradition" it was possible for a person to declare all his possessions to be **Corban** and thereby absolve himself from the fifth commandment.

"Corban" is the Greek (and Eng.) transliteration of a Hebrew term used to refer to **a gift devoted to God.** It was a dedicatory formula pronounced over money and property donated to the temple and its service by an inviolable vow. Such gifts could only be used for religious purposes.

If a son declared that the resources needed to support his aging parents were "Corban" then, according to scribal tradition, he was exempt from this command of God, and his parents were legally excluded from any claim on him. The scribes emphasized that his vow was unalterable (cf. Num. 30) and held priority over his family responsibilities. So they **no longer let him do anything for** his parents.

7:13. By their **tradition** they nullified the **Word of God. Nullify** translates *akyrountes,* from *akyroō,* used in the papyri for annulling contracts. To sanction religious donations at the expense of violating God's command regarding one's duty to parents was to set human tradition above God's Word.

The "Corban" vow was only one example of **many** other **things like** it (e.g., restrictive Sabbath rules; cf. 2:23–3:5) where scribal tradition distorted and obscured the Old Testament.

c. Jesus' explanation of real defilement (7:14-23)
(Matt. 15:10-20)

At this point Jesus gave a more direct reply to the defilement question (cf. Mark 7:5). He addressed the crowd first (vv. 14-15) and gave a general principle applicable to everyone. Then He explained the principle to His disciples privately (vv. 17-23).

7:14-16. Following a solemn call to attentive hearing and careful consideration by **everyone** (cf. 4:3), **Jesus** disclosed to **the crowd** the true source of defilement. Negatively, **Nothing outside a man** (generic, "person") by going into him **can make him "unclean"** (cf. 7:2). Jesus spoke in a moral not a medical sense. A person is *not* defiled morally by what he eats even if his hands are not ceremonially washed.

Positively **What comes out of a man** (person; cf. vv. 21-23) **makes him "unclean."** A person *is* defiled morally by what he thinks in his heart even though he may scrupulously observe outward purity rituals. So Jesus contradicted the Rabbinic view by stating that sin proceeds from within and not from without (cf. Jer. 17:9-10). He also demonstrated the true spiritual intent of the laws regarding clean and unclean food in the Mosaic Law (cf. Lev. 11; Deut. 14). A Jew who ate "unclean" food was defiled not by the food, but by His disobeying God's command.

7:17. After they **left the crowd and entered the house** (probably in Capernaum; cf. 2:1-2; 3:20), **His disciples asked** for an explanation of the **parable** given in 7:15. Their failure to understand Jesus' words and works is emphasized throughout 6:32–8:26 and is traced to their hardness of heart (cf. 6:52; 8:14-21).

7:18-19. Jesus' question, **Are you so dull?** is literally, "So then are you *also* without understanding?" It showed that they, like the crowd, did not comprehend His teaching despite the instruction He already gave them.

Jesus amplified the negative truth that **nothing . . . from the outside** of a person **can** defile **him** morally (cf. v. 15a). The reason is that food (or any other item) does not enter **his heart,** the control center of the human personality, and thereby affect his moral nature. Rather, it enters **his stomach** (a nonmoral agent).

The concluding sentence of verse 19 is an editorial comment by Mark (cf. 2:10, 28; 3:30; 13:14), to emphasize the significance of Jesus' statement for his Christian readers in Rome, some of whom may have been confused over Jewish food laws (cf. Rom. 14:14; Gal. 2:11-17; Col. 2:20-22). He simply pointed out that **Jesus declared all foods "clean"** for Christians. The early church was slow to grasp this truth (cf. Acts 10; 15).

7:20-23. Jesus repeated and amplified the positive truth that **what comes out of a** person **is what** defiles **him** morally (cf. v. 15b). This is confirmed by noting what things come **from within, out of** a person's heart (cf. v. 19).

The general term translated **evil thoughts** precedes the verb in the Greek text and is viewed as the root of various evils which follow. Evil thoughts generated in a heart unite with one's will to produce evil words and actions.

The catalog of evil Jesus gave has a strong Old Testament flavor and consists of 12 items. First, there are six *plural* nouns (in Gr.) depicting wicked acts viewed individually: **sexual immorality** (*porneiai,* "illicit sexual activities of various kinds"); **theft** (*klopai*); **murder** (*phonoi*); **adultery** (*moicheiai,* illicit sexual relations by a married person); **greed** (*pleonexiai,* "covetings"), insatiable cravings for what belongs to another; **malice** (*ponēriai,* "wickednesses"), the many ways evil thoughts express themselves.

Second, there are six singular nouns depicting evil dispositions: **deceit** (*dolos*), cunning maneuvers designed to ensnare someone for one's personal advantage; **lewdness** (*aselgeia;* cf. Rom. 13:13; Gal. 5:19; Eph. 4:19; 2 Peter 2:2, 7), unrestrained and unconcealed immoral behavior; envy (*opthalmos poneros*, lit., "an evil eye," a Heb. expression for stinginess; cf. Prov. 23:6), a begrudging, jealous attitude toward the possessions of others; slander (*blasphemia*), injurious or defaming speech against God or man; arrogance (*hyperephania*, used only here in the NT), boastfully exalting oneself above others who are viewed with scornful contempt; and folly (*aphrosyne*), moral and spiritual insensitivity.

All these evils defile a person, and have their source from inside, from one's heart. So Jesus took the focus of attention away from external rituals and placed it on the need for God to cleanse one's evil heart (cf. Ps. 51).

5. THE CURE OF THE SYROPHOENICIAN WOMAN'S DAUGHTER (7:24-30)
(MATT. 15:21-28)

This is the first of three events Mark recorded from Jesus' third excursion beyond the borders of Galilee (for the three excursions see Mark 4:35; 5:20; 6:32-52; 7:24–8:10). On this journey He actually went out of Palestine, apparently for the only time. These events in Gentile territory are an appropriate sequel to Jesus' teaching in verses 1-23 and a fitting preview of the proclamation of the gospel to the Gentile world (cf. 13:10; 14:9).

7:24. Jesus left that place, probably Capernaum and went to the vicinity of Tyre, a Mediterranean seaport city in Phoenicia (modern Lebanon) about 40 miles northwest of Capernaum. Because of excellent, early Greek manuscript support, the words "and Sidon" (cf. NIV marg.) should be included (cf. v. 31).

Jesus went there not to minister publicly to the people but to secure privacy, previously interrupted (cf. 6:32-34, 53-56), in order to instruct His disciples. That is why He did not want anyone to know He was there. But He could not conceal His presence since news of His healing power had preceded Him (cf. 3:8).

7:25-26. An unnamed woman, whose little daughter was demon-possessed (cf. 1:23; 5:2), came immediately (*euthys*; cf. 1:10) and fell at His feet, an expression of deep respect as well as personal grief over her daughter's condition (cf. 9:17-18, 20-22, 26). She kept asking Jesus to drive the demon out of her daughter.

Mark stressed the woman's non-Jewish identity: she was a Greek, not from Greece, but a Gentile by culture and religion. She was a Syrophoenician born in Phoenicia, part of the province of Syria. Matthew called her a "Canaanite woman" (Matt. 15:22).

7:27. Jesus' reply was appropriate to His purpose for being there (cf. v. 24), and was on a level the Gentile woman could grasp. It was cast in figurative language: the children represented His disciples (cf. 9:35-37); the children's bread represented the benefits of His ministry to them; and the dogs (lit., "little dogs," house pets, not outdoor scavengers) represented the Gentiles (not in a derogatory sense here).

Jesus was telling the woman that His first priority in being there was to instruct His disciples. It is not appropriate to interrupt a family meal to give the dogs food from the table. So it was not appropriate for Him to interrupt His ministry to His disciples to give His services to her, a Gentile. But Jesus' reluctance to help stimulated her faith.

Other interpreters understand a broader theological meaning in Jesus' words: the children (unbelieving Israel) must be fed (Jesus' mission); their bread (special privileges including first claim on Jesus' ministry) must not be thrown to the dogs (Gentiles) because their time for feeding (worldwide proclamation of the gospel) had not yet come. Though this view is true theologically, it overplays Mark's point.

7:28. The woman accepted Jesus' statement with the words, Yes, Lord ("Sir," a title of respect). She realized He had the right to refuse her request. However, feeling no insult in the analogy He used, she pressed it a little further: Even the dogs under the table eat the children's crumbs.

Her point was that the dogs get some food *at the same time* as the children and thus do not have to wait. There need be no interruption in His instructing the disciples for all she humbly requested was a crumb, a small benefit of His grace for her desperate need.

7:29-30. Because of such a reply, which demonstrated her humility and faith, Jesus told her to go home (cf. 2:11; 5:34; 10:52), and assured her that the demon had left her daughter. The words "has left" (perf. tense) indicate the cure was already complete.

When **she** returned **home,** she **found** that **her child** was resting peacefully **and the demon** was **gone.** This is the only miracle recorded in Mark that Jesus performed at a distance without giving any vocal command.

6. THE HEALING OF THE DEAF MAN WITH DEFECTIVE SPEECH (7:31-37)

This miracle is recorded only by Mark. It concludes a narrative cycle, 6:32-7:37, with the people's confession about Jesus (7:37). This event prefigured the opening of the disciples' "ears" (cf. 8:18, 27-30). A second narrative cycle begins in 8:1 and climaxes in the disciples' confession (8:27-30).

7:31-32. Jesus left . . . Tyre (cf. v. 24) **and went** north 20 miles **through Sidon,** a coastal city, and then turned southeastward, avoiding Galilee, to a place on the eastern side of **the Sea of Galilee** within **the region of the Decapolis** (cf. 5:20).

Some people there **begged** Jesus **to place His hand** (cf. 5:23) **on a man** who **was deaf and could hardly talk** (*mogilalon,* "speaking with difficulty"). This rare word occurs only here and in the Septuagint of Isaiah 35:6, a passage promising the coming of God's rule on earth. This promised intervention was already taking place in Jesus' ministry (cf. Mark 7:37; 1:15).

7:33-35. In healing this man, Jesus used sign language and symbolic acts (which Mark did not explain) that uniquely suited the man's needs and caused him to exercise faith. Jesus **took him aside** privately (cf. 6:32) in order to communicate one-to-one with him apart **from the crowd.** By touching his **ears** and **tongue,** spitting (on the ground) and looking **up to heaven** (to God; cf. 6:41), Jesus conveyed what He was going to do. His **deep sigh** may have reflected compassion for the man but it was likely Jesus' strong emotion as He battled the satanic powers that enslaved the suffering man.

Then Jesus gave the Aramaic command **Ephphatha!** meaning **Be opened!** (lit., "be completely opened") This word could easily be lip-read by a deaf person. This Aramaic word may indicate that the man was not a Gentile.

Immediately (*euthys;* cf. 1:10) **at** Jesus' command **the man's ears were opened, his tongue was loosened, and he** could **speak** clearly. Defective speech usually results from defective hearing, both physically and spiritually.

7:36. The more **Jesus commanded** (lit., "kept commanding") the people to be silent, **the more they kept** proclaiming the news (cf. 1:44-45; 5:20, 43). He wanted to minister in the Decapolis region without being regarded as a popular "Miracle-worker."

7:37. Jesus' miracle left the people **overwhelmed with amazement** (*exeplēssonto;* "struck out, overwhelmed"; cf. 1:22; 6:2; 10:26; 11:18) beyond all measure (*hyperperissōs,* a forceful adverb used only here in the NT).

The crowd's climactic confession is a general statement about their understanding of Jesus, based on previous reports (cf. 3:8; 5:20). The words **the deaf** and **the dumb** are plural in Greek, viewing them as two classes of people. **Even** should be rendered "both." Mark probably intended an allusion to Isaiah 35:3-6 in the crowd's confession.

7. THE FEEDING OF THE 4,000 (8:1-10) (MATT. 15:32-39)

In Mark 8:1-30 Mark presented a series of events that parallels his sequence in 6:32-7:37. Despite the replay of events and teaching, the disciples were still slow to "see and hear" who Jesus really is (cf. 8:18). In both narrative cycles the feeding of a multitude played an important role (cf. 6:52; 8:14-21).

8:1-3. During Jesus' ministry in the Decapolis region (cf. 7:31), **another large crowd gathered** (cf. 6:34), probably both Jews and Gentiles.

After listening to Jesus' teaching **three days,** they had **nothing to eat.** They were weakened by hunger so that **if** Jesus would **send them home hungry, they** would **collapse on the way** as **some** had **come a long distance.**

Jesus had **compassion** on them in their physical need (cf. 6:34) and called the disciples' attention to it (contrast 6:35-36). He took the initiative to feed the multitude who chose to forgo food in order to be nourished by His words.

8:4-5. The disciples' question highlighted their slowness in comprehending the significance of Jesus' presence with them in a new crisis. It also showed their inadequacy to meet the need; yet they indirectly referred the matter back to Jesus (contrast 6:37).

Jesus' question concerning the amount of **bread** available clearly indicated His intentions, and was an invitation for the **disciples** to use the resources they had—**seven** loaves. They also had "a few small fish" (cf. 8:7; Matt. 15:34).

8:6-7. The feeding of this crowd occurred much like the feeding of the 5,000 (cf. 6:39-42). The Greek participles translated **taken** and **given thanks** (*eucharistēsas;* cf. 14:23), and the verb **broke** are in the aorist tense, expressing decisive acts, whereas the verb **gave** is in the imperfect, showing that Jesus "kept on giving" the bread **to His disciples** for distribution (cf. 6:41). He did the same thing with **a few small fish.**

8:8-9a. In abrupt fashion Mark stressed the sufficiency of the miracle (all **ate and were satisfied**), the abundance of the provision (**seven basketfuls of** food **remained**), and the large size of the crowd (**about 4,000 men** besides women and children; cf. Matt. 15:38).

The baskets (*spyridas*) on this occasion differed from those used in feeding the 5,000 (*kophinoi,* Mark 6:43; cf. 8:19-20). They were rope or mat baskets sometimes large enough to carry a man (cf. Acts 9:25). Thus the 7 basketfuls (perhaps a basket for each loaf used) of Mark 8:8 likely held more than the 12 basketfuls of 6:43.

8:9b-10. Dismissing the crowd, Jesus immediately (*euthys;* cf. 1:10) entered a **boat with His disciples** and crossed the Sea of Galilee **to the region of Dalmanutha,** a town (also called Magadan; cf. Matt. 15:39) near Tiberias on the lake's western side (cf. Mark 8:13, 22).

8. THE PHARISEES' DEMAND FOR A SIGN
(8:11-13)
(MATT. 16:1-4)

8:11. The religious authorities (cf. 3:22-30; 7:1-5) **came and began to question** (*syzētein,* "to dispute, debate") Him. They wished **to test** (from *peirazō;* cf. 1:13; 10:2; 12:15) **Him,** to get Him to prove the source of His authority (cf. 3:22-30; 11:30; Deut. 13:2-5; 18:18-22). They were seeking (from *zēteō;* cf. Mark 11:18; 12:12; 14:1, 11, 55) from Him **a sign from heaven,** one with divine

authorization. In the Old Testament a "sign" was not so much a demonstration of power as an evidence that an utterance or action was authentic and trustworthy (cf. TDNT, s.v. *"sēmeion,"* 7:210-6, 234-6). The Pharisees did not demand a spectacular miracle, but that Jesus give unmistakable proof that He and His mission were authorized by God. They believed quite the opposite (cf. 3:22).

8:12. Jesus **sighed deeply** (cf. 7:34) and asked a rhetorical question that reflected His distress at their obstinate unbelief. The words **this generation** denoted the nation of Israel represented by those religious leaders (cf. 8:38; 9:19; 13:30). They continually rejected God's gracious dealings with them (cf. Deut. 32:5-20; Ps. 95:10). **Miraculous** is not in the Greek text.

With a solemn introductory formula (**I tell you the truth;** cf. Mark 3:28) and a Hebrew idiom of strong denial (cf. Ps. 95:11; Heb. 3:11; 4:3, 5), Jesus rejected their demand: **No sign will be given to** "this generation." Matthew cited the only exception, "the sign of Jonah" (Matt. 16:4), that is, Jesus' resurrection (cf. Matt. 12:39-40).

In Mark, there is a distinction between a miracle (*dynamis*) and a sign (*sēmeion*). The former evidences God's presence and power in Jesus. An appeal for a miracle can be a legitimate expression of one's faith (e.g., Mark 5:23; 7:26, 32). But such an appeal is illegitimate if it arises out of unbelief, as was true of the Pharisees.

8:13. Jesus' indignation was evident by His abrupt departure. He **crossed** the Sea of Galilee **to the** northeastern shore once more. This ended His public ministry in Galilee.

9. THE DISCIPLES' FAILURE TO UNDERSTAND
JESUS' WORDS AND DEEDS (8:14-21)
(MATT. 16:5-12)

8:14. Their hasty departure (v. 13) probably accounts for the disciples' failure **to bring bread.** They had no food in the boat **except for one loaf,** a sufficient amount with Jesus on board (cf. 6:35-44).

8:15. With the encounter near Tiberias (vv. 11-13; the site of Herod's palace) still fresh in His mind, **Jesus warned** (lit., "kept giving orders to"; cf. 7:36) **them to be** continually on guard against **the yeast**

of the Pharisees and that of Herod Antipas.

A small amount of yeast can affect a large amount of bread dough when they are mixed. Yeast was a common Jewish metaphor for an invisible, pervasive influence. It often, as here, connoted a corrupting influence. In this context the yeast referred to a gradual increase of unbelief. This lay behind the Pharisees' request for a sign even though their minds were already made up (cf. 8:11-12; 3:6). So it was with Herod (cf. 6:14-16; Luke 13:31-33; 23:8-9). As indicated by Jesus' question (Mark 8:12), this attitude had affected the whole nation of Israel, and He warned His disciples against it. In contrast, He called them to faith and understanding without signs (cf. vv. 17-21).

8:16. The disciples totally ignored Jesus' reference to the Pharisees and Herod. They heard "yeast" and assumed Jesus spoke of their **bread** shortage.

8:17-18. Jesus' rebuke is expressed in five penetrating questions that showed their persistent lack of spiritual understanding (cf. 4:13, 40; 6:52). Since He was **aware of their discussion** (cf. 8:16), His rebuke was not because of their failure to grasp the meaning of His warning (v. 15), but at their failure to **understand** the meaning of His presence with them. Their **hearts** were **hardened** (cf. 6:52). They had **eyes but** failed **to see and ears but** failed **to hear** (cf. Jer. 5:21; Ezek. 12:2). In this sense, they were no better than those "outside" (cf. Mark 4:11-12). They also had short memories.

8:19-20. The questions about the two miraculous feedings (cf. 6:35-44; 8:1-9) indicated that the disciples had failed to comprehend the meaning of what they had seen, and to discern who Jesus really is.

8:21. The climactic question, **Do you still not understand?** was more of an appeal than a rebuke. The emphasis on "understanding" (vv. 17-18, 21) expressed the goal of Jesus' words and works which had not yet been reached.

10. THE HEALING OF THE BLIND MAN AT BETHSAIDA (8:22-26)

This miracle and its structural parallel (7:31-37) are the only miracles recorded in Mark alone. It is the only recorded two-stage miracle which Jesus

performed. Sight was a widely used metaphor for understanding. This miracle depicts the correct but incomplete understanding of the disciples.

8:22. When **Jesus** and the disciples arrived in **Bethsaida** Julias (cf. v. 13; 6:32), **some people brought a blind man and begged** Him **to touch him** with healing (cf. 5:23; 7:32).

8:23-24. Jesus **led** the man **outside the village**, probably to establish a one-to-one relationship with him (cf. 7:33) and to avoid publicity (8:26). In general Jesus' miracles were public events (cf. 1:23-28; 32-34; 3:1-12; 6:53-56; 9:14-27; 10:46-52). But there are three exceptions in Mark (5:35-43; 7:31-37; 8:22-26). The latter two may teach that a true understanding of Jesus comes through a personal relationship with Him apart from the crowd's opinions.

The touch of saliva and Jesus' **hands** (cf. 7:33) conveyed His intentions and stimulated the blind man's faith. At first the healing was only partial: **He looked up** (cf. 8:25) **and** saw **people** (lit., "the men," perhaps the Twelve) moving in a blur **like trees walking around.** Jesus' unusual question, **Do you see anything?** indicated that this was intentional on His part (not a weakness in the man's faith). It was a fitting follow-up to His rebuking the disciples (vv. 17-21). The man was no longer totally blind, but his sight was still poor. How like him were the disciples!

8:25. Then **Jesus put His hands on the man's eyes** again. He looked intently (from *diablepō*; v. 24 has a form of *anablepō*); **his sight was restored, and he** began to see (from *emblepō*) **everything clearly.** Now his sight was perfect. This was the outcome the disciples could anticipate despite difficulties in the process.

8:26. Apparently the man did not live in Bethsaida since **Jesus sent him** home with the admonition, **Don't go into the village** (i.e., "Don't go there first"). This is likely another instance of a command for silence in order to safeguard His planned activity (cf. 1:44-45; 5:43; 7:36).

D. Conclusion: Peter's confession that Jesus is the Christ (8:27-30) (Matt. 16:13-20; Luke 9:18-21)

At the center of his Gospel Mark placed Peter's confession that Jesus is the

Messiah. Up to this point the underlying question had been, "Who is He?" After Peter's declaration on behalf of the Twelve, Mark's narrative is oriented toward the Cross and the Resurrection. From now on, the underlying double question was, "What kind of Messiah is He, and what does it mean to follow Him?" This crucial passage is the point to which the first half of the book leads and from which the second half proceeds.

8:27. Jesus took **His disciples** about 25 miles north of Bethsaida (cf. v. 22) **to the villages around Caesarea Philippi,** a city located at the source of the Jordan River on the southern slopes of Mount Hermon. It was in the tetrarchy of Herod Philip, who gave it his own name to distinguish it from the Caesarea on the Mediterranean coast.

On the way (*en tē hodō*; cf. 1:2; 9:33-34; 10:17, 32, 52) Jesus **asked** the disciples what **people** were saying about Him. Often Jesus' questions were springboards for new teaching (cf. 8:29; 9:33; 12:24-25).

8:28. Their response was the same as that given in 6:14-16: **John the Baptist . . . Elijah . . . one of the prophets.** All three responses were wrong, indicating that Jesus' identity and mission remained veiled from the people.

8:29. Then more directly and personally Jesus **asked** the disciples, **Who do you say I am?** The emphasis is on **you,** those He had chosen and trained. **Peter,** acting as the Twelve's spokesman (cf. 3:16; 9:5; 10:28; 11:21; 14:29), declared openly, **You are the Christ,** the Messiah, God's Anointed One (cf. 1:1).

Their open confession of Him at this point (cf. John 1:41, 51) was necessary because people in general were failing to discern His true identity, the religious leaders were strongly opposed to Him, and He was about to give the disciples additional revelation about Himself that would have costly implications for them. It was essential that the question of His identity be firmly settled. This affirmation of faith in Jesus was the anchor of their discipleship despite their temporary failures and defections (cf. Mark 14:50, 66-72).

Mark gave Peter's confession in its simplest, most direct form (cf. Matt. 16:16-19) to focus on Jesus' teaching on

the nature of His messiahship (cf. Mark 8:31; 9:30-32; 10:32-34, 45).

8:30. Jesus sternly **warned** (lit., "ordered"; cf. 1:25; 3:12) **them not to tell anyone** He is the Messiah. People had thought up many false ideas about the concept of the "Messiah." The promised Davidic Messiah (cf. 2 Sam. 7:14-16; Isa. 55:3-5; Jer. 23:5) was commonly thought to be a political, nationalistic figure destined to free the Jews from Roman domination (cf. Mark 11:9-10). But Jesus' messianic mission was broader in scope and far different in nature. So He was reluctant to use this title (cf. 12:35-37; 14:61-62), and the disciples were not yet ready to proclaim the true meaning of His messiahship.

Jesus knew He is God's Anointed One (cf. 9:41; 14:62), so He accepted Peter's declaration as correct. However, because of the disciple's misunderstandings (cf. 8:32-33), He commanded silence (cf. 1:44) until He could explain that as Messiah it was necessary for Him to suffer and die in obedience to God's will (cf. 8:31).

VI. Jesus' Journey to Jerusalem (8:31-10:52)

The fourth major section of Mark's Gospel is set in the framework of His journey from Caesarea Philippi in the north, where Jesus was confessed as Messiah, to Jerusalem in the south, where He fulfilled His messianic mission (cf. 8:27; 9:30; 10:1, 17, 32; 11:1; also cf. 14:28; 16:7).

Jesus explained the nature of His messianic vocation and its implications for those who wish to follow Him. There is a balanced tension between His veiledness in suffering and His future revelation in glory. The structure of this section revolves around three Passion predictions: 8:31-9:29; 9:30-10:31; 10:32-52. Each unit includes a prediction (8:31; 9:30-31; 10:32-34); a reaction by the disciples (8:32-33; 9:32; 10:35-41); and one or more lessons in discipleship (8:34-9:29; 9:33-10:31; 10:42-52).

A. The first Passion prediction unit (8:31-9:29)

1. JESUS' FIRST PREDICTION OF HIS DEATH AND RESURRECTION (8:31)
(MATT. 16:21; LUKE 9:22)

8:31. After Peter declared that Jesus

is the Messiah (v. 29), **He . . . began to teach them** what this meant. This marked a turning point to new content in His teaching.

Contrary to popular messianic expectations, Jesus had not come to establish an earthly messianic kingdom *at that time*. Instead He declared **that the Son of Man must suffer many things** (cf. Isa. 53:4, 11), **be rejected by the** Jewish authorities, **be killed, and after three days** ("on the third day"; cf. Matt. 16:21; Luke 9:22) **rise again** (Isa. 52:13; 53:10-12). This introduced to the disciples a new element in God's kingdom program for which they were not prepared (cf. Mark 8:32). "Must" (*dei*, "it is necessary") denotes compulsion. In this context it refers to the compulsion of God's will, the divine plan for Jesus' messianic mission (cf. 1:11). This prediction shows His submission to it (cf. 14:35-36).

Three groups—the **elders** (influential lay leaders), **chief priests** (Sadducees, cf. 12:18, including former high priests), **teachers of the Law** (scribes, mostly Pharisees)—constituted the Sanhedrin, the Jewish supreme court which met in Jerusalem (cf. 11:27; 14:53).

Though Peter identified Him as "the Christ" (8:29), Jesus did not discuss the title or the issue of His identity. Rather, He focused on His mission and used the designation "the Son of Man." This expression has appeared only twice before in Mark (cf. 2:10, 28). Both times Mark used it to show the significance of an event for his Christian readers. From now on it occurs more often but only when Jesus talked about Himself (cf. 8:31, 38; 9:9, 12, 31; 10:33, 45; 13:26; 14:21 [twice], 41, 62).

This title especially suited Jesus' total mission. It was free of political connotations, thus preventing false expectations. Yet it was sufficiently ambiguous (like a parable) to preserve the balance between concealment and disclosure in Jesus' life and mission (cf. 4:11-12). It combined the elements of suffering and glory in a way no other designation could. It served to define His unique role as Messiah.

2. PETER'S REBUKE AND JESUS'
COUNTERREBUKE (8:32-33)
(MATT. 16:22-23)

8:32-33. In contrast with previously

veiled allusions (cf. 2:20), Jesus **spoke plainly,** in unambiguous terms, **about** the need for His death and resurrection.

Peter clearly understood Jesus' words (8:31), but could not reconcile his view of "Messiah" (v. 29b) with the suffering and death Jesus predicted. So Peter **began to rebuke Him** for this defeatist approach.

Peter's reaction, which the other disciples probably shared, was a satanic attempt similar to the wilderness temptation (cf. 1:12-13), to divert Jesus from the Cross. **Jesus . . . rebuked** (cf. 8:32) **Peter** for the benefit of them all. This was not a personal attack. The words, **Out of My sight,** are literally, "Go away behind (after) Me." This is probably not a command to Peter to take his proper place as a disciple (contrast 1:17; 8:34), for Jesus named **Satan** as the source of Peter's thoughts.

Peter was an unwitting spokesman for Satan because he was setting his **mind** (*phroneō* means "to have a mental disposition for"; cf. Col. 3:2) **not on the things of God,** His ways and purposes (cf. Isa. 55:8-9), **but on the things of men,** human values and viewpoints. The way of the Cross was God's will and Jesus refused to abandon it.

3. JESUS' TEACHING ON THE MEANING OF
DISCIPLESHIP (8:34–9:1)
(MATT. 16:24-28; LUKE 9:23-27)

A suffering Messiah had important implications for those who would follow Him. This section contains a series of short sayings concerning personal allegiance to Jesus (cf. Mark 9:43-50; 10:24-31). The main statement (8:34) is followed by four explanatory (*gar*, "for") clauses (vv. 35-38) and a concluding assurance (9:1). This instruction was part of the disciples' preparation for future ministry. It also provided encouragement for Mark's readers who were facing persecution in Rome.

8:34. Jesus summoned **the crowd,** interested onlookers (cf. 4:1, 10-12; 7:14-15), **along with His disciples and** addressed them both. His words, **If anyone** (not just the Twelve) **would come after Me** (cf. 1:17) indicated that Jesus was talking about their following Him as disciples (cf. 1:16-20). He then stated two requirements which, like repent and believe (cf. 1:15), are bound together.

Negatively, one **must deny himself** decisively ("deny" is an aorist imper.) saying no to selfish interests and earthly securities. Self-denial is not to deny one's personality, to die as a martyr, or to deny "things" (as in asceticism). Rather it is the denial of "self," turning away from the idolatry of self-centeredness and every attempt to orient one's life by the dictates of self-interest (cf. TDNT, s.v. *"arneomai,"* 1:469-71). Self-denial, however, is only the negative side of the picture and is not done for its own sake alone.

Positively, one must **take up his cross,** decisively ("take up" is also an aorist imper.) saying yes to God's will and way. Cross-bearing was not an established Jewish metaphor. But the figure was appropriate in Roman-occupied Palestine. It brought to mind the sight of a condemned man who was forced to demonstrate his submission to Rome by carrying part of his cross through the city to his place of execution. Thus "to take up one's cross" was to demonstrate publicly one's submission/obedience to the authority against which he had previously rebelled.

Jesus' submission to God's will is the proper response to God's claims over self's claims. For Him it meant death on the cross. Those who follow Him must take up *their* (not His) cross, whatever comes to them in God's will as a follower of Jesus. This does not mean suffering as He did or being crucified as He was. Nor does it mean stoically bearing life's troubles. Rather, it is obedience to God's will as revealed in His Word, accepting the consequences without reservations for Jesus' sake and the gospel (cf. 8:35). For some this includes physical suffering and even death, as history has demonstrated (cf. 10:38-39).

In Jesus' words, **Follow Me,** "follow" is a present imperative: "(So) let him keep following Me" (cf. 1:17-18; 2:14; 10:21, 52b; cf. "daily" in Luke 9:23). Saying no to self and yes to God is to continue all through one's following Jesus (cf. Rom. 13:14; Phil. 3:7-11).

8:35. Verses 35-38 each begin with the explanatory Greek *gar* (**for,** trans. only once in the NIV). These verses explain Jesus' requirements in verse 34, focusing on entrance into discipleship, leaving one's old allegiance to this life

(the crowd), and pledging allegiance to Jesus as a disciple.

Paradoxically a person **who wants to save** (from *sōzō,* "preserve") **his life** (*psychēn,* "soul, life") **will lose it;** he will not be saved to eternal life. **But** a person who **loses** (lit., "will lose") **his life** (*psychē*) **for** the sake of Jesus and **the gospel** (cf. 1:1) **will save** (from *sōzō,* "preserve") **it;** he will be saved to eternal life (cf. comments on 10:26-27; 13:13).

Jesus made a word play on the terms "lose" and "life" (*psychē*). The *psychē* on one hand is one's natural physical life but it also refers to one's true self, the essential person that transcends the earthly sphere (cf. 8:36; Matt. 10:28; TDNT, s.v. *"psychē,"* 9:642-4). One who decides to maintain a self-centered life in this world by refusing Jesus' requirements (Mark 8:34) will ultimately lose his life to eternal ruin. Conversely a person who will "lose" (give over, "deny himself") his life (even literally, if necessary) in loyalty to Jesus and the gospel (cf. 10:29) by accepting His requirements (8:34) will actually preserve it forever. As a follower of Jesus, he is heir to eternal life forever with God (cf. 10:29-30; Rom. 8:16-17).

8:36-37. Jesus used penetrating rhetorical questions and economic terms to show the supreme value of eternal life and to reinforce the paradox of verse 35.

For (*gar,* confirming v. 35) **what good** (lit., "benefit, profit") **is it for a man** (generic, "person") **to gain the whole world,** all earthly pleasures and possessions, if this were possible, and **yet forfeit** (lit., "suffer the loss of") **his soul** (*psychēn*) not gaining eternal life with God? The expected answer: "It is no good!" (Cf. Ps. 49, esp. vv. 16-20.)

For (*gar,* confirming Mark 8:36) **what can a man** (generic, "person") **give in exchange for his soul** (*psychēs*), for eternal life with God? The answer: Nothing, because having "gained the world" he has in the end irrevocably lost eternal life with God, with nothing to compensate for it.

8:38. Structurally this verse parallels and complements verse 35 by carrying the thought to its ultimate consequence.

For (*gar,* confirming v. 35) a person who **is ashamed of** (denies) Jesus **and His words** (cf. 13:31) **in this adulterous** (spiritually unfaithful) **and sinful genera-**

tion (*genea;* cf. 8:12; Matt. 12:39; Isa. 1:4; Hosea 1:2), **the Son of Man** (cf. comments on Mark 8:31) **will** also **be ashamed of him when** (lit., "whenever") **He comes in His Father's glory** (visibly invested with God's splendor), **with the holy angels** (cf. 13:26-27).

Clearly Jesus (cf. "Me, My") and the Son of Man are the *same* Person (cf. 14:41b-42, 62). The veiled reference to His future role as Judge was appropriate because of the crowd's presence.

To be "ashamed" of Jesus is to reject Him (cf. 8:34-35a) and to retain allegiance to "this generation" because of unbelief and fear of the world's contempt. In return, when Jesus comes in glory as the awesome Judge, He will refuse to claim those as His own (cf. Matt. 7:20-23; Luke 13:22-30), and they will experience shame (cf. Isa. 28:16; 45:20-25; Rom. 9:33; 10:11; 1 Peter 2:6, 8).

9:1. This verse is the positive side of 8:38 (cf. Matt. 10:32-33; Luke 12:8-9) and provides a reassuring conclusion to this section (Mark 8:34–9:1).

The words **And He said to them** (cf. 2:27) introduce an authoritative statement by Jesus. He predicted that **some who** stood there listening to Him would **not** (lit., "by no means," *ou mē*) **taste death before** (lit., "until") **they** saw a powerful display of God's kingdom. The words "taste death" are a Hebrew idiom for experiencing physical death, like a fatal poison that all must take sooner or later (cf. Heb. 2:9).

Several interpretations have been suggested for the meaning of **the kingdom of God come with power:** (a) Jesus' transfiguration, (b) Jesus' resurrection and Ascension, (c) the coming of the Holy Spirit at Pentecost (Acts 2:1-4) and the spread of Christianity by the early church, (d) the destruction of Jerusalem by Rome in A.D. 70, and (e) the second coming of Jesus Christ.

The first of these is the most reasonable view in this context. The specific time reference in the following account of Jesus' transfiguration (Mark 9:2a) indicates that Mark understood a definite connection between Jesus' prediction (v. 1) and this event. Jesus' transfiguration was a striking preview and guarantee of His future coming in glory (cf. 2 Peter 1:16-19).

4. JESUS' TRANSFIGURATION (9:2-13) (MATT. 17:1-13; LUKE 9:28-36)

a. His glory displayed (9:2-8)

This event confirmed Peter's confession (8:29) and fulfilled Jesus' prediction (9:1). It also served as a prelude to Jesus' Passion (14:1–16:8). Despite His impending death (8:31-32), He assured them by this event that His return in glory (8:38b) was certain and that their commitment to Him was well-founded (8:34-37). Future glory would follow present suffering for Him *and* them.

9:2-4. The words, **after six days** link the transfiguration to Jesus' prediction in verse 1. The event occurred on the *seventh* day after the prediction—a day reminiscent of fulfillment and special revelation (cf. Ex. 24:15-16).

Matthew gave the same time sequence but Luke stated that the transfiguration occurred "about eight days" later (Luke 9:28). Luke's general reference reflects an alternate method of measuring time in which part of a day was counted as a whole day (see comments on Luke 9:28).

Jesus selected **Peter, James, and John** (cf. Mark 5:37; 14:33) **and took them up a high mountain where they were all alone** (*kat' idian;* cf. 4:34). The unnamed location was probably a southern ridge of Mount Hermon (ca. 9,200 feet) about 12 miles northeast of Caesarea Philippi (cf. 8:27; 9:30, 33). This is preferable to Mount Tabor in Galilee. The "high mountain" was an appropriate site in view of God's previous self-disclosure to Moses and Elijah on Mount Sinai (Horeb; cf. Ex. 24:12-18; 1 Kings 19:8-18).

Jesus **was transfigured** in the presence of the three disciples (cf. 2 Peter 1:16). "Transfigured" (*metemorphōthē,* cf. Eng. "metamorphosis") means "to be changed into another form," not merely a change in outward appearance (cf. Rom. 12:2; 2 Cor. 3:18). For a brief time Jesus' human body was transformed (glorified) and the disciples saw Him as He will be when He returns visibly in power and glory to establish His kingdom on earth (cf. Acts 15:14-18; 1 Cor. 15:20-28; Rev. 1:14-15; 19:15; 20:4-6). This was dramatically portrayed by the supra-earthly whiteness of **His clothes**—a comment unique to Mark, probably reflecting Peter's eyewitness report.

Two significant Old Testament men, **Elijah and Moses,** appeared miraculously and were conversing **with Jesus** (cf. Luke 9:31). Mark's mentioning Elijah first is likely due to his emphasis on Elijah in this context (cf. Mark 8:28; 9:11-13). Moses, in the role of Israel's deliverer and lawgiver, represented the Law. Elijah, defender of Yahweh worship and the future restorer of all things (Mal. 4:4-5), represented the Prophets. Both were prominent mediators of God's rule to the nation of Israel (cf. Ex. 3:6; 4:16; 7:1; Deut. 18:15-18; 1 Kings 19:13; Acts 7:35). Their presence attested Jesus' role as the Messiah.

9:5-6. Peter's impulsive response, using the Hebrew title **Rabbi** (cf. 11:21; 14:45; also cf. "Teacher" in 4:38; 9:17; 10:35; 13:1), indicates that he did not understand this event. He said **it was good for** them **to be** there, implying that he wished to prolong the glorious experience. His idea that they build **three shelters** (tents of meeting, booths; cf. Lev. 23:33-43), **one** each **for** Jesus, **Moses,** and **Elijah,** confirms this and may imply that he viewed all three as being equal in importance. Thinking the kingdom had come, **Peter** felt it appropriate to build booths for the Feast of Tabernacles (Zech. 14:16). Unwittingly or not, Peter (cf. Mark 8:32) was again resisting the suffering which Jesus had said would precede the glory.

Mark's explanatory (*gar,* "for") comment is set off as a parenthesis. It shows that Peter, as spokesman, responded inappropriately because (*gar*) **they were so frightened** (*ekphoboi,* "terrified," a strong adjective used only here and in Heb. 12:21 where it is trans. "fear"; cf. the verb *phobeomai,* "be afraid," in Mark 4:41; 16:8) by this dazzling display of supernatural glory.

9:7-8. God the Father's response to Peter's suggestion set forth the true meaning of this event. The **cloud** that **enveloped them** (Jesus, Moses, Elijah) signified God's awesome presence (cf. Ex. 16:10; 19:9) and from it came His commanding **voice.** Once again, as at Jesus' baptism, the Father placed His unqualified endorsement on His beloved **Son** (cf. comments on Mark 1:11). Jesus' sonship

sets Him above all other men including Moses and Elijah.

Listen to Him (pres. imper.), actually means, "Be obedient to Him." This reflects the prophecy of Deuteronomy 18:15 (cf. Deut. 18:19, 22 also) and serves to identify Jesus as the new and final Mediator of God's rule in its present and future form (cf. Ps. 2:4-7; 2 Peter 1:16-19). Jesus succeeded Moses and Elijah, who suddenly disappeared leaving no one **except Jesus.** Their work was done and they were superseded. Jesus, not Moses or Elijah, is now God's authorized Ruler and Spokesman.

b. His command to silence (9:9-10)

9:9. On their descent from **the mountain Jesus** told the three disciples to keep silent about **what they had seen** till after His resurrection. Their misunderstanding of His messianic mission (8:29-33) was still evident at the transfiguration (cf. 9:5-6, 10; and comments on 8:30).

This was Jesus' last command to silence recorded by Mark and the only one on which He set a time limit. This implied that a time of proclamation (cf. 13:10; 14:9) would follow this period of silence. Only from the perspective of the Resurrection would they understand the transfiguration and thus be able to proclaim its meaning correctly.

9:10. The three disciples were perplexed by Jesus' command. **They kept** discussing among **themselves . . . what "rising from the dead"** meant. They believed in a future resurrection, but were puzzled by the unexpected announcement of Jesus' death and resurrection.

c. His declaration about Elijah (9:11-13)

9:11. The presence of Elijah at the transfiguration (v. 4), the confirmation of Jesus as Messiah (8:29; 9:7), and His reference to the Resurrection (v. 9) suggested that the end of all things was near. If so, where was **Elijah** who **must come first** to prepare the nation spiritually for the Messiah's coming? (cf. Mal. 3:1-4; 4:5-6) Perhaps the disciples thought Elijah's work of renewal would mean the Messiah would not need to suffer.

9:12-13. In reply, **Jesus** made two things clear. First, He acknowledged on the one hand that **Elijah does come** (lit., "is coming") **first** (before the Messiah) and restores ("is going to restore") all things through spiritual renewal (Mal. 4:5-6). On the other hand this does not remove the necessity for the Son of Man to suffer much and be rejected (cf. Ps. 22; Isa. 53, esp. v. 3).

Second, however (but in Gr. is a strong adversative), Jesus declared that indeed Elijah has come already. In a veiled way Mark recorded how Jesus identified John the Baptist as the one who fulfilled at Jesus' First Advent the role function expected of the end-time Elijah (cf. Mark 1:2-8; Matt. 17:13; Luke 1:17). Jesus gave John his true significance which John did not even recognize about himself (cf. John 1:21; comments on Matt. 11:14).

The expression, They have done to him everything they wished, denotes the ruthless, arbitrary suffering and death John experienced at the hands of Herod Antipas and Herodias (cf. Mark 6:14-29). In like manner Elijah suffered persecution at the hands of Ahab and Jezebel (cf. 1 Kings 19:1-3, 10). What these antagonists did to Elijah and John, people hostile to God would do to Jesus.

John the Baptist fulfilled the Elijah prophecy (Mal. 4:5-6) typically at Christ's First Advent. Yet Malachi's prophecy (Mal. 4:5-6) indicates that Elijah himself will also appear just before Christ's Second Advent (cf. Rev. 11).

5. THE CURE OF A DEMON-POSSESSED BOY (9:14-29)

(MATT. 17:14-21; LUKE 9:37-43)

This episode of desperate human need and the disciples' failure contrasts sharply with the glory of the transfiguration. It shows the reality of living in the world in the absence of Jesus.

The disciples from whom help could be expected (cf. Mark 6:7) were powerless. Mark 9:28-29 provides the key to understanding this incident. In Jesus' absence they must live and work by faith in God, expressed through prayer. The extended account (in contrast with Matt. and Luke) and the vivid details once again suggest the input of Peter's eyewitness report.

9:14-15. When Jesus and the three disciples (cf. v. 2) returned to the other nine disciples, they saw a large crowd gathered around the nine and Law

teachers arguing with them. The subject of the dispute is not stated.

As soon as (euthys; cf. 1:10) the crowd saw Jesus they became greatly amazed (exethambēthēsan, "alarmed"; cf. 14:33; 16:5-6) and ran to greet Him. Their astonishment was not due to some afterglow from the transfiguration (cf. 9:9) but to the unexpected yet opportune presence of Jesus in their midst.

9:16-18. Jesus asked the nine what the argument was about. A man in the crowd, the father of the demon-possessed boy, explained the situation to Jesus. Respectfully addressing Jesus as Teacher (cf. v. 5), the father said he had brought his son to Jesus for healing because the boy was possessed by a spirit (cf. comments on 1:23-24) who deprived him of his power of speech (and hearing; cf. 9:25). Also the demon often convulsed him with violent seizures symptomatic of epilepsy. The demon's attempts to destroy the lad (cf. vv. 18, 21-22, 26) show again the purpose of demon possession (cf. comments on 5:1-5).

The father's appeal to the disciples to exorcise the demon was legitimate because Jesus had given them authority over evil spirits (cf. 6:7).

9:19. Jesus addressed the crowd but especially His disciples with deep emotion (cf. 3:5; 8:12). O unbelieving generation emphasizes the characteristic cause of all spiritual failure—lack of faith in God (cf. 9:23; 10:27). The rhetorical questions further reflect Jesus' continued distress over His disciples' spiritual dullness (cf. 4:40; 6:50-52; 8:17-21). Yet He intended to act with power where they had failed, so He commanded, Bring the boy to Me.

9:20-24. When the demonic spirit saw Jesus, he immediately (euthys; cf. 1:10) threw the lad into a violent seizure, reducing him to utter helplessness (cf. 9:18).

In reply to Jesus' compassionate inquiry, the father said his son had experienced such pathetic and near-fatal convulsions from childhood. The lad's condition was long-standing and critical. The words, If You can do anything, indicate that the disciples' inability to expel the demon (v. 18) had shaken the father's faith in Jesus' ability.

Jesus took up the father's words of doubt, If You can, to show that the point was not His ability to heal the boy but the father's ability to trust in God who can do what is humanly impossible (cf. 10:27). Jesus then challenged the father not to doubt: **Everything is possible for him who believes** (cf. 9:29). Faith sets no limits on God's power and submits itself to His will (cf. 14:35-36; 1 John 5:14-15).

The father's response was immediate (*euthys*). He declared his faith (**I do believe**), but also acknowledged its weakness: **Help me overcome my unbelief!** This brings out an essential element of Christian faith—it is possible only with the help of the One who is its Object.

9:25-27. When Jesus saw that a curious **crowd was** converging on **the scene** (apparently He had withdrawn briefly), **He rebuked** ("ordered"; cf. 1:25) **the evil** (lit., "unclean"; cf. 1:23, 34) **spirit** with two commands: **come out . . . and never enter him again.**

With a final burst of violence on his victim and a scream of rage (cf. 1:26), the demon fled. **The boy lay** limp in utter exhaustion looking **like a corpse so that many** concluded, **He's dead. But Jesus . . . lifted him . . . up.** Mark's parallel wording in the account of the raising of Jairus' daughter (cf. 5:39-42) suggests that breaking from Satan's power is like passing from death to life. To accomplish this in a final, irreversible sense necessitated the death and resurrection of Jesus Himself.

9:28-29. These verses conclude this incident and explain why the disciples failed. **After going indoors** (lit., "into the house"; cf. 7:17; the location is unnamed) **the disciples asked** Jesus **privately** (*kat' idian*; cf. 4:34) **why** they could not expel the demon.

Jesus explained, **This kind**—probably demonic spirits in general rather than a special type of demon—**can come out only** (lit., "is not able to come out by anything except . . .") **by prayer.** The disciples had failed because they had not prayerfully depended on God's power. Apparently they had trusted in past successes (cf. 6:7, 13) and had failed.

Nearly all major ancient Greek manuscripts have "prayer and fasting" at the end of 9:29 (NIV marg.). Perhaps the words were added early by some scribes to the textual tradition to support asceticism. But the words, if original, refer to a practical means of focusing one's atten-

tion more fully on God for a specific purpose, for a limited period of time.

B. The second Passion prediction unit (9:30–10:31)

1. JESUS' SECOND PREDICTION OF HIS DEATH AND RESURRECTION (9:30-31) (MATT. 17:22-23A; LUKE 9:43B-44)

9:30-31. Jesus and His disciples **left that place** (cf. vv. 14, 28, probably near Caesarea Philippi) **and** were passing **through** northeastern **Galilee** (cf. 1:9), heading toward Capernaum (9:33). This was the first leg of their final journey southward to Jerusalem. **Jesus** wanted to keep their presence from becoming known **because** His public ministry in Galilee had ended and now **He** wished to prepare **His disciples** for the future.

His coming death was a constant theme of His **teaching** on this journey. He said that He, **the Son of Man** (cf. 8:31) would **be betrayed** to both Jews and Gentiles. "Betrayed" (*paradidotai*) means "deliver up" or "hand over." It was used both of Judas' betrayal of Jesus (3:19; 14:41; Luke 24:7) and of God's delivering up Jesus to death for the redemption of sinners (Isa. 53:6, 12; Acts 2:23; Rom. 8:32). The latter idea is probably intended here, suggesting that the implied Agent of the passive verb is God, not Judas.

2. THE DISCIPLES' LACK OF UNDERSTANDING (9:32) (MATT. 17:23B; LUKE 9:45)

9:32. The disciples failed to **understand what** Jesus **meant** (cf. v. 10) **and were afraid to** inquire further. Perhaps this was because they remembered Jesus' rebuke of Peter (8:33) or, more likely, because His words had a devastating effect on their hopes for a reigning Messiah.

3. JESUS' LESSONS ON THE MEANING OF DISCIPLESHIP (9:33–10:31)

This section has two geographical settings. First, Jesus taught His disciples in a house in Capernaum, Galilee (9:33-50). Second, Jesus resumed a public as well as a private teaching ministry in Judea and Perea (10:1-31).

a. The essence of true greatness (9:33-37) (Matt. 18:1-5; Luke 9:46-48)

9:33-34. Jesus and His disciples **came to Capernaum** for the last time after

145

an absence of several months (cf. 8:13, 22, 27). **When they were in the house** (cf. 2:1-2; 3:20; 7:17) Jesus candidly **asked them what they were . . . arguing about on the road** (en tē hodō, "on the way"; cf. comments on 1:2). Once again His pointed question opened the way for additional teaching (cf. 8:27, 29).

The disciples were ashamed to admit **they had argued about who was the greatest** among them. Matters of rank were important to the Jews (cf. Luke 14:7-11) so it was natural for the disciples to be concerned about their status in the coming messianic kingdom. Perhaps the privileges given to Peter, James, and John (cf. Mark 5:37; 9:2) fueled the argument. Whatever its cause, it showed that the Twelve did not understand or accept what Jesus' Passion prediction (cf. v. 31) meant for them.

9:35. After **sitting down,** the recognized position of a Jewish teacher (cf. Matt. 5:1; 13:1), **Jesus summoned the Twelve.** He taught them the essence of true greatness: **If anyone wants** (cf. Mark 8:34) **to be first,** to have the highest position among the "great" in God's kingdom, **he must be the very last** (lit., "he shall be last of all," by deliberate, voluntary choice) **and the servant of all.** Here "servant" (diakonos) depicts one who attends to the needs of others freely, not one in a servile position (as a doulos, a slave). Jesus did not condemn the desire to improve one's position in life but He did teach that greatness in His kingdom was not determined by status but by service (cf. 10:43-45).

9:36-37. To illustrate servanthood Jesus set **a little child** from the home (cf. v. 33, perhaps Peter's child) **among the** disciples. To be a "servant of all" included giving attention to a child, the least (cf. "the very last," v. 35) significant person in Jewish as well as Greco-Roman society which idealized the mature adult (cf. TDNT, s.v. "pais," 5:639-52).

Jesus took the child **in His arms** (cf. 10:13-16). To welcome, that is, to serve or show kindness to (cf. 6:11; Luke 9:53) **one of these little children,** who represented the lowliest disciple (cf. Mark 9:42), **in** Jesus' **name** (on His behalf) is equivalent to welcoming Jesus Himself (cf. Matt. 25:40 and comments on Mark 6:7). But to do this was not to **welcome** Jesus only but also the heavenly Father **who sent** Him to

earth (cf. John 3:17; 8:42). This gives dignity to the task of serving others.

b. *The rebuke of a sectarian attitude (9:38-42)*
(Luke 9:49-50)

9:38. Jesus' words (v. 37) prompted **John** (cf. 3:17; 5:37; 9:2), addressing Him as **Teacher** (cf. 4:38; 9:5), to report an attempt by the disciples **to stop** an anonymous exorcist from **driving out demons in** Jesus' **name** (cf. comments on 1:23-28; 5:6-7). They did this **because he was not one of** them; he was a disciple but not one of the Twelve commissioned by Jesus to do this work (cf. 6:7, 12-13). It was not the man's misuse of Jesus' name (as in Acts 19:13-16) that troubled them but rather his *unauthorized* use of the name. Furthermore, he was successful (in contrast with the nine; Mark 9:14-18). This incident revealed the Twelve's narrow exclusivism.

9:39-40. Jesus told them to **stop** hindering this exorcist because **no one** performs **a miracle** (dynamin, a mighty "deed") **in** His **name** and then immediately turns around and publicly speaks evil of Him.

Jesus' acceptance of this man was reinforced by the maxim, **Whoever is not against us is for us** (cf. the reverse of this in Matt. 12:30). "Against us" and "for us" leave no room for neutrality. If one is working for Jesus, in His name (cf. Mark 9:38), he cannot work against Him at the same time.

Though this man did not follow Jesus in exactly the same way as the Twelve, he nevertheless followed Him truly and stood against Satan.

9:41. With a solemn affirmation (**I tell you the truth**; cf. 3:28) Jesus broadened His words (in 9:39-40) to include activity besides exorcism. Even one who performs the smallest act of hospitality in Jesus' name (cf. v. 37), such as giving **a cup of water** to someone **because** he **belongs to Christ will certainly not** (ou mē, emphatic negation) **lose his reward.** He will ultimately be recompensed by participation in God's kingdom (cf. v. 47; 10:29-30; Matt. 25:34-40), not on the basis of merit (a good deed) but because of God's gracious promise to people of faith (cf. Luke 12:31-32). Jesus' use of the title "Christ" instead of "Son of Man" is rare in the Synoptic Gospels.

9:42. This verse concludes the thought in verses 35-41 and sets the stage for verses 43-50. Jesus sternly warned **anyone** who would deliberately turn somebody away from believing in Him. The punishment for such an offense was so severe that **it would be better for him to be drowned** in **the sea** before he could cause **one of these little ones who believe** in Jesus (i.e., lowly disciples, including children, who are immature in faith; cf. vv. 37, 41) **to sin.**

The verb "cause to sin" (*skandalisē*; cf. v. 43) must be understood from a future judgment viewpoint (cf. vv. 43-48). It refers to enticing or provoking a disciple to turn away from Jesus, resulting in serious spiritual damage. The undeveloped faith of the exorcist (v. 38) or anyone else who acts in Jesus' name (v. 41) should be encouraged rather than ruined by harsh criticism or sectarian bias.

The **large millstone** (*mylos onikos*, lit., "donkey millstone") was a heavy, flat stone turned by a donkey when it was grinding grain; this differed from the small hand mill (*mylos*) used by women (Matt. 24:41). Punishment by drowning someone this way was no doubt familiar to Jesus' disciples (cf. Josephus *The Antiquities of the Jews* 14. 15. 10).

c. The snare of sin and the radical demands of discipleship (9:43-50) (Matt. 18:7-9)

9:43-48. These strong words warn disciples about the danger of letting *themselves* be led astray. Jesus reinforced the demands of discipleship (cf. 8:34-38; 10:24-31) in hyperboles (cf. TDNT, s.v. "*melos*," 4:559-61).

If (*ean*, "whenever," indicating a real possibility) the activity of **your hand**, an instrument of inward inclinations (cf. 7:20-23), **causes you to sin** (*skandalisē*, "should entice you to fall away"; cf. 9:42) then **cut it off.** Jesus meant a disciple should take prompt, decisive action against whatever would draw him away from his allegiance to Him. The same is true of the **foot** and the **eye,** for temptations come through various means. Whatever *tempts* a disciple to cling to this world's life must be removed much as a surgeon amputates a gangrenous limb.

It is better to be a disciple and **to enter** eternal **life** (cf. 10:17, 30) in God's future **kingdom** (9:47), and to do so **maimed,** minus earthly possessions that have been renounced, **than to** be an unbeliever. An unbeliever retains his allegiance to this world, refuses eternal **life** with God on His terms, **and** so will be **thrown into hell** (*geennan*; vv. 45, 47).

The Greek word *geenna* ("Gehenna," trans. "hell") is transliterated from two Hebrew words meaning "Valley of Hinnom," a place south of Jerusalem where children were once sacrificed to the pagan god Molech (2 Chron. 28:3; 33:6; Jer. 7:31; 19:5-6; 32:35). Later, during the reforms of Josiah (2 Kings 23:10) the site became Jerusalem's refuse dump where fires burned continually to consume regular deposits of worm-infested garbage. In Jewish thought the imagery of fire and worms vividly portrayed the place of future eternal punishment for the wicked (cf. the apocryphal Judith 16:17 and Ecclesiasticus 7:17). Jesus used the word *geenna* in 11 of its 12 New Testament occurrences (the one exception is James 3:6).

Where the fire never goes out is probably Mark's explanation of Gehenna for his Roman readers. The **worm** (internal torment) and **the** unquenchable **fire** (external torment) (quoted from the LXX of Isa. 66:24) vividly portray the unending, conscious punishment that awaits all who refuse God's salvation. The essence of hell is unending torment and eternal exclusion from His presence.

9:49. This enigmatic statement, unique to Mark, is difficult to interpret. About 15 possible explanations have been suggested.

An explanatory "for" (*gar*, not trans. in the NIV) and the word "fire" link this verse to verses 43-48. **Everyone** may be explained in one of three ways: (1) It could refer to every unbeliever who enters hell. They **will be salted with fire** in the sense that as salt preserves food so they will be preserved throughout an eternity of fiery judgment. (2) "Everyone" could refer to every disciple living in this hostile world. They will be "salted with fire" in the sense that Old Testament sacrifices were seasoned with salt (Lev. 2:13; Ezek. 43:24). Disciples, living sacrifices (cf. Rom. 12:1), will be seasoned with purifying fiery trials (cf. Prov. 27:21;

Isa. 48:10; 1 Peter 1:7; 4:12). The trials will purge out what is contrary to God's will and preserve what is consistent with it. (3) "Everyone" could refer to every person in general. All will be "salted with fire" in a time and manner appropriate to their relationship with Jesus—for nonbelievers, the preserving fire of final judgment; for disciples, the refining fire of present trials and suffering. This last view seems preferable.

9:50. "Salt" links this verse to verse 49. **Salt is good,** useful. Salt as a condiment and a preservative was common in the ancient world. It was a necessity of life in Palestine, so it had commercial value.

The main source of salt in Palestine was from the area southwest of the Dead (Salt) Sea. The coarse, impure salt from the saline deposits of this area was susceptible to deterioration, leaving savorless saltlike crystals as residue. If (*ean,* "whenever"; cf. v. 43) **it loses its saltiness,** its savory quality, it cannot be regained so such salt is worthless. **Have salt in yourselves** (pres. imper.) points to the disciples' need to "have salt" which is good (not worthless) *within* themselves continually. Here "salt" depicts what distinguishes a disciple from a nondisciple (cf. Matt. 5:13; Luke 14:34). A disciple is to maintain his allegiance to Jesus at all costs and to purge out destructive influences (cf. Mark 9:43-48).

The second command, **Be at peace** (pres. imper.) **with each other** is based on the first command and rounds out the discussion provoked by the disciples' strife (vv. 33-34). In essence Jesus said, "Be loyal to Me and then you will be able to maintain peace with one another instead of arguing about status" (cf. Rom. 12:16a; 14:19).

d. The permanence of marriage (10:1-12) (Matt. 19:1-12; Luke 16:18)

10:1. On Jesus' final journey to Jerusalem, He **left that place,** Capernaum in Galilee (cf. 9:33), **and went into . . . Judea** west of the Jordan River **and** then **across the Jordan** into Perea on the east side.

Because of His popularity in these areas (cf. 3:8) He drew **crowds of people** around Him **again** and **as was His custom** (cf. 1:21-22; 2:13; 4:1-2; 6:2, 6b, 34; 11:17;

12:35) **He taught them** again. The second "again," left untranslated in the NIV, was included for emphasis. Thus He resumed His public ministry (cf. 9:30-31).

Though Jesus' later Judean and Perean ministries covered a span of about six months, Mark recorded only some of the closing events which probably occurred in Perea (cf. 10:2-52 with Luke 18:15–19:27).

10:2. A group of **Pharisees** questioned Jesus about **divorce** in order to test (from *peirazō;* cf. 8:11; 12:15b) **Him.** They wanted Him to give a self-incriminating answer that would arouse opposition against Him. Perhaps He would contradict Deuteronomy 24:1-4 (cf. Mark 10:4). All Pharisees agreed that this Old Testament passage permitted divorce, that only the husband could initiate it, and that divorce implied the right to remarry. But they disagreed on the grounds of divorce. The strict view of Rabbi Shammai allowed divorce only if a wife were guilty of immorality; the lenient view of Rabbi Hillel allowed a husband to divorce his wife for almost any reason (cf. Mishnah *Gittin* 9. 10). Perhaps Jesus would take sides in this dispute and thereby split the ranks of His followers. Or perhaps He would offend Herod Antipas as John the Baptist had done (cf. 6:17-19) and be arrested since He was under Herod's jurisdiction in Perea. Herod had married his half-niece Herodias despite the decrees in Leviticus 18.

10:3-4. Jesus' counterquestion set aside the casuistry of Rabbinic interpretation and directed the Pharisees to the Old Testament (cf. 7:9, 13). The verb **command** indicates **He** asked about Mosaic legislation on the divorce issue.

In response, they summarized Deuteronomy 24:1-4, the basis for their divorce practices. They believed that **Moses permitted a** husband to divorce his wife if he protected her from the charge of adultery by writing out **a certificate of divorce** in the presence of witnesses, signing it, and giving it to her (cf. Mishnah *Gittin* 1. 1-3; 7. 2). In ancient Israel adultery was punishable by death, usually stoning (cf. Lev. 20:10; Deut. 22:22-25), when guilt was clearly established (cf. Num. 5:11-31). By Jesus' time (ca. A.D. 30) the death penalty was dropped (cf. Matt. 1:19-20; TDNT, s.v.

"*moicheuō*," 4:730-5), but Rabbinic law compelled a husband to divorce an adulterous wife (cf. Mishnah *Sotah* 1. 4-5; *Gittin* 4. 7).

10:5. Moses wrote . . . this Law (Deut. 24:1-4), **Jesus** said, **in view of their hardheartedness**, their obstinate refusal to accept God's view of marriage. Moses *acknowledged* the presence of divorce in Israel but did not institute or authorize it.

10:6-8. Jesus then contrasted their view of marriage with God's view **from the beginning of Creation** (Jesus quoted both Gen. 1:27 and 2:24). **God made them,** the first couple, Adam and Eve, distinctly **male and female** yet fully complementary to each other. **A man shall leave** behind **his** parents, shall **be united to his wife, and the two**—man and woman—**will become one flesh.** As "one flesh" they form a new unit comprising a sexually intimate, all-encompassing couple just as indissoluble in God's present Creation order as a blood relationship between parent and child.

So (*hōste*, "so then") **they are no longer two, but one** (lit., "one flesh," a one-flesh unit). Marriage is not a contract of temporary convenience which can be readily broken; it is a covenant of mutual fidelity to a lifelong union made before God (cf. Prov. 2:16-17; Mal. 2:13-16).

10:9. Jesus then added a prohibition. **Therefore,** in light of verses 6-8, **what God has joined together** as one flesh, **let man not separate** (*chōrizetō*, pres. tense; cf. this Gr. verb in 1 Cor. 7:10, 15). "Man" (*anthrōpos*, probably meaning the husband) is to stop disrupting marriage through divorce. Marriage is to be a monogamous, heterosexual, permanent one-flesh relationship. Jesus indirectly confirmed John the Baptist's courageous pronouncement (cf. Mark 6:18), contradicting the Pharisees' lax views.

10:10-12. Later, **when Jesus' disciples** questioned Him privately **about this** subject **in the house** (cf. 7:17), He added, **Anyone who divorces** (*apolysē*, "releases," same word in 15:6, 9, 15) **his wife and marries another woman commits adultery against her,** his first wife (cf. Ex. 20:14, 17). According to Mark 10:12, which is unique to Mark, the same applies to a woman who **divorces her husband and marries another man.** These words were significant for Mark's

Roman readers since under Roman law a wife could initiate divorce. Though not allowed under Jewish law such action was sometimes practiced in Palestine (e.g., Herodias, 6:17-18).

Divorce violates God's Creation ordinance, but does not dissolve it. Jesus left open the possibility of divorce for sexual immorality as demanded by Jewish law in New Testament times (10:4). But remarriage, though permitted under Rabbinic law, was here forbidden by Jesus (cf. TDNT, s.v. "*gameō, gamos,*" 1:648-51; "*moicheuō,*" 4:733-5). (Many interpreters believe that Jesus gave one exception to this. See comments on Matt. 5:32; 19:1-12.) God's desire for a "broken" marriage is forgiveness and reconciliation (cf. Hosea 1–3; 1 Cor. 7:10-11).

e. *The reception of God's kingdom in childlike trust (10:13-16) (Matt. 19:13-15; Luke 18:15-17)*

This episode complemented Jesus' teaching on marriage and offset the Pharisees' opposition (Mark 10:2-12). It probably took place "in the house" (v. 10). The incident came to be used in later church history in connection with infant baptism but without clear warrant from the passage.

10:13. People—mothers, fathers, older children, and others—**were bringing little children** (*paidia,* those ranging from babies to preteens, cf. same word in 5:39; a different word *brephē,* meaning infants and young children, is used in Luke 18:15) **to Jesus** in order that He might **touch them,** a visible means of conveying God's blessing on their future lives (cf. Mark 10:16). **The disciples rebuked them** (cf. 8:30, 32-33) and tried to keep them from going to Jesus. They probably thought children were unimportant (cf. 9:36-37) and should not waste His time—another instance where they thought only in human-cultural categories (cf. 8:32-33; 9:33-37).

10:14. Jesus . . . was indignant (cf. v. 41) at the disciples' interference (cf. 9:38). This verb of strong emotional reaction is unique to Mark who highlighted Jesus' emotions more than the other Gospel writers (cf. 1:25, 41, 43; 3:5; 7:34; 8:12; 9:19). Jesus' sharp double command—**Let** (lit., "start allowing") **the little children come to Me, and do not hinder** (lit., "stop preventing") **them**—was a rebuke to the disciples (who had rebuked the people!). Jesus welcomed the children because **the kingdom of God,** God's present spiritual rule in people's lives (cf. comments on 1:14-15), **belongs** as a possession **to such as these.** All, including children, who come to Jesus in childlike trust and dependence, are given free access to Jesus.

10:15. In a solemn pronouncement (**I tell you the truth**; cf. 3:28) Jesus developed the truth in 10:14. Whoever **will not receive** God's **kingdom** as a gift now with the trustful attitude of a **child will never** (emphatic negative, *ou mē,* "by no means") **enter it.** He will be excluded from its future blessings, specifically eternal life (cf. vv. 17, 23-26). God's kingdom is not gained by human achievement or merit; it must be received as God's gift through simple trust by those who acknowledge their inability to gain it any other way (cf. comments on 1:15).

10:16. Jesus' loving action (cf. 9:36) vividly illustrated that His blessing is freely given to those who receive it trustingly. The intensive compound verb **blessed** (*kateulogei,* imperf., occurring only here in the NT) emphasizes the warmhearted fervor with which Jesus blessed each child who came to Him.

f. The rejection of God's kingdom by trust in riches (10:17-27)
(Matt. 19:16-26; Luke 18:18-27)

This event probably took place as Jesus was leaving the house (cf. Mark 10:10) somewhere in Perea. The rich man illustrated those who fail to acknowledge their own inability to gain eternal life and to receive it as God's gift (cf. vv. 13-16).

10:17. As Jesus was setting out on **His way** (cf. comments on 8:27) to Jerusalem (10:32) **a man,** influential, wealthy, and young (cf. Matt. 19:20, 22; Luke 18:18), came running **to Him.** His eager approach, kneeling posture, sincere form of address (**Good Teacher,** not used by Jews to address a Rabbi), and profound question revealed his earnestness and respect for Jesus as a spiritual Guide.

This man's question indicated that he viewed **eternal life** as something to be achieved by doing good (in contrast with Mark 10:15; cf. Matt. 19:16) and also that he felt insecure about his future destiny. References to **eternal life** (mentioned in

Mark only in 10:17, 30), "entering God's kingdom" (vv. 23-25), and being "saved" (v. 26) all focus on the future possession of life with God, though a person enters it now by accepting God's rule in his earthly life. John's Gospel emphasizes the *present* possession of eternal life.

10:18. Jesus challenged the man's faulty perception of **good** as something measured by human achievement. **No one is good,** absolutely perfect, **except God alone,** the true Source and Standard of goodness. The man needed to see himself in the context of God's perfect character. Jesus' response did not deny His own deity but was a veiled claim to it. The man, unwittingly calling Him "good," needed to perceive Jesus' true identity. (Later, however, he dropped the word "good," v. 20.)

10:19-20. In answering the man's question directly, Jesus quoted five **commandments** from the so-called "second table" of the Decalogue (cf. Ex. 20:12-16; Deut. 5:16-20) but in a different order. Obedience to those commands dealing with human relationships are more easily verified in a person's conduct than are the earlier commands (Ex. 20:3-8). The command, **Do not defraud,** not a part of the Decalogue and occurring only in Mark, may represent the 10th commandment (Ex. 20:17). But more likely, it is an appropriate supplement to the 8th and/or 9th commandments (Ex. 20:15-16) applicable to a wealthy person (cf. Lev. 6:2-5; Mal. 3:5).

The man's reply shows he firmly believed he had **kept** these commandments perfectly (cf. Phil. 3:6) **since he was a boy,** since age 12 when he assumed personal responsibility for keeping the Law as a "son of the Law" (*bar Mitzvah;* cf. Luke 2:42-47). Perhaps he had expected Jesus to prescribe something meritorious that he needed to do to make up for any lack.

10:21-22. With a penetrating look (from *emblepō;* cf. 3:5), **Jesus** saw beneath the rich man's religious devotion to his deepest need **and loved him,** something mentioned only in Mark (cf. comment on 10:14). The one necessary **thing** he lacked was unrivaled allegiance to God, since wealth was his god (v. 22). He was devoted to it rather than God, thereby breaking the first commandment (Ex. 20:3).

Jesus commanded two things: (1) The man was to go, sell all his assets, and give to the poor, thereby removing the obstacle blocking him from eternal life, namely, self-righteous achievement coupled with a love for money. (2) Also Jesus told him to follow (pres. imper.) Him to Jerusalem and the Cross. The way to eternal life was in turning from trust in self-attainments and earthly securities to trust in Jesus (cf. Mark 10:14-15).

The man, saddened by Jesus' directives, went away. This particular *form* of self-denial—to sell all—was appropriate in this situation but is not a requirement for all prospective disciples.

10:23-25. When **Jesus** told the **disciples** that it is **hard . . . for the rich to enter** God's **kingdom,** they **were amazed** (*ethambounto,* "surprised"; cf. 1:27; 10:32) because in Judaism riches were a mark of God's favor and thus an advantage, not a barrier, in relation to God's kingdom. Only here in the Synoptic Gospels did **Jesus** address the Twelve as **children** (cf. John 13:33), reflecting their spiritual immaturity.

In light of their surprise Jesus repeated and clarified His original statement. If the words "for those who trust in riches" (NIV marg.) are omitted, Mark 10:24 (which is unique to Mark) applies to everybody who is confronted with the demands of God's **kingdom.** If included, they explain the rich man's difficulty and expose the danger of trusting in riches.

The humorous comparison (v. 25) employs a memorable Jewish proverb to depict the impossible. **It is easier** by comparison **for a camel,** the largest animal in Palestine at that time, **to go through the eye of a** common sewing **needle** (the smallest opening) **than for a rich man** who trusts in his riches **to enter** God's **kingdom.**

10:26-27. Jesus' statement (v. 25) greatly **amazed** (*exeplēssonto,* "astounded, struck out of their senses, overwhelmed"; cf. 1:22; 6:2; 7:37; 11:18) **the disciples.** They carried it to its logical conclusion: If it is impossible for a rich man to enter God's kingdom, **Who then can be saved?** (delivered to life eternal; cf. 10:17, 30)

Jesus offset their concern by declaring **that** salvation **is impossible** with men—beyond their human merit or achievement—**but not with God.** It is not beyond His power to bring about because

all things necessary for people's salvation—rich and poor alike—**are possible with God** (cf. Job 42:2). What people cannot effect, God can and does by His grace (cf. Eph. 2:8-10).

g. The rewards of discipleship (10:28-31) (Matt. 19:27-30; Luke 18:28-30)

10:28. Acting as spokesman (cf. 8:29) **Peter** presumptuously reminded Jesus that the Twelve, unlike the rich man (**we** is emphatic in Gr., suggesting the contrast), had **left everything to follow** Him (cf. 1:16-20; 2:14; 10:21-22). The implication was, "What recompense shall we get?" (cf. Matt. 19:27) Again this reflected the disciples' tendency to think of material honors in God's kingdom (cf. Mark 9:33-34; 10:35-37; Matt. 19:28-29).

10:29-30. In another solemn affirmation (**I tell you the truth;** cf. v. 15; 3:28) Jesus acknowledged that their allegiance to Him **and the gospel** (cf. 1:1; 8:35) entailed a break with old ties—**home,** loved ones, or property (**fields**), as the case may be (cf. 13:11-13; Luke 9:59-62). But to everyone who makes the break Jesus promised that all these things will be replaced a hundredfold by new ties with fellow disciples (cf. Mark 3:31-35; Acts 2:41-47; 1 Tim. 5:1-2) **in this present Age,** the time period between Jesus' First and Second Advents. Then **in the Age to come,** the future Age following Jesus' return (from a NT viewpoint), each will receive the ultimate recompense—**eternal life** (cf. Mark 10:17).

In verse 30 the word "father" (cf. v. 29) is omitted since God is the Father of the new spiritual family (cf. 11:25). The words **with them** (the rewards), **persecutions** are added realistically by Mark alone. As Jesus said later (10:43-45) discipleship involves service, which often includes suffering. This was relevant to Mark's Roman readers who faced persecution. This fact helped remove the temptation to associate with Jesus simply for the rewards (cf. v. 31).

10:31. This "floating saying" (cf. these same words in other contexts: Matt. 20:16; Luke 13:30) could be intended as (a) a warning against Peter's presumption (Mark 10:28), (b) a confirmation of Jesus' promise (vv. 29-30), or most likely, (c) a summary of Jesus' teaching about the servant nature of discipleship (cf. 9:35;

10:43-45). Rewards in God's kingdom are not based on earthly standards such as rank, priority, or duration of time served, personal merit, or sacrifice (cf. Matt. 20:1-16), but on commitment to Jesus and following Him faithfully.

C. The third Passion prediction unit (10:32-45)

1. JESUS' THIRD PREDICTION OF HIS DEATH AND RESURRECTION (10:32-34) (MATT. 20:17-19; LUKE 18:31-34)

10:32a. **Jesus** and His disciples continued **on their way up** from the Jordan Valley (cf. v. 1) **to Jerusalem,** the first mention of their destination. **Jesus** was **leading** them, in accord with Rabbinic custom. This detail unique to Mark points to Jesus as the One who leads His people both in suffering and in triumph (the same verb is trans. "go[ing] ahead of" in 14:28 and 16:7).

His steadfast determination in the face of impending danger **astonished** (ethambounto, "surprised"; cf. 10:24; 1:27) **the disciples; indeed those who followed were afraid** (ephobounto; cf. 4:40-41; 6:50; 11:18; 16:8). Here Mark probably had one group—the Twelve—in mind. In 10:46, he indicated the presence of another group.

10:32b-34. Once **again** Jesus gathered **the Twelve** (cf. 3:13-15) around Him **and** revealed **what** would soon **happen to Him.** This third prediction is the most precise and comprehensive of the three Mark recorded (cf. comments on 8:31; 9:30-31; also see 9:12). Because He understood the Old Testament (cf. Ps. 22:6-8; Isa. 50:6; 52:13-53:12; Luke 18:31) and was aware of the contemporary religio-political climate (cf. Mark 8:15), He was well capable of making this explicit prediction.

Jesus used eight future-tense verbs, implying certainty, in describing the coming events. The new elements were that **the Son of Man** (cf. comments on 8:31) **will be betrayed** (cf. 9:31) into the hands of the **Jewish** leaders, the Sanhedrin (cf. 8:31). **They** would **condemn Him to death** (cf. 14:64) at the hands of **the Gentiles** (the Romans) since the Sanhedrin lacked the power to exercise capital punishment (cf. 15:1, 9-10). Before executing Him (15:24-25), the Romans would **mock Him** (cf. 15:18, 20), **spit on**

Him (cf. 15:19), and **flog Him** (cf. 15:15)—indications that His death would be by crucifixion (cf. Matt. 20:19). But the promise of resurrection offered hope for the future.

2. THE ESSENTIAL MEANING OF DISCIPLESHIP (10:35-45) (MATT. 20:20-28)

10:35-37. **James and John** (cf. 1:19; 5:37; 9:2) approached Jesus privately, addressing **Him** as **Teacher** (cf. 4:38; 9:5). They asked for the places of highest honor and authority **in His glory,** the messianic kingdom rule which they expected He was about to establish openly (cf. 8:38; 9:1-2; 13:26). One of them wished to **sit at** His **right,** the highest assigned position, **and the other at** His **left,** the next highest place in a royal court (Josephus *The Antiquities of the Jews* 6. 11. 9).

Matthew added that their mother came with them and spoke for them (Matt. 20:20-21). She was Salome, probably a sister of Jesus' mother (cf. Matt. 27:56; Mark 15:40; John 19:25). If so, then James and John were Jesus' first cousins. Perhaps they hoped their family ties would help their cause.

10:38-39. **Jesus** told them they did **not** realize **what** was involved in their ambitious request. To ask for a place of honor in His glory was also a request to share His suffering since the one is a requisite to the other.

Jesus' question called for a negative response because the sufferings and death facing Him were unique to fulfilling His messianic mission. **The cup** was a common Jewish metaphor either for joy (cf. Pss. 23:5; 116:13) or for divine judgment against human sin, as here (cf. Pss. 75:7-8; Isa. 51:17-23; Jer. 25:15-28; 49:12; 51:7; Ezek. 23:31-34; Hab. 2:16; Zech. 12:2). Jesus applied this figure to Himself for He was to bear the wrath of God's judgment against sin in place of sinners (cf. Mark 10:45; 14:36; 15:34). He would **drink** the "cup" voluntarily.

The figure of **baptism** expresses a parallel thought. Being under water was an Old Testament picture of being overwhelmed by calamity (cf. Job 22:11; Ps. 69:2, 15; Isa. 43:2). Here the "calamity" Jesus faced was bearing the burden of God's judgment on sin which involved

New Testament Words for Redemption

Greek Words	English Meanings	References
agorazō (verb)	To buy, to purchase in the market (or slave market)	(1 Cor. 6:20; 7:23; 2 Peter 2:1; Rev. 5:9; 14:3-4)
exagorazō (verb)	To buy out, to purchase out of the market (or slave market)	(Gal. 3:13; 4:5; Eph. 5:16; Col. 4:5)
lytron (noun)	Ransom, price of release	(Matt. 20:28; Mark 10:45)
lytroomai (verb)	To ransom, to free by paying a ransom price	(Luke 24:21; Titus 2:14; 1 Peter 1:18)
lytrōsis (noun)	Act of freeing by paying a ransom price	(Luke 1:68; 2:38; Heb. 9:12)
apolytrōsis (noun)	A buying back, a setting free by paying a ransom price	(Luke 21:28; Rom. 3:24; 8:23; 1 Cor. 1:30; Eph. 1:7, 14; 4:30; Col. 1:14; Heb. 9:15; 11:35)

overwhelming sufferings culminating in His death (cf. Luke 12:50). He was to be baptized by God who placed these sufferings on Him (Isa. 53:4b, 11). James and John may have thought Jesus was describing a messianic battle and their confident reply, We can, showed their willingness to fight in it. But their reply also showed that they had not understood Jesus' words. So Jesus applied the same cup and baptism figures to them but in a different sense. In following Him they would share His sufferings (cf. 1 Peter 4:13) even to death but not in a redemptive sense. His prediction was fulfilled: James was the first apostle to be martyred (cf. Acts 12:2), whereas John, who endured many years of persecution and exile, was the last apostle to die (cf. John 21:20-23; Rev. 1:9).

10:40. Jesus denied their request for positions of honor. Such places were not within His jurisdiction to give. But He assured James and John that God the Father (cf. Matt. 20:23) will assign those positions to those for whom the places of honor have been prepared.

10:41-44. When the other 10 disciples found out about James and John's private attempt to gain preferential status, they became indignant (cf. v. 14) with them. This jealous reaction indicates that they also harbored those selfish ambitions. To avert disharmony among the Twelve and to reemphasize the meaning of true greatness (cf. 9:33-37) Jesus contrasted greatness in this world's kingdoms with that in God's kingdom. The contrast is not between two ways of ruling but between ruling (good or bad) and serving.

Gentile **rulers . . . lord it over them,** dominating and oppressing their subjects, and **exercise authority over them,** exploiting them. But it is not to be this way **with** Jesus' followers who are under God's rule. **Whoever** aspires **to become great among you,** let him **be your** (pl.) house **servant** (diakonos), one who voluntarily renders useful service to others.

153

Whoever aspires to be first (lit., "first among you") let him be a slave (doulos), one who forfeits his own rights in order to serve any and all (cf. comments on 9:35-37). A disciple is to serve others, not his own interests, voluntarily and sacrificially.

10:45. Jesus Himself is the supreme Example of true greatness (in contrast with v. 42). **The Son of Man** (cf. comments on 8:31) voluntarily veiled His glory (cf. 8:38; 13:26) and came as God's Servant (cf. Ps. 49:5-7; Isa. 52:13-53:12; Phil. 2:6-8) **not . . . to be served** by others **but to serve** them (cf. Mark 2:17; 10:46-52; Luke 22:27). The climax of His service was His death **as a ransom for many.** He did this voluntarily, sacrificially, vicariously, and obediently (cf. comments on Mark 15:34).

"Ransom" (lytron) occurs only here and in Matthew 20:28 in the New Testament. As "the price of release" it refers to a payment to effect the release of slaves or captives from bondage. It also includes the concept of substitution (cf. TDNT, s.v. "lyō," 4:328-35). People are captives under the power of sin and death (cf. Rom. 5:12; 6:20) from which they cannot free themselves. Jesus' substitutionary death paid the price that sets people free (cf. Rom. 6:22; Heb. 2:14-15). (See the chart, "New Testament Words for Redemption.")

The preposition "for" (anti), used in Mark only here, reinforces the idea of substitution. It means "instead of, in the place of" (cf. Matt. 2:22; Luke 11:11; 1 Peter 3:9). Jesus gave His life (psychēn) in the place of many (cf. Mark 14:24 where hyper, "for," is used).

"Many" is used in the inclusive sense of "all" (cf. 1:32-34; Isa. 53:10-12). It emphasizes how a large number derive redemptive benefit from the single sacrifice of the One Redeemer (cf. Rom. 5:15, 18-19). Jesus' death as a ransom extended beyond His own people to all peoples (cf. 1 Tim. 2:5-6).

D. Conclusion: The faith of blind Bartimaeus (10:46-52)
(Matt. 20:29-34; Luke 18:35-43)

This is the last healing miracle Mark recorded. It concludes his special section on discipleship (Mark 8:31–10:52) and is an excellent illustration of its meaning (cf.

10:52b). It also signifies that the disciples, despite their misunderstandings (cf. 8:32-33; 9:32; 10:35-41), would have clear sight (i.e., understanding) as Jesus opened their eyes to the full implications of His messiahship.

The vividness of the account (e.g., v. 50) suggests that it was an eyewitness report from one such as Peter. The three Synoptic Gospels record this event with some divergent details. Matthew mentioned two blind men (Matt. 20:30), and Luke placed the incident at Jesus' approach to Jericho instead of His exit (Luke 18:35). Probably two blind men were involved but Mark and Luke focused on one, perhaps the more vocal or well known. Also there were two Jerichos—an old and a new city—and the healings could have occurred as the crowd was leaving old Israelite Jericho (Matt. 20:29; Mark 10:46) and entering new Herodian Jericho (Luke 18:35), though the evidence that old Jericho was inhabited at that time is not certain.

10:46. **Jesus and His disciples** left Perea (cf. v. 1), crossed the Jordan, and **came to Jericho** in Judea. The Jericho of New Testament times, built by Herod the Great as the site for his winter palace, was about 5 miles west of the Jordan River, 1 mile south of the Old Testament city (Josh. 6; 2 Kings 2:4-5, 15-18), and 18 miles northeast of Jerusalem.

As they and **a large crowd,** probably Passover pilgrims en route to Jerusalem (cf. Ps. 42:4; Mark 14:1-2), **were leaving** Jericho, presumably **the** old **city,** they saw **a blind** beggar, **Bartimaeus,** an Aramaic name meaning **the Son of Timaeus.** Only Mark recorded his name, suggesting that perhaps Bartimaeus was known in the early church. He **was sitting** beside **the** road **begging,** a common sight near wealthy Jericho.

10:47-48. When Bartimaeus was informed that **Jesus of Nazareth** (cf. 1:24) was passing by, he clamored for His attention and relentlessly shouted for **Jesus** to **have mercy on** him (cf. Pss. 4:1; 6:2). No doubt he had heard reports that Jesus restored sight. When **many** people kept rebuking (cf. Mark 10:13) **him** to silence him, he cried out **more** intensely. They probably regarded him as a nuisance and may have resented any possible delay. They may also have been opposed to what he was shouting.

Son of David, occurring here for the first time in Mark, designated the Messiah as David's Descendant (2 Sam. 7:8-16) and became a recognized title of the Messiah-King (cf. comments on Mark 12:35-37; also cf. Isa. 11:1-5; Jer. 23:5-6; Ezek. 34:23-24; Matt. 1:1; 9:27; 12:23; 15:22; Rom. 1:3). Bartimaeus' using that title probably indicated that despite his physical blindness he believed Jesus of Nazareth was Israel's Messiah, in contrast with the blind unbelief of most Jews. Later he addressed Jesus more personally ("Rabbi," Mark 10:51) and followed Him (cf. v. 52b). Jesus did not silence him, implying He accepted the title.

10:49-52a. Jesus did not ignore Bartimaeus but directed that he be called, a reproof to those (perhaps including the disciples) who were attempting to silence him (cf. v. 14). In Jesus' determined movement toward Jerusalem He had time to serve someone in need (cf. vv. 43-45). The crowd encouraged the beggar: **Cheer up!** (*tharsei,* "be courageous"; cf. 6:50) **On your feet!** (lit., "rise") **He's calling you.** This motivated Bartimaeus to toss aside his outer **cloak** which was spread before him to collect alms, jump up, **and** come **to Jesus.**

Jesus' question was not designed to get information but to encourage Bartimaeus to articulate his need and express his faith. Bartimaeus' simple response, **Rabbi, I want to see,** declared his confident trust in Jesus' ability. "Rabbi" (*Rhabbouni*) is an emphatic, personal form meaning, "My Lord, my Master" (cf. John 20:16).

Jesus acknowledged his faith: **Go ... your faith has healed** (*sesōken,* "saved") **you.** Faith was the necessary means, not the efficient cause of his healing (cf. comments on Mark 5:34). Bartimaeus' physical "salvation" (i.e., deliverance from darkness [blindness] to light [sight]) was an outward picture of his spiritual "salvation" (cf. Ps. 91:14-16; Luke 3:4-6).

10:52b. Immediately (*euthys,* cf. 1:10; contrast 8:22-26) Bartimaeus **received his sight and** began to follow **Jesus along the road** (*en tē hodō,* "on the way"; cf. comments on 1:2). Though he accompanied Jesus to Jerusalem, perhaps to offer a thanksgiving sacrifice in the temple, he also became a "follower" in the sense of a loyal disciple (cf. 8:34). Bartimaeus pictured discipleship clearly.

He recognized his inability, trusted Jesus as the One to give him God's gracious mercy, and when he could "see" clearly he began to follow Jesus.

VII. Jesus' Ministry in and around Jerusalem (11:1–13:37)

The fifth major section of Mark's Gospel presents Jesus' ministry in and around Jerusalem. He denounced the Jewish religious leaders for rejecting God's messengers, especially the last One, God's Son. Jesus also warned of God's impending judgment on Jerusalem and the nation.

The section revolves around three or four days (11:1-11, Sunday; 11:12-19, Monday; 11:20–13:37, Tuesday and probably Wednesday). Precise temporal links are missing between 11:20 and 13:37, suggesting that Mark arranged this material topically, not in strict chronological order (cf. 2:1–3:6). If so, he intended it to be a select summary of Jesus' teaching, some of which took place on Tuesday and some on Wednesday of His Passion Week (cf. 14:49). The Passion narrative opens with a new chronological starting point (cf. 14:1). The chronological framework for 11:1–16:8 is one week, extending from Palm Sunday to Easter Sunday.

A. Jesus' entry into Jerusalem (11:1-11)
(Matt. 21:1-11; Luke 19:28-44; John 12:12-19)

Mark's account of this event exhibits vivid detail but is somewhat restrained in proclaiming Jesus as the Messiah (cf. comments on Mark 1:43-44; 8:30-31). Only later (probably after Jesus' resurrection) did His disciples fully understand.

11:1a. Less than a mile southeast of **Jerusalem** was the village of **Bethphage** (lit., "house of unripe figs") **and** about two miles out was **Bethany** (lit., "house of dates or figs") on the eastern side of **the Mount of Olives,** a high ridge about two miles long known for its many olive trees. In Bethany, the last stopping place on the desolate and unsafe road from Jerusalem to Jericho (cf. 10:46), was the home of Mary, Martha, and Lazarus (John 11:1), which generally served as Jesus' abode when He was in Judea (cf. Mark 11:11). Bethany was also the home of Simon the Leper (14:3-9).

11:1b-3. Jesus sent two . . . disciples (cf. 14:13) into **the village ahead of** (*katenanti*, "opposite," perhaps across the Mount of Olives from Bethany) them, presumably Bethphage, to find immediately (*euthys;* cf. 1:10) on entry, an unbroken **colt** of a donkey. They were to **untie it and bring it** to Jesus. Matthew included mention of the mother with her colt (see comments on Matt. 21:2).

If anyone challenged them they were to say, **The Lord needs it and will send it back here** (to the village) **shortly** (*euthys,* "without delay"; cf. Mark 1:10). It is generally assumed that Jesus here referred to Himself by the title "Lord" (*kyrios;* cf. 5:19) not to the colt's owner.

11:4-6. Mark recorded the disciples' carrying out Jesus' instructions (cf. vv. 2-3), demonstrating the detailed accuracy of His prediction. This highlighted the **untying** of the **colt,** which **Jesus** may have intended as a messianic sign (cf. Gen. 49:8-12).

Had Jesus made prearranged plans with the colt's owner, or did this event reflect His supernatural knowledge? A later parallel situation (cf. Mark 14:13-16) may support the first view, but the large amount of detail Mark included on securing the colt (11:2-6) convincingly favors the second view. Even so, the colt's owner probably had had previous contact with Jesus.

The amount of detail Mark recorded here implies an eyewitness report; possibly Peter was one of the two disciples sent on this errand (cf. *Introduction*).

11:7-8. The disciples put **their** outer **cloaks** on **the colt** as a makeshift saddle. **Jesus** mounted the previously unridden colt and began His ride into Jerusalem. **Many people** entered into the excitement of the moment and spontaneously paid Him tribute by spreading **their** outer **cloaks** before Him **on** the dusty **road** (cf. 2 Kings 9:12-13). **Others spread** green **branches** (*stibadas,* "leaves or leafy branches") **cut** from surrounding **fields.** Palm branches are mentioned in John 12:13.

11:9-10. The chiastic (*a-b-b'-a'*) arrangement of these verses suggests antiphonal chanting by two groups— **those who went ahead** of Jesus **and those who followed** Him. They chanted Psalm 118:25-26. At the annual Passover festival (cf. Mark 14:1), the Jews chanted the six "ascent" psalms (Pss. 113-118) to express thanksgiving, praise, and petitions to God.

Hosanna, a transliteration of the Greek word which is itself a transliteration of the Hebrew *hôšî 'âh nā',* originally was a prayer addressed to God, meaning "O save us now" (cf. Ps. 118:25a). Later it came to be used as a shout of praise (like "Hallelujah!") and then as an enthusiastic welcome to pilgrims or to a famous Rabbi. **Hosanna in the highest,** in highest places, likely means "Save us, O God, who lives in heaven." Its use here probably reflects a mixture of all these elements due to the nature of the crowd.

The acclamation, **Blessed** (lit., "May . . . be blessed") calls for God's gracious power to attend someone or to effect something. **He who comes in the name of the Lord** (as God's representative and with His authority) originally referred to a pilgrim coming to the festival. Though these words are not a messianic title, this crowd of pilgrims applied them to Jesus, perhaps with messianic overtones (cf. Gen. 49:10; Matt. 3:11) but they stopped short of identifying Jesus as the Messiah.

The coming kingdom (cf. comments on Mark 1:15) in association with **David** reflected the peoples' messianic hope for the restoration of the Davidic kingdom (cf. 2 Sam. 7:16; Amos 9:11-12). But their enthusiasm was for a ruling Messiah and a political kingdom, not realizing and not accepting the fact that the One peaceably riding on the colt was their Messiah (cf. Zech. 9:9), the suffering Messiah whose kingdom stood near because of His presence with them. For most people, then, this moment of jubilation was simply part of the traditional Passover celebration—it did not alarm the Roman authorities or initiate a call for Jesus' arrest by the Jewish rulers.

11:11. After entering **Jerusalem Jesus . . . went to the temple** (*hieron,* "the temple precincts"; cf. vv. 15, 27), not the central sanctuary (*naos;* cf. 14:58; 15:29, 38). **He** carefully surveyed the premises to see if they were being used as God intended. This led to His action the next day (cf. 11:15-17). **Since it was** near sunset when the city gates were closed, Jesus **went out to Bethany** (cf. v. 1a) **with the Twelve** for the night.

B. Jesus' prophetic signs of God's judgment on Israel (11:12-26)

This section has a "sandwich" structure (cf. 3:20-35; 5:21-43; 6:7-31). The account of Jesus' judgment on the fig tree (11:12-14, 20-26) is divided by the account of His cleansing the temple precincts (vv. 15-19). This structure suggests that each episode helps explain the other. Like the fig tree, Israel flourished with the "leaves" of ritual religion but lacked the "fruit" of righteousness God demanded. Both episodes signify God's impending judgment on Israel for religious hypocrisy (cf. comments on 7:6). Matthew telescoped the incidents into two separate, successive accounts without the precise time intervals Mark noted (Matt. 21:12-17, 18-22).

1. JESUS' JUDGMENT ON THE UNPRODUCTIVE FIG TREE (11:12-14) (MATT. 21:18-19)

11:12-13. Next day, early Monday morning, after **leaving Bethany** for Jerusalem (cf. v. 1a) **Jesus was** (lit., "became") **hungry.** From a **distance** Jesus saw **a** wayside **fig tree in leaf,** with full green foliage, and **went to** see **if it had any fruit.** But it had **nothing but leaves.** Mark explained that **it was not the season for figs.**

The time of year was Passover (cf. 14:1), the middle of the month of Nisan (April). In Palestine fig trees produced crops of small edible buds in March followed by the appearance of large green leaves in early April. This early green "fruit" (buds) was common food for local peasants. (An absence of these buds despite the tree's green foliage promising their presence indicated it would bear no fruit that year.) Eventually these buds dropped off when the normal crop of figs formed and ripened in late May and June, the fig season. Thus it was reasonable for Jesus shortly before Passover (mid-April) to expect to find something edible on that fig tree even though it was not the season for figs.

11:14. Jesus' strong denunciation of the tree, which Peter later regarded as a curse (v. 21), was a dramatic prophetic sign of God's impending judgment on Israel, not an angry reaction because Jesus was hungry and found no food. The

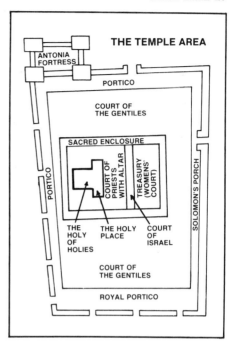

THE TEMPLE AREA

ANTONIA FORTRESS

PORTICO

COURT OF THE GENTILES

SACRED ENCLOSURE

PORTICO

COURT OF PRIESTS WITH ALTAR

TREASURY (WOMENS COURT)

SOLOMON'S PORCH

THE HOLY OF HOLIES

THE HOLY PLACE

COURT OF ISRAEL

COURT OF THE GENTILES

ROYAL PORTICO

promising but unproductive fig tree symbolized Israel's spiritual barrenness despite divine favor and the impressive outward appearance of their religion (cf. Jer. 8:13; Hosea 9:10, 16; Micah 7:1). This is aptly illustrated in Mark 11:27-12:40.

2. JESUS' JUDGMENT ON THE MISUSE OF THE TEMPLE (11:15-19) (MATT. 21:12-17; LUKE 19:45-46)

This event is recorded in all three Synoptic Gospels. John recorded an earlier cleansing of the temple at the beginning of Jesus' public ministry (cf. comments on John 2:13-22).

11:15-16. When **Jesus** arrived in **Jerusalem,** He went into **the temple area** (hieron; cf. v. 11), the large outer court of the Gentiles surrounding the inner sacred courts of the temple itself. (See the sketch of the temple.) No Gentile was allowed beyond this outer court. In it the high priest Caiaphas had authorized a market (probably a recent economic innovation) for the sale of ritually pure items necessary for temple sacrifice: wine, oil, salt, approved sacrificial animals and birds.

Money from three sources circulated in Palestine in New Testament times: imperial money (Roman), provincial money (Greek), and local money (Jewish). Money changers provided the required

Tyrian (Jewish) coinage for the annual half-shekel temple tax (Ex. 30:12-16) required of all male Jews 20 years of age and up. This was in exchange for their Greek and Roman currency, which featured human portraits considered idolatrous. Though a small surcharge was permitted in these transactions, dealings were not free from extortion and fraud. In addition (according to Mark 11:16) people loaded with **merchandise** were taking shortcuts **through** this area, making it a thoroughfare from one part of the city to another.

Jesus was outraged by this blatant disregard for the temple area specifically set apart for Gentile use. So He **overturned the** money changers' **tables** and the dove-sellers' **benches, and would not allow** people to use the area as a thoroughfare. Other certified markets were available elsewhere in the city.

11:17. Jesus' daring action captured peoples' attention and **He taught** (lit., "began teaching") **them** about God's purpose for the temple. Using a question expecting a positive answer, He appealed to Old Testament authority for His action (quoting Isa. 56:7b verbatim from the LXX).

Only Mark extended the quotation from Isaiah to include the words **for all nations.** God desired that both Gentiles and Jews use the temple as a place of worship (cf. John 12:20). This was especially relevant to Mark's readers in Rome.

By contrast **you** (emphatic), the insensitive Jews, **have made it, the** court of the Gentiles, **a den of robbers.** It was a refuge for fraudulent traders (cf. Jer. 7:11) instead of **a house of prayer** (cf. 1 Kings 8:28-30; Isa. 60:7) for both Jews and Gentiles.

By this action Jesus as the Messiah claimed greater authority over the temple than that of the high priest (cf. Hosea 9:15; Mal. 3:1-5).

11:18-19. When the religious leaders (cf. comments on 8:31; 11:27; 14:1, 43, 53) **heard** about **this,** they **began** seeking (cf. 12:12; 14:1, 11) the best **way to kill Him** without creating a major uprising. Mark alone explained (*gar,* **for**) that **they** were afraid of **Him because** of His authoritative appeal to the crowds. **The whole crowd** of Passover pilgrims from all parts

of the ancient world **was amazed** (*exeplēsseto,* "astounded, struck out of their senses, overwhelmed"; cf. 1:22; 6:2; 7:37; 10:26) **at** the content of **His teaching** (cf. 1:27). His popularity with the people kept the Jewish authorities from arresting Him immediately. That **evening** (Monday) **they,** Jesus and the Twelve, left Jerusalem and presumably went to Bethany (cf. 11:11).

3. THE WITHERED FIG TREE AND A LESSON ON FAITH AND PRAYER (11:20-26) (MATT. 21:20-22)

11:20-21. These verses form the sequel to verses 12-14. Next **morning,** Tuesday, **as** Jesus and His disciples were returning to Jerusalem, **they saw the** same **fig tree** (v. 13) but it was **withered from the roots,** completely dried up, fulfilling Jesus' words (v. 14).

Addressing **Jesus** as **Rabbi** (cf. 9:5), **Peter** spoke of the tree's condition with great surprise probably because the tree's total destruction was much more severe than Jesus' words the previous day (11:14) indicated. Though Jesus did not explain the meaning of the event, many believe that it was a vivid picture of God's impending judgment on Israel (cf. comments on vv. 12-14).

11:22-24. Jesus exhorted the disciples, **Have faith in God.** Faith that rests in God is unwavering trust in His omnipotent power and unfailing goodness (cf. 5:34).

Following a solemn introduction (**I tell you the truth;** cf. 3:28), Jesus said in a hyperbole that whoever **says to this mountain,** the Mount of Olives representing an immovable obstacle, **Go, throw yourself** (lit., "be uprooted" and "be thrown") **into the sea** (the Dead Sea, visible from the Mount of Olives), **it will be done for him** by God. The one condition is, negatively, absence of **doubt** and positively, belief, unwavering trust in God, that the petition will be granted. Such faith contrasted with Israel's lack of faith.

Therefore, because believing **prayer** taps God's power to accomplish the humanly impossible (cf. 10:27), Jesus exhorted His disciples to **believe that** they **have** already **received** whatever they request **in** prayer. Faith accepts it as good as done even though the actual answer is still future.

Jesus made this promise on the recognized premise that petitions must be in harmony with God's will (cf. 14:36; Matt. 6:9-10; John 14:13-14; 15:7; 16:23-24; 1 John 5:14-15). This enables faith to receive the answers God gives. God is always ready to respond to obedient believers' prayers, and they can petition Him knowing that no situation or difficulty is impossible for Him.

11:25-26. A forgiving attitude toward others as well as faith in God is also essential for effective prayer. When a believer stands to pray, a common prayer posture among Jews (cf. 1 Sam. 1:26; Luke 18:11, 13), and if he has **anything against anyone**, a grudge against an offending believer or nonbeliever, he is to **forgive** that one of the offense.

This is to be done in order that his **Father in heaven** (the only Marcan occurrence of this phrase, but frequent in Matt.) **may** "also" (*kai* in Gr.) **forgive** him his **sins** (lit., *paraptōmata*, "trespasses," only occurrence in Mark), acts that sidestep or deviate from God's truth.

Divine forgiveness toward a believer and a believer's forgiveness toward others are inseparably linked because a bond has been established between the divine Forgiver and the forgiven believer (cf. Matt. 18:21-35). One who has accepted God's forgiveness is expected to forgive others just as God has forgiven him (Eph. 4:32). If he does not, he forfeits God's forgiveness in his daily life.

C. Jesus' controversy with the Jewish religious leaders in the temple courts (11:27–12:44)

Mark likely packaged the five episodes in 11:27–12:37 around the theme of conflict between Jesus and various influential religious groups (similarly, cf. 2:1–3:5). A contrast between self-righteous religion and wholehearted devotion to God concludes the section (12:38-44). The temple area was the focal point of Jesus' ministry during His final week (cf. 11:11, 15-17, 27; 12:35, 41; 13:1-3; 14:49). The controversies serve as a summary of Jesus' teaching during Tuesday and Wednesday of that week. They depict the religious leaders' growing hostility toward Him.

1. THE QUESTION CONCERNING JESUS' AUTHORITY (11:27–12:12)

Jesus' credentials were questioned by representatives of the Sanhedrin. His response placed them in an embarrassing dilemma (11:27-33) and His Vineyard Parable exposed their rejection of God's messengers (12:1-12).

a. Jesus' counterquestion about John's baptism (11:27-33)

11:27-28. On Tuesday morning (cf. v. 20) Jesus and His disciples entered **Jerusalem** again (cf. vv. 11-12, 15). In the temple courts (*heirō;* cf. vv. 11, 15) **Jesus** was confronted by representatives of the Sanhedrin (cf. comments on 8:31; 14:43; 53; 15:1). As guardians of Israel's religious life they asked two questions: (1) **What** was the nature of His **authority** (cf. 1:22, 27); what were His credentials? (2) **Who** was the source of His **authority?** Who authorized Him **to do this?** "This" (lit., **these things**) refers to His purging the temple the previous day (cf. 11:15-17) and probably more generally to all His authoritative words and deeds which drew much popular acclaim (cf. v. 18; 12:12, 37). Their questions indicate that Jesus had not openly stated that He is the Messiah, a significant point in view of Mark's "secrecy motif" (cf. comments on 1:43-45; 12:1, 12).

11:29-30. Jesus' counterquestions, a common Rabbinic debating technique (cf. 10:2-3), made His answer to them depend on their answer to Him. It focused the issue: Was **John's baptism** and his whole ministry (cf. 1:4-8; 6:14-16, 20) **from heaven** (of divine origin; cf. 8:11), **or from men?** (of human origin) Jesus implied that His own authority came from the same source as John's which indicates there was no rivalry between them. The leaders' conclusion about John would reveal their conclusion about Him.

11:31-32. Jesus' question placed these religious leaders in a dilemma. If they answered, **From heaven,** they would incriminate themselves for not believing John and supporting his ministry (cf. John 1:19-27). They would stand self-condemned for rejecting God's messenger. They would also be forced to acknowledge that Jesus' authority came from God (cf. Mark 9:37b). This answer, though true, was unacceptable because of their unbelief.

But if they answered, From men (lit., "But shall we say, 'From men'?"), the implications were obvious: they would deny that John was commissioned by God and discredit themselves before the people. Mark explained, **They feared the people** (cf. 12:12) because **everyone** regarded **John** as a genuine **prophet,** God's spokesman (cf. Josephus *The Antiquities of the Jews* 18. 5. 2). The people viewed Jesus this way too (cf. Matt. 21:46). This latter answer, though false, was the one they preferred but found unacceptable because of the people.

11:33. Since neither option was acceptable they pleaded ignorance in an attempt to save face. So **Jesus was not obligated** to answer their question. His question (cf. v. 30) implied that His **authority,** like John's, was from God.

By suspending judgment, these religious leaders showed that they really rejected John and Jesus as God's messengers. Throughout their history most leaders of Israel repeatedly rejected God's messengers, a point Jesus made in the following parable (12:1-12).

b. Jesus' Parable of the Vineyard Owner's Son (12:1-12)
(Matt. 21:33-46; Luke 20:9-19)

This parable reflects the social situation of first-century Palestine, especially Galilee. Wealthy foreign landlords owned large land estates which they leased to tenant farmers. The tenants agreed to cultivate the land and care for the vineyards when the landlords were away. A contract between them designated that a portion of the crop was to be paid as rent. At harvesttime the owners sent agents to collect the rent. Inevitably tension arose between the absentee owners and the tenants.

12:1a. This brief summary statement (cf. introduction to 2:1-2) introduces the single parable (cf. introduction to 4:1-2) Mark recorded here. Jesus addressed it **to them,** the Sanhedrin interrogators who were plotting against Him (cf. 11:27; 12:12). It exposed their hostile intentions and warned them of the consequences.

12:1b. The details of the vineyard's construction are derived from Isaiah 5:1-2 (part of a prophecy of God's judgment on

Israel), as the vineyard is a familiar symbol for the nation of Israel (cf. Ps. 80:8-19).

A man, a landlord (cf. Mark 12:9), **planted a vineyard,** analogous to God's relationship to Israel. The **wall** for protection, **a pit** beneath **the winepress** to gather the juice of the pressed grapes, and **a watchtower** for shelter, storage, and security, show the owner's desire to make this a choice vineyard. **Then he** leased it **to** tenant **farmers,** vinegrowers, representing Israel's religious leaders, **and went away on a journey** probably to live abroad. He was an absentee owner.

12:2-5. The owner sent three servants—agents representing God's servants (the prophets) to Israel—**to the** tenant farmers to receive a share **of the fruit** as rent **at harvesttime** (lit., "at the right time," i.e., the vintage season of the fifth year; cf. Lev. 19:23-25). **But the** tenant farmers behaved violently. **They seized the first servant . . . beat him, and sent him away empty-handed. They** seriously wounded the second **servant** and insulted him. **They killed** the third **servant.**

The long-suffering owner also **sent many others, some of** whom were beaten **and others . . . killed.** Time and again God had sent prophets to Israel to gather fruits of repentance and righteousness (cf. Luke 3:8) but His prophets were abused, wounded, and killed (cf. Jer. 7:25-26; 25:4-7; Matt. 23:33-39).

12:6-8. The owner still **had one** messenger **to send, a son, whom he loved** (lit., "a beloved son"—a designation representing God's Son, Jesus; cf. 1:11; 9:7). **Last of all,** a phrase unique to Mark, **he sent** his **son,** expecting the tenant farmers to give *him* the honor denied his servants.

The son's arrival may have caused **the tenants** to assume that the owner had died and **this** son was his only **heir.** In Palestine at the time, a piece of land could be possessed lawfully by whoever claimed it first if it was "ownerless property," unclaimed by an heir within a certain time period (cf. Mishnah *Baba Bathra* 3. 3). The tenant farmers assumed that if they killed the son they could acquire the vineyard.

So they conspired together **and killed him and threw him out of the vineyard.** Some say this predicts what would happen to Jesus: He would be crucified outside of Jerusalem, expelled from Israel in a climactic expression of the leaders' rejection of Him. But this presses the parable's details too far here. It is better to see the throwing of the son's dead body over the wall without burial as a climax to their wicked indignities. Mark's emphasis of their rejection and murder of the son took place *within* the vineyard, that is, within Israel.

12:9. Jesus' rhetorical question invited His audience to share in deciding what action **the owner** should take. He affirmed his listeners' answer (cf. Matt. 21:41) by alluding to Isaiah 5:1-7 again. This was a strong appeal for those plotting His death to consider the serious consequences of their actions. He saw Himself as the "only Son" sent by God (John 3:16).

The rejection of the owner's son was really a rejection of the owner who would **come** with governmental authority **and kill the murderous tenants and give the vineyard to others.** Likewise the Jewish leaders' rejection of John the Baptist and of Jesus, God's final Messenger, was a rejection of God Himself. This would inevitably bring His judgment on Israel and would transfer their privileges to others temporarily (cf. Rom. 11:25, 31).

12:10-11. Jesus sharpened the application of the parable to Himself as the Son and extended its teaching by quoting verbatim Psalm 118:22-23 (Ps. 117 in the LXX), a familiar text recognized as messianic elsewhere (Acts 4:11; 1 Peter 2:4-8). The figure changed from the son/tenants of the parable to the stone/builders of the psalm, making possible a parabolic allusion to Jesus' resurrection and exaltation. A slain son cannot be revived but a rejected stone can be retrieved and used.

The quotation begins where the parable ended. **The stone** (Jesus, like the son), which **the builders** (the Jewish religious leaders, like the tenant farmers) **rejected has become the capstone** ("cornerstone," NIV marg.; lit., "head of the corner"). This was considered the most important stone of a building. This dramatic reversal of the builders' decision and exaltation of the rejected stone was God's sovereign doing, a remarkable thing. God overrules in amazing ways

rebellious human attempts to block His purposes.

12:12. They, the Sanhedrin representatives (11:27), were seeking (cf. 11:18) **to arrest Him because they** realized Jesus **had** addressed **the parable against them** ("with reference to" or directed "toward" them). **But** fearing **the** excitable Passover **crowd, they left Him** alone **and** departed.

The fact that Jesus' adversaries understood this parable is a new development (cf. 4:11-12), suggesting that at Jesus' initiative the "secret" of His true identity would soon be openly declared (cf. comments on 1:43-45; 14:62).

2. THE QUESTION CONCERNING THE POLL TAX (12:13-17)
(MATT. 22:15-22; LUKE 20:20-26)

12:13. Despite Jesus' warning to His Sanhedrin adversaries in the preceding parable, **they** continued their campaign against Him by sending some . . . **Pharisees** (cf. 2:16) **and Herodians** (cf. 3:6) **to catch Him in His words** (lit., "by means of a word," i.e., an unguarded statement they could use against Him; cf. 10:2). The word translated "catch" (*argeusōsin,* found only here in the NT) was used to describe catching wild animals with a trap. **Later** (NIV), though implied, is not in the Greek text; no time reference is given.

12:14-15a. Addressing Jesus as **Teacher** (cf. 4:38; 9:5), they used carefully chosen remarks designed to hide their true motives and to prevent Jesus from evading their difficult question. They acknowledged He was honest and impartial, courting no one's favor, **because** He paid **no attention to who they are** (lit., "You do not look at the face of men," a Heb. expression; cf. 1 Sam. 16:7). Then they asked, **Is it right,** legally permitted by God's Law (cf. Deut. 17:14-15), **to pay taxes to Caesar,** the Roman emperor, **or not? Should we pay** (*dōmen,* "Shall we give") **or shouldn't we?**

"Taxes" (*kēnson*) was a Latin loanword meaning "census." It referred to the annual poll tax (head tax) demanded by the Roman emperor from all Jews since A.D. 6, when Judea became a Roman province (Josephus *The Antiquities of the Jews* 5. 1. 21). The money went directly into the emperor's treasury. This tax was unpopular because it typified the Jews' subjugation to Rome (cf. Acts 5:37).

The Pharisees objected to the tax, but expediently justified its payment. They were concerned about the *religious* implications of their question. The Herodians supported foreign rule through the Herods and favored the tax. They were concerned about the *political* implications of their question. Obviously the question was designed to place Jesus in a religious and political dilemma. A yes answer would antagonize the people and discredit Him as God's Spokesman. No messianic claimant could sanction willing submission to pagan rulers. A no answer would invite retaliation from Rome.

12:15b-16. Jesus immediately detected **their hypocrisy,** the malicious intent beneath their pretense of an honest inquiry. He exposed it with a rhetorical question about **why** they were **trying to trap** (*peirazete,* "test"; cf. 10:2) Him. Then **He asked** them to **bring** Him **a denarius** (cf. 6:37) so He might **look at it,** to use it as a visual aid. **The** common Roman denarius, a small silver **coin,** was the only coin acceptable for imperial tax payments.

When Jesus **asked them** to tell Him **whose portrait** and **inscription** were on it, they replied, **Caesar's.** The portrait (*eikōn,* "image") was probably that of Tiberius Caesar (reigned A.D. 14–37; see the list of Roman emperors at Luke 3:1) and the inscription read in Latin: "Tiberius Caesar Augustus, Son of the Divine Augustus" and on the reverse side: "Chief Priest." This inscription originated in the imperial cult of emperor worship and was a claim to divinity, which was particularly repulsive to Jews.

12:17. But to use Caesar's coinage was to acknowledge his authority and the benefits of the civil government it represented and consequently the obligation to pay taxes. So **Jesus** declared, **Give** (*apodote,* "give back"; cf. v. 14) **to Caesar what is Caesar's** (lit., "the things belonging to Caesar"). This tax was a debt they owed to Caesar for use of his money and the other benefits of his rule.

Jesus had made His point but significantly He added, **and** give back **to God what is God's** (lit., "the things belonging to God"). This could refer to "paying" God the temple tax due Him (cf. Matt. 17:24-27), but Jesus probably meant it as a protest against the emperor's claim to deity. Indeed the emperor must receive

his due, but not more than that; he must not receive the divine honor and worship he claimed. Those are due only to God. People are "God's coinage" because they bear His image (cf. Gen. 1:27) and they owe Him what belongs to Him, their allegiance. This, not the poll tax, was the crucial issue to Jesus. His questioners continued to be greatly **amazed** (*exethaumazon,* imperf. tense of a strong compound verb found only here in the NT) **at Him.** This incident was especially relevant to Mark's Roman readers for it indicated that Christianity did not foster disloyalty to the state.

3. THE QUESTION CONCERNING THE RESURRECTION (12:18-27) .
(MATT. 22:23-33; LUKE 20:27-40)

12:18. The Sadducees . . . came to Jesus **with a question** in another attempt to discredit Him (cf. 11:27; 12:13). It is generally believed that they were the Jewish aristocratic party whose members came largely from the priesthood and the upper classes. Though less numerous and popular than the Pharisees, they occupied influential positions on the Sanhedrin, the Jewish supreme court and generally cooperated with the Roman authorities. They denied the truths of the **resurrection,** future judgment, and the existence of angels and spirits (cf. Acts 23:6-8). They accepted only the Books of Moses (the Pentateuch) as authoritative and rejected the oral traditions observed as binding by the Pharisees. This is Mark's only reference to the Sadducees.

12:19-23. After formally addressing Jesus as **Teacher** (cf. v. 14), they gave a free rendering of the Mosaic regulation concerning levirate (from Latin, *levir,* "husband's brother") marriage (cf. Deut. 25:5-10). If a husband **died** without leaving a male heir his (unmarried) **brother** (or, if none, his nearest male relative) was to **marry** his **widow.** The first son of that union was given the name of the dead **brother** and was considered **his** child. This was to prevent extinction of a family line and thereby kept the family inheritance intact.

The Sadducees made up a story about **seven brothers** who successively fulfilled the duty of levirate marriage to their first brother's wife but all seven **died** childless. Then **the woman died** also. They asked Jesus, **At the resurrection**

whose wife will she be? Clearly they were ridiculing belief in the resurrection.

12:24. Using a two-pronged counterquestion expecting a positive answer in Greek, **Jesus** cited two reasons why they **were in error** (*planasthe,* "you are deceiving yourselves"; cf. v. 27): (a) they did **not know the Scriptures**—their true meaning, not merely their contents; and (b) they did not know **the power of God**—His power to overcome death and give life. Then Jesus amplified each reason starting with the second (v. 25) and then the first (vv. 26-27).

12:25. The Sadducees wrongly assumed that marriages would be resumed after the resurrection. In resurrection-life people **will neither marry** (contract a marriage) **nor be given in marriage** (have a marriage arranged by parents). Rather, **like the angels in heaven** they will be immortal beings in God's presence.

Marriage is necessary and suitable for the present world order, in which death prevails, in order to continue the human race. But angels, whose existence the Sadducees denied (cf. Acts 23:8), are deathless and live in a different order of existence where they have no need for marital relations or reproduction of offspring. Their lives center totally around fellowship with God. So it will be in the afterlife for human beings rightly related to God.

The Sadducees did not grasp that God will establish a whole new order of life after death and resolve all apparent difficulties connected with it. In short, their question was irrelevant.

12:26-27. The Sadducees wrongly alleged that the idea of a resurrection was absent from the Pentateuch. But Jesus, using a question expecting a positive answer, appealed to **the Book of Moses,** the Pentateuch, and spoke of **the** burning **bush** (Ex. 3:1-6).

In this passage God identified Himself to Moses, affirming, **I am the God of Abraham . . . Isaac, and . . . Jacob** (Ex. 3:6). God implied that the patriarchs were still alive and that He had a continuing relationship with them as their covenant-keeping God, even though they had died long before. This demonstrates, Jesus concluded, that **He is not the God of the dead,** in the Sadducean understanding of death as extinction, **but of the living.** He is still the patriarchs' God which would

not be true had they ceased to exist at death, that is, if death ends it all. And His covenant faithfulness implicitly guarantees their bodily resurrection.

Jesus' answer clearly affirmed the fact of life after death. Apparently He assumed that this was enough to prove that the resurrection of the body will occur as well. In Hebrew thought people are regarded as a unity of the material (body) and immaterial (soul/spirit). One is incomplete without the other (cf. 2 Cor. 5:1-8). Thus authentic human existence in the eternal order of life demands the union of soul/spirit with the body (cf. Phil. 3:21). Both bodily resurrection and life after death depend on the faithfulness of "the God of the living."

Jesus' final remark, recorded only by Mark, emphasized how seriously **mistaken** (*planasthe,* "you are deceiving yourselves"; cf. Mark 12:24) they were to deny the resurrection and life after death.

4. THE QUESTION CONCERNING THE GREATEST COMMANDMENT (12:28-34) (MATT. 22:34-40)

12:28. One of the Law **teachers** (cf. 1:22), had **heard** Jesus' discussion with the Sadducees (12:18-27) and was impressed with His **good answer to them.** This suggested he was probably a Pharisee.

He came with no apparent hostile or hidden motive to appraise Jesus' skill in answering a much-debated subject in scribal circles. Traditionally the scribes spoke of 613 individual commandments of the Mosaic Law—365 negative ones and 248 positive ones. While they believed all were binding, they assumed a distinction between weightier and lighter statutes and often attempted to sum up the whole Law in a single unifying command.

In light of this debate, this **Law** teacher **asked** Jesus, **Which** (*poia,* "what kind of") commandment **is the most important** (*prōtē,* "first") of them all?

12:29-31. Jesus' reply went beyond the debated lighter/weightier classifications to a statement of **the most important** command and its inseparable companion, which together summarize the whole Law.

He began with the opening words of the *Shema* (from Heb., "Hear!" [*š^ema'*], the first word of Deut. 6:4). This creed

163

(Num. 15:37-41; Deut. 6:4-9; 11:13-21) was recited twice daily—morning and evening—by devout Jews. It asserted the basis of Jewish faith: **The Lord** (Heb., *Yahweh*), namely, **our God,** Israel's covenant-keeping God, **the Lord is One,** that is, unique (cf. Mark 12:32).

The command, **Love** (lit., "you shall love") **the Lord your God** (Deut. 6:5), calls for a volitional commitment to God that is personal, comprehensive, and wholehearted. This is emphasized by the repeated words **with** (*ex,* "out of," denoting source), **all** (*holēs,* "the whole of"), **your** (sing.), and the various terms relating to the human personality—**heart** (control center; cf. Mark 7:19), **soul** (self-conscious life; cf. 8:35-36), **mind** (thought capacity), and **strength** (bodily powers). The Hebrew text does not mention "mind"; the Septuagint omits "heart"; but Jesus included both terms, stressing the comprehensive nature of the command (cf. 12:33; Matt. 22:37; Luke 10:27).

Jesus then spoke of a similar commitment to one's neighbor by quoting a **second** inseparable (cf. 1 John 4:19-21) and complementary command. **Love** (lit., "you shall love") **your neighbor** (*plēsion,* "one who is nearby," a generic term for fellowman) **as,** in the same way as, **yourself** (Lev. 19:18). The love a person has naturally for himself is not to focus solely on himself—a constant tendency—but should be directed equally toward others.

No (Gr., "no other") **commandment is greater than these** two because whole-hearted love to God and one's neighbor is the sum and substance of the Law and the Prophets (cf. Matt. 22:40). To fulfill these commands is to fulfill all others.

12:32-34a. These verses are unique to Mark. Apparently they instructed his readers who struggled with the relationship between spiritual reality and cere-monial ritual (cf. comments on 7:19).

The scribe (cf. 12:28) recognized the accuracy of Jesus' answer and voiced his approval, viewing Him as an excellent **Teacher** (cf. vv. 14, 19). He restated Jesus' answer, carefully avoiding mention of **God** (not in the Gr. text but supplied in the NIV) in keeping with the typical Jewish practice of avoiding unnecessary use of the divine name out of great respect for it. The words, **There is no other but Him,**

come from Deuteronomy 4:35. He also substituted the word **understanding** for "soul" and "mind" (cf. Mark 12:30).

He made the bold statement that the double command of love **is** much **more important than all burnt offerings** (fully consumed sacrifices) **and sacrifices** (those partly consumed and partly eaten by worshipers; cf. 1 Sam. 15:22; Prov. 21:3; Jer. 7:21-23; Hosea 6:6; Micah 6:6-8).

He had responded **wisely,** and Jesus probably stimulated further thought by declaring, **You are not far** ("not far" is emphatic in Gr.) **from the kingdom of God** (cf. Mark 1:15; 4:11; 10:15, 23). This man had the kind of spiritual understanding (cf. 10:15) and openness to Jesus that brought him near to embracing God's kingdom, His spiritual rule over those related to Him by faith. Whether he entered this relationship is not known.

12:34b. Jesus had effectively thwarted all attempts to discredit Him and had exposed the hostile motives and errors of His opponents so skillfully that nobody else **dared ask Him any more questions.**

5. JESUS' QUESTION CONCERNING MESSIAH'S SONSHIP (12:35-37) (MATT. 22:41-46; LUKE 20:41-44)

12:35. Later while **teaching in the temple courts** (*tō hierō;* cf. 11:11), **Jesus** asked what **the Law teachers** meant when they said **that the Christ,** the expected Messiah, **is** ("simply" is implied) **the Son** (Descendant) **of David,** who would be the triumphant Deliverer (cf. 10:47). The Davidic sonship of the Messiah was a standard Jewish belief (cf. John 7:41-42) firmly based on the Old Testament Scriptures (cf. 2 Sam. 7:8-16; Ps. 89:3-4; Isa. 9:2-7; 11:1-9; Jer. 23:5-6; 30:9; 33:15-17, 22; Ezek. 34:23-24; 37:24; Hosea 3:5; Amos 9:11). Jesus added that it is equally true that the Messiah is David's Lord. The Law teachers' view was correct but incomplete (cf. similarly, Mark 9:11-13). The scriptural view held far more than just their narrow nationalistic hopes.

12:36-37a. To prove that the Messiah is David's Lord, Jesus quoted what **David himself speaking by** (under the controlling influence of) **the Holy Spirit** declared in Psalm 110:1. This clearly argues for both the Davidic authorship and the divine inspiration of this psalm. He said: **The Lord** (Heb., *Yahweh,* God the Father; cf. Mark 12:29) **said to my** (David's) **Lord** (Heb., *'Ăḏōnāy,* the Messiah): **Sit at My** (the Father's) **right hand,** the place of highest honor and authority, **until** (or "while"; cf. 9:1; 14:32) I (the Father) **put Your** (the Messiah's) **enemies under Your** (the Messiah's) **feet,** bringing about their subjugation (cf. Josh. 10:24; Heb. 10:12-14).

The unassailable fact was that **David** called the Messiah **Lord.** This raised a problem: **How then,** or in what sense, **can** (*estin,* "is") **He** (the Messiah, David's Lord) **be his** (David's) **Son?** Jesus' rhetorical question pointed His listeners to the only valid answer: the Messiah is David's Son *and* David's Lord at the same time. This strongly implies that the Messiah is both God (David's Lord) and man (David's Son; cf. Rom. 1:3-4; 2 Tim. 2:8). He will restore the future Davidic kingdom on earth (2 Sam. 7:16; Amos 9:11-12; Matt. 19:28; Luke 1:31-33).

No doubt Jesus deliberately raised this issue so that His listeners might relate it to Him. It carried a bold yet veiled reference to His true identity which the Jewish leaders probably caught but did not accept (cf. comments on Mark 12:12; 14:61-62). (Interestingly the NT has more references and allusions to Ps. 110 than to any other single OT passage [cf., e.g., Acts 2:29-35; Heb. 1:5-13; 5:6; 7:17, 21].)

12:37b. In contrast with the Jewish leaders who had been trying to trap Jesus with subtle questions (cf. v. 13), **the large** Passover **crowd** was listening all along to His teaching **with delight,** though not necessarily with comprehension.

6. CONCLUSION: JESUS' CONDEMNATION OF HYPOCRISY AND COMMENDATION OF TRUE COMMITMENT (12:38-44)

Jesus' denunciation of the Law teachers' conduct (vv. 38-40) concludes Mark's account of His public ministry and signals Jesus' final break with the Jewish religious authorities. This contrasts sharply with His recognition of a widow's genuine devotion to God (vv. 41-44) which resumes His teaching to His disciples (cf. v. 43) and forms a transition to His prophetic discourse (chap. 13).

a. Jesus' condemnation of hypocrisy (12:38-40)
(Matt. 23:1-39; Luke 20:45-47)

12:38-39. Jesus kept warning people to **Watch out** (cf. 8:15) **for** those (implied in the Gr. construction) Law **teachers** who sought praise from men and abused their privileges. Many but not all Law teachers acted this way (cf. 12:28-34).

They liked to (a) go **around in flowing robes,** long white linen garments with fringes worn by priests, Law teachers, and Levites; (b) **be greeted in the marketplaces** with formal titles—Rabbi (teacher), master, father (cf. Matt. 23:7; Luke 20:46)—by the common people who respected them highly; (c) **have the most important** synagogue **seats,** those reserved for dignitaries, situated in front of the chest containing the sacred scrolls of Scripture and facing the whole congregation; **and** (d) have **the places of honor at banquets,** special evening meals at which they were seated next to the host and received preferential treatment.

12:40. Since first-century Law teachers got no pay for their services (Mishnah *Aboth* 1. 13; *Bekhoroth* 4. 6) they depended on the hospitality extended to them by many devout Jews. Unfortunately there were abuses. The charge, **they devour widows' houses,** was a vivid figure of speech for exploiting the generosity of people of limited means, especially widows. They unethically appropriated people's property. In addition, they made **lengthy prayers** in order to impress people with their piety and gain their confidence.

Jesus condemned their ostentatious conduct, greed, and hypocrisy. Instead of pointing people's attention to God they claimed it for themselves under the pretense of piety. Teachers such as these **will be punished most severely** (lit., "will receive greater condemnation"; James 3:1) at God's final judgment.

b. Jesus' commendation of a widow's commitment to God (12:41-44)
(Luke 21:1-4)

12:41-42. From the court of the Gentiles (cf. 11:15) where He conducted His public teaching, **Jesus** entered the court of the women. Against the wall of this court were 13 trumpet-shaped collection receptacles for receiving worshipers' freewill **offerings** and contributions (Mishnah *Shekalim* 6. 5).

From a vantage point **opposite** (*katenanti;* cf. comments on 11:2) one of these receptacles Jesus was observing how (*pōs,* "in what way") the Passover **crowd** was **putting their money into the temple treasury** (lit., "the receptacle").

In contrast with **many** wealthy **people** who gave **large amounts** (lit., "many coins" of all kinds—gold, silver, copper, and bronze), one unnamed **poor widow** gave **two** *lepta* (Gr.). A *lepton* was the smallest bronze Jewish coin in circulation in Palestine. Two *lepta* were worth 1/64 of a Roman denarius, a day's wage for a laborer (cf. 6:37). For his Roman readers Mark stated their value in terms of Roman coinage, namely, **a fraction of a penny.**

12:43-44. With solemn introductory words (**I tell you the truth;** cf. 3:28) **Jesus said** that she had given **more . . . than all the others.** The reason was (*gar,* "for, because") the others **gave out of their** material **wealth** at little cost to them, **but** the widow **out of her poverty** gave **everything.** Proportionally she had given the most—**all she had to live on.** In giving to God sacrificially she completely entrusted herself to Him to provide her needs.

She could have kept back one coin for herself. A Rabbinic rule stating that an offering of less than two *lepta* was not acceptable related to charitable gifts and does not apply here. Jesus used her example to teach His disciples the value God places on wholehearted commitment. Their own commitment to Jesus would soon be severely tested (cf. 14:27-31). This incident also illustrates Jesus' total self-giving in death.

D. *Jesus' prophetic Olivet Discourse to His disciples (chap. 13)*
(Matt. 24:1-25:46; Luke 21:5-36)

This chapter, known as the Olivet Discourse as Jesus gave it on the Mount of Olives, is the longest unit of His teaching recorded by Mark (cf. Mark 4:1-34).

Jesus predicted the destruction of the temple in Jerusalem (13:2) which prompted the disciples to inquire about the timing of "these things" (v. 4). Apparently they associated the destruc-

tion of the temple with the end of the Age (cf. Matt. 24:3). In reply Jesus skillfully wove together into a unified discourse a prophetic scene involving two perspectives: (a) the near event, the destruction of Jerusalem (A.D. 70); and (b) the far event, the coming of the Son of Man in clouds with power and glory. The former local event was a forerunner of the latter universal event. In this way Jesus followed the precedent of Old Testament prophets by predicting a far future event in terms of a near future event whose fulfillment at least some of His hearers would see (cf. Mark 9:1, 12-13).

This indicates Jesus anticipated a period of historical development between His resurrection and His second coming (cf. 13:10; 14:9). Nearly two millennia have passed since the fall of Jerusalem, and the end has not yet come. This prophetic information was set within a framework of (a) warnings against deception and (b) exhortations to vigilant obedience during the intervening time of missionary outreach, persecution, and socio-political upheavals. There are 19 imperatives in 13:5-37, and in each case the hortatory element (second person verbs: vv. 5b, 7a, 9a, et al.) arises out of Jesus' instruction about the future (third person indicative verbs: vv. 6, 7b-8, 9b-10, et al.). The verb "be on guard" (*blepete*) occurs four times at significant points throughout the discourse (vv. 5 ["Watch out," NIV], 9, 23, 33). This was to encourage His followers to maintain steadfast faith and obedience to God throughout the present Age.

In Mark's narrative, the Olivet Discourse is a bridge between Jesus' controversies with the religious authorities (11:27-12:44) and the Passion narrative (14:1-15:47) which culminated in His arrest and death. It disclosed to His disciples that the religious establishment which opposed Him and would eventually condemn Him to death would itself fall under God's judgment.

1. SETTING: JESUS' PREDICTION OF THE TEMPLE'S DESTRUCTION (13:1-4)
(MATT. 24:1-3; LUKE 21:5-7)

13:1. As Jesus **was leaving the temple** area (*hierou;* cf. 11:11) probably on Wednesday evening of Passion Week (cf. the introduction to 11:1-13:37) **one of His disciples** addressed **Him** as **Teacher**

(cf. 4:38; 9:5) and with awe and admiration called attention to the **massive stones** (lit., "Behold, what manner of stones") and the **magnificent buildings** in the temple, that is, the sanctuary itself with its various courts, balconies, colonnades, and porches.

The Jerusalem temple (not fully completed until ca. A.D. 64) was built by the Herodian dynasty to win Jewish favor and to create a lasting Herodian monument. It was considered an architectural wonder of the ancient world. It was built with large white stones, polished and generously decorated with gold (Josephus *The Antiquities of the Jews* 15. 11. 3-7). It covered about 1/6 of the land area of old Jerusalem. To the Jews nothing was as magnificent and formidable as their temple.

13:2. Jesus' response was a startling prediction of the total destruction of **all these great buildings.** The whole complex would be completely leveled— literally, **"stone will** certainly **not** (*ou mē*) **be left** here upon stone." Jesus' use of the emphatic double negative (*ou mē*) twice stressed the certainty of His words' fulfillment.

This ominous prediction is the sequel to Jesus' judgment on the misuse of the temple (cf. 11:15-17; Jer. 7:11-14). As in Jeremiah's day so again the destruction of the temple by a foreign power would be God's judgment on rebellious Israel.

This prediction was fulfilled literally within the span of a generation. In A.D. 70, after the temple area was burned contrary to Titus' directives, he ordered his Roman soldiers to demolish the whole city and level its buildings to the ground (Josephus *Jewish Wars* 7. 1. 1).

13:3-4. Going across the Kidron Valley to the top of the **Mount of Olives** (cf. 11:1a), **Jesus** and His disciples sat down **opposite the temple.** The Mount of Olives rises about 2,700 feet above sea level but is only about 100 feet higher than Jerusalem. West of the mount lay the temple and the city.

The four disciples Jesus called first (cf. 1:16-20) **asked Him privately** (*kat' idian;* cf. 6:32) for more information about His prediction. Only Mark recorded their names. Often in Mark a question from the disciples introduced a section of Jesus' teaching to them (cf.

4:10-32; 7:17-23; 9:11-13, 28-29; 10:10-12).

The disciples' question, perhaps voiced by **Peter** (cf. 8:29), is expressed in two parts: (a) **When will these things** (destruction of the temple [13:2] and other future events [note the pl.]) **happen, and** (b) **What will be the sign that they** (lit., "these things") **are all about to be fulfilled?** The verb "fulfilled" (*synteleisthai,* "be accomplished") denotes the final consummation, the end of the present Age (cf. v. 7; Matt. 24:3).

Having only the perspective of Old Testament prophecy (e.g., Zech. 14), the disciples saw no long interval between the temple's destruction and the end-time events climaxing in the coming of the Son of Man. They assumed that the destruction of Jerusalem and the temple were some of the events at the end of the present Age and would inaugurate the messianic kingdom. They wanted to know *when* this would happen and *what* visible sign would indicate that fulfillment was about to take place.

2. PROPHETIC DISCOURSE IN JESUS' ANSWER TO HIS DISCIPLES' QUESTIONS (13:5-32)

The conditions associated with the impending local crisis of Jerusalem's fall foreshadow those connected with the worldwide end-time crisis. Thus Jesus' words, relevant to His first disciples, remain so for all disciples who face similar conditions throughout this Age.

He first answered their *second* question regarding "the sign" (v. 4b) in two ways: negatively, by warning them against false signs of the end (vv. 5-13), and positively, by stating the notable event that inaugurates unparalleled tribulation and by describing the Second Advent (vv. 14-27). Then He answered their *first* question regarding "when" (v. 4a) in a parable (vv. 28-32).

a. His warnings against deception (13:5-8) (Matt. 24:4-8; Luke 21:8-11)

13:5-6. Watch out (*blepete,* "take heed, be on guard") is a call to vigilance repeated throughout the discourse (cf. vv. 9, 23, 33; v. 35 has a different verb). **Jesus** warned His disciples to be on guard against messianic impostors. **Many** false messiahs (cf. v. 22) **will** arise in crisis times, making use of His **name** (His title and authority), **claiming, I am He** (lit., *egō eimi*, "I am"). This claim to deity is expressed in the formula of God's own self-revelation (cf. 6:50; Ex. 3:14; John 8:58). They **will** lead **many** people astray (cf. Acts 8:9-11).

13:7-8. Second, Jesus warned His disciples against misinterpreting contemporary events such as **wars** and natural disasters as indications that the end is at hand. They were **not** to **be alarmed** and thereby diverted from their work whenever they would **hear of** wars (sounds of battle close at hand) **and rumors** (lit., "reports") **of wars** far away. It is necessary (*dei*, by divine compulsion; cf. 8:31; 13:10) that these things come about. They fall within God's sovereign purposes, which include permitting wars as a consequence of human rebellion and sin. **But the end**—of the present Age and the establishing of God's rule on earth—**is still to come** (lit., "is not yet").

This is confirmed (*gar*, "for") and expanded: **Nation will rise** (lit., "shall be raised," i.e., by God; cf. Isa. 19:2) in armed aggression **against nation.** In addition **there will be earthquakes and famines,** suggesting divine judgment. Yet **these** ("these things") **are** just **the** (lit., "a") **beginning of birth pains.** The words "birth pains," the sharp pains preceding childbirth, picture divine judgment (cf. Isa. 13:6-8; 26:16-18; Jer. 22:20-23; Hosea 13:9-13; Micah 4:9-10). They refer to the period of intense suffering preceding the birth of the new Age, the messianic kingdom.

This emphasis—"the end is still to come" (Mark 13:7d) and "these [things] are the beginning of birth pains" (v. 8c)—suggests that an extended period of time will precede "the end." Each generation will have its own wars and natural disasters. Yet all these events fall within God's purposes. Human history is heading toward the birth of the new Messianic Age.

b. *His warnings about personal dangers while under persecution (13:9-13)*
(Matt. 24:9-14; Luke 21:12-19)

These "floating sayings" (cf. their use in other contexts: Matt. 10:17-22; Luke 12:11-12) are linked by the word *paradidōmi* ("to hand over," Mark 13:9, 11 ["arrested," NIV], 12 ["betray," NIV]).

Jesus probably said these words several times, not just here on the Mount of Olives. His purpose here was to prepare His disciples for suffering because of their allegiance to Him.

13:9. With the admonition, **Be on your guard** (*blepete*; cf. v. 5), Jesus warned His disciples to be alert against wrongful retaliation under persecution. They would **be handed over** for trial **to the local councils** (lit., "sanhedrins"), local Jewish courts held in the synagogues. **And** they would be publicly **flogged,** that is, beaten with 39 strokes (cf. 2 Cor. 11:24), **in the synagogues** as heretics (cf. Mishnah *Makkoth* 3. 10-14). Because of their loyalty to Jesus Christ they **will stand** (lit., "be made to stand") **before** Gentile civil authorities, that is, provincial rulers (cf. Acts 12:1; 23:24; 24:27), **as witnesses to them** (cf. comments on Mark 1:44; 6:11). Their witness to the gospel during their defenses would become, in God's final judgment, incriminating evidence against their persecutors.

13:10. The gospel must (*dei*, "out of [divine] necessity"; cf. v. 7; 8:31) **first be preached** ("proclaimed") **to all nations** (emphatic word position in Gr.), all peoples worldwide (cf. 11:17; 14:9).

In proclaiming the gospel the disciples would be persecuted but they must not despair and give up. Despite all opposition, it is a priority in God's plan for this Age and will be accomplished in accordance with His purposes. It is the responsibility of each generation (cf. Rom. 1:5, 8; 15:18-24; Col. 1:6, 23). But preaching the gospel worldwide does not require or guarantee its worldwide acceptance before or at the end of the Age (cf. Matt. 25:31-46).

13:11. Whenever the disciples **are arrested** (from *paradidōmi*; cf. v. 9) **and brought to trial** for preaching the gospel, they are **not** to be anxious **beforehand about what to say** in giving a defense. They are to speak **whatever** God (implied) gives them to say **at** that moment (cf. Ex. 4:12; Jer. 1:9). **The Holy Spirit** would do the **speaking;** He would enable them to say the right things at the right times with boldness despite their natural fears. This assistance, however, did not guarantee acquittal.

13:12-13. Opposition will come through official channels (vv. 9, 11) and also through close personal relationships.

It will be so severe that family members—**brother** versus **brother, father** versus **child,** and **children** versus **parents—will betray** (from *paradidōmi;* cf. vv. 9, 11) each other to hostile authorities, thereby causing Christian members to be **put to death.** Because of their allegiance to Jesus (lit., "on account of My name"; cf. v. 9), His disciples will be hated continually by **all men,** that is, all kinds of people, not just hostile authorities or family members (cf. Phil. 1:29; 3:11; Col. 1:24; 1 Peter 4:16). **He who stands firm** (lit., "he who has endured," viewing one's life as completed), who has remained loyal to Jesus Christ and the gospel (cf. Mark 8:35) **to the end** (*eis telos,* adverbial phrase, an idiom meaning "completely, to the limit"; cf. John 13:1; 1 Thes. 2:16) of his life on earth, **will be saved** (cf. Mark 8:35; 10:26-27). This "saved" one will experience God's salvation in its final form—glorification (contrast usage in 13:20; cf. Heb. 9:27-28). Perseverance is a result and outward sign, not the basis, of spiritual genuineness (cf. Rom. 8:29-30; 1 John 2:19). A person genuinely saved by grace through faith (cf. Eph. 2:8-10) endures to the end and will experience the consummation of his salvation.

These words of warning were pertinent to Mark's Roman readers who were threatened by persecution for their allegiance to Jesus. Such suffering could be more readily endured when viewed in the context of God's plan for worldwide evangelism and vindication. (Cf. comments on Matt. 24:13.)

c. Jesus' portrayal of the coming crisis (13:14-23)

(Matt. 24:15-28; Luke 21:20-24)

Jesus then answered the disciples' second question (Mark 13:4b) positively (vv. 14-23).

Some interpreters limit the events of this section to the chaotic years preceding Jerusalem's fall (A.D. 66-70). Others relate them exclusively to the Great Tribulation at the end of this Age. But the details suggest that *both* events are in view (cf. Matt. 24:15-16, 29-31; Luke 21:20-28). The conquest of Jerusalem is theologically (not chronologically) attached to the end-time events (cf. Dan. 9:26-27; Luke 21:24). The expression "the abomination that causes desolation" is the link between the historical and eschatological perspectives (cf. Dan. 11:31 with Dan. 9:27; 12:11). These "near" tribulations foreshadowed the "far" Tribulation of the end time.

13:14. The sign that "these things" were about to be fulfilled (cf. v. 4b) was the appearance of **the abomination that causes desolation** (lit., "the abomination of desolation"; cf. Dan. 9:27; 11:31; 12:11; Matt. 24:15), **standing where it does not belong,** a reference to the temple sanctuary. More precise identification may have been politically dangerous for his readers. Mark's exhortation, **Let the reader understand,** was a decoding signal urging them to recognize the significance of Jesus' words in light of their Old Testament context (cf., e.g., Dan. 9:25-27).

The word "abomination" denoted pagan idolatry and its detestable practices (Deut. 29:16-18; 2 Kings 16:3-4; 23:12-14; Ezek. 8:9-18). The phrase "the abomination of desolation" referred to the presence of an idolatrous person or object so detestable that it caused the temple to be abandoned and left desolate.

Historically, the first fulfillment of Daniel's prophetic use of the expression (Dan. 11:31-32) was the desecration of the temple in 167 B.C. by the Syrian ruler Antiochus Epiphanes. He erected an altar to the pagan Greek god Zeus over the altar of burnt offering and sacrificed a pig on it (cf. apocryphal 1 Maccabees 1:41-64; 6:7; and Josephus *The Antiquities of the Jews* 12. 5. 4).

Jesus' use of "the abomination of desolation" referred to another fulfillment—the temple's desecration and destruction in A.D. 70. **When** (lit., "whenever") His disciples, those present and future, **see** this desecration take place, it is a signal for people **in Judea** to escape **to the mountains** beyond the Jordan River in Perea.

Josephus recorded the occupation and appalling profaning of the temple in A.D. 67-68 by Jewish Zealots, who also installed a usurper, Phanni, as high priest (Josephus *Jewish Wars* 4. 3. 7-10; 4. 6. 3). Jewish Christians fled to Pella, a town located in the Transjordanian mountains (Eusebius *Ecclesiastical History* 3. 5. 3).

The events of 167 B.C. and A.D. 70 foreshadow a final fulfillment of Jesus' words just prior to His Second Advent (cf. Mark 13:24-27). Mark used the *masculine* participle "standing" (*hestēkota,* masc. perf. part.) to modify the *neuter* noun "abomination" (*bdelygma*; v. 14). This suggests that "the abomination" is a future person "standing where he (NIV marg.) does not belong."

This person is the end-time Antichrist (Dan. 7:23-26; 9:25-27; 2 Thes. 2:3-4, 8-9; Rev. 13:1-10, 14-15). He will make a covenant with the Jewish people at the beginning of the seven-year period preceding Christ's second coming (Dan. 9:27). The temple will be rebuilt and worship reestablished (Rev. 11:1). In the middle of this period (after 3½ years) the Antichrist will break his covenant, stop temple sacrifices, desecrate the temple (cf. Dan. 9:27), and proclaim himself to be God (Matt. 24:15; 2 Thes. 2:3-4; Rev. 11:2). This launches the terrible end-time events of the Great Tribulation (Rev. 6; 8-9; 16). Those who refuse to be identified with the Antichrist will suffer severe persecution and be forced to flee for refuge (Rev. 12:6, 13-17). Many—both Jews and Gentiles—will be saved during this period (Rev. 7) but many will also be martyred (Rev. 6:9-11).

13:15-18. When this crisis breaks, the person **on the roof of his house** (cf. 2:2-4) must not take time to **go** inside to retrieve any possessions. The person working out **in the field** must not take time to **go back** to another part of the field or his house **to get his cloak**, an outer garment that protected against cold night air.

Jesus expressed compassion **for pregnant women and nursing mothers** forced to flee under such difficult circumstances. He exhorted His disciples (cf. 13:14) to **pray that this** (lit., "it"; cf. v. 29)—the coming crisis necessitating their flight—**will not happen during the winter**, the rainy season when swollen streams would be difficult to cross.

13:19. The reason their flight was urgent and hopefully would be unhindered is that **those** (lit., "those days") **will be days of distress** (lit., "will be a tribulation," *thlipsis*; cf. v. 24) **unequaled from the beginning** of Creation **until now** . . . **never** (*ou mē*; cf. v. 2) **to be equaled again**. At no time in the past, present, or future has there been or will there be such a severe tribulation as this.

This unprecedented distress was true of but not restricted to the destruction of Jerusalem (cf. Josephus *Jewish Wars*

preface; 1. 1. 4; 5. 10. 5). Jesus looked beyond A.D. 70 to the final Great Tribulation (*thlipsis*; cf. Rev. 7:14) prior to the Second Advent. This is supported by these facts: (a) Mark 13:19 echoes Daniel 12:1, an end-time prophecy; (b) the words "never to be equaled again" indicate that another crisis will never be like this one; (c) "those days" link the "near" future with the "far" future (cf. Mark 13:17, 19-20, 24; Jer. 3:16, 18; 33:14-16; Joel 3:1) (d) the days will be terminated (Mark 13:20).

13:20. If the Lord (*Yahweh* God; cf. 12:29), **had not** already decided in His sovereign plan to **cut short** (terminate, not reduce the number of) **those days** (lit., "the days"; cf. 13:19), **no one would survive** (*esōthē*, "would be saved"; cf. 15:30-31), that is, be delivered from physical death; this is in contrast with 13:13. **But** God set limits on the duration of the end-time Tribulation, because **of the elect**, those redeemed during "those days," **whom He has chosen** for Himself (cf. Acts 13:48). While all this proved true indirectly in A.D. 70, the language of this verse suggests God's *direct* intervention in judgment, an unmistakable characteristic of the end-time Tribulation (cf. Rev. 16:1).

13:21-22. At that time (*tote*, "then"; cf. vv. 26-27) in the middle of "those days" (cf. v. 19) of severe affliction and flight, **if** someone should claim that **the Christ** (Messiah) was **here** or **there**, His disciples were **not** to **believe it** (the fallacious claim, or possibly "him," the person), and turn aside from taking refuge. Jesus explained that many **false Christs** (messiahs; cf. v. 6) **and false prophets** would **appear and perform** miraculous deeds that would seem to validate their claims. Their purpose would be **to mislead the elect** (cf. v. 20), believers in the true Messiah. The clause **if that were possible** shows that they will not succeed.

13:23. Again Jesus exhorted His disciples, **Be on . . . guard** (*blepete*; cf. vv. 5, 9) for deceptive pitfalls in crisis days.

d. Jesus' portrayal of His triumphant return (13:24-27)
(Matt. 24:29-31; Luke 21:25-28)

13:24-25. The word **But** (*alla*) introduces a sharp contrast between the appearance of false messiahs who will perform miraculous signs (v. 22) and the dramatic coming of the true Messiah **in those days** (cf. vv. 19-20; Joel 2:28-32) **following that distress** (*thlipsin*, "tribulation"; cf. Mark 13:19). These phrases indicate a close connection with verses 14-23. If these verses apply exclusively to the events of A.D. 70 then Jesus Christ should have returned shortly thereafter. That He did not return then supports the view that verses 14-23 refer to both the destruction of Jerusalem and the future Great Tribulation before Christ will return.

A variety of cosmic disorders involving **the sun . . . moon,** and **stars** will immediately precede the Second Advent. Jesus' description is fashioned from Isaiah 13:10 and 34:4 without His quoting exactly from either passage. This vividly refers to observable celestial changes in the physical universe.

The last statement—**the heavenly bodies** (lit., "the powers that are in the skies") **will be shaken**—may refer to: (a) physical forces controlling the movements of the celestial bodies which will be thrown out of their normal course, or (b) spiritual forces of evil, Satan and his cohorts, who will be greatly disturbed by these events. The first view is preferred.

13:26. **At that time** (*tote*, "then"; this Gr. word is also used in vv. 21, 27 though the NIV does not trans. it in v. 27) when the cosmic events just mentioned have taken place, **men** (generic, "people") living on the earth then **will see the Son of Man** (cf. 8:31, 38) **coming in clouds** or "with clouds." The "clouds of heaven" signify divine presence (cf. 9:7; Ex. 19:9; Ps. 97:1-2; Dan. 7:13; Matt. 24:30b). He will exercise **great power and** display heavenly **glory** (cf. Zech. 14:1-7). This is Jesus' personal, visible, bodily return to the earth as the glorified Son of Man (cf. Acts 1:11; Rev. 1:7; 19:11-16). Jesus described it in the familiar but elusive language of Daniel 7:13-14. His triumphant return will bring an end to the veiled nature of God's kingdom in its present form (cf. comments on Mark 1:15; 4:13-23).

13:27. **Also at that time** (*tote,* "then," omitted in the NIV; cf. vv. 21, 26) the Son of Man **will send** forth (cf. 4:29) **His angels** (cf. 8:38; Matt. 25:31) **and gather His elect** (cf. Mark 13:20, 22) **from the**

four winds. The "four winds" means from all directions, a reference to people living in all parts of the world, as emphasized by the last two phrases (v. 27). None of the elect will be left out. Though not stated, this would appear to include a resurrection of Old Testament saints and believers martyred during the Tribulation (cf. Dan. 12:2; Rev. 6:9-11; 20:4). Nothing is said here about those not among the elect (cf. 2 Thes. 1:6-10; Rev. 20:11-15).

The Old Testament often mentioned God's regathering of dispersed Israelites from the remotest parts of the earth to national and spiritual unity in Palestine (Deut. 30:3-6; Isa. 11:12; Jer. 31:7-9; Ezek. 11:16-17; 20:33-35, 41). At the time of the Second Advent Israelites will be regathered around the triumphant Son of Man, judged, restored as a nation, and redeemed (Isa. 59:20-21; Ezek. 20:33-44; Zech. 13:8-9; Rom. 11:25-27). Also all the Gentiles will be gathered before Him (Joel 3:2) and like a shepherd He will separate "the sheep" (the elect) from "the goats" (Matt. 25:31-46). These redeemed Jews and Gentiles will enter the millennial kingdom, living on the earth in natural bodies (Isa. 2:2-4; Dan. 7:13-14; Micah 4:1-5; Zech. 14:8-11, 16-21).

Identifying "the elect" in this context as Gentiles and Jews who come to believe in Jesus as the Messiah *during* the final Tribulation period (cf. Rev. 7:3-4, 9-10) is compatible with a pretribulational view of the Rapture of the church, the body of Christ (cf. 1 Cor. 15:51-53; 1 Thes. 4:13-18). Since the church will be spared from God's final judgment on the earth (cf. 1 Thes. 1:10; 5:9-11; Rev. 3:9-10), the church will not go through the Tribulation. This preserves the imminence of the Rapture for present-day believers and gives added emphasis to Jesus' exhortation, "Watch!" (cf. Mark 13:35-37) But since Jesus' disciples had no clear understanding of the coming church (cf. Matt. 16:18; Acts 1:4-8), He did not mention this initial phase of God's end-time program separately.

Some interpreters, however, hold to a posttribulational view of the Rapture. They identify "the elect" here as the redeemed of all ages—past, present, and future. This requires the resurrection of all the righteous dead at the end of the Tribulation and together with all living believers they will be caught up (raptured) to meet the returning Son of Man who descends to the earth at that time. Thus the church, the body of Christ, *remains* on earth during the Tribulation period, is supernaturally protected as an entity through it, is raptured at the end of it, and immediately returns to the earth to participate in the Millennium. But in light of the preceding discussion on Mark 13:17 and the following discussion on verse 32, the pretribulational viewpoint is preferred.

e. His parabolic lesson from the fig tree (13:28-32)
(Matt. 24:32-36; Luke 21:29-33)

13:28. The disciples' first question (v. 4a) was, "When will these things happen?" Jesus exhorted them to **learn** a **lesson** (lit., "the parable"; cf. introduction to 4:1-2) **from the fig tree.** Though the fig tree was sometimes used as a symbol for Israel (11:14), Jesus did not intend such a meaning here (in Luke 21:29 the words "and all the trees" are added). In contrast with most of Palestine's trees, fig trees lose their leaves in winter and bloom later in the spring. Thus whenever the stiff, dry, winter **twigs** become **tender,** softened due to the rising sap, and **leaves** appear, then observers **know that** winter is past and **summer is near.**

13:29. This verse applies the lesson of verse 28. Whenever **you** (emphatic position in Gr.), the disciples in contrast with others, **see these things** (cf. vv. 4, 23, 30), the events described in verses 14-23, then **you know that** the impending crisis (cf. v. 14) **is near** in time, in fact, **right at the door.** This was a common figure for an imminent event. If alert to these events the disciples have sufficient insight to discern their true meaning.

The unstated subject of the Greek verb "is" could be rendered "He" (the Son of Man) or preferably **it** ("the abomination that causes desolation," v. 14).

13:30-31. With solemn introductory words (**I tell you the truth;** cf. 3:28) Jesus declared that **this generation will certainly not** (*ou mē,* emphatic double negative; cf. 13:2) come to an end **until** (lit., "until which time") **all these things** (cf. vv. 4b, 29) **have** taken place. "Generation" (*genea*) can refer to one's "contem-

poraries," all those living at a given time (cf. 8:12, 38; 9:19), or to a group of people descended from a common ancestor (cf. Matt. 23:36). Since the word "generation" is capable of both a narrow and a broad sense, it is preferable in this context (cf. Mark 13:14) to understand in it a double reference incorporating both senses. Thus "this generation" means: (a) the Jews living at Jesus' time who later saw the destruction of Jerusalem, and (b) the Jews who will be living at the time of the Great Tribulation who will see the end-time events. This accounts best for the accomplishment of "all these things" (cf. vv. 4b, 14-23).

Jesus' assertion (v. 31) guarantees the fulfillment of His prophecy (v. 30). The present universe will come to a cataclysmic end (cf. 2 Peter 3:7, 10-13) **but** Jesus' **words**—including these predictions—**will never** (*ou mē;* cf. Mark 13:2, 30) **pass away.** They will have eternal validity. What is true of God's words (cf. Isa. 40:6-8; 55:11) is equally true of Jesus' words, for He is God.

13:32. Though it will be possible for some to discern the proximity of the coming crisis (vv. 28-29), yet **no one knows** the precise moment when **that day or hour** will arrive (cf. v. 33) except **the Father. Not even the angels** (cf. 1 Peter 1:12) **nor the Son** know. This openly expressed limitation on Jesus' knowledge affirms His humanity. In His Incarnation Jesus voluntarily accepted human limitations, including this one (cf. Acts 1:7), in submission to the Father's will (cf. John 4:34). On the other hand Jesus' use of "the Son" title (only here in Mark) instead of the usual "Son of Man" revealed His own awareness of His deity and sonship (cf. Mark 8:38). Nevertheless He exercised His divine attributes only at the Father's bidding (cf. 5:30; John 8:28-29).

The words "that day or hour" are widely understood to refer to the Son of Man's second coming (Mark 13:26). But that event will climax a series of preliminary events. In light of Old Testament usage and this context (vv. 14, 29-30) it is preferable to understand "that day" as referring to "the day of the Lord."

The "day of the Lord" includes the Tribulation, the Second Advent, and the Millennium (cf. Isa. 2:12-22; Jer. 30:7-9; Joel 2:28-32; Amos 9:11; Zeph. 3:11-20;

Zech. 12–14). It will begin suddenly and unexpectedly (cf. 1 Thes. 5:2), so no one except the Father knows the critical moment.

In the pretribulational view of the future (cf. comments on Mark 13:27) the coming of the Lord for His own (the Rapture) will occur before the 70th week of Daniel. The Rapture is not conditioned by any preliminary events. It is therefore an imminent event for each generation. The Parable of the Absent House Owner (vv. 34-37) along with Matthew's corresponding account (cf. Matt. 24:42-44) support this view. It precludes all date-setting and lends urgency to Jesus' exhortations to be watching and working till His return.

3. JESUS' EXHORTATION TO VIGILANCE (13:33-37)
(MATT. 24:42-44; LUKE 21:34-36)

13:33. Because no one knows **when** (cf. v. 4a) **that time,** the appointed time of God's intervention ("that day," v. 32), **will come,** Jesus repeated His admonition, **Be on guard!** (*blepete*; cf. vv. 5, 9, 23) and added, **Be alert!** (*agrypneite,* "be constantly awake")

13:34-37. The Parable of the Absent House Owner, unique to Mark, reinforces the call to constant vigilance and defines it as a faithful fulfillment of assigned tasks (cf. Matt. 25:14-30; Luke 19:11-27).

Before **going away** on a journey the Owner put **his servants** (collectively) **in charge of** carrying on the work of **his house.** He gave **each** one **his** own **task** and ordered the doorkeeper who controlled all access to the house **to keep watch** (*grēgoreite,* pres. tense; cf. Mark 13:33).

Jesus applied this parable to His disciples (vv. 35-37) without distinguishing between the doorkeeper and the other servants. They all are responsible to **keep watch,** to be alert to spiritual dangers and opportunities (cf. vv. 5-13) **because** no one knows **when** (cf. v. 33) **the Owner** (*kyrios*) **of the house,** who indirectly represents Jesus Himself, **will** return. The night represents the time of the Owner's (Jesus') absence (cf. Rom. 13:11-14). He could return at any time, so they should be constantly watching in view of the danger that **if** (lit., "when") the Owner, Jesus, **comes suddenly,** He should **find**

them **sleeping** (spiritually negligent), not watching for His return. Such vigilance is the responsibility not only of the Twelve (cf. Mark 13:3) but also of every believer in every generation during this present Age. Believers should be watching and working (cf. v. 34) in light of the certainty of His return, though its time is unknown except to the Father.

The reference to the four watches corresponds to the Roman system of reckoning time. **The evening** was 6–9 P.M.; the **midnight** watch was 9 P.M. till midnight; **when the rooster crows** was the third watch (midnight till 3 A.M.); and **dawn** was 3–6 A.M. (These names of the watches were derived from their termination points.) This differs from the Jewish system of dividing the night into three watches. Mark used the Roman system for his readers' benefit (cf. 6:48).

VIII. Jesus' Suffering and Death in Jerusalem (chaps. 14–15)

The sixth major section of Mark's Gospel, the Passion narrative, includes Jesus' betrayal, arrest, trial, and death by crucifixion. It provides the necessary historical and theological perspective for various themes mentioned earlier in the Gospel: (a) Jesus as the Christ, the Son of God (1:1; 8:29); (b) His conflicts with the religious authorities (3:6; 11:18; 12:12); (c) His rejection, betrayal, and abandonment by those close to Him (3:19; 6:1-6); (d) His disciples' failure to understand His messianic office clearly (8:31–10:52); (e) His coming as the Son of Man to give His life a ransom for many (10:45).

The narrative reflects how the early Christians turned to the Old Testament (esp. Pss. 22; 69; Isa. 53) to understand the meaning of Jesus' suffering and death and to explain the ignominious course of events to their Jewish and Gentile contemporaries (cf. 1 Cor. 1:22-24).

A. Jesus' betrayal, the Passover meal, and His disciples' desertion (14:1-52)

This division consists of three cycles of events (vv. 1-11, 12-26, 27-52).

1. THE PLOT TO KILL JESUS AND HIS ANOINTING IN BETHANY (14:1-11)

Like other passages in Mark the first cycle of events in this division also has a "sandwich" structure (cf. 3:20-35; 5:21-43; 6:7-31; 11:12-26; 14:27-52). The account of the conspiracy by the religious leaders and Judas (vv. 1-2, 10-11) is divided by the account of Jesus' anointing in Bethany (vv. 3-9). In this way Mark emphasized the striking contrast between the hostility of those who plotted His death and the loving devotion of one who recognized Him as the suffering Messiah.

a. The leaders' plot to arrest and kill Jesus (14:1-2)
(Matt. 26:1-5; Luke 22:1-2)

14:1a. Mark's Passion narrative begins with a new chronological starting point (cf. introduction to 11:1-11), the first of several time notations that link the following events. The chronology of the Passion Week events is complicated partly because two systems of reckoning time were in use, the Roman (modern) system in which a new day starts at midnight and the Jewish system in which a new day begins at sunset (cf. 13:35).

The Passover, observed in Jerusalem (cf. Deut. 16:5-6), was an annual Jewish festival (cf. Ex. 12:1-14) celebrated on Nisan (March-April) 14-15 (which most say was Thursday-Friday of Jesus' Passion Week). Preparations for the Passover meal (cf. Mark 14:12-16)—the highlight of the festival—included the slaughter of the Passover lamb which took place near the close of Nisan 14 by Jewish reckoning, Thursday afternoon. The Passover meal was eaten at the beginning of Nisan 15, that is, between sunset and midnight Thursday evening. This was followed immediately by the festival **of Unleavened Bread** celebrated from Nisan 15-21 inclusive, to commemorate the Jews' exodus from Egypt (cf. Ex. 12:15-20).

These two Jewish festivals were closely related and in popular usage were often designated as the "Jewish Passover Feast" (an eight-day festival, Nisan 14-21 inclusive; cf. Mark 14:2; John 2:13, 23; 6:4; 11:55). So Nisan 14, the day of preparation, was commonly called "the first day of the Feast of Unleavened Bread" (cf. Mark 14:12; Josephus *The Antiquities of the Jews* 2. 15. 1). The words **only two days away** are literally, "after two days." To the Jews, with their inclusive way of counting, "after two days" would mean

"on the day after tomorrow." Reckoning from Nisan 15 (Friday) two days prior would be Nisan 13 (Wednesday), and "after two days" means "after Wednesday and Thursday."

14:1b-2. The Jewish religious leaders, Sanhedrin members (cf. 8:31; 11:27; Matt. 26:3), had already decided that **Jesus** must be put to death (cf. John 11:47-53). But their fear of a popular uprising kept them from seizing Him openly. So they kept seeking (*ezētoun,* imperf. tense; cf. Mark 11:18; 12:12) for **some sly way** (lit., "how to seize Him by deceit"), by a cunning covert strategy, to do it. However, because of the large Passover crowds it was still unwise to risk a **riot** by many potential supporters of Jesus, especially impetuous Galileans. So the leaders determined **not** to seize Him **during the Feast,** the full eight-day festival, Nisan 14-21 inclusive (cf. 14:1a). Apparently they planned to arrest Him after the crowds had gone, but Judas' unexpected offer (cf. vv. 10-11) expedited matters. Thus God's timetable was followed.

b. Jesus' anointing in Bethany (14:3-9)
(Matt. 26:6-13; John 12:1-8)

This anointing episode is not to be equated with an earlier anointing in Galilee (Luke 7:36-50). However, it is the same episode recorded in John 12:1-8 though there are some significant differences. One difference concerns when the event occurred. John stated that it happened "six days before the Passover," that is, the beginning of the Passover festival, Nisan 14 (Thursday). This means it occurred the previous Friday. Mark's placement seems to suggest that the episode occurred on Wednesday of Passion Week (cf. Mark 14:1a). In light of this it seems reasonable to follow John's chronology and to conclude that Mark used the incident thematically (cf. introduction to 2:1-12; 11:1-11) to contrast responses of this woman and Judas. Consequently the time reference in 14:1 governs the leaders' concern to arrest Jesus, not *this* event.

14:3. While . . . in Bethany (cf. comments in 11:1a) Jesus was being honored with a festive meal **in the home of . . . Simon the Leper,** a man apparently cured by Jesus previously (cf. 1:40) and well known to the early disciples. The unnamed **woman** was Mary, sister of Martha and Lazarus (cf. John 12:3). She **came with an alabaster jar,** a small stone flask with a long slender neck, containing about a pint **of** costly **perfume** (lit., "ointment") **made of pure** (unadulterated) **nard,** an aromatic oil from a rare plant root native to India.

Mary **broke** the slender neck of **the** stone flask **and poured the perfume** over Jesus' **head.** John wrote that she poured it on Jesus' feet and wiped them with her hair (cf. John 12:3). Both are possible since Jesus was reclining on a dining couch at the table (cf. Mark 14:18). Anointing a guest's head was a common custom at festive Jewish meals (cf. Ps. 23:5; Luke 7:46) but Mary's act had a greater meaning (cf. Mark 14:8-9).

14:4-5. Some of the disciples, led by Judas (cf. John 12:4), voiced angry (cf. Mark 10:14) criticism of this apparent wasteful extravagance. In their view the act was uncalled for because the **perfume . . . could have been sold for more than a year's wages** (lit., "more than 300 denarii," roughly a year's wages; cf. comments on 6:37) **and the money given to the poor.** This was a legitimate concern (cf. John 13:29), but here it concealed the disciples' insensitivity and Judas' greed (cf. John 12:6). So they were scolding (same verb in Mark 1:43) **her,** a comment unique to Mark.

14:6-8. **Jesus** rebuked Mary's critics and defended **her** action, calling it **a beautiful thing** (lit., "a good [*kalon,* 'noble, beautiful, good'] work"). Unlike them, He saw it as an expression of love and devotion to Him in light of His approaching death as well as a messianic acclamation.

The contrast in verse 7 is not between Jesus and **the poor** but between the words **always** and **not always.** Opportunities to **help** the poor will always be present and the disciples should take advantage of them. But Jesus would not be in their midst much longer and opportunities to show Him love were diminishing rapidly. In a sense **she** had anointed His **body beforehand** in preparation for its **burial.**

14:9. Prefaced by a solemn introductory saying (**I tell you the truth;** cf. 3:28) Jesus promised Mary that **wherever the gospel** (cf. 1:1) **is preached throughout the world** (cf. 13:10) her deed of love would **also be told** along with the gospel **in memory of her.** This unique promise looked beyond His death, burial, and resurrection to the present period of time when the gospel is being preached.

c. Judas' agreement to betray Jesus (14:10-11)
(Matt. 26:14-16; Luke 22:3-6)

14:10-11. These verses complement verses 1-2 and heighten the contrast with verses 3-9. **Judas Iscariot** (cf. 3:19), **one of the Twelve** (cf. 3:14), **went to the** influential **chief priests** (cf. 14:1) and offered **to betray** (*paradoi*; cf. v. 11; 9:31) **Jesus to them.** He suggested doing it "when no crowd was present" (Luke 22:6). This would avoid a public disturbance, which was the priests' primary concern (cf. Mark 14:2). **They** welcomed this unexpected offer, one they would have never dared solicit. They **promised to give him money** (30 pieces of silver, in response to his demand; cf. Matt. 26:15). **So** Judas was seeking (*ezētei;* cf. Mark 14:1) the right **opportunity,** without the presence of a crowd, **to hand Him over** (*paradoi;* cf. v. 10; 9:31) into their custody.

Why did Judas offer to betray Jesus? Various suggestions have been made, each of which may contain an element of truth: (1) Judas, the only non-Galilean member of the Twelve, may have responded to the official notice (John 11:57). (2) He was disillusioned by Jesus' failure to establish a political kingdom and his hopes for material gain seemed doomed. (3) His love for money moved him to salvage something for himself. Ultimately he came under satanic control (cf. Luke 22:3; John 13:2, 27).

In Judas' life one finds an intriguing combination of divine sovereignty and human responsibility. According to God's plan Jesus must suffer and die (Rev. 13:8); yet Judas, though not compelled to be the traitor, was held responsible for submitting to Satan's directives (cf. Mark 14:21; John 13:27).

2. THE PASSOVER MEAL AS THE LAST SUPPER (14:12-26)

The second cycle of events in this chapter also has three parts (vv. 12-16, 17-21, 22-26).

a. *The preparation of the Passover meal*
(14:12-16)
(Matt. 26:17-19; Luke 22:7-13)

14:12. The time designation, **on the first day of the Feast of Unleavened Bread,** would be Nisan 15 (Friday), strictly speaking. However, the qualifying clause (a common feature in Mark's time notations; cf. 1:32, 35; 4:35; 13:24; 14:30; 15:42; 16:2) referring to the day **Passover** lambs were slaughtered indicates that Nisan 14 (Thursday) was meant (cf. comments on 14:1a).

Since the Passover meal had to be eaten within Jerusalem's walls, the **disciples asked** Jesus **where** He wanted them **to go and make preparations** (cf. v. 16) **for** the meal. They assumed they would eat this "family feast" with Him (cf. v. 15).

14:13-15. This episode is structurally parallel to 11:1b-7. It may reflect another instance of Jesus' supernatural knowledge. However, the need for security (cf. 14:10-11), the disciples' question (v. 12), and Jesus' subsequent directives seem to indicate that He had carefully reserved a place in advance where they could eat the Passover meal together undisturbed.

Jesus and **His disciples** were probably in Bethany (cf. 11:1a, 11). Thursday morning **He sent two of** them—Peter and John (cf. Luke 22:8)—into Jerusalem with instructions for locating the reserved room. For security reasons (cf. Mark 14:11; John 11:57) the participants remained anonymous and the location was kept secret.

A man carrying a jar of water would **meet** the two disciples, presumably near the eastern gate. This unusual, eye-catching sight suggests that it was a prearranged signal because normally only women carried water jars (men carried wineskins). They were to **follow** this man, apparently a servant, who would lead them to the right **house.** They were to tell the **owner . . . The Teacher** (cf. Mark 4:38) **asks: Where is My guest room. . . ?** The single self-designation "Teacher" implies Jesus was well known to the owner and the possessive pronoun "My" implies His prior arrangement to use the room.

He (*autos,* the owner "himself") would **show** them **a large Upper Room,** built on the flat ceiling, **furnished** (with a dining table and reclining couches), and set up for a banquet meal. The owner also may have secured the necessary food including the Passover lamb. The two disciples were to prepare the meal for Jesus and the other disciples (cf. 14:12) **there.** Tradition claims this was Mark's home (cf. comments on vv. 41-52; also Acts 1:13; 12:12) and the owner was Mark's father.

14:16. Presumably preparing **the Passover** meal involved roasting the lamb, setting out the unleavened bread and wine, and preparing bitter herbs along with a sauce made of dried fruit moistened with vinegar and wine and combined with spices.

These Passover preparations on Nisan 14 (Thursday) imply that Jesus' last meal with His disciples was the regular Passover meal held that evening (Nisan 15 after sunset) and that He was crucified on Nisan 15 (Friday). This is the consistent witness of the Synoptic Gospels (cf. Matt. 26:2, 17-19; Mark 14:1, 12-14; Luke 22:1, 7-8, 11-15). The Gospel of John, however, indicates that Jesus was crucified on "the day of preparation" (John 19:14). This was the Passover proper and also the preparation for the seven-day Feast of Unleavened Bread, which was sometimes called the Passover Week (cf. Luke 22:1, 7; Acts 12:3-4; see comments on Luke 22:7-38).

b. *Jesus' announcement of His betrayal*
(14:17-21)
(Matt. 26:20-25; Luke 22:21-23;
John 13:21-30)

14:17. That (Thursday) **evening,** the beginning of Nisan 15 (cf. v. 1a), **Jesus** and **the Twelve** arrived in Jerusalem to eat the Passover meal which began after sunset and had to be finished by midnight. Mark abbreviated the events of the meal (cf. Luke 22:14-16, 24-30; John 13:1-20) in order to focus attention on two incidents: (a) Jesus' announcement of His betrayal as they dipped bread and bitter herbs into a bowl of fruit sauce together (Mark 14:18-21), and (b) His new interpretation of the bread and wine just after the meal (vv. 22-25).

14:18-20. It was customary to recline on dining couches during a festive meal (cf. 14:3; John 13:23-25); in fact, it was a first-century requirement for the Passover meal, even for the poorest people (cf.

Mishnah *Pesachim* 10. 1). **While they were . . . eating,** dipping bread into the bowl (cf. Mark 14:20) before the meal itself, Jesus, with solemn introductory words (**I tell you the truth;** cf. 3:28), announced that **one of the Twelve** would **betray Him** (cf. 14:10-11). The added words, **one who is eating with Me,** unique to Mark, allude to Psalm 41:9 where David laments that his trusted friend Ahithophel (cf. 2 Sam. 16:15–17:23; 1 Chron. 27:33), who shared table fellowship with him, had turned against him. To eat with a person and then betray him was the height of treachery.

This thought is reinforced in Mark 14:19-20. The disciples were deeply grieved. **One by one** (even Judas; cf. Matt. 26:25) **they** sought to clear themselves. The form of their question in Greek (lit., "It is **not I,** is it?") expects a reassuring negative answer from Jesus. But He declined to name the offender to the group. (The identification in Matt. 26:25 was doubtless made only to Judas.) Jesus repeated His disclosure that His betrayer was **one of the Twelve . . . one who** was dipping **bread into the** same **bowl with Him.** His announcement emphasized the treachery of the betrayal and also gave the betrayer an opportunity to repent.

14:21. On the one hand (Gr., *men*) **the Son of Man** (cf. 8:31) **will go,** that is, He must die, in fulfillment of Scripture (e.g., Ps. 22; Isa. 53). His death was according to God's plan not simply because of the betrayer's action. **But** on the other hand (Gr., *de*) **woe,** a lament denoting heartfelt pity, **to that man,** literally, "through whom **the Son of Man is being betrayed."** The betrayer was acting as Satan's agent (cf. Luke 22:3; John 13:2, 27). So awful a destiny awaited him that **it would** have been **better for him if he** (lit., "that man") **had not been born.** Though he acted within God's plan, the betrayer remained morally responsible (cf. Mark 14:10-11). This woe contrasts sharply with Jesus' promise in verse 9.

c. The institution of the Lord's Supper (14:22-26)

(Matt. 26:26-30; Luke 22:19-20)

This is the second key incident Mark selected from the events of the Passover

meal (cf. comments on Mark 14:17). Before this meal was eaten in Jewish homes the head of the house explained its meaning regarding Israel's deliverance from slavery in Egypt. As host, Jesus probably did so to prepare His disciples for a new understanding of the bread and wine.

14:22. While they were eating (cf. v. 18), apparently before the main part of the meal but after Judas had left (John 13:30), **Jesus took bread** (*arton,* an unleavened flat cake), **gave thanks** (*eulogēsas;* cf. Mark 6:41), **broke it** to distribute it, **and gave it to** them with the words, **Take it** (and "eat" implied); **this is My body.**

Jesus spoke of literal things—the bread, wine, His physical body (*sōma*), and blood—but the relationship in them was expressed figuratively (cf. John 7:35; 8:12; 10:7, 9). The verb "is" means "represents." Jesus was physically present as He spoke these words, so the disciples did not literally eat His body or drink His blood, something abhorrent to Jews anyway (cf. Lev. 3:17; 7:26-27; 17:10-14). This shows the impropriety of the Roman Catholic view of the eucharist (transubstantiation), that the bread and wine are changed into Christ's body and blood.

14:23. Similarly, after the meal (cf. 1 Cor. 11:25), Jesus **took the cup** containing red wine mixed with water, **gave thanks** (*eucharistēsas;* cf. Mark 8:6-7; hence the word "eucharist"), **and offered** (lit., "gave") **it to them, and they all drank from it.** Assuming Jesus followed the established Passover ritual this was the third of four prescribed cups of wine ("the cup of thanksgiving"; cf. 1 Cor. 10:16) which concluded the main portion of the meal. Presumably He did not drink the fourth cup, the cup of consummation. Its significance still lies in the future when Jesus and His followers will be together again in His kingdom (Luke 22:29-30; see comments on Mark 14:25).

14:24. Jesus explained the meaning of the cup: **This** (the wine) **is** (represents) **My blood of** (i.e., which inaugurates) **the covenant, which** (blood) **is poured out for** (*hyper,* "in behalf of, instead of") **many,** a reference to His vicarious, sacrificial death for mankind (cf. 10:45). Just as sacrificial blood ratified the Old (Mosaic) Covenant at Sinai (cf. Ex.

24:6-8), so Jesus' blood shed at Golgotha inaugurated the New Covenant (Jer. 31:31-34). This promises forgiveness of sins and fellowship with God through the indwelling Spirit to those who come to God by faith in Jesus.

The word *diathēkē* ("covenant") refers not to an agreement between two equals (denoted by *synthēkē*) but rather to an arrangement established by one party, in this case God. The other party—man—cannot alter it; he can only accept or reject it. The New Covenant is God's new arrangement in dealing with people, based on Christ's death (cf. Heb. 8:6-13). The spiritual blessings Israel expected God to grant in the last days are *now* mediated through Christ's death to all who believe. The *physical* blessings promised to Israel, however, are not being fulfilled now. They will be fulfilled when Christ returns and establishes His millennial reign with Israel in her land.

14:25. Jesus seldom spoke about His death without looking beyond it. Using solemn introductory words (**I tell you the truth;** cf. 3:28) He vowed that He would **not** (*ouketi ou mē*, "certainly not any more"; cf. 13:2) **drink again of the fruit of the vine,** in this festive way **until that day** (cf. 13:24-27, 32) in the future **when** He will **drink it anew.** He will enjoy renewed table fellowship with His followers in a qualitatively new (*kainon*) existence (cf. Isa. 2:1-4; 4:2-6; 11:1-9; 65:17-25) **in the kingdom of God** (cf. comments on Mark 1:15), the Millennium established on earth when Jesus Christ returns (cf. Rev. 20:4-6).

14:26. The Hallel (praise) Psalms were **sung** or chanted antiphonally in connection with the Passover—the first two (Pss. 113–114) before the meal, the remaining four (Pss. 115–118) after it to conclude the evening observance. Such verses as Psalm 118:6-7, 17-18, 22-24 gain added significance on Jesus' lips just before His suffering and death.

Since their conversation after the meal included Jesus' discourse and prayer (John 13:31–17:26), it was probably near midnight when He and the Eleven (minus Judas) finally left the Upper Room and the city. **They** crossed the Kidron Valley (cf. John 18:1) **to the** western slopes of the **Mount of Olives** (cf. Mark 11:1a) where Gethsemane was located (14:32).

3. JESUS' PRAYER BEFORE HIS ARREST AND THE DISCIPLES' DESERTION (14:27-52)

The third cycle of events in this division has a "sandwich" structure like many other passages in Mark (cf. 3:20-35). The account of Jesus' prediction of His disciples' desertion (14:27-31) and its fulfillment at His arrest (vv. 43-52) is interrupted by the account of Jesus' prayer in Gethsemane (vv. 32-42). In this way Mark emphasized that Jesus faced His final hour of testing alone with His Father, without human sympathy or support.

a. Jesus' prediction of the disciples' desertion and Peter's denial (14:27-31) (Matt. 26:31-35; Luke 22:31-34; John 13:36-38)

Whether this episode took place in the Upper Room (as Luke and John indicate) or on the way to Gethsemane (as Matt. and Mark imply) is difficult to determine. Mark apparently used it thematically without an explicit chronological connection in anticipation of the subsequent events he wished to highlight (e.g., Mark 14:50-52, 66-72). Matthew, however, included a temporal connection (Matt. 26:31, *tote*, "then"). Perhaps Jesus gave this prediction in the Upper Room relating it only to Peter (as in Luke and John), and repeated it on the way to Gethsemane (as in Matt.) telling it to the Eleven and especially to Peter.

14:27. The verb translated **fall away** (*skandalisthēsesthe*) means to take offense at someone or something and thereby turn away and fall into sin (cf. 4:17; 6:3; 9:42-47). **Jesus** predicted that **all** 11 disciples would take offense at His sufferings and death. To avoid the same treatment they would "fall away," denying association with Him (cf. 14:30) and desert Him (cf. v. 50). Their loyalty would temporarily collapse.

Jesus applied Zechariah 13:7 to this situation: I (God the Father) **will strike** (put to death) **the Shepherd** (Jesus), **and the sheep** (the disciples) **will be scattered** in all directions. The interpretive change from the command "Strike" (Zech. 13:7) to the assertion "I will strike" suggests that Jesus viewed Himself as God's suffering Servant (cf. Isa. 53: esp. Isa. 53:4-6).

14:28. Jesus immediately countered His desertion prediction with the promise of a post-Resurrection reunion (cf. 16:7; Matt. 28:16-17). As the **risen** Shepherd He would precede His flock **into Galilee,** where they had lived and worked and were called and commissioned by Jesus (Mark 1:16-20; 3:13-15; 6:7, 12-13). They were to "follow" the risen Lord who would continue to lead His people in their future tasks (cf. 13:10; 14:9).

14:29-31. As before (cf. 8:32) **Peter** focused on the first part of Jesus' prediction (14:27), ignoring the second part (v. 28). He insisted that he was an exception—**all** the rest might **fall away** as Jesus predicted (v. 27) but he would **not** (lit., "but not I," the word "I" is emphatic by position). Peter claimed greater allegiance to Jesus than all the others (cf. "more than these"; John 21:15).

Prefaced by solemn introductory words (**I tell you the truth**; cf. Mark 3:28) **Jesus** emphatically told Peter that his failure would be greater than the others despite his good intentions. That same night **before the rooster crows twice,** before dawn, Peter would not only desert Jesus but actually **disown** (*aparnēsē,* "deny"; cf. 8:34) Him **three times.** The "cockcrow" was a proverbial expression for early morning before sunrise (cf. 13:35). Only Mark mentioned the rooster crowing twice, a detail probably due to Peter's clear recollection of the incident. (The major Gr. ms. evidence is split over including the word "twice" but the more strongly attested words "the second time" in 14:72 provide confirmation that Mark wrote "twice" here.)

Jesus' pointed reply caused **Peter** to protest even more **emphatically** (an adverb used only here in the NT) that he would **never** (*ou mē,* emphatic negation) **disown** Jesus **even if** he must (*deē;* cf. 8:31) **die with** Jesus. **The others** echoed Peter's affirmation of loyalty. They implied Jesus' prediction was wrong, but a few hours later they showed He was right (14:50, 72).

b. Jesus' prayer in Gethsemane (14:32-42) (Matt. 26:36-47; Luke 22:39-46)

This is the third time Mark portrayed Jesus in prayer (cf. Mark 1:35; 6:46). In each case Jesus reaffirmed His commitment to God's will. Though Satan is not mentioned directly, he was no

doubt present, giving the event the character of a temptation scene (cf. 1:12-13). The Synoptics give five renderings of Jesus' prayer, all similar but with minor variations. Jesus probably repeated the same request in different ways (cf. 14:37, 39).

14:32-34. Jesus and the 11 disciples came to **Gethsemane** (lit., "press of oils," i.e., a press for crushing oil out of olives). It was a gardenlike enclosure in an olive orchard near the foot of the Mount of Olives (cf. v. 26; John 18:1). This secluded spot known also to Judas was one of their favorite meeting places (cf. Luke 22:39; John 18:2).

Jesus told **His disciples**—perhaps as He often had done—to **sit** down near the entrance and wait, literally, "until I have prayed." Then **He** selected **Peter, James, and John** (cf. Mark 5:37; 9:2) to go **along with Him.**

As the four walked into the "garden" Jesus became noticeably **distressed** (from *ekthambeō,* "to be alarmed"; cf. 9:15; 16:5-6) **and troubled** (from *adēmoneō,* "to be in extreme anguish"; cf. Phil. 2:26). He told the three that His **soul** (*psychē,* inner self-conscious life) was **overwhelmed with** such **sorrow** (*perilypos,* "deeply grieved"; cf. Mark 6:26) that it threatened to extinguish His life. This prompted Him to tell them to remain where they were **and keep watch** (*grēgoreite;* cf. 14:38), be alert. The full impact of His death and its *spiritual* consequences struck Jesus and He staggered under its weight. The prospect of alienation from His Father horrified Him.

14:35-36. Moving forward a short distance from the three and gradually prostrating Himself on **the ground** (cf. Matt. 26:39; Luke 22:41) Jesus **prayed** (*proseucheto,* "was praying") aloud with great emotion (Heb. 5:7). His prayer lasted at least an hour (cf. Mark 14:37) but Mark recorded only a brief summary of it, first in narrative form (v. 35b), then in a direct quotation (v. 36).

In essence Jesus requested that **if possible the hour might pass from Him.** The words "if possible" (first-class condition in Gr.) do not express doubt but a concrete supposition on which He based His request. He made His request on the assumption that the Father was able to grant it. The issue remained whether it was God's will to do so (cf. Luke 22:42).

The metaphor "the hour" denoted God's appointed time when Jesus would suffer and die (cf. Mark 14:41b; John 12:23, 27). The corresponding metaphor, **this cup,** referred to the same event. The "cup" means either human suffering and death or more likely, God's wrath against sin, which when poured out includes not only physical but also spiritual suffering and death (cf. Mark 10:38-39; 14:33b-34). In bearing God's judgment the sinless Jesus endured the agony of being "made sin" (cf. 15:34; 2 Cor. 5:21).

The double title **Abba** (Aram., "My Father") **Father** (Gr., *patēr*) occurs only two other times (Rom. 8:15; Gal. 4:6). "Abba" was a common way young Jewish children addressed their fathers. It conveyed a sense of familial intimacy and familiarity. The Jews, however, did not use it as a personal address to God since such a familar term was considered inappropriate in prayer. Thus Jesus' use of *Abba* in addressing God was new and unique. He probably used it often in His prayers to express His intimate relationship with God as His Father. *Abba* here suggests that Jesus' primary concern in drinking the cup of God's judgment on sin necessarily disrupted this relationship (cf. Jesus' words of address, Mark 15:34).

What did Jesus mean by requesting that the hour "might pass" and that the Father **take** the cup **from** Him? The traditional answer is that Jesus asked to avoid "the hour" hoping, if possible, that it would bypass Him and that the cup would be removed *before* He must drink it. According to this view Jesus prayed a prayer of submission to God's will as He went to the cross. Some interpreters, however, contend that Jesus asked to be restored following "the hour," hoping, if possible, that it would pass on by *after* it came and that the cup would be removed *after* He had drained it (cf. Isa. 51:17-23). In this view, Jesus prayed a prayer of faith that the Father would not abandon Him forever to death under divine wrath but would remove it and resurrect Him.

Though not problem-free (e.g., John 12:27), the traditional view is preferred in light of the contextual factors just discussed, other passages (Matt. 26:39, 42; Luke 22:41-42; Heb. 5:7-8), and the final qualifying statement in Mark 14:36: **Yet** (lit., "but") the final answer, is **not what I** (emphatic) **will but what You** (emphatic)

will. Jesus' human will was distinct from but never in opposition to the Father's will (cf. John 5:30; 6:38). So He acknowledged that the answer to His request was not governed by what He desired but by what the Father willed. God's will entailed His sacrificial death (cf. Mark 8:31) so He resolutely submitted Himself to it. His deep distress passed from Him but "the hour" did not (cf. 14:41b).

14:37-41a. The emphasis in Mark's narrative now shifts from Jesus' prayer to the three disciples' failure to stay awake (cf. vv. 33-34). Thrice Jesus interrupted His praying and **returned to** where they were only to find **them sleeping.** The first time He addressed **Peter** as **Simon,** his old name (cf. 3:16), and chided him for his failure to **watch for** even **one hour.** Then Jesus exhorted all three, **Watch,** be alert to spiritual dangers, **and pray,** acknowledge dependence on God, **so that you will not fall** (lit., "come") **into temptation.** This anticipated the testings they would face at His arrest and trial (cf. 14:50, 66-72). On the one hand (Gr., *men*) **the spirit** (one's inner desires and best intentions) **is willing** or eager (e.g., Peter, vv. 29, 31), **but** on the other hand (Gr., *de*) **the body** (lit., "flesh"; a person in his humanness and inadequacies) **is weak,** easily overwhelmed in action (e.g., Peter, v. 37).

After going back and praying **the same** petition (cf. v. 36) Jesus returned and **again found them sleeping.** To His words of rebuke they had nothing appropriate **to say** (cf. 9:6).

Following **a third** prayer session, Jesus returned and again found them sleeping. His words (**Are you still sleeping and resting?**) could be a convicting question (NIV), an ironic but compassionate command (KJV), or an exclamation of surprised rebuke. In light of verses 37, 40, the first option seems preferable. Three times Peter failed to watch and pray; three times he would fall into temptation and disown Jesus. This warning applies to all believers, for all are susceptible to spiritual failure (cf. 13:37).

14:41b-42. Probably a short time occurred between verse 41a and 41b. Jesus' word **Enough!** (i.e., of sleeping) aroused the disciples. Then He announced, **The hour** (cf. v. 35) **has come. The Son of Man** (cf. 8:31) was about to be **betrayed** (cf. 9:31) **into the hands**

(control) of sinners, specifically, hostile Sanhedrin members. His betrayer, Judas, had arrived. Instead of fleeing, Jesus and the three disciples (no doubt now joined by the other eight) advanced to meet Judas. The issue that prompted Jesus' prayer had been settled (cf. 14:35-36).

c. Jesus' betrayal and arrest and the disciples' desertion (14:43-52) (Matt. 26:47-56; Luke 22:47-53; John 18:2-12)

14:43. Immediately (euthys; cf. 1:10), while Jesus was still speaking to His disciples, Judas came with . . . a crowd of Roman soldiers (cf. John 18:12) armed with short hand swords and the temple police armed with clubs (cf. Luke 22:52). Judas had guided them to Gethsemane (cf. John 18:2) and to Jesus (cf. Acts 1:16) at night so He could be arrested without commotion (cf. Mark 14:1-2). The Sanhedrin (cf. comments on 8:31) issued the warrant for His arrest. The high priest likely secured the aid of the Roman troops.

14:44-47. Judas had given the armed band a signal (a kiss) that would identify the One they were to arrest. They were to lead Him away under guard to prevent His escape. When Judas entered the "garden," he at once (euthys; cf. 1:10) went to Jesus, greeted Him as Rabbi (cf. 4:38; 9:5) and kissed Him fervently (intensive compound verb). A kiss on the cheek (or hand) was a common gesture of affection and reverence given to a Rabbi by his disciples. But Judas used it as a token of betrayal.

Since Jesus offered no resistance He was easily seized and arrested. No charges are stated in Mark's account; nevertheless the legality of His arrest according to Jewish criminal law was assumed since the Sanhedrin authorized it. His apparent defenselessness continued to veil His true identity publicly.

Mark recorded a single-handed attempt at armed resistance by an unnamed bystander (Peter; cf. John 18:10). The Greek wording implies Mark knew who it was. As one of two disciples with a sword (cf. Luke 22:38), Peter drew it and struck Malchus, the servant of the high priest, Caiaphas. But Peter managed to cut off only his right ear (cf. John 18:10, 13). Only Luke recorded that Jesus

restored it (cf. Luke 22:51). Peter's attempted defense of Jesus was a wrong deed in a wrong place.

14:48-50. Though He offered no resistance Jesus did protest to the religious authorities for the excessive display of armed force marshaled against Him as if He had been leading a rebellion (lit., "as though they came out against an armed robber"). He was not a revolutionary who acted in stealth but a recognized religious Teacher. Every day that week He appeared openly among them in Jerusalem teaching (cf. 11:17) in the temple courts (hierō; cf. 11:11) but they did not arrest Him (cf. 12:12; 14:1-2). Their arresting Him like a criminal at night in a secluded place showed their cowardice. But this happened so that the Scriptures would be fulfilled (cf. Isa. 53:3, 7-9, 12).

When Jesus' response made it clear that He would not resist His arrest, the disciples' loyalty and their confidence in Him as the Messiah collapsed. Everyone ("all," emphatic by position) deserted Him and fled (cf. Mark 14:27). No one remained with Jesus to share His suffering—not even Peter (cf. v. 29).

14:51-52. This unusual episode, unique to Mark, supplements verse 50 emphasizing the fact that all fled, leaving Jesus completely forsaken. Most interpreters believe that this young man (neaniskos, a person in the prime of life, between 24 and 40 years of age) was Mark himself. If so, and if he was the son of the house owner (vv. 14-15; cf. Acts 12:12) that night's events may have occurred as follows. After Jesus and His disciples left Mark's father's house after the Passover, Mark removed his outer cloak (cf. Mark 13:16) and went to bed wrapped in a linen sleeping garment (lit., "cloth"). Shortly afterward a servant may have aroused him with the news about Judas' treachery since Judas and the arresting force had come there looking for Jesus. Without stopping to dress Mark rushed to Gethsemane perhaps to warn Jesus, who had already been arrested when Mark arrived. After all the disciples fled, Mark was following Jesus and His captors into the city when some of them seized Mark, perhaps as a potential witness, but he fled from them naked, leaving his linen sleeping garment in someone's hands. So no one remained with Jesus—not even a courageous young man who intended to follow Him.

B. Jesus' trials, crucifixion, and burial (14:53-15:47)

This division also consists of three cycles of events: Jesus' trials (14:53-15:20), crucifixion (15:21-41), and burial (15:42-47).

1. JESUS' TRIALS BEFORE THE SANHEDRIN AND PILATE (14:53-15:20)

Jesus was tried first by the religious authorities and then by the political authorities. This was necessary because the Sanhedrin did not have the power to exercise capital punishment (John 18:31). Each of the two trials had three hearings. (See the chart, "Jesus' Six Trials," at Matt. 26:57-58.)

a. Jesus' trial before the Sanhedrin and Peter's threefold denial (14:53-15:1a)

Jesus' trial before the Jewish religious authorities included a preliminary hearing by Annas (John 18:12-14, 19-24), an arraignment before Caiaphas, the high priest, and the Sanhedrin at night (Matt. 26:57-68; Mark 14:53-65), and a final verdict by the Sanhedrin just after dawn (cf. Matt. 27:1; Mark 15:1a; Luke 22:66-71).

(1) Jesus in the high priest's residence and Peter in the courtyard (14:53-54; Matt. 26:57-58; Luke 22:54; John 18:15-16, 18, 24). **14:53.** Jesus' captors led Him under guard from Gethsemane back into Jerusalem **to the** residence of the **high priest,** Joseph Caiaphas (cf. Matt. 26:57), who held this office from A.D. 18 to 36 (see the chart on Annas' family at Acts 4:5-6).

The 71-member Sanhedrin (cf. comments on Mark 8:31), including the presiding high priest, was hastily assembled in an upstairs room (cf. 14:66) for a plenary night session. This was an "informal" trial that required a "formal" ratification after dawn (cf. 15:1) to satisfy strict Jewish legal procedure allowing trials only in the daytime. A quorum consisted of 23 members (Mishnah Sanhedrin 1. 6) but on this occasion the majority were probably there even though it was around 3 A.M. on Nisan 15 (Friday), a feast day.

This hasty night meeting was deemed necessary because: (1) In Jewish criminal law it was customary to hold a trial immediately after arrest. (2) Roman legal trials were usually held shortly after sunrise (cf. 15:1) so the Sanhedrin needed a binding verdict by daybreak in order to get the case to Pilate early. (3) With Jesus finally in custody they did not want to delay proceedings, thereby arousing opposition to His arrest. Actually they had already determined to kill Him (cf. 14:1-2); their only problem was getting evidence that would justify it (cf. v. 55). Perhaps also they wished to have the Romans crucify Jesus to avoid the people's blaming the Sanhedrin for His death.

Some have questioned the legality of a capital trial on a feast day in light of certain Rabbinic legal ordinances. However, the Rabbis justified the trial and execution of serious offenders on a major feast day. That way, they argued, "all the people will hear and be afraid" (Deut. 17:13; cf. Deut. 21:21; cf. TDNT, s.v. "pascha," 5:899-900). Normally in capital cases a conviction verdict could not be legally determined until the following day.

14:54. Peter (cf. vv. 29, 31, 50) regained enough courage to follow Jesus **at a distance, right** inside **the courtyard of the high priest.** This was a central quadrangle with the high priest's residence built around it (cf. John 18:15-18). Peter **sat** there **with the guards,** the temple police, and **warmed himself at** a charcoal **fire** (lit., "facing the light" of the fire, so his face was illuminated; cf. Mark 14:67) because of the cold night air. He wanted to know what would happen to Jesus (cf. Matt. 26:58).

(2) Jesus' trial before the Sanhedrin (14:55-65; Matt. 26:59-68). The material in this section probably rests on the report of one or more Sanhedrin members who were secretly sympathetic to Jesus or who were against Him originally but later came to believe in Him (cf. Acts 6:7).

14:55-56. The **Sanhedrin** began their deliberations by seeking **evidence** (lit., "testimony") **against Jesus** in order to justify a **death** sentence **but they** found none (lit., "were **not** finding **any**"). They did not lack witnesses because **many** were testifying **falsely against Him, but their** testimony was invalid because their statements (lit., "testimonies") did not agree (lit., "were not equal"). Various unverified charges were made and numerous discrepancies arose in testimony on the same charge. Perhaps these witnesses were already on call prior to Jesus' arrest but did not coordinate their stories. In Jewish trials the witnesses served as the prosecution, giving their testimonies separately. Convicting a person for a crime, the Mosaic Law required precise agreement in the testimony of at least two witnesses (Num. 35:30; Deut. 17:6; 19:15).

14:57-59. In due time **some** witnesses ("two"; cf. Matt. 26:60) declared they had heard Jesus say: I (*egō*, emphatic) **will destroy this man-made temple** (*naon*, "the sanctuary"; cf. Mark 11:11), **and in three days will build another** (*allon*, "another" of a different kind), **not made by man.** Yet even in this **testimony** there were unspecified discrepancies, so Mark labeled it **false.**

Jesus had made a cryptic statement similar to this (John 2:19) but He was referring to the "temple" of His body (cf. John 2:20-22). These witnesses, like those present at the time, misinterpreted His words as a reference to the Jerusalem temple. Destruction of a worship place was a capital offense in the ancient world (Josephus *The Antiquities of the Jews* 10. 6. 2). Though their testimony was invalid, it opened the way for questions about Jesus' identity (Mark 14:61) and led to the taunt recorded in 15:29.

14:60-61a. The high priest Caiaphas **asked Jesus** two questions to get information that could be used against Him. In Greek the first question expects a positive answer: "**You are going to answer** Your accusers, aren't You?" The second question expected an explanation from Him: "**What is** the meaning of the charges **these** witnesses are making **against You?**" But Jesus remained silent and gave no defense (cf. Isa. 53:7). His silence frustrated the court and brought its proceedings to a standstill.

14:61b-62. The high priest changed tactics and **asked** (lit., "kept asking") Jesus pointedly, **Are You** (emphatic) **the Christ** (the Messiah; cf. 1:1; 8:29), **the Son of the Blessed One?** The title "Blessed One," found in this sense only here in the New Testament, is a Jewish substitute for "God" (cf. Mishnah *Berachoth* 7. 3). These

two titles of Jesus both refer to His claim to be the Messiah.

Jesus unequivocally answered, **I am,** that is, "I am the Messiah, the Son of God." This is the first time in Mark's Gospel that He openly declared He is the Messiah (cf. comments on 1:43-44; 8:29-30; 9:9; 11:28-33; 12:12). In proof of this—something the Jews expected the true Messiah to provide—Jesus made a startling prediction. Applying words from Psalm 110:1 and Daniel 7:13 to Himself, He stated, **And you** (His human judges) **will see the Son of Man** (cf. Mark 8:31, 38) **sitting at the right hand,** exalted to the place of highest honor and authority (cf. 12:36), **of the Mighty One** (lit., "the Power"), a Jewish substitute title for "God" (cf. 14:61), **and coming on** (lit., "with") **the clouds of heaven** to judge (cf. 8:38; 13:26). The fact that they "will see" this did not mean Jesus would return in their lifetimes. Rather it referred indirectly to bodily resurrection in judgment before the exalted Son of Man who will one day judge those who were judging Him. Then it will be unmistakably clear that He is God's Anointed One, the Messiah.

14:63-64. By tearing **his clothes,** probably his inner garments rather than his official robes, **the high priest** showed that he regarded Jesus' bold declaration as **blasphemy.** To him, Jesus' words dishonored God by claiming rights and powers belonging exclusively to God (cf. 2:7). This symbolic expression of horror and indignation was required of the high priest whenever he heard blasphemy. His reaction also expressed relief since Jesus' self-incriminating answer removed the **need** for **more witnesses.**

The Mosaic Law prescribed death by stoning for blasphemy (Lev. 24:15-16). Without further investigation the high priest called for a verdict from the Sanhedrin. Since there were no objections **they all condemned Him** (cf. Mark 10:33) **as worthy** (*enochon*, "guilty, liable"; cf. 3:29) **of death.**

14:65. **Some** Sanhedrin members showed their contempt through mockery and physical abuse. To **spit** in someone's face was an act of total repudiation and gross personal insult (cf. Num. 12:14; Deut. 25:9; Job 30:10; Isa. 50:6). On account of His messianic claims **they blindfolded Him, struck Him with their**

fists and demanded that He prophesy who hit Him. This reflects a traditional test of messianic status based on a Rabbinic interpretation of Isaiah 11:2-4. The true Messiah could judge such matters without the benefit of sight (cf. Babylonian Talmud *Sanhedrin* 93b). But Jesus refused to submit to their test and remained silent (cf. Isa. 53:7; 1 Peter 2:23). When He was returned to the temple guards (cf. Mark 14:54), they followed their superiors' example and continued beating Him with open-handed slaps on the face (cf. Luke 22:63-65).

(3) Peter's threefold denial of Jesus (14:66-72; Matt. 26:69-75; Luke 22:55-62; John 18:15-18, 25-27). All four Gospels record this episode with variations, but without contradicting each other. Mark's vivid account probably came from Peter. It resumes Mark 14:54, showing that Peter's ordeal coincided with Jesus' interrogation before the Sanhedrin. After this denial account Mark resumed his report of the Sanhedrin's action (cf. 15:1a).

14:66-68. One of the high priest's **servant girls**, presumably the inner courtyard's doorkeeper (cf. John 18:16) approached **Peter** while he warmed himself by the fire **in the courtyard** (cf. Mark 14:54; 15:16) which apparently **was below** the upstairs room where Jesus' trial was taking place. After **she looked closely** (from *emblepō*; cf. 10:21) **at him,** she blurted out contemptuously, **You** (emphatic sing. pronoun) **also** (John was there too; cf. John 18:15) **were with** (cf. Mark 3:14) **that Nazarene** (cf. 1:24; 10:47), **Jesus.**

Her charge correctly identified Peter as a disciple **but he denied** (*ērnēsato*; cf. 8:34; 14:30) **it,** refusing to acknowledge his relationship to Jesus out of fear for his safety. His denial was a common Jewish legal expression, literally, "I neither **know** nor **understand what** you (emphatic) are saying." To avoid further exposure he **went out into the entryway,** the covered passageway leading to the street.

Nearly all major ancient Greek manuscripts and early versions include the words "and the rooster crowed" (NIV marg.; KJV) at the end of verse 68. This evidence plus the strongly attested words "the second time" in verse 72 favor inclusion of these words. Since only one

rooster-crowing is mentioned in the parallel passages (cf. Matt. 26:74; Luke 22:60; John 18:27) these words were probably omitted from Mark very early by some scribes to conform to the parallels. But Mark was simply more specific than the other Gospels, probably because of Peter's vivid recollection. Apparently this first rooster-crowing held no significance for Peter since it happened every morning (cf. Mark 13:35b; 14:72).

14:69-71. The same **servant girl** along with others (cf. Matt. 26:71; Luke 22:58) **saw** Peter in the entryway and **again** identified him **to** the bystanders as **one of** Jesus' disciples. **Again he denied** (lit., "kept denying," imperf.) **it.**

About an hour later (cf. Luke 22:59) the bystanders (again, in Gr.) confronted **Peter** with the charge, **Surely** (lit., "truly," despite his denials) **you are one of them** (the disciples), **for** ("because") **you are** ("also," in Gr.) **a Galilean.** Galileans spoke an Aramaic dialect with noticeable differences in pronunciation (cf. Matt. 26:73). So they concluded he was a follower of that heretic Galilean, Jesus.

The fact that Peter **began to call down curses on himself and** that **he swore to them** does not mean he used profanity. Rather he placed himself under God's curse if he were lying to them and put himself under oath, as in a courtroom, to confirm the veracity of his denial. Carefully avoiding the use of Jesus' name Peter emphatically denied any knowledge of **this Man** they were **talking about.**

14:72. Peter's third denial in less than two hours was **immediately** (*euthys;* cf. 1:10) punctuated by the rooster's **second** crowing (cf. 14:68, NIV marg.). This time he suddenly **remembered** Jesus' prediction of his denial made earlier that night (vv. 29-31). Peter also saw **Jesus** looking down at him (Luke 22:61). Overwhelmed, **he broke down and wept.**

In contrast with Judas (Matt. 27:3-5) Peter's remorse opened the way for true repentance and a reaffirmation of his loyalty to Jesus as the risen Lord (cf. Mark 16:7; John 21:15-19). Peter had a faith in Jesus that could be renewed, but Judas did not.

(4) The Sanhedrin's verdict at dawn (15:1a; Matt. 27:1; Luke 22:66-71). **15:1a.** Immediately (*euthys;* cf. 1:10) after daybreak—between 5 and 6 A.M., prob-

ably on Friday, April 3, A.D. 33—the whole Sanhedrin (cf. 14:53) led by the chief priests formalized their condemnation of Jesus and reached a decision, a plan of action for getting a guilty verdict from the Roman governor.

Though the Sanhedrin could pronounce a death sentence it could not exercise capital punishment. So a condemned prisoner had to be turned over to the Roman authorities for a death sentence to be carried out (cf. John 18:31; TDNT, S.V. "synedrion," 1:865-6). The Roman governor could either ratify or rescind the Sanhedrin's death sentence (cf. John 19:10). If rescinded, a new trial had to be conducted before a Roman court in which the Sanhedrin had to prove that the defendant had committed a capital crime under Roman law. Since the charge of blasphemy (cf. Mark 14:64) was not punishable by Roman law it was not mentioned in the following trial. In its place the Sanhedrin substituted a charge of treason, turning Jesus' acknowledgment that He was the Messiah into a traitorous political claim that He is "the King of the Jews" (cf. 15:2; Luke 23:2). The Roman court surely could not ignore that charge.

b. Jesus' trial before Pilate and the Roman soldiers' abuse (15:1b-20)

Jesus' trial before the Roman political authorities also had three hearings: (a) an initial interrogation by Pilate (cf. Matt. 27:2, 11-14; Mark 15:1b-5; Luke 23:1-5; John 18:28-38); (b) an interrogation by Herod Antipas (cf. Luke 23:5-12); (c) a final arraignment before Pilate, Barabbas' release, and the crucifixion verdict (cf. Matt. 27:15-26; Mark 15:6-20; Luke 23:13-25; John 18:39–19:16).

Before the Sanhedrin Jesus was condemned for blasphemy under Jewish law, but here He was tried for treason under Roman law. On both occasions He was sentenced to die, in conformity with God's will (cf. Mark 10:33-34).

(1) Pilate's interrogation and Jesus' silence (15:1b-5; Matt. 27:2, 11-14; Luke 23:1-5; John 18:28-38). **15:1b.** The Sanhedrin had Jesus **bound** and led through the city from Caiaphas' residence (cf. 14:53) probably to Herod's palace where they **handed Him over to Pilate** for execution of the death sentence.

Pontius Pilate, the fifth Roman prefect (a title later changed to "procurator," i.e., imperial magistrate) of Judea held office A.D. 26–36. He was a harsh governor who despised the Jews (cf. Luke 13:1-2). Normally he resided in Caesarea by the Mediterranean Sea, but he came to Jerusalem on special occasions such as the Passover festival to help maintain order. Presumably he stayed in Herod's palace as was customary for provincial governors rather than in the Antonia Fortress near the temple. If so, Jesus' civil trial was held there.

15:2. Pilate had sole responsibility for the Roman court's decisions. The proceedings, usually held in public, opened with an indictment by the plaintiff followed by the magistrate's interrogation and further testimony from the defendant and other witnesses. When all the evidence was in, the magistrate usually consulted with his legal advisers and then pronounced the sentence, which had to be carried out immediately.

Instead of confirming the Sanhedrin's death sentence (cf. John 18:29-32) Pilate insisted on hearing the case. Only one of three accusations that had already been made (cf. Luke 23:2) merited Pilate's attention, namely, Jesus' alleged claim to be "a king." So Pilate **asked** Jesus, **Are You** (emphatic) **the King of the Jews?** To Pilate such a claim was tantamount to treason against Caesar, a crime punishable by death.

Jesus gave a cryptic reply, literally, **You** (emphatic) **say** (so), that is, "The designation is yours." It is best understood as a **yes** answer but with a qualification attached. As Messiah, Jesus is the King of the Jews but His concept of kingship differed from that implied in Pilate's question (cf. John 18:33-38).

15:3-5. Since Jesus' initial response provided no solid basis for a capital conviction under Roman law Pilate returned to His accusers to gain more information. **The chief priests** (cf. v. 1a) seized the opportunity to bolster their case by pressing multiple charges against Jesus.

Again Pilate tried to get Jesus to respond to His accusers and defend Himself against their charges **but** to his utter amazement **Jesus** remained absolutely silent (cf. Isa. 53:7; lit., "He

185

answered no longer nothing"; *ouketi ouden*, emphatic negative). Such silence was rare in a Roman court. It seemed to confirm Pilate's initial feeling that Jesus was not guilty.

Mark included only two short utterances by Jesus—one to Caiaphas (Mark 14:62) and one to Pilate (15:2). Jesus' silence highlights the fact that He, the Son of Man, suffered and died within God's sovereign plan (cf. comments on 8:31).

Learning that Jesus was a Galilean and hoping to avoid making a judgment against Him, Pilate sent Him to Herod Antipas, governor of Galilee (cf. 6:14), also in Jerusalem at the time. But Herod soon returned Him to Pilate. Only Luke recorded this middle phase of the civil trial (cf. Luke 23:6-12).

(2) Pilate's futile attempts to gain acquittal for Jesus (15:6-15; Matt. 27:15-26; Luke 23:13-25; John 18:39-40; 19:1, 13-16). **15:6.** Each year during the Passover festival **it was the** governor's **custom** as a sign of goodwill **to release a prisoner** selected by **the people** (cf. v. 8). Though no explicit reference to the custom occurs outside the New Testament it was consistent with Rome's conciliatory attitude toward subject peoples on local matters. Instead of granting Jesus an acquittal, Pilate chose to grant the customary Passover amnesty, thinking the people would request Jesus' release (cf. v. 9).

15:7. While suppressing an **uprising** in Jerusalem, the Roman authorities had arrested **Barabbas** (from *Bar Abba*, "son of the father"), a notorious freedom fighter, robber (John 18:40), and murderer, along **with** other **insurrectionists.** He may have been a Zealot, a nationalist who stirred up opposition against Rome. Now he was awaiting execution.

15:8-11. During the trial proceedings a sizable **crowd** had gathered in the palace forum (cf. v. 16). The people approached Pilate's elevated judgment seat **and asked** him **to** grant the annual Passover amnesty (cf. v. 6). Many of them were probably supporters of Barabbas.

Pilate saw this as an opportunity to show his contempt for the Jews, especially their leaders. He offered **to release to them the King of the Jews** (cf. v. 2). He recognized **that the chief priests had** turned **Jesus over to him** not out of loyalty to Rome but **out of envy** and

hatred. **Pilate** hoped to achieve Jesus' release and thus undo the religious leaders' scheme.

But Pilate's plan did not work. **The chief priests** incited **the** emotional **crowd** to pressure him into releasing **Barabbas instead** of Jesus. Apparently they knew that the Sanhedrin had already condemned Jesus (cf. 14:64). Strangely, Pilate failed to consider that the crowd would never side with him against their own leaders (cf. John 19:6-7).

15:12-14. Since the crowd had rejected Pilate's offer and requested the release of Barabbas, he inquired ("again" is in the Gr.) about **what** they wanted done **with the One** they called **the King of the Jews. Pilate** did not accept this title for Jesus but his question implied he was willing to release Jesus *also* if they wished. But without hesitation **they shouted** back, **Crucify Him!** The punishment that once awaited Barabbas was now thrust on Jesus.

Pilate challenged them to state the **crime** which made Jesus guilty enough to be crucified. **But they** persistently cried out **all the louder, Crucify Him!** Pilate considered the clamor of the crowd an acclamation, legally indicating a decision by popular demand. Thus Jesus must be pronounced guilty of high treason, a capital offense normally punishable by crucifixion in Roman provinces.

15:15. Though he believed Jesus was innocent (cf. v. 14) **Pilate** followed political expedience rather than justice. Wishing **to satisfy the** people lest they complain to Emperor Tiberius—thereby putting his position in jeopardy (cf. John 19:12)—Pilate **released Barabbas to them . . . had Jesus flogged, and** sentenced **Him** to death by crucifixion.

A Roman flogging was a brutal beating that always preceded the execution of a capital sentence on male offenders, though it could also be a separate punishment (cf. TDNT, s.v. *"mastigoō,"* 4:517-9). The prisoner was stripped, often tied to a post, and beaten on the back by several guards using short leather whips studded with sharp pieces of bone or metal. No limit was set on the number of blows. Often this punishment was fatal.

Pilate had Jesus flogged in hope that the people would take pity and be satisfied. But this also failed; they still insisted He be crucified (cf. John 19:1-7). (3) The Roman soldiers' mockery of Jesus (15:16-20; Matt. 27:27-31; John 19:2-12). **15:16.** After the flogging of **Jesus,** presumably outside in the public square, **the** Roman **soldiers** took Him, battered and bleeding, **into** (*esō*, "inside") **the palace** (lit., "courtyard"; cf. same word in 14:54, 66). The rendering "palace" is justified due to Mark's explanatory comment, **that is, the Praetorium,** equating the two places. The Latin loanword, *Praetorium,* meant the governor's official residence (cf. Matt. 27:27; John 18:28, 33; 19:9; Acts 23:35). Once inside they summoned **the whole company** (*speiran,* Gr. for the Latin "cohort") **of soldiers.** Ordinarily a cohort was 600 men, ¹/₁₀ of a 6,000-soldier legion. But in this case it may have been an auxiliary battalion of 200-300 soldiers that had accompanied Pilate to Jerusalem from Caesarea.

15:17-19. In ludicrous imitation of a vassal king's regal robes and gilded headwreath, the soldiers dressed Jesus in **a purple robe,** a faded military cloak, and pressed **a crown of thorns,** perhaps palm spines, on His head. With this "crown" the soldiers unwittingly pictured God's curse on sinful humanity being thrust on Jesus (cf. Gen. 3:17-18). Matthew noted that they also placed a staff in His hand as a mock scepter (Matt. 27:29).

Then they ridiculed Him with contemptuous words and insulting actions in mock homage to a king. The derisive greeting **Hail** (Rejoice), **King of the Jews,** paralleled the formal Roman plaudit, "Ave, Caesar." The NIV words, **again and again** reflect the imperfect tense of the Greek verbs. The soldiers kept striking Jesus **with a staff,** probably His mock scepter, on His thorn-crowned **head.** They kept spitting **on Him** (cf. Mark 14:65) and bending **their knees** in mock submission to royalty. In all this they acted out of contempt not so much for Jesus personally but for their subject nation which had long desired a king of its own.

15:20. The soldiers then removed the mock royal attire and dressed Him in **His own clothes.** Then they, a four-soldier execution squad (cf. John 19:23) under the command of a centurion, **led Him** outside the city **to crucify Him.**

Jesus' suffering before the Roman authorities was exemplary for Mark's readers who would be subjected to similar ridicule before pagan authorities (cf. comments on Mark 13:9-13).

2. JESUS' CRUCIFIXION AND DEATH (15:21-41)

Death by crucifixion was one of the cruelest forms of capital punishment ever devised. Mark's account of Jesus' physical sufferings is vivid but restrained. They were secondary to His overwhelming spiritual anguish (cf. 14:36; 15:34). (For the order of events, see the "Harmony of Events at Jesus' Crucifixion," at Matt. 27:32-38.)

a. *Jesus' crucifixion and the crowd's mockery (15:21-32)*
(Matt. 27:32-44; Luke 23:26-43; John 19:17-27)

15:21-22. Customarily a condemned man carried the *patibulum* of his own cross, that is, the crossbeam weighing about 100 pounds, through the city streets out to the place of crucifixion. Jesus started to carry His (cf. John 19:17) but was so weak from being flogged that His strength gave out near the city gate. The soldiers randomly seized **a** passerby named **Simon** and **forced him to carry the** beam the rest of the way.

Simon was a native of **Cyrene,** an important coastal city of North Africa that had a large Jewish colony (Acts 2:10). He was either an immigrant living near Jerusalem or more likely, a pilgrim who had come to Jerusalem for the Passover festival but had to stay in **the country** at night because there was no room in the city. Only Mark mentioned Simon's sons, **Alexander and Rufus,** suggesting that they were disciples known to his readers in Rome (cf. Rom. 16:13).

The soldiers took **Jesus to the place** outside but near the city wall (cf. John 19:20) **called Golgotha,** a Greek transliteration of an Aramaic word meaning **The Place of the Skull.** The word "Calvary" comes from the Latin Vulgate rendering *Calvaria,* a variation of *calva,* "a skull." Golgotha was a rounded, rocky knoll (not a hill or mountain) vaguely resembling the shape of a human skull. Its exact location is uncertain. It was either at the present Church of the Holy Sepulchre, the traditional site dating from the fourth century, or "Gordon's Calvary," a more recent suggestion. The traditional site is more probable.

15:23-24. According to Rabbinic tradition certain Jerusalem women provided sedative drinks for those about to be crucified, to decrease their pain (cf. Prov. 31:6-7). On arrival at Golgotha, **they,** presumably the Roman soldiers, **offered** (lit., "were attempting to give") Jesus such a drink, **wine mixed with myrrh,** a plant's sap having anesthetic properties. But after He had tasted it (cf. Matt. 27:34) He refused **it,** choosing rather to face suffering and death in full control of all His faculties.

With restrained simplicity Mark wrote, **And they crucified Him.** His Roman readers needed no elaboration and he offered none. Normally a condemned man was stripped (except possibly for a loincloth), laid on the ground, and both outstretched forearms were nailed to the crossbeam. Then this beam was raised and fastened to an upright post already stuck in the ground and the victim's feet were nailed to it. A wooden peg partway up the post on which the victim sat helped support his body. Death from extreme exhaustion and thirst was painful and slow and usually came after two or three days. Sometimes death was hastened by breaking the victim's legs (John 19:31-33).

A victim's personal belongings became the property of the execution squad. In Jesus' case the four-man squad (cf. John 19:23) **cast lots,** probably dice, for **His clothes**—an inner and outer garment, a belt, sandals, and perhaps a head covering—**to see what each one would get.** Unwittingly they fulfilled Psalm 22:18, another aspect of Jesus' humiliation.

15:25. Using the Jewish method of counting hours from sunrise (and sunset) Mark alone recorded that Jesus' crucifixion took place at **the third hour,** that is, 9 A.M. This seems to conflict with the time reference "the sixth hour" in John 19:14. But John probably used the Roman (modern) method of counting hours from midnight (and noon); thus he put Jesus' trial before Pilate at "about the sixth hour," that is, approximately 6 A.M. The interval between 6 and 9 A.M. was filled with the soldiers' mockery (cf. Mark 15:16-20), Pilate's verdict on the two robbers (cf. 15:27), and preparations for the crucifixions.

15:26. It was a Roman custom to write the name of the condemned man and a description of his crime on a board and attach it to his cross (John 19:19). All four Gospels record the words of Jesus' notice but with minor variations, probably because it was written in three languages (John 19:20). Mark recorded only the official **charge against Him . . . THE KING OF THE JEWS** (cf. Mark 15:2, 12). Pilate's wording was intended as an insult to Jewish aspirations for independence (cf. John 19:21-22).

15:27-28. Pilate had Jesus **crucified** between **two robbers** who, like Barabbas, were perhaps guilty of insurrection (cf. v. 7; John 18:40). They may have been convicted of treason at the same time as Jesus because they were familiar with His case (Luke 23:40-42).

Unwittingly Pilate's action fulfilled Isaiah 53:12, which is cited in Mark 15:28 (NIV marg.; KJV; cf. Luke 22:37).

15:29-30. Again Jesus was subjected to verbal abuse (cf. 14:65; 15:17-19). Passersby **hurled insults at Him** (lit., "kept slandering Him"). **Shaking their heads** refers to a familiar gesture of derision (cf. Pss. 22:7; 109:25; Jer. 18:16; Lam. 2:15). They taunted Him for His alleged claim regarding **the temple** (cf. Mark 14:58). If He could rebuild the temple **in three days** (a great feat), then surely He could **save** (from *sōzō,* "deliver or rescue"; cf. 5:23, 28, 34) Himself from death by coming **down from the cross** (a lesser feat).

15:31-32. Similarly the Jewish religious leaders **mocked** Jesus indirectly in conversations **among themselves.** Their long-standing desire to kill Him was successful at last (cf. 3:6; 11:18; 12:12; 14:1, 64; 15:1, 11-13). Their words **He saved** (from *sōzō*) **others** refer to His healing miracles, which they could not deny (cf. 5:34; 6:56; 10:52). **But** they ridiculed Him because **He** seemed powerless to **save** (from *sōzō;* cf. 15:30) **Himself.** Ironically their words expressed a profound spiritual truth. If Jesus was to save others, delivering them from the power of sin, then He could not save (rescue)

Himself from the sufferings and death appointed to Him by God (cf. 8:31). They also mocked Jesus' messianic claims (cf. comments on 14:61-62) replacing Pilate's words "King of the Jews" (cf. 15:26) with **King of Israel.** They challenged Him to prove His messianic claim by a miraculous descent **from the cross** so they could **see** the compelling evidence **and believe** that He is God's Messiah. The issue, however, was not lack of evidence but unbelief.

The two men **crucified with** Jesus **also** joined in reviling Him. But one of them soon stopped and asked Jesus to remember him in His kingdom (Luke 23:39-43).

b. Jesus' death and the accompanying phenomena (15:33-41)
(Matt. 27:45-56; Luke 23:44-49; John 19:28-30)

Climactically Mark recorded five phenomena that accompanied Jesus' death: (a) darkness (Mark 15:33), (b) Jesus' cry, "My God . . ." (v. 34), (c) Jesus' loud cry (v. 37), (d) the temple curtain torn from top to bottom (v. 38), and (e) the Roman centurion's confession (v. 39).

15:33. Jesus hanged on the cross for three hours in the daylight (9 A.M. till noon) and then **at the sixth hour** (noon) total **darkness** engulfed **the whole land** (Palestine and environs) **until the ninth hour** (3 P.M.; cf. comments on v. 25). The darkness, whether caused by a sudden dust-laden wind, or thick clouds, or, more likely, a miraculous solar eclipse, was probably a cosmic sign of God's judgment on human sin (cf. Isa. 5:25-30; Amos 8:9-10; Micah 3:5-7; Zeph. 1:14-15) which was placed on Jesus (cf. Isa. 53:5-6; 2 Cor. 5:21). Specifically it pictured God's judgment on Israel who rejected His Messiah, the Sin-Bearer (cf. John 1:29). The darkness visualized what Jesus' cry (Mark 15:34) expressed.

15:34. Mark (and Matthew) recorded only this one of Jesus' seven sayings from the cross. **At the ninth hour** (3 P.M.), **Jesus cried . . . Eloi, Eloi** (Aram. for the Heb., *'Ēlî, 'Ēlî*), **lama sabachthani?** (Aram.; from Ps. 22:1) Mark translated the saying into Greek for his readers, **which** in English **means, My God, My God, why** (lit., "for what [reason]") **have You forsaken** (lit., "did You abandon") **Me?**

This was more than the cry of a righteous Sufferer affirming His faith that God would cause Him to triumph (contrast Ps. 22:1 with Ps. 22:28). Nor did Jesus merely *feel* abandoned. Instead, Jesus' cry combined (a) abandonment by God the Father in a judicial not relational sense, and (b) a genuine affirmation of Jesus' relationship to God. Bearing the curse of sin and God's judgment on sin (cf. Deut. 21:22-23; 2 Cor. 5:21; Gal. 3:13) He experienced the unfathomable horror of separation from God, who cannot look on sin (cf. Hab. 1:13). This answers Jesus' question, "Why?" Dying for sinners (Mark 10:45; Rom. 5:8; 1 Peter 2:24; 3:18), He experienced separation from God.

Also Jesus' cry affirmed His abiding trust, reflected in the words, "My God, My God." This is the only one of Jesus' recorded prayers in which He did not use the address "Abba" (cf. Mark 14:36). Far from renouncing Him, Jesus claimed the Father as His God. He died forsaken by God so that His people might claim God as their God and never be forsaken (cf. Heb. 13:5).

15:35-36. Some Jewish bystanders apparently misunderstood or more likely, as a mockery, deliberately misinterpreted Jesus' cry as a call to **Elijah.** Popular Jewish belief held that Elijah came in times of distress to deliver righteous sufferers.

Probably in response to Jesus' additional words "I thirst" (John 19:28-29) a bystander, likely a Roman soldier, soaked **a sponge with wine vinegar** diluted with a mixture of eggs and water, a common inexpensive beverage, and raised **it on a stick** to Jesus' mouth so He could extract some refreshment from it (cf. Ps. 69:21). Jesus' cross was probably higher than normal, holding Him two or three feet off the ground. If the drink prolonged His life, the spectators would have a chance to **see if Elijah** would **take Him down.**

In Mark the words **Leave Him alone** were spoken by the soldier to the bystanders just before he offered a drink to Jesus. The verb is plural, "You (pl.) leave. . . ." In Matthew 27:49 the same words are spoken by bystanders to the soldier apparently while he was giving Jesus the drink. The verb is singular, "You (sing.) leave. . . ." Both expressed the taunt about Elijah coming to rescue Him.

15:37. Jesus' **loud cry** (Luke 23:46) before He **breathed His last** indicated that He did not die the ordinary death of one who was crucified (cf. Mark 15:39). Normally such a person suffered extreme exhaustion for a long period (often two or three days) and then lapsed into a coma before dying. But Jesus was fully conscious to the end; His death came voluntarily and suddenly. This accounts for Pilate's surprise (cf. v. 44).

15:38. Simultaneous with Jesus' death **the curtain** (veil) **of the temple** (*naou*, "sanctuary"; cf. 11:11) **was torn in two from top to bottom.** The passive verb and the direction of the tear indicate that this was God's action. It was no doubt observed and reported by the priests (cf. Acts 6:7) who at that moment were conducting the Jewish evening sacrifice. This could have been the outer curtain hung between the sanctuary itself and the forecourt (Ex. 26:36-37) or the inner curtain separating the holy place from the most holy place (Ex. 26:31-35). If it was the outer curtain, then the tear was a public sign confirming Jesus' words of judgment on the temple, later fulfilled in A.D. 70 (cf. Mark 13:2). Probably the inner curtain was torn, for it was a sign that Jesus' death ended the need for repeated sacrifices for sins, and opened a new and living way of free and direct access to God (Heb. 6:19-20; 9:6-14; 10:19-22).

15:39. The centurion who stood nearby facing **Jesus** and observing these unusual happenings (cf. vv. 33-37) was the *Gentile* Roman officer in charge of the execution squad (cf. v. 20) and thus accountable to Pilate (cf. v. 44). Only Mark used the Greek word *kentyriōn* ("centurion"), a transliteration of the Latin word referring to a commander of 100 soldiers (also vv. 44-45). All other New Testament writers used the equivalent Greek word *hekatontarchos*, also translated "centurion" (e.g., Matt. 27:54). This provides additional evidence that Mark wrote to a Roman audience (see *Introduction*).

The manner of Jesus' death, especially His last loud **cry** (cf. Mark 15:37), prompted the centurion to declare, **Surely** (lit., "truly," despite all insults to the contrary; cf. Matt. 27:40; John 19:7), **this Man was,** from the centurion's perspective, **the Son of God.**

The Roman officer probably did not use the phrase "the Son of God" in its distinctive Christian sense, as a reference to Jesus' deity (cf. Luke 23:47). Because of his pagan background he probably viewed Jesus as an extraordinary "divine man" much like the Roman emperor who was acclaimed "son of God" (cf. comments on Mark 12:16). Consequently some interpreters translate the phrase with an indefinite article, "a son of God" (NIV marg.). However, Mark regarded the declaration in its distinctive Christian sense; the centurion unwittingly said more than he knew.

The centurion's confession is the climax of Mark's revelation of Jesus' identity (cf. comments on 1:1; 8:29-30). This confession by a *Gentile* Roman officer contrasts with the mocking response of those mentioned in 15:29-32, 35-36. This Gentile's confession also exemplifies the truth of the torn curtain.

15:40-41. In addition to the mocking crowd and the Roman soldiers, **some** devoted **women were** also (in Gr.) carefully observing **from a distance** all that occurred. Earlier in the day—probably before the sixth hour (noon; v. 33)—they had stood "near the cross" (John 19:25-27).

Mary Magdalene's surname indicates she was from Magdala, a village on the Sea of Galilee's western shore. Jesus had released her from demon possession (Luke 8:2; she is not the sinful woman of Luke 7:36-50). The second **Mary** (the "other Mary"; Matt. 27:61) is distinguished from the others by the names of her sons **James the younger** (lit., "the small one," in stature and/or age) and **Joses,** who apparently were well known in the early church. **Salome,** whose name appears only in Mark (Mark 15:40; 16:1), was the mother of Zebedee's sons, the disciples James and John (Matt. 20:20; 27:56). She was probably the sister of Jesus' mother whom Mark did not mention (John 19:25).

When Jesus was **in Galilee these** three **women** used to follow (imperf. tense) **Him** from place to place and used to care **for** ("serve," imperf.) **His** material **needs** (cf. Luke 8:1-3). **Many other women who** did not accompany Him regularly **were also there.** They had **come . . . to Jerusalem** for the Passover festival with Jesus, perhaps hoping He would establish His messianic kingdom (cf. Mark 10:35-40; 15:43).

Mark mentioned the women as eyewitnesses of the Crucifixion in anticipation of their eyewitness role at Jesus' burial (15:47) and His resurrection (16:1-8). Their devotion surpassed that of the 11 disciples who had deserted Him (14:50). Mark may have intended these words as an encouragement to faithful discipleship among women in the church at Rome.

3. JESUS' BURIAL IN A NEARBY TOMB (15:42-47)
(MATT. 27:57-61; LUKE 23:50-56; JOHN 19:38-42)

15:42-43. Jesus' burial officially confirmed His death, an important point in early Christian preaching (cf. 1 Cor. 15:3-4). The designation **Preparation Day** is used here as a technical name for Friday, **the day before the Sabbath** (Saturday) as Mark explained to his non-Jewish readers. Since no work was allowed on the Jewish Sabbath, Friday was used to prepare for it. This reference confirms that Jesus was crucified on Friday, Nisan 15 (cf. comments on Mark 14:1a, 12, 16). "Evening" referred to the hours between mid-afternoon (3 P.M.) and sunset, when Friday ended and the Sabbath began.

Under Roman law the release of a crucified man's corpse for burial was determined only by the imperial magistrate. Usually such a request by a victim's relatives was granted, but sometimes a body would be left on a cross to decay or be eaten by predatory animals or birds and the remains were thrown into a common grave. Jewish law required a proper burial for all bodies, even those of executed criminals (cf. Mishnah *Sanhedrin* 6. 5). It also dictated that those hanged were to be taken down and buried before sunset (cf. Deut. 21:23).

Aware of these regulations, **Joseph of Arimathea** went **to Pilate and** requested **Jesus' body** for burial. He did this **as evening approached** (lit., "when evening had already arrived," i.e., probably about 4 P.M.). This gave urgency to his intended action.

Though Joseph probably lived in Jerusalem he was originally from Arimathea, a village 20 miles northwest of the city. He was a wealthy (Matt. 27:57), reputable **member of the Council** (*bouleutēs*), a non-Jewish designation for the Sanhedrin. He had not approved of the Sanhedrin's decision to kill Jesus (Luke 23:51). He was personally **waiting for the kingdom of God** (cf. Mark 1:15) which suggests he was a devout Pharisee. He regarded Jesus as the Messiah though so far he was a secret disciple (John 19:38).

But he took courage and **went to** Pilate **boldly,** a description unique to Mark. His action was bold because: (a) he was not related to Jesus; (b) his request was a favor that would likely be denied on principle since Jesus had been executed for treason; (c) he risked ceremonial defilement in handling a dead body; (d) his request amounted to an open confession of personal loyalty to the crucified Jesus which would doubtless incur his associates' hostility. He was a secret disciple no longer—something Mark impressed on his readers.

15:44-45. Pilate was amazed (*ethaumasen,* "astonished"; cf. 5:20) **that** Jesus had **already** died (cf. comments on 15:37). He summoned **the centurion** in charge of the Crucifixion (v. 39) to find out from a trusted source if the report were true. Once he was assured that Jesus was **dead,** Pilate **gave** (lit., "gave as a gift," i.e., without requiring a fee) **the body** (*ptōma,* "the corpse") **to Joseph.** Pilate's favorable response to Joseph's request was exceptional; perhaps it arose from his belief that Jesus was innocent (cf. vv. 14-15). Only Mark recorded Pilate's questioning of the centurion, thereby highlighting to his Roman readers that Jesus' death was confirmed by a Roman military officer.

15:46-47. Joseph undoubtedly had servants help him to accomplish a proper burial before sunset, a time span of about two hours. Nicodemus, a fellow Sanhedrin member, joined in, presumably by prearrangement (John 19:39-40).

After Jesus' **body** was removed from the cross, it was probably washed (cf. Acts 9:37) before it was wrapped tightly in strips of **linen cloth** with aromatic spices placed between the wraps. All this was in accord with Jewish burial customs (John 19:39-40).

Then the body was carried to a nearby garden **and placed** on a stone shelf inside Joseph's own previously unused tomb (Matt. 27:60; John 19:41-42) hewn out of rock. The tomb was sealed shut with a circular flat stone that rolled down a sloping groove till it was securely in front of the entrance to keep out intruders. To roll that stone back up again would require the strength of several men.

Two women who had witnessed Jesus' death (cf. Mark 15:40) saw (lit., "were observing," imperf. tense) with interest where He was buried. Apparently the other women had returned home to prepare for the Sabbath, a day on which they rested (Luke 23:56).

IX. Jesus' Resurrection from the Dead near Jerusalem (16:1-8) (Matt. 28:1-8; Luke 24:1-12; John 20:1-10)

The four Gospel accounts of the Resurrection contain various differences in recorded details (e.g., the number and names of the women who came to the tomb, the number of angelic messengers who appeared, and the women's reactions to the Resurrection announcement). None of the writers reported all the data; they were free (within veritable limits) to summarize, particularize, and emphasize different aspects of the same event. The various recorded differences reflect the natural effect of this unique event on different eyewitnesses, thereby confirming the Resurrection as a historical event. (See the chart, "Forty Days—from Resurrection to Ascension," at Matt. 28:1-4.)

A. The women's arrival at the tomb (16:1-5)

16:1. The Sabbath, Saturday (Nisan 16), concluded at sunset and the new Jewish day, Sunday (Nisan 17), began. That evening after sunset the women who had witnessed Jesus' death and burial (cf. 15:40, 47) bought spices, aromatic oils, to anoint Jesus' body (lit., "Him") the next morning. This indicates that they did not expect Jesus to rise from the dead (cf. 8:31; 9:31; 10:34).

Spices were poured over a dead body to counteract the odor of decay and as a symbolic expression of loving devotion. Embalming was not a Jewish custom.

16:2-3. Very early on the first day of the week (Sunday, Nisan 17) just after sunrise the women went to the tomb. They left home while it was still dark (cf. John 20:1) and got to the tomb shortly after sunrise.

Two of them knew that a large stone had been rolled in front of the tomb's entrance (cf. Mark 15:47). Only Mark recorded their concern over the practical problem of getting it rolled back. Evidently they were not aware of the official sealing of the tomb or the posting of a guard (cf. Matt. 27:62-66).

16:4-5. When the women arrived on the scene, they looked up toward the tomb and immediately noticed that the stone . . . had been removed, for (gar; cf. 1:16) it was very large and thus easily seen.

The women entered the tomb's outer room that led to the inner burial chamber. They were startled to see a young man (neaniskon; cf. 14:51) sitting to their right probably in front of the burial chamber. The unique circumstances, the accompanying description, and the revelatory message (16:6-7) indicate that Mark viewed him as an angelic messenger sent from God even though Mark called him a young man, as he appeared to the women. The white robe pictured his heavenly origin and splendor (cf. 9:3).

Luke (24:3-4) and John (20:12) mentioned the presence of two angels, the number necessary for a valid witness (cf. Deut. 17:6); but Matthew (28:5) and Mark referred to only one, presumably the spokesman.

The women were alarmed (exethambēthēsan; cf. Mark 9:15; 14:33) when they encountered the divine messenger. This compound verb of strong emotion (used only by Mark in the NT), expresses overwhelming distress at what is highly unusual (cf. 16:8).

B. The angel's announcement (16:6-7)

16:6. Sensing the women's distress, the angel commanded them, Don't be alarmed (cf. same verb, v. 5). They were looking for (zēteite, "seeking") the dead body of Jesus, the Man from Nazareth who had been crucified, expecting to anoint it (cf. v. 1). But the angel announced, He has risen! ("He was raised"; ēgerthē, pass.) indicating that the Resurrection was God's act, a New Testament emphasis (cf. Acts 3:15; 4:10; Rom. 4:24; 8:11; 10:9; 1 Cor. 6:14; 15:15; 2 Cor. 4:14; 1 Peter 1:21). His body was **not** there as they could easily see. The tomb was empty!

The angel's message clearly identified the Risen One as the Crucified One, both referring to the same historical Person, and it revealed the meaning of the empty tomb. The certainty of the Resurrection rests on the angel's message from God which people then and now are called on to believe. The historical fact of the empty tomb confirms it.

16:7. The women were given a task. They were to **go** and **tell** Jesus' **disciples** that they would be reunited with Him in **Galilee.** The words **and Peter,** unique to Mark, are significant since much of Mark's material likely came from Peter. He was singled out not because of his preeminence among the disciples but because he was forgiven and still included in the Eleven despite his triple denial (cf. 14:66-72).

The message that Jesus was **going ahead of** (from *proagō*) them **into** Galilee recalled the reunion He had promised (cf. the same verb in 14:28). His followers would **see Him** there which implies a Resurrection appearance (cf. 1 Cor. 15:5). This does not refer, as some say, to His second coming. Mark's journey motif (cf. introduction to Mark 8:31; also 10:32a) did not end with Jesus' death, for the risen Jesus continued to lead His followers.

These women were the first to hear the news of Jesus' resurrection but their reports were disregarded initially as women were not considered eligible witnesses under Jewish law. The disciples did not go to Galilee immediately. Jesus' additional appearances to them in the Jerusalem vicinity were necessary to convince them of the reality of His resurrection (cf. John 20:19-29).

C. The women's response to the news of Jesus' resurrection (16:8)

16:8. The women . . . fled from the tomb because (*gar;* cf. 1:16) they were **trembling** (*tromos,* a noun) **and bewildered** (astonishment, *ekstasis;* cf. 5:42). For a time **they said nothing to anyone** (Matt. 28:8) a double negative expression

in Greek unique to Mark, **because** (*gar*) **they were afraid** (*ephobounto;* cf. Mark 4:41; 5:15, 33, 36; 6:50-52; 9:32; 10:32).

Their response was similar to Peter's at the transfiguration (cf. 9:6). The object of their fear was the awesome disclosure of God's presence and power in raising Jesus from the dead. They were overwhelmed with reverential fear and reduced to silence.

Several interpreters believe that Mark concluded his Gospel at this point. The abrupt ending is consistent with Mark's style and punctuates his development of the themes of fear and astonishment throughout his Gospel. The reader is left to ponder with awe the meaning of the empty tomb as interpreted by the angel's revelatory message (cf. the following comments on 16:9-20).

X. Disputed Epilogue (16:9-20)

The last 12 verses of Mark (16:9-20) known as "the longer ending of Mark" constitute one of the most difficult and most disputed textual problems in the New Testament. Were these verses included or omitted in Mark's original text? Most modern English translations call attention to the problem in some way such as adding an explanatory footnote at verse 9 (NASB), setting this section apart from verse 8 with an explanatory note (NIV), or printing the whole section in the margin (RSV).

The *external* evidence includes the following: (1) The two earliest (fourth century) uncial manuscripts (Sinaiticus and Vaticanus) omit the verses though their respective scribes left some blank space after verse 8, suggesting that they knew of a longer ending but did not have it in the manuscript they were copying. (2) Most all other manuscripts (fifth century on) as well as early versions support the inclusion of verses 9-20. (3) Several later manuscripts (seventh century on) and versions supply a "shorter ending" after verse 8 which is clearly not genuine but all these manuscripts (except one) continue on with verses 9-20. (4) Early patristic writers—such as Justin Martyr (*Apology* 1. 45, ca. A.D. 148), Tatian (*Diatessaron,* ca. A.D. 170), and Irenaeus who quoted verse 19 (*Against Heresies* 3. 10. 6)—support the inclusion of these verses. However, Eusebius

(*Questions to Marinus 1*, ca. A.D. 325) and Jerome (*Epistle* 120. 3; *ad Hedibiam*, ca. A.D. 407) said verses 9-20 were missing from Greek manuscripts known to them. (5) An Armenian manuscript of the 10th century attributed verses 9-20 to "the presbyter Ariston," probably Aristion, a contemporary of Papias (A.D. 60–130) who was purportedly a disciple of the Apostle John. (6) If Mark ended abruptly at verse 8, then it is easy to see why some early copyist(s) wanted to provide a "suitable" ending for the Gospel from other authoritative sources. However, if verses 9-20 were part of the original, it is difficult to see why the early copyists would have omitted it.

Internal evidence includes this data: (1) The transition from verse 8 to verse 9 involves an abrupt change of subject from "women" to the presumed subject "Jesus" since His name is not stated in verse 9 of the Greek text. (2) Mary Magdalene is introduced with a descriptive clause in verse 9 as though she had not been mentioned already in 15:40, 47 and 16:1. (3) About ⅓ of the significant Greek words in verses 9-20 are "non-Marcan," that is, they do not appear elsewhere in Mark or they are used differently from Mark's usage prior to verse 9. (4) The Greek literary style lacks the vivid, lifelike detail so characteristic of Mark's historical narrative. (5) Mark would have been expected to include a Resurrection appearance to the disciples in Galilee (14:28; 16:7), but the appearances in verses 9-20 are in or near Jerusalem. (6) Matthew and Luke parallel Mark until verse 8 and then diverge noticeably, suggesting that Mark began its literary existence without verses 9-20.

Equally astute and conscientious interpreters differ widely in their evaluations of this data and reach opposing conclusions. Those who include these verses in light of the preponderance of early and widespread external support must still account satisfactorily for the internal evidence which appears to distinguish these verses from the rest of the Gospel. And those who omit these verses must still account for their early and widespread attestation externally and give a suitable reason for Mark's seemingly abrupt conclusion at verse 8. Four possible solutions for this have been suggested: (1) Mark finished his Gospel but the original ending was lost or destroyed in some way now unknown before it was copied. (2) Mark finished his Gospel but the original ending was deliberately suppressed or removed for some reason now unknown. (3) Mark was unable to finish his Gospel for some reason now unknown—possibly sudden death. (4) Mark purposely intended to end his Gospel at verse 8.

Of these options, numbers 1 and 2 are unlikely even though the view that the original ending was accidentally lost is widely accepted. If Mark's Gospel was a scroll manuscript rather than a codex (leaf form of book) the ending would normally be on the inside of the scroll and less likely to be damaged or lost than the beginning of the scroll. If the incompleteness of Mark is assumed, number 3 is the most probable option but due to its very nature it cannot be confirmed. In light of Mark's use of the theme "fear" in relation to Jesus' followers (cf. v. 8), many modern interpreters incline toward option 4.

A final conclusion to the problem probably cannot be reached on the basis of presently known data. A view which seems to account for the relevant evidence and to raise the least number of objections is that (a) Mark purposely ended his Gospel with verse 8 and (b) verses 9-20, though written or compiled by an anonymous Christian writer, are historically authentic and are part of the New Testament canon (cf. similarly the last chapter of Deut.). In this view, very early in the transmission of Mark's Gospel (perhaps shortly after A.D. 100) verses 9-20 were added to verse 8 without any attempt to match Mark's vocabulary and style. Possibly these verses were brief extracts from the post-Resurrection accounts found in the other three Gospels and were known through oral tradition to have the approval of the Apostle John who lived till near the end of the first century. Thus the material was included early enough in the transmission process to gain recognition and acceptance by the church as part of canonical Scripture. These verses are consistent with the rest of Scripture. The development of the theme of belief and unbelief unifies the passage.

A. *Three of Jesus' post-resurrection appearances (16:9-14)*

This section contains three of Jesus' post-resurrection appearances before His Ascension. (See the chart, "Forty Days— from Resurrection to Ascension," at Matt. 28:1-4.)

1. HIS APPEARANCE TO MARY MAGDALENE AND HIS FOLLOWERS' UNBELIEF (16:9-11) (JOHN 20:14-18)

16:9-11. These verses turn abruptly to **Mary** Magdalene's return visit to the tomb while it was still **early** (cf. "very early," v. 2) that same morning. Though mentioned three times previously in Mark (cf. 15:40, 47; 16:1), she was described here for the first time as the Mary **out of whom** Jesus had expelled **seven demons** (cf. Luke 8:2). Jesus **appeared,** made Himself visible, to her **first.** This suggests that people could not recognize **Jesus** in His resurrected state unless He deliberately revealed Himself to them (cf. Luke 24:16, 31).

Mary **went and told those who had been with Him** that she had seen Jesus. This designation for Jesus' followers was not used earlier in Mark or in the other Gospels (but cf. Mark 3:14; 5:18). The clause probably refers to Jesus' disciples in general (cf. 16:12), not just the Eleven (cf. Acts 1:21). They all **were mourning and weeping** over Jesus' death, a description unique to this account.

On hearing **that Jesus was alive and . . . had** been **seen** (*etheathē*, not used elsewhere in Mark) by Mary, the disciples refused to **believe** (*ēpistēsan*, a verb not used elsewhere in Mark) her report (cf. Luke 24:11). Apparently a short time later Jesus appeared to the other two women, confirming the angel's announcement and urging them to tell His disciples (cf. Matt. 28:1, 9-10).

2. HIS APPEARANCE TO TWO FOLLOWERS AND THE UNBELIEF OF THE REST (16:12-13)

16:12-13. These verses summarize the story about the two Emmaus disciples (Luke 24:13-35). The words **two of them** indicate that they were part of the group who disbelieved Mary's report (cf. Mark 16:10-11). **While they were** out **walking,** going from Jerusalem into **the country,**

Jesus **appeared** (cf. v. 9) to them **in a different form** (*hetera morphē,* "a form of a different kind"). This could mean that He took on a form different from that in which He appeared to Mary Magdalene or, more likely, that He appeared to them in a form different from that in which they had previously recognized Him as **Jesus.** When they **returned** to Jerusalem **and reported** the event **to the rest** of the disciples, **they did not believe** their report **either** (cf. v. 11). Apparently, despite affirmative statements (cf. Luke 24:34), the disciples initially seemed to regard Jesus' post-resurrection appearances as apparitions (cf. Luke 24:37).

3. HIS APPEARANCE TO THE ELEVEN AND HIS REBUKE OF THEIR UNBELIEF (16:14) (LUKE 24:36-49; JOHN 20:19-25)

16:14. Later (*hysteron,* a comparative adverb not used elsewhere in Mark) on the evening of the same day (cf. v. 9) **Jesus appeared to the Eleven** themselves while **they** sat **eating** (their evening meal is implied in Luke 24:41-43). **He rebuked** (*ōneidisen,* a strong verb not used of Jesus elsewhere) their unbelief and hardness of heart (*sklērokardian;* cf. Mark 10:5) because they refused **to believe** the testimony of eyewitnesses to His resurrection earlier that day. By hearing about Jesus' resurrection (before seeing **Him**) they learned what it was like to believe the testimony of eyewitnesses. This would be necessary for all those to whom they would preach in their coming missionary outreach.

B. *Jesus' commission to His followers (16:15-18)* *(Matt. 28:16-20)*

16:15. Later Jesus gave His disciples His great missionary commission: **Go into all** (*hapanta,* "the whole," emphatic form) **the world and preach** (*kēryxate,* "proclaim"; cf. 1:4, 14) **the good news** (*euangelion,* "gospel"; cf. 1:1) **to all creation,** that is, to all people.

16:16. In response to the preaching of the gospel, **whoever believes and is baptized,** a baptized believer (lit., "the one who believed and was baptized"), **will be saved** (*sōthēsetai;* cf. comments on 13:13) by God (implied) from spiritual death, the penalty of sin. A single Greek article governs both substantival participles, linking them together in describing the inward, efficacious reception of the gospel by faith (believing) and the outward, public expression of that faith in water baptism.

Though the New Testament writers generally assume that under normal circumstances each believer will be baptized, 16:16 does not mean that baptism is a necessary requirement for personal salvation. The second half of the verse indicates by contrast that one who **does not believe** the gospel **will be condemned** by God (implied) in the day of final judgment (cf. 9:43-48). The basis for condemnation is unbelief, not the lack of any ritual observance. Baptism is not mentioned because unbelief precludes one's giving a confession of faith while being baptized by water. Thus the only requirement for personally appropriating God's salvation is faith in Him (cf. Rom. 3:21-28; Eph. 2:8-10).

16:17-18. These verses list five kinds of **signs** (*sēmeia*; cf. comments on 8:11) which would attend **those who believe.** "Signs" are supernatural events attesting the divine origin of the apostolic message (cf. 16:20). The signs authenticated the faith the early believers proclaimed, not the personal faith that any one of them exercised. In light of this and historical evidence it is reasonable to conclude that these authenticating signs were normative only for the apostolic era (cf. 2 Cor. 12:12; Heb. 2:3-4).

In fulfilling their commission (cf. Mark 16:15) believers would be given the ability to do miraculous things **in Jesus' name** (cf. comments on 6:7, 13; 9:38-40). **They** would **drive out demons,** thereby demonstrating Jesus' victory over Satan's realm. The Twelve (cf. 6:13) and the Seventy had already expelled demons, and this ability continued in the apostolic church (cf. Acts 8:7; 16:18; 19:15-16). **They** would **speak in new tongues,** presumably a reference to intelligible foreign languages not previously known to the speakers. This was demonstrated at Pentecost (cf. Acts 2:4-11) and later in the life of the early church (cf. Acts 10:46; 19:6; 1 Cor. 12:10; 14:1-24).

In the Greek the first two clauses in Mark 16:18 may be understood as conditional clauses with the third clause

as the conclusion. An interpretive rendering would be, "And if **they** be compelled to **pick up snakes with their hands and** if **they** should be compelled to **drink deadly poison, it** shall by no means (*ou mē,* emphatic negative; cf. 13:2) harm **them.**" This promise of immunity by divine protection in either situation refers to occasions when persecutors would force believers to do these things. This does not warrant voluntary snake-handling or drinking of poison, practices not attested in the early church. Since Paul's encounter with a snake at Malta was unintentional (cf. Acts 28:3-5), the New Testament records no actual instance of either of the experiences described here.

As a final kind of authenticating sign **they** would put **their hands on sick people and they** would **get well.** Healing by this means is mentioned in Acts 28:8 and the gift of healing was exercised in the early church (cf. 1 Cor. 12:30).

C. Jesus' Ascension and the disciples' ongoing mission (16:19-20) (Luke 24:50-51; Acts 1:9-11)

16:19-20. These verses consist of two closely related parts. On the one hand (Gr., *men*) **the Lord Jesus**—a compound title not found in the Gospels except in Luke 24:3—**after** His post-resurrection ministry (a 40-day period; cf. Acts 1:3) **was taken up into heaven** (by God the Father, implied). There **He sat** down **at the right hand of God,** His place of honor and authority (cf. comments on Mark 12:36-37a). The reality of this was confirmed to the early believers by Stephen's vision (cf. Acts 7:56). In one sense Jesus' work on earth was finished.

On the other hand (Gr., *de*) His work on earth in another sense continued through **the disciples** who **went out** from Jerusalem **and preached** (*ekēryxan,* "proclaimed"; cf. Mark 1:4, 14; 16:15) the gospel **everywhere.** At the same time **the** risen **Lord** was working **with them** by empowering them, **and** confirming **His Word,** the gospel message, **by the signs** (cf. 16:17-18) **that accompanied it.** The signs authenticated their message (cf. Heb. 2:3-4). This task of proclaiming the gospel still goes on through disciples empowered by the risen Lord.

BIBLIOGRAPHY

Alford, Henry. *Alford's Greek Testament.* Vol. 1. Reprint. Grand Rapids: Baker Book House, 1980.

Anderson, Hugh. *The Gospel of Mark.* The New Century Bible Commentary. Grand Rapids: Wm. B. Eerdmans Publishing Co., 1976.

Burdick, Donald W. "The Gospel according to Mark." In *The Wycliffe Bible Commentary.* Chicago: Moody Press, 1962.

Cole, R.A. *The Gospel according to St. Mark.* The Tyndale New Testament Commentaries. Grand Rapids: Wm. B. Eerdmans Publishing Co., 1961.

Cranfield, C.E.B. *The Gospel according to Saint Mark.* Cambridge Greek Testament Commentary. Rev. ed. New York: Cambridge University Press, 1972.

Earle, Ralph. *Mark: the Gospel of Action.* Everyman's Bible Commentary. Chicago: Moody Press, 1970.

Hendriksen, William. *Exposition of the Gospel according to Mark.* New Testament Commentary. Grand Rapids: Baker Book House, 1975.

Hiebert, D. Edmond. *Mark: A Portrait of the Servant.* Chicago: Moody Press, 1974.

Lane, William L. *The Gospel according to Mark.* The New International Commentary on the New Testament. Grand Rapids: Wm. B. Eerdmans Publishing Co., 1974.

Lenski, R.C.H. *The Interpretation of St. Mark's Gospel.* Reprint. Minneapolis: Augsburg Publishing House, 1961.

Martin, Ralph P. *Mark: Evangelist and Theologian.* Grand Rapids: Zondervan Publishing House, 1973.

—————. *Mark.* Knox Preaching Guides. Atlanta: John Knox Press, 1981.

Stonehouse, Ned B. *The Witness of the Synoptic Gospels to Christ.* 1944. Reprint. Grand Rapids: Baker Book House, 1979.

Swete, Henry Barclay. *The Gospel according to St. Mark.* 3rd ed. 1909. Reprint. Grand Rapids: Kregel Publishing Co., 1978.

Swift, C.E. Graham. "Mark." In *The New Bible Commentary: Revised.* Grand Rapids: Wm. B. Eerdmans Publishing Co., 1970.

Taylor, Vincent. *The Gospel according to St. Mark.* 2nd ed. Thornapple Commentaries. 1966. Reprint. Grand Rapids: Baker Book House, 1981.

Vos, Howard F. *Mark: A Study Guide Commentary.* Grand Rapids: Zondervan Publishing House, 1978.

Wilson R. McL. "Mark." In *Peake's Commentary on the Bible.* New York: Thomas Nelson & Sons, 1962.

LUKE

John A. Martin

INTRODUCTION

Author. The two books attributed to Luke (Luke and Acts) make up about 28 percent of the Greek New Testament. Luke is not mentioned by name in either book. The only places where his name occurs in the New Testament are in Colossians 4:14; 2 Timothy 4:11; and Philemon 24. Luke also referred to himself directly in the "we" sections of Acts (16:10-17; 20:5–21:18; 27:1–28:16).

Luke must have been a Gentile for Paul differentiates him from the Jews (Col. 4:10-14). Paul wrote that, of his fellow-workers, Aristarchus, Mark, and John were the only ones who were Jews. The others (Epaphras, Luke, and Demas) were therefore probably Gentiles. Paul referred to Luke as a physician (Col. 4:14), a fact which many try to corroborate from passages in Luke and Acts. Until modern times church tradition uniformly has held Luke to be the author of Luke and Acts. According to tradition Luke was from Antioch, but it is impossible to verify this claim.

Sources. Luke claimed to be a historian (Luke 1:1-4). He carefully researched his material for specific reasons. He consulted eyewitnesses for information (1:2). He may have gathered certain details, such as facts on Jesus' youth, from Mary herself (cf. 2:51). Luke also seemed to have had contacts with the Herodian court (cf. 3:1, 19; 8:3; 9:7-9; 13:31; 23:7-12). Scholars do not agree on which sources Luke used in writing his Gospel. He may have reworked various source materials at his disposal in order to create a unified whole, written in his style, which reflected his purpose. All this, of course, was done under the inspiration of the Holy Spirit.

Date and Place. A number of dates have been suggested for the writing of Luke. If Acts were written before the time of Nero's persecution (A.D. 64)—which seems evident by the fact that Acts closed with Paul still alive and in prison—then the Book of Luke must have been written several years before that, for Acts was subsequent to Luke. Though it is impossible to pinpoint a specific date, a time of composition between A.D. 58 and 60 fits well.

Luke gave no clues as to the place where he wrote his Gospel. Thus any statement on the matter would be mere speculation. Some suggest that Luke wrote from either Caesarea or Rome.

Purposes. Luke had two purposes in writing this book. One was to confirm the faith of Theophilus, that is, to show that his faith in Christ rested on firm historical fact (1:3-4). His other purpose was to present Jesus as the Son of Man, who had been rejected by Israel. Because of this rejection, Jesus was also preached to Gentiles so that they could know the kingdom program of God and attain salvation.

Gentile Character of the Book. Several lines of evidence point to the conclusion that Luke wrote primarily for Gentiles. First, Luke frequently explained Jewish localities (4:31; 8:26; 21:37; 23:51; 24:13). This would be unnecessary if he were writing to Jews. Second, he traced Jesus' genealogy (3:23-38) all the way back to Adam (rather than to Abraham, as in Matthew's Gospel). The implication is that Jesus was representing all mankind rather than just the Jewish nation. Third, Luke referred to Roman emperors in designating the dates of Jesus' birth (2:1) and of John the Baptist's preaching (3:1). Fourth, Luke used a number of words which would be more familiar to Gentile readers than the comparable Jewish terms

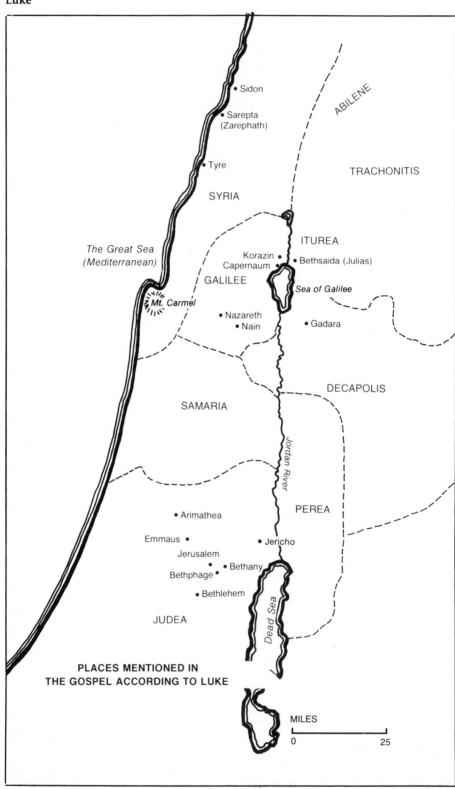

**PLACES MENTIONED IN
THE GOSPEL ACCORDING TO LUKE**

found in Matthew's Gospel. An example is Luke's use of the Greek *didaskalos* rather than *rabbi* for "teacher."

Fifth, Luke used the Septuagint when quoting from the Old Testament. He has relatively few direct quotations, though the book is filled with allusions. The quotations and references are in 2:23-24; 3:4-6; 4:4, 8, 10-12, 18-19; 7:27; 10:27; 18:20; 19:46; 20:17, 28, 37, 42-43; 22:37. All these except 7:27 are based on the Septuagint. The quotation in 7:27 appears to be taken neither from the Greek Septuagint nor the Hebrew Masoretic text but from some other text. Sixth, little is said about Jesus' fulfilling prophecies because that theme was not nearly so important to Gentile readers as it was to Jewish readers. Luke has only five direct references to fulfillment of prophecy and all but one (3:4) are found in the teaching of Jesus to Israel.

Luke's Relationship to Matthew and Mark. Luke is one of the Synoptic Gospels, having much material in common with Matthew and Mark. However, Luke has a lengthy section in which much of the material is unique to his book (9:51–19:27). He also presented unique material in the birth narratives of John and Jesus and the record of Jesus at age 12 (1:5–2:52). It is assumed that Luke knew of and used both Matthew and Mark or sources common to Matthew and/or Mark. The differences in narrative sequence and accounts presented can be explained on the basis of the purposes of the various authors. Though the accounts are historical, the purpose of each of the writers was theological. (For more on the relationships of the Synoptic Gospels see the *Introduction* to the Book of Matt. and the *Introduction* to the Book of Mark.)

Characteristics of the Book. 1. Luke emphasized the universal message of the gospel more than the other Gospel writers. He often wrote about sinners, the poor, and outcasts from Jewish society. He also referred many times to Gentiles who shared in the blessings of the Messiah. Samaritans were presented as coming to faith in the Messiah. And Luke wrote frequently of women and children and their faith.

2. Luke's Gospel gives a reader a more comprehensive grasp of the history of the period than the other Gospels. He presented more facts about the earthly life of Jesus than did Matthew, Mark, or John.

3. Luke emphasized forgiveness (3:3; 5:18-26; 6:37; 7:36-50; 11:4; 12:10; 17:3-4; 23:34; 24:47).

4. Luke emphasized prayer. At many points in His ministry Jesus prayed (3:21; 5:16; 6:12; 9:18, 29; 22:32, 40-41).

5. Luke noted the individual's place in coming to repentance. He stressed the action which must come from each individual who followed Jesus. Examples include Zechariah, Elizabeth, Mary, Simeon, Anna, Martha, Mary, Simon, Levi, the centurion, the widow of Nain, Zacchaeus, and Joseph of Arimathea.

6. Luke said more about material things than did any other author in the New Testament. He did not always present the poor as being righteous, but he did say that the self-sufficient rich, who regarded riches more highly than Jesus, were unable to enter into the salvation Jesus offered.

7. Luke often spoke of joy that accompanies faith and salvation (1:14; 8:13; 10:17; 13:17; 15:5, 9, 32; 19:6, 37).

OUTLINE

and surrounding cities (chaps. 7-8)

E. Jesus' teaching of His disciples (9:1-50)

V. The Journey of Jesus toward Jerusalem (9:51-19:27)

A. The rejection of Jesus by most on His journey toward Jerusalem (9:51-11:54)

B. Jesus' teaching of His followers in view of the rejection (12:1-19:27)

VI. The Ministry of Jesus in Jerusalem (19:28-21:38)

A. Jesus' entry into Jerusalem as Messiah (19:28-44)

B. Jesus in the temple (19:45-21:38)

VII. The Death, Burial, and Resurrection of Jesus (chaps. 22-24)

A. The death and burial of Jesus (chaps. 22-23)

B. The resurrection and appearances of Jesus (chap. 24)

COMMENTARY

I. The Prologue and Purpose of the Gospel (1:1-4)

1:1-4. Luke is the only one of the four Gospel writers who stated his method and purpose at the beginning of his book. He was familiar with other writings about Jesus' life and the message of the gospel (v. 1). His purpose was to allow **Theophilus** to **know the certainty of the things** he had **been taught** by writing out **an orderly account** (v. 3; cf. v. 1) of the events in Christ's life.

Luke carefully identified himself with the believers (v. 1). Some have suggested that Luke may have been among the 72 Jesus sent out on the missionary journey (10:1-24) because of his notation that the things were **fulfilled among us.** However, the next statement that these "things" (i.e., accounts and teachings) **were handed down** orally by the **eyewitnesses** of Jesus would negate that possibility. Luke implied that he was not an eyewitness but a researcher. He was thorough and exact in his research, having **investigated** for his account **everything from the beginning,** that is, from the first of Christ's life.

"Theophilus" (lit., "lover of God") was a common name during the first century. Who this man was is open to

conjecture. Though it has been suggested that Luke used the name for all who are "lovers of God" (i.e., the readers of his Gospel narrative), it is better to suppose that this was a real individual who was the first recipient of Luke's Gospel and who then gave it wide circulation in the early church. Apparently he was an official of some kind, for he was called **most excellent** (cf. Acts 23:26; 24:3; 26:25, which use the same Gr. term, *kratiste*).

II. The Births and Maturations of John and Jesus (1:5-2:52)

A. The announcements of the births (1:5-56)

Luke arranged the material in this section and the following sections in a form which compared John's birth and maturation with Jesus' birth and maturation. In both cases the parents were introduced (vv. 5-7 and 26-27), an angel appeared (vv. 8-23 and 28-30), a sign was given (vv. 18-20 and 34-38), and a woman who had no children became pregnant (vv. 24-25 and 42).

1. THE ANNOUNCEMENT OF THE BIRTH OF JOHN (1:5-25)

a. The introduction of John's parents (1:5-7)

1:5-7. John's parents were **a priest named Zechariah** and **Elizabeth,** who **was also a descendant of Aaron.** John therefore was by lineage one who was to become a priest. His parents lived when **Herod** the Great ruled as **king of Judea,** from 37 to 4 B.C. (See chart on the Herods.) They were godly people, or **upright** (*dikaioi*, "righteous"), **observing all the Lord's commandments.** They were **both well along in years** and thus had no prospect of children. This fact was a constant embarrassment to Elizabeth as is evident from her statement later on (v. 25). God's allowing a barren woman to have children occurred several times in the Old Testament (e.g., the mothers of Isaac, Samson, and Samuel).

b. The angel's announcement to Zechariah (1:8-23)

1:8-9. Luke recorded that **Zechariah's division was on duty.** This division was one of 24 groups of priests, drawn up in David's time (1 Chron. 24:7-18). The priests in each division were on duty twice a year for a week at a time.

Herod the Great
King of Palestine, 37–4 B.C. (Luke 1:5)
Killed Bethlehem baby boys (Matt. 2:1-17)

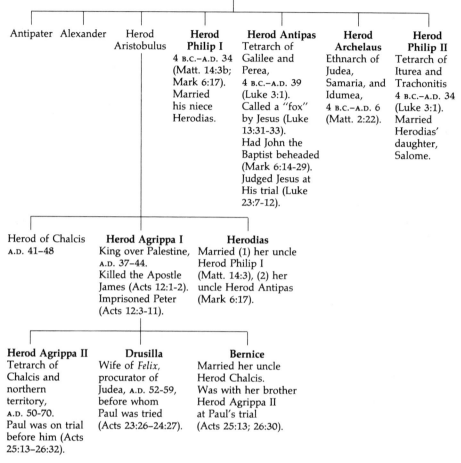

Antipater	Alexander	Herod Aristobulus	**Herod Philip I** 4 B.C.–A.D. 34 (Matt. 14:3b; Mark 6:17). Married his niece Herodias.	**Herod Antipas** Tetrarch of Galilee and Perea, 4 B.C.–A.D. 39 (Luke 3:1). Called a "fox" by Jesus (Luke 13:31-33). Had John the Baptist beheaded (Mark 6:14-29). Judged Jesus at His trial (Luke 23:7-12).	**Herod Archelaus** Ethnarch of Judea, Samaria, and Idumea, 4 B.C.–A.D. 6 (Matt. 2:22).	**Herod Philip II** Tetrarch of Iturea and Trachonitis 4 B.C.–A.D. 34 (Luke 3:1). Married Herodias' daughter, Salome.

Herod of Chalcis A.D. 41–48	**Herod Agrippa I** King over Palestine, A.D. 37–44. Killed the Apostle James (Acts 12:1-2). Imprisoned Peter (Acts 12:3-11).	**Herodias** Married (1) her uncle Herod Philip I (Matt. 14:3), (2) her uncle Herod Antipas (Mark 6:17).

Herod Agrippa II Tetrarch of Chalcis and northern territory, A.D. 50–70. Paul was on trial before him (Acts 25:13–26:32).	**Drusilla** Wife of *Felix*, procurator of Judea, A.D. 52-59, before whom Paul was tried (Acts 23:26–24:27).	**Bernice** Married her uncle Herod Chalcis. Was with her brother Herod Agrippa II at Paul's trial (Acts 25:13; 26:30).

Names in boldface appear in the New Testament.

Zechariah was of the division of Abijah (Luke 1:5; cf. 1 Chron. 24:10).

Zechariah **was chosen by lot** (*elache*) to be the **priest** who offered the **incense**. Because of the large number of priests this would be the only time in Zechariah's life when he was allowed to perform this task. As elsewhere in Scripture (e.g., Es. 3:7), the sovereignty of God is stressed even in matters which seem like chance, as in the casting of a lot.

1:10-11. While Zechariah was inside at the altar of **incense,** a crowd gathered to pray. The incense for which Zechariah was responsible symbolized the prayers of the entire nation. At that particular moment Zechariah was thus the focal point of the entire Jewish nation.

At that unique moment in Zechariah's life **an angel of the Lord appeared** . . . **standing** where Zechariah was praying beside **the altar of incense.**

1:12-13. The purpose of the appearance of the **angel** of the Lord was to announce the birth of **a son** to **Zechariah** and **Elizabeth.** Zechariah **was gripped with fear** (lit., "fear fell on him"). In Luke, many people responded with fear or awe (*phobos*) when confronted with mighty acts of God (cf. 1:30, 65; 2:9-10; 5:10, 26; 7:16; 8:25, 37, 50; 9:34, 45; 12:4-5, 32; 21:26; cf. 23:40). Because of the angel's response, **Do not be afraid, Zechariah; your prayer has been heard,** it may be inferred that Zechariah was praying for a son, or possibly even for the coming of the Messiah and that the birth of John would be a partial answer to his prayer. The angel told Zechariah what to name his son. This was also the case when the angel appeared to Mary (1:31).

1:14-17. The angel not only gave the name of the son, but also detailed six aspects of John's character.

1. **He will be a joy and delight to you** (v. 14). Luke frequently used the word "joy" in his accounts in Luke and Acts, often linking it closely with salvation. An illustration of this is in Luke 15, where three times joy and rejoicing came because something lost had been found, a picture of salvation. And John the Baptist's ministry brought joy to the Israelites who believed his message of repentance for the forgiveness of sins (3:3).

2. **He will be great in the sight of the Lord.** The expression "in the sight of" (*enōpion*) is characteristic of Luke. Though it appears 35 times in Luke and Acts, it is used only one other time in the other Gospels (John 20:30).

3. **He is never to take wine or other fermented drink.** Later John voluntarily took on himself a Nazirite vow, refusing to drink anything fermented (Num. 6:1-21). Luke did not specifically state that John would fulfill all aspects of the Nazirite vow. Instead, John would avoid taking any wine perhaps to support his contention that his message was urgent. Another way he emphasized the urgency of his message was to dress, act, and eat like Elijah the prophet (cf. Matt. 3:4; 2 Kings 1:8).

4. **He will be filled with the Holy Spirit even from birth.** "From birth" is literally "from his mother's womb." When Mary visited Elizabeth before John was born, the baby leaped in her womb. The ministry of the Holy Spirit was important to Luke, and he often went to great length to show His empowering and enabling ministry. Both of John's parents were filled with the Spirit (Luke 1:41, 67).

5. **Many of the people of Israel** would **he bring back to . . . God.** Crowds of Israelites did turn to the Lord through John's ministry (Matt. 3:5-6; Mark 1:4-5).

6. **He will go on before the Lord.** John the Baptist was the Lord's forerunner, announcing His coming **in the spirit and power of Elijah.** Luke here referred to two passages in Malachi which speak of messengers: a messenger was to be sent to clear the way before the Lord (Mal. 3:1), and Elijah's return was promised before the day of the Lord (Mal. 4:5-6) to restore **the hearts of the fathers to their children.** Zechariah apparently understood that the angel was identifying John the Baptist with the messenger in Malachi 3:1, for in his song of praise he noted that John would "go on before the Lord to prepare the way for Him" (Luke 1:76; cf. 3:4-6). Jesus affirmed that John was the fulfillment of Malachi 3:1 (Matt. 11:10) and stated that John *would have* fulfilled Malachi 4:5-6 if the people had accepted his message (Matt. 11:14).

1:18-20. Zechariah had doubts that such a thing could take place because both he and Elizabeth were **old.** But **the angel,** identifying himself as **Gabriel,** reassured Zechariah that this **good news** was from the Lord. When Gabriel appeared twice to Daniel (Dan. 8:16; 9:21), both times he gave Daniel instruction and understanding. He did the same here with Zechariah, as can be inferred from the song of praise and trust which Zechariah uttered later (Luke 1:67-79). Zechariah's inability **to speak** till the fulfillment of Gabriel's message was, to some degree, a punishment for his unbelief. But it was also a sign. A sign in the Old Testament was often associated with a confirming observable phenomenon which accompanied a word of prophecy. For the next nine months Zechariah's attempts to speak would prove the reality of Gabriel's message.

1:21-23. When **Zechariah** finally **came out** of **the temple,** he was able to make the waiting **people** realize that **he had seen a vision.** He then **returned home** in Judah's hill country after completing his temple duty.

c. Elizabeth's pregnancy (1:24-25)

1:24-25. After . . . Elizabeth became **pregnant . . . for five months** she **remained in seclusion.** Most likely, this was because of the excitement of the surrounding **people** to her pregnancy

(v. 25). Mary may have been the first person other than Zechariah and Elizabeth to know the news which the angel had delivered (v. 36).

Luke did not say in verse 25 if Elizabeth knew about the destiny of her son at this time. However, because she knew that his name was to be John (v. 60) even before Zechariah was able to speak, he probably communicated his entire vision in writing. Elizabeth was overjoyed that she was finally able to have a baby.

2. THE ANNOUNCEMENT OF THE BIRTH OF JESUS (1:26-56)

a. The introduction of Mary and Joseph (1:26-27)

1:26-27. In the sixth month, that is, when Elizabeth was in her sixth month of pregnancy, **God sent . . . Gabriel to Nazareth.**

Mary had not yet had sexual contact with a man, for Luke called her **a virgin** (*parthenon;* cf. 1:34) and noted that she was **pledged to be married to . . . Joseph** (cf. 2:5). In Jewish culture then a man and woman were betrothed or pledged to each other for a period of time before the actual consummation of their marriage. This betrothal was much stronger than an engagement period today, for the two were considered husband and wife except that they did not live together till after the wedding.

b. The angel's announcement of Jesus' birth to Mary (1:28-38)

1:28-31. The angel said that **Mary** was **highly favored** (*kecharitōmenē,* a part. related to the noun *charis,* "grace"; the verb *charitoō* is used elsewhere in the NT only in Eph. 1:6). Also Mary had **found favor** (*charis,* "grace") **with God.** Obviously God had bestowed a special honor on her. She was a special recipient of His grace.

Gabriel's admonition (Luke 1:30-31) was the same as to Zechariah: **Do not be afraid, for you** will have **a Son** (cf. v. 13). As with John (v. 13b), the naming was by the angel (v. 31).

1:32-33. The angel predicted five things about Mary's Son.

1. **He will be great.**
2. **He will be called the Son of the Most High** (cf. v. 76). The Septuagint often used the term "Most High" (*hypsistou*) to translate the Hebrew *'elyôn* (cf. v.

76). Mary could not have missed the significance of that terminology. The fact that her Baby was to be called the "Son of the Most High" pointed to His equality with Yahweh. In Semitic thought a son was a "carbon copy" of his father, and the phrase "son of" was often used to refer to one who possessed his "father's" qualities (e.g., the Heb. trans. "son of wickedness" in Ps. 89:22 [KJV] means a wicked person).

3. He will be given **the throne of His father David.** Jesus, as David's descendant, will sit on David's throne when He reigns in the Millennium (2 Sam. 7:16; Ps. 89:3-4, 28-29).

4. **He will reign over the house of Jacob forever.** Jesus' reign over the nation Israel as her King will begin in the Millennium and continue on into the eternal state.

5. **His kingdom will never end.** These promises must have immediately reminded Mary of the promise of Yahweh to David (2 Sam. 7:13-16). David understood the prophecy as referring not only to his immediate son (Solomon) who would build the temple, but also to the future Son who would rule forever. David stated that Yahweh had spoken of the distant future (2 Sam. 7:19). Mary would have understood that the angel was speaking to her of the Messiah who had been promised for so long.

1:34-38. Mary did not seem surprised that the Messiah was to come. Rather, she was surprised that she would be His mother since she was **a virgin** (lit., "since I do not know a man"). But **the angel** did not rebuke Mary, as he had rebuked Zechariah (v. 20). This indicates that Mary did not doubt the angel's words but merely wanted to know how such an event would be accomplished. The answer was that **the Holy Spirit** would creatively bring about the physical conception of Jesus (v. 35). This miraculous conception and Virgin Birth of Jesus Christ was necessary because of His deity and preexistence (cf. Isa. 7:14; 9:6; Gal. 4:4).

Like Zechariah, Mary was given a sign: **Elizabeth . . . is going to have a child.** Mary affirmed her part in her Son's subsequent birth by assenting to the plan of God: **May it be to me as You have said.** She willingly submitted to God's plan, calling herself **the Lord's servant** (*doulē,* "slave"; cf. Luke 1:48).

c. Mary's visit to Elizabeth and her
return home (1:39-56)

1:39-45. After learning of the sign,
Mary . . . hurried to see Elizabeth.
Elizabeth and Zechariah lived in **a town
in the hill country,** which probably
referred to the hilly region surrounding
Jerusalem. As Mary arrived, Elizabeth's
baby **leaped in her womb** for joy, **and
Elizabeth was filled with the Holy Spirit.**
Zechariah also was later filled with the
Holy Spirit (v. 67). Prior to the day of
Pentecost, believers were filled with the
Holy Spirit for specific tasks.

Elizabeth's loudly spoken words,
Blessed (eulogēmenē, lit., "well spoken
of") **are you among women,** carry the
idea that Mary is the most honored of all
women. Elizabeth called her **the mother
of my Lord.** In Luke the term "Lord"
(kyrios) often describes Jesus. It has a
double meaning. "Lord" would be more
important for a Greek reader than would
the term "Christ" (meaning "Messiah"),
for the Gentiles had not been anxiously
awaiting the Messiah. On the other hand
the Septuagint often used the word
"Lord" (kyrios) to translate Yahweh.
Again (v. 45) Elizabeth said Mary was
blessed (makaria, "happy") because she
believed what God had told **her.** This
suggests that Mary visited Elizabeth not
with a skeptical attitude but rather
joyously, to confirm what had been
announced to her.

1:46-55. In response to the situation
at hand **Mary** recited a song which
praised God's favor on her and her
people. "The Magnificat," as the song is
called, consists almost entirely of Old
Testament allusions and quotations. The
same is true of the songs of Zechariah
and Simeon (vv. 1:68-79; 2:29-32). Mary's
song has similarities to Hannah's song
(1 Sam. 2:1-10). First, Mary praised God
for His special favor on her (Luke
1:46-50). Mary saw herself as part of the
godly remnant that had served Yahweh.
She called God **my Savior** (sōtēri mou)
showing an intimate acquaintance with
Him. She spoke of His faithfulness
(v. 48), power (v. 49), holiness (v. 49), and
mercy (v. 50). Second, Mary praised God
for His special favor on Israel (vv. 51-55).
Through the Child that she was to bear,
God was being **merciful to Abraham and
his descendants.** Mary was aware that the

birth of her Child was a fulfillment of the
covenant promises to Abraham and his
people.

**1:56. Mary stayed with Elizabeth
for about three months,** apparently until
John was born (cf. v. 36). Mary **then
returned home.** The Greek has the words
"her home," indicating that she was still a
virgin and was not yet married to Joseph.

**B. The births and boyhoods of John
and Jesus (1:57-2:52)**

As in the previous section (1:5-56)
here also the records of the births were
arranged by Luke in a parallel fashion.
The emphasis is on the birth of Jesus,
which is described in greater detail than
the birth of John.

1. THE BIRTH AND MATURATION OF JOHN
(1:57-80)

a. John's birth (1:57-66)

1:57-66. The record of John's birth is
given in a single verse (v. 57), with friends
sharing in the **joy.** Several verses then
focus on and emphasize the obedience of
Zechariah and Elizabeth. The old couple
was careful to follow the Law in the
circumcision of the boy. Though others
objected, Elizabeth said that he was to be
named **John,** which Zechariah confirmed
in **writing.** The fact that Zechariah
immediately was able **to speak** amazed
the crowd. As was true of each person in
the account, Zechariah was praising
(eulogōn, "was blessing"; cf. eulogēmonē in
v. 42) **God.** Word then spread through **the
whole hill country** (in the Jerusalem area)
that this was an unusual child. The people
continued to note that **the Lord's hand
was with him.** Years later, when John
began his preaching ministry, many went
out from this district who no doubt
remembered the amazing events surrounding his birth (Matt. 3:5).

b. Zechariah's prophesy and psalm
(1:67-79)

1:67-79. This psalm, known as "the
Benedictus," is filled with Old Testament
quotations and allusions. Zechariah
expounded four ideas.

1. **Zechariah** gave an exhortation to
praise . . . God (v. 68a).

2. Zechariah noted the reason God
should be praised—**He has come and has
redeemed His people** (v. 68b).

3. Zechariah described the deliver-

Roman Emperors in New Testament Times

Augustus (27 B.C.—A.D. 14)
Ordered the census that involved Joseph and Mary going to Bethlehem (Luke 2:1)

Tiberius (A.D. 14–37)
Jesus ministered and was crucified under his reign (Luke 3:1; 20:22, 25; 23:2; John 19:12, 15)

Caligula (A.D. 37–41)

Claudius (A.D. 41–54)
An extensive famine occurred in his reign (Acts 11:28). He expelled Jews from Rome, including Aquila and Priscilla (Acts 18:2).

Nero (A.D. 54–68)
He persecuted Christians, including the martyrdoms of Paul and Peter. He is the Caesar to whom Paul appealed for a fair trial (Acts 25:8, 10-12, 21; 26:32; 27:24; 28:19).

Galba (A.D. 68–69)

Otho (A.D. 69)

Vitellius (A.D. 69)

Vespasian (A.D. 69–79)
Crushed the Jewish revolt, and his son Titus destroyed the Jerusalem temple in A.D. 70.

---

ance for Israel through the Messiah (vv. 69-75). The Messiah was to be Israel's **horn of salvation** (v. 69). The horns of an animal symbolized its power. Thus the Messiah would be strong and would deliver the nations **from her enemies** (v. 74). Of special import in these verses is the mention of **His holy covenant, the oath** God **swore to our father Abraham** (vv. 72-73; cf. Gen. 22:16-18).

4. Zechariah prophetically described the ministry John would have (Luke 1:76-79). Zechariah had understood the message of the angel, so he foretold that John would be the one to **go on before the Lord to prepare the way for Him** (cf. Isa. 40:3; Mal. 3:1). He would be a **prophet of the Most High** (Luke 1:76; cf. v. 32). Verse 77 may refer to the Lord rather than to John. However, John did preach the same message of **forgiveness of . . . sins** (cf. 3:3).

c. John's growth and seclusion (1:80)

1:80. As John **grew,** he **became strong in spirit,** that is, in human spirit he had an inner vitality and fortitude. His living **in the desert** till the time of his public appearance was not normal for a young person. But because of the special mission which John knew from an early age he would perform, he chose to follow the role of Elijah (cf. v. 17) by living in a desolate area. For in only a brief period of time John's ministry would catapult him into prominence.

2. THE BIRTH AND MATURATION OF JESUS (CHAP. 2)

a. Jesus' birth (2:1-7)

2:1-2. Jesus' birth was dated by Luke as falling in the reign of **Caesar Augustus,** who was officially made the ruler of the Roman Empire in 27 B.C. and ruled to A.D. 14. (See the list of Roman emperors.) Because Herod the Great's reign ended in 4 B.C., Jesus was born before that time. The mention of **Quirinius** as **governor of Syria** poses a problem. He was governor in A.D. 6-7, much too late for Jesus' birth. Therefore does the word **first** (*prōtē*) refer, as in the NIV, to a first, that is, an earlier, **census** by Quirinius? If so, one would have to posit a previous governorship for Quirinius at about 4 B.C. Perhaps a better solution is to take "first" to mean "before," as it does, for example, in John 15:18. Luke 2:2 would then read, "this was the census that took place before Quirinius was governor of Syria" (i.e., before A.D. 6).

2:3-5. For the census **Joseph** and **Mary** went **to Bethlehem,** Joseph's ancestral home. Joseph was a descendant **of David** (cf. 1:27), who was born in Bethlehem. Some have argued that it seems strange that people were not registered in the places where they currently lived. However, other instances of the same practice are known (see I. Howard Marshall, *The Gospel of Luke*, pp. 101-2). Mary accompanied Joseph for several reasons. The couple knew she would have the Baby during the time Joseph was gone, and they most likely did not want to be separated at that event. Also both of them knew that the Child was the Messiah. They also would have known that the Messiah was to be born in Bethlehem (Micah 5:2).

2:6-7. The Child was born during their time in Bethlehem. The fact that Jesus was called Mary's **firstborn** implies that later she had other children. The couple was housed in quarters which were not private. According to tradition, they were in a cave near the inn. The Child was **placed . . . in a manger,** from which livestock fed. Being wrapped **in strips of cloth** was important, for this was the way the shepherds would recognize the infant (v. 12). Some infants were bound up in that way to keep their limbs straight and unharmed.

b. The shepherd's worship of the baby (2:8-20)

2:8-14. An announcing **angel** and other angels appeared **at night** to a group of **shepherds** and heralded the birth of the **Savior** in **the town of David,** that is, Bethlehem (v. 4). The shepherds may have been caring for lambs which were destined for sacrifice during the time of Passover. The appearance of the angel and of the radiant **glory of the Lord . . . terrified** them. The Greek for "terrified" (lit., "they feared a great fear") stresses the intensity of this fear.

The angels' message was comforting. The shepherds were told **not** to **be afraid** (cf. 1:13, 30). The message was that "a Savior," **Christ the Lord,** was **born.** This was **good news of great joy.** Throughout Luke "joy" (*chara*) is often associated with salvation. This news was to be proclaimed to **all the people.** These were specifically the people of Israel, but perhaps Luke also hinted that the Savior would be for all mankind. The **angel** was then joined by **a great company** of other angels engaged in **praising God** in the highest. The NIV's **on earth peace to men on whom His favor rests** is preferred to the KJV's "good will toward men." God's peace is not given to those who have good will, but to those who are recipients of God's good will or favor.

2:15-20. The **shepherds** went to see **the Baby,** and they told what **the angels** had related to them. The shepherds understood that the angels were speaking for **the Lord.** They believed the message and went to confirm it for themselves. This was much like the action of Mary after she had heard the message of Elizabeth. Such an attitude contrasts sharply with that of the religious leaders who knew where the Baby was to be born but did not take the time or the effort to confirm it for themselves (Matt. 2:5).

After seeing the Baby, the shepherds were the first messengers to proclaim the arrival of the Messiah: **they spread the word.** Those **who heard . . . were amazed** (*ethaumasan*). The theme of amazement at the proclamation of the Messiah runs throughout the Book of Luke. (The Gr. verb *thaumazō*, "to be amazed, to wonder, to be astonished," occurs in Luke 1:21, 63; 2:18, 33; 4:22; 8:25; 9:43; 11:14, 38; 20:26; 24:12, 41. Two other words for amazement were also used by Luke; see 2:48.) **Mary** reflected on this momentous event in history. Of all the women of Israel *she* was the mother of the Messiah! The **shepherds returned glorifying and praising God,** much as the angels had done (vv. 13-14).

c. Jesus' circumcision (2:21)

2:21. Mary and Joseph carried out the pronouncement of **the angel** by naming their Son according to the word which had come to her before the Baby's conception (1:31) and to him after the Baby's conception (Matt. 1:18-21). The name **Jesus** is very fitting for it is the Greek form of the Hebrew name Joshua which means "Yahweh is salvation" (cf. Matt. 1:21). As was the custom, Jesus was circumcised **on the eighth day** (Lev. 12:3), perhaps in Bethlehem.

d. The presentation of Jesus to the Lord (2:22-38)

(1) Mary and Joseph's offering. **2:22-24.** The couple was required by the Law not only to have Jesus circumcised (Lev. 12:3), but also to present their **firstborn** to God (Ex. 13:2, 12) 33 days later and to bring an offering for Mary's **purification** after childbirth (Lev. 12:1-8). The offering which they presented for her purification showed that they were a poor couple. They could not afford a lamb, so they bought a pair of doves or pigeons, which were all they could afford. They traveled the short distance from Bethlehem **to Jerusalem** for the presentation and purification at the temple.

(2) Simeon's prophecy and blessing of the family (2:25-35). **2:25-26.** Simeon had been told **by the Holy Spirit that he would not die** till he had seen the Messiah. Simeon was **righteous** (*dikaios*) **and devout** (*eulabēs*, "reverent") before God. Unlike the religious leaders, **he was waiting for the consolation of Israel,** that is, the Messiah, the One who would bring comfort to the nation (cf. "the redemption of Jerusalem," v. 38). The notation that **the Holy Spirit was upon** Simeon reminds one of the Old Testament prophets on whom the Holy Spirit came. Since Anna was "a prophetess" (v. 36), Simeon was probably also in the godly prophetic tradition of Israel. The special revelation from the Holy Spirit about seeing the Messiah was apparently unique and perhaps came because of Simeon's intense desire for the Promised One.

2:27-32. On seeing **the Child** and picking Him up, **Simeon . . . praised God,** the response of godly people toward the Messiah throughout the Gospel of Luke. He then uttered a psalm of praise extolling God for fulfilling His promise by bringing **salvation.** The Messiah is the Source of salvation, as His name Jesus indicates. In all three of the hymns of thanksgiving and praise recorded by Luke in his first two chapters (1:46-55, 68-79; 2:29-32) lie the deep significance of the births of John and Jesus for the salvation of Israel and the world. Simeon noted that the Messiah was to be for **the Gentiles** as well as for **Israel.** The idea of salvation for the Gentiles is set forth many times in the Gospel of Luke.

2:33. The words of Simeon caused Mary and Joseph to marvel (*thaumazontes;* cf. comments on v. 18). Though they had been told that their Son was the Messiah, perhaps they had not comprehended the scope of His ministry to the entire world—to the Gentiles as well as to the people of Israel.

2:34-35. Simeon revealed **to Mary** that her Son would be opposed (**a sign . . . spoken against**) and that she would be hurt greatly. Her grief would be like **a sword** piercing her **soul.** The Son would **cause the falling and rising of many in Israel.** Throughout His ministry Jesus proclaimed that the only way to the kingdom, something the nation had long sought, was to follow Him. The ones who did so would receive salvation; they would "rise." But the ones who did not believe Him would not receive salvation; they would "fall." These consequences would reveal what they thought about Mary's Son.

(3) Anna's thanks to God. **2:36-38.** This godly woman from the prophetic tradition continued the work Simeon had started. Anna **was 84** years old and had devoted herself completely to the Lord's service in **the temple** since her husband had died years before. She announced **to all who were looking forward to the redemption of Jerusalem** (cf. v. 25) that the Messiah had come. The word about Jesus was likely known throughout the entire city as people either believed or disbelieved the words of the old prophet and the widowed prophetess.

e. Jesus' growth in Nazareth (2:39-40)

2:39-40. Joseph and Mary then **returned** with Jesus to their home in **Nazareth of Galilee,** about 65 miles north of Jerusalem, where Jesus **grew** up. Luke omitted Jesus' sojourn in Egypt from his account (cf. Matt. 2:13-21) since it was not his purpose to show the early rejection of the Messiah. In Nazareth He was first rejected after He publicly declared that He was the Messiah. The preparation for His ministry took place in that town as He continued to grow up. Luke noted that He **became strong** and **was filled with wisdom** (*sophia*). His growth in wisdom was mentioned later (Luke 2:52). Luke also portrayed Jesus as the Source of wisdom for His followers (21:15). Jesus had **the grace** or favor (*charis*) **of God . . .**

upon Him. Luke also reiterated that characteristic in 2:52. The wisdom and favor from God were evident before He reached the age of 12.

f. Jesus' visit to the temple (2:41-50)

2:41-50. By the time Jesus was 12 years old, He understood His mission on earth. As was their custom, Mary and Joseph went yearly to Jerusalem to observe the Feast of the Passover. The one-day Passover was followed by the seven-day Feast of Unleavened Bread (Ex. 23:15; Lev. 23:4-8; Deut. 16:1-8). The entire eight-day festival was sometimes called the Passover (Luke 22:1, 7; John 19:14; Acts 12:3-4). On the return home from their trip to Jerusalem, His parents did not realize He was not with them until they had gone some distance. After three days they found Him in the temple courts. The "three days" refer to the time since they had left the city. They had traveled one day's journey away from the city (Luke 2:44); it took them a second day to get back; they found Him on the following day. When Jesus was found, He was interacting with the teachers of the Law, listening and asking intelligent questions. Everyone . . . was amazed (*existanto*, "beside themselves in amazement"; cf. 8:56) at His understanding and His answers. When Mary and Joseph saw Him, they were astonished (*exeplagēsan*, "struck out of their senses," perhaps with joy; cf. 4:32; 9:43). In response to Mary's question about why He had treated them in this manner, Jesus drew a sharp distinction between them and God, His true Father (2:49). His statement confirmed that He knew His mission and that His parents also should have known about His mission. However, His parents did not understand this.

g. Jesus' continued growth (2:51-52)

2:51-52. Luke was careful to point out that Jesus was obedient to Joseph and Mary in case his readers would think otherwise from the previous paragraph. Mary treasured all these things in her heart, reflecting on and remembering her 12-year-old's words, even though she did not understand them. Perhaps Luke received these details about the early years of Jesus from Mary herself or from someone in whom she had confided. Jesus continued to grow (*proekopten*, lit.,

"cut one's way forward," i.e., "increased") in every way (spiritually, mentally, and physically) and had favor with God and men (cf. v. 40).

III. The Preparation for Jesus' Ministry (3:1–4:13)

This section paves the way for the major message of the Gospel of Luke—Jesus' ministry in Galilee and His ministry on the way to Jerusalem (4:14–19:27).

A. The ministry of John the Baptist (3:1-20)
(Matt. 3:1-12; Mark 1:1-8)

As noted earlier (Luke 1:80) John the Baptist lived a life of seclusion till his meteoric rise in public prominence and his sudden fall by the edict of Herod.

1. THE INTRODUCTION OF JOHN (3:1-6)

3:1-2. John's message began in the 15th year of the reign of Tiberius Caesar, that is, A.D. 29. Tiberius ruled over the Roman Empire from A.D. 14 to A.D. 37. Pontius Pilate was appointed governor of Judea in A.D. 26 and ruled to A.D. 36. He was generally opposed to the Jewish people over whom he ruled. The Herod here is Herod Antipas who ruled from Tiberius over Galilee from 4 B.C. to A.D. 39. His brother Philip ruled to the east of the Jordan from 4 B.C. to A.D. 34. (See chart on the Herods at 1:5.) Herod's capital was at Caesarea Philippi. Little is known about Lysanias who ruled in Abilene, northwest of Damascus. John's ministry also began in the time of Annas and Caiaphas. Annas was the high priest from A.D. 6 to A.D. 15 but was deposed by the Roman authorities. Eventually his son-in-law, Caiaphas, was placed in the position (A.D. 18-36). The Jews continued to recognize Annas as the rightful high priest though Caiaphas functioned in that role (cf. comments on Acts 4:5-6, and see chart there on Annas' family; also cf. comments on Luke 22:54; Acts 7:1).

Luke noted that the word of God came to John . . . in the desert. The Old Testament is filled with similar phrases as God called specific prophets to perform tasks. Luke had previously noted that John remained in the desert until his public appearance (1:80).

3:3-6. John's message was a baptism of repentance for the forgiveness of sins. John's baptism was associated with repentance, that is, it outwardly pictured an inner change of heart. The word "for" (eis) refers back to the whole "baptism of repentance." The baptism did not save anyone, as is clear from what follows (vv. 7-14). Repentance was "unto" (lit. rendering of eis; cf. comments on Acts 2:38) or resulted in sins forgiven. Since John's function was to be Christ's forerunner, so also his baptism prefigured a different baptism (Luke 3:16). Luke noted that John's baptizing work was in the country around (perichōron) the Jordan. Because John was visibly taking on himself the role of Elijah, it is possible that he picked this area on the lower Jordan because that was where Elijah spent his last days (cf. 2 Kings 2:1-13). Luke quoted from Isaiah 40:3-5 concerning John's ministry. Isaiah was writing of God's smoothing the way for the return of the exiles from Babylon to Judah. But all three Synoptic Gospel writers applied Isaiah's words to John the Baptist.

Isaiah wrote, "A voice of one calling: 'In the desert, prepare the way for the Lord.'" But Matthew, Mark, and Luke each wrote, A voice of one calling in the desert—the words "in the desert" going with the "voice" rather than with the preparing of the way. Why? Because they quoted from the Septuagint. Of course both are true—the voice (of John the Baptist) was in the desert, and the desert was to be smoothed.

When a king traveled the desert, workmen preceded him to clear debris and smooth out the roads to make his trip easier. In Luke the leveling of the land was a figurative expression denoting that the way of the Messiah would be made smooth because through John a large number of people were ready to receive Jesus' message (cf. Luke 1:17).

Typical of Luke's emphasis on the universal availability of the gospel are his words in 3:6, And all mankind will see God's salvation.

2. THE MESSAGE OF JOHN (3:7-14)

Luke recorded the message of John in ethical terms. John's teaching was that one's life proves whether or not he has truly repented (cf. the Book of James). Ethical teaching was important to Luke for he wrote frequently about helping the oppressed and the poor.

3:7-9. John challenged the people to bring forth fruit as an indication of their belief. John's address to the people was harsh: You brood of vipers! Apparently some were coming with the belief that baptism alone could insure salvation. John was alerting them to the stark realities of life. One must face the fact that wrath was coming. John was clear that being a member of the nation of Israel would not save anyone (v. 8; cf. John 8:33-39; Rom. 2:28-29). An ax is ready to cut down trees that do not bear good fruit so they can be burned. Likewise judgment was extremely close to anyone who did not evidence ("produce good fruit") a genuine repentance (Luke 3:8).

3:10-14. The crowd, tax collectors, and soldiers all asked, What should we do (vv. 10, 12, 14) to give evidence of genuine repentance? (Cf. similar questions in 10:25; 18:18.) In response John told the people to be (a) generous (3:11), (b) honest (v. 13), and (c) content (v. 14).

A person showed his repentance by being generous with the necessities of life—clothing and food. A tunic (chitōn) was a shirtlike garment. Often people wore two if they had them.

Tax collectors, notorious for their dishonesty in collecting more than required and pocketing it for themselves (cf. 5:27-32), exemplified the need for honesty. And soldiers, known and hated for always trying to get more money (by extorting it and blaming others for it), were examples of the need to be content and gentle.

3. THE ROLE OF JOHN (3:15-17)

3:15-17. Luke had previously explained what John's function was to be (1:17, 76). But the crowds who thronged out to hear John began to wonder if John might possibly be the Christ. John distinguished between his own baptism and the Messiah's baptism: John's baptism was with water, but the Messiah would baptize with the Holy Spirit and with fire. The Apostle John presented Jesus not only as the Spirit-baptized One but also as the baptizing One (John 20:22). Ultimately the fulfillment of the baptizing work of the Spirit was seen on the day of Pentecost (Acts 2:1-4). The baptizing "with fire" may refer to the purifying aspect of the baptism of the Spirit (Acts 2:3), or it may refer to the purifying work of judgment that the

Messiah will accomplish (Mal. 3:2-3). The latter seems more probable in view of the work of judgment described in Luke 3:17 (cf. v. 9).

4. THE PREACHING AND IMPRISONMENT OF JOHN (3:18-20)

3:18-20. Scholars debate the dates of John the Baptist's imprisonment and death. It is likely that John began his ministry about A.D. 29 (cf. v. 1), that he was imprisoned the following year, and that he was beheaded not later than A.D. 32. His entire ministry lasted no more than three years—about one year out of prison and two years in prison. (For details on John's imprisonment and death by beheading see Matt. 14:1-12; Mark 6:14-29; Luke 9:7-9, 19-20.)

B. The baptism of Jesus (3:21-22) (Matt. 3:13-17; Mark 1:9-11; John 1:29-34)

All four Gospels record this momentous occasion in the life of Jesus which signaled the beginning of His public ministry. Luke condensed the account more than the other Gospel writers. The purpose of the baptism was to anoint Jesus with the Spirit and to authenticate Him by the Father for beginning His ministry. Each Person of the Godhead was involved in the activity of the Son on earth, including His baptism. The Son was baptized, the Holy Spirit descended on Him, and the Father spoke approvingly of Jesus. In His baptism Jesus identified Himself with sinners though He was not a sinner.

3:21. Only Luke stated that at Jesus' baptism **He was praying.** Luke presented Jesus as praying in or before many occasions in His life (v. 21; 5:16; 6:12; 9:18, 29; 22:32, 40-44; 23:46). When Luke recorded that **heaven was opened,** he was conveying the idea that God was breaking into human history with revelation—sovereignly declaring that Jesus is His Son.

3:22. Since the dove was a symbol of peace or freedom from judgment (Gen. 8:8-12), the Holy Spirit's presence **like a dove** signified that Jesus would bring salvation to those who turn to Him. The **voice** of God authenticated Jesus by alluding to Psalm 2:7 and Isaiah 42:1.

C. The genealogy of Jesus (3:23-38) (Matt. 1:1-17)

The genealogy of Jesus, recorded by Luke immediately after His authentication in baptism by the Father, further shows the sovereign hand of God in preparing the events of the world so that the Messiah could accomplish the Father's will.

3:23. Luke recorded that **Jesus . . . was about 30 years old when He began His ministry.** Luke was not unsure of the age of Jesus when the ministry began. Luke had carefully investigated everything from the beginning (1:3), so it is unlikely that he would not have uncovered the age at which Jesus began His ministry. Though Bible students debate when Jesus' ministry began, the year A.D. 29 may be the best. Luke apparently used the term "about 30" to indicate that He was well prepared for ministry. In the Old Testament 30 was often the age when one's ministry began (Gen. 41:46; Num. 4; 2 Sam. 5:4; Ezek. 1:1). Luke's clarity on the fact of the Virgin Birth is seen in his notation that Jesus **was the Son, so it was thought, of Joseph.**

3:24-38. Verses 23-38 list 76 names including Jesus and Adam and excluding God. Contrary to Matthew's genealogy, Luke's genealogy begins with Jesus and works back to God. Matthew began with Abraham and worked forward to Jesus in three sets of 14 generations. Other differences exist between the two genealogies. Luke included 20 names prior to Abraham, and he stated that Adam was "the son of God."

In addition Luke's and Matthew's lists from David to Shealtiel (during the time of the Exile) differ. That is because the lists trace different lines. Luke traced David's line through Nathan, whereas Matthew traced it through Solomon. Following Shealtiel's son, Zerubbabel, the lists once again differ until both lists unite at Joseph whom, Luke noted, "thought" to be the father of Jesus. Little doubt exists that Matthew's genealogy traced the kingly line of David—the royal legal line. The question is, What is the significance of Luke's genealogy? Two main possibilities exist.

1. Luke was tracing the line of Mary. Many interpreters argue that Luke was giving the genealogy of Mary, showing

that she also was in the line of David and that therefore Jesus was qualified as the Messiah not only through Joseph (since he was the oldest legal heir) but also through Mary.

2. Luke was tracing the actual line of Joseph. This view maintains that the legal line and the actual line of David through which Jesus came met at Joseph, the supposed father of Jesus. In this view Jacob, Joseph's uncle, would have died childless and therefore Joseph would have been the closest living heir. Thus Joseph and then Jesus would have been brought into the royal line.

Both views have problems which are difficult to answer, not the least of which is the fact that the two genealogies meet at Shealtiel and Zerubbabel and then split a second time only to come together at Joseph and Jesus. (Cf. comments on Matt. 1:12.) Regardless of one's view it is important to note an important aspect of the theology Luke expressed in his genealogy. He related Jesus not only to Abraham but all the way back to Adam and to God. This is an indication of the universal offer of salvation, which is common to his Gospel—that Jesus came to save all people—Gentiles as well as the nation of Israel (cf. Luke 2:32).

D. The temptation of Jesus (4:1-13) (Matt. 4:1-11; Mark 1:12-13)

1. JESUS' LEADING BY THE SPIRIT INTO THE DESERT (4:1-2)

4:1-2. Luke then picked up the account of the preparation of the Lord's ministry where he left off in 3:23. **Jesus was full of the Holy Spirit** (cf. 3:22; 4:14, 18). Interestingly **the Spirit** led Him into **the desert, where for 40 days He was tempted by the devil.** The traditional site of Jesus' temptation is a barren area northwest of the Dead Sea. The "40 days" motif is prominent in the Old Testament (cf. Gen. 7:4; Ex. 24:18; 1 Kings 19:8; Jonah 3:4). It is not by accident that Jesus' temptation continued for 40 days, just as Israel's wanderings and temptation continued for 40 years in the wilderness. Jesus' responses to Satan's temptations by quoting from Deuteronomy, chapters 6 and 8, confirm that He was thinking about the experience of the nation in the wilderness. And yet, though the Israelites were miraculously fed in the desert, Jesus **ate nothing.**

2. JESUS' TEMPTATION IN THE AREA OF PHYSICAL NEED (4:3-4)

4:3-4. Since Jesus was extremely hungry and in need of food (v. 2), it is not surprising that **the devil** first tempted Jesus to turn a **stone** into **bread** for His sustenance. Jesus countered this temptation by quoting Deuteronomy 8:3, in which Moses had reminded the people of the manna which God had given them. Though the manna was on the ground, it still was a test of faith for the people. They had to believe that God's Word was trustworthy for their existence. If it was not God's will for them to live they certainly would have died; therefore they did not live by bread alone. Likewise **Jesus,** knowing God's Word, knew of the plan which was before Him and was trusting in the Father and His Word for sustenance. Jesus knew He would not die in the wilderness.

3. JESUS' TEMPTATION IN THE AREA OF GLORY AND DOMINION (4:5-8)

4:5-8. What Matthew recorded as the second and third temptations were reversed by Luke. This may indicate that there were continual temptations in these areas. The second temptation Luke recorded was an appeal to Jesus to be in control of **all the kingdoms of the world.** The condition was that Jesus must **worship** (*proskynēsēs,* lit., "bend the knee to") the devil. Though Jesus would have world rulership, He would be depending on Satan—rather than on God the Father and His plan. Jesus again referred to Moses to combat a temptation. In that passage (Deut. 6:13) Moses warned the people about their attitude when they finally were to get into the land and achieve some glory and dominion. The temptation for them would be to praise themselves and forget to worship God. **Jesus,** by quoting the verse, showed that He would not make that mistake. He would give **God** the credit and not take it for Himself. He would not fail as Israel had failed.

4. JESUS' TEMPTATION IN THE AREA OF THE TIMING OF HIS MINISTRY (4:9-12)

4:9-12. **The devil** tried to get Jesus to change the timing and structure of His ministry. Jesus knew He must go to the cross and die for the sins of the world. He knew that He was the Suffering Servant (Isa. 52:13–53:12). The devil challenged Jesus to throw Himself off **the highest point of the temple.** This was perhaps at the southeastern corner of the wall overlooking the deep Kidron Valley below. Satan meant that the nation, seeing Jesus' miraculous protection from such a jump, would immediately accept Him. The devil even quoted Psalm 91:11-12 to show that the Messiah would be kept safe from harm.

However, Jesus was aware of the implication. To receive the acceptance of the people without going to the cross would be to question whether God was really in the plan at all. That was exactly the situation Moses wrote about in Deuteronomy 6:16, which Jesus quoted. Moses referred back to a time when the people wondered whether God was really with them (Ex. 17:7). But Jesus was confident of the fact that God was with Him and that the Father's plan and timing were perfect. So Jesus would not fall for Satan's temptation.

5. SATAN'S DEPARTURE FROM JESUS (4:13)

4:13. The **devil** departed, not permanently, but only **until** a latter more **opportune time.**

IV. The Ministry of Jesus in Galilee (4:14–9:50)

Jesus' early ministry was primarily in Galilee, though from John 1–4 it is known that He did have an early ministry in Judea and Jerusalem before His Galilean ministry. Two purposes of the Galilean ministry were to authenticate Jesus and to call the disciples who would follow Him.

A. *The initiation of Jesus' ministry (4:14-30)*
(Matt. 4:12-17; Mark 1:14-15)

These 17 verses serve as Luke's summary of what happened throughout the entire ministry of Jesus: Jesus declared Himself to be the Messiah (Luke 4:21); the Jewish hearers proved themselves to be unworthy of God's blessings (vv. 28-29), and the gospel would also go to the Gentiles (vv. 24-27).

1. JESUS' RECEPTION IN GALILEE (4:14-15)

4:14-15. Returning **to Galilee,** Jesus was **in the power** (*dynamei,* "spiritual ability") **of the Spirit.** The Spirit had

descended on Him (3:21-22), He had been led by the Spirit into the desert (4:1), and now He ministered "in the power of the Spirit." The Spirit's power was the source of Jesus' authority, which Luke set forth in chapters 4–6. The initial response was positive. The **news about Him spread** and as they heard Him teach **in their synagogues . . . everyone praised Him.**

2. JESUS' REJECTION IN HIS HOMETOWN, NAZARETH (4:16-30)
(MATT. 13:53-58; MARK 6:1-6)

4:16-30. Jesus initially was a popular Teacher, so when He went back to His hometown, it was natural for Him to teach in synagogues. It was the custom in the synagogue for a man to stand while he was reading the Scriptures but then to sit while explaining the portion he had read. The portion of Scripture Jesus read was **Isaiah 61:1-2,** a messianic passage. He concluded His reading with the words, **to proclaim the year of the Lord's favor**—stopping in the middle of the verse without reading the next line in Isaiah 61:2 about God's vengeance. When Jesus added, **Today this Scripture is fulfilled in your hearing,** the implication was clear. Jesus was claiming to be the Messiah who could bring the kingdom of God which had been promised for so long—but His First Advent was not His time for judgment. The crowd was fascinated at His teaching—**The eyes of everyone . . . were fastened on Him** (Luke 4:20). Jesus' words plainly stated that the offer of the favorable year of the Lord (i.e., the kingdom time) was being made to them through Him (v. 21).

The people **were amazed** (*ethaumazon,* "wondered, marveled"; cf. comments on 2:18) at His **gracious words** (lit., "words of grace"), but they immediately began to question the authority with which He could say these things. How could **Joseph's Son**—the Boy they saw grow up in their town—be the Messiah? Jesus, sensing their opposition (4:23-24), noted two instances in which God's prophets ministered miraculous acts of grace to Gentiles while Israel was in unbelief—**Elijah** and the **widow of Zarephath** (vv. 25-26; cf. 1 Kings 17:8-16), and **Elisha** and **Naaman the Syrian** leper (Luke 4:27; cf. 2 Kings 5:1-19).

Jesus' mention of Gentiles rather than Jews having God's blessing caused the people to be **furious** (Luke 4:28). They attempted to kill Him, **but He walked right through the crowd** (v. 30). Luke no doubt described a miraculous escape from the angry crowd. This pattern is seen throughout the rest of Jesus' ministry: Jesus went to the Jews; they rejected Him; He told of Gentile participation in the kingdom; some Jews wanted to kill Him. But He was not killed until the proper time, when He chose to die (23:46; cf. John 10:15, 17-18).

B. The authentication of Jesus' authority (4:31–6:16)

The people of Nazareth and others in Galilee who heard of Him wondered by what authority He made His statements. So Jesus authenticated His authority by healing and teaching. And because of who He is and what He taught, He had the authority to call disciples. In this section Jesus performed three sets of healings, and after each one He called one or more disciples (5:1-11, 27-32; 6:12-16).

1. JESUS' DEMONSTRATION OF HIS AUTHORITY BY HEALING AND TEACHING (4:31-44)

a. Jesus' healing of a man with an unclean spirit (4:31-37)
(Mark 1:21-28)

4:31-37. Jesus went . . . to Capernaum, which He later made His home since His own hometown, Nazareth, had rejected Him. Capernaum was also the home of Peter and Andrew (v. 38). Again the people were **amazed** (*exeplēssonto*, lit., "struck out of their senses" [also used in 2:48; 9:43]; cf. *ethaumazon*, "wondered, marveled," 4:22, cf. v. 36) **at His teaching** (v. 32) for **His message had authority.** To authenticate that authority, Jesus performed a series of healing miracles which showed that His teaching in Nazareth was true (cf. vv. 18-19). **A man** with **a demon, an evil spirit,** was **in the synagogue.** It has been suggested that since Luke was most likely writing to people with a Greek background, he was clarifying the fact that this demon was evil since the Greeks thought there were both good and evil demons. This demon recognized Jesus, calling Him not only **Jesus of Nazareth** but also **the Holy One of God** (v. 34). In the Gospels crying out with a loud voice seems to be characteristic of those who were demon-possessed. Jesus'

exorcism of **the demon** (v. 35) **amazed** the crowd (lit. "amazement [*thambos*] came on all," v. 36). The crowd noted that Jesus had **authority** *(exousia)* **and power** *(dynamei)* over demons (cf. 9:1), and this caused His fame to **spread** (4:37). This was Jesus' third miracle. (See the list of His miracles at John 2:1-11.)

b. Jesus' healing of Simon's mother-in-law (4:38-39)
(Matt. 8:14-15; Mark 1:29-31)

4:38-39. Both Mark and Luke related that the next miracle occurred immediately after the first miracle in **the synagogue. Simon's mother-in-law** had a severe **fever.** At Jesus' word **the fever . . . left her.** In each of these cases the cause of the difficulty was removed and the person had no side effects. The demon left without hurting the man (v. 35), and the fever left so that Simon's mother-in-law could immediately serve them (v. 39). She was not left in a weakened condition.

c. Jesus' healing of the sick and the demon-possessed (4:40-41)
(Matt. 8:16-17; Mark 1:32-34)

4:40-41. The news about Jesus' authority over sickness spread quickly so that same night **people** began coming to Him for healing. They came **when the sun was setting,** when the Sabbath Day was ending. It would have been unlawful to carry the sick before then. As the **demons came out of many people,** they were **shouting, You are the Son of God!** The reason for Jesus' rebuke was that He did not come to earth so that demons could acknowledge Him as **the Christ,** that is, the Messiah. Instead, He came to be acknowledged by *people.*

d. Jesus' statement about His wider ministry (4:42-44)
(Mark 1:35-39)

4:42-44. Jesus pointed out to the people that He had a ministry to fulfill (cf. v. 18). He had a mission to the rest of the nation of Israel. The reception Jesus received at Capernaum contrasted greatly with His reception in His hometown of Nazareth. The people of Capernaum wanted Him to stay, but He needed to **preach the good news of the kingdom of God** elsewhere **also.**

The main emphasis in Jesus' ministry was on preaching, not healing. Though

He had compassion on people, His healing ministry was usually to authenticate what He was saying (cf. Matt. 11:2-6). Luke's point that **He kept on preaching in the synagogues of Judea** should be interpreted in that light. "Judea" (*Ioudaias*) probably refers to the whole nation (the land of the Jews), not just the southern portion. Luke's point was that wherever Jesus went He constantly taught that He was the Messiah who had come to proclaim the favorable year of the Lord (Luke 4:18-19).

2. JESUS' DEMONSTRATION OF HIS AUTHORITY BY CALLING HIS FIRST DISCIPLES (5:1-11) (MATT. 4:18-22; MARK 1:16-20)

The incident recorded here is obviously not the first time Jesus had been in contact with the men whom He called to be His disciples. Luke already had stated that Jesus had healed Simon's mother-in-law which denotes previous contact with Simon and Andrew. This seems to be at least the third time Jesus had contact with these men. In John 1:41 Andrew told Peter that he had found the Messiah. Apparently the men at first did not follow Jesus on a "full-time" basis, for in Mark 1:16-20 (also Matt. 4:18-22) Jesus called Simon, Andrew, James, and John. Mark recorded that that call was before Jesus entered the synagogue in Capernaum and healed a man who was demon-possessed. It is no wonder Peter invited Jesus home after the synagogue incident.

Now, sometime later, Peter and the others were still fishermen. It was at this point, now that Jesus had established His authority (Luke 4:31-44), that He called these men to full-time discipleship.

5:1-3. The large throng **crowding around** Jesus prevented His teaching effectively as He stood **by the Lake of Gennesaret,** another name for the Sea of Galilee, by a village on the northwest shore. So He went out a short distance in the water in Simon's boat so that they could all listen **to the Word of God.**

5:4-7. On Jesus' request, **Simon** put out his **nets** and **caught . . . a large** amount **of fish.** Though **Simon,** an experienced fisherman, was sure he would not catch anything at that time of the day when the fish were deeper in the lake, he obeyed Jesus' word. This showed a significant amount of faith. The result-

ing catch **began to break** the **nets, so they filled** Simon's and another **boat** with the fish till **both boats . . . began to sink.**

5:8-11. The miracle of the fish brought two responses in **Peter** and the others. They **were astonished** (lit., "amazement [*thambos*] seized him and all those with him," v. 9; cf. 4:36) **at the** large **catch of fish,** and Peter realized his sinfulness before Jesus (5:8). The result was that Jesus made the fishermen fishers of **men.** Jesus' teaching, combined with His miraculous acts, showed that He had the authority to call the men and have them respond by leaving **everything.**

3. JESUS' DEMONSTRATION OF HIS AUTHORITY BY FURTHER HEALING (5:12-26)

The next two healings brought about a confrontation with the religious establishment—the first such conflict recorded in Luke. Both healings authenticated Jesus' claim to be the Messiah (cf. 4:18-21).

a. Jesus' healing of a leper (5:12-16) (Matt. 8:1-4; Mark 1:40-45)

5:12-16. Jesus encountered **a man . . . covered with leprosy** (lit., "full of leprosy"). Perhaps he was in the final stages of leprosy—a fact which would have been easily discernible in the man's home community. The Law (Lev. 13) commanded strict segregation of a person who had leprosy, for it was a graphic picture of uncleanness. A leprous person could not worship at the central sanctuary; he was ceremonially unclean and therefore cut off completely from the community.

This leper addressed **Jesus** as **Lord** (*kyrie*) as Simon had also done (Luke 5:8). Though the term was often used as one would today use "sir," it seems to have stronger import here. The leper did not doubt the ability of Jesus to heal him, for he said, **If You are willing You can make me clean.** His only reservation seemed to be Jesus' willingness. According to the Mosaic Law one who was leprous was not to be touched by anyone who was ceremonially clean. When someone clean touched something unclean, the clean became unclean. Luke, in describing Jesus' actions, showed that Jesus was the Source of ceremonial cleansing. If He was the Source of cleansing for that leper, He would also be the Source of ceremonial cleansing for the nation. This theme is carried on into the next healing (vv. 17-26) and into the call of Levi (vv. 27-39). At the touch of Jesus, **immediately the leprosy left him.** The immediacy of the healing brings to mind 4:35 and 4:39. Healing from leprosy was rare. The Scriptures record only Miriam (Num. 12) and Naaman (2 Kings 5) as having been healed of leprosy (cf. Moses; Ex. 4:6-7). Thus it would have been extremely unusual for a person to present himself before **the priest and offer the sacrifices . . . for . . . cleansing.** Instructions for an offering for cleansing from leprosy are given in Leviticus 14:1-32. Luke 5:14 emphasized the phrase **as a testimony to them.** The fact that a man would go to the priest claiming healing from leprosy would alert the religious leaders that something new was afoot in Israel. Why did **Jesus** command **him** not to **tell anyone?** Perhaps for two reasons: (a) The man was to go immediately to the priest to be a testimony. (b) When **the news** of Jesus' healing power **spread,** He was constantly besieged by people, which caused Him to have to withdraw (vv. 15-16).

b. Jesus' healing and forgiveness of a paralytic (5:17-26)
(Matt. 9:1-8; Mark 2:1-12)

5:17-26. The healing and forgiving of a paralyzed man was further evidence of Jesus' authority and power to make others ceremonially clean. Luke noted that a number of religious officials were present at the occasion, including some from **Jerusalem** who perhaps were the most influential. Luke did not portray this healing as happening immediately after the preceding event he had recorded. It is evident that he placed the two accounts side by side as a development in his argument.

The statement, **the power** (*dynamis,* "spiritual ability") **of the Lord was present for Him to heal the sick,** is unique to Luke (cf. Matt. 9:1-8; Mark 2:1-12). Luke used *dynamis* on several occasions to describe Jesus' healing (cf. Luke 4:36; 6:19; 8:46). A large number of people now accompanied Jesus everywhere because of His works of healing. Thus a group of **men** who were **carrying a paralytic** had to take him to **the roof** of

the house, remove some **tiles,** and let him down **in front of Jesus. Jesus** linked **faith** with the miracle (5:20), which was also the case in 7:9; 8:25, 48, 50; 17:19; and 18:42. Presumably the faith of which **Jesus** spoke (i.e., **their** faith) also included the paralyzed man (5:20).

Surprisingly Jesus did not immediately heal the man's body; instead, He first forgave his **sins.** This is extremely important for the argument of this section, for Luke's point was that Jesus had the authority to call disciples, including people (such as Levi) who were not thought of as being righteous (vv. 27-39). The religious leaders immediately began to think that Jesus' words were **blasphemy** for they rightly associated forgiveness with **God** (cf. 7:49). Jesus pointed out that the religious leaders were absolutely right. His subsequent healing of the man was incontrovertible proof that He did have the **authority . . . to forgive sins** and therefore should be accepted as God. Anyone could *say,* **Your sins are forgiven.** In that sense it was **easier** than saying, **Get up and walk,** for if He did not have the power to heal, all would know it **immediately.** The result of the forgiveness and the healing was that **everyone was amazed** (lit., "received amazement") and was full of **awe** (*phobou,* "reverential fear,") realizing that they had seen remarkable **things** (*paradoxa,* "things out of the ordinary").

4. JESUS' DEMONSTRATION OF HIS AUTHORITY BY CALLING A TAX COLLECTOR (5:27-39)
(MATT. 9:9-17; MARK 2:13-22)

5:27-39. The call of **Levi** was the culmination of the previous two miracles. (Levi is named Matthew in Matt. 9:9.) Jesus had shown that He had the authority to make a person ceremonially clean and to forgive sins. Now those two authorities were brought to bear on one who was to become His disciple.

Luke did not mention Levi's duties as **a tax collector.** But his position alienated him from the religious community of his day (cf. Luke 5:29-31). He was seen as one who betrayed his nation for material gain, for tax collectors gathered money from the Jews to give to the Romans, who were Gentiles, who then did not have to work (cf. 3:12-13). Seemingly Levi would be an unlikely candidate for a disciple of the One who claimed to be the Messiah. Jesus simply spoke the words, **Follow Me.** Levi broke with his way of life; he **left everything and followed** Jesus. Levi's response was the same as that of the fishermen (5:11).

Luke's point would have been clear even if he had stopped with the account of Levi's decision to follow Jesus. But in order to drive the point home Luke related events which occurred at a reception which Levi, Jesus' new follower, gave for Jesus. Levi must have been a wealthy man, for **a great banquet** was prepared at his house and many guests were invited, including **a large crowd of tax collectors.** The same group of religious leaders who had previously questioned Jesus' authority (v. 21) questioned the propriety of Jesus' association **with tax collectors and "sinners."** Not only was Jesus associating with people to whom the Pharisees objected, but He also was eating and drinking with them. Eating and drinking with others denotes a fellowship or camaraderie with them. Though the religious leaders **complained to** Jesus' **disciples . . .** Jesus **answered** their objections (vv. 31-32). He noted that it was not His purpose **to call the righteous, but sinners to repentance.** Here Jesus was not concerned about discussing who were "the righteous." His point was simply that His mission was to those in need of "repentance"—a change of heart and a change of life (cf. 3:7-14). **The Pharisees** sensed no need for such a change. Because He had shown authority in the two healings which preceded this account, the implication is that He was also able to fulfill His mission to sinners.

The sentence addressed to Jesus in 5:33 causes some difficulty. If the Pharisees and religious leaders were still talking, it seems strange that they would refer to their own disciples as **disciples of the Pharisees.** It is possible that this teaching of Jesus is from a different setting but that Luke included it here because it continued the purpose of this section. The accusation was that Jesus and His disciples refused to fast, in contrast with the disciples of John and of the Pharisees, who were seen as righteous people. Jesus' response was that the new way (His way) and the old way (the way of John and the Pharisees) simply do not mix. He gave three examples.

1. A bridegroom's **guests** (cf. John 3:29) do not **fast while he is with them** because it is a joyous occasion. They **fast** later after he is gone.

2. A **new** unshrunk **patch** of cloth is not put on an **old** garment because it will shrink and the tear will be worse.

3. **New wine** is not put **into old wineskins** for as it ferments it will break **the** old **skins,** which have lost their elasticity, and both the **wine** and the skins **will be ruined.**

In each case two things do not mix: a time of feasting and a time of fasting (vv. 34-35), a new patch and an old garment (v. 36), and new wine and old wineskins (vv. 37-38). Jesus was noting that His way and the way of the Pharisees simply are unmixable. The Pharisees would refuse to try the new way for they assumed that their old way was better. Jesus' teaching was considered by the Pharisees and religious leaders to be like **new** wine, and they wanted no part in it (v. 39).

5. JESUS' DEMONSTRATION OF HIS AUTHORITY OVER THE SABBATH (6:1-11)

In 6:1-11 Luke recorded two incidents that occurred on the Sabbath: " One Sabbath" (v. 1) and "On another Sabbath" (v. 6). Luke's point in bringing the accounts together to form a unit was to show that Jesus had authority over the Sabbath.

a. The disciples' picking of grain on the Sabbath (6:1-5)
(Matt. 12:1-8; Mark 2:23-28)

6:1-5. Jesus' **disciples began to pick some heads of grain, rub them in their hands, and eat.** God allowed people to pick grain from a neighbor's field as they passed through (Deut. 23:25). But the **Pharisees,** interpreting the Law strictly, held that rubbing the heads together in order to eat the grain constituted threshing, which was not allowed **on the Sabbath. Jesus** responded to the Pharisees' objection by referring to 1 Samuel 21:1-9. **David** had approached the priests at Nob and asked for bread. The only food available at the moment was the **consecrated bread** that **only** the **priests** were allowed **to eat.** David was given the bread, and **he** and **his companions** ate it. The parallel in Jesus' teaching was clear. In the interest of survival David and his companions were allowed to be above the

Law with the priest's blessing. Christ and His companions were also above the man-made law which the Pharisees proclaimed. Another parallel implicit in Jesus' teaching should not be missed. David, as God's anointed, was being hounded by the forces of a dying dynasty—the dynasty of Saul. Jesus was God's new Anointed One who was being hounded by the forces of a dying dynasty (cf. Luke 5:39). The ultimate conclusion was that Jesus **is Lord of the Sabbath,** that is, He has authority even over matters of the Law.

b. Jesus' healing of a man on the Sabbath (6:6-11)
(Matt. 12:9-14; Mark 3:1-6)

6:6-11. This second contention about the **Sabbath** (cf. the first one in vv. 1-5) seems to have been brought about purposely by **the Pharisees and the teachers of the Law.** As Jesus **was** teaching in the synagogue, He encountered **a man . . . whose right hand was shriveled.** The religious leaders were observing Jesus because they **were looking for a reason to accuse** Him. As was the case when He was opposed previously by religious leaders, **Jesus knew what they were thinking** (5:22). He used the situation to show that He has authority over **the Sabbath. Jesus said . . . I ask you, which is lawful on the Sabbath: to do good or to do evil, to save life or to destroy it?** By this question He showed that refusing to do good on the Sabbath was tantamount to doing evil. If suffering is not alleviated, then one is doing evil to the sufferer.

As the man stretched out his **hand** at Jesus' command, it **was completely restored. Jesus** performed no "work" on the Sabbath—He simply spoke a few words and a hand was completely restored. He humiliated the religious leaders and healed the man all at the same time without even breaking the Pharisees' law. It is no wonder that the religious establishment was **furious** and sought a way to get rid of Him.

6. JESUS' DEMONSTRATION OF HIS AUTHORITY BY CALLING THE TWELVE (6:12-16)
(MATT. 10:1-4; MARK 3:13-19)

6:12-16. Before **Jesus** chose the 12 **disciples,** He **spent** an entire **night** in

prayer. Jesus had a large number of disciples and from those He picked **12** who were to be close **to Him.** These were specifically called **apostles** (*apostolous*) as opposed to the term disciples (*mathētas*). Disciples were followers, but apostles were those sent out as messengers with delegated authority (cf. "apostles" in 9:10; 17:5; 22:14; 24:10). In Luke's list of the Twelve (as well as Matthew's and Mark's lists) **Peter** is listed first and **Judas Iscariot** is last. **Bartholomew** must be Nathanael (John 1:45), Levi and **Matthew** are the same man, and Thaddaeus (Mark 3:18) is **Judas, son of James.** They were now willing to be sent out as apostles, being with Jesus on a full-time basis.

C. Jesus' sermon on the level place (6:17-49)
(Matt. 5–7)

1. INTRODUCTION TO THE SERMON (6:17-19)

6:17-19. The sermon recorded in verses 17-49 is a shorter version of the Sermon on the Mount recorded in Matthew 5–7. Both sermons are addressed to disciples, begin with beatitudes, conclude with the same parables, and have generally the same content. However, in Luke the "Jewish parts" of the sermon (i.e., the interpretation of the Law) are omitted. This fits well with Luke's purpose. The problem in seeing these accounts as reflecting the same sermon is the place in which the sermon was given. Matthew recorded that Jesus was "on a mountainside" (Matt. 5:1), whereas Luke said Jesus was **on a level place** (Luke 6:17). The sequence of events solves the problem easily. Jesus went up in "the hills" near Capernaum to pray all night (v. 12). He called 12 disciples to be His apostles. He then went down on a level place to talk and to heal **diseases** (vv. 17-19). Following that, He went up higher to get away from the crowds and to teach His disciples (Matt. 5:1). The multitudes (Matt. 7:28; Luke 7:1) climbed the mountain and heard His sermon, which explains Jesus' words at the end of the sermon (Matt. 7:24; Luke 6:46-47).

2. THE BLESSINGS AND THE WOES (6:20-26)

Jesus began His sermon with a series of blessings and woes on His listeners. The items are placed in two sets of four—

219

four blessings and four woes which parallel each other.

a. The blessings (6:20-23)

6:20-23. The term "blessed" (*makarioi*) was common in the Gospels; it occurs more than 30 times. All but 2 of the occurrences are in Matthew and Luke. Originally in Greek usage the word described the happy estate of the gods above earthly sufferings and labors. Later it came to mean any positive condition a person experienced. Unlike the biblical authors, the Greek authors drew happiness from earthly goods and values. In the Old Testament the authors recognized that the truly blessed (or happy) individual is one who trusts God, who hopes for and waits for Him, who fears and loves Him (Deut. 33:29; Pss. 2:12; 32:1-2; 34:8; 40:4; 84:12; 112:1). A formal beatitude was an acknowledgement of a fortunate state before God and man (Ps. 1:1; Prov. 14:21; 16:20; 29:18).

Beatitudes in the New Testament have an emotional force. They often contrast a false earthly estimation with a true heavenly estimation of one who is truly blessed (Matt. 5:3-6, 10; Luke 11:28; John 20:29; 1 Peter 3:14; 4:14). All secular goods and values are subservient to one supreme good—God Himself. This is a reversal of all human values. The Beatitudes present the present in the light of the future (cf. Luke 23:29).

Jesus spoke of four conditions in which people are blessed or happy when they are following Him. **Blessed are you who are poor . . . blessed are you who hunger now . . . blessed are you who weep now,** and **blessed are you when men hate you** (6:20-22). In each case a clause is added that explains why such a person is blessed or happy. A poor person is happy because his **is the kingdom of God.** Matthew referred to "the poor in spirit" (Matt. 5:3), but Luke simply wrote "poor." Jesus' hearers were physically poor. Luke already mentioned twice that those who followed Jesus left everything (Luke 5:11, 28).

Jesus' explanation about their inclusion in "the kingdom of God" is mentioned because they were following the One who was proclaiming His ability to bring in the kingdom. They were staking everything they had on the fact that Jesus

was telling the truth. They were following His new way (5:37-39). Jesus' words were not a promise that every poor person had a part in the kingdom of God; instead His words were a statement of fact for His followers. They were poor and theirs was the kingdom of God. They were much better off being poor, following Jesus, and having a part of the kingdom of God than being rich and not having a part of the kingdom. That is why they were blessed.

The next two explanatory phrases have future fulfillments. The hungry **will be satisfied,** and the ones who weep **will laugh.** The apostles who would hunger and weep because they followed Jesus would eventually be vindicated for their faith in Him.

The final beatitude concerned persecution **because of the Son of Man.** This was to become a natural course of events for the apostles. They would be hated, excluded, insulted, and rejected. Yet they would be happy ("blessed") because of their **reward in heaven** and because they were following in the train of **the prophets** (i.e., those who spoke for God; cf. 6:26).

b. The woes (6:24-26)

6:24-26. In contrast with the disciples who had given up everything to follow Jesus were the people who would refuse to give up anything to follow Him (cf. 18:18-30). These were the **rich, well-fed,** the ones **who laugh,** who were popular. They did not understand the gravity of the situation which confronted them. They refused to follow the One who could bring them into the kingdom, and therefore Jesus pronounced woes on them. These woes were the exact reversal of their temporal benefits. And they are the exact opposites of the blessings and rewards of Jesus' followers, cited in 6:20-23.

3. TRUE RIGHTEOUSNESS (6:27-45)

a. True righteousness revealed by love (6:27-38)

6:27-38. Jesus mentioned seven aspects of unconditional love. These actions, not done naturally by human nature, require supernatural enabling—and are thus proof of true righteousness:

(1) **Love your enemies.**
(2) **Do good to those who hate you.**
(3) **Bless those who curse you.**

(4) **Pray for those who mistreat you.**
(5) Do not retaliate (v. 29a).
(6) Give freely (vv. 29b-30).
(7) Treat **others** the way you want to be treated (v. 31). This kind of **love** marks one off as distinctive (vv. 32-34), and as having the same characteristics as the heavenly Father (v. 35).

Jesus then taught His followers a fundamental principle of the universe—what one sows he will reap (vv. 36-38; cf. Gal. 6:7). Jesus outlined five areas which were proof of the sowing and reaping theme, mentioned so often in Scripture: (1) Mercy will lead to mercy (Luke 6:36). The disciples were exhorted to have the same merciful attitude God displayed toward them.

(2) Judgment will lead to judgment (v. 37a).

(3) Condemnation will lead to condemnation (v. 37b).

(4) Pardon will lead to pardon (v. 37c).

(5) Giving will lead to giving (v. 38). It is simply a fact of life that certain attitudes and actions often reflect back on the individual.

b. True righteousness revealed by one's actions (6:39-45)

6:39-45. Jesus explained that a person is not able to hide his attitude toward righteousness. It is obvious that if a person is **blind** he will lead another **into a pit** (v. 39). He will not be able to hide the fact that he is not righteous for he will lead others astray. Jesus also noted that a person becomes like the one whom he emulates (v. 40). Therefore His disciples should emulate Him. One must rid himself of a sin before he can help his **brother** with that sin (vv. 41-42). And often one's own sin is greater than the one he criticizes in someone else—a **plank** compared with a **speck of sawdust.** The point is that one cannot help someone else become righteous if he is not righteous himself. To seek to do so is to be a **hypocrite.**

Jesus also pointed out that a man's words will eventually tell what kind of **man** he is (vv. 43-45). Just as people know the kind of **tree** by the **fruit** it bears, so people know from what a person says whether he is righteous or not. In this case **fruit** stands for what is said, not

what is done: **out of the overflow of his heart his mouth speaks.**

4. TRUE OBEDIENCE (6:46-49)

6:46-49. Outward expression is not nearly so important as obedience (v. 46). It is not enough to call Jesus **Lord, Lord.** A believer must do what He says. Those who hear His words and act on them are secure—**like a man building a house . . . on rock** (vv. 47-48), and those who hear His words and do not act on them are destroyed—**like a man who built a house . . . without a foundation** (v. 49). The disciples had already acted on His words to some extent by following Him. (This is the first of Jesus' parables recorded in the Gospel of Luke. See the list of Jesus' 35 parables at Matt. 7:24-27.)

D. Jesus' ministry in Capernaum and surrounding cities (chaps. 7–8)

In this section is an interchange between the ministry of Jesus in miraculous signs (which again authenticated that He is the Messiah: 7:1-17, 36-50; 8:22-56) and His teaching (which has authority based on the message He was proclaiming: 7:18-35; 8:1-21). Luke emphasized His teaching, which has authority because of the symbolic miraculous events which show that Jesus is the Messiah.

1. JESUS' MINISTRY IN THE MIDST OF SICKNESS AND DEATH (7:1-17)

Here Luke recorded two miracles—a centurion's servant healed and a dead boy raised—as a basis for belief in authority (vv. 22-23).

a. Healing a centurion's servant (7:1-10) (Matt. 8:5-13; John 4:43-54)

7:1-10. After Jesus' sermon (chap. 6), which was given outside of town, **He entered Capernaum,** His adopted hometown where He performed many of His messianic signs. **A centurion** in the Roman army was a commander of a century, a group of 100 soldiers. This centurion in Capernaum, unlike most Roman soldiers, was well liked and respected by the Jewish people in and around Capernaum because he loved them and **built** them a **synagogue** (7:4-5). This **centurion's servant . . . was** extremely **sick and about to die** (v. 2). **The centurion** had faith that **Jesus** would **heal** the servant. Perhaps the reason he sent

Jewish **elders** to present his request was that he doubted that Jesus would have heeded a Roman soldier's request. Matthew 8:5-13 records the same event, but Matthew did not record the sending of messengers. He presented the account as if the centurion were present himself. Matthew was reflecting what the centurion meant when he noted that his messengers do his bidding as if he were there himself (Luke 7:8).

The centurion realized that his request was brash and that he really was not **worthy** to see Jesus (v. 7). Jesus **was amazed** (*ethaumasen;* cf. comments on 2:18) at the centurion and said, **I have not found such great faith even in Israel.** The concept of faith is extremely important throughout chapters 7 and 8. It is vital to believe who Jesus is (i.e., the Messiah) and what He said. The exercise of faith by Gentiles also becomes prominent later in Luke's book.

b. Raising a widow's son (7:11-17)

7:11-17. Luke recorded the raising of the widow's son from the dead so that the ensuing interchange between Jesus and John the Baptist's disciples (vv. 18-23) would have more force.

A large crowd went along with Jesus as He traveled from Capernaum to **Nain** (v. 11). Nain was about 25 miles southwest of Capernaum. **A large crowd** was also with the funeral procession carrying the coffin of a **dead** young man, **the only son of his mother.** The woman was now completely alone and seemingly unprotected, without a close male relative. Help for widows is a major theme in both the Old and the New Testaments, especially under the covenant as related in Deuteronomy. Jesus' **heart went out to her** and He immediately began to comfort her. The verb "heart went out" translates *esplanchnisthē,* a verb used numerous times in the Gospels to mean pity or sympathy. It is related to the noun *splanchna,* "inner parts of the body," which were considered the seat of the emotions. This noun is used 10 times (Luke 1:78; 2 Cor. 6:12; 7:15; Phil. 1:8; 2:1; Col. 3:12; Phile. 7, 12, 20; 1 John 3:17). The woman and the others in the funeral procession must have had faith in Jesus for when **He touched the coffin . . . those carrying it stood still.** At Jesus' command the previously **dead man sat up and**

began to talk—solid proof that he was truly alive. As a result the people **were all filled with awe** (*phobos;* cf. comments on 1:12), they **praised God,** they thought Jesus was **a great prophet** (thinking, no doubt, of the ministries of Elijah and Elisha), they noted that God had **come to help His people** (cf. Isa. 7:14), and the **news about Jesus spread.**

2. JESUS' TEACHING THAT HIS DEEDS AUTHENTICATE HIS MINISTRY (7:18-35) (MATT. 11:2-19)

Luke's purpose in recording the two previous miracles (7:1-17) was to lead up to the interchange between John's disciples and Jesus. It was important for people to believe in Jesus—His works and His words—for both showed that He is the Messiah.

a. John the Baptist's request for clarification of Jesus' ministry (7:18-23)

7:18-23. This event happened while John was in prison (Matt. 11:2). John had had a meteoric ministry which lasted for no more than a year. John expected that the Messiah would set up the kingdom as he had been announcing. But suddenly John found himself in prison and in danger of being put to death, and still the kingdom had not come. Thus John was anxious concerning the Messiah. He knew the Old Testament well and knew of the works of the Messiah—but he did not see the kingdom coming. He sent two **disciples** to ask Jesus, **Are You the One who was to come, or should we expect someone else?** The disciples of John approached Jesus at the **very time Jesus cured many who had diseases, sicknesses, and evil spirits, and gave sight to many who were blind.** Jesus, who was performing messianic miracles, reminded John's disciples of Isaiah 61:1-2 which He had read in Nazareth. Jesus' miraculous deeds pointed to the fact that He is the Messiah. His point was that one should not **fall away** (*skandalisthē,* lit., "to be trapped" and thus "to let oneself be ensnared away from") **on account of** Him. One had to have faith in His message and His works. Neither Matthew nor Luke recorded the reaction of John the Baptist after his disciples returned to him.

b. Jesus' condemnation of Israel for rejecting John's ministry and His ministry (7:24-35)

7:24-28. Jesus used the occasion of John the Baptist's inquiry to teach the people about John's ministry and to commend him. He noted that John was not convictionless, like a **reed** blowing in **the wind.** Nor was he **dressed** luxuriously. Instead, he was rightly understood by the people to be **a prophet.** Jesus added that John was **more than a prophet** in that he, as prophesied in Malachi 3:1, was also the Messiah's forerunner. In Malachi 3:1-2 two messengers are spoken of. One is the forerunner, revealed here as John the Baptist, and the other is "the Messenger of the Covenant" who will purify His people, that is, the Messiah Himself.

Jesus paid John a great compliment by stating that **no one** was **greater than John.** And **yet the one who is least in the kingdom of God is greater than he.** Jesus was not declaring that John was not a part of "the kingdom of God," for John had been preaching the same message of repentance for the forgiveness of sins. Jesus was saying that being a great prophet is not nearly so great as being a member of the kingdom. Implied also is the fact that citizens of the kingdom have a distinct advantage over the prophets who were seen as great men of God in the Old Testament. Citizens of the kingdom will be under the New Covenant and have the Law of God written on their hearts (Jer. 31:31-34). Even the least person in the kingdom will have a greater spiritual capacity than John the Baptist himself.

7:29-30. Luke showed deep division in the thinking of **the people** who listened to **Jesus' words.** Those who **had been baptized by John,** that is, had repented of their sins and had been baptized to show their sincerity, agreed with Jesus and **acknowledged that God's way was right.** In contrast, **the Pharisees and experts in the Law rejected God's purpose for themselves.** By refusing to be **baptized by John** they showed that they did not accept his message of repentance or accept the kingdom. Thus they rejected God's plan of salvation for them. The ironic fact was that the Pharisees and the experts in the Law were the ones who should have known best about the ministry of the forerunner (John) and the Messiah (Jesus).

7:31-35. The editorial interjection by Luke (vv. 29-30) into the narrative account explains the following five verses. Since the religious leaders were rejecting the message of John and of Jesus, the Lord told a short parable to explain their treatment. When Jesus mentioned the **people** (*anthrōpous*) **of this generation** He was not speaking of the people (*laos*) mentioned in verse 29 who accepted His message. Instead the people in His parable were the religious leaders of verse 30, the rejecters of John and Jesus. Jesus described them as capricious **children** who wanted others to respond to their music. They were not satisfied with the behavior of either **John** or Jesus. John was too much of an ascetic, and Jesus was too much of a libertine (in the Pharisees' definition of the term). Neither extreme could make the religious leaders happy. Jesus applied the parable by stating that **wisdom is proved right by all her children.** The ones who were following Jesus and John were proof enough of the correctness of their teaching.

3. JESUS' MINISTRY TO A SINFUL WOMAN (7:36-50)

This passage illustrates the principle Jesus laid down in verse 35. A Pharisee named Simon is contrasted with a sinful woman, who received forgiveness (v. 47) and salvation (v. 50).

7:36-38. Simon (v. 40), a Pharisee, invited **Jesus to . . . dinner,** perhaps to trick Him in some way. It was the custom of the day when one had a dinner party to provide for the guests' feet to be cleaned before the meal. Because most roads were unpaved and the normal foot attire was sandals, it was common for people's feet to be dusty or muddy. As pointed out later in the episode, Simon did not provide for Jesus' feet to be cleaned at the beginning of the dinner party (v. 44). For special dinner parties recliners or couches were provided for the guests to use while eating.

A woman arrived at the dinner after she **learned that Jesus was eating** there. She **had lived a sinful life,** and was probably a prostitute in the community. Her life was known enough for the Pharisee to characterize her as a sinner (v. 39). She was not an invited guest at the dinner gathering, but came in anyway with a **jar of perfume.** Her presence was not unusual for when a Rabbi was invited to someone's house others could stop by and listen to the conversation. As the woman **stood behind** Jesus, **her tears** began to fall on **His feet.** It was a normal sign of respect to pour oil or **perfume** on someone's head. Perhaps the woman felt unworthy to anoint Jesus' head, so she anointed His feet. Such an act would have amounted to a large financial outlay for the woman who apparently was not wealthy. She also bent over Jesus and **wiped** her tears off **His feet . . . with her hair.** She constantly **kissed** His feet (the Gr. verb *katephilei* is the imperf. tense suggesting continuous past action), a sign of the utmost respect, submission, and affection. Jesus pointed out later that the host, in contrast, had done none of these things to His head (v. 46) or even given Him water for His feet (v. 44), whereas the woman was constantly anointing His feet.

The passage does not state why she was weeping. It may have been because she was seeking repentance. Or she may have been weeping for joy at the opportunity of being around the One she obviously considered to be the Messiah.

7:39. The host thought that Jesus could not possibly be **a prophet,** for if He were **He would** have known that the **woman was a sinner.** And He then would not have let her touch Him, for a touch by a sinner brought ceremonial uncleanness.

7:40-43. Jesus, knowing Simon's thoughts (cf. 5:22), taught in a parable that a person who is forgiven much loves more than a person who is forgiven little. In the parable one man was forgiven a debt 10 times greater than another man—**500 denarii** compared with **50** denarii. These were huge debts, for one denarius coin was worth a day's wages. When asked **which** one would **love** the lender **more, Simon** rightly responded that **the one who** was forgiven the larger **debt** would naturally be more inclined to greater love. Jesus then applied the parable to the woman.

7:44-50. The woman had been **forgiven** much and therefore **she loved** Jesus very **much.** Jesus was not implying that the Pharisee did not have much need for forgiveness. His point was that "a sinner" who is forgiven is naturally going

to love and thank the One who has forgiven her. Simon's treatment of Jesus differed vastly from the woman's. She was evidencing that she loved Jesus for she realized that she had been forgiven much. She realized that she was a sinner and in need of forgiveness. In contrast, Simon saw himself as pure and righteous and therefore did not need to treat Jesus in a special manner. In fact, he did not even extend to Jesus the normal courtesies of that day: greeting a male by **a kiss** on the cheek, and anointing a guest's **head** with a small portion of **oil.** In effect he did not seem to think Jesus could do anything for him, for he did not consider Jesus a prophet (v. 39).

But the woman was not forgiven because of her love; rather, she loved because she was forgiven (vv. 47-48). Her faith brought her salvation: **Your faith has saved you; go in peace** (cf. 8:48). Her faith in turn caused her to respond in love. **The other** dinner **guests** wondered **who** Jesus **is** since He forgave **sins** (cf. 5:21). Though Jesus in this interchange with Simon never explicitly stated His claim to be the Messiah, He spoke as He did because He is the Messiah.

4. JESUS' TEACHING ABOUT VARIOUS RESPONSES TO HIS MINISTRY (8:1-21)

a. *A close band of followers who responded positively (8:1-3)*

8:1-3. Much as the woman had responded positively to **Jesus,** in contrast with Simon the Pharisee (7:36-50), so others responded positively to the message **of the kingdom** which Jesus was **proclaiming** and some responded negatively (8:4-15). The believers included **the Twelve** and a number of **women** who had been recipients of Jesus' healing power, including **Mary (called Magdalene;** i.e., Mary from Magdala in Galilee) **from whom seven demons had come out.** Often in Scripture the number seven is used to denote completion. Apparently Mary had been totally demon-possessed. **Joanna,** who was the **wife of** one **of Herod's** officials, was also singled out, as was **Susanna.** These three and many other **women were helping to support them** (i.e., Jesus and the Twelve) **out of their own means.** This would have been viewed as a scandalous situation in Palestine in that day. However, like the forgiven woman (7:36-50), these women had also been forgiven much and they loved much. They were responding positively to Jesus' message about His kingdom.

b. *Various responses illustrated by the Parable of the Sower (8:4-15) (Matt. 13:1-23; Mark 4:1-20)*

8:4. Jesus gave this parable and its explanation to show that a number of responses are possible to the Word of God. Luke noted that **a large crowd was gathering** from many towns. The crowd presumably included people who would respond in the four different ways which Jesus was going to set forth in the **parable.** This parable is perhaps a warning to His hearers that obstacles would be ahead of them.

8:5-8. Farmers sowed seed by scattering it by hand over plowed soil. The **seed** of this **farmer** landed on four kinds of soil. **Some** of the seed **fell along the path** and was eaten by **birds.**

Other seed **fell on rock** (i.e., thin soil covering a ledge of rock) and therefore **withered** (v. 6).

Still **other seed fell** on soil which also supported **thorns** and therefore the **plants** were **choked** out (v. 7).

Still other seed fell on good soil and brought forth a good **crop** (v. 8).

Jesus ended His parable by calling out, **He who has ears to hear, let him hear.** The term **called out** denotes that Jesus was making the major point of His short discourse. Jesus used "He who has ears to hear, let him hear" on several occasions when telling parables (Matt. 11:15; 13:9, 43; Mark 4:9, 23; Luke 8:8; 14:35). The expression describes the fact that spiritual people can discern the intended spiritual meaning of a parable. The implication is that unspiritual people would understand no more than the parable's surface meaning.

8:9-10. Jesus' disciples had asked Him **what the parable meant.** But before He told them its meaning, He explained why He used the parabolic form of teaching. People who were spiritually discerning, that is, were following Him and acknowledging His message as true (such as those in 7:36-8:3) would have **the knowledge of the secrets of the kingdom of God.** But others who were not responding to Jesus' message of the kingdom would not understand the parable

(cf. 1 Cor. 2:14). In support of this Jesus quoted Isaiah 6:9—the people heard what He said but did **not understand** it. Jesus' speaking **in parables** was actually an act of grace to those listening to Him. If they refused to acknowledge Him as Messiah, their judgment would be less severe than if they had understood more (cf. Luke 10:13-15).

8:11-15. Jesus explained **the parable** to His disciples. **The seed is the Word of God.** The words which were being preached by the Living Word, Jesus, was the same message John the Baptist had been preaching. The people's responsibility was to accept the message which both Jesus and John were preaching.

Four kinds of people are represented by the four soils. All four kinds receive the same news. The first group consists of those **who hear** but do not **believe** at all, because of the work of the devil (v. 12).

The second group are those who listen and rejoice **but** then do not stick with the truth of the message for **they have no root** (v. 13). The fact that **they believe for a while but . . . fall away** means that they only accept the facts of the Word mentally and then reject it when "the going gets rough." It does not mean they lose their salvation, for they had none to lose.

The third group are those who listen but never come to maturity (v. 14). These may be those who are interested in Jesus' message but who cannot accept it because of their devotion to material things— **life's worries, riches, and pleasures.**

The fourth group consists of those who listen, **retain** the Word, **and . . . produce a crop** (v. 15), that is, they bear spiritual fruit, evidence of their spiritual life. Their hearts were changed for they were **noble and good.**

As Jesus' ministry progressed, it was evident that each of these groups surfaced: (1) The Pharisees and religious leaders refused to believe. (2) Some people rallied around Jesus because of His miracles of healing and feeding but refused to stay with His message (e.g., John 6:66). (3) Others, such as the rich ruler (Luke 18:18-30), were interested in Jesus but would not accept Him because of the strong pull of materialism. (4) Others followed Him and were committed to His Word regardless of the cost (e.g., 8:1-3).

c. The need to respond positively to His teaching (8:16-18)
(Mark 4:21-25)

8:16-18. This short parable is a logical extension of the Parable of the Sower. The emphasis is once again on hearing or, as it is put here, on listening (v. 18). If one understands the Word of God his life should reflect that understanding (cf. v. 15). Just as one does not light **a lamp** in order to hide **it** (cf. 11:33-36), so also a person is not **given** "the secrets of the kingdom of God" (8:10) in order to keep them secret. The disciples were to make **known** the things Jesus was telling them. The people who followed Jesus were to **consider carefully** (v. 18) **how** they listened. If they heard and responded with genuine belief (cf. v. 15), then they would receive **more** truth. If they did not receive what they heard, they would lose it.

d. The response of Jesus' earthly family (8:19-21)
(Matt. 12:46-50; Mark 3:31-35)

8:19-21. The logical outcome of the preceding teaching (vv. 1-18) is that a person who understands (and therefore puts into practice) the things Jesus was saying was rightly related to Him. **Jesus' mother and brothers** arrived **to see Him.** These brothers were undoubtedly sons of Mary and Joseph who were born after Jesus. Joseph had no sexual relations with Mary until after the birth of Jesus (Matt. 1:25). The implication is that after Jesus' birth Mary and Joseph engaged in normal marital relations and had a number of children. Thus these "brothers" were Jesus' half-brothers.

Jesus was informed that some blood relatives wanted **to see** Him (Luke 8:20). In His answer Jesus did not negate His relationship with His family. Rather, He positively stated that His affiliation with those **who hear** the Word of God **and put it into practice** is like a family relationship. In addition, Jesus' remarks showed that the gospel is not limited to a people, the Jews, but is for all who believe, including Gentiles. Once again the importance of hearing **God's Word** is central; this time, however, the admonition is that the Word must be "put . . . into practice." James, Jesus' half brother, must have learned the lesson well, for he

wrote about obeying the Word instead of merely listening to it (James 1:22-23).

5. JESUS' MINISTRY THROUGH A SERIES OF MIRACLES (8:22-56)

Luke had previously recorded events that authenticated Jesus' authority (4:31–6:16). Here again an authentication was necessary. Jesus had been teaching that one must listen carefully to His words and carry them out. Now He authenticated His words in ways that only the Messiah could do. Jesus showed His power over three aspects of the created world: the natural realm (8:22-25), the demonic realm (vv. 26-39), and sickness and death (vv. 40-56).

a. Jesus' power over the natural realm (8:22-25)
(Matt. 8:23-27; Mark 4:35-41)

8:22-25. While **Jesus** and **His disciples** were sailing across the Sea of Galilee to a less-inhabited area, a storm arose which caused their boat to take on water and to be in peril. Sudden storms would whip the lake into a frenzy very quickly. Jesus was **asleep** so **the disciples went and woke Him** for they were afraid of drowning. Jesus **rebuked** the storm, and chided them for their fear and their lack of **faith** in Him. He had already told them they would be crossing **over to the other side of the lake** (v. 22). This was an excellent opportunity for them to act on God's Word that Jesus had been teaching (vv. 1-21). When Jesus rebuked the storm, the lake calmed immediately (which normally does not occur after a storm). The disciples were in **fear and amazement** (cf. vv. 35, 37).

b. Jesus' power over the demonic realm (8:26-39)
(Matt. 8:28-34; Mark 5:1-20)

8:26. Whereas Matthew wrote that Jesus met two demon-possessed men (Matt. 8:28-34), Luke wrote about only one of the two. There is some confusion as to the place where the miracle occurred. What is meant by **the region of the Gerasenes?** Apparently the area was named for the small town Gersa (now the ruins of Khersa) on the eastern shore, **across the lake from Galilee.** Matthew mentioned "the region of the Gadarenes" (Matt. 8:28), which was named for the town Gadara, about six miles southeast of the lower tip of the Sea of Galilee. Perhaps the territory around Gersa belonged to the city of Gadara (cf. comments on Mark 5:1). **8:27-29. When Jesus stepped ashore, He was** confronted by **a man who was demon-possessed.** The man's manner of life showed that he was totally under the demon's control. He did not take part in normal human amenities (v. 27) and was often forced **by the demon** to go **into solitary places** (v. 29). As with most "demonized" individuals in the Gospels, this man was **shouting at the top of his voice.** The demon recognized Jesus, for the man called Him **Jesus, Son of the Most High God.** The words, **Don't torture me** show that the demon recognized that Jesus had control over him even though men could not (v. 29).

8:30-33. In answer to **Jesus** the demon said that his **name** was **Legion,** a Latin term denoting a group of about 6,000 Roman soldiers. The point of the name was that a large number of demons were inhabiting the man. The demons asked that Jesus not torment them (Matt. 8:29 adds "before the appointed time") by asking that they not be sent **into the abyss,** which was thought of as a place of the dead. The abyss was also thought of as a "watery place," which made the outcome of this encounter all the more ironic and climactic. At the request of **the demons** Jesus let them enter into **a large herd of pigs** nearby which immediately **rushed** over a cliff **into the lake** and were **drowned.** Thus the request not to be sent into the abyss was granted by Jesus, but they were sent to a watery place anyhow.

8:34-37. The effect of the miracle on **the people** of the area was **fear** (vv. 35, 37; cf. 7:16; 8:25). This fear was enough to cause them to ask **Jesus to leave.**

8:38-39. In contrast with those people the previously demon-possessed **man** was, on Jesus' command, spreading the news of what had happened to him. This was the first recorded witness of Jesus in a Gentile area.

c. Jesus' power over sickness and death (8:40-56)
(Matt. 9:18-26; Mark 5:21-43)

This section (chaps. 7–8) begins with Jesus ministering to people in sickness and death (7:1-17). It closes with the same theme. However, the healings described in 8:40-56 bring the section to a climax because of the rich symbolism concerning Jesus' ability to make others clean while not becoming ceremonially unclean Himself.

8:40-42. Jairus, a ruler of the synagogue, pled with Jesus for the life of **his only daughter, who was dying.** The fact that a ruler of a synagogue would come to Jesus showed that people were beginning to acknowledge who Jesus is—that He is indeed the Messiah. A synagogue ruler was in charge of the synagogue services and was responsible for maintaining and cleaning the building. Other synagogue rulers in the New Testament were Crispus (Acts 18:8) and Sosthenes (Acts 18:17).

8:43-48. The story of Jairus is momentarily broken off by Luke who recorded what happened on the way to heal Jairus' daughter. **A woman** in the crowd **had been subject to bleeding for 12 years.** Interestingly, Jairus' only daughter was about 12 years old, and this woman's illness had extended for 12 years. Her hemorrhaging made the woman ceremonially unclean (Lev. 15:25-30), and anyone who touched her would also be ceremonially unclean. In contrast to the fact that **no one could heal her** is the fact that when she **touched** Jesus' **cloak . . . immediately her bleeding stopped.** Jesus' question, **Who touched Me?** does not imply that He was ignorant of the situation. He wanted the woman to reveal herself and openly express the faith which caused her to touch Him. The woman's faith became public when she **fell at His feet.** (This reminds one of another woman who expressed her faith at the feet of Jesus [Luke 7:36-50].) The woman's **faith** had **healed** her (8:48)—faith that Jesus could make her ceremonially clean and therefore faith that He really is the Messiah. Jesus told her, **Go in peace,** just as He had recently said to a sinful woman (7:50).

8:49-56. The story now returned to **Jairus.** Jesus had just been touched by someone who was considered ceremonially unclean. In spite of the fact that Jairus was informed that his **daughter** had died, he had faith that she would be resurrected (v. 50). That faith was partly expressed in the fact that he allowed Jesus to come into his **house** after He had touched an unclean woman.

After Jesus had raised Jairus' daughter from the dead, she was given **something to eat.** This proved that she was restored to normal health and not to a long convalescence (cf. a similar situation with Peter's mother-in-law; 4:39). In this case the **parents were astonished** (*exestē-san,* "beside themselves in amazement"; cf. 2:47), but were not fearful. Jesus' command **not to tell** others about the miracle must have stemmed from His desire not to be openly proclaimed as the Messiah until His formal proclamation in Jerusalem.

E. Jesus' teaching of His disciples (9:1-50)

Luke's section on Jesus' Galilee ministry closes with several important events through which Jesus taught His disciples. For Luke, the events in this chapter, though important, are not the crux of his argument. Jesus' journey to Jerusalem is, for Luke, the highlight of His ministry. The events recorded in this chapter form a climax to this portion of Jesus' ministry (4:14–9:50) and a bridge to His journey to Jerusalem, which begins in 9:51.

1. THE SENDING OF THE TWELVE (9:1-6)
(MATT. 10:5-15; MARK 6:7-13)

9:1-6. Jesus gave **the Twelve** two assignments on the mission to which He sent them. They were **to preach the kingdom of God and to heal the sick.** They were able to carry out that mission because Jesus **gave them power** (*dynamin,* "spiritual ability"; cf. 4:14, 36; 5:17; 6:19; 8:46) **and authority** (*exousian,* "the right to exercise the power") over the demonic realm and the physical realm of **diseases.** Jesus had just shown His power over both of these realms (8:26-56). Their healing ministry was to authenticate their preaching ministry. The fact that the Twelve healed in Jesus' authority and power showed that He was the Messiah who could bring in the kingdom. Therefore it was necessary that people believe the Twelve. People would evidence their belief in the Twelve—and thus in the Messiah—by showing hospitality to these men who were ministering in Jesus' authority.

This helps explain Jesus' rather strange instructions (9:3-5) concerning a method of their ministry. The mission was not to be long—they came back to report to Jesus (v. 10). Why were the Twelve not to take supplies or **money** with them? This was because of the brevity of their mission and also because people's reactions to them would indicate whether or not the nation was accepting Jesus' claim as the Messiah. People who believed the message and the messianic healings would be glad to share with the Twelve. People who did not believe would be judged (vv. 4-5). If a **town** rejected the Twelve the latter were to **shake the** town's **dust off** their **feet.** When Jews returned home from a Gentile country, they would shake the dust off their feet to signify their breaking ties with the Gentiles. In this way the Twelve signified that certain Jewish townspeople were like Gentiles who would not listen or believe. Jesus was thus giving the entire area opportunity to believe His message and mission. Luke stated that the Twelve **went . . . everywhere,** presumably everywhere in the Galilean region rather than everywhere in the nation.

2. HEROD'S QUERY ABOUT JESUS (9:7-9)
(MATT. 14:1-2; MARK 6:14-29)

9:7-9. As the Twelve went through the villages and towns, their ministry attracted much attention. Even **Herod** who was responsible for the region of Galilee as **tetrarch** (cf. 3:1), **heard about** their ministry but did not understand it. Herod, who apparently did not believe in resurrection, knew that Jesus could not be **John** the Baptist for he had previously killed John. **Others** were saying **that** Jesus might be **Elijah** or another of **the** Old Testament **prophets** raised from the dead. Luke's point in the account seems to be that everyone, even in the highest levels of government, was talking about the ministry of Jesus and the Twelve.

3. JESUS' FEEDING OF THE 5,000 (9:10-17)
(MATT. 14:13-21; MARK 6:30-44; JOHN 6:1-14)

The feeding of the 5,000 is the only miracle of Jesus which is recorded in all four Gospels. In many ways it is the climax of Jesus' ministry of miracles. It was designed to produce faith in His disciples.

9:10-11. Luke now called the Twelve **apostles** (*apostoloi*). **Jesus** had so named them previously (6:13). Presumably the apostles **returned** to Jesus' home base at Capernaum. Jesus **took them to Bethsaida,** across the Jordan River to the northeast on the Sea of Galilee. (Others, however, say Bethsaida was a town now known as Tabgha, southwest of Capernaum.) As usual, **the crowds . . . followed Him.** Jesus continued to preach the message of **the kingdom of God.** He had sent the Twelve to preach, and He **healed those who needed healing.** The miracle which immediately followed showed climactically that Jesus is the Messiah, fully able to provide for His people. Herod had raised the issue as to who Jesus is (9:7-9). Later Jesus again raised the same issue (vv. 18-20). The feeding of the 5,000 (vv. 10-17) clinched the truth for the disciples that Jesus truly is the Messiah.

9:12-17. The people who had gathered were apparently not local people for the disciples wanted Jesus to **send the crowd away so** that **they** could **find food and lodging.** This would not have been necessary if the people had lived nearby and could have returned to their homes. When Jesus told His disciples to **give** the people **something to eat,** He was showing His men that it was humanly impossible to satisfy the crowd. The disciples admitted this and noted that **food** would have to be bought for the people if they were to feed them. The disciples stated that there were only **five loaves of bread and two fish,** clearly inadequate for such a large group of people. The **5,000 men** (*andres,* "males") is no doubt a round figure, not counting the women and children who were present (Matt. 14:21). If the latter were also counted, the total might have been over 10,000.

After having the people **sit down in groups of** 50s, for ease in distributing the food, Jesus thanked God the Father and gave out the food, using the disciples as waiters. **Twelve basketfuls of broken** food **pieces** were collected at the end of the meal, perhaps thus providing a basket of food for each disciple to eat. The word used for baskets (*kophinoi*) was considered typical of Jewish commerce. The seven baskets from the feeding of the 4,000 (Mark 8:8) were a different kind of basket. Jesus, by this act of provision, had shown Himself sufficient for the nation Israel. He is the One who could provide prosperity if the people would believe His message. This miracle is reminiscent of Elisha when he spoke the Word of the Lord and a small amount of food fed many people, with some left over (2 Kings 4:42-44).

4. JESUS' TEACHING ABOUT HIS IDENTITY AND MISSION (9:18-27)
(MATT. 16:13-28; MARK 8:27–9:1)

For the first time in this section Jesus taught His disciples about His ultimate mission—the fact that He had to die. **9:18-21.** On this occurrence, which Mark said was on the way north to Caesarea Philippi (Mark 8:27), Jesus initiated the questioning about **who** people said He was (cf. Luke 9:7-9). Jesus was specifically interested in who the **disciples** thought He was. **Peter,** answering for the entire group, affirmed that He is **the Christ** (i.e., the Messiah) **of God.** Though some time had passed since the incident of the loaves and fish, the implication from Luke seems to be that it was Jesus' sufficiency in that instance which clinched His identification as Messiah in the disciples' minds. Jesus did not want others to know of this (v. 21) because it was not time for Him to be proclaimed publicly as Messiah. The public proclamation would come about at a later time and it was that proclamation which Jesus spoke about next.

9:22-27. The subject of these verses is death—Jesus' death and His followers' deaths. He pointed out that the Jewish leaders would play a prominent part in His death (v. 22). Jesus also gave His first indication that He would be resurrected (v. 22). Jesus then discussed the deaths of His followers. They were to have the same attitude toward death and life that He had. Each one **must deny himself,** that is, not think about his own good. Also he must **take up his cross daily,** that is, admit that the One for whom he carried the cross was right (see comments on 14:27). And he must **follow** Jesus, even to death.

The words Jesus spoke in this setting must be understood in their historical context. Not long before this the disciples had been actively engaged in telling the nation about the Messiah and His kingdom program. No doubt many thought the disciples were throwing their lives away. They had given up their sources of income and were in danger because they associated with Jesus. Jesus assured His disciples that they were doing the right thing. They had chosen the proper values (9:24-25). People were to respond in faith and identify with that program (v. 4). Those who did not identify with the kingdom program would be rejected (v. 5). In the same manner Jesus noted that if one **is ashamed of** Him (i.e., will not identify with Him or believe on Him) **and** His **words** (i.e., His message), **the Son of Man will be ashamed of him** in the future. It was vital that the people of that generation side with Jesus and His disciples in order to escape future judgment. That judgment will occur **when He comes in His glory and in the glory of the Father and of the holy angels** (cf. 2 Thes. 1:7-10).

Jesus added, **Some who are standing here will not taste death before they see the kingdom of God.** Over the centuries many views on this statement have been suggested. The four most common views are these: (1) Jesus was talking about the beginning of Christian missions at Pentecost. Surely most of the apostles did see the activities on the day of Pentecost for only Judas was dead at that time. However, to identify Pentecost with the kingdom violates much of the Old Testament teaching about the kingdom. (2) Jesus was speaking about the destruction of Jerusalem. However, it is difficult to see in what way that would even symbolize the kingdom of God. (3) Jesus meant that the disciples would not die with Him but would continue to spread the gospel after His death. But it is difficult to see how this would be related to the kingdom in light of the Old Testament with which the disciples were familiar. (4) Jesus was speaking of the three apostles who would accompany Him up the mountain of transfiguration. The transfiguration was a foretaste of the glories of the kingdom. This seems the best view. Luke linked this teaching (Luke 9:27) with the transfiguration account (vv. 28-36).

5. JESUS' TRANSFIGURATON BEFORE THREE
   DISCIPLES (9:28-36)
   (MATT. 17:1-8; MARK 9:2-8)

9:28-31. About eight days later

Jesus . . . took three of His apostles **up onto a mountain to pray.** But Mark wrote that the event occurred after *six* days (Mark 9:2). The two accounts are not contradictory if one understands Mark as speaking of the intervening days and Luke as including the days of Jesus' teaching as well as the day on which the transfiguration took place. The transfiguration may have occurred on Mount Hermon near Caesarea Philippi (cf. Mark 8:27), though some say it was Mount Tabor. At the transfiguration three events occurred:

1. Jesus' **face** and **clothes became as bright as a flash of lightning.** This would have immediately reminded those present of Moses' face shining with a bright light when he received the tablets of the Law (Ex. 34:29-35).

2. **Moses and Elijah appeared** and spoke **with Jesus.** The bodies of Moses and Elijah were never found. God buried Moses' body (Deut. 34:5-6), and Elijah did not die but was taken up to heaven (2 Kings 2:11-12, 15-18). These two men represent the beginning and the end of Israel, for Moses, as the Lawgiver, founded the nation, and Elijah is to come back before the great and terrible day of the Lord (Mal. 4:5-6).

3. Moses and Elijah **spoke about His departure** (*exodon,* "going out or away") **which He was about to bring to fulfillment at Jerusalem.** "Departure" referred to Jesus' leaving the world through which He would bring salvation—much as Yahweh had brought deliverance to Israel in its Exodus (departure) from Egypt. This departure was to be fulfilled in Jerusalem. From this point on, Jesus indicated several times that He was headed toward Jerusalem (Luke 9:51, 53; 13:33; 17:11; 18:31). Jesus did not want His miracles widely publicized at that time, for the fulfillment had to be at Jerusalem. This was confirmed by Elijah's and Moses' words.

9:32-33. Three disciples were with Jesus. This number is reminiscent of Moses' three companions—Aaron, Nadab, and Abihu—who saw God (Ex. 24:9-11). **Peter,** James, and John **were very sleepy** at the beginning of the transfiguration. Later these three and the others fell asleep while Jesus was praying in the garden (Luke 22:45). As the disciples woke up, they were overwhelmed with the **glory** of the situation.

They realized they were in a kingdom setting which triggered Peter's idea that they build **three shelters**. **Peter** may have been thinking of the Feast of Booths, a feast of ingathering long associated with the coming kingdom (cf. Zech. 14:16-21). Peter seemed to have assumed that the kingdom had arrived.

Luke editorially inserted that Peter **did not know what he was saying**. The thought is not that Peter misunderstood the significance of the kingdom setting— he was correct in that. The problem was that he forgot Jesus' prediction that He would suffer (Luke 9:23-24).

9:34-36. While Peter **was speaking, a cloud . . . enveloped them**. Grammatically the word "them" could refer to the three disciples or to all six people (Jesus, Moses, Elijah, and the three disciples). But more likely it refers to Jesus and the heavenly visitors, with the disciples being those who **were afraid**. A **cloud** was often a symbol of God's divine presence (Ex. 13:21-22; 40:38). Perhaps the disciples thought Jesus was being taken away from them, and they would never see Him again.

As was the case at Jesus' baptism (Luke 3:22), so here a voice spoke to those witnessing the event: **This is My Son, whom I have chosen; listen to Him.** Those familiar with the Old Testament, as the disciples were, doubtless immediately recognized the reference (in the words "listen to Him") to Deuteronomy 18:15 with its messianic prediction of a Prophet greater than Moses. The people were to listen to (i.e., obey) the Prophet.

Suddenly **the disciples** saw **that Jesus was alone.** At that time they did not tell anyone **what they had seen.** The experience at the transfiguration fulfilled Jesus' prediction (Luke 9:27). Three of the disciples did see a manifestation of the kingdom of God before they died (cf. 2 Peter 1:16-19).

6. JESUS' HEALING OF THE EPILEPTIC BOY (9:37-43)

(MATT. 17:14-18; MARK 9:14-27)

9:37-43. The transfiguration may have occurred at night, for Luke noted that **the next day** the four descended **from the mountain** and a **crowd met** Jesus. A **man** begged Jesus **to look** at his demon-possessed **son,** whom the other **disciples** had been unable to help. In

stark contrast with the disciples, only Jesus could help the boy—just as He is the only One who can help the world. The disciples were powerless without Him. After the boy was healed, the crowd was **amazed** (*exeplēssonto,* "struck out of their senses"; cf. 2:48; 4:32) **at the greatness of God.**

7. JESUS' TEACHING OF HIS DEATH (9:44-45)

9:44-45. In the midst of the amazement by the crowd, Jesus taught the disciples a second time that He would die by being **betrayed into the hands of men. But they did not understand** as it was **hidden from them.** Apparently the disciples were still confused as to how Jesus, with His glorious power, could experience a humiliating death. Nor could they put together the crowd's reaction to His miracles and His prediction that the nation would turn against Him and kill Him.

8. JESUS' TEACHING ABOUT GREATNESS (9:46-50)

(MATT. 18:1-5; MARK 9:33-40)

9:46-50. This section (9:1-50) ends with Jesus' teaching concerning the disciples' attitude toward greatness. He had been revealed to them as the Messiah who would bring in the kingdom. Perhaps this fact precipitated the disciples' argument about their greatness in that kingdom. Jesus set forth the principle that the one who is **the greatest** is the one **who is least among you.** This same attitude of service characterized Him, the Messiah who was willing to go to the cross for all people.

Coupled with this discussion on greatness was John's attempt **to stop** someone else who was **driving out demons** in Jesus' **name.** John's reason was that the **man** was **not one of us.** John must have thought that the disciples' own greatness was diminished if others who were not of the Twelve could also cast out demons. Jesus' reply, **Whoever is not against you is for you,** suggested that the Twelve were not to see themselves as God's exclusive representatives. Rather they should have rejoiced that the power of God was being manifested on earth by others as well. If they manifested that attitude, it would show that they were truly trying to be of service to the Messiah.

V. The Journey of Jesus toward Jerusalem (9:51–19:27)

This lengthy section of Luke comprises two parts: (1) the rejection of Jesus by most on His journey toward Jerusalem (9:51–11:54) and (2) Jesus' teaching His followers in view of that rejection (12:1–19:27).

The previous section (4:4–9:50) dealt with Jesus' authentication in His Galilean ministry. In this next section authentication was no longer the issue. The issue was now acceptance. Jesus was not accepted by most of the nation. Therefore He began to teach His followers how they should live in the face of opposition.

A. The rejection of Jesus by most on His journey toward Jerusalem (9:51–11:54)

This section begins with Jesus' rejection by people in a Samaritan village (9:51-56). Of course it was expected that Samaritans would reject Him, but that rejection set the pattern for what followed. The rejection climaxed when Jesus was accused of having demonic power (11:14-54).

1. JESUS AND THE SAMARITANS (9:51–10:37)

a. *Jesus' rejection by a Samaritan city (9:51-56)*

9:51-56. After the transfiguration (vv. 9:28-36), in which Moses and Elijah spoke with the Lord concerning His departure *from* Jerusalem, **Jesus resolutely set out *for* Jerusalem.** Jesus made several trips to Jerusalem, but Luke telescoped them to make his point that Jesus had to get to Jerusalem to present Himself as the Messiah and then depart. On His way, **He sent messengers on ahead,** but the Samaritans **did not welcome Him, because He was heading for Jerusalem.** Conflict between Jews and Samaritans had been going on for several hundred years. The reaction of **the disciples, James and John** in particular, was **to destroy them** by **fire . . . from heaven.** They were thinking, no doubt, of Elijah (2 Kings 1:9-12), who destroyed by fire those who were opposing God's work. Jesus, on the other hand, called for tolerance. The implication is not that it was right to oppose Jesus and His followers. The Samaritans who rejected Jesus would be judged for their rejection.

However, there were more important things to take care of. Jesus had to move along toward Jerusalem.

b. *Jesus' teaching that discipleship takes radical commitment (9:57-62) (Matt. 8:19-22)*

Luke introduced three people who wanted to join Jesus on His journey to Jerusalem.

9:57-58. A **man** approached and wanted to **follow** where they were going. Jesus' response was that a person desiring to follow Him must give up what others consider necessities. Jesus had no home of His own nor did His followers. They were on their way to Jerusalem where Jesus would be put to death.

9:59-60. Jesus called the next **man** with the same words with which He had called His disciples (5:27). The man's reply that he **first** wanted to **go and bury** his **father** has been variously interpreted. Some maintain that the man's father was dead already. It would seem strange if that was the case for he would certainly have been engaged in the burial procedure already. It is more likely that the man's father is ready to die. His request was to let him wait just a little while before following Jesus. Perhaps the man also wanted to receive the inheritance from his father's estate. Jesus' response, **Let the dead bury their own dead,** implies that the spiritually dead can bury the physically dead. The point was that proclaiming **the kingdom of God** was so important that it could not wait. Of course if the man had left and followed Jesus, it would have caused a scandal in the community. But that was less important than proclaiming the kingdom and following the Messiah. A disciple must make a radical commitment.

9:61-62. The third man simply wanted to **go** home and **say good-by to** his **family.** Elijah had allowed Elisha to do this very thing when Elisha was plowing (1 Kings 19:19-20). Jesus' words underscore the fact that His message of the kingdom of God was more important than anything else—even family members. The message and the Messiah cannot wait. Jesus' message was more important than Elijah's message and demanded total allegiance. Jesus' servants should not have divided interests, like a farmer who begins plowing **and looks**

back. Since Jesus was on His way to Jerusalem, the man had to make up his mind right then as to what he was going to do. Interestingly Luke did not record the outcome of any of Jesus' conversations with the three men.

c. *Jesus' sending of the messengers to spread the Word (10:1-24)*

This section contains instructions similar to those given to the Twelve in 9:1-6. On His way to Jerusalem Jesus was sending out messengers to all the towns in order to give people opportunities to accept His message. Only Luke records this incident.

(1) The choosing of the 72 (10:1-16). **10:1-12.** Jesus gave instructions to the **72.** Some Greek manuscripts in verses 1 and 17 have "70" and others have "72." Both readings have strong support. The 72 were people other than the Twelve, who apparently remained with Jesus on His journey. The 72 were to prepare the way so that when Jesus came into a **town,** it would be ready for Him. When Jesus stated, **Ask the Lord . . . to send out workers,** He implied that the ones asking were also to be workers (v. 2). Their mission was dangerous (v. 3) and required haste (v. 4). The 72 were supported by those who accepted their message (v. 7). Through hospitality people would show whether or not they believed the message of the kingdom. To the believing cities the message was to be, **The kingdom of God is near you.** The Messiah was coming, and He could bring in the kingdom. Even the cities that rejected the message were to be told that **the kingdom** was **near.** (For the meaning of wiping **dust** off their **feet,** see comments on 9:5).

10:13-16. Jesus warned the surrounding towns against rejecting the 72 because that meant rejecting Jesus and the Father (v. 16). Jesus singled out two cities—**Korazin** and **Bethsaida,** both of which were located in the area of Jesus' early ministry of miracles on the north side of the Sea of Galilee. He also singled out His adopted hometown, **Capernaum,** which also had been a site of His miraculous works. The message was clear: those cities (no doubt representative of others as well) were to be more severely judged than pagan cities, such as

Tyre and Sidon (cf. Sodom, v. 12) which did not have the benefit of the Lord's miraculous works and words.

(2) The return of the 72. **10:17-20.** When the messengers came back, they were excited that **even the demons** had submitted to them in Jesus' **name.** This was true because of the **authority** Jesus had **given** them. They had such authority because Satan's power had been broken by Jesus. He answered them, **I saw Satan fall like lightning from heaven.** Jesus was not speaking of Satan being cast out at that precise moment, but that his **power** had been broken and that he was subject to Jesus' authority. However, Jesus said the cause for their **joy** should not be what they could do in His name but in the fact **that** their **names** were **written in heaven.** The personal relationship of a believer with God should be the cause of his joy. The authority given to these workers and the promise of no harm from **snakes and scorpions** was given for this particular situation.

(3) Jesus' rejoicing in the Spirit (10:21-24; Matt. 11:25-27). **10:21-24.** Jesus was **full of joy through the Holy Spirit** (cf. the joy of the 72, v. 20). Luke frequently mentioned the Holy Spirit's ministry in Jesus' life. The three Persons of the Godhead are clearly seen: Jesus **the Son** was doing the Father's will in the power of the Holy Spirit. Each had a specific function (vv. 21-22).

The people who were following Jesus were not the important people of the nation; they were not considered **the wise and learned.** They had become like **little children** to enter into the kingdom, and thus they knew **the Son** and **the Father.** The disciples were living in an opportune day which **many** Old Testament **prophets and kings** longed **to see**— the day of the Messiah.

d. *Jesus' teaching on one's neighbor (10:25-37)*

10:25-37. The Parable of the Good Samaritan is perhaps the most well-known Lucan parable. It must be interpreted on two levels. The first level is the plain teaching that a person, like the Samaritan, should help others in need (v. 37). If one has the heart of a **neighbor,** he will see and help a neighbor. However, in the context of the rejection of Jesus, it should also be noted in this parable that the Jewish religious leaders rejected the man who fell among the robbers. A Samaritan, an outcast, was the only one who helped the man. Jesus was like the Samaritan. He was the outcast One, who was willing to seek and to save people who were perishing. He was directly opposed to the religious establishment. The theme is reminiscent of Jesus' words to the Pharisees (7:44-50). The theme of Jesus' going to those who needed Him became more and more evident.

An expert in the Law asked Jesus, **Teacher . . . what must I do to inherit eternal life?** This question surfaced on several occasions (Matt. 19:16-22; Luke 18:18-23; John 3:1-15). The question in this case was not sincere, as can be seen from two points in the text: (1) The lawyer wanted **to test Jesus.** (He called Jesus "Teacher," *didaskale,* Luke's equivalent of a Jewish Rabbi.) (2) After Jesus answered the man's question, Luke recorded that the man wished **to justify himself** (Luke 10:29).

Jesus answered his question with two other questions (v. 26), driving the Law expert back to **the** Old Testament **Law.** The expert answered **correctly** by quoting from Deuteronomy 6:5 and Leviticus 19:18. One must **love . . . God** and one's fellowman in order to keep the Law properly. **Jesus** affirmed that if the man did **this,** he would **live.**

The man's response should have been to ask, "How can I do this? I am not able. I need help." Instead, he tried "to justify himself," that is, to defend himself against the implications of Jesus' words. So he tried to move the focus off himself by asking, **And who is my neighbor?**

Jesus answered by telling the Parable of the Good Samaritan. The road **from Jerusalem to Jericho** descends approximately 3,000 feet in about 17 miles. It was a dangerous road to travel for **robbers** hid along its steep, winding way. **A priest,** one expected to love others, avoided **the** wounded **man,** probably a fellow Jew.

Levites were descendants of Levi but not of Aaron, and they assisted the priests (Aaron's descendants) in the temple.

The Samaritans were scorned by the Jews because of their mixed Jewish and Gentile ancestry. It is ironic, then, that **a Samaritan** helped the **half-dead** man, dressing **his wounds,** taking **him to an inn,** and paying his expenses. By asking

Which . . . was his **neighbor?** (Luke 10:36) Jesus was teaching that a person should be a neighbor to anyone he meets in need. The ultimate Neighbor was Jesus, whose compassion contrasted with the Jewish religious leaders who had no compassion on those who were perishing. Jesus wrapped up His teaching with the command that His followers were to live like that true neighbor (v. 37).

2. JESUS' TEACHING THAT ATTENTION TO HIM IS THE MOST IMPORTANT THING IN LIFE (10:38-42)

10:38-42. The focus of this passage is not that people should be unconcerned with household chores, but that the proper attitude toward **Jesus** is to listen to Him and obey His words. The **village** where **Martha opened her home to Him** was Bethany (John 11:1–12:8), a few miles east of Jerusalem. Jesus stayed in Bethany during His final week on earth. A sharp contrast was portrayed between the two sisters. **Mary . . . sat** and listened to Jesus, while **Martha** made **preparations** for a meal. The phrase, **only one thing is needed** (Luke 10:42), refers to listening to His words, which **Mary** had **chosen** to do. The same theme is seen in 8:1-21.

3. JESUS' TEACHING ABOUT PRAYER (11:1-13)

11:1. **Jesus** prayed at every major crisis point in His life. He prayed at the time of His baptism (3:21), and at the time of the choosing of His disciples (6:12). He **was** often alone **praying** (5:16; 9:18) and also prayed with others around (9:28-29). He prayed for Simon (22:32), and He prayed in the garden before His betrayal (22:40-44). He even prayed on the cross (23:46). **One of His disciples,** impressed with Jesus' life of prayer, asked Jesus to **teach** them **to pray.**

a. Jesus' model prayer (11:2-4)
(Matt. 6:9-15)

11:2-4. In this model prayer Jesus began with an intimate direct address, **Father.** This was somewhat characteristic of the way Jesus referred to God in His prayers (cf. 10:21). He then made five requests. The first two dealt with God's interests. The first request was that God's **name** be **hallowed** (*hagiasthētō,* from *hagiazō,* "to set apart or sanctify" or, as here, "to treat as holy"). Thus the request was for God's reputation to be revered by men.

The second request was **Your kingdom come.** John the Baptist, Jesus, the Twelve, and the 72 had been preaching about the coming of God's kingdom. When a person prays for the coming of the kingdom, he is identifying with the message of Jesus and His followers.

The third request was for **daily bread.** Bread is a general term denoting nourishing and filling food. Thus the request is for food that is necessary to sustain life for the day.

The fourth request concerned man's relationship to God—the forgiveness of **sins.** Luke had already linked the forgiveness of sins to faith (7:36-50). In asking for forgiveness of sins a person expresses his faith that God will forgive him. Such a person then evidences his faith by forgiving others.

The fifth request is, **lead us not into temptation.** But why pray such a prayer since God does not want people to sin? The meaning is that Jesus' followers are to pray that they be delivered from *situations* that would cause them to sin. His disciples, contrary to the Law experts (10:25-29), realized that they were easily drawn into sin. Therefore Jesus' followers need to ask God for help to live righteous lives.

b. Jesus' teaching about prayer through two parables (11:5-13)

11:5-8. The first parable concerns **persistence** in prayer. It is common in Luke for good lessons to be taught from bad examples (cf. 16:1-9; 18:1-8). In contrast with the man who did not want to be bothered, God wants His people to pray to Him (11:9-10). So Jesus encouraged people to be persistent in prayer— not to change God's mind but to be steadfast in praying and to receive their **needs.**

11:9-13. The second parable noted that the heavenly Father gives His children what is **good** for them, not what harms them. Jesus encouraged the people of God to **ask.** He noted that natural **fathers** give **good** food to their children rather than something that would harm them (some **fish** may look like snakes, and the body of a large white **scorpion** could be mistaken **for an egg**). **How**

much more **will** the heavenly **Father** give what is good to His children.

Jesus stated that this good gift is **the Holy Spirit,** the most important gift that followers of Jesus would receive (cf. Acts 2:1-4). The heavenly Father gives both heavenly gifts and earthly gifts. Believers today are not to pray for the Holy Spirit because this prayer of the disciples (for the Holy Spirit) was answered at Pentecost (cf. Rom. 8:9).

4. THE INCREASED REJECTION OF JESUS (11:14-54)

This section contains a record of the high point of the rejection of Jesus and His message. After the record of this rejection Luke began to record Jesus' words as to how disciples should live in the midst of rejection.

a. Jesus accused of demonic power (11:14-26)
(Matt. 12:22-30; Mark 3:20-27)

In Luke the terms "demon" and "demons" occur 16 times and "evil spirit(s)" ("unclean spirit[s]" in KJV) occurs 8 times. Jesus always had authority over the demons—a sign of His messianic power (7:21; 13:32). The demons themselves recognized that authority (4:31-41; 8:28-31), and Jesus' enemies did too (11:14-26). Jesus gave others power over demons (9:1), and His authority over demons amazed the crowds (4:36; 9:42-43).

11:14-16. After seeing **Jesus** cast out a demon from a person who **was mute . . . some** among **the crowd** suggested that He did it by demonic power, that is, by the power of **Beelzebub.** This name given to **the prince of demons,** clearly Satan, originally meant "lord of the princes," but had been corrupted to a pun denoting "lord of the flies" (cf. 2 Kings 1:2). The charge was that Jesus was possessed by Satan himself. A second group wanted Jesus to show **a sign from heaven.** They were probably not sincere in their request as Luke linked them with the former group and noted that they were testing Him.

11:17-20. Jesus gave a twofold response. First, He said it would be ridiculous for **Satan** to **drive out** his own **demons,** for then he would be weakening his position and **kingdom.** Second, Jesus pointed out the double standard of those who were accusing Him. If their **followers** drove **out** demons, they claimed it was done by the power of God. Thus since Jesus cast **out demons,** it too must be **by** God's **finger,** that is, His power. Therefore **the kingdom of God has come to you.**

11:21-22. Jesus' parable of the **strong man** and the **stronger** man has been variously interpreted. In view of the context (vv. 17-20) the strong man refers to Satan, and the stronger man to Christ Himself. When it was that Christ attacked and overpowered Satan is not stated by Luke. Luke may have had in mind Jesus' temptation experience, or the Resurrection, or perhaps the ultimate binding of Satan. The point of the parable, however, is that Jesus is the stronger One, and therefore He has the right to divide **up the spoils.** In this case the spoils include formerly demon-possessed people who no longer belong to Satan.

11:23-26 (Matt. 12:43-45). Jesus stated that it was impossible to be neutral in the battle between Christ and Satan. The people who were watching had to make up their minds. If they thought Jesus was casting out demons by the power of Satan, then they were actively **against** Him.

Jesus' words recorded in Luke 11:24-26 are difficult. Probably He was referring to the man who was formerly demon-possessed and was making him a symbol of everyone who was demon-possessed. It was vital that this man also accept what Jesus was saying about His being the Messiah, or he would end up in a **condition . . . worse than the first.** Matthew recorded that Jesus compared this situation to what would happen to the generation of people who were listening to Him (Matt. 12:45).

b. Jesus' teaching on the observance of God's Word (11:27-28)

11:27-28. This teaching is similar to that in 8:19-21. Family relationships are not the most important things in life. A **woman** noted that it must have been wonderful to have been Jesus' **mother.** The idea of physical relationship was more important in that day. The whole nation took pride in the fact that they descended from Abraham (cf. John 8:33-39). **Jesus** pointed out that a physical relationship was unimportant compared

with hearing and obeying **the Word of God.** As Luke emphasized, the gospel is not limited to Israel but is for all who trust in Christ.

c. Jesus' refusal to give a sign (11:29-32) (Matt. 12:38-42; Mark 8:11-12)

11:29-32. The Pharisees asked Jesus for a sign (Matt. 12:38; Mark 8:11) which Luke did not mention. A **sign** was a confirming miracle which showed that the spoken message was true. The crowds were not willing to believe Jesus' words without external confirmation.

Jesus' response was that no sign would **be given . . . except the sign of Jonah** (Luke 11:29). This sign has been interpreted in at least two ways: Many say it was the physical appearance of Jonah, for perhaps his skin was bleached white by the sea monster's inner juices. However, nothing in the context hints at this. "The sign of Jonah" must have been the words (cf. "preaching," v. 32) Jonah spoke about his miraculous preservation by God when he was at the point of death. The people **of Nineveh** believed what Jonah said, even if they had no physical evidence. Jesus' words about the **Queen of the South** lend strength to this interpretation. The queen traveled a great distance **to listen to Solomon's wisdom** (1 Kings 10). She acted on what she heard, without any external confirmation. The point is clear: the generation that was listening to Jesus' words did not have as much faith as some Gentiles who listened to the words of God in previous eras. Therefore even Gentiles **will stand up at the judgment with this generation and condemn it.** Jesus affirmed that something (neut., not masc.) **greater than Solomon** (Luke 11:31) and **greater than Jonah** was present (v. 32). That something was the kingdom of God, present in the person of Jesus. Thus the people should listen and believe without a sign.

d. Jesus' stress on responding to His teachings (11:33-36)

11:33-36. Jesus often taught His disciples through parables. Because they had been listening to Him they had **light** shining **on** them (v. 36). Thus they should share that **light** (v. 33). When a person's eyes (like lamps) react properly to **light,** he can function normally. Being receptive to Jesus' teachings would show that they were **full of light** (vv. 34, 36) and were benefiting from His teachings (cf. comments on 8:16-18).

e. Jesus accused and questioned by the Pharisees (11:37-54)
(Matt. 23:1-36; Mark 12:38-40)

11:37-41. A Pharisee invited Jesus to dinner. **Jesus did not** engage in the ritual washing **before the meal,** which completely **surprised . . . the Pharisee.** Jesus focused on **greed,** a characteristic of the Pharisees, and said that they should be as concerned with the cleansing of **the inside** as they were with washing **the outside** of the body. One indication that they were clean on the inside would be their willingness to give material things **to the poor.** This meant not that their act of giving would atone for their sins, but that it would show a proper relationship to the Law and to God.

11:42-44. Jesus next pronounced three woes (pronouncements of condemnation) on the **Pharisees** for disregarding **justice and the love of God.** They were bound up in the ritual of the Law, tithing even small **garden herbs.** This made them hypocrites (cf. 12:1). They were filled with pride, loving **the most important seats in the synagogues.** And rather than guiding the people aright, they caused people who followed them to be contaminated, just as **unmarked graves,** when walked on, would defile a Jew without his knowing it (Num. 19:16). The Pharisees feared contamination from ritual uncleanness, but Jesus pointed out that their greed, pride, and wickedness contaminated the entire nation.

11:45-52. Jesus then pronounced three woes on the **Law . . . experts** (vv. 46-47, 52). They placed **burdens** on others which effectively kept them away from the way of knowledge. And they built **tombs for the prophets,** thus identifying with their **forefathers who** killed **. . . the prophets.** Outwardly they seemed to honor the prophets, but God knew that inwardly they were rejecting the prophets. So they would **be held responsible for the blood of all the prophets. The blood of Abel** and **the blood of Zechariah** refers to the killing of innocent men involved in serving God. Abel was the first innocent victim (Gen. 4:8), and Zechariah the priest (not the

writing prophet, though see Matt. 23:35) was the last martyr in the Old Testament (2 Chron. 24:20-21; Chron. was last in the OT Heb. order). Jesus' indictment became even more severe when He noted that not only were they themselves staying away from **knowledge** (i.e., Jesus' teaching) but were also taking **away the key,** that is, they were keeping the knowledge from others (cf. Luke 13:14).

11:53-54. The Pharisees and lawyers **began to oppose** Jesus **fiercely.** They were constantly questioning Him, plotting against Him, and hoping **to catch Him** saying something wrong.

B. Jesus' teaching of His followers in view of the rejection (12:1–19:27)

Jesus first taught several truths to His inner circle of disciples (12:1-53), and then taught several things to the multitudes (12:54–13:21). Jesus taught about people of the kingdom (13:22–17:10), and about the attitude of the disciples in view of the coming kingdom (17:11–19:27).

1. JESUS TEACHING HIS INNER CIRCLE OF DISCIPLES (12:1-53)

a. Jesus' teaching about witnessing without fear (12:1-12)

12:1-3. Jesus first stated that it is foolish to be hypocritical because eventually everything will **be made known** (cf. 8:17). So the disciples should be open, not two-faced, about the way they lived. He warned them to **guard against the yeast of the Pharisees,** that is, their teaching, for it **is hypocrisy.** In the Scriptures yeast often refers to something evil (cf. Mark 8:15).

12:4-12 (Matt. 10:28-31). Jesus went on to teach that His disciples (**My friends**) should be fearless (Luke 12:4, 7; cf. v. 32) because God would take care of them. Instead of fearing men who could kill their bodies (cf. 11:48-50), they should **fear** God, the One who **has the power to throw** one **into hell.** This follows as a natural corollary of 12:2-3—God knows everything. The disciples were far more valuable to **God** than **sparrows,** which were sold for a small amount (**five** birds **for two pennies**). The word for "penny" is *assarion,* a Roman copper coin worth about $1/16$ of a denarius (a day's wage), and used only here and in Matthew 10:29. Since God takes care of common little birds (cf. Luke 12:22), He will also care for His own, even knowing the number of their **hairs.**

The point of verses 8-10 is that disciples must make a choice. To **acknowledge** denotes the fact that the disciples recognized Him as the Messiah and therefore they had access to the way of salvation. Those who did not acknowledge Him were denying themselves the way of salvation. Jesus carried the logic one step further, noting that one **who blasphemes against the Holy Spirit will not be forgiven.** In Matthew 12:32 Jesus linked this activity with the Pharisees who were rejecting the work of Jesus. Apparently the Pharisees were being convicted by the Holy Spirit that Jesus was indeed the Messiah, but were rejecting His witness. They could never be forgiven because they were rejecting God's only means of salvation. (In contrast to that, a number of Jesus' own brothers who initially rejected Him [John 7:5] later came to faith [Acts 1:14] and were forgiven even though they had spoken **against the Son of Man.**)

Jesus then promised the disciples (Luke 12:11-12) that when they were arraigned and **brought before** officials because of their preaching and teaching (cf. Acts 4:1-21), **the Holy Spirit** would **teach** them **what** to **say.** In contrast to Jesus' enemies, who blasphemed the Holy Spirit, Jesus' followers would be helped by the Holy Spirit.

b. Jesus' teaching about greed (12:13-21)

12:13-21. This passage explains Jesus' teaching to **guard against all kinds of greed.** Someone wanted Jesus to instruct his **brother to divide** up **the inheritance** which was due him in an equitable way. Jesus' point was that **life does not consist in** having many **possessions.** The disciples needed to learn the lesson that life is more important than material things. To explain this teaching Jesus told a parable about a **rich man** who continued to build **bigger** and bigger **barns** to **store all** his **grain and . . . goods.** His attitude was that he would have an easy life because he had everything he could possibly want or need. God's response in the parable was that the man was foolish (**You fool!**) because when he died that **night** his goods would do

nothing for him. They would simply pass on to someone else. Such a person **is not rich toward God** (cf. 1 Tim. 6:6-10; James 1:10). Luke returned to this subject in chapter 16.

c. Jesus' teaching about anxiety (12:22-34)
(Matt. 6:25-34)

The section builds to a climax in verse 31 when the disciples were instructed to seek God's kingdom. In building to that climax Jesus said three things about anxiety.

12:22-24. Jesus first noted that anxiety is foolish because **life** consists of far **more** than what one eats or wears (cf. v. 15). Jesus again referred to **birds** (cf. vv. 6-7) to point out that since His disciples were **more valuable** than **ravens,** which **God feeds,** He cares for them. (Unlike sparrows, ravens were not sold for they are scavengers.)

12:25-28. Jesus next pointed out that **worry** is foolish because it cannot change the situation. Not one **hour** can be added to one's **life** so it is ridiculous to worry. Again Jesus went to the natural realm (**lilies** and **grass**) to point out that **God** takes care of what belongs to Him.

12:29-31. Finally Jesus pointed out that **worry** is foolish because worry is the attitude of pagans. **The pagan world** is concerned with the material things of life and not with life's ultimately important spiritual realities. On the other hand one who pursues spiritual matters (seeking God's **kingdom**) will also receive from God material provisions.

12:32-34. Jesus then told His disciples not to fear (cf. vv. 4, 7). He compared them to a **little flock,** a seemingly defenseless group which could be preyed on. To make them even more defenseless Christ instructed, **Sell your possessions and give to the poor.** (Luke later came back to this subject in chaps. 16 and 19.) This is also what the early church did (Acts 2:44-45; 4:32-37). Jesus' point was that if His followers had a treasure on earth they would think about it. But if they instead had **a treasure in heaven,** which is safe from theft and decay by moths, and were "rich toward God" (Luke 12:21), they would be concerned with matters pertaining to **the kingdom** and therefore would not be in a state of anxiety.

d. Jesus' teaching about readiness (12:35-48)
(Matt. 24:45-51)

In this section Jesus told two parables (vv. 35-40 and 42-48) which were joined by a question by Peter (v. 41). The second parable expands and explains the first.

12:35-40. Jesus taught that the disciples should **be ready because the Son of Man will come at** a time when they will **not** be expecting **Him.** The parable describes a scene in which several servants were **waiting for their master to return from a wedding banquet.** The point was that they had to remain constantly vigilant so that the **master** would be able to come into the house whenever he might arrive at home. If they are **watching** (v. 37) and **ready** (v. 38), their master will **serve** them. **The second watch** was from 9 P.M. to midnight, and the **third watch** was from midnight to 3 A.M. The point of the words about **the thief** (v. 39) is the same—the disciples must "be ready" for "the Son of Man will come" unexpectedly.

12:41. Peter's question holds the two parables together. **Peter** wanted to know the extent of the first parable's meaning. Was it addressed only to the disciples **or to everyone?**

12:42-48. Jesus did not answer Peter's question directly. Instead these verses indicate that He was talking primarily about the leadership of the nation at that time. The religious leaders were supposed to be managing the nation for God until He brought in the kingdom. However, they failed in that task; they were not looking expectantly toward the kingdom. Because of the penalty exacted (vv. 46-47), Jesus must not have been speaking about believers who were not **ready.** He seems to have been referring to the nation's leaders who would be present at the time of the coming of the Son of Man. Faithless ones (v. 47) will be judged more severely than those who, though wicked, do **not know** about the coming of the Son of Man (v. 48a). Unbelievers with a great knowledge of God's revelation will have to answer for their lack of response to that revelation.

e. Jesus' teaching about being misunderstood (12:49-53)
(Matt. 10:34-36)

12:49-53. To be Jesus' disciple might mean being misunderstood even by one's own **family.** Ultimately His ministry would bring not **peace . . . but division** because some would accept what He was saying and others would reject it. His ministry would be like a **fire** which devours (v. 49). Jesus longed for the purpose of His ministry to be accomplished. His life and death would be the basis for His judging Israel. That judgment, like fire, would purify the nation. The **baptism** He spoke of no doubt referred to His death which He said would be **completed** (v. 50). Jesus' mission actually did result in the kind of family divisions of which He spoke here (vv. 52-53). Families have been **divided** and loyalties broken. Jewish believers are still ostracized from their families and friends. However, to be a disciple one must be willing to undergo such problems.

2. JESUS' TEACHING OF THE MULTITUDES (12:54–13:21)

After Jesus spoke directly to His disciples, He turned His attention to the multitudes. In this section six events occurred in which the crowds played a major part. They were now the focal point in Jesus' ministry.

a. Jesus' teaching about signs (12:54-56)
(Matt. 16:2-3)

12:54-56. Jesus taught the crowds that they needed to be sensitive **to interpret** the things they were seeing. Though they had been observing His ministry they were not able to ascertain that He was truly the Messiah. He made the point that they, with no trouble, could **interpret** natural signs (western clouds and **south** winds—**the appearance of the earth and the sky**). But they could not discern spiritual signs. They should discern what was going on right in their midst—He was offering the kingdom and they were not responding properly to His offer.

b. Jesus' illustration of the law court (12:57-59)

12:57-59. Jesus used an illustration of a law court to drive home the point that people need to be rightly related to God. Even in the earthly sphere it makes sense to **try hard to be reconciled** with an opponent—even **on the way . . . to the magistrate**—in order to avoid being thrown **into prison** and having to pay **the last penny.** How much more important it is to "be reconciled" when the opponent is God! (The word for "penny" is *leptos*, used only here and in Mark 12:42; Luke 21:2. It was a Jewish copper coin worth about ⅛ of a cent.)

c. Jesus' teaching on perishing (13:1-5)

13:1-5. Jesus taught the crowds that calamity can happen to anyone because all are human. **Jesus** cited two common instances about destruction. The first concerned some **Galileans** who were killed by **Pilate** while they were offering **sacrifices.** The second concerned **18** seemingly innocent bystanders **in Siloam** who were killed when a **tower . . . fell on them.** Jesus' point was that being killed or not being killed is no measure of a person's unrighteousness or righteousness. Anyone can be killed. Only God's grace causes any to live. This point is brought out in verses 3 and 5—**unless you repent, you too will all perish.** Death is the common denominator for everyone. Only repentance can bring life as people prepare to enter the kingdom.

d. Jesus' parable of the fig tree (13:6-9)

13:6-9. To illustrate His point Jesus taught in a **parable** that if **fruit** does not show in one's life, judgment will come. A **fig tree** requires **three years** to bear figs, but since this one did not produce, the owner said, **Cut it down.** His **vineyard** keeper asked him to give it **one more year.** This parable illustrates the point made in verses 1-5 that judgment comes on those who do not repent. Here Jesus took the thought one step further and noted that **fruit** must be present (cf. Matt. 3:7-10; 7:15-21; Luke 8:15). A visible change must be seen in the life of one who claims to trust the Messiah. If there is no visible change that person, like the figless fig tree, is judged.

e. Jesus' healing of a woman (13:10-17)

Jesus illustrated His teaching by healing a woman on a Sabbath. This episode is the last time in the Gospel of Luke Jesus taught in a synagogue. The term "hypocrites" is extremely important in the narrative. Toward the beginning of this section (12:54–13:21) Jesus had called

the crowds and the leaders of the people "hypocrites" (12:56). Here at the end of the section He again called them "hypocrites" (13:15). Jesus' point was that the crowds and the leaders were not really interested in what God could and would do in their lives.

13:10-13. Luke described the **woman** as one **who had been crippled by a spirit for 18 years** and "bound" by "Satan" (v. 16). Without denying the historicity of the event, it must be pointed out that there is obvious symbolic value in Luke's placing this miracle at this point in the narrative. It was Jesus' mission among the people of the nation to loose them from crippling influences and bring them to uprightness. Here was a graphic example of Jesus' touch, bringing the woman to a position of uprightness. Jesus healed **her** by His words (**Woman, you are set free from your infirmity**) and by touching **her. Immediately she straightened up and praised God.** This act of praising God was the proper response to the work of Jesus (cf. 2:20; 5:25-26; 7:16; 17:15; 18:43; 23:47). It showed that people were understanding His mission.

13:14. In contrast to the proper response which the woman evidenced, **the synagogue ruler** was **indignant because Jesus had** not followed the Law as that ruler interpreted it. He appealed to the crowd to reject Jesus' miracle. This attitude supports what Jesus had already said about religious leaders keeping others from entering the kingdom (11:52).

13:15-17. Jesus pointed out that a person is much more important than an animal, and His enemies saw nothing wrong in helping their animals **on the Sabbath** (cf. 14:5). The total hypocrisy and foolishness of the thinking of the religious leaders was obvious. As a result Jesus' **opponents were humiliated but** the crowds **were delighted.**

f. Jesus' teaching about the kingdom of God (13:18-21)
(Matt. 13:31-33; Mark 4:30-32)

13:18-21. This passage is actually a hinge between Jesus' teaching of the multitudes (12:54–13:21) and His teaching about the people of **the kingdom** (13:22–17:10). Some feel that in these brief parables about the **Mustard Seed** (a mustard tree, from a tiny seed, grows as tall as 12-15 feet in one season!) and the

Yeast Jesus was teaching something positive about the kingdom. It seems better, however, to understand these parables as teaching something undesirable. Like pervading yeast, evil will enter the Age and become all-pervasive. This seems to be true since Luke placed this teaching immediately after the synagogue leader's rejection of Jesus' work on the Sabbath.

3. JESUS' TEACHING ABOUT THE PEOPLE OF THE KINGDOM (13:22-17:10)

In this section Luke recorded Jesus' teachings concerning who is and who is not a member of the kingdom. Throughout this section the theme of entering into the kingdom is often symbolized as taking part in a feast or banquet (13:29; 14:7-24; 15:23; 17:7-10). The kingdom was yet to come. Those who enter are those who respond positively to God by accepting the Messiah and His kingdom message.

a. Jesus' teaching that most of Israel will be excluded from the kingdom (13:22-35)

13:22-30. Jesus taught that many from Israel will not be in **the kingdom** whereas many from outside Israel will be. **Someone asked** Jesus if **only a few people** were **going to be saved.** Apparently His followers were somewhat discouraged that His message of the kingdom was not sweeping the nation as they thought it would. They saw that Jesus continually met opposition as well as acceptance. Jesus' teaching was clear—a person must accept what He was saying in order to enter the kingdom. To a Jewish mind salvation was related to the kingdom, that is, a person was saved in order to enter into God's kingdom.

Jesus responded to the person's question with a story of a man who was giving a **feast** (symbolic of the kingdom, v. 29). After he closed **the door** to the banquet, no one else could come in for they were too late (v. 25). In fact, the host of the feast actually called them **evildoers** (v. 27). The latecomers responded that they had eaten and drunk with the host and that he had **taught in** their **streets** (v. 26), an obvious reference to Jesus' ministry among the people of that generation. Jesus' point in telling the story was that the people had to respond to His

invitation at that time, for a time would come when it would be too late and they would not be allowed in the kingdom.

Jesus spoke directly, telling the crowds that judgment would come on those who refused His message: **There will be weeping . . . and gnashing of teeth** and they will be **thrown out,** that is, not allowed to enter the kingdom. (On "weeping and gnashing of teeth" see comments on Matt. 13:42.) But godly ones in the nation (represented by **Abraham, Isaac, and Jacob, and all the prophets**) will be **in the kingdom of God.**

These remarks were revolutionary to Jesus' hearers. Most of them assumed that because they were physically related to Abraham they would naturally enter into the promised kingdom. However, His next words were even more revolutionary—in fact devastating—to those who assumed that *only* the Jewish nation would be involved in the kingdom. Jesus explained that Gentiles would be added to the kingdom in place of Jewish people (Luke 13:29-30). **People** coming from the **four corners of the world** represent various population groups. Those listening to Jesus' words should not have been surprised by this teaching because the prophets had often said the same thing. However, Jews in Jesus' day believed that Gentiles were inferior to them. When Jesus had begun His ministry in Nazareth, His teaching of Gentile inclusion had so maddened the crowd that they tried to kill Him (4:13-30). The Jewish people considered themselves to be **first** in every way, but they would be **last,** that is, they would be left out of the kingdom. In contrast, some Gentiles, considered **last,** would be in the kingdom and would really be **first** in importance (13:30).

13:31-35 (Matt. 23:37-39). In response to a warning from **some Pharisees . . . Jesus** said that He had to reach **Jerusalem** because He was appointed to **die** there. There is debate concerning the Pharisees' report about **Herod** wanting **to kill** Jesus. Throughout Luke, the Pharisees are presented in a negative light. Why would the Pharisees have wanted to protect Jesus in this instance? It seems best to understand the incident as the Pharisees' pretext to get rid of Jesus. Jesus had publicly stated that His **goal** was to reach Jerusalem, and He was well on His way. Thus the Pharisees were apparently trying to deter Him from His task, to scare Him into setting aside His goal.

Jesus' response, **Go tell that fox,** indicates that He saw the Pharisees as Herod's messengers who would report back to him. Jesus stated that He had a mission to perform (Luke 13:32). This Herod was Herod Antipas (see the chart on the Herods at 1:5).

When Jesus said, **Today and tomorrow and the next day,** He was not saying that He would arrive in Jerusalem in three days. The point was that He had a mission in mind and that He would continue on the schedule He had set for Himself. The goal was Jerusalem where He would die. He must present Himself publicly to the religious authorities and then be put to death.

It was at this point that Luke recorded the rejection of **Jerusalem** (representing the nation) by Jesus (13:34-35). Jesus lamented for the city and **longed to** protect it **as a hen gathers her chicks under her wings,** that is, tenderly and lovingly, even though the people **were not willing.** His entire ministry up to this point had been to offer the kingdom to the nation. But since the nation, which had even killed **the prophets,** had rejected His words, He would now reject them. Jesus stated, **Your house is left to you desolate** (*aphietai*, "abandoned"). "House" probably refers not to the temple, but to the whole city. Though He would continue to offer Himself as the Messiah, the die was now cast. The city was abandoned by the Messiah.

Jesus noted (quoting Ps. 118:26) that the people of the city would **not see** Him **again** till they said that He was the Messiah. The crowd did quote this verse when Jesus entered the city in His Triumphal Entry (Luke 19:38), but their religious leaders disapproved. Ultimately this truth will be proclaimed when Jesus **comes** again and enters the city as the millennial Ruler.

b. *Jesus' teaching that many outcasts and Gentiles will be in the kingdom (14:1-24)*

This section continues the thought of 13:22-35 but explains it from another angle. Rather than the excluded ones being the main subject, the ones included in the kingdom are now discussed. Contrary to His hearers' expectations,

Jewish outcasts and Gentiles will make up a large portion of the kingdom's population.

14:1-6. Jesus had been invited **to eat** on the **Sabbath** at the **house of a prominent Pharisee** where there **was** also **a man** who was **suffering from dropsy.** Dropsy is a condition of excess fluid in the tissues of the body, caused perhaps by a type of cancer or possibly liver or kidney problems. The man was probably invited to the Pharisee's house in order to see what Jesus would do. **Jesus** immediately took the initiative in the situation and asked the host and other guests whether it would be **lawful to heal** the man **on the Sabbath.** Apparently Jesus' question disarmed the crowd, for all of them **remained silent.** Jesus went ahead and **healed** the man. He said that the guests would help **a son or an ox** in distress **on the Sabbath,** so it was totally appropriate to heal this poor individual. Jesus was setting the stage for the discussion to follow concerning those who were considered ceremonially unclean and therefore unable to enter the kingdom.

14:7-11. Looking around, Jesus **noticed how the guests picked the places of honor.** The closer a person was to the host, the greater was that guest's position of honor. As people entered the room in the Pharisee's house where the table was spread, they must have scrambled for seats at the head of the table. The parable Jesus then told was designed to get them to think about spiritual realities in relation to the kingdom message He had been preaching.

Verse 11 records the point of Jesus' parable: **Everyone who exalts himself will be humbled, and he who humbles himself will be exalted.** This recalls Jesus' earlier statement that those who are last will be first and those who are first will be last (13:30). The Pharisees, assuming they would have important positions in the kingdom, would be **humiliated** if they were pushed aside for someone else (14:9). However, if they would humble themselves, then they would perhaps **be honored** (v. 10).

14:12-14. Then Jesus spoke to **His host,** telling him that if he would **invite** the outcasts of society (**the poor, the crippled, the lame, the blind**)—people who could never **repay** him for his generosity—this would show that he was ministering to them for the Lord's sake and not his own (cf. Matt. 6:1-18; James 1:26-27). He would be laying up for himself treasures in heaven (Matt. 6:20) and would be becoming rich toward God (Luke 12:21). Inviting the outcasts would not make the man righteous; it would testify that he was in a righteous standing before God. This is shown by Jesus' statement that the repayment would not come at the present time but **at the resurrection of the righteous.**

14:15-24 (Matt. 22:1-10). Jesus then told a parable about **a great banquet.** One of the diners expressed a blessing on everyone who would **eat . . . in the kingdom.** This person was assuming that he and the other people present would all be present in the kingdom. **Jesus** took the opportunity to use the feast motif to explain that many of the people there would *not* be present in God's kingdom. In their places would be many outcasts and Gentiles. The host in the parable **invited many guests.** However **all** those invited **began to** give **excuses** for not going. The excuses were supposedly valid—the need to **see** about a recently purchased **field,** or to **try** out recently purchased **oxen,** or to be with one's recently **married** bride (Luke 14:18-20).

The host **became angry** and commanded that people in **the streets and alleys of the town . . . the poor, the crippled, the blind, and the lame**—be invited. Jesus was referring to those members of the Jewish community who were considered inferior and ceremonially unclean as was the man with dropsy He had just healed (vv. 2-4).

When the host learned that there was **still room** for more, he commanded that others be invited from **the roads and country lanes** (v. 23). These people outside the city were probably Gentiles, those outside the covenant community. The host then stated that none of the originally invited guests would **get a taste of** his **banquet.**

This parable at a banquet about another banquet reinforced His previous teaching that He would abandon Jerusalem (13:34-35). The people who originally had been offered a share of the kingdom had rejected it, so now the message was going out to others including Gentiles. The excuses seemed good to those who gave them, but they were inadequate for refusing Jesus' kingdom offer. Nothing was so important as accepting His offer of the kingdom, for one's entire destiny rests on his response to that offer.

c. Jesus' warning against thoughtless discipleship (14:25-35)

14:25-27. The setting then changed: **large crowds were traveling with Jesus.** Jesus intended to impress on the people their need to examine their resolve to follow Him. He was on His way to die on the cross. Ultimately everyone did desert Him when He was alone in the garden and then arrested and put on trial.

To emphasize that discipleship is difficult, Jesus said that one must **hate his** own family and **even his own life** in order to **be** His **disciple.** Literally hating one's family would have been a violation of the Law. Since Jesus on several occasions admonished others to fulfill the Law, He must not have meant here that one should literally hate his family. The stress here is on the priority of love (cf. Matt. 10:37). One's loyalty to Jesus must come before his loyalty to his family or even to life itself. Indeed, those who did follow Jesus against their families' desires were probably thought of as hating their families.

The second difficult qualification Jesus stressed was that one must **carry his** (i.e., his own) **cross and follow** Jesus (Luke 14:27; cf. 9:23). When the Roman Empire crucified a criminal or captive, the victim was often forced to carry his cross part of the way to the crucifixion site. Carrying his cross through the heart of the city was supposed to be a tacit admission that the Roman Empire was correct in the sentence of death imposed on him, an admission that Rome was right and he was wrong. So when Jesus enjoined His followers to carry their crosses and follow Him, He was referring to a public display before others that Jesus was right and that the disciples were following Him even to their deaths. This is exactly what the religious leaders refused to do.

14:28-33. Using two illustrations, Jesus then taught that discipleship must include planning and sacrifice. The first illustration concerned **a tower** (vv. 28-30). Before a person begins **to build,** he should be sure he will be able to pay the full **cost** of the project. Jesus' followers must also be sure they are willing to pay the full price of discipleship.

The second illustration concerned **a king** who went out to battle. The king should be willing to sacrifice a desired victory if he senses he is unable to win. This principle of sacrifice is also important in the realm of discipleship: one must be willing to **give up everything** for Jesus. The people who were following Jesus throughout the countryside of Israel had done that. They had given up possessions and employment, knowing that the message Jesus was proclaiming was the most important thing on earth.

14:34-35. Jesus climaxed His teaching on discipleship by proclaiming that **salt is good** only as long as it contains the characteristics of saltiness. If **it loses its saltiness,** it has no value at all and **is thrown out.** The same is true of disciples. They must contain the characteristics of discipleship—planning and willing sacrifice—or they are of no value at all.

d. Jesus' teaching about the hopeless and sinners in the kingdom (chap. 15)

Jesus combated the religious leaders by teaching again that some who were considered to be hopeless and sinners will be in the kingdom. Here are perhaps the best known of Jesus' parables—The Lost Sheep, The Lost Coin, and The Prodigal Son. All three parables teach the same message—that God is vitally concerned with the repentance of sinners. But the third story goes beyond the others, applying that truth to the situation in which Jesus found Himself—being accepted by the outcasts of society while being rejected by the religious leaders.

15:1-2. Much to the disgust of the religious leaders, Jesus associated with those who were thought of as hopeless and **"sinners."** The opposition to Jesus was once again, as almost always in Luke, **the Pharisees and the teachers of the Law.** Because of this opposition Jesus told three parables. All three speak of things or a person being lost and then found, and of rejoicing when the lost is found.

Some view these parables as teaching a believer's restoration to fellowship with God. One cannot lose something he does not own, they reason, so the first two parables must represent children of God who come back to Him. Also, a son is

already a son, so the third parable must be teaching that people who are believers can be restored to fellowship with God.

Others understand the parables to teach that lost people (i.e., people who are not believers) can come to Christ. This view seems preferable for two reasons: (1) Jesus was speaking to Pharisees who were rejecting the message of the kingdom. Their objection was that sinners were coming to Jesus and believing His message. In no way could these two groups be adequately represented in the third parable if the point of the parable is a restoration to fellowship by a believer. (2) Verse 22 indicates that the son who came back received a new position which he did not have before. The Jews were God's "children" in the sense that they had a special covenant relationship to Him. But each individual still had to become a believer in God. It was their responsibility to accept the message Jesus was preaching—that He was the Messiah and that He would bring in the kingdom for the nation.

15:3-7. The Parable of the Lost Sheep teaches that **there is . . . rejoicing in heaven** when a **sinner . . . repents.** Jesus was not saying **the** other **99** sheep were not important. Instead, He was emphasizing that the one **sheep** not in the fold corresponded with the sinners with whom Jesus was eating (vv. 1-2). The **99 righteous persons** refer to the Pharisees who *thought* themselves righteous and therefore in no **need to repent.**

15:8-10. The Parable of the Lost Coin teaches that **there is rejoicing in the presence of the angels** when a **sinner . . . repents.** This is the same message as the first but it emphasizes the thoroughness of the search. The woman continued to **sweep the house and search carefully until she** found the **coin** which was a thing of great value. A *drachma,* a Greek silver coin referred to only here in the New Testament, equaled about a day's wages. The point would have been clear to Jesus' listeners: the sinners with whom He was associating were extremely valuable to God. (Cf. similar wording in vv. 6, 9.)

Jesus then told the Parable of the Lost Son and His Older Brother to explain that God is inviting *all* people to enter the kingdom.

15:11. A man . . . had two sons; the

contrast between his sons is the point of the parable.

15:12-20a. This section of the parable describes the actions of **the younger son.** He requested an unusual thing when he asked **his father** to **give** him his **share of the estate.** Normally an estate was not divided and given to the heirs until the father could no longer manage it well. This father acquiesced to his son's demand and gave him his share of the inheritance. **The younger son** took that wealth, went far away, and **squandered it in wild living,** involving himself presumably, as his older brother said, with prostitutes (v. 30). The hearers immediately would have begun to understand the point of the story. Jesus had been criticized for associating with sinners. The sinners were considered people who were far away from God, squandering their lives in riotous living. In contrast with the younger son, the older son continued to remain with the father and did not engage in such practices.

A **famine** occurred and the second son ran out of money so that he had to work for a foreigner feeding **pigs,** something detestable to a Jew. Perhaps the far **country** was east of the Sea of Galilee where Gentiles tended **pigs** (cf. 8:26-37). In his hunger he **longed** for the **pods**—the food he fed **the pigs.** As a Jew, he could have stooped no lower. The pods were probably carob pods, from tall evergreen carob trees.

In this low condition, **he came to his senses** (15:17). He decided to **go back to** his **father** and work for him. Surely he would be better off to work for his **father** than for a foreigner. He fully expected to be **hired** by **his father** as a servant, not to be taken back as his son.

15:20b-24. The third section of the parable describes the father's response. He had been waiting for his son to return, for **while he was still a long way off the father saw him.** The father, full of **compassion for** his son, **ran to** him, and **hugged and kissed him.** The father would not even listen to all of the young son's rehearsed speech. Instead **the father** had **his servants** prepare a banquet to **celebrate** the son's return. He gave the son a new position with a **robe . . . a ring . . . and sandals.** Jesus intentionally used the banquet motif again. He had previously spoken of a banquet to symbolize the

coming kingdom (13:29; cf. 14:15-24). Jesus' hearers would have easily realized the significance of this feast. Sinners (whom the young son symbolized) were entering into the kingdom because they were coming to God. They believed they needed to return to Him and be forgiven by Him.

15:25-32. The parable's final section describes the attitude of the older brother, who symbolized the Pharisees and the teachers of the Law. They had the same attitude toward the sinners as **the older son** had toward the younger son. **The older brother,** coming home from working **in the field** and hearing what was happening, got **angry.** Similarly the Pharisees and teachers of the Law were angry with the message Jesus was proclaiming. They did not like the idea that people from outside their nation as well as outcasts and sinners in the nation were to be a part of the kingdom. Like the older son who **refused to go** to the feast, the Pharisees refused to enter the kingdom Jesus offered to the nation.

Interestingly the **father went out and pleaded with** the older brother to go to the feast. Likewise, Jesus ate with Pharisees as well as sinners. He did not desire to exclude the Pharisees and teachers of the Law from the kingdom. The message was an invitation to everyone.

The older brother was angry because he had **never** been honored with a feast even though, as he said, **All these years I've been slaving for you and never disobeyed your orders** (v. 29). Those words betrayed the fact that the older brother thought he had a relationship with his father because of his work. He served his father not out of love but out of a desire for reward. He even thought of himself as being in bondage to his father.

The father pointed out that the older son had had the joy of being in the house all the time, and now he should rejoice with the father in his brother's return. The words, **You are always with me and everything I have is yours,** suggest the religious leaders' privileged position as members of God's Chosen People. They were the recipients and guardians of the covenants and the Law (Rom. 3:1-2; 9:4). Rather than feeling angry, they should rejoice that others were joining them and would be a part of the kingdom.

e. Jesus' teaching about wealth and the kingdom (chap. 16)

This chapter includes two parables about wealth. The first parable (vv. 1-13) was spoken primarily to the disciples (v. 1). The second parable (vv. 19-31) was addressed to the Pharisees because of their response (vv. 14-18) to the first parable.

16:1-8a. Jesus told this Parable of the Unjust Manager to teach that His disciples must use their wealth for kingdom purposes. The application (vv. 8b-13) follows the parable (vv. 1-8a).

In the parable **a rich man . . . called** his **manager** to **give an account of** his dealings. The rich man had heard that the manager was not handling the wealthy owner's finances wisely. In Jesus' day managers were often hired by wealthy people to care for the finances of their estates. Such a manager would be comparable to a modern-day financial planner or trustee who controls the finances of an estate for the purpose of making more money for that estate. The money did not belong to the manager but was his to use for the estate. Apparently the manager was **wasting** those goods as the younger son had wasted his father's goods (15:13).

At the beginning of the parable the rich man viewed his manager as irresponsible rather than dishonest (16:2). The manager was fired. But then, in order to make friends who might later hire him, the ex-manager charged the rich man's two **debtors** less than what they actually owed—**400** instead of **800 gallons of olive oil,** and **800** instead of **1,000 bushels of wheat.** The manager's thinking was reflected in his statement, **When I lose my job here, people will welcome me into their houses** (v. 4).

When the rich man heard what he had done, **he commended the dishonest manager because he had acted shrewdly.** The dishonest manager had not done a good thing. But he *had* been careful to plan ahead, using material things to insure a secure future. Jesus was not teaching that His disciples should be dishonest. He was teaching that they should use material things for future spiritual benefit. This was a good lesson from a bad example.

16:8b-13. In three ways Jesus applied the parable to His disciples who had to live with nonbelievers in the world. First, one should use money to win people into the kingdom (vv. 8b-9). Jesus said, **The people of this world are more shrewd in dealing with their own kind than are the people of the light.** Here Jesus set His disciples apart from the dishonest manager. The dishonest manager was a person of "this world," seeking a way to make his life more comfortable. The disciples, "the people of the light" (cf. 11:33-36; Eph. 5:8), should act in a shrewd (wise, not dishonest) manner. Jesus plainly taught that the people of light should **use worldly wealth** (Luke 16:9). Jesus also used the word "wealth" (*mamōna*) later (v. 13) when He affirmed that one "cannot serve both God and money." In verse 9 Jesus was saying that one is to use wealth, not store it up or be a servant of it. Wealth should be a disciple's servant, not vice versa. The disciples were to use wealth **to gain friends,** the same reason the dishonest manager used the rich man's wealth. The disciples would then **be welcomed into eternal dwellings.** The disciples' wise use of wealth would help lead others to believe the message of the kingdom and bring them to accept that message.

Jesus' second application is in verses 10-12. If one is faithful in his use of money, then he **can be trusted** with greater things. **True riches** (v. 11) seem to refer to the kingdom's spiritual riches of which the disciples will partake.

The third application Jesus drew from the parable was that a person **cannot serve both God and money** (v 13). As masters the two are mutually exclusive. Love for money will drive one away from God (1 Tim. 6:10); conversely, loving God will cause one not to make money his primary concern in life.

16:14-18. The Pharisees, who loved money, reacted negatively to Jesus' teaching about it. They **were sneering at Jesus** because they saw Him as a poor man being followed by other poor men and yet having the nerve to teach about money. Jesus responded that **God knows the hearts** of people and is not impressed with their outward appearances or their wealth. Though the Pharisees justified themselves (v. 15; cf. 15:7) **God,** who judges the inward man, will be the ultimate Judge. The Pharisees misunderstood the blessings of God's covenant.

They apparently assumed that a person's wealth was God's blessing in return for his righteous conduct. They completely neglected the fact that many righteous people in the Old Testament lacked material things, while many unrighteous people had plenty.

Luke 16:16-18 is included with Jesus' teaching about money to the Pharisees because it illustrates what Jesus had just said about the Pharisees justifying themselves but really being judged by God. Jesus stated that since the time of John the Baptist, He had been announcing God's **kingdom**. People, including the Pharisees (cf. 14:15 and comments on Matt. 11:12), were attempting to force their **way into it.**

However, in spite of justifying themselves, the Pharisees were still not living according to **the Law.** Jesus spoke of divorce as an example. To divorce and remarry constituted **adultery.** (Jesus gave one exception to this. See comments on Matt. 5:32; 19:1-12.) Some Pharisees took a loose view of divorce. It was acknowledged that a **man** should not commit adultery. But if a man wanted another **woman,** many of the Pharisees condoned divorcing his present wife for no good reason and marrying the desired woman. In this way they thought **adultery** did not take place. However, as Jesus pointed out, this was a perfect example of justifying themselves in the eyes of men but not being justified before God (Luke 16:15). The religious leaders were not actually living according to the Law. Jesus pointed out the importance **of the Law** (v. 17), which showed that the people should live by it.

16:19-21. Jesus then told the Parable of the Rich Man and Lazarus to show that being rich should not be equated with being righteous. The **rich man** had everything he wanted. **Purple** referred to clothes dyed that color, **and fine linen** was worn for underclothes; both were expensive.

A poor man, **a crippled beggar named Lazarus,** had nothing. One **lived in luxury** for himself, the other in abject poverty with hunger and poor health (**sores**). Perhaps Jesus picked the name Lazarus because it is the Greek form of the Hebrew name which means "God, the Helper." Lazarus was righteous not

because he was poor but because he depended on God.

16:22-23. In the course of **time** both men **died.** Lazarus went **to Abraham's side** while **the rich man . . . was buried** and was **in hell,** a place of conscious torment (vv. 24, 28). *Hadēs,* the Greek word often translated "hell," is used 11 times in the New Testament. The Septuagint used *hadēs* to translate the Hebrew *šᵉ'ôl* (the place of the dead) on 61 occasions. Here *hadēs* refers to the abode of the unsaved dead prior to the great white throne judgment (Rev. 20:11-15). "Abraham's side" apparently refers to place of paradise for Old Testament believers at the time of death (cf. Luke 23:43; 2 Cor. 12:4).

16:24-31. The rich man was able to converse with **Abraham.** He first begged to have **Lazarus** sent over to give him some **water. Abraham replied** that that was not possible and that he should **remember that** during life he had everything he wanted **while Lazarus** had had nothing. Even so, the rich man had never helped Lazarus during the course of his life. Furthermore, **a great chasm** separated paradise and hades so that no one could **cross** from one to the other. The rich man next begged that **Lazarus** be sent to earth to **warn** his **brothers.** It was his contention that if one came back **from the dead** then his brothers would **listen** (v. 30). **Abraham** replied that if they refused to **listen to** the Scriptures (**Moses and the Prophets** represent all the OT; cf. v. 16), then they would refuse to listen to one who came back **from the dead.**

Jesus was obviously suggesting that the rich man symbolized the Pharisees. They wanted signs—signs so clear that they would compel people to believe. But since they refused to believe the Scriptures, they would not believe any sign no matter how great. Just a short time later Jesus did raise a man from the dead, another man named Lazarus (John 11:38-44). The result was that the religious leaders began to plot more earnestly to kill both Jesus and Lazarus (John 11:45-53; 12:10-11).

f. Jesus' teaching about obligations toward men and God (17:1-10)

17:1-4. **Jesus** taught about the obligations **His disciples** had toward other people (vv. 1-4) and God (vv. 6-10). Followers of Jesus are not to **cause people to sin.** In this life sin cannot be eradicated—such things **are bound to come.** But a disciple would be better off drowned by a **millstone** (a heavy stone for grinding grain) **tied around his neck, than** to bring spiritual harm (*skandalisē,* "to cause to sin") to **these little ones** (people who, like little children, are helpless before God; cf. 10:21; Mark 10:24). Presumably the sinning referred to is lack of faith in the Messiah. Jesus had already noted that the Pharisees were not only refusing to enter the kingdom but were also keeping others from entering (Luke 11:52).

Not only are Jesus' followers not to cause others to sin; they also are to counteract sin by forgiving others (17:3-4). One should **rebuke a brother** if he **sins. If he repents,** he is to be forgiven even if he **sins** and repents over and over. The words **seven times in a day** denote a completeness—as often as it happens.

17:5-10. Jesus also taught that His followers have responsibilities toward God. The first responsibility is to **have faith.** When the disciples asked Jesus for more **faith,** He answered that they needed not more faith but the right kind of faith. Even the smallest amount of faith (like **a mustard seed,** the smallest seed; cf. 13:19) could do amazingly miraculous things, such as uprooting a **mulberry tree,** a tree with deep roots (17:6).

The disciples' second responsibility toward God was humble service (vv. 7-10). They should not expect special praise for doing things they were expected to do. A **servant** does not get special praise from his master for doing his job. Likewise disciples have certain responsibilities which they are to fulfill in humility as God's **unworthy** (*achreioi,* "good for nothing," used elsewhere only in Matt. 25:30) **servants.**

4. JESUS' TEACHING ABOUT THE KINGDOM AND THE ATTITUDES OF HIS DISCIPLES (17:11-19:27)

In this section Luke brought together a series of events in the life of Jesus on His way to Jerusalem. The events teach the kind of attitude disciples should have in view of the coming kingdom.

a. A leper returned (17:11-19)

17:11-14. Jesus was **on His way to Jerusalem . . . along the border between Samaria and Galilee.** When asked for help by **10** lepers, He healed them from **a distance.** This was the second time in the Book of Luke that lepers were healed (cf. 5:12-16). As in the former case, Jesus instructed the men to **show** themselves **to the priests.** On their way **they were cleansed** from the disease and were made ceremonially clean.

17:15-19. Only **one of** the men—a **foreigner,** that is, **a Samaritan**—came back to thank Jesus. This one understood the significance of what had been done for him. He was **praising God** and **he threw himself at Jesus' feet,** a posture of worship. He apparently understood that Jesus is God, for he placed **faith** in Him. Whether or not he understood that Jesus is the Messiah is not mentioned by Luke. The lack of gratitude by **the other nine** was typical of the rejection of His ministry by the Jewish nation. He alone had the power to cleanse the nation and make it ceremonially clean. However, the nation did not respond properly to Him. The nation accepted the things that Jesus could do (such as heal them and feed them), but it did not want to accept Him as Messiah. However, those outside the nation (such as this Samaritan leper—a person doubly repulsive to the Jews) were responding.

b. Jesus's teaching about the presence of the kingdom (17:20-37) (Matt. 24:23-28, 37-41)

17:20-21. Jesus was **asked by the Pharisees when the kingdom of God would come.** This was a logical question to ask, for He had been preaching for quite some time that the kingdom was at hand. **Jesus** responded to the question in two ways. First, He said that the Pharisees would not be able to tell of the coming of **the kingdom** through their observations. Second, he told them that the **kingdom** was in their midst. The term **within you** is often misunderstood. The Pharisees were rejecting Him as the Messiah and were not believers. (They were distinct from the disciples Jesus addressed beginning in v. 22.) Thus it would not make sense for Jesus to have told the Pharisees that the kingdom of God was within them as if it were some sort of spiritual kingdom. It is better to translate the phrase "within you" (*entos hymōn*) as "in your midst." Some feel that the force of the expression is "within your possession or within your reach." Jesus' point was that He was standing right in their midst. All they needed to do was acknowledge that He is indeed the Messiah who could bring in the kingdom—and then the kingdom would come.

17:22-25. Jesus then gave **His disciples** several facts about the kingdom. First, He said that a **time** would come when the disciples would **long to see** Him return, but they would not see it (v. 22). Second, He said that when the kingdom would come everyone would know it (vv. 23-24). It will not be a hidden (i.e., only an inner, spiritual) kingdom. It will be a kingdom that the whole world will know. His appearing **will be like the lightning** (cf. Matt. 24:27, 30). Third, Jesus told the disciples **He must suffer** before the kingdom comes (Luke 17:25).

17:26-27. Next Jesus compared the coming of the kingdom to the coming of the flood in Noah's day and to the coming of judgment on Sodom (v. 29). By bringing up these two events, Jesus was stressing the judgmental aspect of the kingdom. When He will establish His kingdom, people will be judged to see if they will be allowed to enter it. In this section (17:26-35) Jesus was not speaking about the Rapture but about the judgment before entering the kingdom.

Jesus reminded His disciples that people in Noah's day were not prepared for **the Flood,** and therefore they were completely **destroyed** (Gen. 6).The same problem will exist when the kingdom comes—people will not be ready.

17:28-33. In **the same** way the materialistic, indifferent **people** of **Sodom** (**eating and drinking, buying and selling, planting and building**) were not prepared for God's judgment (Gen. 19). They were living in sin, oblivious to God. Therefore they were **destroyed.** Jesus reminded His followers that people should not be attached to their material things at the time of the coming of the kingdom for they, like **Lot's wife,** will be judged accordingly. People who are working or relaxing on their roofs (many of which are flat in Palestine) should not try to get things out of their houses. Nor

should those working in the fields go to their houses to save their possessions. Any delay could be fatal. Thus **whoever tries to keep his life** (Luke 17:33) by going back for his goods (v. 31) **will lose it.**

17:34-36. Jesus stated that some will be **taken** into judgment. In some parts of the world it will be nighttime (**people will be in . . . bed**); in other parts it will be daytime (people will be doing daily tasks, such as **grinding grain**). The taking away means **taken** into judgment, not taken up in the Rapture. The ones left are those who will enter into the kingdom. (Some mss. add the words of v. 36, "Two men will be in the field; one will be taken and the other left." Most likely the verse was inserted to harmonize this passage with Matt. 24:40.)

17:37. The disciples questioned **where** these people would be taken. Jesus' cryptic answer, **Where there is a dead body, there the vultures will gather**—has been interpreted variously. It seems best to understand that Jesus was reaffirming that these people would be taken into judgment. Much as a dead body causes vultures to "gather" on it, so dead people are consigned to judgment if they are not ready for the kingdom (cf. Matt. 24:28; Rev. 19:17-19).

c. Jesus' teaching about prayer (18:1-14)

These verses include two of Jesus' parables about prayer. One was addressed to the disciples (vv. 1-8), and the other (vv. 9-14) to "some who were confident of their own righteousness."

18:1-8. Jesus told the **Parable** of the Unjust Judge to teach persistence in prayer: **that they,** His disciples, **should always pray and not give up.** Verses 2-5 contain the parable itself. A **widow** continued to go before an unjust **judge** to plead for **justice** in her case. He continually **refused** to "hear" her case, **but finally he** decided to give her **justice so that she** would not **wear** him **out with her** complaining. Jesus interpreted the parable (vv. 6-8), pointing out that if **the unjust judge** would give **justice,** then imagine how **God** (the just Judge) **will see that they get justice, and quickly.** Jesus' question, **When the Son of Man comes, will He find faith on the earth?** was not spoken out of ignorance. Nor was He questioning whether all believers would be gone when He returns. Instead, He asked the question to spur the disciples on to faithfulness in prayer, to encourage them to keep on in their praying. This is another good lesson from a bad example (cf. 16:1-13).

18:9-14. The purposes of the **Parable** of the Prayers of the **Pharisee** and the **Tax Collector** were to show that one cannot trust in himself for **righteousness** and should not view others with contempt (v. 9). The Pharisee's prayer was concerned with telling God what a good man he was, for not only did he keep the Law by fasting and tithing (v. 12), but also he considered himself better than other people (v. 11). He was using other people as his standard for measuring righteousness.

On the other hand **the tax collector** used **God** as his standard for measuring righteousness. He realized that he had to throw himself on the **mercy** of **God** for forgiveness.

Jesus' application of the parable echoed His teaching in 13:30. It is necessary for people to humble themselves before God to gain forgiveness, and those who are proud (**everyone who exalts himself**) will be brought low (**humbled**) by God.

d. Jesus' teaching about childlikeness (18:15-17)
(Matt. 19:13-15; Mark 10:13-16)

18:15-17. Luke placed this short section here to follow up on the message of the previous parable. **Jesus** had taught that it was necessary to be humble before God. In these verses He compared that humility to childlikeness: **Let the little children come to Me, and do not hinder them, for the kingdom of God belongs to such as these.** In these words Jesus was stating that a person must come to Him in humility in order to enter **the kingdom. Children** come with expectation and excitement. They come realizing that they are not sufficient in themselves. They depend totally on others. If these same attitudes are not present in adults, they can **never enter** into the kingdom.

e. Jesus' teaching that wealth is a hindrance to the important issues of life (18:18-30)
(Matt. 19:16-30; Mark 10:17-31)

18:18-20. A certain ruler (who was very wealthy, v. 23) came to **Jesus** to talk about how **to inherit eternal life.** This man was perhaps a member of the Sanhedrin or perhaps an official in a local synagogue. "To inherit eternal life" meant to enter the kingdom of God (cf. John 3:3-5). The man wanted to know what actions (**what must I do**) would make him right with God.

The man had called Jesus **Good Teacher.** Jesus responded that **God alone** is **good,** that is, only God is truly righteous. Apparently the man thought Jesus had gained a measure of status with God by His good works. Jesus was implying that if He were truly good, then it would be because He is God. This, then, is another of Jesus' claims of deity.

Jesus responded to the man's question by instructing him to keep the seventh, sixth, eighth, ninth, and fifth commandments (Ex. 20:12-16), each of which pertain to man's relationship to man. (The first four of the Ten Commandments pertain to man's relationship with God.)

18:21-22. The ruler's reply that **he** had **kept** all these since childhood was probably correct. He may have been a model citizen.

Jesus then told the man **one** other **thing** he needed to do: he needed to **follow** Jesus, and in order to do that he had to **give** the money from his possessions **to the poor.** This action would touch on the 10th commandment against coveting, which included the idea of greed and holding onto things which are one's own as well as wanting things that belong to others. It was at this point that the man faltered.

Jesus' reasoning was clear: (a) one must keep the Law perfectly in order to inherit eternal life (cf. James 2:10). (b) Only God was good—truly righteous. (c) Therefore nobody can obtain eternal life by following the Law (cf. Rom. 3:20; Gal. 2:21; 3:21). The only course of action left to an individual is to follow Jesus in order to obtain eternal life.

18:23-25. The ruler was not prepared to take that step (but contrast Zacchaeus, 19:8). The ruler was more attached to his wealth than to the idea of obtaining "eternal life" which he had so nobly asked about at the beginning of his conversation with the Lord. **Jesus** responded that riches are a hindrance to one's obtaining eternal life. Riches often cloud a person's thinking about what is truly important in life. Jesus used a common hyperbole of something that is impossible—a camel going through the eye of a needle (belonēs, a sewing needle, not a small door in a city gate). Likewise it is most difficult (but not impossible; cf. Zaccheus, 19:1-10) for a rich person to be saved.

18:26-27. The disciples were dumbfounded. They had the mistaken impression, like the Pharisees, that wealth was a sign of God's blessing. If a person such as the ruler could not be saved, **Who then can be saved?** Jesus, by His reply, did not rule out all wealthy people from salvation. He noted that **God** can do the **impossible.**

18:28-30. In response to the disciples' sacrifice in following Him, expressed by **Peter,** Jesus affirmed that they would be amply rewarded. Though they had **left** their families (cf. 14:26-27), their reward would consist of **many times as much in this age and** also **eternal life.** Jesus was obviously referring to the community of believers who would share with the disciples during their ministries. Those believers became a closely knit family, all sharing together, so that none had any need (Acts 2:44-47; 4:32-37).

f. Jesus' teaching about His resurrection (18:31-34)
(Matt. 20:17-19; Mark 10:32-34)

18:31-34. Each time **Jesus . . . told** His followers about what would happen to Him in **Jerusalem,** He got more explicit. At this point He laid out the events which would come to pass. He clearly stated the involvement of **Gentiles** in His trial and death. This was important because Luke did not want his readers to think that the Gentiles were guiltless in Jesus' death. The whole world was guilty of the death of the Savior. But **the disciples** could **not** comprehend any of this. They still thought the kingdom would come almost immediately. So **they did not know what He was talking about.**

g. Jesus and a blind man (18:35-43)
(Matt. 20:29-34; Mark 10:46-52)

In this passage and the next (Luke 19:1-10) are two examples of how the nation should have responded to the

Messiah. In each case the person who did respond was an outcast from the mainstream of Judaism.

18:35-38. Near **Jericho** a certain **blind man,** hearing all the commotion around him as **Jesus** was **passing by . . .** **asked** those around him **what was** going on. When he was **told** it was **Jesus of Nazareth,** he immediately realized that the Messiah was there, for his words, **Jesus, Son of David, have mercy on me!** presupposed that he knew Jesus is the Messiah.

Great symbolic value is here in Luke's account. The man was a beggar **sitting by the** side of the road, waiting for something to happen. He was blind and could do nothing to improve his condition. The Messiah came through his town (as He had walked through many towns). Immediately the blind man recognized Him as the Messiah, the One who could save him from his blindness. Spiritual outcasts, unable to help themselves, far more readily recognized the Messiah and asked for His help than did the Jewish religious leaders.

18:39. Those in front tried to make **him** keep **quiet.** Similarly the religious leaders tried to keep people from believing on Jesus. **But** the opposition caused the man to be even more adamant in his faith.

18:40-43. In stating his desire **to see,** the man was confident that **Jesus, the** Messiah, had the power to heal him. When **Jesus** said, **Your faith has healed you,** He was not saying that the man's faith possessed some power. The man had faith in the Messiah, and it was the Messiah's power that had healed him (cf. 7:50; 17:19). In the same way, if the nation had faith in the Messiah, their faith would have healed them of their spiritual blindness. As a result of the man's healing, **he** and **all the people** who **saw** the miracle **praised God.**

h. Jesus and Zacchaeus (19:1-10)

A second person in Jericho came to faith in Jesus. Zacchaeus, like the blind man, was considered outside the normal Jewish system because of his activities for Rome as a tax collector (cf. 5:27; 18:9-14). Zacchaeus responded to Jesus' message in precisely the opposite way the rich ruler had responded (18:18-25). Zacchaeus, also wealthy (19:2), knew he was a sinner.

When Jesus called on him, he responded with a greater enthusiasm than Jesus had asked for. This account is also a commentary on Jesus' words that with God all things are possible (18:25-27), for Zacchaeus was a wealthy person who found salvation.

19:1-4. This incident seems ludicrous. Here was **Zacchaeus, a wealthy** and probably influential man, running **ahead of the crowd** and climbing **a sycamore-fig tree** (cf. Amos 7:14) to get a chance **to see . . . Jesus.** Luke may have been presenting Zacchaeus' actions as a commentary on Jesus' words that unless people become like little children they cannot enter the kingdom of God (Luke 18:17).

19:5-6. Jesus already knew Zacchaeus' name and all about him. He instructed the tax man to **come down immediately** for Jesus wanted to **stay at his house.** This was more than Zacchaeus had hoped for, so he **welcomed Him gladly.** The word "gladly" (*chairōn*) is literally "rejoicing." Luke used this verb (and the noun *chara*) nine times (1:14; 8:13; 10:17; 13:17; 15:5, 9, 32; 19:6, 37) to denote an attitude of joy accompanying faith and salvation.

19:7-10. As usual, many complained (**began to mutter**) because Jesus had **gone to be the guest of a "sinner"** (cf. 15:1). But **Zacchaeus stood up and** voluntarily announced that he would **give half of** what he owned **to the poor** and repay fourfold all he had wronged. He publicly wanted the people to know that his time with Jesus had changed his life. Interestingly he parted with much of his wealth, similar to what Jesus had asked the rich ruler to do (18:22).

Jesus' words, **Today salvation has come to this house,** did not imply that the act of giving to the poor had saved Zacchaeus, but that his change in lifestyle evidenced his right relationship before God. Zacchaeus, **a son of Abraham** by birth, had a right to enter the kingdom because of his connection with **Jesus.** That was Jesus' mission—**to seek and to save** those who are **lost** (cf. 15:5, 9, 24).

i. Jesus' teaching on stewardship of responsibilities (19:11-27)
(Matt. 25:14-30)

This parable brings to a close the section of Jesus' teaching in response to

rejection (Luke 12:1-19:27). It also concludes the subsection of Jesus' teaching about the coming kingdom and the attitudes of His disciples (17:11-19:27). Jesus' disciples should be like the grateful ex-leper (17:11-19), persistent in prayer (18:1-14), childlike (18:15-17), like the former blind man (18:35-43), and like Zacchaeus (19:1-10) as opposed to the rich ruler (18:18-25).

This Parable of the 10 Minas sums up Jesus' teaching to the disciples. Each disciple had duties given to him by Jesus, and each was to carry out his responsibilities. But the parable was addressed not only to disciples. It was also addressed to the nation at large, to show that it too had responsibilities. If the nation did not turn to Jesus, it would be punished.

19:11. Jesus gave this **parable because . . . the people** with Him **thought** He was **going to** reinstitute **the kingdom** immediately. Since they were close to **Jerusalem,** Jesus wanted to dispel any disappointment on the part of His followers.

19:12-14. The **man of noble birth** obviously represented Jesus. Because His followers thought the kingdom was to be set up immediately, Jesus said the nobleman in the parable had to go **to a distant country to have himself appointed king and then to return.** He would have to leave before the kingdom would be set up. Before leaving, **he called 10 of his servants and gave them 10 minas,** 1 apiece. A mina was about three months' wages, so its value was considerable. They were to invest the **money** while he was gone. Another group of people, **His subjects,** did not **want** him **to be . . . king.** Obviously this group represented the religious leaders in particular and the nation in general.

19:15-26. When the **king . . . returned,** he called **the servants in to find out what they had** done with **the money** he had entrusted to them. **The first** two servants had used the money to be productive for the king. One had earned another **10** minas (v. 16), and the second had earned another **5** minas (v. 18). Each of these servants was commended by the king and given a reward commensurate with the amount of money earned (vv. 17, 19).

Another servant had done nothing with the **mina** given to him. His **words** to the king, **You are a hard man; you take out what you did not put in and reap what you did not sow,** were used against him by the **master** (v. 22). If he were right then he should have at least banked the **money**—then the king would have received his money back **with interest.** The implication was that the servant did not really expect the king to come back. He was not at all concerned about the king's return so he did not bother with the king's business. Matthew related that the third servant was thrown out of the kingdom (Matt. 25:30). This indicates that this servant really belonged to the group of people who did not want the king to reign over them (Luke 19:14). His money was taken away and given **to the one who** had done the most for the king.

19:27. In contrast with the two servants who had expected the king's return, the **enemies** of the **king** were put to death in the king's presence. The analogy of this parable was clear to Jesus' hearers. Jesus was going away to receive a kingship. When He returned, He would establish His kingdom. Until that time His followers were to fulfill the responsibilities He gave them. On His return He would reward the faithful commensurate with their service to Him, and His enemies would be judged before Him.

VI. The Ministry of Jesus in Jerusalem (19:28–21:38)

Jesus' goal was to go to Jerusalem to present Himself to the religious leaders as the Messiah. Now he arrived in Jerusalem and ministered there. This section is divided into two parts: (1) Jesus entered Jerusalem and was presented as the Messiah (19:28-44); (2) He entered the temple and taught there for several days (19:45–21:38). Those present would have clearly understood that He was presenting Himself as the Messiah, capable of bringing in the kingdom.

A. Jesus' entry into Jerusalem as Messiah (19:28-44) (Matt. 21:1-11; Mark 11:1-11; John 12:12-19)

Up to this time Jesus had not sought to be openly called Messiah. But now He allowed it and even encouraged it. Everything He did over the course of these days was designed to call attention to the fact that He is the Messiah.

1. THE PREPARATION FOR ENTRY (19:28-34)

19:28-34. Luke noted that it was now time for **Jesus** to go **up to Jerusalem** and He prepared His way for the entry. Jesus had come from Jericho (18:35–19:10) and was a short distance from Jerusalem at **Bethphage and Bethany.** At that point He stopped until the way could be prepared so that when He entered the city people would know He was presenting Himself as the Messiah. His command to **two of His disciples** was to **find a colt** and **bring it here.** Jesus was fulfilling Zechariah 9:9-10, which predicted the Messiah would ride on a donkey (cf. comments on Matt. 21:2, which refers to a donkey *and a* colt). As is evident (Luke 19:38) the crowds would understand the message behind the symbolism. Apparently even the **owners** of **the colt** understood for they allowed the donkey to go with the disciples when they were told, **The Lord needs it.**

2. JESUS' ADVANCE INTO THE CITY (19:35-40)

19:35-40. Jesus advanced **down** the west side of **the Mount of Olives** (v. 37) toward the city and was praised by the crowd as their Messiah. The act of spreading **their cloaks on the road** (v. 36) in front of **Jesus** was a sign of respect. **The whole crowd of disciples** (*mathētōn*) **began joyfully to praise God . . . for all the miracles** (*dynameōn,* "evidences of spiritual power") **they had seen.** These believers quoted (v. 38a) from Psalm 118:26, a messianic psalm of praise. **The Pharisees** understood the meaning of what was going on, for they told **Jesus** to **rebuke** His followers, so they would stop calling him Messiah or King.

Jesus responded that there must be some proclamation that He is the Messiah. If not, even inanimate objects (**stones**) would be called on to testify for Him. All history had pointed toward this single, spectacular event when the Messiah publicly presented Himself to the nation, and God desired that this fact be acknowledged.

3. JESUS' PROPHECY ABOUT JERUSALEM (19:41-44)

19:41-44. Jesus showed compassion on **Jerusalem** but He also foretold that

253

days would come when it would lie in ruins. Jesus rejected Jerusalem because Jerusalem rejected Him. **He wept over** the city because its people did not understand the significance of what was going on that day—that national acceptance of Him on that day **would bring** them **peace.** Because the people **did not recognize the time of God's coming to** them (v. 44), the city would be totally destroyed. Roman soldiers did this starting in A.D. 70.

B. Jesus in the temple (19:45–21:38)

Jesus cleansed the temple, disputed there with the religious leaders (20:1–21:4), and then told His disciples what would happen in the end times (21:5-36).

1. JESUS' CLEANSING OF THE TEMPLE
(19:45-46)
(MATT. 21:12-13; MARK 11:15-17)

19:45-46. Jesus cleansed **the temple** twice—once at the beginning of His ministry (John 2:13-22), and again at the end of His ministry. Matthew, Mark, and Luke recorded the latter but said nothing of the former. Because of Jesus' role as Messiah, His bringing ceremonial cleanliness to the nation was logical at both the beginning and the end of His ministry. In both cases His teaching in the temple was disregarded by the religious leaders.

Jesus quoted from Isaiah 56:7 and Jeremiah 7:11 as **He** was **driving out** the people **who were selling** in the temple. Mark adds that the buyers and money changers were also driven out, as well as people who were apparently taking shortcuts through the temple compound in their business dealings (Mark 11:15-16). Money changing was done because only certain coinage was then accepted in the temple from those who bought animals for sacrifices. The religious leaders made money off the system of buying and selling animals for sacrifice (thus making the temple **a den of robbers**). Also they led the people into mere formalism. A pilgrim traveling to Jerusalem could go to the temple, buy an animal, and offer it as a sacrifice without ever having anything to do with the animal. This led to an impersonalization of the sacrificial system. The commercial system was apparently set up in the area of the temple which had been designated for devout Gentiles to pray and so was disrupting Israel's witness to the surrounding world.

2. JESUS' TEACHING IN THE TEMPLE
(19:47–21:38)

The two parts of this section—Jesus disputing in the temple (20:1–21:4) and His teaching His disciples (21:5-36)—are bracketed by an introduction (19:47-48) and a conclusion (21:37-38). The introduction and conclusion show that the people were amazed at His teaching and liked to listen to Him, whereas in contrast the chief priests, leaders, and teachers of the Law wanted to kill Him (19:47).

a. The crowd's delight (19:47-48)

19:47-48. Jesus taught daily in **the temple** to the delight of the crowds. They **hung on His words,** but the religious **leaders** wanted **to kill Him. Yet they** feared the crowds (cf. 20:19; 22:2; Acts 5:26).

b. Jesus' disputing in the temple
(20:1–21:4)
(Matt. 21:23–23:37; Mark 11:27–12:44)

As a logical outcome of Jesus' cleansing of the temple, the religious leaders again rejected Him, and conflict arose. Jesus had upset the normal "religious" atmosphere of the temple, which led the religious leaders to question His authority.

20:1-8 (Matt. 21:23-27; Mark 11:27-33). The religious leaders asked Jesus where His authority came from. **The chief priests** were the temple officials; **the teachers of the Law,** often called "scribes," were made up of both Pharisees and Sadducees; and **the elders** may have been laymen who were political leaders. They asked two questions: **By what authority** was He acting, and **who gave** Him **this authority?** (Luke 20:2) The first question dealt with the kind of authority Jesus was using. Was He a prophet, a priest, or a king? No doubt the words **doing these things** referred to His cleansing the temple. The second question dealt with who was backing Him. Did Jesus believe that He was acting on His own or was He acting for some group?

Jesus responded with **a question.** He asked them about the authority behind

John's baptism. The religious leaders had disapproved the baptizing work of John, for John had humiliated them and had taken away some allegiance from their religious system (Matt. 3:7-10). Because the crowds venerated John the Baptist, the religious leaders were afraid to deny his authority and therefore refused to answer Jesus' question (Luke 20:7; cf. 19:48). So Jesus therefore refused to tell . . . by what authority He had cleansed the temple. The implication was that He was doing His work with the same authority—God in heaven—by which John the Baptist baptized.

20:9-19 (Matt. 21:33-46; Mark 12:1-12). Jesus then told a **parable** to describe His authority. A parable about a vine was not new for Israelites. Isaiah had used the figure to refer to the nation (Isa. 5:1-7), and the symbolism would have been clear to the hearers. The owner of a **vineyard** sent three servants to gain **fruit** from his **vineyard** (Luke 20:10-12). But the tenant **farmers . . . beat** each of the three. Finally he sent his **son,** whom they **killed** so that they could gain **the inheritance** (vv. 13-15). Jesus then asked his listeners a rhetorical question, **What then will the owner of the vineyard do to them?** He answered His own question—**He** would **kill those tenants and give the vineyard to others** (v. 16).

This culminated all of Jesus' messages concerning the fact that Gentiles and outcasts would be added to the kingdom whereas many from Israel would not be allowed to enter. The crowd responded with a strong statement of negation—**May this never be!** (*mē genoito;* used several times by Paul in Rom.) They understood the implications of what Jesus was saying: the Jewish system was being set aside because the religious leaders were rejecting Him. Luke pointed out the seriousness of the situation by recording that **Jesus looked directly at them** and quoted from Psalm 118:22, a verse which noted that a seemingly insignificant thing (a **stone** thrown away by stone masons) was really the most important thing (this stone became **the capstone**).

Jesus' point was that He, the most important element in the Jewish nation, was being rejected, but ultimately would be supreme. He also would be the means of judgment (Luke 20:18). The severity of Jesus' words struck home. **The teachers of the Law and the chief priests** wanted to kill Him **because they knew He had spoken this parable against them. But** again **they** feared to take any action because **of the people** (cf. 19:47-48; 22:2).

20:20-26. Since the religious leaders were afraid to do anything to Jesus because of the people (v. 19), they kept a **close watch on Him. They** were hoping **to catch** Him in some teaching that the crowds would not like, which would allow them to prosecute Him legally. Some **spies** asked Jesus a question about taxes: **Is it right for us to pay taxes to Caesar or not?** But this question was not merely about money. It pertained to politics and religion as well. If Jesus gave either a yes or a no answer He would lose support. If He said it was proper to pay taxes to Caesar, a foreign ruler (viz., Tiberius Caesar, A.D. 14-37), the zealots (who opposed Roman rule and favored Jewish autonomy) would be offended by His answer. If He answered that it was not proper to pay taxes (which the religious leaders might have suspected because He had been teaching about the kingdom), then the Romans would be displeased and the religious leaders would be able to turn **Him** over to their authority.

Jesus, pointing to the **portrait and inscription** of Caesar on **a denarius** coin (cf. 7:41; 10:35), answered in the affirmative: **Give to Caesar what is Caesar's.** But He also used the occasion to teach that one should give to God the thing that bears His image—oneself (**and to God what is God's**).

This astonishing answer silenced the spies (20:26). Interestingly the religious leaders used this incident against Jesus in His trial. But they totally misrepresented His position, charging that Jesus opposed payment of taxes to Caesar (23:2).

20:27-40. The Sadducees denied all supernatural occurrences including **resurrection** (v. 27; cf. Acts 23:8). Their **question** on resurrection, therefore, was not to elicit information but to find a way to make **Jesus** look foolish by presenting an extreme hypothetical case. They posited a situation in which **a woman** married each of **seven brothers** after each previous brother had died. The idea behind such an occurrence was the Hebrew concept of the Levirate marriage (Deut. 25:5-10) in which an unmarried man would marry his dead brother's **widow** who was **childless** in order to **have children** in his name. Then the Sadducees asked, **At the resurrection whose wife will she be?**

First, Jesus said, there will be no **marriage** in **the resurrection** (Luke 20:34-36). This showed (a) that the present **Age** contrasts sharply with the **Age** to come; and (b) when **people** are resurrected, **they** will be **like the angels,** being **God's children** and **children of the resurrection.** Jesus did not say that resurrected people become angels. His point was that they, like angels, will be immortal. Thus there will be no further need for procreation, and the marriage relationship will not be necessary.

Second, Jesus pointed out that there certainly will be a resurrection (vv. 37-38). He referred to an incident when the Lord told Moses that He is the God of the patriarchs (Ex. 3:6). Jesus appealed to **Moses** because the Sadducees wrongly taught that Moses' teachings did not reveal a resurrection. The statement that **the Lord** is **the God of** the patriarchs should have shown the Sadducees that the patriarchs were still alive (**He is . . . the God . . . of the living**), even though those words were uttered several hundred years after the last patriarch's death. **God** was preserving them **alive** for future resurrection.

The teachers of the Law and the Sadducees were at odds with each other because of conflicting beliefs. The former applauded Jesus' refutation of the Sadducees' doctrine (Luke 20:39). The result of the conversation was that everyone was afraid **to ask** Jesus **any more questions.**

20:41-44. Jesus then took the offensive and asked a question of the people around Him. The question concerned the nature of the Messiah—**How is it that they say the Christ is the Son of David?** Jesus then quoted from Psalm 110:1, in which **David** called the Messiah **my Lord** and said that He was exalted by being at Yahweh's **right hand,** the place of prominence. Two points are evident in these words of Jesus. First, the Son of David is also David's **Lord** (Luke 20:44) by the power of the resurrection. (In Acts 2:34-35 Peter used the same verse from Ps. 110 to prove that Jesus' superiority is based on His resurrection.) Second, David must have realized that the Son, who was

to be the Messiah, would be divine, for **David** called **Him Lord.**

20:45-47. Jesus' words were designed not only to teach **His disciples** but also to instruct the crowds (v. 45). Jesus pointed out the dichotomy between what **the teachers of the Law** taught and what they practiced. Their lives were bound up in greed and pride—they desired: (a) display (**flowing robes**), (b) attention (**greeted in the marketplaces**), (c) prominence (**important seats in the synagogues and . . . at banquets**), and (d) more money, taking from those who did not have much (e.g., widows). Their pompous **lengthy prayers** were thus hypocritical. Jesus stated that these teachers would **be punished most severely.** Those who have greater knowledge are held more accountable (James 3:1).

21:1-4. Following naturally what **Jesus** had just said about the teachers of the Law and their attitude toward widows, He pointed to **a poor widow** who was putting into the collection all her meager resources (**two** *lepta,* each worth about ⅛ cent; cf. 12:59; Mark 12:42). The percentage of what she gave was larger than **all the others.** So Jesus' point was that her gift, though small, was more because she gave **out of her poverty . . . all she had to live on.**

c. *Jesus' teaching in the temple about the end times (21:5-36)*
(Matt. 24:1-44; Mark 13:1-31)

In this section, which parallels the Olivet Discourse (Matt. 24–25), Jesus taught His followers what would happen immediately before His return to set up the kingdom. Being ready for the kingdom was the purpose of this teaching (Luke 21:34-36); thus the Rapture is not in view in this passage. As with all prophecy in Scripture, the teaching had immediate application to the hearers. They were to live righteous lives because of events which would occur in the future.

21:5-7. Some of the **disciples** were impressed with **the temple** and were **remarking** about its **beautiful** craftsmanship. Jesus' **comment** that a **time** was coming **when not one stone will be left on another** immediately brought a question to the disciples' minds. Their question, recorded by Luke, concerned the destruction of the temple (v. 7). Matthew also recorded another question about the signs of the end of the Age (Matt. 24:3). The disciples wanted to know **what** things would **take place** before the temple complex fell. **21:8-19.** Jesus told His disciples about three things that would start to occur before the destruction of the temple, by Titus and the Roman army in A.D. 70, and one that would occur later. First, Jesus said others would claim to be Messiah (v. 8). He gave this warning so that the disciples would **not** be **deceived.**

Second, Jesus said that **wars** would occur (vv. 9-10). When **these things** happened, the disciples were **not** to **be frightened,** for **the end** would **not come right away.**

Third, Jesus added that tremendous **earthquakes** would occur, causing **famines** (*loimoi*) **and pestilences** (*limoi*; v. 11). But these events do not fit between Jesus' day and the fall of Jerusalem. These **fearful events and great signs from heaven** refer to the Great Tribulation which will precede the return of the Lord to the earth.

Fourth, Jesus taught that persecution of believers would be common and severe. The disciples did undergo persecution by the authorities (cf. Acts 2-4). Because of Jesus' prediction in Luke 21:9-11, it seems that His words in verses 12-17 refer not only to the situation which would confront the disciples before the fall of Jerusalem but also to what will confront believers during the time of the Great Tribulation (cf. vv. 25-36). The same kinds of persecution would be present at both times—imprisonment (vv. 12-15), betrayal (v. 16), and hatred (v. 17). The persecution the original disciples would experience was a precursor to the ultimate persecution which future disciples would undergo.

Jesus' next two statements (**But not a hair of your head will perish,** and **By standing firm you will save yourselves;** vv. 18-19) have confused many. Some interpret these phrases as speaking of spiritual realities in a believer's life. Ultimately even though a believer dies, he or she will be protected eternally by God. However, it appears that Jesus was speaking here of salvation as entering into the kingdom alive (cf. Matt. 24:9-13). To "save yourselves" by "standing firm" means that believers show that they are

members of the believing community in opposition to those who turn away from the faith during times of persecution (Matt. 24:10). The ones who are saved are those who are preserved by God's sovereign power (cf. Matt. 24:22).

21:20-24. Jesus then returned to the disciples' original question about when the temple would be destroyed. In these five verses He noted that Gentile domination included the destruction of **Jerusalem** which would come about when the city was **surrounded by armies.** Gentile domination would continue **until the times of the Gentiles are fulfilled** (v. 24). The times of the Gentiles' domination over Jerusalem actually began when the Babylonians took the city and the nation into Captivity in 586 B.C. Jerusalem will again fall under Gentile domination in the Tribulation (Zech. 14:1-2) just before Messiah returns to restore Jerusalem. It is that restoration of which Jesus spoke next (Luke 21:25-28).

21:25-28. Here Jesus first noted that cosmic **signs** will precede the **coming** of **the Son of Man** and will cause people to be terrified. **The sun, moon, and stars . . . will be shaken,** and **the sea** will roar and toss, signifying that the world will be in a chaotic state, out of control. Second, Jesus told about the coming of the Son of Man Himself. He drew His terminology from Daniel 7:13-14, in which Daniel saw "one like a Son of Man" coming with clouds and **glory** and receiving the kingdom from the Ancient of Days (i.e., God the Father). Jesus' point was that the Son of Man will come to receive the kingdom— the same kingdom He had been proclaiming since the beginning of His ministry. When these things **begin to** occur, His followers will **lift up** their **heads,** a symbol of rejoicing, **because** their **redemption** (i.e., safety in the kingdom brought by the returning King) will be **drawing near.**

21:29-33. In the **Parable** of the **Fig Tree** Jesus taught that one can tell what is coming by watching the signs. By looking at fig **leaves** sprouting in April, they know **that summer is near.** Similarly when the Great Tribulation comes, people will **know that the kingdom of God is near.**

The clause, **this generation** (*genea*) **will certainly not pass away until all these things have happened,** has caused much controversy. Some think Jesus was telling His disciples that their generation would see the destruction of the temple. That interpretation stems primarily from verses 5-7 in which the discussion pertained to the temple's destruction. However, because of verse 31 (in which Jesus spoke of the coming of the kingdom of God), and because of Matthew 24:34, it seems preferable to say His words refer to the generation living at the time of the cosmological events that will just precede His second coming. That generation will actually see the founding of the kingdom of God—something every generation of Jewish citizens has longed for throughout the nation's history.

21:34-36. Jesus warned His disciples to be ready at all times. Though a believer will be able to anticipate the coming of the kingdom by the signs, it is possible to get so entangled with the affairs **of life** that some will not be ready for the kingdom when it comes—**unexpectedly** (v. 34) and universally (v. 35)—and therefore will not enter the kingdom. It was against this wrong attitude that Jesus said, **Be careful** (v. 34) and **be always on the watch** (v. 36).

d. The crowd's reaction (21:37-38)

21:37-38. The crowd reacted to Jesus' **teaching** with amazement. Jesus spent the nights on **the Mount of Olives,** and each morning returned to **the temple** in Jerusalem to teach. The people were so taken with His teaching that they would arrive **early in the morning** to get an opportunity **to hear Him.** Apparently they were understanding His teachings about the coming of the kingdom in a way they had not understood before.

VII. The Death, Burial, and Resurrection of Jesus (chaps. 22–24)

A. The death and burial of Jesus (chaps. 22–23)

In this section Luke brought out the highpoint of the Messiah's rejection by the religious leaders of the nation, acting for the entire nation and for the world. Luke also emphasized Jesus' innocence in a number of ways not mentioned by the other Gospel writers: (a) Luke recorded that Pilate three times declared Jesus' innocence (23:4, 14, 22). (b) To Pilate's words Luke added the witness of Herod

(23:15). (c) Luke contrasted Jesus with Barabbas, who had been put into prison because of insurrection and murder (23:25). (d) Jesus was declared to be innocent by the thief who confessed his sin and the justice of his own punishment (23:39-43). (e) The centurion confessed that Jesus was righteous (23:47). (f) The multitude beat their breasts, an act which showed that they knew He was innocent (23:48).

1. THE AGREEMENT BY JUDAS TO BETRAY JESUS (22:1-6)
(MATT. 26:1-5, 14-16; MARK 14:1-2, 10-11; JOHN 11:45-53)

22:1-6. Luke recorded that the death of Christ occurred at the time of **the Passover,** the annual celebration of the time lambs had been slain in Egypt, when God spared the Israelites but punished the Egyptians (Ex. 12:1-28). On the relationship of **the Feast of Unleavened Bread** to the Passover, see comments on Luke 22:7 and John 19:14. The religious leaders **were afraid of the people** (cf. Luke 19:47-48; 20:19), but were still trying **to get rid of Jesus.** The initiative for the betrayal rested on Judas. **Satan entered Judas** (cf. John 13:27) and he was willing to **betray Jesus** for **money.** Satan's taking part in Jesus' death was actually his own downfall, for through dying Jesus conquered Satan and death (Col. 2:15; Heb. 2:14).

2. THE PREPARATION BY JESUS FOR DEATH (22:7-46)

Luke's account of Jesus' preparation for His death includes two parts: Jesus' final ministry to His close disciples at the Passover meal (vv. 7-38), and Jesus' final hours praying alone in the garden (vv. 39-46).

a. Jesus at the Passover meal (22:7-38) (Matt. 26:17-35; Mark 14:12-31; John 13:1-38)

The Synoptic Gospels speak of the meal Jesus ate with His disciples as the Passover meal. But the Gospel of John indicates Jesus died on the cross at the exact time that lambs were slain in preparation for the nation's Passover meals (John 19:14). But this can be explained by the fact that the Feast of Unleavened Bread was a seven-day feast following the one-day Feast of the

Passover, but sometimes all eight days were called "the Passover" (Luke 2:41; 22:1; Acts 12:3-4) or the seven days were the "Passover Week" (John 19:14) A different explanation is that Jews in the first century followed two calendars in observing the Passover. According to this view Jesus and His disciples observed one date, eating the Passover meal before His crucifixion, whereas most of the nation, including the Pharisees, followed the other calendar in which the Passover lambs were slain on the very day of Jesus' death.

(1) The disciples' preparation for the meal. **22:7-13.** Even during these final preparations for His death **Jesus** was doing miraculous things. In this instance He told **Peter and John** exactly what they would find when they went about the **preparations of the Passover.** It would be easy to recognize **a man carrying a jar of water** because women usually carried the water from the wells to their houses. The two disciples were to tell the person who owned **the house** that **the Teacher** wanted to use **the guest room** to **eat the Passover with** His **disciples.** The owner of the house must have been a believer in Jesus, for he let the disciples **make preparations** for the meal at his house.

(2) Jesus' teaching during the meal (22:14-38). **22:14-20.** Jesus taught His men that His death would mean the beginning of the **New Covenant.** The symbolism about the **bread** and **the fruit of the vine** was given to show that Jesus' **body** and **blood** were necessary to institute the New Covenant.

Jesus' final teaching about the kingdom occurred at this final feast. Throughout the Book of Luke feasting has symbolic value. **Jesus and His** disciples, now called **apostles** (cf. 6:13; 9:10; 17:5; 24:10), were **reclined at the table.** Jesus enjoyed the fellowship of those men who had believed His message of the kingdom. They were the ones who had followed Him, knowing that He was truly the Messiah. They were the ones who had left everything in order to follow Him. They had been called to a radical form of discipleship. Jesus announced that this was the last **Passover** He would **eat** with them **until** all that **it** means would find **fulfillment in the kingdom of God** (22:16; cf. v. 18). Many events in the Old Testament, including the Passover,

pointed toward the ministry of Jesus and the kingdom He was to inaugurate. When His kingdom would arrive, the Passover would be fulfilled for God would have brought His people safely into their rest.

The bread and the wine were common, not only at Passover meals but also at every meal in that culture. Those elements symbolized His "body," the sacrifice for the entire nation, and His "blood." He was the sacrificial Lamb who was to take away the sin of Israel and of the entire world (John 1:29). The New Covenant (spoken of many times in the OT but highlighted in Jer. 31:31-34), which was a prerequisite for the Kingdom Age, was instituted by Jesus' sacrifice (Luke 22:20). The New Covenant provided for the regeneration of the Israelite nation and the Holy Spirit's indwelling individuals in the nation. Believers in the Church Age also participate in those spiritual blessings of regeneration and the indwelling Spirit (1 Cor. 11:25-26; 2 Cor. 3:6; Heb. 8:6-7).

22:21-23. Jesus now revealed that the betrayer was one of the gathered disciples who was eating the Passover meal. Judas' accountability and God's sovereign plan for Jesus' death are seen together (v. 22). Jesus had to die, for His death was the basis of salvation for all mankind and the only means for lifting the curse of sin. But the betrayer was accountable for his actions. Apparently the disciples had trusted Judas completely, for they had no idea **who would do** such a thing (v. 23).

22:24-30. The disciples' arguing about **which of them was considered to be greatest** is surprising in view of what Jesus had just said about one of them betraying Him. **Jesus** then told them that such thinking is like that of pagans. The followers of the Messiah should not think about such things. Rather than wanting to be **the greatest,** His followers should each desire to be **the one who serves.** For Jesus was **among** them **as One who serves** (*diakonōn,* "serves in a lowly way," v. 27). The disciples should desire to be like Jesus. Ultimately they will have places of honor in the **kingdom** because they were with Jesus **in** His **trials.** They will fellowship with Him, **and sit on thrones judging** Israel's **12 tribes** (cf. Matt. 19:28).

22:31-34. Jesus revealed that **Peter** would deny Him three times that same night, **before the rooster crows.** However, He assured Peter that in spite of Satan's desire to **sift** the disciples (**you** is pl. in the Gr.) like **wheat** (i.e., to put them through difficult times), Peter's faith would not fail. He would be restored (**turned back**), and would be the leader of the disciples (i.e., the leader of the group of **brothers**). Peter protested, thinking that he was strong, stating that he would even go **to prison** or **to death** for Jesus.

22:35-38. Jesus pointed out to His disciples that they had never lacked **anything** while they were with Him and were sent out to minister for Him (cf. 9:3). However, now that He was to be taken away from them, they would have to make preparations for their ministries including **a purse . . . a bag, and . . . a sword** for personal protection. Jesus was about to die and be **numbered with the transgressors,** a quotation from Isaiah 53:12.

When the disciples responded that they had **two swords,** Jesus replied, **That is enough.** This response has been interpreted in at least four ways: (1) Some understand the words as a rebuke to the disciples. If that were the case, then Jesus was saying, "Enough of this kind of talk!" (Leon Morris, *The Gospel according to St. Luke: An Introduction and Commentary,* p. 310) (2) Others understand the words to denote the fact that even two swords are enough to show human inadequacy at stopping God's plan for the death of Christ. Swords could not stop God's purpose and plan. (3) Jesus may simply have been saying that two swords were adequate for the 12 of them. (4) Others see the clause in conjuction with the quotation from Isaiah and understand Jesus to mean that by possessing two swords they would be classified by others as transgressors or criminals. This fourth view seems preferable.

b. Jesus on the Mount of Olives (22:39-46)
(Matt. 26:36-46; Mark 14:32-42)

The account of Jesus' praying in Gethsemane is recorded in the Synoptic Gospels but not in John. However, John recorded that Jesus went to "an olive grove" because Jesus "often met there with His disciples" and Judas "knew the place" (John 18:1-2). There may be deep signficance to the fact that in some of His final hours Jesus faced temptation (Luke 22:46) in a garden. Man fell into sin because of temptation in a garden (Gen. 3). And man's deliverance from sin comes about in spite of further temptation in a garden. Jesus, the "last Adam" (1 Cor. 15:45), did not fall into temptation but followed the will of God which the first Adam failed to do.

22:39-44. Luke says the place was **the Mount of Olives.** Matthew and Mark refer to the place as Gethsemane, which means "olive press." The "garden" was a grove of olive trees on the Mount of Olives (John 18:1, 3).

Jesus . . . prayed fervently for the trial to pass, but He submitted Himself to His **Father.** Because the **disciples** slept, Jesus was alone praying and being buffeted by the temptation to forsake the Father's plan, which was that the Son must go to death and bear the sins of the whole world. The words of His prayer showed that He was concerned **not** with His own interests but with the interests of the Father (Luke 22:42). Only Luke recorded that **an angel** ministered to Jesus in the garden (v. 43). Jesus was **in anguish** with His **sweat** being **like drops of blood falling to the ground.** Luke may have been alluding to God's words to Adam that he would earn his food by the sweat of his brow (Gen. 3:19).

22:45-46. Jesus **found** His **disciples . . . asleep, exhausted from sorrow.** The disciples were most depressed because of Jesus' teaching that He would die. They were not only in physical danger, which was bound to come on them, but also they may have faced spiritual danger as the temptation raged in the garden. Twice Jesus told them to pray that *they* would **not fall into temptation** (vv. 40, 46).

3. THE BETRAYAL OF JESUS (22:47-53)
(MATT. 26:47-56; MARK 14:43-50; JOHN 18:3-11)

22:47-53. Luke recorded three elements in the betrayal and arrest of Jesus. First, **Jesus** knew that **Judas** would betray Him (vv. 47-48). A large **crowd** including the religious leaders (v. 52) and soldiers (John 18:12) came into the grove with Judas **leading them.** Judas had agreed on a sign for the people who had come with him—he would **kiss** the One they were to arrest. Jesus, by His words, showed that

He already knew all about the betrayal, including Judas' secret sign.

Second, **Jesus** had compassion for people even in the midst of His own arrest (Luke 22:49-51). After Peter cut off the ear of the high priest's servant (named Malchus, John 18:10), using one of the two swords the disciples possessed (Luke 22:38), Jesus **healed** the man.

Third, **Jesus** pointed up the hypocrisy of the religious leaders (vv. 52-53). Jesus asked them why they had not arrested Him during the **day** as He taught **in the temple.** The reason was obvious, that out of fear of the people they looked for a way to arrest Him secretly (19:48; 20:19; 22:2). Thus He could tell them, **This is your hour—when darkness reigns** (v. 53). Not only were they coming out under the cover of darkness, but they were also acting as the forces of darkness to kill the Messiah. The garden experience must have ended by about 2:30 A.M., for the six trials of Jesus were completed by morning and Jesus was on the cross by 9:00 A.M. The arrest in the garden was illegal for it was done at night and was accomplished through a hired accuser.

4. THE TRIALS OF JESUS (22:54–23:25)

Jesus faced six trials in all: three before Jewish officials, and three before Roman officials (see the list of these trials at Matt. 26:57-58). Luke recorded only two of the three Jewish trials.

a. At the house of the high priest
   (22:54-65)
   (Matt. 26:57-75; Mark 14:53-54,
   65-72; John 18:12-18, 25-27)

22:54. Jesus was taken **into the house of the high priest,** who was Caiaphas (Matt. 26:57; John 18:13; cf. comments on Luke 3:2, and see the chart on Annas' family at Acts 4:5-6). But Jesus first was taken to Caiaphas' influential father-in-law, Annas (John 18:13). **Peter,** remaining true to his word up to this point (Luke 22:33), **followed** the Lord even though it could have meant death for him.

22:55-62. Within several hours **Peter** denied Jesus three times, as He had foretold (v. 34). Peter's denials got progressively more vehement (vv. 57-58, 60). After **the rooster crowed,** Jesus **turned and looked straight at Peter.** The combination of events along with Jesus' look caused Peter to remember the words Jesus spoke earlier in the evening. Peter realized what he had done. His bitter weeping showed he was heartbroken over the fact he had **denied** Jesus.

22:63-65. While at the house of the high priest, **Jesus** began to be mistreated by **the men who were guarding** Him. They mocked Him and beat Him. Blindfolding Him, they mockingly asked Him to **prophesy** by telling **who hit** Him. Apparently they knew of His claims, but they had a misunderstanding of true prophecy.

b. At the council of the elders (22:66-71)
   (Matt. 26:59-66; Mark 14:55-64;
   John 18:19-24)

22:66-67a. **The council of the elders** (also known as the Sanhedrin) was the Jewish nation's official judicial body. This council was their final court of appeals. If the council found **Jesus** guilty, it was the last word—the nation found Him guilty. They met **at daybreak** since it was illegal to assemble at night. The council wanted to know **if** Jesus was **the Christ,** that is, if Jesus was truly presenting Himself as the Messiah. At this point they were not interested in other charges. Since the council knew that Jesus had been presenting Himself as the Messiah, they may have been giving Him an opportunity to recant. Or perhaps they were trying to shame Him in front of His followers.

22:67b-70. **Jesus** affirmed His authority as Messiah, the One who, after His death, resurrection, and Ascension, would **be seated at the right hand of the mighty God,** the place of honor (cf. Ps. 110:1; Acts 2:33; 5:31; Eph. 1:20; Col. 3:1; Heb. 1:3; 8:1; 10:12; 12:2; 1 Peter 3:22). Also He plainly told the council that He is **the Son of God.**

22:71. The council decided they had received all the **testimony** they needed. In their view Jesus was guilty of blasphemy. So they were ready to hand Him over to the Roman authorities. The council could give a guilty verdict, but the Jews at that time were not allowed to impose the death penalty. Only Rome could sentence to death. Even though Jesus had performed messianic miracles, the leaders of the nation refused to believe. They acted on behalf of the nation in rejecting Christ.

c. Before Pilate (23:1-7)
(Matt. 27:1-2, 11-14; Mark 15:1-5; John 18:28-38)

23:1-7. The council agreed to take Jesus to the Roman authorities. On arriving before **Pilate,** governor of Judea (3:1; cf. 13:1), the Jewish authorities charged Him falsely. They said He opposed paying **taxes to Caesar,** but Jesus had said the opposite (20:25). And the blasphemy charge—He **claims to be Christ, a king**—was worded to sound as if Jesus was an insurrectionist (23:2). Pilate stated clearly that Jesus was innocent (v. 4). However, because the Jewish leaders kept insisting that Jesus was guilty, Pilate **sent Him to Herod,** "tetrarch of Galilee" (3:1), **who was also in Jerusalem at that time.**

d. Before Herod (23:8-12)

23:8-12. Jesus had told Pilate who He is (v. 3), but He repeatedly refused to answer **Herod** who merely wanted **to see Him perform some miracle.** Herod showed his true feelings toward Jesus by joining in the mockery, dressing Him up as a false king. Herod then **sent** Jesus **back to Pilate,** without passing any judgment on the case.

e. Before Pilate for sentencing (23:13-25)
(Matt. 27:15-26; Mark 15:6-15; John 18:39–19:16)

23:13-17. Pilate told **the people** there was really nothing he could do but **punish** Jesus and **release Him** because he **found no basis for** the **charges against Him.** Jesus had **done nothing to deserve death.** (V. 17, missing from many mss., is not in the NIV.)

23:18-25. In spite of the fact that **Jesus** had been proved by the Roman authorities to have done nothing deserving of death, the Jews yelled out that a known insurrectionist, **Barabbas,** should be **released** in place of Jesus. Amazingly the people were willing to have an insurrectionist and a murderer in their midst rather than the Messiah. They would rather be with a well-known sinner than with the One who could forgive their sins. **Pilate** desired **to release Jesus,** affirming His innocence for a **third time,** but he finally gave in to **their demand . . . and surrendered Jesus to their will.**

5. THE CRUCIFIXION OF JESUS (23:26-49)
(MATT. 27:32-56; MARK 15:21-41; JOHN 19:17-30)

Crucifixion was a common method of carrying out the death sentence in the Roman Empire. It was probably the most cruel and painful method of death the Romans knew. Crucifixion was reserved for the worst criminals; by law a Roman citizen could not be crucified. Crucifixion was usually a long slow process, but Jesus died in a remarkably short period of time for He voluntarily "breathed His last" (v. 46).

23:26-31. A man named **Simon, from** the town of **Cyrene** in North Africa, was forced to carry Jesus' **cross** part of the way to the Crucifixion site. On the way Jesus warned the people of their coming persecution. Because Jesus was going to the cross, the kingdom was being postponed and times of tribulation would come on the nation (cf. Hosea 10:8; Rev. 6:15-17). Jesus' message was being rejected when He was physically present. How much more it would be rejected in coming years! (Luke 23:31)

23:32-43. Luke did not state, as did Matthew and John, how the events of Jesus' death fulfilled Old Testament Scriptures. Luke's purpose, instead, was to show that **Jesus** was the forgiving Messiah even as He died. Jesus asked the **Father** to **forgive** those who were killing Him (v. 34), and He forgave one of the men sentenced to die with Him (v. 43). Even in death Jesus had power to make people right with God. And yet **the rulers . . . sneered** (v. 35) **the soldiers . . . mocked** (vv. 36-37), and **one of the criminals** crucified with Him insulted **Him** (v. 39).

23:44-49. Luke noted four things that occurred at the time Jesus died. First, two symbolic events took place while Jesus was on the cross. **Darkness came over the whole land** for three hours, from **the sixth hour** (noon) **until the ninth hour** (3:00 P.M.). Jesus had already told those who arrested Him that "this is your hour—when darkness reigns" (22:53). Darkness was reigning because of His crucifixion. The other symbolic event was the tearing **in two of the curtain of the temple,** which separated the holy of holies from the rest of the temple. The curtain divided people from the place where God had localized His presence. The tearing from top to bottom (Matt. 27:51) symbolized the fact that now, because of Jesus' death, people had freer access to God as they no longer had to go through the sacrificial system (cf. Rom. 5:2; Eph. 2:18; 3:12). Jesus was the only Sacrifice needed to enable people to have a proper relationship with God.

Second, Luke noted that Jesus' death occurred because He willed it. Breathing **His last** (Luke 23:46), He voluntarily gave up His life (John 10:15, 17-18).

Third, even a Roman **centurion** noted that Jesus **was a righteous Man,** that is, not guilty (Luke 23:47). He too **praised God,** as did many others in Luke's Gospel.

Fourth, **the people** who witnessed His death mourned (vv. 48-49).

6. THE BURIAL OF JESUS (23:50-56)
(MATT. 27:57-61; MARK 15:42-47; JOHN 19:38-42)

23:50-56. All four Gospel writers presented details about Jesus' burial in order to demonstrate that Jesus was truly dead. All the preparations for His burial would have been unnecessary if Jesus had not really died. The death of the Messiah was needed or there could not have been the Resurrection.

Interestingly whereas **the council** had demanded Jesus' death one **member . . . Joseph,** disagreed. **Waiting for the kingdom of God,** he believed that Jesus is the Messiah. He was a secret disciple of Jesus (Matt. 27:57; John 19:38). Out of love for Jesus, he buried Him in his own **tomb** (Matt. 27:60).

Jesus died on the **Preparation Day** (which most assume was Friday) before **the Sabbath.**

B. The resurrection and appearances of Jesus (chap. 24)

The final chapter of Luke records the experiences of a number of people who had firsthand experiences with the risen Messiah. In each case the people were depressed because of Jesus' death. But after meeting with Him, they were joyful and praised God. (See the list of Jesus' post-resurrection events at Matt. 28:1-4.)

1. THE WOMEN AND THE APOSTLES (24:1-12)
(MATT. 28:1-10; MARK 16:1-8; JOHN 20:1-10)

24:1-9. The first people to learn of the resurrection of Jesus were **the women** who had been faithful in following Him. They found out about the Resurrection first because of their devotion to Him. For after His death they brought more **spices** for His burial **on the first day of the week** (cf. 23:55-56). **They did not find the body** they were looking for. Instead they saw **two men in clothes that gleamed like lightning,** an obvious reference to angelic beings. These **men** reminded them of the words Jesus had spoken about His crucifixion and resurrection (9:31; 18:31-34). The women went to report to the apostles and **others** what they had seen (24:9).

24:10-12. The apostles **did not believe** the report **the women** brought them **because their words seemed . . . like nonsense.** This was because they had seen Jesus' death and had seen His body placed in the grave. But **Peter ran to the tomb** and found what the women had described. Still he did not understand **what had happened.**

2. JESUS' APPEARANCES TO HIS FOLLOWERS (24:13-49)

In these two appearances—to two men (vv. 13-35) and to the gathered disciples (vv. 36-49)—Jesus taught His followers from the Old Testament the things that had been accomplished among them. It was not until after Jesus had explained from the Old Testament that the Messiah had to die that His followers began to understand what had occurred the past few days.

a. Jesus' appearance to the two men (24:13-35)
(Mark 16:12-13)

24:13-16. Two of Jesus' followers were walking to **Emmaus,** which is **about seven miles** (northwest) **from Jerusalem. They were talking . . . about** the things **that had happened,** that is, the report that Jesus had been resurrected (vv. 19-24). When **Jesus** joined them, they did not recognize **Him.**

24:17-24. When Jesus asked them to tell Him what they were **discussing,** the men related the view about Jesus that most of the nation believed at that time. The men, **one of** whom was **Cleopas,** said they were talking **about Jesus of Nazareth.** Cleopas commented that their fellow companion must be **the only one**

living in all of Jerusalem who did not know what had happened. By this question Luke got across the point that Jesus' ministry and death were known to everyone in the city and in most of the nation. The entire nation was responsible to accept the Messiah.

The two men added that the chief priests and our rulers handed Him over to . . . death. Along with many others these two men thought that Jesus was the One who was going to redeem Israel, that is, be the Messiah and bring in the kingdom (cf. Simeon's words in 2:30 and Anna's in 2:38). They even related that they had heard a report of the Resurrection directly from some . . . women. But despite all this, their faces were downcast (24:17).

24:25-27. Jesus chided them for not understanding and believing. He explained from Moses and all the Prophets what had been said about Him. He implied that these disciples should have understood from the Old Testament what had happened.

24:28-35. It was not until after Jesus had broken bread with them that their eyes were opened and they recognized Him. Their experience with Jesus caused them to hurry back to Jerusalem (seven miles) and affirm the Resurrection to the Eleven and others who were meeting together. The two men now acknowledged the truth of the reports about Jesus' resurrection for they had recognized Him themselves. The disciples who were meeting together now had at least three reports of the Resurrection: the women, Peter, and Cleopas and his companion. But still they did not understand (cf. v. 38).

b. *Jesus' appearance to the gathered followers (24:36-49)*
(Matt. 28:16-20; Mark 16:14-18; John 20:19-23)

In this appearance three things about Jesus are evident.

24:36-43. First, Jesus proved to His followers that He had really been resurrected. Not only did He stand in their presence so they could see Him and His wounds (vv. 39-40), but He also ate food (a piece of broiled fish) before them to show that He was not a ghost.

24:44-47. Second, Jesus showed His followers all the facts written . . . in the

Old Testament about the Messiah. The Law of Moses, the Prophets, and the Psalms are the three divisions of the Old Testament sometimes referred to in Jesus' day. (More often, however, Moses and the Prophets were said to comprise the OT; e.g., v. 27.) In other words He showed them from different parts of the Old Testament (e.g., Deut. 18:15; Pss. 2:7; 16:10; 22:14-18; Isa. 53; 61:1) that He is the Messiah and that He must suffer and rise from the dead (Luke 24:46; cf. v. 26). Because of His death and resurrection, the message of repentance and forgiveness of sins could be preached in His name to all nations, beginning at Jerusalem for they were witnesses of His death and His rising from the dead. This became the outline for Luke in his second book (cf. Acts 1:8).

24:48-49. Jesus commanded His followers to remain in the city of Jerusalem until they had received power from on high, a clear reference to the Holy Spirit (cf. Acts 1:8), who was promised by the Father.

3. JESUS' PARTING FROM HIS FOLLOWERS (24:50-53)
(MARK 16:19-20)

24:50-53. In the vicinity of Bethany, that is, on the Mount of Olives, Jesus was taken up into heaven (cf. Acts 1:9-11). The disciples responded with worship and great joy and kept praising God in the temple. As seen frequently in Luke, believers repeatedly responded to Jesus with joy (cf. comments on Luke 2:18) and praise. This attitude set the stage for Luke's next volume which began with Jesus' followers remaining in Jerusalem until the Holy Spirit came (Acts 1:4-14).

BIBLIOGRAPHY

Caird, G.B. *Saint Luke*. Westminster Pelican Commentaries. Philadelphia: Westminster Press, 1978.

Danker, Frederick W. *Jesus and the New Age according to St. Luke: A Commentary on the Third Gospel*. St. Louis: Clayton Publishing House, 1980.

Ellis, E. Earle. *The Gospel of Luke*. The New Century Bible Commentary. Rev. ed. Grand Rapids: Wm. B. Eerdmans Publishing Co., 1974.

Fitzmyer, Joseph A. *The Gospel according to Luke (I–IX).* The Anchor Bible. Garden City, N.Y.: Doubleday & Co., 1981.

Geldenhuys, J. Norval. *Commentary on the Gospel of Luke.* Grand Rapids: Wm. B. Eerdmans Publishing Co., 1951.

Godet, F. *A Commentary on the Gospel of Saint Luke.* 2 vols. 5th ed. Reprint. Greenwood, S.C.: Attic Press, 1976.

Hendriksen, William. *Exposition of the Gospel according to Luke.* New Testament Commentary. Grand Rapids: Baker Book House, 1978.

Ironside, H.A. *Addresses on the Gospel of Luke.* 2 vols. New York: Loizeaux Brothers, 1946.

Marshall, I. Howard. *The Gospel of Luke.* The New International Greek Testament Commentary. Grand Rapids: Wm. B. Eerdmans Publishing Co., 1978.

Morgan, G. Campbell. *The Gospel according to Luke.* Old Tappan, N.J.: Fleming H. Revell Co., 1931.

Morris, Leon. *The Gospel according to St. Luke: An Introduction and Commentary.* The Tyndale New Testament Commentaries. Grand Rapids: Wm. B. Eerdmans Publishing Co., 1974.

Plummer, Alfred. *A Critical and Exegetical Commentary on the Gospel according to St. Luke.* The International Critical Commentary. Edinburgh: T. & T. Clark, 1901. Reprint. Greenwood, S.C.: Attic Press, 1977.

Safrai, S., and Stern, M., eds. *The Jewish People in the First Century.* 2 vols. Assen: Van Gorcum & Co., 1974, 1976.

JOHN

Edwin A. Blum

INTRODUCTION

Authorship

Internal evidence. In the strict sense of the term, the Fourth Gospel is anonymous. No name of its author is given in the text. This is not surprising because a Gospel differs in literary form from an epistle or letter. The letters of Paul each begin with his name, which was the normal custom of letter writers in the ancient world. None of the human authors of the four Gospels identified himself by name. But that does not mean one cannot know who the authors were. An author may indirectly reveal himself within the writing, or his work may be well known in tradition as coming from him.

Internal evidence supplies the following chain of connections regarding the author of the Fourth Gospel. (1) In John 21:24 the word "them" refers to the whole Gospel, not to just the last chapter. (2) "The disciple" in 21:24 was "the disciple whom Jesus loved" (21:7). (3) From 21:7 it is certain that the disciple whom Jesus loved was one of seven persons mentioned in 21:2 (Simon Peter, Thomas, Nathanael, the two sons of Zebedee, and two unnamed disciples). (4) "The disciple whom Jesus loved" was seated next to the Lord at the Last Supper, and Peter motioned to him (13:23-24). (5) He must have been one of the Twelve since only they were with the Lord at the Last Supper (cf. Mark 14:17; Luke 22:14). (6) In the Gospel, John was closely related to Peter and thus appears to be one of the inner three (cf. John 20:2-10; Mark 5:37-38; 9:2-3; 14:33). Since James, John's brother, died in the year A.D. 44, he was not the author (Acts 12:2). (7) "The other disciple" (John 18:15-16) seems to refer to the "disciple whom Jesus loved" since he is called this in 20:2. (8) The "disciple whom Jesus loved" was at the cross (19:26), and 19:35 seems to refer to him.

(9) The author's claim, "We have seen His glory" (1:14), was the claim of someone who was an eyewitness (cf. 1 John 1:1-4).

Putting all of these facts together makes a good case for the author of the Fourth Gospel having been John, one of the sons of a fisherman named Zebedee.

External evidence. The external evidence is the traditional ascription of authorship which has been well known in the church. Polycarp (ca. A.D. 69–ca. A.D. 155) spoke of his contact with John. Irenaeus (ca. 130–ca. 200), the bishop of Lyons, heard Polycarp and testified that "John, the disciple of the Lord, who also had leaned upon His breast, had himself published a Gospel during his residence in Ephesus in Asia" (*Against Heresies* 3. 1). Polycrates, Clement of Alexandria, Tertullian, and other later fathers support this tradition. Eusebius was specific that Matthew and John of the apostles wrote the two Gospels which bear their specific names (*The Ecclesiastical History* 3. 24. 3-8).

Place of Origin. The external tradition is strong that John came to Ephesus after Paul had founded the church and that he labored in that city for many years (cf. Eusebius *The Ecclesiastical History* 3. 24. 1). Supporting this tradition is the evidence of Revelation 1:9-11. When John was in exile on Patmos, an island off the coast of Asia Minor, he wrote to seven Asian churches, the first of which was Ephesus. That the Fourth Gospel was originally published at Ephesus is a good probability.

Date. The date for the Gospel of John was probably between A.D. 85 and 95. Some critics have attempted to assign a date as late as A.D. 150 on the basis of the book's alleged similarities to Gnostic writings or because of a supposed long development of church theology. Archeological finds supporting the authenticity of the text of John (e.g., John 4:11; 5:2-3), word studies (e.g., *synchrōntai*, 4:9), manuscript discoveries (e.g., P[52]), and the Dead Sea Scrolls have given powerful support to an early dating for John. So it is common today to find nonconservative scholars arguing for a date as early as A.D. 45-66. An early date is possible. But this Gospel has been known in the church as the "Fourth" one, and the early church fathers believed that it was written when John was an old man. Therefore a date between 85 and 95 is best. John 21:18, 23 require the passing of some time, with Peter becoming old and John outliving him.

Purpose. The purpose of the Gospel of John, stated in 20:31, was to record Jesus' "signs" so that readers would come to believe in Him. Doubtless the author had other purposes as well. Some have argued that John wrote against synagogue Judaism, or the Gnostics, or the followers of John the Baptist. Some think John wrote to supplement the other Gospels. John's Gospel has a clear evangelistic purpose (as do the other Gospels), so it is no accident that it has been greatly used in the history of the church for that purpose.

The Glory of the Fourth Gospel. In introductions to the Fourth Gospel many writers have a section entitled "The Problem of the Fourth Gospel." The Fourth Gospel has been *the* great problem in modern New Testament studies. But what is that problem? One critic claimed many years ago that Jesus in the Synoptics (Matthew, Mark, Luke) is historical but not divine, and that in the Fourth Gospel He is divine but not historical. This, however, is clearly an unwarranted distinction, for the Gospel of John begins with a plain statement of the full deity of the Word made flesh (1:1, 14). And the Gospel nearly ends with Thomas' confession, "My Lord and my God" (20:28). Jesus Christ is both "divine" (Deity) and historical (One who actually lived on the earth). So what is a problem to many critics is actually the chief glory of the church.

Also, contrary to what some have argued, the Synoptic writers, as well as John, present a divine Messiah. But John's Gospel is so clear and pointed in his Christology that his theology has greatly enriched the church. The text, "the Word became flesh" (1:14), became the central focal point of the early church fathers' meditation and study. John presented the Incarnation—God manifest in the flesh—as the foundation of the gospel. This is the "glory," not the "problem," of the Fourth Gospel.

John's Distinctive Portrait. When one compares the Gospel of John with the other three Gospels, he is struck by the distinctiveness of John's presentation. John does not include Jesus' genealogy, birth, baptism, temptation, casting out of demons, parables, transfiguration, instituting of the Lord's Supper, His agony in Gethesemane, or His Ascension. John's presentation of Jesus stresses His ministry in Jerusalem, the feasts of the Jewish nation, Jesus' contacts with individuals in private conversations (e.g., chaps. 3-4; 18:28-19:16), and His ministry to His disciples (chaps. 13-17). The major body of the Gospel is contained in a "Book of Signs" (2:1-12:50) which embraces seven miracles or "signs" which proclaim Jesus as the Messiah, the Son of God. This "Book of Signs" also contains great discourses of Jesus which explain and proclaim the significance of the signs. For example, following the feeding of the 5,000 (6:1-15), Jesus revealed Himself as the Bread of Life which the heavenly Father gives for the life of the world (6:25-35). Another notable and exclusive feature of the Fourth Gospel is the series of "I am" statements that were made by Jesus (cf. 6:35; 8:12; 10:7, 9, 11, 14; 11:25; 14:6; 15:1, 5).

The distinctiveness of this Gospel must be kept in perspective. The Gospels were not intended as biographies. Each Gospel writer selected from a much larger pool of information the material which would serve his purpose. It has been estimated that if all the words from the lips of Jesus cited in Matthew, Mark, and Luke were read aloud, the amount of time taken would be only about three hours. Since the ministry of Jesus lasted about three years, a three-hour sample of His teaching is a small amount. Each Gospel records certain miracles or parables and

Jesus' Seven "Signs" in the Gospel of John

1. Changing water into wine in Cana (2:1-11)
2. Healing an official's son in Capernaum (4:46-54)
3. Healing an invalid at the Pool of Bethesda in Jerusalem (5:1-18)
4. Feeding the 5,000 near the Sea of Galilee (6:5-14)
5. Walking on the water of the Sea of Galilee (6:16-21)
6. Healing a blind man in Jerusalem (9:1-7)
7. Raising dead Lazarus in Bethany (11:1-45)

Jesus' Seven "I Am's" in the Gospel of John

1. "I am the Bread of Life" (6:35).
2. "I am the Light of the world" (8:12).
3. "I am the Gate for the sheep" (10:7; cf. v. 9).
4. "I am the Good Shepherd" (10:11, 14).
5. "I am the Resurrection and the Life" (11:25).
6. "I am the Way and the Truth and the Life" (14:6).
7. "I am the true Vine" (15:1; cf. v. 5).

omits others. The focus of the Gospels is the good news of Jesus' death and resurrection. The Gospels have been called "Passion narratives with extended introductions." That is, they center on Christ's death (e.g., Mark 11–16) with only enough information (e.g., Mark 1–10) to explain the nature of the One who ministered and died.

The following facts are known about John's relationship to the Synoptic Gospels. John, Zebedee's son, was Peter's co-worker in Jerusalem during the early years of the church (Acts 3:1–4:23; 8:14; 12:1-2). Further, John was called one of the "reputed . . . pillars" of the Jerusalem church (Gal. 2:9). The Jerusalem church was led by the apostles, and James the brother of Jesus with Peter and John often took the initiative (Acts 3:1; 4:3-21; 8:14-24; 15:7-11, 13-21). During the early years of the Jerusalem church a certain fixed core of apostolic teaching and preaching developed. After a great multitude were converted, "they devoted themselves to the apostles' teaching" (Acts 2:42). Later the number of men who believed grew to about 5,000 (Acts 4:4). It would be necessary for a system of instruction to be set up. This would center around Jesus' messianic fulfillment

of Old Testament prophecies, particularly His ministry and Passion. In particular the commands of Jesus—His "oral Torah"—were to be taught (Matt. 28:20).

According to fairly strong church tradition, Mark's Gospel is directly related to Peter's preaching. Acts 10:36-43 seems to reinforce this tradition, for many have seen the Marcan outline in this example of Peter's preaching. Since Peter's preaching is basically the outline and content of the Gospel of Mark, John—having been with Peter for many years—would have been completely familiar with this body of truth.

This core of early apostolic Jerusalem preaching and teaching came to be written down by Mark who helped Peter in his later ministry. After John was in Jerusalem for many years (perhaps 20) he went to Asia Minor and settled in Ephesus. When John wrote his Gospel he provided, by the Spirit of God, a rich supplement to the early Jerusalem core. Thus John's distinctive portrait of Jesus contains 93 percent original material in comparison to the Synoptics. As John wrote, he was aware that even his contribution contained only a small fraction of what could be said (John 20:30-31; 21:25). (For more on the interrelatedness of the Gospels see the *Introduction* to Matthew and the *Introduction* to Mark.)

The Text. The Greek text of the Fourth Gospel, as well as that of the entire New Testament, is in very good condition. The reader of the NIV will notice certain changes in some places in comparison to the KJV. This reflects the fact that in the years since the publication of the KJV in 1611 new manuscripts and new theories pertaining to textual transmission have enabled scholars to do a better job in ascertaining what the original writings, though not extant, actually said. The two most notable places where the NIV varies from the KJV in John are 5:3b-4 (which is in the NIV marg.) and 7:53–8:11 (which is set off from the main body of the NIV text). These will be discussed in the commentary.

The Structure and Theme. The key word in the Gospel of John is "believe" (*pisteuō*), which occurs 98 times. The Greek noun "faith" (*pistis*) does not occur. (A few times, however, the NIV translates the Gr. verb with the Eng. "put . . . faith in.") The Greek verb *pisteuō* is frequently used in the present tense and in participial forms. Apparently John wanted to stress an active, continuous, and vital trust in Jesus. The book can be divided into the following main sections: Prologue (1:1-18), Book of Signs (1:19–12:50), Farewell Instructions (chaps. 13–17), Passion and Resurrection (chaps. 18–20), Epilogue (chap. 21). The Prologue sets forth the theological introduction, which enables readers to understand that the words and deeds of Jesus are the words and deeds of God manifest in the flesh. The Book of Signs records seven miracles which reveal the Father's glory in the Son. The miracles with their explanatory discourses progressively draw out two responses: faith, and unbelief and hardening in sin.

As Jesus' public ministry closed, irrational unbelief was the people's major response (12:37). Jesus in His farewell instructions prepared His own for His coming death and His followers' future ministry. The culmination of unbelief is evident in the Passion section, and the faith of the disciples is evident in the Resurrection account. The Epilogue completes the Gospel by showing the plans of the Lord for His disciples.

OUTLINE

I. The Prologue (1:1-18)
   A. The Logos in eternity and time (1:1-5)
   B. The witness of John the Baptist (1:6-8)
   C. The coming of the Light (1:9-13)
   D. The Incarnation and revelation (1:14-18)
II. Jesus' Manifestation to the Nation (1:19–12:50)
   A. Jesus' early ministry (1:19–4:54)
   B. Jesus' controversy in Jerusalem (chap. 5)
   C. Jesus' revelation in Galilee (6:1–7:9)
   D. Jesus' return to Jerusalem and the resumption of hostility (7:10–10:42)
   E. The great sign at Bethany (11:1-44)
   F. The plot to kill Jesus (11:45-57)
   G. The conclusion of Jesus' public ministry (12:1-36)
   H. Jewish national unbelief (12:37-50)
III. Jesus' Preparation of His Disciples (chaps. 13–17)
   A. The Last Supper (13:1-30)
   B. Jesus' coming departure (13:31-38)
   C. Jesus, the Way to the Father (14:1-14)
   D. Jesus' promise of the Counselor (14:15-31)
   E. The Vine and the branches (15:1-10)
   F. Jesus' friends (15:11-17)
   G. The world's hatred (15:18–16:4)
   H. The Spirit's work (16:5-15)
   I. The prediction of changes (16:16-33)
   J. Jesus' intercession (chap. 17)
IV. Jesus' Passion and Resurrection (chaps. 18–20)
   A. The arrest of Jesus (18:1-11)
   B. The religious trial and Peter's denials (18:12-27)
   C. The civil trial (18:28–19:16)
   D. The Crucifixion (19:17-30)
   E. The burial (19:31-42)
   F. The empty tomb (20:1-9)

COMMENTARY

I. The Prologue (1:1-18)

All four Gospels begin by placing Jesus within a historical setting, but the Gospel of John is unique in the way it opens. The Book of Matthew begins with the genealogy of Jesus that connects Him to David and Abraham. Mark starts with the preaching of John the Baptist. Luke has a dedication of his work to Theophilus and follows that with a prediction of the birth of John the Baptist. But John begins with a theological prologue. It is almost as if John had said, "I want you to consider Jesus in His teaching and deeds. But you will not understand the good news of Jesus in its fullest sense unless you view Him from this point of view. Jesus is God manifest in the flesh, and His words and deeds are those of the God-Man."

The prologue contains many of the major themes of the Gospel which are later reintroduced and developed more fully. The key terms include "life" (v. 4), "light" (v. 4), "darkness" (v. 5), "witness" (v. 7), "true" (v. 9), "world" (v. 9), "Son" (v. 14), "Father" (v. 14), "glory" (v. 14), "truth" (v. 14). Two other key theological terms are "the Word" (v. 1) and "grace" (v. 14), but these important words are used in John only in this theological introduction. "Word" (*Logos*) does occur elsewhere in the Gospel but not as a Christological title.

A. The Logos in eternity and time (1:1-5)

1:1. As far back as man can think, **in the beginning . . . the Word** was existing. The term "Word" is the common Greek word *logos*, which meant "speaking, a message, or words." "Logos" was widely used in Greek philosophical teaching as well as in Jewish wisdom literature and philosophy. John chose this term because it was familiar to his readers, but he invested it with his own meaning, which becomes evident in the prologue.

The Word was with God in a special relationship of eternal fellowship in the Trinity. The word "with" translates the Greek *pros*, which here suggests "in company with" (cf. the same use of *pros* in 1:2; 1 Thes. 3:4; 1 John 1:2). John then added that **the Word was God.** Jehovah's Witnesses translate this clause, "The Word was a god." This is incorrect and logically is polytheism. Others have translated it "the Word was divine," but this is ambiguous and could lead to a faulty view of Jesus. If this verse is correctly understood, it helps clarify the doctrine of the Trinity. The Word is eternal; the Word is in relationship to God (the Father); and the Word is God.

1:2. The Word has always been in a relationship **with God** the Father. Christ did not at some point in time come into existence or begin a relationship with the Father. In eternity past the Father (God) and the Son (the Word) have always been in a loving communion with each other. Both Father and Son are God, yet there are not two Gods.

1:3. Why is there something rather than nothing? That is a great question in philosophy. The Christian answer is God. He is eternal, and He is the Creator of **all things.** And the Word was the agent of Creation (cf. 1 Cor. 8:6; Col. 1:16; Heb. 1:2). All Creation was **made** by the Word in relation with the Father and the Spirit. John stressed the work of the Word. He came to reveal the Father (John 1:14, 18); and the work of revelation began in Creation for Creation reveals God (Ps. 19:1-6; Rom. 1:19-20).

1:4. Life is man's most important asset. To lose life is tragic. John affirmed that in the ultimate sense, **life is in** Christ. Man's spiritual and physical **life** come from Him. (For John's teaching on life, cf. 5:26; 6:57; 10:10; 11:25; 14:6; 17:3; 20:31.) Jesus, the Source of "life" (cf. 11:25), is also **the light of men** (cf. 8:12). Light is commonly used in the Bible as an emblem of God; darkness is commonly used to denote death, ignorance, sin, and separation from God. Isaiah described the coming of salvation as the people living in darkness seeing a great light (Isa. 9:2; cf. Matt. 4:16).

1:5. Light's nature is to shine and dispel **darkness.** Darkness is almost personified in this verse: darkness is unable to overpower light. By this, John summarized his Gospel record: (a) **Light** will invade the dominion of **darkness.** (b) Satan the ruler and his subjects will resist the light, but they will be unable to frustrate its power. (c) The Word will be victorious in spite of opposition.

B. The witness of John the Baptist (1:6-8)

1:6. In addition to the eternal Word, **a man** came on the stage of history: **his name was John.** This John did not author this Gospel but was the great forerunner of Jesus known as John the Baptist. He **was sent from God,** which was the secret of his importance. Like the Old Testament prophets he was equipped and commissioned by God for special ministry.

1:7. The word **witness** (both as a noun [*martyria*] and verb [*martyreō*]) is important in this Gospel (cf. v. 15, 32, 34; 3:11, 26; 5:31-32, 36-37; 18:37; 19:35; etc). (See the chart with the comments on 5:33-34.) John the Baptist was sent for people's benefit to be an additional pointer to the truth of Jesus, the Revealer of the Father. People in sin are in such darkness that they need someone to tell them what is **light.** John's goal was that **all men might** come to trust in Jesus.

1:8. John the Baptist was great, but **he . . . was not the Light.** Some evidence suggests that the movement begun by John the Baptist continued after his death and even after the death and resurrection of Jesus (4:1; cf. Mark 6:29; Luke 5:33). Twenty years after Jesus' resurrection (cf. Acts 18:25; 19:1-7) Paul found about 12 disciples of John the Baptist in Ephesus. A Mandaean sect still continues south of Baghdad which, though hostile to Christianity, claims an ancestral link to the Baptist.

C. The coming of the Light (1:9-13)

1:9. This has been called the Quaker's text because of that group's erroneous use of it and their stress on the "inner light." The words **was coming** (*erchome-*non) may refer to every man (as in the NIV marg.) or to Christ, **the true Light** (as in the NIV text). The latter is preferred, for it suggests the Incarnation.

Christ **gives light to every man.** This does not mean universal salvation or general revelation or even inner illumination. Instead, it means that Christ as the Light shines (*phōtizei*) on each person either in salvation or in illuminating him with regard to his sin and coming judgment (3:18-21; 9:39-41; cf. 16:8-11).

1:10. The **world** (*kosmos*) means the world of men and human society which is now in disobedience to God and under the rulership of Satan (cf. 14:30). The *Logos* came among people in the Incarnation, but mankind **did not recognize** its Maker (cf. Isa. 1:2-3). The failure to recognize (*egnō*, "know") **Him** was not because God's nature was somehow "hidden" in people, as some suggest. Rather, it is because of human ignorance and blindness, caused by sin (John 12:37).

1:11. In some ways this is one of the saddest verses in the Bible. The *Logos* went to **His own** home **but** He had no welcome. Jesus went to **His own** people, the nation Israel, but they as a whole rejected Him. In rejecting **Him,** they refused to accept Him as the Revelation sent by the Father and refused to obey His commands. Isaiah long before had prophesied of this Jewish national unbelief: "Who has believed our message?" (Isa. 53:1)

1:12. That unbelief, however, was not universal. Some **received** Jesus' universal invitation. **To all who** accepted Jesus as the Revealer of the Father's will and as the Sacrifice for sin, **He gave the right to become children of God.** The word "right" (*exousian*) is a needed improvement over the KJV's "power," and "children" (*tekna*) is better than the KJV's "sons." People are not naturally children of God but can become so by receiving the gift of the new birth.

1:13. The new birth does **not** come by **natural descent** (lit., "of bloods"), **nor** is it the result **of a human decision** (lit., "the will of the flesh," i.e., the natural human desire for children), nor is it the result of **a husband's will.** The birth of a child of God is not a natural birth; it is a supernatural work **of God** in regeneration. A person welcomes Jesus and responds in faith and obedience to Him, but the mysterious work of the Holy Spirit is "the cause" of regeneration (3:5-8).

D. The Incarnation and revelation (1:14-18)

1:14. The Word (*Logos*; cf. v. 1) **became flesh.** Christ, the eternal *Logos*, who is God, came to earth as man. Yet in doing so, He did not merely "appear" like a man; He became one (cf. Phil. 2:5-9). Humanity, in other words, was added to Christ's deity. And yet Christ, in becoming "flesh," did not change; so perhaps the word "became" (*egeneto*) should be understood as "took to Himself" or "arrived on the scene as."

"Flesh" in this verse means a human nature, not sinfulness or weakness. In the Greek the words **lived for a while among us** recall God's dwelling with Israel in the Old Testament. The word "lived" is *eskēnōsen*, from *skēnē* ("tabernacle"). Much as God's presence was in the tabernacle (Ex. 40:34), so Jesus dwelt among people.

We have seen most naturally implies that the author was an eyewitness. **His glory** refers to the unique splendor and honor seen in Jesus' life, miracles, death, and resurrection. **The one and only Son** (*monogenous*; cf. John 1:18; 3:16, 18; 1 John 4:9) means that Jesus is the Son of God in a sense totally different from a human who believes and becomes a child of God. Jesus' sonship is unique for He is eternal and is of the same essence as **the Father.** The glorious revelation of God which the *Logos* displayed was **full of grace and truth,** that is, it was a gracious and truthful revelation (cf. John 1:17).

1:15. John the Baptist gave a continuing testimony to Jesus. The present tense of the Greek verbs **testifies** and **cries out** stresses this. Jesus was younger and began His ministry later than John. But John said that because of His preexistence (and thus His true nature) **He . . . has surpassed me.**

1:16. The Word made flesh is the source of grace (*charin*), which is the sum total of all the spiritual favors God gives to people. The words **we . . . all** refer to Christians and include John the author. Because of **the fullness of His grace . . . one blessing after another** (*charin anti charitos*, lit., "grace in place of grace") comes to Christians as waves continue to

come to the shore. The Christian life is the constant reception of one evidence of God's grace replacing another.

1:17. The greatness of the old dispensation was the giving of **the Law** by God **through** His servant **Moses.** No other nation has had such a privilege. But the glory of the church is the revelation of God's **grace and truth . . . through Jesus Christ** (cf. v. 14).

1:18. The statement **No one has ever seen God** (cf. 1 John 4:12) may seem to raise a problem. Did not Isaiah say, "My eyes have seen the King, the LORD Almighty"? (Isa. 6:5) God in His essence is invisible (1 Tim. 1:17). He is One "whom no one has seen or can see" (1 Tim. 6:16). But John 1:18 means, "no one has ever seen God's essential nature." God may be seen in a theophany or anthropomorphism but His inner essence or nature is disclosed only in Jesus.

God the only Son is literally "the unique God" or "the only begotten God" (*monogenēs theos*; cf. *monogenous*, "the one and only" in v. 14). John was probably ending his prologue by returning to the truth stated in verse 1 that the Word is God. Verse 18 is another statement affirming Christ's deity: He is unique, the one and only God. The Son **is at the Father's side,** thus revealing the intimacy of the Father and the Son (cf. the Word was "with God," vv. 1-2). Furthermore, the Son **has made . . . known** (*exēgēsato*, whence the Eng. "exegeted") the Father. The Son is the "exegete" of the Father, and as a result of His work the nature of the invisible Father (cf. 4:24) is displayed in the Son (cf. 6:46).

II. Jesus' Manifestation to the Nation (1:19–12:50)

This major part of John's Gospel describes the public ministry of Jesus to the nation Israel. It is a "book of signs," a narrative of seven of Jesus' miracles that point to Him as the Messiah. Along with the signs are public discourses explaining the significance of the signs and two long private interviews (chaps. 3–4).

A. Jesus' early ministry (1:19–4:54)

1. EARLY TESTIMONIES TO JESUS (1:19-34)

a. John's first witness (1:19-28)

1:19. As in the Synoptic Gospels, the ministry of John the Baptist was so influential that the authorities in **Jerusalem** decided to investigate him. **The Jews** is the author's title for the city's leaders. The **priests and Levites** went **to ask** about his baptism and what he claimed for himself.

1:20-21. John said, **I am not the Christ** (i.e., the Messiah). (See comments on vv. 40-41 about the meaning of the title "Messiah.") This was his confession, as stressed by the repetition of the verb (in Gr.) **confessed.**

Interestingly in response to their questions John's answers were progressively shorter: "I am not the Christ" (v. 20); **I am not** (v. 21); **No** (v. 21). He did not want to talk about himself, for his function was to point to Another. John had an Elijah-type ministry. He appeared on the scene suddenly and even dressed like **Elijah.** He sought to turn people back to God as Elijah did in his day. And Malachi had predicted that Elijah would return before Messiah's coming (Mal. 4:5). Therefore many speculated that John was Elijah. **The Prophet** was expected because of Deuteronomy 18:15 (referring to Christ; cf. John 1:45). Some wrongly understood that the coming "prophet" was to be distinct from the Messiah (v. 24; 7:40-41).

1:22-23. John replied that he was not any of the expected prophetic figures. He explained, however, that his ministry was described in the Old Testament. He was **the voice** (*phōnē*), while Jesus is the Word (*Logos*). John's function was one of preparation, and it was carried on in **the desert.** (On the meaning of John's quotation from Isa. 40:3, see the comments on Matt. 3:3.)

1:24-25. The **Pharisees** were an important sect of Judaism. They numbered about 6,000 and were most influential. They held a strict interpretation of the Law and embraced many oral traditions. The Pharisees were the only minor group to survive the Jewish war of A.D. 66-70, and their teachings formed the basis for Talmudic Judaism. Their question to the Baptizer was, in essence, "Since you have no official title, **why** are you baptizing?"

1:26-27. John knew that his baptizing work was only anticipatory. He explained that another **One** was coming who was unknown to them. That coming **One** is so great that John considered himself unworthy to do even the lowliest service for Him (such as untying His **sandals**).

1:28. The site of **Bethany on the other side of the Jordan** River is now unknown. (It is not to be confused with another Bethany, home of Mary, Martha, and Lazarus, near Jerusalem.) As early as A.D. 200, Origen, when visiting Palestine, could not find it. A probable site is opposite Jericho.

b. John's second witness (1:29-34)

1:29. John's second witness started at the beginning of a series of days (cf. **The next day** in vv. 29, 35, 43; and "On the third day" in 2:1) when Jesus' first disciples were called and came to faith. **John** identified **Jesus** as **the Lamb of God** (cf. 1:36; 1 Peter 1:19). The connection to the Old Testament sacrifices is probably general. The sin offering which bore the sins of the nation on the Day of Atonement was a goat (Lev. 16). Daily offerings were normally lambs, but they did not atone for sin. The Passover lamb (Ex. 12) and Isaiah's mention of the Messiah's likeness to a lamb (Isa. 53:7) may have been in John's mind. John, by the Holy Spirit, saw Jesus as the sacrificial Victim who was to die for **the sin of the world** (cf. Isa. 53:12).

1:30-31. John repeated here what he had said earlier about Jesus (vv. 15, 27). John's fame was to be superseded by that of Jesus, whose priority stems from His preexistence: **He was before me.** But why did John say, **I myself did not know Him?** Though John and Jesus were related, as Mary and Elizabeth were relatives (Luke 1:36), nothing is known of any contacts between them in their years of childhood and adolescence. John did not know that Jesus was the coming One until He was revealed by the Father. All John knew was that he was to prepare the way for Him by **baptizing with water.** God would send His Man **to Israel** in His good time.

1:32. The baptism of Jesus is not recorded in John's Gospel, but the material of the Synoptic Gospels is assumed (see "John's Distinctive Portrait" in the *Introduction*). The Fourth Gospel does not state that this descent of **the Spirit** like **a dove** occurred at Jesus' baptism. The significant thing is that the invisible Spirit came **from heaven** and manifested Himself in a bodily (dovelike) form. John saw the Spirit as a dove **remain on** Jesus (cf. Isa. 11:2; Mark 1:10).

1:33. John had been **told** by God **(the One who sent** him) that when this sign of the dove would occur, the Person so marked out by the Spirit's coming and presence would be the One who would **baptize** by that same **Holy Spirit.** Cleansing by water is one thing, but the cleansing produced by the Spirit is of another order. Later at Pentecost, 50 days after Jesus' resurrection, the baptism with the Holy Spirit brought in a new Age (Acts 1:5; 2:1-3), the Church Age, the "Age of the Spirit" (cf. 1 Cor. 12:13).

1:34. John's testimony was **that this is the Son of God.** The prophesied Davidic King was God's Son (2 Sam. 7:13), and the messianic King is uniquely the Son of God (Ps. 2:7). The title "Son of God" goes beyond the idea of obedience and messianic King to that of Jesus' essential nature. In the Fourth Gospel this title is not applied to believers. They are called "children" (*tekna*; e.g., John 1:12) while "Son" (*hyios*) is used only of Jesus.

2. THE DISCIPLES OF JESUS (1:35-51)

a. Jesus' first disciples (1:35-42)

1:35-36. The next day refers to the second day in this series (cf. vv. 29, 35, 43; 2:1). The most likely reason for this chronological notation is that the author had a particular interest in narrating how some disciples came from their positions as adherents in John's party to faith in **Jesus.** The verb tenses in 1:35-36 are unusual. **John was there** (lit., "stood," perf. tense) while Jesus was **passing by** (pres. tense). The action in God's economy was shifting from John's baptism to the ministry of Jesus. John pointed **his disciples** to Jesus as God's **Lamb** (cf. comments on v. 29).

1:37. Two of John's **disciples heard** the witness of the Baptist and **followed Jesus.** The word "followed" probably has a double meaning here. They followed Him in the sense of literal walking and also as His disciples, that is, they turned their allegiance to Jesus that day.

1:38. The first words the disciples heard from **Jesus** were, **What do you want?** In one sense Jesus was asking a simple question and the disciples responded with a request for information as

to **where** He lived. But the author seemed to imply more. Perhaps Jesus was also asking, "What are you seeking in life?" The word translated **staying** (*menō*) is a favorite word of John's. This Greek word occurs here in his writings for the first time. Of the 112 New Testament passages in which it occurs, 66 are in his writings— 40 in the Gospel of John, 23 in 1 John, and 3 in 2 John (William F. Arndt and F. Wilbur Gingrich, *A Greek-English Lexicon of the New Testament and Other Early Christian Literature.* Chicago: University of Chicago Press, 1957, pp. 504-5). Sometimes, as here, it means "to stay or dwell" in a place; a few times it means "to last or continue"; but more often it has a theological connotation: "to remain, continue, abide" (e.g., John 15:4-7).

1:39. Jesus' words of invitation were, **Come . . . and you will see.** A person must first come to Him; then he will see. In addition to their seeing where He stayed, these words may possibly also have a deeper theological implication. The two disciples remained with Him **that day,** beginning at **the 10th hour.** That hour was 4 P.M. or 10 A.M., depending on whether the Fourth Gospel counted days from 6 A.M. (as the Synoptics customarily did) or from midnight or noon. The 10 A.M. times seems better and was the official Roman usage (cf. comments on 4:6; 19:14).

1:40-41. Andrew, one of the two disciples who **followed Jesus,** was the first proclaimer of Jesus as **the Messiah.** In Hebrew, "Messiah" means "the anointed One," which in Greek is translated **Christ** (*ho Christos*). The idea of "the anointed One" comes from the Old Testament practice of anointing priests and kings with oil. This was symbolic of the Spirit and pointed to the future One who would come (cf. Isa. 61:1). The title "Messiah" came to be used of the future Davidic King (cf. Matt. 1:1; John 6:15). In bringing **his brother Simon** Peter to Christ, no man did the church a greater service than Andrew. Andrew appeared two more times in John (6:4-9; 12:20-22); both times he was bringing someone to Jesus. The unnamed disciple is commonly held to be John the son of Zebedee, a brother of James and author of this Gospel. In Mark 1:16-20 two pairs of brothers (Simon and Andrew, James and John) who were fishermen were called by Jesus.

1:42. When **Jesus . . . looked at** Simon (cf. v. 47), He knew the man's character and destiny. Jesus gave him the Aramaic name **Cephas. Peter** is the Greek translation of Cephas ("rock"). Simon's name in Hebrew was probably Simeon (Gr. in Acts 15:14; 2 Peter 1:1; cf. NIV marg.). No reason is given here for the change of his name from Simon to Cephas. The common understanding is that his name indicates what God by His grace would do through him. He would be a rock-like man in the church during its early years (cf. Matt. 16:18; Luke 22:31-32; John 21:15-19; Acts 2–5; 10–12).

b. Jesus' call of Philip and Nathanael (1:43-51)

1:43-44. Though the first disciples were from Galilee, **Jesus** had called them in Judea where they were with the Baptist. On His way north to **Galilee, He** called **Philip** to be His disciple. Philip's hometown **of Bethsaida** was on the northeast side of the Sea of Galilee (called "Bethsaida in Galilee" in 12:21). Also **Andrew and Peter** were born there. Politically, Bethsaida in lower Gaulonitis in the territory of Herod Philip (Josephus *The Antiquities of the Jews* 18. 2. 1). Philip's name is Greek but his nationality cannot be inferred from that fact.

1:45. Philip's testimony to **Nathanael** stressed that Jesus is **the** Promised **One** of whom **Moses** (Deut. 18:18-19; cf. John 1:21, 25) and **the prophets** (Isa. 52:13–53:12; Dan. 7:13; Micah 5:2; Zech. 9:9) **wrote.** Surprisingly Philip called **Jesus . . . the son of Joseph.** But this is what the disciples would have believed at this time. Yet Nathanael would soon recognize that He is "the Son of God" (John 1:49).

1:46. Nathanael momentarily stumbled over the lowly origin of the Messiah. **Nazareth! Can anything good come from there?** Nathanael knew of the poor reputation of Nazareth. Surely the Messiah would come from Jerusalem, Hebron, or some other prominent city. Jesus' condescension still remains a puzzle to many people. How can the *Logos* be a Man? **Philip** was wise enough not to argue, he gently invited his friend to meet Jesus: **Come and see.** He knew

that Nathanael's questions would then be resolved.

1:47. Jesus, having supernatural knowledge (cf. v. 42), called **Nathanael . . . a true Israelite, in whom there is nothing false** (*dolos,* "deceitful") unlike Jacob (cf. v. 51 with Gen. 28:12).

1:48. Nathanael was puzzled as to **how** Jesus knew about him. **Jesus** said He knew exactly what Nathanael was doing **before Philip** came up to him; he was **under the fig tree.** This expression often meant to have safety and leisure (cf. 1 Kings 4:25; Micah 4:4; Zech. 3:10). Perhaps here the fig tree was a place for meditation (cf. comments on John 1:50-51). Psalm 139 elaborates on the theme of God's knowledge of a person's life in every detail.

1:49. Jesus' supernatural knowledge moved **Nathanael** to confess Him as **the Son of God** and **the King of Israel.** This does not mean that Nathanael at this early date fully understood the Trinity or the Incarnation. Rather He understood Jesus to be the Son of God in the messianic sense (cf. Ps. 2:6-7). This future Davidic King would have God's Spirit on Him (Isa. 11:1-2) and thus would have supernatural knowledge.

1:50-51. Jesus promised Nathanael a **greater** basis for belief, probably referring to the miracles in chapters 2–13. From 1:48, 51 it can be inferred that Nathanael was meditating on Jacob's life, particularly on the incident recorded in Genesis 28:12. Jacob saw the angels going up and down a ladder. But Nathanael would **see . . . the angels of God ascending and descending on the Son of Man.** Just as Jacob saw angels from heaven communicating with earth, so Nathanael (and the others; though **you** is sing. in John 1:50, the **you** in v. 51 is pl.) would see Jesus as the divine Communication from heaven to earth. The Son of Man, replacing the ladder, is God's link with earth (cf. Dan. 7:13; Matt. 26:64). Perhaps Jesus was also indicating that He is the new "Bethel," God's dwelling place (Gen. 28:17; John 1:14).

As the Son of Man, Jesus left heaven to come to the earth. Jesus used the term "Son of Man" of Himself more than 80 times. It speaks of His humanity and suffering and His work as "the ideal Man." **I tell you the truth** ("Verily, verily," KJV; lit., "Amen, Amen") occurs

THE MIRACLES OF JESUS

Order	Miracle	Place	Matthew	Mark	Luke	John
1	Turning water into wine	Cana				2:1-11
2	Healing an official's son	Capernaum				4:46-54
3	Delivering a demoniac in the synagogue	Capernaum		1:21-28	4:33-37	
4	Healing Peter's wife's mother	Capernaum	8:14-15	1:29-31	4:38-39	
5	First miraculous catch of fish	Sea of Galilee			5:1-11	
6	Cleansing a leper	Galilee	8:2-4	1:40-45	5:12-15	
7	Healing a paralytic	Capernaum	9:1-8	2:1-12	5:17-26	
8	Healing an infirm man at the Pool of Bethesda	Jerusalem				5:1-15
9	Healing a withered hand	Galilee	12:9-13	3:1-5	6:6-11	
10	Healing a centurion's servant	Capernaum	8:5-13		7:1-10	
11	Raising a widow's son	Nain			7:11-17	
12	Casting out a blind and dumb spirit	Galilee	12:22-32		11:14-23	
13	Stilling a storm	Sea of Galilee	8:18-27	4:35-41	8:22-25	
14	Delivering a demoniac of Gadara	Gadara	8:28-34	5:1-20	8:26-39	
15	Healing a woman with a hemorrhage	Capernaum	9:20-22	5:25-34	8:43-48	
16	Raising Jairus' daughter	Capernaum	9:18-26	5:22-43	8:41-56	
17	Healing two blind men	Capernaum	9:27-31			
18	Casting out a dumb spirit	Capernaum	9:32-34			
19	Feeding the 5,000	Near Bethsaida	14:13-21	6:32-44	9:10-17	6:1-14
20	Walking on the water	Sea of Galilee	14:22-33	6:45-52		6:15-21
21	Casting out a demon from a Syrophoenician's daughter	Phoenicia	15:21-28	7:24-30		
22	Healing a deaf person with a speech impediment	Decapolis		7:31-37		
23	Feeding the 4,000	Decapolis	15:32-38	8:1-9		
24	Healing a blind man of Bethsaida	Bethsaida		8:22-26		
25	Casting out a demon from a lunatic boy	Mount Hermon	17:14-21	9:14-29	9:37-42	
26	Finding money in a fish's mouth	Capernaum	17:24-27			
27	Healing a man born blind	Jerusalem				9:1-7
28	Healing a woman infirm for 18 years	Perea(?)			13:10-17	
29	Healing a man with dropsy	Perea			14:1-6	
30	Raising Lazarus	Bethany				11:1-44
31	Cleansing 10 lepers	Samaria			17:11-19	
32	Healing blind Bartimaeus	Jericho	20:29-34	10:46-52	18:35-43	
33	Cursing a fig tree	Jerusalem	21:18-19	11:12-14		
34	Healing Malchus' ear	Jerusalem			22:49-51	
35	Second miraculous catch of fish	Sea of Galilee				21:1-13

25 times in John and always calls attention to important affirmations: 1:51; 3:3, 5, 11; 5:19, 24-25; 6:26, 32, 47, 53; 8:34, 51, 58; 10:1, 7; 12:24; 13:16, 20-21, 38; 14:12; 16:20, 23; 21:18. Interestingly this double "Amen" does not occur in the Synoptic Gospels.

3. JESUS' FIRST SIGN (2:1-11)

Jesus' first miracle in the Gospel of John was a private one, known only to His disciples, some servants, and probably Jesus' mother. If Matthew had not yet been called to be one of the Twelve, this may explain why the miracle is not recorded in the Synoptics. Of the four Gospel writers only John was there. John used the word "signs" (*sēmeiōn,* v. 11) because he was seeking to draw attention away from the miracles as such and to point up their significance. A miracle is also a "wonder" (*teras*), a "power" (*dynamis*), and a "strange event" (*paradoxos*).

This turning water into wine was the first of 35 recorded miracles Jesus performed. (See the chart listing those miracles, the places where they happened, and the references in the Gospels.)

2:1. On the third day probably means three days after the calling of Philip and Nathanael. (Cf. the sequence of days suggested by "the next day" in 1:29, 35, 43.) It would take a couple of days to reach **Cana in Galilee** from Bethany near Jericho of Judea (1:28). Cana was near Nazareth, though its exact location is unknown. **Jesus' mother was there,** but John did not give her name (cf. 2:12; 6:42; 19:25-27). In his Gospel, John never named himself or the mother of Jesus. (Jesus' mother went to the home of the beloved disciple John [19:27].)

2:2-3. Oriental wedding feasts often lasted seven days. The feast followed the groom's taking of his bride to his home or his father's house, before the consummation of the marriage. When the supply of **wine** was used up, Mary turned to Jesus in hope that He could solve the problem. Did Mary expect a miracle? In the light of verse 11 this is not likely. Mary had not yet seen any miracles done by her Son.

2:4-5. The word **woman** applied to His mother may seem strange to a modern reader, but it was a polite, kind expression (cf. 19:26). However, the clause, **Why do you involve Me?** was a

common expression in Greek that referred to a difference in realms or relations. Demons spoke these words when they were confronted by Christ ("What do You want with us?" [Mark 1:24]; "What do You want with me?" [Mark 5:7]). Mary had to learn a painful lesson (cf. Luke 2:35), namely, that Jesus was committed to God the Father's will and the time for His manifestation was in the Father's hand. **My time has not yet come** or similar words occur five times in John (2:4; 7:6, 8, 30; 8:20). Later the fact that His time had come is mentioned three times (12:23; 13:1; 17:1). Mary's response **to the servants (Do whatever He tells you)** revealed her submission to her Son. Even though she did not fully understand, she trusted Him.

2:6-8. The water in the **six . . . water jars** (of **20 to 30 gallons** each) was **used** for Jewish purification rites before and after meals (cf. Matt. 15:1-2). The contrast between the old order and the new way is evident (cf. John 4:13; 7:38-39).

Probably the water jars were outside. **The master of the banquet,** in charge of the festivities, would not know he was drinking from the purification jars. For a Jew this would be unthinkable. The servants dipped out the water, which had become wine.

2:9-10. As **the master of the banquet tasted the . . . wine,** he found it to be superior to what they had been drinking. In contrast with a common custom in which the best **wine** was served **first** and the lesser quality later, he affirmed that this wine, served last, was the **best.** The significance of this miracle is that Christianity is an advance over Judaism. God has kept the best gift—His Son—until **now.**

2:11. The significance of the miracle was explained by John as a manifestation of Christ's **glory.** In contrast with the ministry of Moses who turned water into blood as a sign of God's judgment (Ex. 7:14-24), Jesus brings joy. His first miracle was a gracious indication of the joy which He provides by the Spirit. The sign points to Jesus as the Word in the flesh, who is the mighty Creator. Each year He turns water to wine in the agricultural and fermentation processes. Here He simply did the process immediately. The 120 gallons of fine wine were His gift to the young couple. The first miracle—a transformation—pointed to the kind of transforming ministry Jesus would have (cf. 2 Cor. 5:17). **The disciples put their faith in Him.** This initial faith would be tested and developed by a progressive revelation of Jesus, the *Logos*. At this point they did not understand His death and resurrection (John 20:8-9) but they did know His power.

4. JESUS' CAPERNAUM VISIT (2:12)

2:12. Jesus' move **to Capernaum** on the northwest shore of the Sea of Galilee **for a few days** marks an interlude in His life. Though Capernaum is northeast of Cana, **He went down** because of the decline in land elevation toward the sea. Capernaum became His home base (cf. Matt. 4:13; Mark 1:21; 2:1). From this point on He seemed to be alienated from His family (Mark 3:21, 31-35; John 7:3-5) and His hometown of Nazareth (Mark 6:1-6; Luke 4:14-30).

5. JESUS' FIRST MINISTRY IN JERUSALEM (2:13–3:21)

a. Jesus' cleansing of the temple (2:13-25)

John recorded a cleansing of the temple at the beginning of Jesus' ministry whereas the three Synoptics recorded a temple cleansing toward the end of His public ministry (Matt. 21:12-13; Mark 11:15-16; Luke 19:45-46). Probably there were two cleansings, for there are differences in the narrations. John was undoubtedly aware of the Synoptics, and he supplemented them. The first cleansing caught the people by surprise. The second cleansing, about three years later, was one of the immediate causes of His death (cf. Mark 11:15-18).

2:13-14. As was the custom for the **Jewish** people (Ex. 12:14-20, 43-49; Deut. 16:1-8) **Jesus went up to Jerusalem** to celebrate the **Passover** (cf. two other Passover feasts—one in John 6:4 and one in John 11:55; 12:1; 13:1). This reminded them of God's grace in delivering them from the bondage in Egypt. It was a fitting time for His ministry.

The temple courts refer to a large courtyard, the Court of the Gentiles, surrounding the temple enclosure. (See the sketch of the temple.) The buying and **selling** of animals in the area was probably rationalized as a convenience for the pilgrims coming into Jerusalem. But abuses developed, and the pilgrim

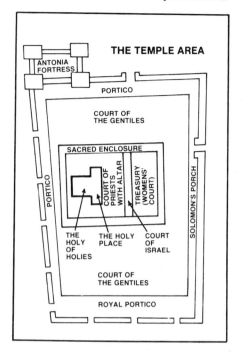

THE TEMPLE AREA

ANTONIA FORTRESS

PORTICO

COURT OF THE GENTILES

SACRED ENCLOSURE

PORTICO

COURT OF PRIESTS WITH ALTAR

TREASURY (WOMENS' COURT)

SOLOMON'S PORCH

THE HOLY OF HOLIES

THE HOLY PLACE

COURT OF ISRAEL

COURT OF THE GENTILES

ROYAL PORTICO

traffic became a major source of income for the city. With **money** to be made, worship easily became corrupted. The money changers were another convenience for the pilgrims. Temple dues had to be paid in the acceptable Tyrian coinage, and a high percentage was charged for changing coins.

2:15. Malachi predicted that One would come suddenly to **the temple** to purify the religion of the nation (Mal. 3:1-3). In moral indignation Jesus started a small stampede of the **sheep and cattle,** and **overturned** the **tables.**

2:16. Jesus protested the turning of His **Father's house into a market.** He did not protest the sacrificial system itself. The purpose of the sacrifices was in danger of being lost. In the second cleansing of the temple toward the end of His ministry, Jesus' attack was sharper. Then He called the temple area "a den of robbers" (Luke 19:46; cf. Jer. 7:11). Jesus frequently referred to God as "My Father." Only through Jesus can the Father be known. "No one knows the Father except the Son and those to whom the Son chooses to reveal Him" (Matt. 11:27).

2:17. Jesus' **disciples remembered** Psalm 69:9, which speaks of the fact that the Righteous One would pay a price for

His commitment to God's temple. This **zeal for** God would ultimately lead Him to His death.

2:18-19. The Jews—either the Jewish authorities or the merchants—**demanded** some proof for His right **to** challenge the existing order ("Jews demand miraculous signs," 1 Cor. 1:22). But instead of giving in to their demand, **Jesus** gave a veiled saying. As with His parables in the Synoptics, one purpose of an enigmatic saying was to puzzle the hearers who opposed Him. He desired that His hearers ponder the saying in order to perceive its significance. **Destroy this temple** is in the form of a command, but the sense is ironic or conditional. At Jesus' trial He was accused of saying He could destroy the temple and **raise it again in three days** (Matt. 26:60-61). A similar charge was made against Stephen (Acts 6:14).

2:20-21. Herod the Great decided to replace the temple of Zerubbabel because it was not of the same glory as that of Solomon's (Hag. 2:3). Since work on Herod's **temple** began in 20 or 19 B.C., **46 years** bring the date to A.D. 27 or 28. The work on the whole temple complex continued until around A.D. 63. The statement of **the Jews** meant either that the sanctuary was completed in 46 years or else one phase had been completed. How then, the Jews asked, could He rebuild **it in three days?** That would be impossible! The Greek words for **and You** are emphatic, suggesting their contempt for Him. Of course by **the temple** Jesus meant **His body** which, after his death, would be resurrected in three days.

2:22. Even Jesus' own **disciples** did not understand His enigmatic saying at first. It took the light of the Resurrection to illuminate it. They did not see the need for His death, so they did not think along these lines until after the event. Nor did they understand the Scriptures which speak of the Messiah's suffering and death (Isa. 52:12–53:12; Luke 24:25-27).

2:23. While . . . **in Jerusalem** during **the Passover,** Jesus did other **signs** which John chose not to describe. The effect of these miracles (which were probably healings) was to elicit faith on the part of **many people.** They **believed in His name,** that is, they trusted in Him. This was not necessarily saving faith as the next verse implies. They believed He was a great Healer, but not necessarily a great Savior from sin.

2:24-25. Jesus knew that a temporary excitement or a faith based on signs was not sufficient. Many of the early followers later turned back when He did not take up the role of a political king (cf. 6:15, 60, 66). Until His death and resurrection and the coming of the Holy Spirit, the foundation for faith was not fully laid. Having supernatural knowledge, Jesus does **not need** human help to evaluate **men.** As God, He sees beyond the superficial to people's hearts (1 Sam. 16:7; Ps. 139; Acts 1:24). John 3 and 4 give illustrations of this truth. He knew Nicodemus' need, and He told the Samaritan woman about her past (4:29). The connection of chapter 3 to chapter 2 is evident (cf. **in a man** [2:25], and "Now there was a man" [3:1]).

b. Jesus' interview with Nicodemus (3:1-21)

3:1. Nicodemus represented the best in the nation. He was a teacher (v. 10), a Pharisee, and **a member of** the Sanhedrin, **the Jewish ruling council.** The Sanhedrin had 70 members who were responsible for religious decisions and also, under the Romans, for civil rule. Two Sanhedrin members who appear in a favorable light in the New Testament are Joseph of Arimathea (19:38) and the Rabbi Gamaliel (Acts 5:34-39; 22:3). The Sanhedrin put Jesus on trial (Luke 22:66). Nicodemus later rebuked the Pharisees for condemning Jesus without hearing Him (John 7:50-51), and he helped Joseph of Arimathea bury Jesus (19:39-40).

3:2. Why did Nicodemus go **to Jesus at night?** Because of fear? Because it was the normal time for visits? Because he wanted a time of uninterrupted conversation without the distractions of the ever-present crowds? John did not say why. And yet nighttime has a sinister tone in the Fourth Gospel (cf. 9:4; 11:10; 13:30; 19:39). Nicodemus began, **Rabbi, we know You are a Teacher who has come from God.** "We" probably means the favorable ones on the council. The titles "Rabbi" and "Teacher" are polite and flattering on one hand, but they showed Nicodemus' inadequate comprehension of who Jesus is. The words "from God" are in an emphatic position in the Greek.

The **signs** had pointed out Jesus as God's Man (**God** was **with Him**), and Nicodemus wanted to talk to Him as one Rabbi to another.

3:3. But **Jesus** was not on the same level with Nicodemus. He is "from above" (*anōthen;* v. 31); therefore Nicodemus must be born "from above" (v. 3, NIV marg.; *anōthen*). To be **born again** or born "from above" (*anōthen* has both meanings; e.g., "from above" in 19:11 and "again" in Gal. 4:9) is to have a spiritual transformation which takes a person out of the kingdom of darkness into **the kingdom of God** (cf. Col. 1:13). The kingdom is the sphere or realm of God's authority and blessing which is now invisible but will be manifested on earth (Matt. 6:10).

3:4. **Nicodemus** was certain Jesus did not mean something absurd (such as a reincarnation or a **second** physical birth), but yet he did not grasp the nature of regeneration.

3:5. Various views are given to explain Jesus' words about being **born of water and the Spirit:** (1) The "water" refers to the natural birth, and the "Spirit" to the birth from above. (2) The "water" refers to the Word of God (Eph. 5:26). (3) The "water" refers to baptism as an essential part of regeneration. (This view contradicts other Bible verses that make it clear that salvation is by faith alone; e.g., John 3:16, 36; Eph. 2:8-9; Titus 3:5.) (4) The "water" is a symbol of the Holy Spirit (John 7:37-39). (5) The "water" refers to the repentance ministry of John the Baptist, and the "Spirit" refers to the application by the Holy Spirit of Christ to an individual.

The fifth view has the merit of historical propriety as well as theological acceptability. John the Baptist had stirred the nation by his ministry and stress on repentance (Matt. 3:1-6). "Water" would remind Nicodemus of the Baptist's emphasis. So Jesus was saying that Nicodemus, in order to **enter the kingdom,** needed to turn to Him (repent) in order to be regenerated by the Holy Spirit.

3:6-7. There are two distinct realms: one is of fallen man (the **flesh**) and the other is of God (**the Spirit**). A fallen person cannot regenerate himself; he needs a divine operation. Only God's Holy Spirit can regenerate a human spirit.

People should not stumble at or reject the importance of Jesus' words. They **must be born** from above. The necessity is absolute and is universally binding.

3:8. This verse contains a wordplay which cannot be adequately expressed in English. The Greek word *pneuma* means both wind and Spirit. The work of **the Spirit** (*pneuma*) is invisible and mysterious like the blowing of **the wind** (*pneuma*). Man controls neither.

3:9-10. Nicodemus asked . . . how this spiritual transformation takes place. **Jesus** answered that Nicodemus, as the **teacher** of Israel (the Gr. has the article "the"), ought to know. The Old Testament prophets spoke of the new Age with its working of the Spirit (Isa. 32:15; Ezek. 36:25-27; Joel 2:28-29). The nation's outstanding teacher ought to **understand** how God by His sovereign grace can give someone a new heart (1 Sam. 10:6; Jer. 31:33).

3:11. But Nicodemus was ignorant of the realm of which Jesus spoke. He represented the nation's unbelief and lack of knowledge. Jesus, like the prophets, spoke to the nation about divine themes but the Jews rejected His witness. "Witness" (or **testimony;** *martyrian*) is a common word in John's Gospel (see the chart at 5:33-34).

3:12. Since Nicodemus could not grasp the basic teaching of regeneration which Jesus presented in **earthly** analogies, how could he understand and **believe** the more abstract **heavenly** matters such as the Trinity, the Incarnation, and Jesus' coming glorification?

3:13. **No one has ever gone into heaven** and then come back to earth, able to give clear teaching about divine matters. The one exception is Jesus who is **the Son of Man** (cf. 1:50-51; Dan. 7:13; Matt. 26:64). He is the "Ladder" between heaven and earth with access to both realms (cf. comments on John 1:50-51). He "descended" in the Incarnation and "ascended" in the Ascension. He also was in **heaven** before the Incarnation, and therefore knows the divine mysteries.

3:14-15. The thought of elevation to heaven (v. 13) leads to the thought of Jesus being **lifted up** (cf. 8:28; 12:32). **Moses** raised a bronze **snake** on a pole as a cure for a punishment due to disobedience (cf. Num. 21:4-9). So Jesus would **be**

lifted up on a cross for people's sin, so that a look of faith gives eternal life to those doomed to die.

3:16. Whether this verse was spoken by John or Jesus, it is God's Word and is an important summary of the gospel. God's motivation toward people is love. God's love is not limited to a few or to one group of people but His gift is for the whole world. God's love was expressed in the giving of His most priceless gift—His unique Son (cf. Rom. 8:3, 32). The Greek word translated one and only, referring to the Son, is *monogenē*, which means "only begotten," or "only born-one." It is also used in John 1:14, 18; 3:18; and 1 John 4:9. On man's side, the gift is simply to be received, not earned (John 1:12-13). A person is saved by believing, by trusting in Christ. Perish (*apolētai*) means not annihilation but rather a final destiny of "ruin" in hell apart from God who is life, truth, and joy. Eternal life is a new quality of life, which a believer has now as a present possession and will possess forever (cf. 10:28; 17:3).

3:17. Though light casts shadows, its purpose is to illuminate. Though those who do not believe are condemned, God's purpose in sending His Son is salvation (to save), not damnation (to condemn). God does not delight in the death of the wicked (Ezek. 18:23, 32). He desires that everyone be saved (1 Tim. 2:4; 2 Peter 3:9).

3:18. The instrumental means of salvation is believing in the finished work of Jesus on the cross. But people who reject the light of the *Logos* are in the dark (1:5; 8:12) and are therefore already under God's judgment. They stand condemned. They are like those sinful, dying Israelites who willfully rejected the divine remedy (Num. 21:4-9). A believer in Christ, on the other hand, is under "no condemnation" (Rom. 8:1); he "will not be condemned" (John 5:24).

3:19. Men love darkness not for its own sake but because of what it hides. They want to continue undisturbed in their evil (*ponēra*, "wicked"; cf. v. 20 which has a different word for evil) deeds. A believer is also a sinner (though a redeemed one), but he confesses his sin and responds to God (cf. 1 John 1:6-7). In the ultimate sense, man's love of darkness rather than God the Light (John 1:5, 10-11; 1 John 1:5) is his love for idols. He

worships and serves "created things rather than the Creator" (Rom. 1:25).

3:20. Just as natural light shows up what is otherwise unseen, so Christ the Light exposes people's deeds as "evil." (The word "evil" here is *phaula* ["worthless"], also used by John in 5:29.) Unbelievers have no ultimate meaning of life, no worthy motivation, no adequate goal, and a destiny of doom. Yet everyone who does evil hates the light (as well as loves darkness, 3:19). He fears that if he comes to the light his deeds will be seen as worthless, and he would need to turn from them.

3:21. Jesus is like a magnet. His people are drawn to Him and welcome His revelation. Though the light rebukes their sin, they respond in repentance and faith. They live by the truth (cf. 2 John 1-2, 4; 3 John 1, 4). By regeneration they live differently than their former lives of darkness. Their new lives are by faith in Jesus and His Word. And the Spirit, working in their lives, gives them new power, goals, and interests (2 Cor. 5:17; Eph. 2:10).

6. THE FINAL TESTIMONY OF JOHN THE BAPTIST (3:22-30)

3:22-24. For a short time the ministry of John the Baptist overlapped Jesus' ministry. Thus the Judean countryside must have been alive with the teaching of both these great preachers of repentance and God's kingdom. Both John and Jesus had disciples, large crowds followed both of them, and both baptized. The statement that Jesus "baptized" (vv. 22, 26) probably means He was overseeing the baptizing done by His disciples (4:2). The site of Aenon near Salim is unknown today but a likely location is about midway between the Sea of Galilee and the Dead Sea (and about three miles east of Shechem). Both groups were baptizing and thus two "reform" movements were popular. This was before John was put in prison (3:24). This statement reveals how the Fourth Gospel supplements the Synoptics. It implies that readers knew about John's imprisonment from reading the other Gospels (Matt. 14:1-12; Mark 6:14-29; Luke 3:19-20) or from common church tradition.

3:25. The zealous disciples of John the Baptist found themselves at a disadvantage in an argument. A certain Jew asked why he should join **John's** group. He (and others; cf. "They" in v. 26) argued about **ceremonial washing.** Since there were Essene lustrations and Pharisaic washings, why should Jews follow another washing, John's baptism? Besides, the group following Jesus was larger (v. 26).

3:26. John's disciples may have been angry and jealous. (They were interested in John's movement and were not committed to Jesus.) They complained that Jesus, of whom **John** had **testified,** had now captured the nation's attention. They longed for the former days when **everyone** went to hear John (Mark 1:5).

3:27. John's greatness is revealed in his reply. He said, **A man can receive only what is given him from heaven.** God is sovereign in bestowing His blessings on one's ministry. If Jesus' movement was expanding, then it must have been in the will of God. This principle of God's sovereignty is stressed in John (cf. 6:65; 19:11) as well as elsewhere in the New Testament (e.g., 1 Cor. 4:7).

3:28. John also reminded his disciples that they were forgetting part of his teaching. For he had clearly taught that he was **not the** promised Messiah **but** was only **sent ahead** by God to do a work of preparation for the Messiah (1:8, 15, 20, 23).

3:29-30. In Jesus' growing influence, John found his own **joy** fulfilled. He illustrated this for his disciples by referring to a custom at Near Eastern weddings. **The friend** of **the bridegroom** was only an assistant, not the main participant in the marriage. The assistant acted on behalf of **the bridegroom** and made the preliminary arrangements for the ceremony. His **joy** came when he heard the bridegroom coming for his bride. John the Baptist's work was to prepare for the arrival of Christ, the "Groom." John baptized only with water, not with the Spirit. Therefore Jesus **must become greater** and John **must become less.** This was not merely advisable or fortuitous; it was the divine order. John willingly and with **joy** accepted Jesus' growing popularity as God's plan.

7. THE TESTIMONY OF JOHN THE EVANGELIST (3:31-36)

The quotation marks in the text of the NIV are a modern innovation and the judgment of translators. The original Greek manuscripts did not have any quotation marks. As the NIV margin indicates, the closing quotation marks could be placed after verse 30 rather than at the end of verse 36. It seems better to view this section (vv. 31-36) as the testimony of John the Evangelist because the theological exposition about the Father and the Son is more a feature of Christian theology than a part of John the Baptist's testimony.

3:31. Here John the Evangelist developed the theme about the supremacy of Jesus, which John the Baptist spoke of to his followers (vv. 28-30). Since Jesus has come from heaven, His words surpass those of any religious teacher. Each human teacher is limited by his earthly boundaries (he **belongs to the earth and** is **from the earth**). But the *Logos* **from heaven is above all;** He is preeminent (Col. 1:18).

3:32. What Jesus spoke came from His previous vision of and communion with the Father in heaven (cf. 1:1, 14). Yet in spite of this clear reliable witness, mankind as a whole has rejected His message (cf. 1:11).

3:33. The message of Jesus has not been universally rejected as verse 32 by itself might indicate. One who receives it gives his attestation or certification to the fact **that God is truthful** (cf. v. 21). To reject this testimony is to call God a liar (1 John 5:10).

3:34. Jesus gives the perfect truth of God as He **speaks the words of God,** because He has the full endowment of the Holy Spirit, **the Spirit without limit.** The Old Testament prophets had the Spirit only for limited times and for limited purposes.

The Apostle John referred to Jesus as **the One whom God has sent.** Thirty-nine times the Gospel of John refers to Jesus being sent from God (vv. 17, 34; 4:34; 5:23-24, 30, 36-38; 6:29, 38-39, 44, 57; 7:16, 28-29; 8:16, 18, 26, 29, 42; 9:4; 10:36; 11:42; 12:44-45, 49; 13:16, 20; 14:24; 15:21; 16:5; 17:3, 18, 21, 23, 25; 20:21). This affirms Jesus' deity and heavenly origin, as well as God's sovereignty and love in initiating the Son's Incarnation (cf. Gal. 4:4; 1 John 4:9-10, 14).

3:35. The relationship between **the Son** and **the Father** is one of loving

CONTRASTS BETWEEN NICODEMUS AND THE SAMARITAN WOMAN (JOHN 3–4)

	Nicodemus	Samaritan Woman
PLACE	(Jerusalem) Judah	Samaria
TIME	By night	About 6 P.M.
OCCASION	Planned visit	By chance
CONTENT	Theological	Practical
INITIATOR	Nicodemus	Jesus
ETHNIC GROUP	Jew	Samaritan (mixed blood)
SOCIAL STATUS	Highly respected ruler, teacher	Despised woman (immoral)
SEX	Male	Female
ATTITUDE	Polite, calling Jesus Rabbi	First hostility, then respect
FORM	Nicodemus faded out, dialogue became monologue	Dialogue carried to the end
RESULT	Not mentioned	Woman converted, witnessed, and people came to believe

intimacy and complete confidence. The Son is endowed with all authority to accomplish the Father's purposes (5:22; Matt. 28:18).

3:36. Man has only two options: trust **in the Son** or reject **the Son** (cf. vv. 16, 18). Unbelief is tragic ignorance but it is also willful disobedience to clear light. **God's wrath** is mentioned only here in the Fourth Gospel (but cf. Rev. 6:16-17; 11:18; 14:10; 16:19; 19:15). "Wrath," God's necessary righteous reaction against evil, **remains** (*menei*) on the unbeliever. This wrath is future but it also exists now. Endless sin and disobedience will result in endless punishment (Matt. 25:46).

8. JESUS' MINISTRY IN SAMARIA (4:1-42)

a. Jesus' interview with a Samaritan woman (4:1-26)

4:1-3. In Greek these verses are one long sentence, introducing the reader to a second long interview by Jesus. The words, **When the Lord learned of this** (v. 3), are actually the first phrase in Greek in verse 1. The sudden prominence of **Jesus,** evidenced by the growth of His followers, caused **the Pharisees** to take special notice of Him. Since Jesus was working on God's schedule, He knew

how His ministry would end. Until that appointed time, He must live carefully, so He withdrew from the conflict until His "hour" (7:6, 8, 30; 8:20; cf. 12:23; 13:1; 17:1). **He left Judea** (cf. 3:22) **and went back . . . to Galilee.**

This second interview is another illustration of the fact that "He knew what was in a man" (2:25). The Samaritan woman contrasts sharply with Nicodemus. He was seeking; she was indifferent. He was a respected ruler; she was an outcast. He was serious; she was flippant. He was a Jew; she was a despised Samaritan. He was (presumably) moral; she was immoral. He was orthodox; she was heterodox. He was learned in religious matters; she was ignorant. Yet in spite of all the differences between this "churchman" and this woman of the world, they both needed to be born again. Both had needs only Christ could meet.

4:4. He had to go through Samaria. This was the shortest route from Judea to Galilee but not the only way. The other route was through Perea, east of the Jordan River. (See the two routes on the map.) In Jesus' day the Jews, because of their hatred for the Samaritans, normally took the eastern route in order to avoid Samaria. But Jesus chose the route through Samaria in order to reach the despised people of that region. As the Savior of the world He seeks out and saves the despised and outcasts (cf. Luke 19:10).

"Samaria" in New Testament times was a region in the middle of Palestine, with Judea to the south and Galilee to the north. Samaria was without separate political existence under the Roman governor. The people were racially mixed and their religion resulted from syncretism and schism from Judaism. Its center of worship was Mount Gerizim. Even today in Israel, a small group of Samaritans maintain their traditions.

4:5-6. The village of **Sychar** was **near** Shechem. Most identify the site with modern Akar but others point to Tell-Balatah. Sychar was between Mount Ebal and Mount Gerizim. A well near Sychar today may be the same as **Jacob's well. The plot of ground** which **Jacob** gave to **Joseph** is mentioned in Genesis 48:21-22. Jacob had purchased it years earlier (Gen. 33:18-20). **Jesus, tired** from walking, **sat down by the well. It was about the sixth hour,** which according to Roman time reckoning would have been 6 P.M. (See comments on John 1:39; 19:14.) Jesus being truly human, experienced thirst, weariness, pain, and hunger. Of course He also possesses all the attributes of Deity (omniscience, omnipotence, etc.).

4:7-8. With His **disciples** in the city buying **food,** Jesus did a surprising thing: He spoke to **a Samaritan woman,** whom He had never met. She was of the region of Samaria, not the town of Samaria. The woman was shocked to hear a Jewish man ask for **a drink** from her. The normal prejudices of the day prohibited public conversation between men and women, between Jews and Samaritans, and especially between strangers. A Jewish Rabbi would rather go thirsty than violate these proprieties.

4:9. Surprised and curious, the **woman** could not understand **how** He would dare **ask** her **for a drink,** since **Jews** did **not associate with Samaritans.** The NIV margin gives an alternate translation to the Greek sentence with the word *synchrōntai* ("associate" or "use together"): the Jews "do not use dishes Samaritans have used." This rendering may well be correct. A Rabbinic law of A.D. 66 stated that Samaritan women were

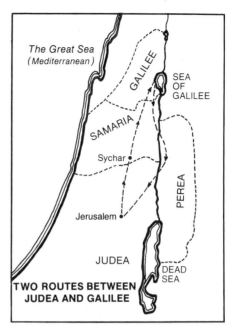

The Great Sea (Mediterranean)

SEA OF GALILEE

GALILEE

SAMARIA

Sychar

PEREA

Jerusalem

JUDEA

DEAD SEA

TWO ROUTES BETWEEN JUDEA AND GALILEE

considered as continually menstruating and thus unclean. Therefore a Jew who drank from a Samaritan woman's vessel would become ceremonially unclean.

4:10. Having captured her attention and stimulated her curiosity, **Jesus** then spoke an enigmatic saying to cause her to think. It was as if He had said, "Your shock would be infinitely greater if you really knew who I am. *You*—not I—would be asking!" Three things would have provoked her thinking: (1) **Who is** He? (2) What is **the gift of God?** (3) What is **living water?** "Living water" in one sense is running water, but in another sense it is the Holy Spirit (Jer. 2:13; Zech. 14:8; John 7:38-39).

4:11-12. She misunderstood the "living water" and thought only of water from **the well.** Since Jacob's **well** was so **deep** how could Jesus **get this living water?** Today this well is identified by archeologists as one of the deepest in Palestine. **Are You greater than our father Jacob?** she asked. In Greek this question expects a negative answer. She could not conceive of Him as greater than Jacob. Her claim "our father Jacob" is interesting in light of the fact that the Jews claim him as the founder of *their* nation. That well had great tradition behind it but, she wondered, *What does this Stranger have?*

4:13-14. **Jesus** began to unveil the

truth in an enigmatic statement. **This water** from Jacob's well would satisfy only bodily thirst for a time. But **the water** Jesus gives provides continual satisfaction of needs and desires. In addition one who **drinks** His living water **will** have within **him a spring of** life-giving **water** (cf. 7:38-39). This inner spring contrasts with the water from the well, which required hard work to acquire. Jesus was speaking of the Holy Spirit who brings salvation to a person who believes and through Him offers salvation to others.

4:15. **The woman** could not grasp this dark saying because of her sin and materialism. All she could understand was that if she had a spring she would not **get thirsty and** would not have to work so hard.

4:16-18. Since she was not able to receive His truth (1 Cor. 2:14), Jesus dealt with her most basic problem. (Apparently she never served Him a drink. He forgot His own physical need in order to meet her spiritual need.) Jesus suggested she get her **husband and** bring him **back** with her. This suggestion was designed to show her that He knew everything about her (cf. John 2:24-25). Her marital history was known to this Stranger, including the fact that she was living in sin. Thus in a few words **Jesus** had revealed her life of sin and her need for salvation.

4:19-20. Her response was most interesting! Jesus was not just a passing Jewish Rabbi. Since He had supernatural knowledge, He must be **a prophet** of God. But instead of confessing her sin and repenting, she threw out an intellectual "red herring." Could He solve an ancient dispute? Samaritan religion held that the one place of divinely ordered **worship** was **on** top of nearby Mount Gerizim, whereas the **Jews** said it was on the temple mount **in Jerusalem.** Who was right in this controversy?

4:21. **A time is coming** (cf. v. 23) referred to the coming death of **Jesus** which would inaugurate a new phase of worship in God's economy. In the Church Age, because of the work of the Spirit, **worship** is no longer centered in temples like those on Mount Gerizim and Mount Zion.

4:22. Jesus was firm in His declaration of the issues involved. The Samaritan religion was confused and in error: **You**

Samaritans worship what you do not know. They were not the vehicle for the salvation of mankind. Israel was the nation chosen by God to have great privileges (Rom. 9:4-5). When Jesus said, **Salvation is from the Jews,** He did not mean that all Jews were saved or were especially pious. "Salvation is from the Jews" in the sense that it is available through Jesus, who was born of the seed of Abraham.

4:23. With the advent of the Messiah the **time** came for a new order of **worship. True worshipers** are those who realize that Jesus is the Truth of God (3:21; 14:6) and the one and only Way to the Father (Acts 4:12). To worship **in truth** is to worship God through Jesus. To worship **in Spirit** is to worship in the new realm which God has revealed to people. **The Father** is seeking true **worshipers** because He wants people to live in reality, not in falsehood. Everybody is a worshiper (Rom. 1:25) but because of sin many are blind and constantly put their trust in worthless objects.

4:24. God is Spirit is a better translation than the KJV's "God is a Spirit." God is not one Spirit among many. This is a declaration of His invisible nature. He is not confined to one location. **Worship** of God can be done only through the One (Jesus) who expresses God's invisible nature (1:18) and by virtue of the Holy **Spirit** who opens to a believer the new realm of the kingdom (cf. 3:3, 5; 7:38-39).

4:25. The Samaritans expected a coming messianic leader. But they did not expect Him to be an anointed king of the Davidic line, since they rejected all the Old Testament except the Pentateuch. Based on Deuteronomy 18:15-18, they expected a Moses-like figure who would solve all their problems. The Samaritan **woman** now understood a part of what Jesus said. She wistfully longed for the messianic days when the **Messiah** would **explain everything.**

4:26. This self-declaration by Jesus Himself—**I . . . am He** (the Messiah)—is unusual. Normally in His ministry in Galilee and Judea (cf. 6:15) because of political implications, He veiled His office and used the title "Son of Man." But with this Samaritan the dangers of revolt by national zealots were not a problem.

b. Jesus' instruction of His disciples (4:27-38)

4:27-30. The woman, excited by Jesus' statement about Himself and because of the arrival of the **disciples,** left and **went** to the village. In her joy of discovery she forgot **her water jar.** It was more important to her now to share her new faith. Her words **A Man who told me everything I ever did,** were bound to stir interest. Perhaps in that village some who heard her had been partners in her past life. Perhaps they wondered, *Could this One also know about us?*

Could this be the Christ? she asked them. More literally, her question was, "This couldn't be the Messiah, could it?" The question expected a tentative negative answer. She framed the question this way, in all probability, because she knew the people would not respond favorably to a dogmatic assertion from a woman, especially one of her reputation. Just as Jesus had captured her attention by curiosity, so she raised the people's curiosity. They decided to investigate this matter.

4:31-32. As the **disciples** spoke with Jesus, they sensed something had happened. Before, He was tired and thirsty. But now food and drink were not important to Him. His mood had changed. They offered Him food, but He gave them instruction. **I have food to eat that you know nothing about** is another of His enigmatic statements.

4:33-34. The disciples' misunderstanding set the stage for Him to clarify His statement. As usual, the **disciples** were confined to thinking materialistically. **Jesus said, My food . . . is to do the will of Him who sent Me.** This does not mean Jesus had no need of physical **food,** but rather that His great passion and desire was to do God's will (cf. 5:30; 8:29). He knows that man does not live by bread alone, but "by every word that comes from the mouth of the Lord" (Deut. 8:3). His priority is spiritual, not material. It is the Father's **work** which must be done (cf. John 17:4).

4:35. Farmers have a period of waiting between their sowing and their reaping. **Four months more and then the harvest** was probably a local proverb. But in the spiritual realm there is no long wait. Jesus has come so now it is the day of opportunity. All that is needed is spiritual vision and perception. If the disciples would **look** around, they would see people with spiritual hunger. The Samaritans in their white garments coming from the village (v. 30) may have visually suggested a wheat field **ripe for harvest.**

4:36-38. As reapers, the disciples had the great and rewarding privilege of leading people to faith in Christ. **Others** had already **done** the **work** of sowing. This perhaps refers to the ministry of the Old Testament prophets or to John the Baptist's ministry of preparation. Both kinds of workers—**the sower and the reaper**—get their pay. Reapers harvest **the crop for eternal life,** that is, Jesus' disciples were involved in ministry to others, in the issue of death and life (2 Cor. 2:15-16).

Harvesttime in the ancient world was a time of joy (Ruth 3:2, 7; Isa. 9:3). There is also great joy at the time of salvation (cf. Luke 15:7, 10, 32). The disciples had the greater joy of seeing the completion of the process (John 4:38). A sower has a harder time because he sees no immediate fulfillment. John the Baptist stirred a nation to repent but he died before the day of Pentecost, when the disciples in great joy saw thousands come to faith in Jesus.

c. The repentance of the Samaritans (4:39-42)

4:39. The little revival among **the Samaritans** is notable because the theme of natural rejection by Israel had been sounded (1:11) as well as the note of a wider ministry (3:16; cf. Acts 1:8). The **testimony** of the woman, though, from one point of view was unnecessary ("not that I accept human testimony," John 5:34); yet it was effective. That Jesus knows what is in a person and that He has comprehensive knowledge of one's life is an indication of His deity (Ps. 139; John 1:47-49; 2:24-25).

4:40-41. The witness of the woman led to the Samaritans' personal confrontation with Jesus. **He stayed** with them **two days.** The word "stayed" (from *menō,* "to remain, to abide") is a favorite Johannine theological term (cf. 3:36; 6:56; 15:4; etc.; and comments on 1:38). **Because of His words many more became believers.**

"Words" is singular in Greek ("His word"). His message was the cause of their faith. Personal testimony plus the message of Jesus is still God's means of salvation.

4:42. Faith based simply on the testimony of another is only secondary. True faith moves to its own experience and confrontation with Jesus. **We have heard for ourselves** is the more adequate basis. Jesus **is the Savior of the world,** not in the sense that everyone will be saved (universalism) but that His light shines for all (1:9). The light is not limited to the nation Israel, but is for "every nation, tribe, people, and language" (Rev. 7:9).

9. THE OFFICIAL'S SON (4:43-54)

4:43-45. After His **two**-day ministry in Samaria, Jesus and His disciples continued north into **Galilee. Now Jesus Himself had pointed out that a prophet has no honor in his own country.** This proverbial saying mentioned by Jesus (cf. Matt. 13:57; Mark 6:4) is cited by the author John. Is His "own country" Judea or Galilee? Or is His "own country" heaven, with His being rejected in His "own land" Israel? Generally Galilee was more favorable to Him, but even there men tried to kill Him (Luke 4:18-30). John was perhaps preparing his readers for the upcoming rejection; he may have been saying that even with the warm reception Jesus received **in Galilee,** He still was not really accepted (cf. John 2:24-25; 4:48). They had been impressed by His clearing the temple **at the Passover feast** (2:13-22) and His miracles (2:23). But the people's enthusiasm for the Healer (cf. Mark 5:21, 24b) did not always indicate they had faith in Him (Mark 6:1-6).

4:46-47. The **certain royal official** is not identified. He could have been a Gentile or a Jew, a centurion, or a minor official in Herod's court. Possibly he was a Jew because Jesus included him among the people who desire signs and wonders (v. 48; cf. 1 Cor. 1:22). **His son** had been **sick,** and undoubtedly he had exhausted all the local means at his disposal. Failure of position and money to solve his problem drove him from **Capernaum** to the village of **Cana,** 20 to 25 miles away, hoping that the Healer would save his **son** from **death.**

4:48. Jesus' address to him, though sharp, was necessary. A faith built only on miraculous signs is not a complete faith (cf. 2:23-25). Many **(you people)** hesitate to **believe** in Jesus apart from seeing **miraculous signs** (*sēmeia*) **and wonders** (*terata*). Faith in **Jesus** is absolutely necessary, but not all believers are given public portents (cf. Matt. 16:1-4; 1 Cor. 1:22).

4:49. The **official** was in no position emotionally to argue his case theologically. All he could plead for was mercy, for his **child** was at the point of death.

4:50. Jesus' calm reply to the official's desperate request created a crisis. **Jesus** announced, **You may go. Your son will live.** If the official really believed that Jesus could make a difference in Capernaum, he must also believe Him now in Cana. So he **took Jesus at His word** and left.

4:51-53. On the way back the official must have pondered Jesus' promise every step of his journey. **His servants met him with** good **news. His boy was living.** The official asked **when** his son recovered. The healing was no accident, for it occurred at **the exact** moment Jesus made His promise to him. It was at the **seventh hour,** which by Roman time was 7:00 in the evening. The man's faith grew, and he brought **all his household** to faith. The lesson of this incident is that Jesus' power is able to save from death even at a great distance. His Word has power to work; people are simply to believe His Word.

4:54. Both signs **in Galilee** (changing the water into wine [2:1-11] and healing the official's son) demonstrate that Jesus is the Promised One. Yet both signs had a certain hidden aspect to them. Only the disciples and some servants saw His miracle at the wedding, and this healing was not in public view.

B. *Jesus' controversy in Jerusalem (chap. 5)*

1. JESUS' HEALING OF A PARALYTIC (5:1-15)

5:1. Jesus . . . later returned **to Jerusalem for a feast.** The feast is not named (some mss. read "the feast"), but it may have been the Passover. Jesus attended three other Passovers (2:23; 6:4; 11:55). John probably intended only to give a reason why Jesus was in Jerusalem.

5:2. To the north of the temple area was **a pool . . . called Bethesda** (see the map showing the pool's location). The excavations of a pool **near the Sheep Gate** have uncovered **five** porticoes or **covered colonnades,** confirming the accuracy of the description given here in the Fourth Gospel. The pool was actually two pools next to each other.

5:3a. The **great number of disabled people** pictures the sad spiritual plight of the world.

5:3b-4. The earliest manuscripts omit these words which appear to be a late insertion to explain why the pool water was "stirred" (v. 7). People believed that an angel came and stirred it. According to local tradition, the first one in the water would be healed. But the Bible nowhere teaches this kind of superstition, a situation which would be a most cruel contest for many ill people. No extant Greek manuscript before A.D. 400 contains these words.

5:5. Jesus picked a certain invalid on a Sabbath Day (v. 9) at a feast time, a man who had been afflicted **for 38 years.** John did not say what kind of physical problem he had or if he was **an invalid** from birth. In any case his condition was hopeless.

5:6. The word **learned** does not mean that **Jesus** received facts from others. It means that He perceived the situation by His knowledge (the Gr. is *gnous,* "knowing"; cf. 1:48; 2:24-25; 4:18). Jesus' seemingly strange question, **Do you want to get well?** was designed to focus the man's attention on Him, to stimulate his will, and to raise his hopes. In the spiritual realm man's great problem is that either he does not recognize he is sick (cf. Isa. 1:5-6; Luke 5:31) or he does not want to be cured. People are often happy, for a while at least, in their sins.

5:7. The man replied that he lacked not the desire but the means to be healed. Without strength and without friends, he could not be helped **when the** pool **water** was **stirred.** He had tried but without success.

5:8. Jesus then **said . . . Get up! Pick up your mat and walk.** His command carried with it the required enablement. As with dead Lazarus (11:43), Jesus' word accomplished His will. This illustrates conversion. When people obey His command to believe, God works in and through His Word.

5:9-10. God's supernatural power

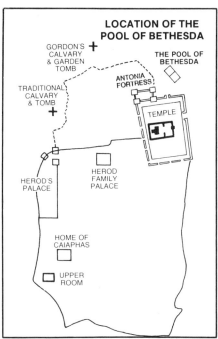

LOCATION OF THE POOL OF BETHESDA

GORDON'S CALVARY & GARDEN TOMB
THE POOL OF BETHESDA
ANTONIA FORTRESS
TRADITIONAL CALVARY & TOMB
TEMPLE
HEROD FAMILY PALACE
HEROD'S PALACE
HOME OF CAIAPHAS
UPPER ROOM

was evident in the man's instantaneous cure. **He picked up his mat and walked.** Muscles long atrophied were completely restored. Isaiah prophesied that in the days of the Messiah the lame would "leap like a deer" (Isa. 35:1-7). Here in Jerusalem was a public sign that the Messiah had come.

The Sabbath was a central issue in the conflicts between Jesus and His opponents (cf. Mark 2:23; 3:4). The Mosaic Law required that work cease on the seventh day. Additional laws were added by later Jewish religious authorities, which became very complicated and burdensome. These human traditions often obscured the divine intention in God's Law. "The Sabbath was made for man" (Mark 2:27) so that he could have rest and a time for worship and joy. The Jews' rigid tradition (not the Old Testament) taught that if anyone carried anything from a public place to a private place on the Sabbath intentionally, he deserved death by stoning. In this case the man who was healed was in danger of losing his life.

5:11. The healed man realized this difficulty and tried to evade any responsibility for violating tradition by saying he was just following orders.

5:12-13. The authorities were naturally interested in the identity of **this**

fellow who told the invalid to violate their rules. But the man . . . had no knowledge of Jesus. This seems to be a case in which healing was done in the absence of faith. The invalid was chosen by **Jesus** as an act of grace because of his need and also to display God's glory in him. Jesus then had slipped away into the crowd (cf. 8:59; 10:39; 12:35), so momentarily He was unknown.

5:14-15. Jesus later found the healed man in the temple area. This implied that Jesus sought him out in order to speak to him. The ex-paralytic seemed to have no gratitude to Jesus: his conduct put him in a bad light. Jesus' warning (**Stop sinning or something worse may happen to you**) does not mean that his paralysis was caused by any specific sin (cf. 9:3), though all disease and death come ultimately from sin. The warning was that his tragic life of 38 years as an invalid was no comparison to the doom of hell. Jesus is interested not merely in healing a person's body. Far more important is the healing of his soul from sin.

2. THE DISCOURSE (5:16-47)

5:16. Jesus was doing these things on the Sabbath. In addition to the case of the invalid's healing (5:1-15), John later recorded the cure of a blind man on the Sabbath (chap. 9). The grain-picking (Mark 2:23-28), the healing of a shriveled hand (Mark 3:1-5), curing a woman who had been crippled for 18 years (Luke 13:10-17), and healing a man with dropsy (Luke 14:1-6)—all these took place on the Sabbath. As seen in these passages, Jesus' theology or philosophy of the Sabbath differed from that of His opponents. His opponents in the controversy were progressively humiliated while the crowds favored Him. The opponents' response was to persecute Jesus by opposing Him and trying to kill Him (John 5:16, 18; 7:19, 25).

5:17. God rested on the seventh day (Gen. 2:2-3) from His work of Creation. But Jesus pointed to the continuous **work** of God as a justification for His Sabbath activity. God sustains the universe, begets life, and visits judgments. It is not wrong for His Son to do works of grace and mercy on the Sabbath. The words **My Father** should be noted. Jesus did not say "your Father" or even "our Father." His

opponents did not miss His claim to Diety.

5:18. The Sabbath controversy was enough to cause them to hate Jesus, but the implication of His claim that God is **His own Father** was impossible for them to accept. To them, God has no equals. Jesus' claim, in their thinking, was a monstrous blasphemy. To be **equal with God** suggested, they thought, two gods and therefore polytheism. To make oneself "equal with God" was a claim of arrogant independence. In the Talmud four persons were branded as haughty because they made themselves equal to God: pagan rulers Hiram, Nebuchadnezzar, Pharaoh, and the Jewish King Joash.

5:19. Jesus explained that He is not independent of or in opposition to **the Father.** His activity is not self-initiated. The **Father** directs and has sent **the Son.** The Son's activity imitates the Father, and the Two always work together. (See comments on 1:51 for the clause I **tell you the truth.**)

5:20. The Son is in no way independent of or in rebellion against **the Father.** Their relationship is one of continuous love. The Son is not doing simply a part of God's will; He has a full disclosure of all the Father's works. By the Father, the Son will do even more amazing works **than** physical healings.

5:21. One of the prerogatives of Deity is the right over **life** and death. (A king of Israel asked Naaman, "Am I God? Can I kill and bring back to life?" [2 Kings 5:7]) One of Jesus' "greater" works (John 5:20) is the giving of life. **The Son gives life to whom He is pleased to give it,** just as He chose to heal one man out of a crowd of disabled people. The giving of life includes spiritual (eternal) life and a resurrected body. The resuscitation of Lazarus (chap. 11) would illustrate both.

5:22. The Son's ability to give life is coupled with His right to judge mankind (cf. v. 27). **The Father** has placed this eschatological prerogative in Jesus' hands.

5:23. Jesus' unity with His **Father** is so complete that the **honor** of God is tied to Jesus. To reject or dishonor God **the Son** is to reject and dishonor God **the Father.**

5:24. Since Jesus has the unity and divine prerogatives mentioned in verses 19-23, to trust His message and His Father is to have in the present time eternal life (cf. 3:36). No judgment will come in the future (he will not be condemned [cf. 3:18; Rom. 6:13; 8:1] because he has already passed from one realm—death—into another—life [cf. Eph. 2:1, 5]). Only once elsewhere (in 1 John 3:14) is the phrase "passed from death to life" used.

5:25. Jesus' life-giving power can call a person out of the grave (11:43), everyone from their tombs (5:28-29), or anyone in spiritual death (v. 24) to eternal life. (The words, a time is coming, occur four times in John: 4:21, 23; 5:25, 28.)

5:26-27. Jesus' discourse now returned to the two central prerogatives of God: life (vv. 21, 24-26) and judgment (cf. vv. 22, 24-25, 27). Jesus has both because the Father . . . has given Him both. This giving is both eternal and temporal. In Himself Christ, the Logos, has life as an eternal gift of the Father (1:4), but in the Incarnation authority to judge was also delegated to Jesus. As the Son of Man (cf. Dan. 7:13), authority is given to Him.

5:28-29. Jesus said His hearers should not be amazed at His claim that right now those who believe pass from death into life (v. 24), because in the future there will be a universal physical resurrection at His command. This universal resurrection is clearly taught in Daniel 12:1-2. Other passages show that the resurrection to life, "the first resurrection," will occur in stages (the church at the Rapture, and Tribulation saints at the Lord's second coming at the end of the Tribulation), and that the resurrection of those who will be condemned will occur at the end of the Millennium (Rev. 20:11-15). John 5:28-29 is one of the few passages in this Gospel which expressly teaches eschatology.

The words those who have done good and those who have done evil (ta phaula, "worthless things"; cf. 3:20) by themselves might imply a salvation by good deeds or damnation because of evil deeds, but a consideration of John's theology as a whole forbids this (cf. 3:17-21; 6:28-29). Those who are truly born again do live a different kind of life. They obey Him (14:15), they abide in Him (15:5-7), and they walk in the light (8:12; 1 John 1:7). They are saved by the Lamb of God who, as their substitutionary Sacrifice, takes away the penalty of their sin. Salvation is by faith in Christ. Damnation is because of rejection of God's Son (John 3:36).

5:30. This verse is transitional; it concludes the section on Jesus' unity with the Father (vv. 19-30). The section ends the way it began, with the point that the Son can do nothing apart from the Father (cf. v. 19). His judgment, as everything He does, is from the express will of the Father. He is the perfect Spokesman for the Father and His effective Executive. Jesus' will is to do the Father's will (cf. 4:34; 8:29), which shows that He has the same nature.

5:31-32. The thought in this discourse moves from that of Jesus' unity with the Father to that of the Father's witness to Jesus. John 5:31 and 8:14 appear to be contradictory. But they speak to different issues. In 5:31, Jesus' point was that if He bore witness to Himself, this witness would not be accepted by the Jewish authorities. They would see it as an arrogant claim of self-exaltation. Yet in another setting (8:14), self-authentication is perfectly valid because an individual is the only one who knows his own full experience. Jesus affirmed that He did not seek an independent self-authentication. He was content to submit to the Father's will and to let the Father authenticate Him.

Number of Occurrences of "Testimony" and "Testify" (in Gr.) in John's Writings

	Gospel	Epistles	Revelation	Total	Total Occurrences in the NT
Noun	14	7	9	30	60
Verb	33	10	4	47	76
Totals	47	17	13	77	136

5:33-34. As stated earlier (see 1:7), the concept of witness or **testimony** is important in John's Gospel. The chart on the preceding page reveals John's stress on this subject in his various writings.

John the Baptist's function was that of a witness. A good witness tells the truth as he knows it. John's witness to Jesus had an abiding character (**has testified** in the Gr. is in the perf. tense). Jesus did not need **human testimony,** but John's work helped people because in their darkness he pointed them to the light. John's work was **that you may be saved.** His great popular movement was only an anticipatory one, in which he pointed to Jesus as the Lamb of God.

5:35. John was only **a lamp,** not the true Light (1:9). The Jewish nation **for a** short **time** was stirred by and rejoiced in his ministry. For a moment they thought the Messianic Age was dawning. Even though his preaching had some stinging rebukes, there was a great popular excitement about his message. The people thought that though Israel might be disciplined, their enemies would be destroyed.

5:36. Though **John** the Baptist was a great voice for God, he did not do any miracles (10:41). The "signs" were specific works which God had assigned for the Son to do. These miracles were predicted in the Old Testament (Isa. 35:5-6). Jesus' **work** was a clear manifestation that God was with Him and that He worked through Him (cf. Nicodemus' words [John 3:2]; Jesus' logic [Mark 3:23-29]; and the lesson from an ex-blind man [John 9:30-33]).

5:37-38. Jesus' witness is His Father. **The Father . . . has Himself testified concerning Me.** But when and how did or does the Father give this witness? The possibilities include: (1) at Jesus' baptism (Matt. 3:17), (2) at the transfiguration (Matt. 17:5), (3) at the Triumphal Entry (John 12:28), (4) in Jesus' works (3:2), (5) in people's minds or hearts (6:45). Most likely Jesus was referring to the inner work of God in which He impresses on people's consciences that Jesus is the Truth (6:45; 1 John 5:9-12). Jesus' opponents are ignorant of God. They have no vision of God and no communication with Him. **His Word** is His message of salvation. This message had not been received by them (does not **dwell** [*menonta,* from *menō,* "remain, abide"] **in** them) because they had rejected Jesus.

5:39-40. The Jewish religious leaders studied the Old Testament with great diligence. They believed that if one could comprehend the words of the text, he would gain a share in the world to come. They considered those ignorant of the Law to be under a curse (7:49). Similarly many people today think Bible study is an end in itself rather than a function leading to the knowledge of God and godliness. Somehow a veil was over the minds of these Jewish scholars (2 Cor. 3:15), and they failed to see that Jesus is the Promised One. He is the fulfillment of the Old Testament sacrificial system, the true righteous Servant of Yahweh, the coming Prophet, the Son of Man, the Davidic King, and the promised Son of God and great High Priest. In spite of the clarity of the revelation, they refused **to come to** Him **for life** (cf. John 3:19-20).

5:41-42. The Jews may have thought that Jesus was upset because He was not officially endorsed by the leaders. But He denied that idea. They thought they knew His motivation, but in contrast He knew them and the cause of their unbelief (cf. 2:24-25): they did **not have the love of God** (i.e., love for God, not love from God) **in** their **hearts.** The great command is that people should love God (Ex. 20:4; Deut. 6:5); the great sin is that they reject Him and love and serve "created things" (Rom. 1:25).

5:43-44. Two things evidenced their lack of love for God. (1) They rejected Christ, the **Father's** "Representative." To insult or reject one's ambassador is the same as rejecting him. (2) They accepted false teachers or prophets. This reveals a lack of affinity with the truth. An additional failure was their desire for acceptance and approval from sinful men while ignoring the favor and the will of **the only God.** True faith was impossible because they were seeking the wrong object: man, not God.

5:45-47. Jesus came as the Savior, not as the Judge (cf. 3:17). It was unnecessary for Him to **accuse** the people. **Moses,** whom they claimed to follow, would condemn them because they had broken the covenant he instituted and missed the Person **he wrote about. On whom your hopes are set**

implies that they thought salvation would come by their good deeds in keeping the Law.

If the Jews really believed Moses, they would believe Christ, for Moses **wrote** about Him. Jesus here did not refer to any specific passage (cf. Gen. 3:15; 22:18; 49:10; Num. 24:17; Deut. 18:15) or to any specific types (such as the Passover, the manna, the rock, the offerings, or the high priesthood). He simply assumed the Old Testament clearly points to Him. Since Moses' revelation was rejected (cf. Luke 16:29-31), Jesus' words were rejected also. Later Jesus said that Isaiah had written about Him (John 12:41).

C. Jesus' revelation in Galilee (6:1–7:9)

1. JESUS' SIGNS ON THE LAND AND THE LAKE (6:1-21)

a. Jesus' feeding of the 5,000 (6:1-15)

The miracle of the feeding of the 5,000 is the only sign recorded in all four Gospels (besides Jesus' resurrection). This fact alone points to its importance. The significance of the sign was expounded by the Lord in a long discourse (vv. 22-71). The miracle was spectacular, and it caused a peak in the people's messianic expectations. But in its aftermath many of His followers no longer followed Him (v. 66).

6:1-2. Though **some time after this** is indefinite, it can be learned from the Synoptics that Herod Antipas had killed John the Baptist (Mark 6:14-29; cf. John 3:24), the disciples had preached throughout Galilee (Mark 6:7-13, 30-31), multitudes of people were curious about Jesus, and Herod Antipas was seeking Jesus (Luke 9:7-9). So the time between the events in John 5 and 6 was probably six months. From verses 1-2 it seems that Jesus had gone to the northeast side of **the Sea of Galilee** with His disciples for rest. This lake was also called the **Sea of Tiberias** (cf. 21:1), named for a town on the lake's west shore built by Herod Antipas. But a **crowd** gathered even in this "solitary" (cf. Matt. 14:13; Mark 6:32) and "remote place" (Matt. 14:15).

6:3-4. The mention of **the hillside** or "the mountain" (NASB) may indicate an intended parallel to Moses' experience on Mount Sinai (cf. vv. 31-32). The notice that **the Jewish Passover feast was near** is theological and only secondarily chronological. The people were thinking in terms of blood, flesh, lambs, and unleavened bread. They longed for a new Moses who would deliver them from Roman bondage.

Since this was the second Passover John mentioned (cf. 2:13, 23), and since he mentioned at least one other Passover (13:1 [5:1 refers to an unnamed feast of the Jews]), Jesus' ministry extended for about three years. The events in chapter 6, then, took place about one year before He was crucified.

6:5-6. Jesus' question **to Philip—Where shall we buy bread for these people to eat?**—was not for information but was part of His program of educating the disciples. Philip was from Bethsaida (1:44) which was the closest town, and he would know the local resources. The answer to Jesus' question was that it was impossible, humanly speaking, for thousands of people to get bread late in the day from the little neighboring villages. John wrote, as he thought back on the incident, that Jesus was asking this **to test** Philip. God tests people to refine their faith, never to tempt them to do evil (cf. Gen. 22:1-18; James 1:2, 13-15; 1 Peter 1:7).

6:7. The amount needed was a large sum of money: literally, "200 denarii." One denarius was the wage for a day's work; this would have been **eight months' wages.** Even if the bread had been available, the disciples did not have nearly that much money. The disciples were supported by people who responded to Jesus' ministry (cf. Mark 6:7-13).

6:8-9. Andrew, in contrast with Philip, had gone into the crowd to determine its resources (cf. Jesus' command, "Go and see"; Mark 6:38). All he could come up with was a little boy's lunch. Man's inability set the stage for a manifestation of Jesus' compassion and power. The **barley loaves** recall the Prophet Elisha's feeding of 100 men with 20 barley loaves (2 Kings 4:42-44). But here was One far greater than Elisha.

6:10-11. As the Good Shepherd, Jesus made the "sheep" (Mark 6:34) **sit down** in green pastures (cf. Ps. 23:2). According to Mark 6:40, the people were seated in groups of 50 and 100. This made the crowd easy to count and the food easy to distribute. **Five thousand men** were there, plus women and children (Matt. 14:21). Thus probably more than 10,000 people were fed.

Since the area was desolate and the time was Passover, **Jesus** was like Moses with the people in the wilderness who needed a miraculous feeding. The miracle itself was not described by John. **Jesus . . . gave thanks,** but no eucharistic implications are obvious as many argue in this chapter. Among devout Jews the giving of thanks was the norm before and after meals. As Jesus **distributed** the food (with the aid of the disciples [Mark 6:41]), the miraculous multiplication took place.

6:12-13. The words, **when they had all had enough to eat,** show that John intended to stress that a miracle took place. Some scholars try to explain away the miracle by saying that this was merely a sacramental or symbolic meal. Others say the "miracle" was in the people's sharing. But these rationalizations are far from the clear meaning of John's words.

The disciples' gathering of the **12 baskets** of fragments was part of their education, to show them that He is more than adequate for their needs. Later He appealed to their spiritual stupidity (cf. Mark 8:17-21). Even though the disciples were closer to Jesus than the crowds, they too were in spiritual blindness (Mark 6:52).

6:14-15. Seeing this **miraculous sign** (*sēmeion*), the people recalled Moses' prediction that a **Prophet** like him would arise (Deut. 18:15). Moses had fed the people. Moses had led them out of bondage. Jesus had fed the people. Jesus could lead the people out of the hated Roman bondage.

The people saw His sign, but they did not perceive its meaning. They wanted to seize Him **and make Him King.** This marks the highpoint of Jesus' popularity and a great temptation for Him. Could He have the kingdom without the Cross? No. Jesus' kingdom would be given to Him by the Father (cf. Ps. 2:7-12; Dan. 7:13-14). It will not come from this world (John 18:36). The path of the Father's will lies in another direction. Before He can be the reigning Lion of Judah, He must be the Lamb who bears the sin of the world (1:29).

b. His walking on the water (6:16-21)

6:16-17. According to Mark 6:45, Jesus compelled His disciples to get **into the boat** and go to Bethsaida while He dismissed the crowds. From Bethsaida they went on toward **Capernaum.** Both villages are at the north end of the Sea of Galilee. **His disciples went down to the lake,** for the land is hilly and high on the east side. As they got out on the lake, the sun went down and the wind picked up. Jesus was up in the hills praying while watching them in their toil (Mark 6:45-48).

6:18-19. The west **wind,** which often picks up at evening, caught them in the open water. They were headed directly into it and found themselves making little progress. They were "straining at the oars" (Mark 6:48). The Sea of Galilee is notable for its sudden and severe storms. **They had rowed three or three and a half miles,** so they were in the middle of the lake. **They were terrified** to see a figure **walking on the water.** They thought it was a ghost (Mark 6:49). Rational explanations have included the idea that Jesus was walking on the sand by the shore or floating on a large beam or log, but neither notion does justice to the text. This occurred in the "fourth watch" of the night, that is, between 3 and 6 o'clock in the morning (Matt. 14:25; Mark 6:48).

6:20-21. The clause **It is I** is literally "I Am," and was used by Jesus (in 8:58) with strong theological meaning. In this setting it seems to mean only that Jesus was identifying Himself. When the disciples recognized Him, they welcomed **Him into the boat.** By the words **and immediately the boat reached the shore** another miracle is probably intended. The two signs on the land and the lake reveal Jesus as the Provider of a "bread" which gives life (as the next section will expound) and as the Savior who intercedes for and protects His own. He intervenes in their times of troubles and brings them to safety.

2. HIS THEOLOGICAL DISCOURSE (6:22-71)

6:22-25. **The crowd** who had been fed were still on the eastern **shore** of the sea. They saw Jesus compel **His disciples** to get into the **one boat** which was there. But since **Jesus** did not get into the boat, the crowd supposed that He had stayed in the area. After some time they **realized** He was no longer **there. Some boats from Tiberias landed,** so the people decided to seek Jesus in the **Capernaum** region and **got into the boats.** The people's question, **When did You get here?** introduces His long discourse in Capernaum (v. 59). Jesus did not explain how or when He crossed the lake, for His walking on the water was a private sign for the disciples only.

6:26. Jesus began with the solemn words, **I tell you the truth** (cf. comments on 1:51). Jesus spoke these words four times in this discourse (6:26, 32, 47, 53). This drew attention to the importance of what He was about to teach. He rebuked them for their materialistic motivation and their lack of spiritual perception. They **saw miraculous signs,** but to them it was only an easy meal. They failed to see what it signified.

6:27. When Jesus said, **Do not work for food that spoils,** He was not condoning laziness. Rather He was saying that people should expend their efforts for what will last forever. "Man does not live on bread alone, but on every word that comes from the mouth of God" (Matt. 4:4). Physical **food** is short-lived but spiritual **food** leads **to eternal life. The Son of Man** (who has access to heaven [John 3:13]) **will give** people this spiritual food, which is ultimately Christ Himself (6:53). **God the Father** Himself authenticated Jesus' claim that He is true heavenly "food."

6:28. The people recognized that Jesus was saying God had a requirement for them. They would do God's requirement if He would inform them what it was. They believed that they could please **God** and thus obtain eternal life by doing good **works** (cf. Rom. 10:2-4).

6:29. Jesus' response to their question was a flat contradiction of their thinking. They could not please God by doing good works. There is only one **work of God,** that **is,** one thing God requires. They need to put their trust **in the One** the Father **has sent.** Because of their sin people cannot please God by doing good works for salvation (Eph. 2:8-9; Titus 3:5). God demands that people recognize their inability to save themselves and receive His gift (Rom. 6:23).

6:30-31. In response the people demanded a **miraculous sign** (*sēmeion;* cf. "Jews demand miraculous signs" [1 Cor. 1:22]). They thought God's order is **see** and **believe.** But the divine order is believe and see (cf. John 11:40). They did not have faith or spiritual perception, but they understood that Jesus was proclaiming something new.

His coming was claimed as an advance over Moses. They reasoned, "If You are more than Moses, do more than Moses." The crowd that asked for a sign from Jesus must have felt that the feeding of the 5,000 did not compare with Moses' gift of **bread from heaven.** They remembered the divine gift of **manna** (Ex. 16; Num. 11:7). They thought Jesus' feeding was less significant because manna fed the whole nation for 40 years. But they missed two things. First, many of the Israelites who were fed 40 years did not believe. The important thing is not the magnitude of the sign but the perception of its significance (cf. Luke 16:29-31). Second, both Moses and Jesus were authenticated by God's signs; therefore both should be listened to and believed.

6:32. In a solemn revelation (**I tell you the truth;** cf. vv. 26, 47, 53) **Jesus** corrected their ideas in three ways. (1) The Father, **not Moses,** gave the manna. (2) The **Father,** was still giving "manna" then, not merely in the past. **(3) The true Bread from heaven** is Jesus, not the manna. Thus the supposed superiorities of Moses and his sign vanish. Manna was food for the body, and it was useful. But Jesus is God's full provision for people in their whole existence. Jesus repeatedly said He had come down from heaven (vv. 32-33, 38, 41-42, 50-51, 58).

6:33. God is the Source of all life. The Son has life in Himself (1:4; 5:26) and He has come to give real and lasting life to people. Sin cuts them off from God, who is Life, and they die spiritually and physically. Christ has come **down from heaven** to give **life to the world.** Jesus is thus **the** genuine **Bread of God.**

6:34. As yet, the crowd did not perceive that Jesus is the genuine **Bread** which He had been describing. Like the woman at the well (4:15), they asked for **this** better food. And they wanted it continually (**from now on**), not like the manna which lasted for 40 years.

6:35. I am the Bread of Life. This corrected two more errors in their thinking: (1) The food of which He spoke refers to a Person, not a commodity. (2) And once someone is in right relationship to Jesus, he finds a satisfaction which is everlasting, not temporal. This "I am" statement is the first in a series of momentous "I am" revelations (cf. 8:12; 10:7, 9, 11, 14; 11:25; 14:6; 15:1, 5). "Bread of Life" means bread which provides life. Jesus is man's necessary "food." In Western culture, bread is often optional, but it was an essential staple then. Jesus promised, **He who comes to Me will never go hungry, and he who believes in Me will never be thirsty.** The "nevers" are emphatic in Greek.

6:36. Jesus then rebuked the crowd for their lack of faith. They had the great privilege of seeing Him and yet they did **not believe.** Seeing does not necessarily lead to believing (cf. v. 30).

6:37. Jesus then gave the ultimate explanation of their lack of faith: **the Father** works sovereignly in people's lives. There is an election of God which is the Father's gift to the Son. The Son has no concern that His work will be ineffective, for the Father will enable people to come to Jesus. Jesus has confidence. But people may have confidence also. (Cf. the crippled man's response to Jesus' question, "Do you want to get well?" [5:6-9]) One who comes to Jesus for salvation will by no means be driven **away** (cf. 6:39).

6:38-39. Jesus then repeated His claim about His heavenly origin. The reason He **came down from heaven** was **to do the will of** the Father **who sent** Him. The Father's **will is that** those whom He gives to the Son will not suffer a single loss and **all** will be raised to life in the resurrection (cf. vv. 40, 44, 54). This passage is strong in affirming the eternal security of the believer.

6:40. This verse repeats and reinforces the ideas of the previous verses. One who **looks** and **believes** on Jesus for salvation has his destiny secure. The divine decree has insured it (cf. Rom. 8:28-30). He has **eternal life** (John 6:47, 50-51, 54, 58) and **will** be raised **at the last day** (cf. vv. 39, 44, 54).

6:41-42. The Jews, hostile unbelievers, grumbled because of Jesus' proclamation of His heavenly origin. Like their ancestors in the wilderness, these Jews murmured (Ex. 15:24; 16:2, 7, 12; 17:3; Num. 11:1; 14:2, 27). Their thinking was seemingly logical: one **whose** parents are known could not be **from heaven** (cf. Mark 6:3; Luke 4:22). They were ignorant of His true origin and full nature. They said He was **the son of Joseph,** but they did not know of the Virgin Birth, the Incarnation. He had come **down** from heaven because He is the *Logos* (John 1:1, 14).

6:43-44. Jesus made no attempt to correct their ignorance other than to rebuke their **grumbling** and to point them to the drawing and teaching ministry of God. They are not in a position to judge Him. Without God's help any assessment of God's Messenger will be faulty. **No one can come to** Jesus or believe on Him without divine help. People are so ensnared in the quicksand of sin and unbelief that **unless** God **draws** them (cf. v. 65), they are hopeless. This drawing of God is not limited to a few. Jesus said, "I . . . will draw all men to Myself" (12:32). This does not mean that all will be saved but that Greeks (i.e., Gentiles; 12:20) as well as Jews will be saved. Those who will be saved will also be resurrected (cf. 6:39-40).

6:45. In support of this doctrine of salvation by God's grace, Jesus cited the Old Testament. The quotation, **They will all be taught by God,** is from **the Prophets,** probably Isaiah 54:13, though Jeremiah 31:34 has the same thought. This "teaching" of God refers to His inner work that disposes people to accept the truth about Jesus and respond to Him. **Everyone who listens to** and **learns from** God will come to and believe in Jesus.

6:46. Yet this secret teaching of God is not a mystical connection of people with God directly. Knowing **God** comes only through Jesus, the *Logos* of God (cf. 1:18). As one is confronted by Him and hears His words and sees His deeds, **the Father** works within him.

6:47-48. These two verses summarize Jesus' teaching in the debate. **I tell you the truth** occurs here for the third of four times in this passage (cf. vv. 26, 32, 53). **He who believes** is in Greek a participial construction in the present tense, meaning that a believer is characterized by his continuing trust. He **has everlasting life,** which is a present and abiding possession. Jesus then repeated His affirmation, **I am the Bread of Life** (see comments on v. 35).

6:49-50. Manna met only a limited need. It provided temporary physical life. The Israelites came to loathe it, and ultimately **they died.** Jesus is a **Bread** of a different kind. He is **from heaven** and gives life. A person who eats of that Bread will **not die.**

6:51. Since Jesus is the **Bread** of Life, what does "eating" this **Bread** mean? Many commentators assume that Jesus was talking about the Lord's Supper. This passage may well illuminate the meaning of the Lord's Supper, in relation to Christ's death. But since the Last Supper occurred one year later than the incidents recorded in this chapter, eating His flesh and drinking His blood should not be thought of as sacramentalism. "Eating" **the living** Bread is a figure of speech meaning to believe on Him, like the figures of coming to Him (v. 35), listening to Him, (v. 45), and seeing Him (v. 40). To eat of this Bread is to **live forever** (cf. vv. 40, 47, 50, 54, 58). Jesus' revelation about the Bread was then advanced in that not only is the Father giving the Bread (Jesus), but also Jesus is giving Himself: **This Bread is My flesh, which I will give for the life of the world.** Salvation is by the sacrificial death of the Lamb of God (1:29). By His death, life came to the world.

6:52. As often happens, Jesus' teaching was not understood (cf. 2:20; 3:4; 4:15; 6:32-34). A violent argument started in the crowd regarding what He meant. Their perception remained at a materialistic level. They wondered, **How can this Man give us His flesh to eat?**

6:53-54. This revelation by **Jesus** is marked out as important by the fourth use of the phrase, **I tell you the truth** (cf. vv. 26, 32, 47). Sacramental interpretations appeal to the words **eat the flesh of the Son of Man and drink His blood** as evidence that Jesus was speaking of the eucharist. As stated earlier, the basic objection to this approach is historical: Jesus did not institute the Communion service until a year later. Drinking "His blood" is another bold figure of speech. The Jews knew the command, "You must not eat . . . any blood" (Lev. 3:17; cf. Lev. 17:10-14). And yet blood was the means of atonement. It is the blood that makes atonement for one's life (Lev. 17:11). Jesus' hearers must have been shocked and puzzled by His enigmatic words. But the puzzle is unlocked by understanding that Jesus was speaking of His making atonement by His death and giving life to those who personally appropriate Him (cf. John 6:63). Faith in Christ's death brings **eternal life** (cf. vv. 40, 47, 50-51) and (later) bodily resurrection (cf. vv. 39-40, 44).

6:55. Just as good food and drink sustain physical life, so Jesus, the **real** (reliable) spiritual **food** and **drink,** sustains His followers spiritually. His **flesh** and **blood** give eternal life to those who receive Him.

6:56-57. One who partakes of Christ enjoys a mutual abiding relationship with Christ. He **remains** (*menei*) in Christ, and Christ remains **in him.** *Menō* is one of the most important theological terms in John's Gospel (cf. comments on 1:38). The Father "remains" in the Son (14:10), the Spirit "remains" on Jesus (1:32), and believers "remain" in Jesus and He in them (6:56; 15:4). The implications of this "remaining" are many. A believer enjoys intimacy with and security in Jesus. Just as He has His life from **the Father, so** believers have life **because of** Jesus.

6:58-59. Jesus gave this discourse on the **Bread** of Life **in the synagogue in Capernaum.** He often spoke in Jewish synagogues, where men had opportunities to give expositions and exhortations (Mark 6:1-6; Luke 4:16-28; Acts 13:15-42). The services were not as formal as those of traditional American churches; "laymen" usually spoke. The conclusion to Jesus' exposition and exhortation, based on the **manna** incident from Exodus 16, repeats the major themes: Moses' bread did not give lasting life (salvation does not come by the Law); God has given the genuine life-giving **Bread . . . from heaven;** those who trust Jesus have eternal life.

6:60. As the people began to understand His teaching, they found it to be totally unacceptable. Besides the hostile Jewish leaders, **many of** the Galilean **disciples** turned away from Him. The popular enthusiasm for Jesus as a political Messiah (v. 15) was then over. They saw that He was not going to deliver them from Rome. He might be a great Healer, but His words were **a hard** (i.e., harsh) **teaching. Who** could **accept it,** that is, obey it? How could they personally appropriate Him?

6:61-62. Jesus knew His audience (cf. 1:47; 2:24-25; 6:15). **Aware that they were grumbling** (cf. v. 41), He asked what was so offensive to **them. (Offend** in Gr. is *skandalizei*.) Paul wrote that the crucified Messiah was a "stumbling block" (*skandalon*) to the Jews (1 Cor. 1:23). The Ascension of **the Son of Man** is also an offense. But His glorification is His heavenly vindication. He was crucified in weakness but He was raised in power (1 Cor. 15:43).

6:63. After His Ascension Jesus gave the Holy Spirit (7:38-39; Acts 1:8-9). **The Holy Spirit,** poured out in the world, **gives life** (salvation) to those who believe. Without the Holy Spirit, man **(flesh)** is utterly unable to understand Jesus' person and His works (John 3:6; 1 Cor. 2:14). Though the crowds assessed Jesus' words as "hard" (John 6:60), actually His **words . . . are spirit and . . . life.** That is, by the work of the Holy Spirit in an individual, Jesus' words provide spiritual life.

6:64. The life **Jesus** gives must be received by faith. The words do not work automatically. From the start Jesus knew **which** followers were believers and which ones were unbelievers. This is another evidence of His supernatural knowledge (cf. 1:47; 2:24-25; 6:15).

6:65. Jesus had taught that divine enablement was necessary for people to **come to** faith (v. 44). The apostasy here (v. 66) should not be surprising. Believers who remain with Jesus evidence the Father's secret work. The unbelieving crowds are evidence that "the flesh counts for nothing" (v. 63).

6:66. His rejecting their desire to make Him their political king; His demand for personal faith; His teaching on atonement; His stress on total human inability and on salvation as a work of God—all these proved to be unpalatable for **many** people. They gave up being His **disciples** ("disciples" here refers to followers in general, not to the 12 Apostles; this is evident in v. 67).

6:67. You do not want to leave too, do you? He framed this question to encourage their weak faith. **The Twelve** were affected by the apostasy of the many, and **Jesus** used that occasion to refine their faith. They did not fully understand His words either and would not until after the Resurrection (20:9).

6:68-69. Peter, as a spokesman, gave his confession of faith. The path may be difficult, but he was convinced that Jesus' **words** lead to life. No one else has the gift **of eternal life.** "We have believed and have known" is a better translation of the Greek perfect tenses (NIV: **We believe and know**). Peter was confident of the apostles' commitment to Jesus as **the Holy One of God.** This title is unusual (a demon addressed Jesus that way; Mark 1:24). It suggests Jesus' transcendence ("the Holy One") and His representation of the Father ("of God"); thus it is another way of confessing Him as Messiah. Peter knew this by a special work of the Father (cf. Matt. 16:17).

6:70-71. Jesus then asked, **Have I not chosen you, the Twelve?** John's Gospel does not record Jesus' choice of the Twelve. He assumed his readers knew the Synoptics or common church tradition (cf. Mark 3:13-19). This choice was not election to salvation, but was Jesus' call to them to serve Him. **Yet,** He said, **one of you is a devil!** In the light of John 13:2, 27, Satan's working in Judas was tantamount to Judas being the devil. In 6:70 the Greek does not have the indefinite article "a," so it could be translated "one of you is Satan (devil)." Jesus' knowledge of **Judas** (who was called Judas Iscariot because his father was **Simon Iscariot**) was still another example of His omniscience (cf. 1:47; 2:24-25; 6:15, 61). **Later** in the Upper Room, Jesus again said **one of the Twelve** would **betray Him** (13:21). John called Judas "the traitor" (18:5). The disciples later could reflect on this prophecy of His and be strengthened in their faith. Judas was a tragic figure, influenced by Satan; yet he was responsible for his own evil choices.

3. THE MINISTRY IN GALILEE (7:1-9)

This section prepares the way for another confrontation of Jesus with His opponents in Jerusalem. This ministry in relative obscurity in Galilee provides a delay in the coming conflict.

7:1. After this is a vague time reference. Since the events recorded in chapter 6 took place shortly before the Passover (6:4), that is, in April, and the Feast of Tabernacles (in October) was now near (7:2), about six months were spent by **Jesus** in His ministry **in Galilee.** Galilee was safer because His enemies were in **Judea . . . waiting to take His life.**

7:2. The **Feast of Tabernacles** was one of the three great **Jewish** feasts. Josephus called it their holiest and greatest feast (*The Antiquities of the Jews* 8. 4. 1). This feast, also called the Feast of Ingathering, was a time of thanksgiving for harvest. It was a happy time; devout Jews lived outdoors in booths made of tree branches for seven days as a reminder of God's provision in the desert during their forefather's wanderings. The feast also signified that God dwells with His people.

7:3. Jesus' brothers, sons of Mary and Joseph after Jesus' birth, were at this time unbelievers (cf. Mark 3:21, 31-35; 6:3; John 7:5). They logically argued that the messianic question could not be settled in Galilee, as Jerusalem was the religious capital. The popular Feast of Tabernacles would be the right time for Jesus to present Himself as the Messiah. If He would display His powers in **Judea,** He might be able to recapture the lost crowds.

7:4-5. It did not seem rational to Jesus' brothers for Him not to show off His glory. If He really was what He claimed to be, they reasoned, He should publicly demonstrate it. They advised Him to display Himself in a powerful, brilliant way: **Show Yourself to the world.** But God's way was a public display on a cross of humiliation. John explained that **even His own brothers did not believe in Him.** This sad note sounds again (cf. 1:10-11; 12:37). Proximity to Jesus, either in a family or as a disciple, does not guarantee faith.

7:6-7. Jesus responded that His time differed from theirs. They could **come** and go without any sigificance; **for** them **any time is right.** But He always pleased the Father, so His time movements were those the Father desired. It was not yet time for the public manifestation (the Cross). Several times John noted that Jesus' **time had not yet come** (2:4; 7:6, 8, 30; 8:20). Then in His intercessory prayer, just before the Cross, He began, "Father, the time has come" (17:1; cf. 12:23, 27; 13:1).

The world was not dangerous to the brothers of Jesus because they were part of it (**the world cannot hate you**). But the world hated Jesus **because** He is not of it.

He had come into it as Light and pointed out its sin and rebellion against the Father. The world has its religions, its programs, its plans, its values, but Christ witnessed **that** it **is** all **evil** (*ponēra,* "wicked"). Partly because of this, He lived carefully in order to fulfill the Father's will.

7:8-9. I am not yet going up to this Feast is clearly the thought in light of verse 10. However, most Greek editions of the New Testament omit the word "yet," because it is considered a difficult reading, but it is more likely in the original. If Jesus said, "I am not going up to the Feast," was He lying since He *did* go to the Feast? (v. 10) No, He simply meant that He was not going up to the Feast "right then," as they suggested. Jesus then for a time **stayed in Galilee,** doing the tasks of ministry which the Father had ordained.

"Going up" may have a geographical meaning (since Jerusalem is in the hills) as well as a theological meaning (going back to the Father).

D. Jesus' return to Jerusalem and the resumption of hostility (7:10–10:42)

1. THE FEAST OF TABERNACLES (7:10–8:59)

a. The anticipation of the feast (7:10-13)

7:10. Because of plots to kill Him (vv. 1, 25) Jesus made a covert entry into the city. It was not yet the time for His messianic manifestation (the Cross).

7:11-13. While Jesus' enemies **were** searching **for Him,** people were debating this controversial Teacher. The opposition against Jesus was growing. A **widespread whispering** (lit., "grumbling"; cf. 6:41, 61), occurred. (Cf. the Israelites' grumbling in the wilderness.) The charge, **He deceives the people,** had ominous tones for the penalty for this, according to Talmudic law, was death by stoning. Since the whole crowd was Jewish, **fear of the Jews** meant fear of the religious leaders.

b. Jesus at the feast (7:14-36)

7:14-15. The first three days passed without anyone seeing **Jesus.** The crowds wondered if He would come and perhaps claim to be the Messiah. Then **halfway through the Feast** He began teaching in **the temple courts.** As the official religious leaders listened to Him along with the crowds they **were amazed** (cf. Mark 1:22). His teaching was learned and spiritually penetrating. Yet He had never been a disciple in any Rabbinic school. They wondered how this could be possible.

7:16-17. The religious authorities figured that either a person studied in a traditional school or else he was self-taught. But Jesus' reply pointed to a third alternative. His **teaching** was **from** God who had commissioned Him (cf. 12:49-50; 14:11, 24). **Jesus** was God-taught, and to know Jesus properly one must be God-taught (6:45). In order to evaluate Jesus' claim, one must desire **to do God's will.** Since Jesus is God's will for man, people must believe in Him (6:29). Faith is the prerequisite for understanding. Without faith it is impossible to please God (Heb. 11:6).

7:18. If Jesus were only self-taught (speaking **on His own**) or a genius, then His ministry would be self-exalting. But He did not seek **honor for Himself.** The true goal of man should be to glorify (**honor**) God and enjoy Him forever. Jesus is what man ought to be. His purpose is to represent His Father correctly (1:18). He **is a Man of truth** (i.e., reliable; cf. 6:28; 8:26) without any injustice.

7:19. The audience boasted in Moses' **Law** (9:28). Jesus attacked their self-confident religion. They assumed they were Law-keepers. But their hearts (inner thoughts) were full of evil (Mark 7:6-7, 20-22; Matt. 5:21-22). He knew them (John 2:24-25), and that their hatred would lead to murder.

7:20. Instead of repenting because His light had rebuked their darkness (3:19-20), they insulted Him, saying He was **demon-possessed.** People had said the same of John the Baptist (Matt. 11:18). Jesus had told His half-brothers the world hated Him (John 7:7), because "everyone who does evil hates the light" (3:20). To call Jesus, who is sent from God, demon-possessed is to call light darkness (cf. 8:48, 52; 10:20). They denied His accusation that they were **trying to kill** Him. But earlier they were in fact trying to do that very thing (5:18). (Cf. Peter who denied he would deny Jesus; Mark 14:29.)

7:21-23. The **one miracle** (lit., "work") Jesus referred to was His healing of the paralytic at the pool of Bethesda, which He had performed in Jerusalem at His last visit (5:1-18). This started a fierce controversy. Circumcision is a religious rite that predated **Moses.** Abraham circumcised as a sign of the covenant (Gen. 17:9-14). But **Moses gave** Israel **circumcision** in the sense of establishing it as part of the Levitical system. Under the Mosaic Law, "On the eighth day the boy is to be circumcised" (Lev. 12:3). If that day fell on a Sabbath, circumcising a boy would seemingly violate the Sabbath Law of rest. Yet the Jews circumcised **on the Sabbath.** Therefore, Jesus argued, if care for one part of the body was permitted, then certainly the **healing** of a **whole** body (that of the paralytic) should be allowed **on the Sabbath.** Hence they had no reason to be **angry** with Him.

7:24. Their problem was that they understood the Scriptures only superficially. They majored in minors and missed the intents of many passages (cf. Matt. 23:23; John 5:39-40). They were **judging by mere appearances.** Their superficial understanding was caused by their hostility against God's Representative. In their darkness they erred. Jesus called them to **make a right judgment;** ultimately this was a call for them to repent.

7:25-26. Some of the local people were amazed at His bold public teaching. They knew of a plot **to kill** Him. Yet the leaders were **not** doing what **they** said they would do. Why? Had **the authorities** changed their minds? People were confused over the lack of leadership in the nation. They felt that if He was a deceiver, He should be locked up, or if He was the Messiah, they should accept Him.

7:27. The crowds assumed that Jesus (**this Man**) was only a Galilean carpenter from the city of Nazareth. They also believed that the Messiah (**the Christ**) would be unknown until His public appearing. A reader of the Gospels recognizes the irony. Jesus is more than a Galilean; He is the *Logos* who was virgin-born in Bethlehem. Yet He was relatively unknown until His manifestation (the Cross and the Resurrection).

7:28-29. Cried out introduced a solemn announcement (cf. 1:15; 7:37; 12:44). He responded to their supposed knowledge of Him (7:27) with irony. He is **from** the Father. God **is true** ("reliable"; cf. v. 18; 8:26) and had **sent** Jesus.

Whereas His enemies did **not know** Jesus or God (1:18; cf. Matt. 11:27), Jesus knows the Father **because** of His origin (John 1:1, 14, 18) and divine mission.

7:30. Jesus' rebuke of the Jerusalemites stirred them to attempt **to seize** (*piazō*, "arrest"; cf. vv. 32, 44; 8:20; 10:39) **Him.** But the Father had ordered a **time** and place for His manifestation (His death), and until then all things would work in concert toward that goal. They could not lay **a hand on Him because** the Father's hand was over Him.

7:31. The exposure of Jesus and His teaching moved **many in the crowd** to believe on **Him.** They logically thought that His **miraculous signs** marked Him out as unusual. Certainly the Messiah could not do any more miracles **than this Man.** But the crowd's faith in Jesus as Messiah was tentative and was not linked to belief in His atoning death.

7:32. Since many in **the crowd** were turning to Jesus, they would set aside the Pharisees' traditional teachings (cf. Mark 7:1-23). **The Pharisees,** as the guardians of Jewish traditions (see comments on the Pharisees, John 1:24-25), realized something needed to be done about Jesus soon. **The chief priests** were leading priests, not just high priests. **Arrest** is the same Greek word (*piazō*) as "seize" in 7:30, 44; 8:20; 10:39.

7:33. While the plan to arrest Him proceeded, **Jesus** continued to teach. The nation had **only a short time** to decide about Him. This time was determined not by the authorities but by God. When He had completed God's plan for His earthly life, He would return to the Father.

7:34. You will look for Me is a prophecy that the Jewish nation will long for her Messiah. She is doing this now, not knowing that Jesus is her Messiah. Later she will weep for Him (Zech. 12:10-13; Rev. 1:7). The time of spiritual opportunity is now. A time will come when it is too late. He went bodily to heaven where unbelievers **cannot come** (cf. John 8:21). So people today do not have the unique opportunity people had when Jesus was speaking to them face to face.

7:35. Once more the words of Jesus were an enigma to **the Jews** (cf. vv. 15, 31, 41-42). **Where** could He possibly **go that** they could not **find Him?** Because they were of the earth, they could think only

earthly thoughts (cf. Isa. 55:8). During some of that period the Jewish people lived in Palestine whereas others migrated throughout the Roman Empire and beyond, as far east as Babylonia. They were **scattered among the Greeks.** "Greeks" means not just people of Greece or Greek-speaking peoples but generally non-Jews or heathen (cf. "Greek" and "Jew" in Col. 3:11). The question then was, Will Jesus go **teach the** heathen? Without the Jews realizing it, this question was prophetic of the spread of the gospel after Jesus' Ascension.

7:36. The crowd, after pondering what Jesus meant, simply repeated their questions. They did not understand His words.

c. The last day of the Feast (7:37-52)

7:37. The Feast of Tabernacles was celebrated with certain festival rituals. One was a solemn procession each day from the temple to the Gihon Spring. A priest filled a gold pitcher with water while the choir sang Isaiah 12:3. Then they returned to the altar and poured out the water. This ritual reminded them of the water from the rock during the wilderness wanderings (Num. 20:8-11; Ps. 78:15-16). It also spoke prophetically of the coming days of Messiah (cf. Zech. 14:8, 16-19). The Feast's seventh and **last** day was its **greatest** (cf. Lev. 23:36). **Jesus stood,** in contrast with the Rabbis' usual position of being seated while teaching. **Said in a loud voice** (cf. John 1:15; 7:28; 12:44) was a way of introducing a solemn announcement. His offer, **Come to Me and drink,** was an offer of salvation (cf. 4:14; 6:53-56).

7:38. Streams of living water will flow from within one who **believes in** Jesus. That is, he will have a continual source of satisfaction, which will provide life continually (cf. 4:14). When Jesus added, **As the Scripture has said,** He did not identify the Old Testament passage(s) He had in mind. But He may have thought of Psalm 78:15-16 and Zechariah 14:8 (cf. Ezek. 47:1-11; Rev. 22:1-2).

7:39. John explained that the "living water" (v. 38) was the coming gift of **the** Holy **Spirit.** The Spirit within a believer satisfies his need of God, and provides him with regeneration, guidance, and empowerment. In the earliest Greek manuscripts, the words, **Up to that time the Spirit had not been given,** are simply, "for there was not yet Spirit." This cannot be taken in an absolute sense since the Spirit had actively worked among people in the Old Testament era. Jesus referred to the special baptizing, sealing, and indwelling work of the Spirit in the Church Age, which would start on the day of Pentecost (Acts 1:5, 8). Jesus said He would "send the Spirit" to His followers (John 15:26; 16:7). "The Spirit had not [yet] been given" to indwell believers permanently (cf. Ps. 51:11). That happened after **Jesus** was **glorified,** that is after His death, resurrection, and Ascension. "Glorified," "glory," and "glorify" are used frequently in John's Gospel (John 7:39; 11:4; 12:16, 23, 28; 13:31-32; 14:13; 15:8; 16:14; 17:1, 4-5, 10).

7:40-41. The crowd continued to debate Jesus' identity. **Some** saw Him as **the Prophet** mentioned by Moses (Deut. 18:15, 18). He would speak God's words to people but not in the awesome display of Mount Sinai from which Moses spoke. Jesus is indeed that predicted Prophet (Acts 3:22), but many rejected Him as such. Some said Jesus **is the Christ,** that is, the Messiah, but **others** rejected that idea because He came **from Galilee** (cf. John 7:52).

7:42. According to Samuel and Isaiah (2 Sam. 7:16; Isa. 11:1) the Messiah was to be born into a Davidic **family.** Micah predicted that He would be born in **Bethlehem . . . David's** hometown (Micah 5:2). Jesus *is* from a Davidic family (Matt. 1:1-17; Luke 3:23-38; Rom. 1:3) and *was* born in Bethlehem (Matt. 2:1-6), but the crowd ignorantly overlooked those facts.

7:43-44. The crowd's **divided** opinion about **Jesus** enabled Him to continue His ministry without immediate arrest (**seize,** *piazō,* is the same word for "arrest" in v. 32, and is also used in v. 30; 8:20; 10:39). Many of the people held a favorable opinion of Jesus even though they did not personally commit themselves to Him (cf. 7:12, 31, 40-41). His enemies had to be careful lest a riot would result. So for a time, **no one** touched **Him.** Twice later the Jews were again divided over Jesus (9:16; 10:19-21).

7:45-46. The temple guards, who were sent to arrest Jesus (v. 32) returned without Him. Responding to the question

Why? the guards answered, **No one ever spoke the way this Man does.** Literally this is, "Never spoke thus a man," which implies that the guards sensed that He was most unusual or perhaps more than a man. The Gospels often reveal Jesus as a most impressive Teacher and Speaker (e.g., Matt. 7:29; 22:46). Though Jesus was opposed, many of those who heard Him were moved by Him (cf. John 7:15; 12:19).

7:47-48. The Pharisees' question to the guards, **Has any of the rulers or of the Pharisees believed in Him?** reveals their pride. They thought they were too educated (v. 15) to be taken in by a deceiver. Ironically a number of the rulers *did* believe (12:42; 19:38-39). The Pharisees were jealous of Jesus' great popularity ("The whole world has gone after Him" [12:19]).

7:49. The Pharisees explained Jesus' popularity among the populace by suggesting that the people were too ignorant to recognize Jesus as a deceiver. The crowd **(this mob),** according to the Pharisees, did not know **the Law.** They did not study it, so they could not obey it. And since they did not obey it, they were under God's **curse** (Deut. 28:15). The irony of the situation was that the Pharisees, not the mob, were under God's wrath because they rejected God's revelation in Jesus (John 3:36).

7:50-51. The Mosaic Law (Deut. 1:16-17) and Rabbinic law stipulated that a person accused of a crime should get a fair **hearing.** Nicodemus appeared as a fair-minded man who did not want the Sanhedrin to make a false or hasty judgment. He had personally spoken with **Jesus** and knew He was from God (John 3:1-3; cf. 12:42; 19:38-39).

7:52. Even though Nicodemus was a respected teacher in the nation (3:10), he was insulted by the other members of the Sanhedrin. Their prejudice and hatred against Jesus were already strong enough to overthrow reason. The Sanhedrin accused Nicodemus of being as ignorant as the Galileans. **A prophet does not come out of Galilee,** they argued. So the messianic Prophet cannot be a Galilean (cf. 7:41).

Note on 7:53–8:11

7:53–8:11. Almost all textual scholars agree that these verses were not part of the original manuscript of the Gospel of John. The NIV states in brackets that

"The earliest and most reliable manuscripts do not have John 7:53–8:11." The style and vocabulary of this passage differ from the rest of the Gospel, and the passage interrupts the sequence from 7:52–8:12. It is probably a part of true oral tradition which was added to later Greek manuscripts by copyists. For more discussion on the subject and an exposition of the passage, see the *Appendix* before the John *Bibliography*.

d. The Light of the world discourse (8:12-59)

A major feature of the Feast of Tabernacles was the lighting of giant lamps in the women's court in the temple (see the diagram). The wicks were made from the priests' worn-out garments. The light illuminated the temple area and the people gathered to sing praises and dance. The light reminded the Jewish people of how God was with them in their wanderings in the wilderness in a pillar of cloud which turned to fire at night (Num. 9:15-23).

8:12. This discourse continues Jesus' public teaching in the city of Jerusalem in the temple area. How fitting that during the Feast of Tabernacles, when the large lamps were burning, **Jesus . . . said, I am the Light of the world** (cf. 1:4, 9; 12:35, 46). The world is in darkness, a symbol of evil, sin, and ignorance (Isa. 9:2; Matt. 4:16; 27:45; John 3:19). "Light" in the Bible is a symbol of God and His holiness (Acts 9:3; 1 John 1:5). Jesus is *"the* Light," not merely a light or another light among many lights. He is the only Light, "the true Light" (John 1:9), for the whole world. When Jesus said, **Whoever follows Me,** He meant whoever believes and obeys Him (cf. 10:4-5, 27; 12:26; 21:19-20, 22). Jesus was speaking of salvation.

Coming to Christ for salvation results in a different kind of life. A believer **will never walk in darkness,** that is, he will not live in it (cf. 12:46; 1 John 1:6-7). He does not remain in the realm of evil and ignorance (John 12:46) for he has Christ as his **Light** and salvation (cf. Ps. 36:9).

8:13. Again **the Pharisees challenged** His claim. Since He appeared **as His own witness,** they said His **testimony** was **not valid.** Self-authentication is sometimes unacceptable. The Law required two witnesses to establish a fact in

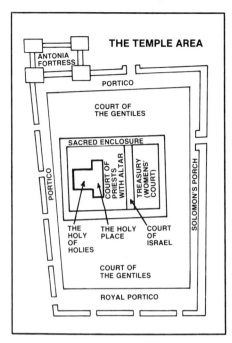

THE TEMPLE AREA

ANTONIA FORTRESS

PORTICO

COURT OF THE GENTILES

SACRED ENCLOSURE

PORTICO

COURT OF PRIESTS WITH ALTAR

TREASURY (WOMENS' COURT)

SOLOMON'S PORCH

THE HOLY OF HOLIES

THE HOLY PLACE

COURT OF ISRAEL

COURT OF THE GENTILES

ROYAL PORTICO

capital offenses (Deut. 17:6; 19:15; John 8:17). Rabbinic tradition rejected self-testimony.

8:14. Sometimes, however, self-authentication is the only way to truth. Sometimes an individual is the only one who knows the facts about himself. And only God can give **testimony** to Himself. **Jesus** was competent to give a true witness of Himself because as God He has a comprehensive knowledge of His origin and destiny (7:29). In spite of what the Pharisees thought they knew about Jesus, they were ignorant of His heavenly origin and destiny (cf. 7:33-34), and thus were invalid judges of Him.

8:15. The Pharisees, Jesus said, judged **by human standards,** that is, they were limited by superficial appearances. They saw only His flesh, not His deity, so they misjudged Him. By contrast, Jesus did not come to **judge** people but to save them (3:17). When He does judge in the future, He will simply execute the Father's will according to truth and the Law (cf. 5:27, 45). He Himself will **pass judgment on no one.**

8:16. Jesus' judging was totally unlike theirs. Theirs was biased and limited. His was not His own because of His unique union **with the Father.** Nor was His witness **alone;** He spoke with divine authority.

8:17-18. In your own Law may refer to Deuteronomy 17:6; 19:15 (or to Rabbinic laws), which speak of the necessity of **two** witnesses. In Jesus' case only God could authenticate Him. God the Son and God **the Father** are the required two Witnesses. The Father **sent** Jesus and authenticated Him by the signs (miracles) He performed.

8:19. Jesus' teaching on God as His **Father** was unique (cf. 5:18), and the Jews were puzzled by His familiar way of talking about Him. The Pharisees **asked Him, Where is Your Father?** Was He talking about God, or (as they supposed) His human father? Their ignorance of Jesus showed their ignorance of God, for Jesus is the Revelation of the **Father** (cf. 1:14, 18; 14:7, 9).

8:20. Jesus **spoke these words while teaching in the temple area near the place where the offerings were put.** This was probably in the women's court (see the diagram at 8:12; cf. Mark 12:41-42). Jesus went there and instructed the people. **No one seized** (*piazō,* "arrested") **Him** (cf. John 7:30, 32, 44, 10:39) **because,** as John repeatedly pointed out, Jesus was working on God's **time** schedule to accomplish the Father's will (cf. 2:4; 7:6, 30; 12:23, 27; 13:1; 17:1).

8:21. Just as His time was short, so their opportunity for trusting in Him was limited. Soon He would go back to His Father and they could not follow Him there (cf. 7:33-34). **You will die in your sin.** The singular "sin" is that of rejecting the One who offers salvation (cf. 16:9). They would "die" because they continued living in the realm of sin, remaining under its power. Physical death would be their prelude to eternal separation from God.

8:22. Their question, **Will He kill Himself?** was both a misunderstanding and an ironic prophecy. They wondered if He would commit suicide and thus be unreachable. (Earlier they thought He meant He would go teach non-Jews in other lands [7:35].) Though Jesus did not kill Himself, He did lay down His own life (10:11, 18).

8:23. Jesus pointed out His heavenly origin and His real home (**from above . . . not of this world**). They belong here (**from below . . . of this world**), but He does not.

8:24. Jesus said twice they **would die**

in their **sins** (cf. this pl. with the sing. "sin" in v. 21). If they would reject the Sin-Bearer (1:29), they would continue in the realm of sin. If they would reject Jesus as the revelation of God, they would miss their only hope for salvation. **I am the One I claim to be** in Greek is the enigmatic "I Am," which is a self-designation for God in certain contexts (cf. Isa. 43:10-11, LXX).

8:25. This revelation of Jesus as "I Am" only confused the Jews. And His words about their sins probably angered them. **Who are You? they asked.** He replied, **Just what I have been claiming all along.** This is the NIV's translation of a problematic Greek sentence. (Other translations make it a question or an exclamation.)

8:26-27. Jesus could have said much more and even condemned His hearers, but His purpose in coming was to give them and **the world** the message from the One **who sent** Him. This message is certainly true because the Sender **is reliable** (cf. 7:18, 28). John added that the people **did not understand that** Jesus **was** referring to the **Father.** God was unknown to them so they missed Jesus (cf. 1:18).

8:28. Jesus was now unknown to them. Only the Crucifixion (when **the Son of Man** would be **lifted up;** cf. 3:14; 12:32) would enable them to see Him for **who** He really is. He did not mean that all will be saved, but that the Cross would reveal that Jesus is God's Word (the *Logos*) to man, and that what He taught was **just what the Father . . . taught** Him.

8:29. Jesus' union with the Father is one of love and continual obedience (cf. 4:34; 5:30). Though people reject Jesus, the Father will never abandon Him. Jesus is never **alone,** and even on the cross the Father glorified Him (cf. 16:32; 17:5).

8:30. In spite of widespread unbelief and official rejection, the ministry of Jesus did bring many to faith (cf. 7:31). Yet this faith would need to be tested and refined. The words **many put their faith in Him** contrast with the next verse. Though large numbers of people responded to Jesus, many people fell away.

8:31-32. Jews who had believed Him indicates that some paid attention to Jesus' words without necessarily committing themselves to Him personally (cf. 6:53). It was possible to "believe" in the message of repentance and the coming kingdom without being born again. Continuing in the truth is the sign of true followers and learners (**disciples**). If they really grasped His message, they would find salvation **truth.** Knowing this salvation truth would liberate them from their bondage in sin.

8:33. Their response indicated that they had not grasped Christ's message. Even though they were under Rome, they insisted that as **Abraham's descendants** they were **free** men. How could Jesus free them when they were not **slaves?** They had no sense of their bondage to sin.

8:34. Three times in this chapter (vv. 34, 51, 58) **Jesus** said, **I tell you the truth** (cf. comments on 1:51). The very act of committing **sin** reveals that the one doing the act is under the power and authority of sin. Sin is personified as a cruel master. Paul used the same illustration (Rom. 6:15-23).

8:35. Just as Ishmael, Abraham's **slave** son, was cast out of the house (Gen. 21:8-21), so those in sin are in danger. Isaac was a **son** who belonged and therefore remained in the house. Were they like Ishmael, or Isaac? The issue was not physical genealogy but spiritual kinship.

8:36. Jesus is **the** true **Son** and seed of Abraham (Gal. 3:16). He remains in the house and is over it (Heb. 3:6). People can become truly **free** by becoming sons of God by faith in Christ, *the* Son (Gal. 3:26).

8:37. Physically the Jews of course **are** the **descendants** of Abraham. **Yet** this same crowd was seeking **to kill** Jesus, Abraham's true Son, thus showing that they were not Abraham's *spiritual* descendants (cf. Rom. 2:28-29; 9:6, 8; Gal. 3:29). They were rejecting His message (**My word**).

8:38. Jesus spoke what He had **seen in the Father's presence** (cf. v. 28). Thus His words are God's truth. But the people had no affinity for His words because they listened to *their* **father** (Satan; v. 44) and followed him. As yet Jesus had not identified their father, but the implication was becoming plain.

8:39. To counter the thrust of Jesus' argument, the Jews claimed **Abraham** as their spiritual **father.** But **Jesus** responded by stating that spiritual descendants of Abraham **do** what **Abraham did,** that is, they believe and obey God. They should respond in faith to the heavenly messenger and do what He says. John the Baptist had earlier warned the Jews against the danger of trusting in their Abrahamic lineage (Luke 3:8).

8:40. But they were rejecting the heavenly Messenger and seeking **to kill** the One who **told** them God's Word. **Abraham did not do** that; he was obedient to God's commands (cf. Gen. 12:1-9; 15:6; 22:1-19).

8:41. The Jews' works were different, so their **father** (cf. v. 38) must also be different. They could seek to evade Jesus' logic only by denying an illegitimate human paternity and claiming a heavenly one. In their denial, **We are not illegitimate children,** they may have been casting aspersions on Jesus' birth.

8:42. Love is a family affair (1 John 5:1). If the Jews really had **God** as their **Father** and really loved Him (the Gr. assumes they did not), then they **would** have loved **Jesus** because He **came from God.** Jesus again affirmed His position as God's Representative: the Father **sent** Him.

8:43. Jesus the *Logos* speaks to people, but their fundamental opposition to Him caused them to misunderstand His **language. Unable to hear** means a spiritual inability to respond. The rendering **what I say** is literally, "My word" (*logos*). Paul later wrote that "the man without the Spirit does not accept the things that come from the Spirit of God, for they are foolishness to him" (1 Cor. 2:14).

8:44. The devil is the enemy of life and **truth.** By a lie he brought spiritual and physical death to mankind (cf. Gen. 3:4, 13; 1 John 3:8, 10-15.) He still distorts truth (**there is no truth in him . . . he is a liar and the father of lies**) and seeks to lead people away from God, the Source of truth and life (2 Cor. 4:4). Since these Jews wanted Jesus' death and since they rejected the truth and embraced the lie, their family solidarity with Satan and his desires was certain. How different from having Abraham as their father!

8:45. Jesus, in contrast with them, lives in **truth** and proclaims it. Since unbelievers love darkness not light (cf. 3:19-20), and falsehood not reality, they reject Jesus.

8:46. Many accusations had been made against Jesus (cf. 7:12b, 20). But He is so committed to doing God's will ("I always do what pleases Him" [8:29]) that it is impossible to show any connection between Jesus and sin: **Can any of you prove Me guilty of sin?** Since this is so, they should have recognized His divine origin. His second question, **Why don't you believe Me?** is answered in the next verse.

8:47. Belonging **to God** is the basis for hearing Him. To **hear** God is **not** a matter of being able to discern audible sounds but of obeying the heavenly commands. Jesus' hearers absolute rejection of the heavenly Word was a clear reflection **that** they did **not belong to God** (lit., "are not of God").

8:48. Samaritans were a mixed race with a religion the Jews considered apostate (cf. comments on 4:4). To call Jesus **a Samaritan** was to use a term of abuse, referring to a heretic or one with a faulty worship. Their charge that Jesus was **demon-possessed** (cf. 7:20; 8:52; 10:20) suggested they thought He was mad, unclean, and evil. How ironic that after He said their father was the devil (8:44), they said He was demon-possessed!

8:49-50. Jesus' claims were not those of a demon-**possessed** person. He was seeking not self-exaltation but the **honor** of His **Father.** Their attempt to **dishonor** Him was an attack on His Father. (Cf. Hanun's attack on David's messengers, which was an insult against the king; 2 Sam. 10:1-6.)

When accused, Jesus did not seek to justify Himself (cf. John 8:54). He committed His case to the heavenly **Judge,** knowing that even if people judge the Son falsely, the Father will reverse their verdict and vindicate Him.

8:51. Again Jesus said, **I tell you the truth** (cf. comments on 1:51). **Keeps My Word** is another way of expressing a positive response to His revelation. (Similar expressions are "hear" His Word [5:24] and "hold" to His teaching [8:31].) It means to observe, pay attention to, or to fulfill. A person who obeys Jesus **will never see death,** that is, **he** will not be eternally separated from God (cf. 3:16; 5:24).

8:52-53. His opponents thought that He meant physical death. To **taste death** means to experience death (Heb. 2:9). So they concluded that since **Abraham** and **the prophets** had **died,** He must be insane or **demon-possessed** (cf. John 7:20; 8:48; 10:19). In Greek their first question in 8:53 expected a negative answer: "You are not **greater than our father Abraham** who died, **are You?"** The irony is that of course He is. But He had not come to proclaim His greatness.

8:54. If He honored Himself (cf. v. 50), His **glory** would have no value. The **Father . . . is the One who** will do the work of vindication. Yet the hostile unbelievers claimed a relationship to **God.** It is obvious that they were in error. Jesus' Father is God; their father was Satan.

8:55. In the deepest intimacy Jesus has a relationship and union wih God but His enemies did not. Jesus knows (*oida*, "to know inherently or intuitively") the Father, but they did **not know** (*ginōskō*, "to come to know by experience or observation") **Him.** For Him to deny this would be to lie just as they were lying. Jesus did **know** the Father and obey Him (**keep His Word;** cf. v. 52).

8:56. The unbelieving Jews were not Abraham's descendants spiritually (v. 39). But here when Jesus referred to **your father Abraham** He meant they were physically related to him. Abraham **rejoiced** to see **My day,** that is, the messianic salvation which God promised ("all peoples on earth will be blessed through you"; Gen. 12:3). Abraham by faith was granted a son Isaac, through whom the Seed (Christ) would come. How much of the messianic times God revealed to His friend Abraham is unknown. But it is clear that he knew of the coming salvation and he rejoiced in knowing about it and expecting it.

8:57. The unbelievers objected that one so young (**not yet 50 years old**) could not have **seen Abraham.** (Nothing should be inferred about Jesus' age from this remark.) They could not understand how Abraham and Jesus could have possibly had any visual contact.

8:58. Jesus then affirmed His superiority over the prophets and Abraham. **Abraham** came into being; but when he **was born,** Jesus was already existing. **I Am** is a title of Deity (cf. Ex. 3:14; Isa. 41:4; 43:11-13; John 8:28); the Jews' response (v. 59) showed they understood it that way. Jesus, because of His equality with God (5:18; 20:28; Phil. 2:6; Col. 2:9), existed from all eternity (John 1:1).

8:59. Jesus' clear affirmation of His deity evoked a crisis. They had to decide whether He was what He claimed or was a blasphemer (cf. 5:18). Stoning was the normal punishment for this sin. The words, **but Jesus hid Himself,** could refer to a supernatural means of escape. The NIV's **slipping away** (lit., "He went out") implies ordinary means (cf. 5:13; 10:39; 12:36). Once again His time had not yet come (cf. 2:4; 7:6, 8, 30; 8:20).

2. THE HEALING OF A MAN BORN BLIND (CHAP. 9)

Isaiah predicted that in messianic times various signs would occur. The Messiah would "open eyes that are blind" (Isa. 42:7; cf. Isa. 29:18; 35:5). Jesus often healed the blind (cf. Matt. 9:27-31; 12:22-23; 15:30; 20:29-34; 21:14). This miracle in John 9 is notable because Jesus had just proclaimed Himself as "the Light of the world" (8:12). As a public demonstration of His claim, He gave sight to a man born blind.

9:1. As He went along in the city of Jerusalem, Jesus **saw a man** with congenital blindness. Jesus' choice of this individual is significant (cf. 5:5-6). He is Sovereign in His works. That the man was **blind from birth** pointed out his seeming hopelessness. This illustrates man's spiritual blindness from birth (9:39-41; 2 Cor. 4:4; Eph. 2:1-3).

9:2-3. The **disciples** faced a theological problem. Believing that sin directly caused all suffering, how could a person be *born* with a handicap? Therefore either **this man . . . sinned** in his mother's womb (Ezek. 18:4) **or his parents** sinned (Ex. 20:5). **Jesus** therefore answered, **Neither this man nor his parents sinned.** These words do not contradict the universal sinfulness of man (cf. Rom. 3:9-20, 23). Instead Jesus meant that this man's blindness was not caused by some *specific* sin. Instead the problem existed **so that . . . God** could display His glory in the midst of seeming tragedy (cf. Ex. 4:11; 2 Cor. 12:9).

9:4-5. Day means the time allotted for Jesus to do God's will (to **do the work of Him who sent Me**). **We** includes the disciples and by extension all believers. **Night** is the limit set to do God's works. In Jesus' case it was His coming death. As

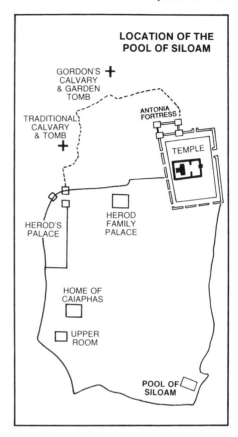

LOCATION OF THE POOL OF SILOAM

the **Light of the world** Jesus gives people salvation (cf. 8:12). After His death, His disciples would be His lights (cf. Matt. 5:14; Eph. 5:8-14), bringing Christ to others.

9:6-7. Jesus placed clay (**mud with . . . saliva) on the man's eyes.** Interestingly man was made from this same substance—the dust of the earth (Gen. 2:7). Jesus probably used the clay as an aid to develop the man's faith, not as a medicine. Jesus' making of clay broke the Rabbinic regulations against kneading clay on the Sabbath (cf. John 9:14). Jesus then **told** the man, **Wash in the pool of Siloam (this word means Sent).** This is located at the southeast corner of Jerusalem (see the map), where Hezekiah's tunnel channeled water inside the city walls from the Gihon Spring. The man was "sent" there and Jesus was the One "sent" by the Father. **The man . . . washed** and went **home seeing!**

9:8-9. People argued over whether he was **the same man who used to sit and beg.** If so, it was incredible that he could see. Perhaps, they said, it was a case of mistaken identity. **But he himself insisted, I am the man.**

9:10-12. But if he were the same man, **how** was this possible? He gave a simple and factual account of how the miracle occurred. He referred to the Lord as **the Man they call Jesus.** Since he was blind at the time of the miracle, he had no idea **where** Jesus went.

9:13-14. Since this miracle was so unusual, the people **brought** the man **to the Pharisees,** who were highly respected in religious matters. To the Pharisees, healing (unless life was in danger) and making or kneading clay violated the **Sabbath** Law.

9:15-16. When **the Pharisees . . . asked him** about his situation, he briefly told what happened (cf. v. 11). **The Pharisees** believed that since Jesus "violated" the Sabbath He was a false prophet turning the people away from God (Deut. 13:3-5). So they concluded, **This Man is not from God.** Later they said Jesus was "a sinner" (John 9:24). **Others** concluded that the **signs** were so impressive that **a sinner** could not do them. (Of course a false prophet could do deceptive signs [cf. 2 Thes. 2:9].) The Pharisees then **were divided** (cf. John 7:43; 10:19).

9:17. The healed **blind** man's opinion was that Jesus **is a prophet.** Old Testament prophets sometimes performed miracles which marked them out as God's men.

9:18-20. The Jews still could **not believe** this man **had been blind.** Surely some mistake had been made. So **they sent for** his **parents,** who affirmed that **he** was their **son** who had been **born blind.**

9:21-23. But the **parents . . . were afraid** to hazard any opinions about the cure or the Healer. The Pharisees and other Jewish authorities **(the Jews)** had **already . . . decided that** Jesus was not the Messiah. Those who held such a heresy would be excommunicated from **the synagogue.** (Some scholars argue that this verse was added later by an editor, but there is nothing unthinkable about this kind of persecution during Jesus' ministry.) The **parents** shifted the pressure from themselves by noting that their son was **of legal age** to testify for himself (vv. 21, 23).

9:24. The authorities tried to pressure the healed **man** into withdrawing his testimony about Jesus: **Give glory to God** (cf. Josh. 7:19; 1 Sam. 6:5; Jer. 13:16) was a call to admit his guilt in siding with Jesus, whom they called **a sinner.** When they said **We know,** they were pressuring him. Unbelief often claims to be scientific, but here it was just stubborn and willful.

9:25-26. His witness was clear, and he refused to deny what he knew for certain: **I was blind, but now I see! They asked him** to go over the story again, hoping to find some contradiction in the man's report.

9:27. The ex-blind man got impatient. He had already **told** how he was healed (v. 15), but they **did not listen** to him. That is, they rejected it. He sarcastically asked if their request for him to repeat his report indicated that they had changed their hearts. Were they inquiring because they were interested in becoming Jesus' disciples?

9:28-29. The idea of this illiterate beggar sarcastically suggesting they were interested in Jesus was more than their pride could take. They insulted **him** and then claimed that they were Moses' **disciples.** Jesus to them was an unknown. **We don't even know where He comes from.** Yet they claimed to know **Moses** who, Jesus said, wrote about Him (5:46).

9:30-33. The beggar proceeded to teach them since they admitted ignorance of Jesus' origin. The irony is strong for the reader knows His origin (1:14, 18). According to the beggar's logic, this miracle was notable and unique. He said that no one had **ever heard of . . . a man born blind** receiving sight. He reasoned that **God** grants **not** the requests of **sinners** but those of the righteous (cf. Elijah, James 5:16-18). Therefore **this Man,** he said, is **from God.** Otherwise He could do no miracles.

9:34. Upstaged by a beggar, they could only insult him again and throw **him out** of the synagogue (cf. v. 22). They reasoned that his blindness must have been due to some specific "sin" (they forgot the Book of Job). But they were irrational. How could anybody be **steeped in sin at birth?** Everybody is born with a sinful nature (Ps. 51:5; Rom. 5:12), but a baby can hardly commit numerous acts of sin moments after it is born!

9:35. Taking the initiative again (cf. v. 6), **Jesus** found the former blind man.

Do you (emphatic in the Gr.) **believe in the Son of Man?** This was a call to commitment. "Son of Man" is a title of Messiah which includes a rich background (cf. Dan. 7:13; and comments on Mark 2:10).

9:36-37. The beggar responded that he was willing to **believe** but he was ignorant. **Jesus** then disclosed Himself and gave the beggar the necessary knowledge for faith. Faith involves an act of the will, based on information.

9:38. After Jesus revealed that *He* is the Son of Man, **the man** responded in faith (**Lord, I believe**) and **worshiped Him.** His worship of Jesus replaced his worship in the synagogue. The Jews had cast him out of the synagogue, but Jesus does not cast out those who come to Him (6:37). One goal of salvation is worship of the One who saves (4:23).

9:39. Does this verse contradict 3:17? According to that verse (and 12:47) Jesus was *not* sent "to condemn the world." But here Jesus said, **For judgment I have come into this world.** Jesus meant He came to pronounce decisions on the ungodly, like a judge (cf. 5:22, 27). **The blind** who come to sight are those who, admitting their helplessness and inability, trust Jesus for salvation. **Those who see and become blind** are those whose self-trust and pride blinds them to the wonders of Jesus. He does not condemn them by *making* them blind; they blind themselves by rejecting Him and Satan contributes to that blinding (2 Cor. 4:4).

9:40-41. Some of the **Pharisees . . . asked,** literally, "**We** also **are** not **blind, are we?**" They expected a negative answer because they assumed that certainly they, of all men, possessed spiritual perception. Sin constantly deceives people so they live in falsehood. **Jesus** replied, If the Pharisees **were blind** to spiritual things absolutely, they might have claimed ignorance as a defense. But their claims and pretentions of spiritual insight (**you claim you can see**) and leadership made them culpable. They were responsible for their sins because they sinned willfully. It is dangerous to be a teacher of spiritual truths (cf. 3:10; Rom. 2:19-24; James 3:1).

3. THE GOOD SHEPHERD DISCOURSE (10:1-21)

The discourse on the Good Shepherd continues the same setting as in chapter 9. Comparing people to a shepherd and his sheep was common in the Middle East. Kings and priests called themselves shepherds and their subjects sheep. The Bible makes frequent use of this analogy. Many of the great men of the Old Testament were shepherds (e.g., Abraham, Isaac, Jacob, Moses, David). As national leaders, Moses and David were both "shepherds" over Israel. Some of the most famous passages in the Bible employ this motif (cf. Ps. 23; Isa. 53:6; Luke 15:1-7).

Jesus developed this analogy in several ways. The connection with the preceding chapter is seen in Jesus' contrast of the Pharisees with the man born blind. The Pharisees—spiritually blind while claiming insight (John 9:41)—were false shepherds. As the True Shepherd, Jesus came to seek and to heal. His sheep hear and respond to His voice.

10:1-2. Verses 1-5 describe a morning shepherding scene. A **shepherd** enters through a **gate** into a walled enclosure which has several flocks in one **sheep pen.** The enclosure, with stone walls, is guarded at night by a doorkeeper to prevent thieves and beasts of prey from entering. Anyone who would climb the wall would do it for no good purpose.

10:3-4. By contrast, the shepherd has a right to enter the sheep pen. **The watchman opens the gate,** and the shepherd comes in to call **his own sheep by name** (out from the other flocks). Shepherds knew their sheep well and gave them names. As **sheep** hear the sound of their owner's familiar **voice,** they go to him. He **leads them out** of the pen till his flock is formed. Then he goes **out** toward the fields with **the sheep** following **him.**

10:5-6. If a **stranger** enters the pen, the sheep **run away from him because** his **voice** is not familiar. The point of **this figure of speech** consists in how a shepherd forms his flock. People come to God because He calls them (cf. vv. 16, 27; Rom. 8:28, 30). Their proper response to His call is to follow Him (cf. John 1:43; 8:12; 12:26; 21:19, 22). But this spiritual lesson was missed by those who heard Jesus, even though they certainly understood the local shepherd/sheep relationship. In their blindness, they could not see Jesus as the Lord who is the Shepherd (cf. Ps. 23).

10:7-9. Jesus then developed the shepherd/sheep figure of speech in another way. After a shepherd's flock has been separated from the other **sheep,** he takes them to pasture. Near the pasture is an enclosure for the sheep. The shepherd takes his place in the doorway or entrance and functions as a door or **gate.** The sheep can go out to the pasture in front of the enclosure, or if afraid, they can retreat into the security of the enclosure. The spiritual meaning is that Jesus is **the** only **Gate** by which people can enter into God's provision for them.

When Jesus said, **All who ever came before Me were thieves and robbers,** He referred to those leaders of the nation who cared not for the spiritual good of the people but only for themselves. Jesus the Shepherd provides security for His flock from enemies (**whoever enters through Me will be saved,** or "kept safe"). He also provides for their daily needs (the sheep **come in and go out, and find pasture**).

10:10. The thief, that is, a false shepherd, cares only about feeding himself, not building up the flock. He steals sheep in order to **kill** them, thus destroying part of the flock. But Christ has **come** to benefit the sheep. He gives **life** which is not constricted but overflowing. The thief takes life; Christ gives **it to the full.**

10:11. Jesus then developed the sheep/shepherd figure in a third way. When evening settled over the land of Palestine, danger lurked. In Bible times lions, wolves, jackals, panthers, leopards, bears, and hyenas were common in the countryside. The life of a shepherd could be dangerous as illustrated by David's fights with at least one lion and one bear (1 Sam. 17:34-35, 37). Jacob also experienced the labor and toil of being a faithful shepherd (Gen. 31:38-40). Jesus said, **I am the Good Shepherd** (cf. John 10:14). In the Old Testament, God is called the Shepherd of His people (Pss. 23:1; 80:1-2; Ecc. 12:11; Isa. 40:11; Jer. 31:10). Jesus is this to His people, and He came to give **His life for** their benefit (cf. John 10:14, 17-18; Gal. 1:4; Eph. 5:2, 25; Heb. 9:14). He is also the "Great Shepherd" (Heb. 13:20-21) and "the Chief Shepherd" (1 Peter 5:4).

10:12-13. In contrast with **the** Good **Shepherd, who owns,** cares, feeds, protects, and dies for His **sheep,** the one who works for wages—**the hired hand**— does not have the same commitment. He is interested in making money and in self-preservation. If a **wolf attacks** (*harpazei,* lit., "snatches away"; cf. this same verb in v. 28), he **runs away** and his selfishness causes **the flock** to be scattered. Obviously he **cares nothing for the sheep.** Israel had many false prophets, selfish kings, and imitation messiahs. The flock of God suffered constantly from their abuse (Jer. 10:21-22; 12:10; Zech. 11:4-17).

10:14-15. In contrast with a hired workman, **the Good Shepherd** has an intimacy with and personal interest in the sheep (cf. vv. 3, 27). **I know My sheep** stresses His ownership and watchful oversight. **My sheep know Me** stresses their reciprocal knowledge of and intimacy with Him. This intimacy is modeled on the loving and trusting mutual relationship of **the Father** and the Son. Jesus' care and concern is evidenced by His prediction of His coming death for the flock. Some shepherds have willingly died while protecting their sheep from danger. Jesus willingly gave His **life for** His **sheep** (vv. 11, 15, 17-18)—on their behalf as their Substitute (Rom. 5:8, 10; 2 Cor. 5:21; 1 Peter 2:24; 3:18). His death gives them life.

10:16. The other sheep . . . not of this flock refers to Gentiles who would believe. His coming death would **bring them also** to the Father. **They too will listen to My voice.** Jesus continues to save people as they hear His voice in the Scriptures. Acts 18:9-11 illustrates how this works out in the history of the church. "I have many people in this city" (i.e., Corinth), the Lord told Paul. **One flock and one Shepherd** speaks of the church with believers from Jewish and Gentile "sheep pens" in one body with Christ as Head (cf. Eph. 2:11-22; 3:6).

10:17-18. Again Jesus predicted His death, saying four times that He would voluntarily **lay down** His **life** (vv. 11, 14, 17-18). The **Father** has a special love for Jesus because of His sacrificial obedience to the will of God. Jesus predicted His resurrection twice (He would **take . . . up** His life **again** [vv. 17-18]) and His sovereignty (**authority**) over His own destiny. His death was wholly voluntary: **No one takes it from Me.** Jesus was not a helpless pawn on history's chessboard.

10:19-21. For the third time Jesus' teaching **divided** the people (cf. 7:43; 9:16). **Many** in this hostile crowd judged Him to be **demon-possessed and raving mad** (cf. 7:20; 8:48, 52). **But others** figured that He was not demon-possessed, for how could **a demon open the eyes of the blind?** (cf. 9:16)

4. THE FINAL PUBLIC TEACHING (10:22-42)

John then recorded a final confrontation of Jesus with the hostile Jerusalem crowd (vv. 22-39), followed by His withdrawal beyond Jordan (vv. 40-42) because of attempts to kill Him.

10:22-23. The Feast of Dedication is nowadays called Hanukkah or the Feast of Lights. It commemorates the reconsecration of the temple by Judas Maccabeus in 165 B.C. after its desecration in 168 B.C. by Antiochus IV (Epiphanes). The time for the eight-day feast was in December. **It was winter.** The feast reminded the Jewish people of their last great deliverance from their enemies. **Solomon's Colonnade** was a long covered walkway on the east side of **the temple.** Two months had elapsed since Jesus' last confrontation with the Jews (7:1–10:21) at the Feast of Tabernacles (7:2), which was in October. Jesus again returned to the temple **area.**

10:24. The Jews gathered around Him. Actually they "closed in (*ekyklōsan*) on Him." The hostile Jerusalem leaders were determined to pin Him down so they surrounded Him. His enigmatic sayings plagued them, and they wanted Him to declare Himself on their terms. **How long will You keep us in suspense?** they asked. "Keep us in suspense" is literally "hold up our soul." They insisted, **If You are the Christ, tell us plainly.**

10:25-26. Jesus responded that **the miracles** (lit., "works"; cf. vv. 32, 38) He had done are clear evidence that He is from the Father (cf. Isa. 35:3-6; John 3:2; 9:32-33). He is the One the Father sent, but He did not match their expectations. He was no Judas Maccabeus nor would His ministry be like Moses'. Their problem was a lack of spiritual perception and faith. **But you do not believe because you are not My sheep** is a simple statement of fact about their conduct. It also reminds one of the ultimate mystery of God's election (cf. 6:37).

10:27. Jesus' flock is responsive to His teaching. They **listen to** His **voice** (vv. 3-5, 16). They have an intimacy with Jesus (**I know them;** cf. vv. 3, 14), they understand His message of salvation, **and they follow** Him (vv. 4-5). To follow Him means to obey the Father's will as Jesus did.

10:28. This is one of the clearest statements in the Bible that one who believes in Jesus for salvation will never be lost. Believers sin and stumble, but Jesus as the perfect Shepherd loses none of His flock (cf. Luke 22:31-32). **Eternal life** is a gift (John 3:16, 36; 5:24; 10:10; Rom. 6:23). If one has it, he has it eternally. **They shall never perish** is a strong affirmation in the Greek: *ou mē apolōntai eis ton aiōna* ("they will indeed not ever perish"; cf. John 3:16, *mē apolētai,* "never perish"). The security of the sheep is found in the ability of the Shepherd to defend and preserve His flock. Such security does not depend on the ability of the frail sheep. **No one can** even **snatch** His sheep **out of** His **hand.** "Snatch" is *harpasei,* related to *harpax* ("ravenous wolves, robbers"). This is a fitting word here for the same verb (*harpazei*) is used in 10:12, "the wolf attacks" (lit., "snatches away").

10:29. My Father, who has given them to Me, is greater than all. That is, **no one** is strong enough to **snatch** any **of** Jesus' flock from the **Father's hand** (or from Jesus' hand, v. 28). As the NIV margin states, verse 29a in many early Greek manuscripts reads, "What My Father has given Me is greater than all." The thought of the verse in either case is that the Father who is omnipotent secures the flock by His power and protection. God's plan of salvation for Jesus' flock cannot be aborted.

10:30. When Jesus said, **I and the Father are One,** He was not affirming that He and the Father are the same Person. The Son and the Father are two Persons in the Trinity. This is confirmed by the fact that the word "One" is neuter. Instead, He was saying They have the closest possible unity of purpose. Jesus' will is identical to the Father's regarding the salvation of His sheep. And yet absolute identity of wills involves identity of nature. Jesus and the Father are One in will (and also in nature for both are God; cf. 20:28; Phil. 2:6; Col. 2:9).

10:31-32. The hostile crowd reacted and attempted **to stone** Jesus (cf. 8:59) because they understood the implications of His claim. Jesus' courage was displayed in His calm question: **Which of His many great miracles** (lit., "works"; cf. 10:25, 38) **from the Father** was their reason for wanting to **stone** Him?

10:33. They claimed that they found no objection in His works. (Yet His healings on the Sabbath had angered them [5:18; 9:16].) They said they objected **because** He, **a mere man,** claimed **to be God.** This, they said, was **blasphemy.** And yet, ironically, Jesus, who *is* God, did become Man (1:1, 14, 18). Jesus did not walk around Palestine saying "I am God," but His interpretation of the Sabbath and His words about His union with the Father revealed His claim of oneness in nature with God.

10:34. Jesus' response to their objection requires a bit of insight into the methods of argument common in Rabbinic discussions. He first directed them to the Old Testament: **in your Law.** Normally "the Law" refers to the first five books. But here it means all the Old Testament, for Jesus quoted from the Psalms. It was "your" Law in the sense that they gloried in their possession of it, and also in the sense that they should submit to its authority over them. Psalm 82 speaks of God as the true Judge (Ps. 82:1, 8) and of men, appointed as judges, who were failing to provide true judgment for God (Ps. 82:2-7). "Gods" in Psalm 82:1, 6 refers to these human judges. In this sense, God **said** to the Jews, **You are gods.** In no way does this speak of a divine nature in man.

10:35. As seen in verse 34, Jesus argued that in certain situations (as in Ps. 82:1, 6) men were **called . . . "gods."** The Hebrew word for **God** or gods is *'ĕlōhîm.* This word is used elsewhere (e.g., Ex. 21:6; 22:8) to mean human judges. Jesus added to His argument the words, **and the Scripture cannot be broken,** so that no one could evade its force by saying an error was in the Scriptures. This important text clearly points up the inerrancy of the Bible.

10:36. Jesus now completed His argument. Since the inerrant Bible called

their judges "gods," the Jews could not logically **accuse** Him **of blasphemy** for calling Himself **God's Son** since He was under divine orders (**set apart**) and on God's mission (**sent into the world**).

10:37-38. Though the Jews were reluctant to **believe** Jesus' words, God was giving them **miracles** (lit., "works"; cf. vv. 25, 32), which he was doing through Jesus. These signs were given for their learning so that by pondering their significance they might recognize Jesus' oneness with the **Father** (**the Father is in Me, and I in the Father**). Nicodemus had recognized this for he said, "No one could perform [those] miraculous signs . . . if God were not with Him" (3:2).

10:39. Again an attempt was made **to seize** (from *piazō*) **Him** (cf. 7:30, 32, 44; 8:20), perhaps to bring Him to trial. Once again, since it was not God's time, **He escaped** (cf. 5:13; 8:59; 12:36). No explanation is given as to how He escaped.

10:40-42. Because of their hostility, **Jesus went . . . across the Jordan to** Perea, which had been the location of **John** the Baptist's activity (1:28). Jesus' ministry here was received much more favorably, probably because the Baptist had prepared the people there. **John,** even though dead, was still having influence in people's lives as they remembered his witness. **Though John never performed a miraculous sign** (*sēmeion*), the people **believed** his witness **about** Jesus. By contrast, the hostile Jerusalem crowd had seen His signs and yet disobeyed. In Perea **many** trusted **Jesus** as Savior.

E. The great sign at Bethany (11:1-44)

This climactic miracle of raising Lazarus from the dead was Jesus' public evidence of the truth of His great claim, "I am the Resurrection and the Life." Death is the great horror which sin has produced (Rom. 5:12; James 1:15). Physical death is the divine object lesson of what sin does in the spiritual realm. As physical death ends life and separates people, so spiritual death is the separation of people from God and the loss of life which is in God (John 1:4). Jesus has come so that people may live full lives (10:10). Rejecting Jesus means that one will not see life (3:36) and that his final destiny is "the second death," the lake of fire (Rev. 20:14-15).

11:1-2. This **Lazarus** is mentioned in the New Testament only in this chapter and in chapter 12. **Bethany** (cf. 11:18) is on the east side of the Mount of Olives. Another Bethany is in Perea (cf. 1:28). Luke added some information on the two sisters **Mary** and **Martha** (Luke 10:38-42). **This Mary . . . was the same one who** later (see John 12:1-10) **poured perfume on the Lord and wiped His feet with her hair.** However, John may be assuming that the original readers of his Gospel already had some knowledge of Mary (cf. Mark 14:3-9).

11:3. **The sisters** assumed, because of the Lord's ability and His **love** for Lazarus, that He would immediately respond to their **word** about Lazarus' illness and come.

11:4. Jesus did not go immediately (see v. 6). But His delay was not from lack of love (cf. v. 5), or from fear of the Jews. He waited till the right moment in the Father's plan. Lazarus' **sickness** would **not end in death,** that is, in permanent death. Instead Jesus would **be glorified** in this incident (cf. 9:3). This statement is ironic. Jesus' power and obedience to the Father were displayed, but this event led to *His* death (cf. 11:50-53), which was His true **glory** (17:1).

11:5-6. In spite of Jesus' love for all three (**Martha and her sister and Lazarus**), **He** waited **two more days.** Apparently (vv. 11, 39) Lazarus was already dead when Jesus heard about him. Jesus' movements were under God's direction (cf. 7:8).

11:7-10. His disciples knew that His going **to Judea,** would be dangerous (10:31). So they tried to prevent Him from going. **Jesus** spoke in a veiled way to illustrate that it would not be too dangerous to go to Bethany. In one sense He was speaking of walking (living) in physical **light** or darkness. In the spiritual realm when one lives by the will of God he is safe. Living in the realm of evil is dangerous. As long as He followed God's plan, no harm would come till the appointed time. Applied to people then, they should have responded to Jesus while He was in the world as its Light (cf. 1:4-7; 3:19; 8:12; 9:5). Soon He would be gone and so would this unique opportunity.

11:11-12. Jesus then said, **Our friend Lazarus has fallen asleep.** The

word "friend" has special significance in Scripture (cf. 15:13-14; James 2:23). This "sleep" is the sleep of death. Since the coming of Christ the death of a believer is regularly called a sleep (cf. Acts 7:60; 1 Cor. 15:20; 1 Thes. 4:13-18). Dead Christians are asleep not in the sense of an unconscious "soul sleep," but in the sense that their bodies appear to be sleeping. The **disciples** wrongly assumed that Jesus meant Lazarus had not died, but was sleeping physically (cf. John 11:13) and was on his way to recovery: **If he sleeps, he will get better.**

11:13-15. As was often the case in the Gospels, **Jesus** was **speaking** about one thing **but the disciples** were thinking about another. The words **Lazarus is dead, and for your sake I am glad I was not there** seem shocking at first. But if Lazarus had not died, the disciples (and readers of all ages) would not have had this unique opportunity to have their faith quickened. Lazarus' death was **so that you may believe.**

11:16. Didymus means "twin." **Thomas** is often called "doubting Thomas" because of the incident recorded in 20:24-25. But here he took the leadership and showed his commitment to Christ, even to death. **That we may die with Him** is ironic. On one level it reveals Thomas' ignorance of the uniqueness of Christ's atoning death. On another level it is prophetic of many disciples' destinies (12:25).

11:17. Apparently **Lazarus had** died soon after the messengers left. **Jesus** was then a day's journey away. Since Palestine is warm and decomposition sets in quickly, a person was usually buried the same day he died (cf. v. 39).

11:18-19. The fact that **Bethany was less than two miles from Jerusalem** points up two things. It explains why **many Jews** from Jerusalem were at the scene of this great miracle (vv. 45-46). It also prepares the reader for the coming climax which was to take place in the great city. When a person died, the Jews mourned for a prolonged period of time. During this period it was considered a pious duty **to comfort** the bereaved.

11:20-22. Martha, the activist, **went . . . to meet** Jesus while **Mary,** the contemplative sister, waited. (Cf. Luke 10:39-42 for a similar portrayal of their personalities.) Martha's greeting is a confession of faith. She really believed that **Jesus** could have healed her brother **if He had been** there. No criticism of Jesus seems to be implied since she knew her **brother** was dead before the messengers got to Jesus. Her words **But I know . . . God will give You whatever You ask** might imply by themselves that she was confident Lazarus would be resuscitated. But her actions in protest at the tomb (John 11:39) and her words to Jesus (v. 24) contradict that interpretation. Her words may be taken as a general statement of the Father's blessing on Jesus.

11:23-24. Your brother will rise again. Since the word "again" is not in the Greek it is better to omit it in the translation. This promise sets the stage for Jesus' conversation with **Martha.** She had no thought of an immediate resuscitation but she did believe **in the** final **resurrection at the last day.**

11:25-26. I am the Resurrection and the Life. This is the fifth of Jesus' great "I am" revelations. The Resurrection and the Life of the new Age is present right now because Jesus is the Lord of life (1:4). Jesus' words about life and death are seemingly paradoxical. A believer's death issues in new life. In fact, the life of a believer is of such a quality that he **will never die** spiritually. He has eternal life (3:16; 5:24; 10:28), and the end of physical life is only a sleep for his body until the resurrection unto life. At death the spiritual part of a believer, his soul, goes to be with the Lord (cf. 2 Cor. 5:6, 8; Phil. 1:23).

11:27. Martha gave a great confession of faith in Christ. She agreed with Jesus' exposition about eternal life for those who **believe** in Him. Then she confessed three things about Jesus. He is (a) **the Christ** ("Messiah"), (b) **the Son of God**—which is probably a title of the Messiah (cf. 1:49; Ps. 2:7)—and (c) the One **who was to come into the world** (lit., "the Coming One"; cf. John 12:13). She believed that Jesus is the Messiah who came to do God's will, but as yet she had no hint of the coming miracle regarding her brother.

11:28-30. Martha then told **Mary** that Jesus **the Teacher** was **asking for** her. He evidently wanted to have a private conversation with Mary. His purpose was probably to comfort and instruct her. "The Teacher" is a notable title for it was unusual for a Jewish Rabbi to instruct a woman (cf. 4:1-42).

11:31-32. Mary's sudden departure to see Jesus caused the crowd of Jewish comforters to follow **her.** So a private session with Jesus became impossible. Reaching **Jesus,** Mary **fell at His feet.** This is significant, for on a previous occasion she had sat at Jesus' feet listening to His teaching (Luke 10:39). Her greeting to Jesus was the same as her sister's (John 11:21). She felt the tragedy would have been averted **if He had been** present. Her faith was sincere but limited.

11:33-34. In great contrast with the Greek gods' apathy or lack of emotion, Jesus' emotional life attests the reality of His union with people. **Deeply moved** may either be translated "groaned" or more likely "angered." The Greek word *enebrimēsato* (from *embrimaomai*) seems to connote anger or sternness. (This Gr. verb is used only five times in the NT, each time of the Lord's words or feelings: Matt. 9:30; Mark 1:43; 14:5; John 11:33, 38.)

Why was **Jesus** angry? Some have argued that He was angry because of the people's unbelief or hypocritical wailing. But this seems foreign to the context. A better explanation is that Jesus was angry at the tyranny of Satan who had brought sorrow and death to people through sin (cf. 8:44; Heb. 2:14-15). Also Jesus was **troubled** (*etaraxen,* lit., "stirred" or "agitated," like the pool water in John 5:7; cf. 12:27; 13:21; 14:1, 27). This disturbance was because of His conflict with sin, death, and Satan.

11:35-37. Jesus' weeping differed from that of the people. His quiet shedding of tears (*edakrysen*) differed from their loud wailing (*klaiontas,* v. 33). His weeping was over the tragic consequences of sin. The crowd interpreted His tears as an expression of love, or frustration at not being there to heal Lazarus.

11:38-39. Disturbed emotionally (cf. comments on **deeply moved,** in v. 33), Jesus **came to the tomb.** Tombs were often cut into limestone making **a cave** in the side of a wall of rock. **A stone** was placed over **the entrance. Jesus** commanded that **the stone** door be taken **away.** To do so was to risk defilement. But obedience was necessary if Jesus' purpose was to be realized. The scene was highly dramatic. The crowd watched and listened. Mary was weeping and **Martha** objected because after **four days** putrefaction had set in.

11:40. **Jesus** reminded Martha of His earlier promise (vv. 25-26; cf. v. 4). If she **believed** His word that He is the Resurrection and the Life and trusted Him, **God** would be glorified. But unless the sisters had trusted Jesus, permission would not have been given to open the tomb.

11:41-42. With **the stone** taken **away,** the tension mounted. What would **Jesus** do? He simply thanked His **Father** for granting His request. He knew He was doing the Father's will in manifesting His love and power. His prayer of thanksgiving was public, not so that He would be honored as a Wonder-Worker but so He would be seen as the Father's obedient Son. The granting of His request by the Father would give clear evidence to the people that He had been **sent** by the Father and would cause the people to **believe** (cf. Elijah's prayer; 1 Kings 18:37).

11:43-44. On other occasions **Jesus** had said that men would hear His voice and come out of their graves (5:28) and that His sheep hear His voice (10:16, 27). After His brief prayer He **called** (*ekraugasen*, lit., "shouted loudly") **in a loud voice.** This verb is used only nine times in the New Testament, eight of them in the Gospels (Matt. 12:19; Luke 4:41; John 11:43; 12:13; 18:40; 19:6, 12, 15; Acts 22:23).

Jesus shouted only three words: **Lazarus come out!** Augustine once remarked that if Jesus had not said Lazarus' name all would have come out from the graves. Immediately, **the dead man came out.** Since he was **wrapped** in **strips of linen,** a special work of God's power must have brought him out. Jesus' directive to the people, **Take off the grave clothes,** enabled Lazarus to move on his own and at the same time gave evidence that he was alive and not a ghost.

This event is a marvelous picture of God's Son bringing life to people. He will do this physically at the Rapture for church saints (1 Thes. 4:16), and at His return for Old Testaments saints (Dan. 12:2) and Tribulation saints (Rev. 20:4, 6). Also He now speaks and calls spiritually dead people to spiritual life. Many who are dead in sins and trespasses believe and come to life by the power of God (Eph. 2:1-10).

F. The plot to kill Jesus (11:45-57)

11:45-47a. Jesus' revelation of Himself always produces two responses. For **many of the Jews,** this miracle was clear proof of Jesus' claim. In response they trusted **Him.** But others were only hardened in sin or confused. They **went to** His enemies, **the Pharisees, and** reported **what** had happened. This miraculous sign was so significant that **the chief priests and the Pharisees** decided to call an emergency session **of the Sanhedrin** (see comments on 3:1 on the Sanhedrin). Doubtless they felt that Jesus was some kind of magician who by secret arts was deceiving the people.

11:47b-48. The council expressed its inability to solve the problem by continuing to do what they had been doing. Official disapproval, excommunication, and counterteaching were not stopping Jesus' influence. The outcome would be insurrection and **the Romans** would crush the Jewish revolt; taking **away both our place** (i.e., the temple) **and our nation.**

11:49-50. **Caiaphas** was the **high priest that year** (cf. 18:13-14, 24, 28). Originally the high priest held his position for a lifetime, but the Romans were afraid of letting a man gain too much power. So the Romans appointed high priests at their convenience. Caiaphas had the office from A.D. 18 to 36. His contempt was expressed in his words, **You know nothing at all!** His judgment was **that** this **Man** must be sacrificed if the **nation** was to continue in Rome's favor. The alternative was destruction of the Jewish nation in war (11:48). But their rejection of Jesus did not solve the problem. The Jewish people followed false shepherds into a war against Rome (A.D. 66-70), which did in fact destroy their nation.

11:51-53. John by God's Spirit recognized a deep irony in Caiaphas' words. As the **high priest,** Caiaphas pointed to the last sacrificial Lamb in a prophecy he did not even know he made. Caiaphas meant **Jesus** had to be killed, but God intended the priest's words as a reference to His substitutionary atonement. Jesus' death would abolish the old system in God's eyes by fulfilling all its types and shadows. His death was not only for Jews but also for the world, thus making a new body from both (cf. Eph.

2:14-18; 3:6). The Sanhedrin then decided to kill Jesus.

11:54. Jesus . . . withdrew from Bethany **to a village** 15 or so miles to the north **called Ephraim.** The little village provided a place for rest and it was close to the wilderness of Judea in case it was necessary to escape.

11:55-57. Jewish pilgrims **went up** to **the Passover** feast at **Jerusalem** and looked **for Jesus.** Previously (2:13-25) He had attended the national festivals during which time He publicly taught **in the temple area.** Would He continue this pattern of ministry? Large crowds gathering in the city **kept looking for** Him. The religious authorities gave **orders** for **anyone** to **report** if he **found out where Jesus was** so **they** could **arrest Him.**

G. The conclusion of Jesus' public ministry (12:1-36)

1. THE ANOINTING (12:1-8)

John in chapter 12 concluded his record of Jesus' public ministry with (a) the account of Mary's anointing of Jesus (which set the stage for His coming sacrifice), (b) His Triumphal Entry, and (c) the prediction of His death.

12:1-2. The time schedule now was more definite and critical: It was **six days before the Passover. Jesus** went back from Ephraim (11:54) to **Bethany, where Lazarus lived,** and attended **a dinner** in His **honor.** Mark wrote that the place was Simon the Leper's home (Mark 14:1-11). The dinner must have been a joyous occasion with Mary, **Martha,** and **Lazarus** there. The relationship of this family to Simon is not known, but it must have been close since Martha **served.**

12:3. The **pure nard** was a fragrant oil prepared from the roots and stems of an aromatic herb from northern India. It was **an expensive perfume,** imported in sealed alabaster boxes or flasks which were opened only on special occasions. Mary's lavish gift (**a pint**) expressed her love and thanks to Jesus for Himself and for His restoring Lazarus to life. **The house was filled with the fragrance.** This is one of John's many side comments which indicate that he was an eyewitness of much of Jesus' ministry.

12:4-5. Judas Iscariot . . . objected to this lavish waste (in his viewpoint). His objection—that **money** from the sale of the **perfume** should have been **given to**

the poor—was not honest (cf. v. 6). According to Mark (14:4-5) the other disciples picked up his criticism and rebuked her harshly. Evil quickly spreads, and even leaders can be carried along by Satan's tools. The value of the perfume was **a year's wages** (lit., "300 denarii") perhaps a lifetime of savings.

12:6. John with the hindsight of history was able to state why Judas said **this.** Judas, evidently the group's treasurer (cf. 13:29), would pocket some of the benevolence **money** for **himself.** Whereas Mary gave openly and sacrificially, Judas wanted to horde money for himself secretly and selfishly. He even betrayed Jesus for money—30 pieces of silver (the price of a gored slave; cf. Ex. 21:32; Zech. 11:12-13).

12:7-8. Normally anointing was something festive. But in this case the anointing was in anticipation of His **burial.** Living by God's Word, **Jesus** knew that as the suffering Servant, He must endure pain, die, and be buried (cf. Isa. 53:9).

So He immediately defended Mary's act of love and devotion. **You will always have the poor among you** is not a divine endorsement of poverty or an encouragement to do nothing about poverty. Instead, Jesus was saying that the causes of poverty are many and people will always have occasions to help the poor (Mark 14:7). But the opportunity to show love to Jesus on earth was limited. **You will not always have Me,** that is, here on earth (cf. John 12:35; 13:33; 14:3-4).

2. THE TRIUMPHAL ENTRY (12:9-19)

12:9-11. Jesus was such a controversial Person that it was impossible for Him to be near Jerusalem and remain unnoticed. From all over the country, people came to the Passover feast. Many sought out **Jesus** (cf. 11:56) and **also . . . Lazarus.** Because Lazarus had been restored, **many . . . Jews** believed in **Jesus. So the chief priests** planned **to kill** two men—Jesus and **Lazarus!**

12:12-13. A wild enthusiasm over **Jesus** broke out. Thousands of Galilean pilgrims **had come** to the Passover, and they had seen many of His mighty works. Previously He had rejected the role of a political Messiah (6:15) but, they thought, perhaps now was the right moment. **Jerusalem** was the city of the great King and He was coming to it. Waving their **palm branches,** symbols of victory, the people were **shouting** (*ekraugazon;* cf. comments on 11:43) **Hosanna!** "Hosanna" in Hebrew means "Please save" or "Save now" (cf. Ps. 118:25). It came to be a shout of praise. Quoting Psalm 118:26, they ascribed messianic titles to Him: **He who comes** (lit., "the Coming One"; cf. John 11:27) and **the King of Israel.**

12:14-15. Jesus' riding into the city on **a young donkey** was a sign of peace (cf. comments on Matt. 21:2, which speaks of Jesus riding on a donkey *and* a colt). He did not ride a war horse or carry a sword or wear a crown. Nor did He ride in a wheeled vehicle, as did many kings. His manner of entry fulfilled Zechariah's prophecy which contrasted Jesus' coming (Zech. 9:9) with the coming of Alexander the Great (Zech. 9:1-8). **Daughter of Zion** is a poetic way of referring to the people of Jerusalem, the city built on Mount Zion. Here, in quoting Zechariah 9:9, John called Jesus Israel's **King.**

12:16. The **disciples,** though close to Jesus and participants in these events, **did not understand** them. They lacked the perspective of the Cross and the Resurrection (when He **was glorified**). They were unaware that Zechariah's prophecy **had been written about Him.** Their faith was weak and they needed the ministry of the Holy Spirit (16:12-14).

12:17-18. The size of **the crowd** kept increasing. The news of the great **miraculous sign—Lazarus** raised **from the dead**—spread through the city, and other groups surged **out to meet Him.** It was a day of great popular acclaim, but sadly the people had little spiritual perception.

12:19. The mass reception of Jesus made the plans of **the Pharisees** impossible. They "were looking for some sly way to arrest Jesus and kill Him. 'But not during the Feast,' they said, 'or the people may riot' " (Mark 14:1-2). Pessimistically they acknowledged, **The whole world has gone after Him.** Irony is again evident, for most of those people did not really believe in Jesus.

3. THE GREEKS AT THE FEAST (12:20-36)

12:20. The mention of **Greeks** is significant. They were the wanderers of the ancient world and the seekers of truth. These Greeks were probably God-fearers who attended Jewish synagogues and feasts. Their coming was symbolic of the coming of Gentiles **to worship** God through Christ (cf. 10:16).

12:21-22. Why did the Greeks approach **Philip** about seeing **Jesus?** Perhaps because Philip had a Greek name. Or he may have had some contact with Greeks from the Decapolis area. **Philip went to . . . Andrew,** and **Andrew and Philip . . . told Jesus.** Since crowds of people probably wanted to speak with Jesus, the disciples may have tried to do some screening (cf. Luke 18:15-16).

12:23-24. **Jesus** had been moving toward His decisive hour (cf. 2:4; 4:21, 23; 7:6, 8, 30; 8:20). The coming of the Greeks confirmed that **the hour has come for the Son of Man to be glorified** (cf. 12:23; 13:1; 17:1). For most people death is their humiliation. But for Jesus death was His means of entry into glory. His willingness to die for others' sins in obedience to the Father (Isa. 53:10, 12) brought Him renown (glory; cf. John 12:16; 17:1, 5). **I tell you the truth** introduces a solemn affirmation. The analogy of **a kernel of wheat** "dying" in **the ground** and producing **many seeds** teaches that death is necessary for a harvest.

12:25-26. The wheat analogy (v. 24) illustrates a general paradoxical principle: death is the way to life. In Jesus' case, His death led to glory and life not only for Himself but also for others.

In the case of a disciple of Jesus, the principle is similar. A disciple must hate **his life in this world.** To "hate his life" means to be so committed to Christ that he has no self-centeredness, no concern for himself. On the other hand **the man who loves his life will lose it.** Anything in life can become an idol including goals, interests, and loves (cf. Luke 12:16-21; 18:18-30). A believer should undergo a spiritual death to self (Rom. 6:1-14; 2 Cor. 5:14-15; Gal. 6:14).

Being a servant of Jesus requires following Him. Many of Jesus' original servants *did* follow Him—in death. According to tradition, the early disciples died as martyrs. Jesus' word was thus a prophecy and also a promise. His true disciples (those who serve Him) **follow** Him in humiliation and later in **honor** or glory (Rom. 8:17, 36-39; 2 Tim. 2:11-13).

12:27-28a. Jesus instructed His disciples on the cost of commitment to the Father's will by disclosing His emotions. He was in turmoil (*tetaraktai,* "stirred, agitated"; cf. 11:33; 14:1) because of the prospect of being made sin (2 Cor. 5:21) in His death. In view of His turmoil, should He shrink back and ask for deliverance **from this hour?** Certainly not, for His Incarnation **was** for the **very** purpose of bringing Him **to this hour** (cf. John 12:23; 13:1; 17:1). Jesus willingly expressed His submission to the will of the Father in the words, **Father, glorify Your name!** So also believers in difficulty should stand and embrace His will—desiring that His name be glorified—in spite of conflicting emotions.

12:28b-29. The Father then spoke **from heaven** in **a** thunderous **voice,** confirming His working in Jesus both in the past and in the future. The voice was audible but not all understood it (cf. v 30; Acts 9:7; 22:9).

12:30-31. The **voice** from heaven confirmed faith in the spiritually perceptive but to the unspiritual it was only a noise (1 Cor. 2:14). Jesus' death on the cross was a **judgment on** the **world.** Evil was atoned for. The world's goals, standards, and religions were shown to be folly. The Cross was also the means of Satan's defeat (Rev. 12:10). **The prince of this world** (i.e., Satan; cf. John 14:30; 16:11), **Jesus** said, **will be driven out.** His power over people by sin and death was defeated and they can now be delivered out of his domain of spiritual darkness and slavery to sin (Col. 1:13-14; Heb. 2:14-15).

12:32-33. Jesus' words, **When I am lifted up from the earth,** refer not to His Ascension but to His crucifixion (cf. 3:14; 8:28). He knew how He would die—by being "lifted up" on a cross. Jews, however, normally stoned those they considered worthy of death (cf. Stephen's death, Acts 7:58-60).

Jesus said that at the cross He would **draw all men to** Himself. He did not mean everybody will be saved for He made it clear that some will be lost (John 5:28-29). If the drawing by the Son is the same as that of the Father (6:44), it means He will draw indiscriminately. Those saved will include not only Jews, but also those from every tribe, language, people, and nation (Rev. 5:9; cf. John 10:16; 11:52).

12:34. The crowd was puzzled. If the Messiah is **the Son of Man,** then He

should be here **forever,** they reasoned. Daniel 7:13-14 spoke of the Son of Man's everlasting dominion. Perhaps the people wondered if He was making a distinction between the Messiah (**Christ**) and **the Son of Man.** Did He use the term "Son of Man" differently than its sense in Daniel 7:13? They seemed to understand that Jesus was predicting His death, but they could not see how that was possible, if He was the Messiah.

12:35-36. The crowd thought on intellectual difficulties, but **Jesus** confronted them with the fact that the issue was moral. Their time of opportunity was limited. He is **the Light** for the world (1:4, 9; 8:12; 12:46), but the day of His public ministry was almost over (v. 23). The **darkness** of night was coming in which evil powers would hold sway over people. **The man who walks in the dark** means an unbeliever who stumbles through life without knowing what life is all about and **where** it **is** headed (cf. 3:19; 8:12; 1 John 1:6). Their privilege was to **trust in the Light** (i.e., in Jesus) and **become sons of Light** (i.e., His disciples; cf. Rom. 13:12; Eph. 5:8, 14; Col. 1:13-14; 1 Thes. 5:5; 1 John 1:7; 2:10). Once again **Jesus** supernaturally vanished **from them** (cf. John 5:13; 8:59; 10:39).

H. Jewish national unbelief (12:37-50)

1. JOHN'S EXPLANATION (12:37-43)

12:37. John from the beginning of his Gospel (1:11) had sounded the theme of national unbelief. John now explained that in spite of **all** Jesus' **miraculous signs** (*sēmeia*), **they still would not believe in Him.** Their unbelief was irrational, as sin always is.

12:38. The Jews' national, irrational unbelief had been predicted by **Isaiah the prophet.** The clearest Old Testament passage concerning the suffering Servant (Isa. 53:1-12) began by stating that Israel would not perceive God's revelation in and through the Servant. **Who has believed our message and** seen His **arm . . . revealed?** implies that only a few have believed (quoting Isa. 53:1).

12:39-40. Then John again quoted from **Isaiah** (6:10) to explain that the nation as a whole was *unable* to believe. Because they constantly rejected God's revelation, He had punished them with judicial blindness **and deadened . . . hearts.** People in Jesus' day, like those in

Isaiah's day, refused to believe. They "would not believe" (John 12:37); therefore **they could not believe** (v. 39). Similar illustrations of God's punishing of persistent sin by hardening are common (Ex. 9:12; Rom. 1:24, 26, 28; 2 Thes. 2:8-12).

12:41. In a vision **Isaiah . . . saw** "the Lord Almighty" (lit., "Yahweh of hosts," or "Yahweh of armies"; Isa. 6:3). John wrote that this glory Isaiah saw was **Jesus' glory.** The implication is startling: Jesus is Yahweh! (Cf. John 1:18; 10:30; 20:28; Col. 2:9.) Jesus in His nature is God (but God the Son is distinct in person from God the Father and God the Spirit). Isaiah **spoke about Him,** for many of Isaiah's prophecies predicted the coming Messiah, Jesus of Nazareth (e.g., Isa. 4:2; 7:14; 9:6-7; 11:1-5, 10; 32:1; 42:1-4; 49:1-7; 52:13-53:12; 61:1-3). Earlier Jesus had said that Moses wrote about Him (John 5:46).

12:42-43. In spite of massive national unbelief, the situation was not hopeless. God always has a remnant. **Many** individuals in high places did believe **in** Jesus, but **for fear** of being **put out of the synagogue** they did **not** openly **confess** Him. They feared men's opinions and **loved** men's **praise . . . more than** God's **praise.**

2. JESUS' EXHORTATION (12:44-50)

When and where Jesus spoke these words is not indicated. This seems to be a general summary of Jesus' manifestation of Himself to the nation.

12:44-46. Cried out (*ekraxen,* "called out," *not* wept; cf. 1:15; 7:28, 37) indicates the importance of the issues before the nation. **Jesus** is the perfect manifestation of God, **the One who sent** Him (1:18; Col. 1:15; Heb. 1:3), so that to **believe in** Jesus is to believe in God. People do not have two objects of faith: God and/or Jesus. When one sees Jesus, he **sees the** Father **who sent** Him (cf. John 12:41; 14:9). Jesus came to lead people out of Satan's kingdom of **darkness** into God's kingdom of love and **light** (cf. 1:4, 9; 8:12; 12:35; Col. 1:13-14).

12:47-50. Since Jesus is God's Word (*Logos*) to people, God **spoke** decisively and finally in Him (Heb. 1:1-3). The issue is the command of **the Father.** To obey **the Father** is to come **to eternal life** (John 12:50). To reject the Father's word—which is Jesus' **very word** (v. 48; cf. v. 50b; 7:16; 14:10, 24)—is to abide in death. Moses predicted the coming of the great Prophet (One who would speak for God). Moses said, "You must listen to Him" (Deut. 18:15). Condemnation **at the last day** is the penalty for rejecting the One whom the Father sent (Deut. 18:18-19; John 3:18, 36; 5:24).

The purpose of God's revelation in Jesus is positive: He came **to save,** not **to judge** (12:47; cf. 3:17 and comments on 9:39). But rejection of God's Revelation inevitably brings a hardening in sin and ultimately God's judgment.

In speaking of Jewish national unbelief John balanced his theological explanation with Jesus' serious exhortation to the nation to repent. In the words of Moses, these "are not just idle words for you—they are your life" (Deut. 32:47).

III. Jesus' Preparation of His Disciples (chaps. 13-17)

A. The Last Supper (13:1-30)

1. JESUS' WASHING OF HIS DISCIPLES' FEET (13:1-17)

John's Gospel reports more of the content of Jesus' instructions to His disciples than do the other three Gospels. Chapters 13-17 concentrate on His teachings on that fateful night in which He was arrested. Before the instruction, Jesus washed His disciples' feet and predicted His betrayal.

13:1. Jesus knew that the time had come (cf. 2:4; 7:6, 8, 30; 12:23, 27; 17:1) **for Him to leave this world and go to the Father.** Jesus' death and resurrection were now imminent. He had come to die in obedience to the Father's will. His coming was also an act of love for all mankind (3:16). But He has a special love for His sheep: He **loved His own.** Then He **showed them the full extent of His love.** His humble service (13:1-17), His teaching (13:18-17:26), and finally His death (chaps. 18-19) are in view. All three revealed His love.

13:2-4. At **the evening meal** before the Passover, **the devil had already prompted Judas Iscariot . . . to betray Jesus. Jesus** had predicted this (6:70-71). Later Satan actually entered Judas (13:27). Yet **God** was in control of all events leading to Jesus' death. Jesus **knew** (cf. vv.

1, 18) His sovereign authority, His origin, and coming destiny; yet He voluntarily took the place of a slave, washing the feet of His disciples. His action contrasts sharply with their self-seeking (cf. Matt. 20:20-24; Mark 9:33-34; Luke 22:24-30) and pictures His whole ministry on earth (cf. Phil. 2:5-8).

13:5. Foot-washing was needed in Palestine. The streets were dusty and people wore sandals without socks or stockings. It was a mark of honor for a host to provide a servant to wash a guest's feet; it was a breach of hospitality not to provide for it (cf. 1 Sam. 25:41; Luke 7:40-50; 1 Tim. 5:10). Wives often washed their husbands' feet, and children washed their parents' feet. Most people, of course, had to **wash** their own **feet.**

13:6-8. Peter sensing Jesus' reversing of their natural roles, asked why He, Peter's **Lord,** should **wash** the **feet** of His servant Peter. In Peter's question the word **You** is emphatic in the Greek. **Jesus** said that **later** (after His death and resurrection) Peter would **understand.**

No . . . You shall never wash my feet, Peter replied. Apparently he did not feel that Jesus should act like a servant toward Peter. This is another case of Peter's thoughtless speech (cf. Mark 8:32; 9:5). **Jesus** responded, **Unless I wash you, you have no part with Me.** This does not mean, "Unless you are baptized you cannot be saved," but, "Unless I wash your sins away by My atoning death (cf. Rev. 1:5) you have no real relationship to Me" (cf. 1 John 1:7).

13:9-10. Peter continued to miss the spiritual lesson, but he was certain of his desire to be joined to Jesus. Therefore he asked Jesus to wash his **hands** and **head as well** as his **feet. Jesus answered, A person who has had a bath needs only to wash his feet; his whole body is clean.** (Some Gr. mss. omit the words "his feet.") Roman Catholics sometimes have interpreted verse 10 to mean that after infant baptism only penance is needed. A preferable interpretation is that after salvation all one needs is confession of sins, the continual application of Jesus' death to cleanse one's daily sins (cf. 1 John 1:7; 2:1-2). When Jesus added that **not every one of you** is **clean,** He was referring to Judas (cf. John 13:11, 18). This suggests that Judas was not converted.

13:11. Judas had rejected the life-giving, cleansing words of Jesus (cf. 6:63; 15:3), so he was yet in his sins. Judas did have his feet literally washed, but he did not enter into the meaning of the event. John stressed Jesus' supernatural knowledge (cf. 2:25; 4:29) of Judas' deception.

13:12-14. After giving this object lesson in humility the Lord questioned the disciples in order to draw out the significance of the lesson: **Do you understand what I have done for you? He asked them** (cf. v. 7). **Teacher** (*didaskalos*) **and Lord** (*kyrios*) show that Jesus is on a higher level than they. Yet He had done a humble service for them. Meeting others' needs self-sacrificially is what they ought to do too.

13:15-16. The foot-washing was **an example** (*hypodeigma*, "pattern"). Many groups throughout church history have practiced literal foot-washing as a church ordinance. However, present culture in many lands does not call for the need to wash dust from the feet of one's guests. Whereas the Lord's Supper was practiced by the early church as an ordinance, it apparently did not practice foot-washing as an ordinance in church gatherings. This passage emphasizes inner humility, not a physical rite. A Christian widow's practice of "washing the feet of the saints" (1 Tim. 5:10) speaks not of her involvement in a church ordinance but of her humble slavelike service to other believers. Not to follow the example of Jesus is to exalt oneself above Him and to live in pride. **No servant is greater than his master** (cf. John 12:26).

13:17. God blesses His servants not for what they **know** but for their responses to what they know. Christian happiness (**you will be blessed**) comes through obedient service (**if you do them,** i.e., **these things** Jesus commanded).

2. JESUS' PREDICTION OF HIS BETRAYAL (13:18-30)

13:18-19. Jesus had just said that blessedness comes through obedience (v. 17). Now He added that there would be no blessedness for one of the disciples. His selection of Judas was not an accident or a failure in God's plan. Jesus chose a betrayer among His 12 disciples (cf. 6:70-71) in order **to fulfill the Scripture,** namely, Psalm 41:9. As David was betrayed by his trusted table companion Ahithophel, who then hanged himself

(2 Sam. 16:20–17:3, 23), so Judas, Jesus' close companion, betrayed Him and then hanged himself. Though Judas' deed was foreknown by God, he was fully culpable. The fact that Jesus knew all this in advance (**before it happens**) and that it fit the Scriptures helped the disciples after the fact to **believe** God sent Jesus (John 13:19; cf. 14:29).

13:20. As Jesus has a high and holy dignity because of His commission from the Father, so the disciples represented Jesus. **Anyone** who accepted the disciples was thus accepting Jesus, the **One** they represented, and in turn that person was also accepting the Father.

13:21. Jesus was troubled in spirit. The word "troubled" is *etarachthē* ("stirred or agitated"), the same word used of Jesus in 11:33; 12:27 (also used by Jesus in 14:1, 27). Being human, Jesus was troubled over Judas' soon betrayal of His love and friendship. Being divine, Jesus knew in advance that it would happen. Jesus sensed the spiritual hardness and deadness which sin had produced in Judas. The word **testified** and the formula **I tell you the truth** stress the solemn announcement of Jesus' words.

13:22. That anyone in this close fellowship could do this to Jesus was almost beyond comprehension. Judas had covered his tracks so well that none of the others suspected him.

13:23-24. Simon Peter, the leader and perhaps the most emotional disciple, wanted to deal with the traitor. Luke (22:38, 49-50) mentioned that the disciples had two swords! **The disciple whom Jesus loved** was evidently John, the author of this Gospel (cf. *Introduction*). John and Judas were **reclining next to** Jesus, but Peter's position at the table was not near enough to ask Jesus privately. So he **motioned to** John and asked him to **ask** Jesus whom He meant.

13:25-27. By **leaning** John could touch **Jesus,** so **he asked . . . Lord, who is it?** Giving the morsel **to Judas** was an uncaught sign of recognition to John, but it was also the Lord's final extension of grace to **Judas.** A host's giving a morsel **of bread** to a guest was a sign of friendship. How ironic that Jesus' act of friendship to Judas signaled Judas' betrayal of friendship.

Satan entered into him (cf. v. 2) is one of the most terrible expressions in the Scriptures. Satan now used Judas as his tool to accomplish his will. **Do quickly** is literally "do it more quickly," which may imply Jesus' words spurred Judas to act in God's proper timing.

13:28-30. Since **no one** grasped the significance of Jesus' words, even the beloved disciple must have missed the intent of the sop until later. As **Judas . . . went out,** no one thought anything but good of him. They assumed that he, as the group's treasurer (cf. 12:6), was going **to buy** food **for the** Passover **feast or to give something to the poor.** He had deceived his peers but not Jesus. **And it was night** in any other Gospel might simply be a time notice, but in John's Gospel it probably also has symbolic significance. Judas was leaving the Light (8:12; 12:35, 46) and going out into the darkness of sin (3:19).

B. Jesus' coming departure (13:31-38)

13:31-32. After the departure of Judas, the events leading to Jesus' death fell into place quickly. **Jesus** was then free from the tension which Satan in Judas had produced. Also the long tension building up toward His death (Luke 12:50) would soon be over. The words **glorified** and **glorify** occur five times in these two verses. Jesus' unique glory was revealed in His death. The Father was also glorified in Jesus' death because God's love, His condescension, and His righteousness were made known (cf. John 1:14; Rom. 3:21-26). The words **God . . . will glorify Him at once** looked ahead to the Resurrection and the Ascension.

13:33. My children translates *teknia,* ("little children"; the diminutive of *tekna,* "children"). This term of love expressed Jesus' concern for them. It is used only here by Jesus in this Gospel. John used it seven times in his first epistle (1 John 2:1, 12, 28; 3:7, 18; 4:4; 5:21), and Paul used it once (Gal. 4:19). Jesus announced once again that He would be gone and they would not be able to find Him (cf. Matt. 23:29; John 7:34; 8:21; 12:8, 35). This was true in both His death and His Ascension.

13:34-35. The 11 disciples would survive in His absence by obeying His example of **love.** The command is **new** in that it is a special **love** for other believers based on the sacrificial love of Jesus: **As I have loved you, so you must love one another.** Christians' love and support for one another enable them to survive in a hostile world. As Jesus was the embodiment of God's love, so now each disciple should embody Christ's love. This love is a sign to the world as well as to every believer (1 John 3:14).

13:36-38. Peter, quick to speak, picked up on what Jesus had said about going away (v. 33). He wanted to know **where** Jesus was **going** (cf. Thomas' similar request; 14:5). Peter's love was such that he wanted to be with Jesus. But **Jesus replied** that it was not possible right then for Peter to be with Him. **Peter** could not conceive of any situation that would make Jesus' words necessary. He was certain that his love and courage were up to any challenge, including death. **I will lay down my life for You,** he affirmed. But Peter did not know himself as well as he thought, nor did he know the satanic power at work against him (cf. Luke 22:31-32). Jesus' prediction of Peter's defection (**you will disown Me three times**) must have completely shocked the other disciples. They may have wondered if Peter was the traitor (cf. John 13:21-25).

C. Jesus, the Way to the Father (14:1-14)

The disciples were completely bewildered and discouraged. Jesus had said He was going away (7:34; 8:21; 12:8, 35; 13:33), that He would die (12:32-33), that one of the Twelve was a traitor (13:21), that Peter would disown Him three times (13:38), that Satan was at work against all of them (Luke 22:31-32), and that all the disciples would fall away (Matt. 26:31). The cumulative weight of these revelations must have greatly depressed them.

14:1-2. To comfort the disciples, Jesus gave them several exhortations along with promises. **Do not let your hearts be troubled,** He said. "Troubled" is *tarassesthō* ("stirred, agitated") from the same verb translated "troubled" in 11:33; 13:21; 14:27. One's heart is the center of his personality. Each believer is responsible for the condition of his heart (cf. Prov. 3:1, 3, 5; 4:23; 20:9). By a firm trust in God the Father and Jesus the Son, they could relieve their soul-sorrow and be sustained in their coming tests. When Jesus said, **Trust in God; trust also in Me,** He was probably giving commands, not making statements (see NIV marg.). Death should not be a terror to them because

Jesus was leaving **to prepare a place for** them in heaven, the **Father's house.**

14:3-4. I will come back refers here, not to the Resurrection or to a believer's death, but to the Rapture of the church when Christ will return for His sheep (cf. 1 Thes. 4:13-18) and they will be **with** Him (cf. John 17:24). Jesus said nothing about the nature of the place where He was going. It is sufficient that believers will be with the Father and Jesus (cf. 2 Cor. 5:8; Phil. 1:23; 1 Thes. 4:17). The disciples knew how to get to heaven. He told them, **You know the way to the place where I am going.** Throughout His ministry, Jesus had been showing them the way, but as Thomas indicated (John 14:5), they did not fully understand.

14:5-6. Thomas' statement (**We don't know where You are going**) and his question (**So how can we know the way?**) reflected the perplexity of the Eleven (cf. Peter's similar question; 13:36). They would remain puzzled until His death and resurrection and until the advent of the Spirit. They had all the information but they could not put it together.

Jesus' words, **I am the Way and the Truth and the Life,** are the sixth of Jesus' seven "I am" statements in the Gospel of John (6:48; 8:12; 10:9, 11; 11:25; 14:6; 15:1). Jesus is the "Way" because He is the "Truth" and the "Life." As the Father is Truth and Life, Jesus is the embodiment of God so people can come to the Father (cf. 1:4, 14, 18; 11:25). By His words, **No one comes to the Father except through Me,** Jesus stressed that salvation, contrary to what many people think, is *not* obtainable through many ways. Only one Way exists (cf. Acts 4:12; 1 Tim. 2:5). Jesus is the only access to the Father because He is the only One from the Father (cf. John 1:1-2, 51; 3:13).

14:7. The first sentence in this verse may either be a promise ("If you really knew Me, you *will* know My Father as well") or a rebuke (**If you really knew Me, you would know My Father as well**). The Lord seems to be rebuking them for a failure to understand His person and mission (cf. 8:19). The following dialogue (14:8-9) indicates a failure on the disciples' part. **From now on, you do know Him** is a promise, which looks beyond the Cross and the

Resurrection (cf. 20:28, "My Lord and my God").

14:8-9. Philip expressed a universal desire of mankind: to see God (cf. Ex. 33:18). In a perverted form this desire leads to idolatry. Philip was probably longing for a theophany (cf. Ex. 24:9-10; Isa. 6:1) or some visible display of God's glory. Jesus' statement, **Anyone who has seen Me has seen the Father** (cf. John 12:45), is one of the most staggering claims He ever made. The Father is in Jesus and Jesus perfectly reveals Him (1:18). Hence no theophany was necessary, for by seeing Jesus they *were* seeing **the Father!**

14:10-11. The proof of the union of Jesus and His Father is threefold. They should **believe** Jesus (a) because of His character (**I am in the Father** [cf. v. 20] **and . . . the Father is in Me**); (b) because His words are the Father's (**The words I say to you are not just My own** (cf. 7:16; 12:49-50; 14:24); and (c) because the miracles reveal God's working through Him (**the Father, living in Me . . . is doing His work. . . . believe on the evidence of the miracles themselves;** cf. 5:36). One of the key elements in John's Gospel is the stress on the signs as gracious pointers to faith (cf. 5:36; 10:25, 38; 11:47; 12:37; 20:30-31).

14:12-14. The apostles would not necessarily do more stupendous miracles than Jesus did (e.g., feeding 5,000) but their outreach would be greater (e.g., Peter in one sermon had 3,000 converts). This was possible **because** Jesus had gone **to the Father** and had sent the Spirit. Miracles are important, but some evangelists have done **even greater things than these** by preaching the good news to many thousands of people.

In My name (vv. 13-14) is not a magical formula of invocation. But the prayers of believers, as Christ's representatives doing His business, will be answered. John expanded this teaching in his first epistle. He wrote, "If we ask anything according to His will . . . we have what we asked of Him" (1 John 5:14-15). To **ask Me for anything in My name** means to ask according to His will (cf. "in My name" in John 15:16; 16:23-24, 26). The word "Me" is omitted in some Greek manuscripts but it is probably correct here. Prayers in the New Testament are usually addressed to God the Father, but prayer addressed to **the Son** is proper also (e.g., Stephen's prayer to the "Lord Jesus" [Acts 7:59]). The goal of answered prayers is to **bring glory to the Father.** Also bearing fruit glorifies the Father (John 15:8).

D. Jesus' promise of the Counselor (14:15-31)

14:15. The disciples' **love** for Christ is revealed in their obeying His commands (cf. vv. 21, 23; 1 John 2:3; 3:22, 24; 5:3). Christ has set the pattern of love and obedience (John 14:31); His disciples are expected to follow (13:15-16).

14:16-17. This is the first of several passages on the Holy Spirit in the Upper Room Discourse. Up to this point in John's Gospel, little has been said about the Holy Spirit. The words to Nicodemus (3:5-8) were private and 7:39 pointed ahead to Pentecost. The Holy Spirit is **to be** the **Counselor** (*paraklētos;* also used in 14:26; 15:26; 16:7; for its meaning see comments on 16:7). In a sense He has now replaced Jesus' physical presence; and He mediates God to believers. The Spirit is in a believer **forever** (cf. Rom. 8:9). He is also **the Spirit of Truth** (lit., "Spirit of *the* truth"; cf. John 15:26; 16:13) and thus would guide the apostles. He is invisible (**the world cannot accept Him because it neither sees Him nor knows Him**), yet He is real and active. Without a radio, radio waves go unnoticed. The Holy Spirit is unnoticed by the unsaved who have no spiritual life. The disciples had some experience with the Spirit (doubtless in preaching and miracle-working) but now His working would be much more intimate.

Why did Jesus say that the Holy Spirit **will be** (fut. tense) **in** them? Because in Old Testament times the Spirit came on some believers for special enablement, but after Pentecost He indwells every believer permanently (Rom. 8:9; 1 Cor. 12:13).

14:18-19. What did Jesus mean when He said, **I will come to you?** Was He referring to (1) His resurrection, (2) the Rapture, (3) the death of a believer, (4) a mystical experience, or (5) the Holy Spirit's coming at Pentecost? Views 1 and 5 seem best. Verse 19 favors view 1 since the disciples did see Him after His resurrection. His resurrection is also the pledge of their resurrection (**Because I**

live, you also will live; cf. 1 Cor. 15:20-21) and the foundation of a new life.

14:20-21. On that day refers to the day of Pentecost when the outpoured Spirit gave evidence of Jesus' Ascension to the **Father.** (Some, however, take the "day" to refer to Jesus' resurrection, the basis for believers' assurance.) The Spirit would come into believers (v. 17), and would teach them of their union with Jesus (**you are in Me, and I am in you**) while He manifested Christ in them.

Christian love is manifested as a believer **obeys** the Lord's words (cf. vv. 15, 23). The rewards of loving Him are great: (a) the **Father** will show His love to him (cf. v. 23), and (b) the Son **will love him and show** Himself **to him.** This passage does not teach a "works" religion, but rather that one who believes and obeys Christ's Word is loved by the Lord. Saving faith results in obedience (cf. "the obedience that comes from faith," Rom. 1:5).

14:22. Judas (not Judas Iscariot) may have been the same man called Thaddaeus (Matt. 10:3; Mark 3:18). He was puzzled that Jesus would manifest Himself to them **and not to the world** (cf. John 14:19a).

14:23-24. Jesus answered that He and the **Father** will not manifest themselves to those who are disobedient to His **teaching.** Obedience grows out of **love** for Jesus and His Word (cf. vv. 15, 21; 1 John 2:3; 3:22, 24; 5:3). And as a result, the Father and the Son abide **(make Our home) with him.** "Home" is *monēn*, the singular of plural *monai*, translated "rooms" in John 14:1. This word occurs in the New Testament only in those two verses. To rebel against Jesus' word is to rebel against God **the Father who sent** Him. Jesus' **words** were **not** His **own**, as He had said previously (12:49; 14:10).

14:25-26. What Jesus said in the days of His earthly ministry was only partially understood. Three things were needed for the apostles to understand Jesus' person and mission: (1) His death had to occur. (2) He had to rise again to vindicate His claim and demonstrate His victory. (3) The **Spirit** had to come (He would be sent by **the Father . . . in My name,** i.e., in Jesus' place and for Him) and interpret the meanings of Jesus' words and deeds. The Spirit, Jesus said,

will teach you all things and will remind you of everything I have said to you. This verse is addressed to the apostles. The context limits the "all things" to the interpretation and significance of His person and work. The Spirit worked in their minds, reminding them of His teaching and giving them insight into its meaning (cf. 2:22; 7:39; 20:9).

14:27. In New Testament times the normal way to say good-bye was **Peace** (*šālôm* in Heb.). In His death Jesus provided a legacy for His disciples: **My peace I give you.** They would have "peace with God" (Rom. 5:1) because their sins were forgiven and the "peace of God" (Phil. 4:7) would guard their lives. **The world** is unable to **give** this kind of peace. Fear of death (Heb. 2:14-15) and fear of the future are removed as Jesus' followers trust in Him. Thus they need not **be troubled** (cf. John 11:33; 13:21; 14:1).

14:28. If the disciples had been more mature in their love for Jesus, they **would** have been **glad** for His departure. But their love was still selfish at this point. Jesus was in His humiliation on earth, but by **going** back **to the Father** He would be exalted in glory (cf. 13:31-32) and He will come **back** (cf. 14:3).

Arians and Jehovah's Witnesses argue from the statement, **The Father is greater than I,** that Jesus is a lesser god. But this would make Jesus a created being or would lead to polytheism, both of which are clearly unbiblical. The Father and the Son share the same essence (cf. 1:1-2; 14:9; 20:28). The Father and the Son are "One" in purpose and essence (10:30). Thus the Father is greater in office or glory than the Son was in His humiliation.

14:29-31. Fulfilled prophecy is a great comfort and support to believers (cf. Isa. 46:8-10). Jesus had predicted His death and resurrection many times (e.g., Mark 8:31-32; 9:31). When this came to pass, after their initial shock, it would greatly help their faith. His teaching time was now limited because Satan, **the prince of this world** (cf. John 12:31; 16:11), was moving his forces against Jesus through Judas (cf. 13:2, 27). And yet Satan had **no hold on** Jesus. Sin leads to death (Rom. 5:12, 21a; 6:16), and sin and death give Satan a hold over people (cf. Heb. 2:14-15; Rev. 12:10). But since Jesus is sinless, Satan cannot claim Him for his kingdom of darkness. Satan thought Jesus' death was a victory for him, but actually it was Jesus' victory over Satan (John 16:11; Col. 2:15).

Because Jesus loves **the Father,** He did **exactly what** the **Father . . . commanded** (cf. John 10:18; 12:49-50) including being "obedient to death" (Phil. 2:8). Then He said, **Come now; let us leave.** Jesus had been with the disciples in the Upper Room. He now prepared to go to the Garden of Gethsemane on the Mount of Olives. Whether Jesus' words in John 15–17 were spoken in the room or on the way to the garden is uncertain, but probably they were given in the room.

E. The Vine and the branches (15:1-10)

Jesus now instructed His disciples on three vital relationships. Disciples are to be rightly related to Jesus (vv. 1-10), to each other (vv. 11-17), and to the world (vv. 18–16:4). Disciples have three respective duties: to remain (abide), to love each other, and to testify.

15:1. **I am the true Vine** (cf. v. 5). This is the last of the seven great "I am" statements in John (cf. comments on 6:35). Israel was God's choice vine on which he lavished care and attention (Ps. 80:8; Isa. 5:1-7; Jer. 2:21; 6:9; Ezek. 15; 17:5-10; 19:10-14; Hosea 10:1; 14:8). He longed for fruit, but the vine (Israel) became degenerate and produced rotten fruit. Therefore Jesus, as "the true Vine," fulfills what God had intended for Israel. The **Father is the Gardener** who cultivates and protects the Vine.

15:2. **He** (i.e., the Gardener, the Father) desires **fruit,** which is mentioned eight times in this chapter (vv. 2 [thrice], 4 [twice], 5, 8, 16). A progression is seen: **fruit** (v. 2), **more fruitful** (v. 2), and "much fruit" (vv. 5, 8). The fruit which God desired from Israel was loving obedience, righteousness, and justice (Isa. 5:1-7). **Every branch in Me that** does not bear fruit **He cuts off.** The phrase "in Me" does not mean the same thing as Paul's words "in Christ." Here it is part of the metaphor of the Vine and seems to mean, "every person who professes to be My disciple (a 'branch') is not necessarily a true follower." A branch **that bears no** fruit is obviously dead. Therefore, like Judas, it is cut off. (See comments on John

15:6.) Every year in Palestine gardeners prune their vines. They cut off the dead wood which has no life in it and trim the living branches so that their yield will be greater.

15:3. The disciples had been cleansed by Jesus and His message, but one, Judas, was not cleansed (cf. 13:10-11).

15:4. Fruitfulness is the result of the Son's life being reproduced in a disciple. The disciple's part is to **remain.** The word **remain,** a key word in John's theology, is *menō* which occurs 11 times in this chapter, 40 times in the entire Gospel, and 27 times in John's epistles. What does it mean to **remain?** It can mean, first, to accept Jesus as Savior (cf. 6:54, 56). Second, it can mean to continue or persevere in believing (8:31 ["hold" is remain]; 1 John 2:19, 24). Third, it can also mean believing, loving obedience (John 15:9-10). Without faith, no life of God will come to anyone. Without the life of God, **no** real **fruit** can be produced: **Neither can you bear fruit unless you remain in Me.**

15:5-6. A disciple's continual abiding with Jesus (**If a man remains in Me**)—and the indwelling of Jesus in a believer (**and I in him**)—result in abundant **fruit** (cf. v. 8). But those who do not believe face disaster. **A branch** without life is dead and cut off (v. 2). It is worthless and therefore is **thrown into the fire and burned.** What did Jesus mean by these symbolic words about vine branches being burned? These words have been interpreted in at least three ways: (1) The "burned" branches are Christians who have lost their salvation. (But this contradicts many passages, e.g., 3:16, 36; 5:24; 10:28-29; Rom. 8:1.) (2) The "burned" branches represent Christians who will lose rewards but not salvation at the judgment seat of Christ (1 Cor. 3:15). (But Jesus spoke here of *dead* branches; such a branch **is thrown away and withers.**) (3) The "burned" branches refer to professing Christians who, like Judas, are not genuinely saved and therefore are judged. Like a dead branch, a person without Christ is spiritually dead and therefore will be punished in eternal fire (cf. Matt. 25:46). Judas was with Jesus; he seemed like a "branch." But he did not have God's life in him; therefore he departed; his destiny was like that of a dead branch.

15:7-8. In contrast with verse 6, the emphasis in these verses is positive: **remain** with Jesus and **bear much fruit.** Effective prayer is based on faith in Christ and on His **words** remaining in believers. Christ's words condition and control such a believer's mind so that his prayers conform to the Father's will. Since his prayer is in accord with God's will, the results are certain—**it will be given you** (cf. 1 John 5:14-15). Fulfilled prayers bring **glory** to the Father because, like Jesus, His **disciples** are doing the heavenly Father's will (cf. "Your kingdom come, Your will be done on earth" [Matt. 6:10]).

15:9-10. A believer is motivated by the wonder of Jesus' **love,** which is patterned after the Father's **love** in its quality and extent. **Remain in My love** might seem to be mystical but Jesus makes it very concrete. Obedience to the **Father's commands** is the same for a disciple as it was for the Son (cf. 14:15, 21, 23; 1 John 2:3; 3:22, 24; 5:3). Active dependence and loving obedience are the proper paths for all of God's children.

F. Jesus' friends (15:11-17)

15:11. Jesus had great **joy** in pleasing His Father by living a fruitful life (cf. Heb. 12:2). The purpose of His teaching is to give man an abundant life, not a joyless existence (John 10:10). The commands for His disciples to obey are for their **joy** (cf. 17:13).

15:12. One primary **command** was given by Jesus to believers: they must have mutual love (**Love each other;** this is repeated in v. 17). Christians grow by caring for and nurturing each other. The standard for that love is Christ's example of humble sacrificial service: **as I have loved you.**

15:13-14. The most a person can do for his friend is to die for him; such a death is a clear demonstration of **love.** Jesus demonstrated His love (v. 12b) by dying **for His friends,** those who obey Him. Abraham was called God's "friend" (2 Chron. 20:7; Isa. 41:8) because he obeyed God. Like close friends, Abraham and God communicated well with each other (cf. Gen. 18:17).

15:15-17. A **servant** (lit., "slave") **does not** have a close relationship with his master, as friends do. Normally, a slave does what he is told without understanding **his master's** mind or **business.** Since Jesus had opened Himself to His disciples, the title "slave" did not fit their relationship. (When Paul spoke of himself as "a servant [lit., slave] of God" [Rom. 1:1], he had a different idea in mind. He meant he willingly and humbly served and obeyed God.) Jesus **called** His disciples **friends** because He had disclosed His Father's revelation to them.

Jesus then reminded them that contrary to the common practice of disciples picking a teacher, Jesus had chosen them (cf. John 15:19). The purpose of His choosing was so that they would produce lasting **fruit.** He **chose** them for a mission, and His **Father** would answer their requests in order to accomplish that mission (**whatever you ask in My name;** cf. v. 7; cf. "in My name" in 14:13-14; 16:23-24, 26). Friendship with Jesus involves the obligation of brotherly love: **Love each other** (cf. 15:12).

G. The world's hatred (15:18–16:4)

15:18. Friendship with God results in enduring the world's hatred. Conversely, being friends with the world is to be God's enemy (James 4:4). Jesus alerted His disciples to the fact of the world's hatred. **The world** in John's Gospel is the system of organized society hostile to God, which is under Satan's power (John 14:30). Believers might be surprised by this hostility (1 Peter 4:12-13), but they should remember that Jesus was **hated** from His birth (when Herod the Great sought to kill Him) to His death on the cross.

15:19. A fundamental reason for the world's hatred of a Christian lies in their differences (cf. 1 Peter 4:4; Rom. 12:2). A believer, having left the kingdom of darkness and having been transferred into the kingdom of God's Son (Col. 1:13), has a different joy, purpose, hope, and love. He now has certainty, truth, and a standard for life. Christians **have** been **chosen** (cf. John 15:16) **out of the world** system by Christ and they now belong to Him. Since they **do not belong to the world . . . the world hates** them.

15:20-21. Jesus reminded His disciples of a statement He had made earlier: **No servant is greater than his master** (cf. 13:16). Previously He was referring to their need to imitate His humble service. But the principle has other applications. Christians are to identify so closely with Jesus that they share in His sufferings (**they will persecute you also**). On the positive side, some people followed and **obeyed** Jesus' **teaching,** so they **also** responded to the apostles' message. The root cause of the world's hatred against the disciples is their identification with Jesus. They hate Jesus because they are ignorant of God, **the One who sent** Him.

15:22-23. Jesus came as the Revelation of God. If Jesus **had not come,** their sin would not be so great. The statement, **they would not be guilty of sin** (cf. v. 24), must not be taken absolutely as 16:9 shows (cf. 3:19; 9:41). Before Jesus' coming people might have pleaded ignorance as an excuse for **sin** (cf. Acts 17:30). But now that the Light has come, those who willfully reject it **have no excuse.** The revelation in Jesus and by Jesus is so tied to the **Father** that to hate Jesus is to hate God (cf. John 15:24b).

15:24-25. These two verses amplify the thought in verses 22-23. Jesus' **miracles** were so distinctive that their import was unmistakable. The Jewish nation should have honestly confessed, "No one could perform the miraculous signs You are doing if God were not with Him" (3:2). But the nation as a whole rejected **both** Jesus **and** the **Father** because in their sins they loved darkness rather than light (3:19). The nation thought it was serving God in rejecting Jesus (16:2-3) but in reality it was serving Satan (8:44). Sin is basically irrational. Their hatred of Jesus was **without** any rational cause which also fits the pattern of hatred for righteous people, as seen in those who hated David (Pss. 35:19; 69:4; 109:3).

15:26-27. In the face of the opposition and hatred of the world a believer might be tempted to try to escape from the world or to be silent in it. Monasticism, extreme separation, and lack of witnessing have been too common in the church's history. Jesus encouraged His disciples by the promise of the Spirit's work in the world. As the work of Jesus was to promote the Father and not Himself, so the Spirit will witness to Jesus as the Messiah (**He will testify about Me**). And what He says is true for He is **the Spirit of Truth** (cf. 16:13). As the

Counselor (cf. 14:26; 16:7), He presents God's truth to the world. The Spirit is sent **from the Father** (cf. 14:26), just as the Son was sent from the Father. Yet this mysterious work of the Spirit is not done in isolation from the church. The apostles were to bear witness to the facts that they came to know: **You also must testify.** As the apostles witnessed, the Holy Spirit persuaded, and people were saved. The same combination of human obedience to the divine command (Acts 1:8) coupled with the witness of the Spirit is needed in every generation.

16:1-2. The disciples may have wondered why Jesus was telling them about the world's hatred and persecution. Jesus, anticipating this question, indicated that expecting trouble beforehand would help them remain in the path of God's will. (He gave a second reason in v. 4.) The disciples would face excommunication and even death. Remembering that Jesus was ostracized and martyred and that He had predicted the same for His apostles would help fortify them. The earliest Christians were Jews (Acts 2:11, 14, 22), but quite soon after the church began to grow and spread, it was quickly thrust outside **the synagogue** (ca. A.D. 90). Persecution unto death occurred in the case of Stephen (Acts 7:59), James (Acts 12:2), and others (Acts 9:1-4). Some people throughout church history have been motivated to persecute believers because of a misguided zeal for God. They **think** they are **offering a service to God** (cf. Rom. 10:2).

16:3-4. The world will persecute Jesus' followers **because they have not known the Father or Me.** They do not recognize the Father at work in the words and deeds of Jesus. The Jewish people, for example, had a certain knowledge of God through the Law, but that knowledge was not a saving knowledge for God said their "hearts go astray and they have not known My ways" (Ps. 95:8-10).

Jesus gave this warning to His disciples about coming persecution in order to strengthen their faith. By recognizing His knowledge of the future they would grow in their confidence in Him. Jesus **did not** give them **this** warning before because the world's hatred was directed against Him. He shielded them with His personal presence, but now they would be His body on earth (Eph. 1:22-23).

H. *The Spirit's work (16:5-15)*

16:5-6. Learning of Jesus' departure brought depression to the disciples. They were obsessed by their coming personal loss of His immediate physical presence. If they could have understood why He was going and to whom He was going, then they would have rejoiced. Later (v. 22) Jesus predicted that their time of sorrow would be suddenly transformed into great joy. Jesus' statement, **Now I am going to Him who sent Me,** should have led the disciples to ask questions, but they didn't (Even Thomas [14:5] did not ask, **Where are You going?**) Their preoccupation with their own problems prevented their understanding the crucial nature of the time ("now") and the momentous significance of the events (His death, burial, resurrection, and Ascension).

16:7. The departure of Jesus was necessary—though painful and difficult—for the disciples. In fact, His leaving was profitable and beneficial (the meaning of the Gr. *sympherei*, here rendered **good**). Without His departing (which included His death, burial, resurrection, and Ascension) there would have been no gospel. Atonement for sin was necessary for Jesus to save His people from their sins (Matt. 1:21). Also **unless** he departed there would have been no glorified Lord to **send . . . the Counselor** (the Holy Spirit) to apply the atonement. "The Counselor" translates the Greek *paraklē-tos.* This word was used of legal assistants who pleaded a cause or presented a case. This Counselor is the promised Spirit who came into the world in a new and distinctive sense on the day of Pentecost.

16:8. One of the Spirit's new ministries was to **convict the world of guilt in regard to sin and righteousness and judgment.** Conviction is not the same as conversion but is necessary to it. The words "convict . . . of guilt" translate the one word *elenxei,* "to present or expose facts, to convince of the truth." The Spirit works on the minds of the unsaved to show them the truth of God for what it is. Normally this process includes human aid (cf. 15:26-27).

16:9. Sin is rebellion against God and this rebellion reached its climax in the crucifixion of Jesus. Today the greatest sin is the failure to **believe in** Jesus (cf. 3:18; 15:22, 24). Most people do not readily admit to being guilty of sin. They will admit to failures or vices or even crimes. However, sin is against God, and people have suppressed the truth of God (cf. Rom. 1:18, 21, 25, 28). The mighty working of the Holy Spirit is necessary to convince and convict people of their desperate plight.

16:10. In crucifying Jesus, the Jewish people showed that they thought He was unrighteous, that only a wicked person would be hanged on a tree and thus be under God's curse (Deut. 21:23; Gal. 3:13). But the Resurrection and the Ascension vindicated Jesus as God's righteous Servant (Acts 3:14-15; Isa. 53:11). The Spirit convicts men of their faulty views of Jesus when the gospel with its stress on the Resurrection is proclaimed (1 Cor. 15:3-4).

16:11. The third area of the Holy Spirit's convicting work concerns **judgment.** The death and resurrection of Jesus were a condemnation of Satan (12:31; Col. 2:15), **the prince of this world** (cf. John 14:30). By Jesus' death, He defeated the devil, who held "the power of death" (Heb. 2:14). (Though defeated at the Cross, Satan is still active [1 Peter 5:8]. But, like a condemned criminal, his "execution" is coming [Rev. 20:2, 7-10].)

People in rebellion should take note of Satan's defeat and fear the Lord who holds the power to judge. As the fact of coming judgment (both Satan's and man's) is proclaimed, the Spirit convicts people and prepares them for salvation (cf. Acts 17:30-31).

16:12-13. The disciples were not able to receive any **more** spiritual truth at that time. Their hearts were hardened, their concern was for their own preeminence in an earthly kingdom, so they saw no need for Jesus' death. Sorrow over His departure and dismay over the prophecy of a traitor among them, along with the prediction of their own desertion, rendered them insensitive to more spiritual truth. **But . . . the Spirit of Truth** (cf. 15:26) would come after Jesus' death to lead the apostles **into the truth** about Jesus and His work.

The Spirit, Jesus said, would **not** teach the disciples **on His own** (i.e., on His own initiative) but would teach **only** what He hears from the Father. This points up the interdependence of the Persons in the Trinity. The Father would **tell** the Spirit what to teach the apostles about the Son.

Also the Spirit would teach **what is yet to come.** This statement helps one understand the promise, **He will guide you into all truth** (lit., "all *the* truth"). This was a promise to the apostles that their partial understanding of the person and work of Jesus as the Messiah would be completed as the Spirit would give them insight into the meanings of the soon-to-come Cross and the Resurrection as well as truths about Jesus' return (cf. 1 Cor. 2:10). The New Testament books are the fulfillment of this teaching ministry of the Spirit.

16:14-15. Because Jesus is the *Logos,* the revelation of the Father (or as Paul expressed it, "the image of the invisible God" [Col. 1:15]), **all that belongs to the Father is** also the Son's. The Spirit of Truth brought **glory to** Jesus as He revealed to the apostles things pertaining to the person and work of the *Logos* **(taking from what is Mine and making it known to you).** The Spirit worked in the apostles' minds so that they could perceive, understand, and teach about the Savior.

I. The prediction of changes (16:16-33)

Jesus' instruction of His disciples shifted at this point from the Spirit's future work to what the immediate future would hold for them. Someday Jesus will reappear, but sorrow, pain, and spiritual failure would be the apostles' lot first. Then, however, joy, prayer, and peace will be their portion.

16:16. The words **in a little while** were bewildering to the disciples (and also possibly to the initial readers of John's Gospel). Also the prediction, **you will see Me,** was not immediately understood. Did Jesus refer (a) to the coming of the Holy Spirit or (b) to His Second Advent or (c) to His brief, 40-day ministry between His resurrection and His Ascension? The last interpretation fits this passage best.

16:17-18. The **disciples** were confused about the time interval. The words **they kept asking** (Gr. imperf. tense) indicate that considerable dialogue took place among the disciples without their

arriving at an answer. They could not reconcile Jesus' statements because He said: (a) In a short time they would not **see** Him, (b) they *would* **see** Him, and (c) He was **going to the Father.** Only His death, resurrection, post-resurrection ministry, and Ascension would make it all clear.

16:19-20. As a Master Teacher, **Jesus** understood the confusion among His students. He did not clarify His teaching; He knew it would all come into focus with the passage of time and with the aid of the Spirit's teaching ministry (cf. vv. 12-13). **I tell you the truth** (cf. comments on 1:51) introduces a solemn prediction that their coming grief would be followed by joy. His death would be bitter agony for them but **the world** would be happy over it. However, the very event, the death of the Messiah, which would cause them to **weep and mourn** would bring them gladness: **your grief will turn to joy.** His resurrection and the Spirit's work of interpretation would enable them to know that He had to die so that they could have forgiveness of sins. Later the church would rejoice in His death (cf. 1 Cor. 1:23; 2:2).

16:21-22. Jesus illustrated the truth of **pain** replaced by **joy** by the pain of childbirth followed by the joy of new life when **a child is born.** The disciples were entering the process of pain (**your time of grief**), **but** the light of **joy** was just ahead. When they saw Him after His resurrection, their joy erupted—joy that will never end since He died to sin once but now lives forever (cf. Rom. 6:9-10; Luke 24:33-52; Heb. 7:24-25).

16:23-24. The forthcoming events brought about changed relations. Since Jesus would not be with them physically (**in that day** means after His Ascension), they would not be able to **ask** Him questions. But the Holy Spirit would help them (vv. 13-15).

I tell you the truth again introduced an important statement. They would be His ambassadors and therefore had the right to **ask** the **Father** for **whatever** they needed to accomplish His will. The words **in My name** are not a magical formula which enable the user to get *his* will done; instead those words tied the requests to the work of the Son in doing the *Father's* will (cf. "in My name" in 14:13-14; 15:16; 16:24, 26). Up to this point the disciples had **not** prayed **in** the **name** of Jesus. Now they are to do this since Jesus' death and the Spirit's coming would enable them to enter into God's new program of the Church Age. Answered prayer brings complete **joy** (cf. 15:11; 16:22) because God is at work in them.

16:25. Though Jesus was a Master Teacher and taught His disciples for three years by example and word, yet their perception of His revelation of the Father remained limited (14:9; cf. 2:22; 6:60; 13:7, 15-17). Veiled utterances (His **speaking figuratively**) would give way to plain speech. In His post-resurrection teaching (cf. Acts 1:3) the Son spoke **plainly about** the **Father** (cf. John 14:25-26).

16:26-27. The coming new **day** would give the disciples intimacy with **the Father** and clarity of understanding. The disciples would have direct personal access to **the Father** by the **name** of, that is, through Jesus (cf. "in My name" in 14:13-14; 15:16; 16:24). Jesus would no longer need to pray **on** their **behalf** since they could ask for themselves. This truth does not negate the promise of Christ's intercessory work in overcoming a believer's sin (cf. Rom. 8:34; 1 John 2:1-2). The disciples were now in a personal love-and-faith relationship with the Father. Only children have this privilege of access to their Father (Rom. 5:2).

16:28. Jesus summarized His mission in one sentence: His Incarnation (**I came from the Father**), His humiliation (**and entered the world**), and His resurrection, Ascension, and exaltation (**now I am leaving the world and going back to the Father**). This is what the disciples had come to believe.

16:29-30. The response of the **disciples** to the Lord's teaching was that **now** they understood and believed. They felt the teaching was so plain that recognizing Jesus' omniscience (**You know all things**) and divine origin (**You came from God**) was their only proper response.

16:31-32. Though the disciples were honest and sincere in their affirmations of faith (v. 30), **Jesus** knew their limitations far better than they did (cf. 2:24-25). The words **You believe at last!** could also be translated "Do you now believe?" (NIV marg.) This seems to capture the thought better. They did believe but it was not complete faith or strong faith until after

the death and resurrection of Jesus and the advent of the Spirit. **You will be scattered** is a fulfillment of Zechariah's words which spoke of the Shepherd (the Messiah) smitten by decree of the Lord Almighty, which resulted in the scattering of the sheep (Zech 13:7). In spite of the disciples' loyalty, faith, and love, they soon failed Him miserably. His prediction, **You will leave Me all alone,** was fulfilled by all His disciples deserting Him (Matt. 26:56) when He was arrested and by Peter's denial (John 18:17, 25-26). Yet the Father had not forsaken Him; **I am not alone for My Father is with Me** (cf. 8:29; Pss. 23:4; 73:25-26), though the Father did forsake Jesus when He was on the cross (Matt. 27:46).

16:33. Jesus' instructions about **these things** (chaps. 14-16) were intended to sustain them, to give them **peace** in Him. Believers have a dual existence: they are **in** Christ and **in this world**. In union with Jesus, His disciples have peace, but the world exerts a hostile pressure. The world system, the enemy of God and His people, opposed Jesus' message and ministry (cf. 1:5, 10; 7:7). **But** Jesus won the victory over the system; He has **overcome the world.** As the "strong man" who came and ruined Satan's kingdom (Matt. 12:25-29), Jesus is the Victor. Jesus wanted the disciples to remember this fact and to rejoice in His victory. **Take heart!** means "Be courageous." (In the NT the word *tharseō* ["take heart, be courageous, cheer up"] was spoken only by the Lord [Matt. 9:2, 22; 14:27; Mark 6:50; 10:49; John 16:33; Acts 23:11].) Because He won they, in union with Him, can win also (Rom. 8:37).

J. Jesus' intercession (chap. 17)

1. JESUS' REQUESTS FOR HIMSELF (17:1-5)

Following the symbolic washing of the disciples' feet (13:1-30) and His private instruction of the apostles (14-16), Jesus prayed. This prayer in John 17 has been called "the Lord's high-priestly prayer," and "the Lord's prayer."

Jesus had ended His teaching of the disciples with a shout of victory: "I have overcome the world" (16:33). This was in anticipation of His work on the cross. Throughout His ministry Jesus' work was done in obedience to the Father's will (cf. Luke 4:42; 6:12; 11:1; Matt. 26:36). As He turned again to His Father, He prayed first for Himself (John 17:1-5), then for His apostles (vv. 6-19), and finally for future believers (vv. 20-26).

17:1. **Jesus** could approach God in prayer because of Their Father-Son relationship. He began His prayer with the word **Father** (cf. Matt. 6:9) and used that word three other times in this prayer (John 17:5, 21, 24) as well as "Holy Father" (v. 11) and "Righteous Father" (v. 25). **The time,** Jesus said, **has come.** The divine plan of redemption was at God's appointment. Several times before this Jesus' time had *not* come (2:4; 7:6, 8, 30; 8:20). But now it had arrived (cf. 12:23; 13:1).

Jesus then prayed, **Glorify Your Son** (cf. 17:5). This request for glorification included sustaining Jesus in suffering, accepting His sacrifice, resurrecting Him, and restoring Him to His pristine glory. The purpose of the request was **that** the Father would be glorified by the **Son,** that God's wisdom, power, and love might be known through Jesus. Believers too are to glorify God (v. 10); in fact, this is the chief end of man (Rom. 11:36; 16:27; 1 Cor. 10:31; Eph. 1:6, 12, 14; cf. *Westminster Larger Catechism,* Question 1).

17:2. The words, **You granted Him authority over all people,** indicate that Jesus' prayer request was in accordance with the Father's plan. The Father has ordained the rule of the Son over the earth (cf. Ps. 2). So the Son has the authority to judge (John 5:27), to take up His life (10:18), and to **give eternal life to all those** whom the Father gave Him. Five times in this prayer Jesus referred to His own as those the Father gave Him (17:2, 6 [twice], 9, 24).

17:3. Eternal life, as defined here by **Jesus,** involves the experience of knowing **the only true God** through His Son (cf. Matt. 11:27). It is a personal relationship of intimacy which is continuous and dynamic. The word **know** (*ginōskōsin*) here in the present tense, is often used in the Septuagint and sometimes in the Greek New Testament to describe the intimacy of a sexual relationship (e.g., Gen 4:1, "lay"; Matt. 1:25, "had . . . union"). Thus a person who knows God has an intimate personal relationship with Him. And that relationship is eternal, not temporal. Eternal life is not simply endless existence. Everyone will exist somewhere forever (cf. Matt. 25:46), but the question is, In what condition or in what relationship will they spend eternity?

17:4-5. Jesus' prayer for Himself was based on His completed **work** (cf. 4:34)— **I have brought You glory** (cf. 17:1)— which assumed His obedience to death (Phil. 2:8). Even though the Cross was future, it was a certainty. He repeated His request for a return to His pristine **glory** with the Father (cf. John 17:1) based on the certainty of the finished work on the cross.

This "work" the Father **gave** Him **to do** is one of five things in Jesus' prayer which the Father "gave" the Son: (a) work (v. 4), (b) believers (vv. 2, 6, 9, 24), (c) glory (vv. 5, 24), (d) words (v. 8), and (e) a name (vv. 11-12). The Son, in turn, gave believers God's words (vv. 8, 14) and God's glory (vv. 22, 24).

2. JESUS' INTERCESSION FOR THE APOSTLES (17:6-19)

Jesus prayed for His disciples before He chose them (Luke 6:12), during His ministry (John 6:15), at the end of His ministry (Luke 22:32), here (John 17:6-19), and later in heaven (Rom. 8:34; Heb. 7:25). This prayer of intercession reveals Jesus' concern and love for His apostles.

17:6-8. The little flock of disciples was given by the Father to the Son (cf. vv. 2, 9, 24). They had been separated **out of the world** ("world" occurs 18 times in this chap.: vv. 5-6, 9, 11 [twice], 13, 14 [thrice], 15, 16 [twice in the Gr.], 18 [twice], 21, 23-25). This separation was by the electing work of the Father, in which the apostles had been given as a gift to Jesus Christ (cf. 6:37). With the words, **They have obeyed Your Word,** Jesus praised His disciples for responding to the message of God in Jesus Christ. The disciples were not perfect, but they had the right commitment. Their faith in Jesus was a trust in His union with the Father (17:8). This faith in Jesus was manifested in their obedience to His words because **they believed** in His divine mission (cf. 16:27).

17:9-10. Christ's prayer (in vv. 6-19) was particularly for the Eleven, though it applies to all believers (cf. v. 20). At this point He was **not praying for the world** in its hostility and unbelief. This prayer is for two things: (a) the disciples' preservation ("protect them," v. 11) and (b) their sanctification ("sanctify them," v. 17). The world is not to be preserved in its rebellion or sanctified in its unbelief. Jesus prayed this request because of God's ownership of them by creation and election (**they are Yours**). Jesus' words, **All I have is Yours, and all You have is Mine,** reveal His claim to unity, intimacy, and equality with the Father.

In the old economy, God dwelt among people and showed His glory. In Jesus, God's glory was displayed (cf. 1:14). Then Christ's disciples glorified Him: **Glory has come to Me through them.** And now in the Church Age the Holy Spirit glorifies the Son (16:14) and believers are also to glorify the Son (Eph. 1:12).

17:11. Jesus would soon depart to the Father and leave His disciples **in the world. They** had to stay in the world to carry out God's plan in spreading the good news of redemption and in planting the church. With the formation of the church, the history of the world has become, in a sense, "a tale of two cities": the city of God and the city of man.

Since the disciples would be **in the world,** Jesus prayed for their protection. The hostility against God which fell on Jesus would now fall on the tiny band of apostles, and subsequently on many of Jesus' followers. Jesus, in calling on His **Holy Father,** pointed up God's distinction from sinful creatures. This holiness is the basis for believers' separation from the world. He would **protect them** from the sin and enmity of the world **by the power of** His **name** (cf. Prov. 18:10). In Bible times a person's name stood for the person. (In John 17:6, 26 the NIV translates the Gr. "Your name" by the word "You.")

Why did Jesus pray for their preservation? It was to promote the unity of the believers, patterned after the unity of the Father and the Son: **so that they may be one as We are One** (cf. vv. 21-22). The unity here seems to be that of will and purpose. By being protected from the world they would be unified in their desires to serve and glorify the Son.

17:12. As the Good Shepherd, Jesus took care of the flock entrusted to Him by the Father. But Judas was an exception. He is here called **the one doomed to destruction** (lit., "the son of perdition").

Judas was never a sheep and his true character was finally manifested (cf. 13:11; 1 John 2:19). He was a "dead branch" (cf. comments on John 15:2, 6). Judas did what he wanted (he sold Jesus). Yet he was an unwitting tool of Satan (13:2, 27). Even people's volitionally free acts fit into God's sovereign plan (cf. Acts 2:23; 4:28). Thus Judas' betrayal of Jesus **fulfilled** (i.e., filled up in a larger sense) the words in Psalm 41:9 about David's betrayal by his friend.

17:13. The words of comfort spoken by Jesus (**I say these things**) to His disciples were of great benefit to them. Following His Passion, **they** would recall His words and experience **the full measure of** His **joy.** Joy came to them because they knew from His words that He had conquered the evil one and brought eternal life to them.

17:14. Jesus' intercession for the disciples continued with a reminder of (a) their value and (b) their coming danger. They were valuable because they had received the Word of God: **I have given them Your Word** (cf. "I gave them the words You gave Me," v. 8). They were in danger because the satanic **world** system **hated them.** It hated them because **they are not** a part **of** it. As believers share Jesus Christ, "Everything in the world— the cravings of sinful man, the lust of his eyes, and the boasting of what he has and does" (1 John 2:16) loses its attractiveness. A believer's commitment shows the world's values to be trash or dung (cf. Phil. 3:8). Therefore **the world** hates the exposure of its sham values (cf. John 3:20).

17:15. God's plan was **not** to remove the disciples from danger and opposition (**take them out of the world**) **but** to preserve them in the midst of conflict. Though Jesus would soon be taken out of the world (v. 11), His followers are to remain in it. Like Daniel in Babylon (Dan. 1–2; 4–6) and the saints in Caesar's household (Phil. 4:22), God intends for His followers to be witnesses to truth in the midst of satanic falsehood. Satan, **the evil one** (cf. Matt. 5:37; 1 John 5:19), as head of the world system, seeks to do everything possible to destroy believers (cf. Rev. 2:10; 12:10) but God's plan will prevail. Christians must not take themselves out of the world but remain in meaningful contact with it, trusting in

God's protection while they witness for Jesus.

17:16-17. Just as Jesus did not belong to the satanic world system (**I am not of it;** cf. v. 14), so believers do not. They belong to the heavenly kingdom (Col. 1:13) because of their new births (cf. John 3:3). Jesus had prayed for protection for His disciples (17:11). Now His second petition for them was for their sanctification. **Sanctify** means "set apart for special use." A believer is to be distinct from the world's sin, its values, and its goals.

The means of this sanctifying work is God's **truth. The truth** is communicated in the **Word,** which is both personal and propositional. As the message about Jesus was heard, believed, and understood, the disciples' hearts and minds were captured. This change in their thinking resulted in changes in their living. The same is true of believers today. As they appropriate God's Word to their lives, they are sanctified—set apart for God and changed in their living in order to honor God (cf. 15:3). God's message set the apostles apart from **the world** so that they would do His will, not Satan's.

17:18. Jesus is the model for every believer. He was in the world but He was not of the world (vv. 14b, 16b). He was **sent . . . into the world** on a mission by His Father. So believers are **sent . . . into the world** on a mission by the Son, to make the Father known (cf. 20:21). Inasmuch as Jesus' prayer for the disciples was not limited to the immediate apostles (cf. 17:20), this passage is similar to the Great Commission (Matt. 28:18-20). Each Christian should view himself as a missionary whose task is to communicate God's truth to others.

17:19. For the benefit of the disciples, Jesus sanctified Himself. In what sense did Jesus need to **sanctify** Himself? Was He not already set apart to God and distinct from the world? Yes, but *this* sanctification refers to His being separated and dedicated to His *death.* And the pupose of His death was **that they too may be truly sanctified.** The words "truly sanctified" are literally "sanctified in truth." This probably means that God's truth is the means of sanctification (cf. comments on v. 17). The purpose of the death of Christ is to dedicate or separate believers to God and His program.

3. JESUS' INTERCESSION FOR FUTURE BELIEVERS (17:20-26)

17:20. The final portion of Jesus' **prayer** (vv. 20-26) was for future believers who would come to Him **through** the **message** of the apostles. In the Church Age all Christians have come to Christ directly or indirectly through the apostles' witness. Jesus knew His mission would succeed. He would die and be raised, He would send forth the Spirit, the apostles would preach, people would be converted, and the church would be formed. As each high priest of Israel bore the names of the tribes before the presence of God in the tabernacle and the temple (cf. Ex. 28:9-12, 21-29), so now Jesus, the great High Priest, carried future believers into the holy presence of His heavenly Father (cf. Heb. 4:14–5:12; 7:24–8:2).

17:21. Jesus requested unity for future believers (cf. vv. 11, 22). This verse is a favorite of promoters of the present ecumenical movement. Admittedly the divided church is in many ways a scandal. The cure, however, is not institutional union. Jesus was not praying for the unity of a single, worldwide, ecumenical church in which doctrinal heresy would be maintained along with orthodoxy. Instead, He was praying for a unity of love, a unity of obedience to God and His Word, and a united commitment to His will. There are great differences between uniformity, union, and unity.

All believers belong to the **one** body of Christ (1 Cor. 12:13) and their spiritual unity is to be manifest in the way they live. The unity Christ desires for His church is the same kind of unity the Son has with the Father: **just as You are in Me and I am in You** (cf. John 10:38; 17:11, 23). The Father did His works through the Son and the Son always did what pleased the Father (5:30; 8:29). This spiritual unity is to be patterned in the church. Without union with Jesus and the Father (**they . . . in Us**), Christians can do nothing (15:5). The goal of their lives is to do the Father's will.

The disciples' union with Jesus as His body will result in people in **the world** believing in the Father: **that You have sent Me** (cf. 17:23).

17:22-23. **The glory** which Christ **gave** the church may refer to the glory of the Cross (cf. vv. 1-5). As the church received and pondered the significance of Jesus' atoning work, it would be united in God's purposes and redemptive plan. Again the union of Christians (that they may be one) is likened to the unity the Son has with the Father (as We are One; cf. vv. 11, 21). This union is further linked by Christ's indwelling of believers (I in them).

The goal of the unity of believers with each other and with God is twofold: (a) that the world will believe in the Son's divine mission (know that You sent Me), and (b) that the world will sense that God's love for believers is deep, intimate, and lasting as is His love for His unique Son (cf. v. 26).

17:24. The communion and fellowship which disciples have with Jesus in this life will increase in eternity. The goal of a believer's salvation is future glorification which includes being with Jesus (cf. 14:3; Col. 3:4; 1 Thes. 4:17). Jesus' last testament and will (I want, *thelō*) is that His disciples enter into (see) His glory (Heb. 2:10). This glory was what Jesus had from the Father and would again have (John 17:5). His testament was sealed by His death and resurrection. Since His will is identical to the Father's (4:34; 5:30; 6:38), it will certainly come to pass.

17:25-26. Jesus' prayer for believers ends with a call to the Righteous Father. The word translated "righteous" here does not occur often in John's Gospel (cf. 5:30; 7:24). Its significance here seems to be in Jesus' praise of the Father for His work of revelation (cf. Matt. 11:25-26). The Father is right (righteous) and the world is in the wrong (the world does not know You). Jesus has known, revealed (John 17:6), and glorified (v. 4) the Father, and so should Christians. The essence of God is love (1 John 4:8). Jesus made the Father and His love known to the world by His death. And the Father made known His love for the Son by raising Him to glory. Jesus' purpose in revealing the Father was that Christians would continue to grow in that love (that the Father's love for the Son may be in them) and to enjoy the personal presence of Jesus in their lives (that I Myself may be in them).

Jesus' petitions for believers are four: preservation (John 17:11), sanctification (v. 17), unity (vv. 11, 21-22), and partici-

pation in Jesus' glory (v. 24). This prayer is sure to be answered (cf. 11:42; 1 John 5:14).

IV. Jesus' Passion and Resurrection (chaps. 18–20)

A. The arrest of Jesus (18:1-11)

18:1. Jesus left the room where He ate the Last Supper with His disciples and crossed the Kidron Valley, to the east. The Kidron, the modern Wodi en-Nar, is a valley or torrent bed which starts north of Jerusalem and passes between the temple mount and the Mount of Olives on its way to the Dead Sea. David was betrayed by a friend (Ahithophel) while crossing the Kidron and going up to the Mount of Olives (2 Sam. 15:23, 30-31). So too Jesus was betrayed by His "trusted friend" Judas while crossing the Kidron and going to the Mount of Olives. The olive grove was a place where Jesus and His disciples came each night to bivouac when they were in Jerusalem (Luke 21:37). During festival times (e.g., the Passover) thousands of Jews flocked to the Holy City and most of them had to stay in tents or other temporary shelters.

18:2-3. "The love of money is a root of all kinds of evil" (1 Tim. 6:10). So it is not surprising that Judas . . . betrayed Jesus for money (John 12:4-6; Matt. 26:14-16). Judas was not an unusual monster but a common man caught in a common sin (greed) which Satan used to accomplish his purpose. Judas knew the habits of Jesus, and his deed stands out in black contrast with Jesus' unselfish love. The soldiers . . . officials from the chief priests, and Pharisees united in their hostility toward Jesus. The detachment of Roman soldiers was a cohort (*speiran*, 10th part of a legion), which here included about 600 men. They were probably commanded to pick up this insurrectionist who claimed to be some kind of king.

18:4. Jesus was conscious of all the events coming on Him. He was not taken by surprise, but was a willing voluntary sacrifice (10:14, 17-18). Earlier in His ministry Jesus was unwilling to be made a popular king (6:15). The scene in 18:4 is one of intense drama and irony. Judas came with soldiers and religious leaders to take Jesus by force. But Jesus stood alone (the disciples had fallen asleep; Luke 22:45-46); though unarmed, He was in command. In the darkness of the night, He could have fled as all the disciples would soon do (cf. Mark 14:50). But instead He gave Himself up.

18:5-6. His words **I am He** (lit., "I Am") startled them and **they . . . fell backward to the ground,** struck no doubt by the majesty of His words (cf. 7:45-46). The phrase **I am** is ambiguous and could refer to Jesus' deity (Ex. 3:14; John 8:58). Or it may simply have been Jesus' way of identifying Himself (as in 9:9).

18:7-9. As the Good Shepherd, Jesus laid down His life for the sheep (10:11). His protection of the apostles was a perfect illustration of His substitutionary atonement. He died not only for them but instead of them. As the Good Shepherd He did not lose any of His sheep but fulfilled His Father's will for the apostles (6:38) and fulfilled His own prophetic Word (6:39).

18:10. **Peter** had promised that he would die for Jesus (Matt. 26:33-35) and he thought he perhaps could save Jesus or at least go down fighting. Undoubtedly he was better at fishing than at swordplay, for he no doubt tried to take off the head of **the high priest's servant . . . Malchus** not just his ear. Both Luke (22:50) and John recorded that it was his **right ear** which is an incidental evidence of the historical reliability of these Gospel books. (Luke added that Jesus healed the man's ear [Luke 22:51], an amazing touch of love for His enemies!) Peter's blind loyalty was touching, but it missed God's plan. Zeal without knowledge in religion often leads men astray (cf. Rom. 10:2).

18:11. Earlier that same night **Jesus** had rebuked **Peter** (13:6-11). Now He rebuked him again, this time for not understanding God's will. In spite of constant teaching about His approaching death (3:14; 8:28; 12:32-33; cf. Luke 9:22) the disciples did not understand its need (cf. Luke 24:25). The cup which the Father had given Jesus refers to the suffering and death He would experience under God's wrath against sin (Ps. 75:8; Isa. 51:17, 22; Jer. 25:15; Ezek. 23:31-33). The words **the cup the Father has given Me** indicated that Jesus saw all the things coming on Him as part of God's sovereign plan. His rhetorical question to Peter was designed to prod Peter's thinking. Jesus had come to do the Father's will and so He must now embrace it.

B. The religious trial and Peter's denials (18:12-27)

18:12-14. When **Jesus** was **arrested,** it was dark and late at night. Jesus had already had a long day. His disciples were so exhausted by the schedule and the pressures that they had fallen asleep. But for Jesus, the time while they were sleeping was a deep crisis in prayer and agony (Mark 14:33-41; Luke 22:44). Now Jesus was **bound** and in the hands of His enemies. He was alone since His disciples had been scattered (Matt. 25:56; John 16:32).

The religious trial began (cf. the list of Jesus' six trials at Matt. 26:57). The words, **They . . . brought Him first to Annas,** provide information not given in the other Gospels. Annas had been appointed high priest by Quirinius, governor of Syria, in A.D. 6 and remained until he was deposed by Valerius Gratus, procurator of Judea, in A.D. 15. According to the Jewish law the high priestly office was for life, but the Romans did not like the concentration of power in one person so they frequently changed high priests. Annas was succeeded by five of his sons and by his son-in-law **Caiaphas** (see the chart at Acts 4:6; cf. Luke 3:2). Evidently Annas remained the power behind the throne; a preliminary investigation was carried out by him before Jesus' formal religious trial. **Caiaphas** was **the high priest that year,** that is, that fateful year of Jesus' death. John reminded his readers of Caiaphas' unconscious prophecy (John 11:49-52).

18:15-16. After the immediate fright in the olive grove, when the mob took **Jesus** and the disciples ran, two disciples returned and followed the Lord and His enemies back across the Kidron and into the city. They were **Simon Peter and another disciple.** The other disciple is unknown but he may well have been John, son of Zebedee (cf. 20:2; 21:20, 24). **This disciple** knew **the high priest** and therefore had access **into the high priest's courtyard.** Thus he was in a unique position to know what was going on and to enable **Peter** to get into the courtyard.

18:17-18. Peter's denial before the servant **girl** was a striking contradiction to his earlier boast to lay down his life for Jesus (13:37), and his show of offense in cutting off Malchus' ear (18:10). Evidently the other disciple was also in danger (perhaps greater) but he did not deny Jesus. **Peter stood by the fire . . . warming himself** in the **cold** spring evening, Jerusalem being about 2,500 feet above sea level. This little detail about the cold evening is another indication that the author of this book was an eyewitness.

18:19. The events in the narrative in verses 12-27 are like a drama presented on two stages. Stage one was set (vv. 12-14) while the action on stage two went on (vv. 15-18). Then the action shifted back to stage one (vv. 19-24), and then returned to the other stage (vv. 25-27).

The preliminary investigation of Jesus may be likened to what might happen today when an arrested person is first brought into a police station. Annas **questioned Jesus about** people who held His views and about the nature of **His teaching.** If an insurrection was feared (cf. 11:48), these would be normal questions.

18:20-21. Jesus responded that He had no secret cult or organization. He had an inner circle of disciples but the character of His teaching was not private. He **taught** in the open and in public places (**in synagogues or at the temple**). The people knew **what** He taught so if there was a **question** concerning what He taught, answers were readily available. Jesus did not have two kinds of truths or teaching. He was innocent unless proven guilty. Therefore they should produce witnesses if they had something substantial against Him. Of course, they had no clear accusation so they sought some way to trick Him or catch Him in a trap.

18:22-24. One of Annas' assistants did not like Jesus' answer so he **struck Him in the face.** The preliminary hearing had several illegalities, and this was one of them. It was improper to try to induce self-accusation, and it was wrong to hit an unconvicted person. Jesus' response concerned not the manner of His speech (**Is that any way . . . ?**) but the substance of His teaching (**If I said something wrong . . .**). It was easier to evade **the truth** or to silence the One who spoke the truth than to attempt to answer the truth. Truth has a self-evident power of persuasion and those who oppose it find it difficult to deny. **Jesus** pressed this point and exposed their hypocrisy. They knew the truth but loved error. They saw the light but loved darkness (cf. 3:19; Rom. 1:18). Following this preliminary interview, **Annas sent** Jesus on to his son-in-law **Caiaphas** (cf. John 18:13). (The NIV text is more probable than the NIV marg.)

18:25-27. In this section **Peter** denied the Lord for the second and third times. Peter's betrayal is reported in all four Gospels, which indicates something of the importance the Gospel writers saw in this defection of the disciples' leader. Since all men fail and even many noted Christians stumble greatly, the record of Peter's denials (and his subsequent restoration; cf. chap. 21) is of great pastoral comfort. The final denial was prompted by a question by **a relative of the man** Malchus, whom **Peter had** tried to kill in the garden. Just after Peter denied Jesus the third time, the Lord looked on him (Luke 22:61) and he went out weeping bitterly (Luke 22:62). Then **a rooster began to crow** (cf. Matt. 26:72-74), which fulfilled Jesus' prophecy (John 13:38). (Mark wrote that a rooster crowed twice; see comments on Mark 14:72.) A rooster crowing and Baalam's donkey speaking reveal God's sovereignty and the movement of all things in His plan and timing.

C. The civil trial (18:28–19:16)

18:28-29. Each of the Gospel writers had a special emphasis in his presentation of Jesus' trial, death, and resurrection. John seems to supplement the material of the first three Gospels. Only he reported the interview with Annas, and he reported the interview with Pilate in much more detail and psychological insight. John did not report the trial before the Jewish Sanhedrin (Mark 14:55-64) with the charge of blasphemy. (See the list of Jesus' six trials at Matt. 26:57.)

Since the Jewish council did not have the legal right to put Jesus to death, the case had to be brought before the Roman governor, Pontius Pilate (A.D. 26–36). Normally the governor lived in Caesarea, but during the great feasts it was prudent for him to come to Jerusalem in case a riot or insurrection took place. **Passover** was particularly dangerous because emotions ran high as the Jews remembered their deliverance from bondage.

The location of **the palace of the Roman governor** is disputed. It could have been at the Antonia Fortress on the north side of the temple area or at one of Herod's two palaces on the west of the city. **The Jews** would **not enter** a Gentile house (in this case **the** governor's **palace**), but they could go into the courtyard or under the colonnades. It is ironic that the Jewish leaders were concerned with ritual **uncleanness** while they planned murder! **So Pilate came out to** the Jews (probably to a courtyard) and began an informal inquiry.

18:30-31. The Jews' reply to **Pilate** revealed the hostility between them. (Pilate was hated by them for his harshness and the fact that he was a Gentile ruling over them. Pilate despised them and eventually in the year A.D. 36 they were able to get Pilate recalled to Rome.) At this time Pilate refused to be their executioner. He knew what was going on. He had seen the Triumphal Entry a few days earlier. He knew that envy was the cause of their accusation against Jesus (Matt. 27:18). So Pilate decided to play a game with the Jews with Jesus' life as the prize. He refused to do anything without a sufficient charge. The Jews' accusation of blasphemy would be difficult to prove and would not impress Pilate as worthy of death under Roman civil law. The Jews seem to have lost the official **right to execute** but in certain cases people were stoned (cf. Acts 6:8–7:60). Jesus was popular, and the Sanhedrin wanted Him dead and, if possible, killed by the Romans. The Sanhedrin could condemn, but only the Romans could execute legally.

18:32. John explained why **Jesus** was delivered by the Jews to the Romans. Jewish executions were normally by stoning, which broke bones. The Roman method of execution was crucifixion. It was necessary for three reasons for Jesus to be crucified by the Romans at the instigation of the Jews: (a) to fulfill prophecies (e.g., that none of His bones be broken; cf. 19:36-37); (b) to include both Jews and Gentiles in the collective guilt for the deed (cf. Acts 2:23; 4:27); (c) by crucifixion, Jesus was "lifted up" like "the snake in the desert" (cf. comments on John 3:14). A person under God's curse was to be displayed (hanged) on a tree as a sign of judged sin (Deut. 21:23; Gal. 3:13).

18:33-34. Pilate had a private inter-

view with **Jesus** (vv. 33-38a). He realized that the Jews would not normally turn over one of their own to the hated Romans so something was strange about this case. According to Luke (23:2) they accused Jesus of three things: subverting the nation, opposing payment of taxes to Caesar, and claiming to be "Christ, a King." Pilate began by asking Jesus if He was **the King of the Jews.** Jesus asked Pilate if he had that **idea** on his **own** or if **others** (Jews) talked **to** him. Jesus here asked Pilate if he was concerned that He was some political threat to Rome, that is, a revolutionary.

18:35-36. Pilate sarcastically **replied** with a question as to whether he was **a Jew** or not. Of course he was not interested in Jewish questions, but only in matters pertaining to civil government. It must have hurt Jesus deeply to have Pilate press the point that **it was** the Jews, His own **people,** and their own religious leaders **who** had accused Him. In his prologue John had sounded this sad theme, "He came to that which was His own, but His own did not receive Him" (1:11). **Jesus** replied that Rome need not fear a political insurrection. He was not a zealot or a revolutionary guerrilla leader. His **kingdom** is not like that. It **is not of this world;** it **is from another place,** that is, heaven. Therefore it comes not by rebellion but by submission to God. Its source was not from men's acts of violence but from a new birth from heaven which transferred a person out of Satan's kingdom into God's **kingdom** (cf. Col. 1:13; John 3:3).

18:37. Since Jesus spoke of a kingdom, **Pilate** seized on the word "king." **You are a king, then? Jesus answered** that question in the affirmative, and then clarified that His kingdom is not like Rome's. It is a kingdom of truth which overshadows all kingdoms. He said, **Everyone on the side of truth listens to Me.** Jesus in a few words asserted His divine origin (**I was born . . . I came into the world**) and ministry (**to testify to the truth**). Later *He* became Pilate's judge.

18:38. Pilate's question, **What is truth?** has echoed down through the centuries. How his question was intended is problematic. Was it a wistful desire to know what no one could tell him? Was it philosophical cynicism concerning the problem of epistemology? Was it indifference to anything so impractical as abstract thought? Or was it irritation at Jesus' response? These are all possible interpretations of his words. But the significant thing is that he suddenly turned away from the *One* who is "the Truth" (14:6) without waiting for an answer. Pilate's declaration of Jesus' innocence is important. He would die like a Passover lamb, a male in its prime without blemish (Ex. 12:5).

18:39-40. Having displayed a lack of interest in truth, Pilate then revealed a lack of commitment to justice. He lacked the courage of his convictions. If Jesus was innocent of all charges, then Pilate should have set Him free. Instead, Pilate began a series of compromising moves to avoid dealing with an inconvenient truth in a difficult circumstance. First, when Pilate found out Jesus was from Galilee, he sent Him to Herod (Luke 23:6-7). Second, Pilate tried to appeal to the crowd (John 18:38), hoping to bypass the desire of the chief priests and elders. Knowing Jesus was popular, he thought the crowd would prefer Jesus to **Barabbas.** But the leaders proved to be persuasive (cf. Matt. 27:20). The offer **to release . . . Barabbas** who was guilty of murder and insurrection showed poor judgment for a person responsible for Rome's interests.

19:1-3. Third, **Pilate . . . had him flogged.** Pilate's action, according to Luke (23:16), was another attempt at compromise. He hoped the crowd would be satisfied with a little blood. Roman flogging was done with a leather whip with bits of metal at the ends. Such flogging often killed a person. The flogging, the mocking **crown of thorns** and **purple robe,** the ridiculing in hailing Him **King of the Jews,** and the physical blows on His **face**—these were all part of Jesus' deep humiliation as He was identified with human sin as the Servant of the Lord (cf. Isa. 50:6; 52:14–53:6). (Matthew and Mark added that the soldiers spit on Jesus [Matt. 27:30; Mark 15:19].) The thorns **on His head** are mindful of the curse of thorns caused by human sin (Gen. 3:18).

19:4-5. Again Pilate's attempt to free Jesus by an appeal to the crowd missed the mark. Their taste for His blood was beyond recall. Pilate's words, **Here is the Man!** (kjv, "Behold the Man!" Latin, *Ecce*

homo) have become famous. It is strange that several of Pilate's statements have become immortal. **Jesus** by that time must have appeared as a pathetic figure, bloody and **wearing the crown of thorns and the purple robe.**

19:6-7. The Jewish leaders displayed their hatred of Jesus and **shouted** for His death. Crucifixion was a shameful death, usually reserved for criminals, slaves, and especially revolutionaries. **Pilate** at first refused to be the executioner, but then the leaders brought forth their real reason: **He claimed to be the Son of God. According to** the **Law** the charge of blasphemy (Lev. 24:16) called for death, if it could be proven. About the same time Pilate's wife sent him strange words: "Don't have anything to do with that innocent Man, for I have suffered a great deal today in a dream because of Him" (Matt. 27:19).

19:8-11. Pilate's response was one of fear. As a pagan he had heard stories of humanlike gods who visited men and judged them. Perhaps the solemn majesty of **Jesus** with His claims of truth began to convict his conscience. Jesus' refusal to **answer** Pilate's question, **Where do You come from?** fulfilled the words of prophecy in Isaiah 53:7.

Pilate had his opportunity for truth and was found wanting. Disturbed by Jesus' silence, he asked, **Don't You realize I have power . . . ?** True, Pilate had some power, but he was a pawn. Yet he was responsible for his decisions (cf. Acts 4:27-28; 1 Cor. 2:8). In reality, God is the only One who has ultimate and full power. Pilate, Jesus said, was under God and therefore responsible to Him: **The one who handed Me over to you is guilty of a greater sin.** In this statement was Jesus referring to Judas, Satan, Caiaphas, the priests, or the Jewish people? Perhaps Caiaphas is the best choice since he is the one who handed Jesus over to Pilate. Pilate was guilty (cf. the words in the Apostles' Creed, "suffered under Pontius Pilate"). But Jesus put more weight on Caiaphas as the responsible one (cf. John 11:49-50; 18:13-14).

19:12-13. Pilate, probably under conviction, wanted to **free** Jesus **but the Jews** now tried a new attack. To let **Jesus** go free, they argued, would be disloyalty to **Caesar.** The title **friend of Caesar** (Latin, *amicus Caesaris*) was an important consideration. Tiberius was on the throne and he was sick, suspicious, and often violent. Pilate had plenty to cover up and he did not want an unfavorable report to go to his boss. If he had to choose between showing his loyalty to Rome or siding with a despised and strange Jew, there was no question in his mind. The dilemma had to be resolved so **Pilate** made the official decision.

19:14-16. The sixth hour, by Roman reckoning of time, could indicate 6 A.M. (some scholars, however, take it to mean noon; cf. comments on 1:39; 4:6). This **was the day of preparation** for the **Passover Week** (i.e., Friday). That day was the Passover proper, the day on which Christ died. But it was also the preparation for the seven-day Feast of Unleavened Bread, which followed immediately after the Day of Passover, and which was sometimes called the Passover Week (cf. Luke 2:41; 22:1, 7; Acts 12:3-4; see comments on Luke 22:7-38).

Pilate said, **Here is your King** (KJV, "Behold your King!"). This is another example of irony. (John is the only Gospel writer who mentioned this incident.) Pilate did not believe Jesus was their King, but to spite the Jews he called Jesus the King of the Jews. John saw this as significant, for Jesus would die for His people as the King of His people, as the Messiah. Pilate could not resist goading the Jews: **Shall I crucify your King?** As if Rome would *not* crucify a Jewish king! The Jewish rejoinder, **We have no king but Caesar,** was full of irony. The rebellious Jews claimed loyalty to Rome while disclaiming their Messiah (cf. Ps. 2:1-3).

D. The Crucifixion (19:17-30)

19:17-18. Carrying His own cross, Jesus **went out.** These words fulfill two Old Testament symbols or types. Isaac carried his own wood for the sacrifice (Gen. 22:1-6) and the sin offering used to be taken outside the camp or city (cf. Heb. 13:11-13). So Jesus was made sin (2 Cor. 5:21). **Golgotha** in **Aramaic (The place of the skull)** was probably called this because the hill with its stony barren top looked like a skull. The **two others** who were crucified with Jesus are mentioned to make understandable the following sequel in which their legs were broken but not those of Jesus (cf. John 19:32-33). Luke added that the two were "criminals" (Luke 23:32-33), and Matthew called them "robbers" (Matt. 27:44).

19:19-20. The game between **Pilate** and the priests continued with the writing of the **notice** (Gr., *titlon;* Latin, *titulus)* which was usually attached to a criminal's **cross. It read, JESUS OF NAZARETH, THE KING OF THE JEWS.** Since **the sign was written in** three languages—**Aramaic, Latin, and Greek**—and the Crucifixion was in a public **place,** all who could **read** saw a clear proclamation.

19:21-22. The chief priests naturally did not want this to be proclaimed as a fact. They wanted Jesus to die for *claiming* to be the Jews' **King.** So they **protested to Pilate** to change the superscription. **Pilate** refused to do so. Doubtless he felt he had done enough dirty work for the leaders of the nation, and he enjoyed his little joke against them. His haughty answer, **What I have written, I have written,** completes a series of amazing utterances by Pilate (cf. 18:38; 19:5, 14-15; Matt. 27:22). Irony was also shown by John, who recognized that Pilate wrote those words but that God wanted His Son to die with this proclamation on His cross. The words in another sense are a fitting judgment on the life of Pilate. He had played his part and had his moment of truth. He, a Gentile, would be judged accordingly by the King of the Jews!

19:23-24. The soldier's activity in stripping **Jesus** and dividing **His clothes** was part of the customary cruelty of those times. Clothes were handmade and therefore expensive in comparison with clothes today. The executioners received the pieces as their due. The **seamless** tunic **(undergarment)** may be significant as the type of garment which the high priest wore, yet John did not expound on this point. John saw the significance in the fulfillment of Psalm 22:18, in which the poetic parallelism in that verse was fulfilled in two separate acts: (a) **They divided My garments** and (b) they **cast lots for My clothing.** That Jesus died naked was part of the shame which He bore for our sins. At the same time He is the last Adam who provides clothes of righteousness for sinners.

19:25-27. In stark contrast with the cruelty and indifference of the soldiers, a group of four women watched with love and grief. The anguish of Jesus' **mother** fulfilled a prophecy of Simeon: "A sword will pierce your own soul too" (Luke 2:35). Seeing her sorrow **Jesus** honored **His mother** by consigning her into the care of John, **the** beloved **disciple.** His brothers and sisters being in Galilee, were not in a position to care for or comfort her. The words of Jesus to Mary and the beloved disciple were His third saying from the cross (the first one recorded by John). In the other Gospels Jesus had already given a respite to the Roman executioners (Luke 23:24) and a pardon to one thief (Luke 23:42-43).

19:28-29. Jesus' fourth of seven sayings from the cross, "My God, My God, why have You forsaken Me?" is not recorded by John (cf. Matt. 27:46; Mark 15:34). John recorded the fifth saying, **I am thirsty.** The wording in John 19:28 indicated that Jesus was fully conscious and was aware of fulfilling the details of prophecies (Pss. 42:1-2; 63:1). The paradox of the One who is the Water of life (John 4:14; 7:38-39) dying in thirst is striking. Giving Him **wine vinegar,** a sour wine, fulfilled Psalm 69:21. Putting the vinegar-soaked **sponge** on the end of a **hyssop plant** stalk seems odd. Perhaps this detail points to Jesus dying as the true Lamb at Passover, for hyssop was used in the Passover ceremonies (cf. Ex. 12:22).

19:30. The sixth word or saying that **Jesus** spoke from the cross was the single Greek work *tetelestai* which means **It is finished.** Papyri receipts for taxes have been recovered with the word *tetelestai* written across them, meaning "paid in full." This word on Jesus' lips was significant. When He said, "It is finished" (not "I am finished"), He meant His redemptive work was completed. He had been made sin for people (2 Cor. 5:21) and had suffered the penalty of God's justice which sin deserved. Even in the moment of His death, Jesus remained the One who gave up His life (cf. John 10:11, 14, 17-18). **He bowed His head** (giving His seventh saying, "Father, into Your hands I commit My spirit" [Luke 23:46]) **and** then dismissed **His spirit.** This differs from the normal process in death by crucifixion in which the life-spirit would ebb away and then the head would slump forward.

E. The burial (19:31-42)

19:31-32. In the only known archeological find of a crucifixion, which came to light in 1968, the skeletal remains revealed that the lower legs had been shattered by a single blow. This illustrates this passage. **Because** of the Law (Deut. 21:22-23) a body was not to remain exposed on a tree (or cross) overnight and certainly not on a **Sabbath.** A person so executed was under God's curse and his body if left exposed would defile the land (cf. Deut. 21:23; Gal. 3:13).

The smashing of the lower leg bones was called in Latin the *crurifragium.* This caused death to occur fairly quickly by shock, loss of blood, and inability to breathe (the chest cavity would bear the pressure of the body's weight after the legs were broken). Without this procedure, a person could live for many hours or even days. This *crurifragium* was done to the two thieves on each side of Jesus.

19:33-34. Jesus had **already** died so **His legs** were not broken. **Instead,** just to make sure, a soldier **pierced Jesus' side with a spear.** The result was **a sudden flow of blood and water.** This flow has been interpreted in various ways. Some have seen this as evidence that Jesus died of a broken heart so that His pericardium was full of blood and serum. Others see a symbolic or sacramental significance of the stream which heals people. More likely, it indicates that Jesus was a real human who died a real death. Possibly the spear struck the stomach and the heart, which accounted for the flow. The one who saw this (v. 35) saw saving significance in the sign. At the time of the writing of this Gospel, Gnosticism and Docetism were current problems. These ideologies denied the reality of the Incarnation and of His death. But the blood and water are firm answers against those heresies.

19:35-37. This section relates the **testimony** of the eyewitness who is also most probably the writer of this Gospel, John the disciple (cf. 13:23; 21:20-24). The value of His **testimony is** an important claim of **truth,** given so that others may grasp the facts and discern their significance (cf. 20:31). John explained that soldiers not administering the *crurifragium* to Jesus but simply piercing His side **fulfilled** two specific prophecies or types.

Jesus, as the true Passover Lamb, did not have any **of His bones . . . broken** (Ex. 12:46; Num. 9:12; Ps. 34:20) and people in the future **will look on the pierced** One (Zech. 12:10; cf. Rev. 1:7).

19:38-39. Joseph of Arimathea was rich (Matt. 27:57) and was waiting for the kingdom (Mark 15:43). (Arimathea was about 20 miles northwest of Jerusalem.) Though a member of the Sanhedrin, the Jewish council, he was "a good and upright man who had not consented to their decision" (Luke 23:50-51). After a crucifixion the Romans usually left the dead body to the beasts of prey. This lack of proper burial was the final humiliation in a crucifixion. But Jews removed exposed bodies (cf. comments on John 19:31-32).

Joseph got **permission** to bury Jesus' **body.** He along with another influential man (**Nicodemus;** cf. 3:1; 7:51) made the necessary arrangements. **About 75 pounds** of **myrrh and aloes** was an extensive amount of spices, used in preparing the body for burial. Perhaps Nicodemus now understood the teaching of Jesus that He would be lifted up and that a man could look in faith to Him and live (cf. 3:14). Both men who had been secret disciples now became manifest.

19:40-42. Because it was almost **the** Sabbath (which began at sundown) the burial had to take place quickly. **Jewish burial customs** did not involve mummification or embalming, which took out the blood and body organs. Their normal process was to wash a body and cover it with cloth and aromatic oils or **spices.** The NIV translation of *othoniois* as **strips of linen** has some support (cf. William F. Arndt and F. Wilbur Gingrich, *A Greek-English Lexicon of the New Testament and Other Early Christian Literature.* Chicago: University of Chicago Press, 1957, p. 558). However, some Roman Catholic scholars argue for the translation "cloth wrappings" since Matthew refers to a linen cloth in which Jesus' body was wrapped (Matt. 27:59, *sindōn*).

Recent discussion on the Shroud of Turin has raised considerable controversy. The translation "strips of linen" would argue against the authenticity of the shroud. But at this time, because of the uncertainties of Jewish burial practices, the meaning of *othoniois,* and the Shroud of Turin, dogmatism should be avoided. Jesus' body was placed in **a new tomb** in a private **garden,** not in a cemetery. Matthew wrote that this was Joseph's "own new tomb that he had cut out of the rock" (Matt. 27:60). Isaiah prophesied that the Messiah, the suffering Servant, though despised and rejected by men, would be with the rich in His death (Isa. 53:9).

The burial of Jesus is part of the gospel ("He was buried," 1 Cor. 15:4). Its significance lies in the fact that it was the completion of Jesus' suffering and humiliation. It also pointed up the reality of His death and set the stage for His coming bodily resurrection. Also, in Jesus' burial He identified with believers who will die and be buried.

Joseph and Nicodemus' act of love and respect for the body of Jesus was for them dangerous, costly, and without any personal gain. The service of Christians for their living Lord should be equally courageous and sacrificial, for their labor is not in vain (1 Cor. 15:58).

F. The empty tomb (20:1-9)

John's Gospel comes to a conclusion with a proclamation of Jesus' victory over death (chap. 20) followed by an epilogue (chap. 21). Each Gospel writer stressed certain aspects of the events. John began with a testimony of how he came to personal faith in the Resurrection by considering the evidence found in the open tomb.

20:1-2. The first day of the week, Sunday, **Mary of Magdala** and other women (cf. **we** in v. 2) came **to the tomb.** "Mary of Magdala" is a translation of the same Greek words which elsewhere are rendered "Mary Magdalene" (Matt. 28:1; Mark 16:1, 9; Luke 24:10). Her devotion to Jesus, living and dead, was based on her gratitude for His delivering her from bondage to Satan. She had been an observer at the cross and now was the first person at the grave. This tomb had been closed with a large rock door (Mark 16:3-4) and had been sealed by the authority of the Roman governor Pontius Pilate (Matt. 27:65-66). The women were amazed to see an open and apparently empty tomb. They ran and told **Peter and the** beloved **disciple** (cf. John 19:26) that a terrible thing had occurred. They assumed that grave robbers had desecrated the tomb.

20:3-9. Peter and John started a footrace to **the tomb.** John beat Peter to the garden and looked in **the tomb.** It was not quite empty for John saw the grave clothes. Perhaps his first thought was that the women had made a mistake! **He bent over and looked** (*blepei*) **in** but **did not** enter the tomb, probably for fear of defilement. When **Peter . . . arrived** he rushed in and **saw** (*theōrei*, "beheld attentively") the grave clothes and the **separate** burial **cloth.** He must have remained inside puzzled at what he saw. After a period of time John **went** in and **saw** (*eiden*, "perceived"—the third Gr. word for "see" in these verses) the significance of the grave clothes **and believed.** Peter must have been thinking, "Why would a grave robber have left the clothes in this order? Why take the body of Jesus?" But John perceived that the missing body and the position of the grave clothes was not due to a robbery. He realized that Jesus had risen from the dead and had gone through the grave clothes. The tomb was open not to let Jesus' body out but to let the disciples and the world see that He rose.

This section of John's Gospel (20:1-9) is a powerful eyewitness testimony which strikes the perceptive reader as being psychologically and historically true. John commented (v. 9) that even after a long period of teaching by Jesus the disciples **still did not understand from Scripture that Jesus had to rise from the dead** (cf. Pss. 16:10-11; 110:1, 4; Isa. 53:11-12).

G. Jesus' appearance to Mary (20:10-18)

20:10-14. Jesus' first resurrection appearance was to **Mary** of Magdala, out of whom He had cast seven demons (Luke 8:2). (For a list of His resurrection appearances see Matt. 28.) **The disciples** returned **to their homes** while Mary remained **outside the tomb crying.** John must not have yet told her that Jesus was risen. He probably was too stunned and puzzled to say anything significant. Mary **looked into the tomb and saw two** individuals who were **angels.** In the Bible when angels appeared to people, the angels looked like men; they did not have halos or wings. In certain visions, winged beings appeared (e.g., Isa. 6) but the norm for angels was that they were in human-like forms.

Because of her grief Mary did not notice anything unusual. Their question and her answer set the stage for the greatest "recognition scene" in all of history (perhaps the second greatest is "I am Joseph"; cf. Gen. 45:1-3). The appearance of **Jesus** to Mary was so unexpected that **she did not realize that it was Jesus.** The fact that He appeared to Mary rather than to Pilate or Caiaphas or to one of His disciples is significant. That a woman would be the first to see Him is an evidence of Jesus' electing love as well as a mark of the narrative's historicity. No Jewish author in the ancient world would have invented a story with a woman as the first witness to this most important event. Furthermore, Jesus may have introduced Himself to Mary first because she had so earnestly sought Him. She was at the cross while He was dying (John 19:25), and she went to His tomb early on Sunday morning (20:1).

20:15-16. Mary talked with Jesus but still did not realize who He was. Some suggest that Jesus' appearance was changed; others say she had a temporary "blindness" as did the Emmaus Road disciples who "were kept from recognizing Him" (Luke 24:16) until His act of disclosure. Others say that possibly the tears in her eyes kept her from recognizing Him.

Jesus said to her, Mary. As the Good Shepherd, He calls His sheep by name (cf. John 10:3) and "they know His voice" (10:4). Immediately she recognized Him! She responded with the cry **Rabboni! (which means** my **Teacher)**

20:17-18. She may have embraced Him physically, for the Lord responded, **Do not hold on to Me, for I have not yet returned to the Father. Go instead to My brothers and tell them. . . .** These words spoke of a new relationship, new relatives, and a new responsibility. Many wanted to "hold onto" Jesus. The KJV translation "Touch Me not," has caused many interpreters to wonder why He could not be "touched." The NIV translation is more accurate, for He certainly was not untouchable (cf. Matt. 28:9; John 20:27). Mary had lost Jesus once before (at His crucifixion) and it was natural to fear the loss of His presence again.

Jesus said, in effect, "This (the physical contact) is not My real presence for the church. A *new relationship* will

begin with My Ascension and the gift of
the Holy Spirit to the church." Jesus then
explained the fact of the *new relatives.* He
called His disciples His brothers. Earlier
He had said they were friends: "I no
longer call you servants . . . instead, I have
called you friends" (15:15). Believers in
Jesus become a part of Jesus' family with
God as their Father (cf. Heb. 2:11-12;
Rom. 8:15-17, 29; Gal. 3:26). Mary's *new
responsibility* was to testify to His risen
presence. She was the recipient of four
special graces: to see angels; to see Jesus
risen; to be the first to see Him alive; and
to be a proclaimer of the good news.
Christians today are also the recipients of
special grace; they too are given this new
responsibility to witness to the world (cf.
Matt. 28:16-20).

Jesus' words, **I am returning to My
Father** indicate His unique sonship. **Mary**
and the other women told **the news** to **the
disciples,** but according to Luke, they did
not believe her or the other women
"because their words seemed to them like
nonsense" (Luke 24:11; cf. Luke 24:23).

H. Jesus' appearance to His disciples (20:19-23)

20:19-20. The disciples had almost
been arrested with Jesus. They remained
under the **fear** of death at the hands of
the Jews (i.e., the Jewish authorities), so
they met in secret at night, with fear,
behind locked doors. (What a contrast
with their boldness about seven weeks
later on the day of Pentecost!) **Jesus**
passed through the door, as indicated by
the fact that when the **doors** were **locked,**
He **came and stood among them** (cf. v.
26). This showed the power of His new
resurrection body. But His body had
substantial form and continuity with His
pre-Cross body (cf. v. 27). His first words,
Peace be with you! were a conventional
greeting similar to *šālôm* in Hebrew. But
the words were now invested with a
deeper and fuller meaning (cf. 14:27;
16:33; Rom. 5:1; Phil. 4:7).

Seeing the wounds in **His** pierced
hands and side, they **were overjoyed**
(though at first they were frightened, as
Luke stated [Luke 24:37-44]). What a
change from their fear and despondency!

20:21-23. Jesus then recommis-
sioned the disciples as His apostles: He
was **sending** them as His representatives,
as the Father had **sent** Him (cf. 17:18).

They were sent with His authority to
preach, teach, and do miraculous signs
(Matt. 28:16-20; Luke 24:47-49). For their
new commission they needed spiritual
power. So **He breathed on them and said,
Receive the Holy Spirit.** The image and
wording of breathing on them recalls
God's creative work in making Adam
(Gen. 2:7). Now this post-Resurrection
"breathing" was a new kind of creative
work for they would soon become new
creations (Eph. 2:8-10). This reception of
the Spirit was in anticipation of the day of
Pentecost and should be understood as a
partial limited gift of knowledge, understanding, and empowerment until Pentecost, 50 days later.

Forgiveness of **sins** is one of the
major benefits of the death of Jesus. It is
the essence of the New Covenant (cf.
Matt. 26:28; Jer. 31:31-34). Proclaiming
the forgiveness of sins was the prominent
feature of the apostolic preaching in the
Book of Acts. Jesus was giving the
apostles (and by extension, the church)
the privilege of announcing heaven's
terms on how a person can receive
forgiveness. If one believes in Jesus, then
a Christian has the right to announce his
forgiveness. If a person rejects Jesus'
sacrifice, then a Christian can announce
that that person is **not forgiven.**

I. Jesus' appearance to Thomas (20:24-29)

20:24-29. In his Gospel, John has
traced the development of unbelief,
which culminated in Jesus' enemies
crucifying Him. Conversely, John also
traced the disciples' development of faith,
which was now climaxed in **Thomas. The
disciples** were affirming Jesus' resurrection to Thomas (**told** in v. 25 is *elegon,* an
imperf. tense which indicates their
continual activity). But **he** remained
unconvinced. He wanted bodily proof of
Jesus' risen state. The reappearance of
Jesus **a week later** provided the opportunity Thomas wanted. **Again . . . Jesus**
miraculously entered a room with **locked**
doors (cf. v. 19). He asked **Thomas** to
touch Him (cf. "showed" in v. 20) and to
stop doubting and believe. This was a
forthright challenge to a personal commitment.

Thomas' response, **My Lord and My
God!** is the high point of the Gospel. Here
was a skeptical man, confronted by the

evidence of Jesus' resurrection. He announced that Jesus, the Man of Galilee, is God manifest in the flesh. Thus the truths in the first chapter were realized personally in this apostle (1:1, 14, 18). The Resurrection (a) demonstrated that what Jesus predicted about His being raised was true (Mark 8:31; 9:9, 31; 10:34; John 2:19), (b) proved that Jesus is the Son of God (Rom. 1:4) and was sent by God ("vindicated by the Spirit," 1 Tim. 3:16), (c) testified to the success of His mission of salvation (Rom. 4:25), (d) entitled Jesus to a position of glory (1 Peter 1:11), and (e) proclaimed that Jesus is the "Lord" (Acts 2:36).

Jesus then pronounced a blessing on all who would come to faith without the help of a visible, bodily manifestation to them (John 20:29; cf. 1 Peter 1:8). This blessing comes to all who believe on the basis of the proclaimed gospel and the evidences for its validity. Believers living today are not deprived by not seeing Him physically; instead, they are the recipients of His special blessing: **Blessed are those who have not seen and yet have believed.**

J. The purpose of the book (20:30-31)

20:30-31. John explained His purpose in writing this Gospel, that people might contemplate and perceive the theological significance of Jesus' miracles (*sēmeia*, "signs"). Many people today ignore, deny, or rationalize Jesus' miracles. Even in Jesus' day some people attributed them to God whereas others attributed them to Satan (3:2; 9:33; Matt. 12:24). To ignore, deny, or rationalize them in that day was impossible because the miracles were manifold and manifest. John indicated He was aware of the Synoptic miracles: **Jesus did many other miraculous signs.** In fact, 35 different miracles are recorded in the four Gospels (see the list at John 2:1-11). John selected 7 for special consideration in order that people might come to **believe that Jesus is the Christ,** the promised Messiah, and **the Son of God.** (The NIV marg. reading, "may continue to believe," is probably not the correct textual reading; the NIV text correctly renders the Gr. by the words **may** believe.)

V. The Epilogue (chap. 21)

John's purposes in this final chapter

are (a) to reveal how Jesus reinstated Peter after his great fall, and (b) to correct a serious error about the Lord's return. The chapter also provides additional clues to the identity of the author. Some critics have argued that this chapter is anticlimactic after the great conclusion in chapter 20, and therefore was written by another (anonymous) writer. But the linguistic evidence does not support this notion. In addition, other great books of Scripture have appendixes after reaching a grand climax (cf., e.g., Rom. 16 following Rom. 15:33). Thus John 21 is neither without value nor out of harmony with other Bible books.

A. Jesus' appearance by the lake (21:1-14)

21:1-3. An angel had promised that **Jesus** would meet with **His disciples** in Galilee (Matt. 28:7). It was significant evidence for Jesus to manifest Himself in a different location and at a later time (cf. Acts 1:3). (**The Sea of Tiberias** is another name for the Sea of Galilee; cf. comments on John 6:1.) The **disciples** had gone to Jerusalem and had experienced a tumultuous series of events: the Triumphal Entry, the expectation of a new kingdom, a betrayal by a trusted friend, near arrest, denial of Jesus by their leader Peter, the agonizing crucifixion of Jesus, the Resurrection, and the manifestations of the risen Lord. Understandably they were confused and unsure of the future.

Peter went fishing since he may have misunderstood the Lord's commission (20:22). **Peter** also had a family to support and undoubtedly had a sense of failure over his sin in denying the Lord. His leadership quality is evident in that six other disciples went **with** him. Their lack of success without Jesus' aid (cf. 15:5) and their great catch with His help gave them direction for their new lives.

21:4-6. **Early in the morning** the **disciples** failed to recognize **Jesus . . . on the shore** either because of distance or lack of light. **He called out to them, Friends, haven't you any fish?** The word "friends" (*paidia*) is literally, "little children" or perhaps "lads." In response to His authoritative voice and instruction (v. 6), they hauled in a huge catch **of fish** (cf. v. 11). This similarity to an earlier miracle (Luke 5:1-11) enabled the disciples to identify the Lord and to recognize

His ability to do great signs after His resurrection.

21:7-9. This revelation of **Jesus** and His power to His disciples dawned first in the beloved **disciple,** who exclaimed, **It is the Lord!** (cf. 20:28) John had also been first to discern the significance of the grave clothes (20:8). Hearing John's word, **Peter** immediately **jumped into the water,** and apparently swam to Jesus. This is typical of his impulsive nature (he went first into the tomb; 20:6). This psychological insight into Peter's character reinforces the historical reliability of John's eyewitness testimony. Peter's action contrasts strikingly with the time he started to sink in the water (Matt. 14:30). Jesus had prepared a breakfast of charcoaled **fish** with **bread** for the hungry disciples.

21:10-11. Mention of the **large fish, 153** in all, has given rise to all kinds of allegorical and symbolic interpretations. But probably John mentioned the number as a matter of historical detail. With a group of men fishing, the common procedure would be for them to count the fish they caught and then divide them equally among the fishermen. A spiritual lesson here is that great blessing comes to one's efforts when he follows the Lord's will.

21:12-14. When **Jesus** invited them to eat with Him, **none of** them asked **who** He was for **they knew it was the Lord.** The fact that both Mary (20:14) and the Emmaus Road disciples (Luke 24:13-35) did not immediately identify the Lord may indicate some difference in the Lord's resurrection appearance here. Yet the identification was so certain that all the disciples knew it was **Jesus.** Their meal together stamped an indelible impression on their minds. Years later in his preaching Peter spoke of himself as a reliable witness who ate and drank with Jesus after His resurrection (Acts 10:41). **The third time** means Jesus' third appearance to the apostles, which John narrated (cf. John 20:19, 24 for the other two appearances).

B. Jesus' reinstating of Peter (21:15-23)

21:15-17. Earlier **Peter** had denied Jesus beside a fire (18:18, 25). Now beside another fire he was restored publicly. **Jesus** called him **Simon Son of John,**

as He had when He first met Peter (1:42). Jesus asked him, **Do you truly love Me more than these?** What did Jesus mean by "these"? Jesus probably was referring to the disciples, in light of Peter's proud statement that he never would fall away no matter what others did (Matt. 26:33, 35; Luke 22:33; John 13:37). Jesus' threefold question and threefold commission of apostolic mission contrast directly with Peter's three denials. Three times Peter said he did not even know the Lord (18:17, 25, 27); now three times he said he loved the Lord (21:15-17). No matter how great a person is, he may fall (cf. 1 Cor. 10:12). But God's grace and forgiveness will restore the repentant. This provision of grace would be important, for the church would soon face great persecution and even church leaders would waver in their commitments.

Three times **Jesus** commissioned **Peter** to care for the flock: **Feed My lambs;** (v. 15); **Take care of My sheep** (v. 16); **Feed My sheep** (v. 17). Some Roman Catholics assume that this asserts Peter's primacy, but this is foreign to the passage (cf. 1 Peter 5:2). In Jesus' three questions of **love** (*agapas, agapas,* and *phileis*) and His three commands of duty (*boske,* "tend"; *poimaine,* "herd, lead to pasture"; *boske*) various Greek synonyms are used. Since it is difficult to see any consistent distinctions that John intended, most scholars see these as stylistic variations.

21:18-19. I tell you the truth (cf. comments on 1:51) introduces a solemn prediction of Peter's coming crucifixion. In old age **Peter** was tied to a cross and had his hands stretched out (cf. 1 Clement 5:4; 6:1; Eusebius *The Ecclesiastical History* 2. 25). Obedience to Jesus' command, **Follow Me,** is the key issue in every Christian's life. As Jesus followed the Father's will, so His disciples should follow their Lord, whether the path leads to a cross or to some other difficult experience.

21:20-23. Peter, having been informed about God's plan for his life, naturally wondered what the future held for his friend John, **the disciple whom Jesus loved. Jesus** sharply rebuked Peter for being curious about God's will for another's life: **What is that to you? You must follow Me.** Some disciples can be easily distracted by unnecessary questions about God's secret will; as a result they neglect God's plainly revealed will. God's plans for Christians vary and His reasons are not often made known. Peter was to commit himself to God's plain commands to him.

John then corrected a faulty inference made by some believers that John **would not die.** Interestingly Jesus' last words recorded by John in this Gospel refer to His **return.** Of course, Jesus gave no indication *when* He would return. **The false rumor** about Jesus' words to Peter show the possibility of misunderstanding God's promises. Christians must seek to understand God's Word accurately.

C. The colophon (21:24-25)

21:24-25. The Fourth Gospel ends with information about its composition. The beloved **disciple** is identified as the author (cf. comments on "Authorship" in the *Introduction*). The first sentence in verse 24 may have been someone other than John, but the wording sounds Johannine (cf. 19:35). **These things** most likely refer to the entire Gospel. The words, **We know that his testimony is true,** were probably written by someone other than John. They are an endorsement, perhaps by the Ephesian church, or a testimony from the early church as a whole. They were certainly in a position to know the facts better than any generation since then.

The final verse—with its statement about the world **not** having **room for** all **the books that** could **be written** about Jesus' deeds—may seem at first glance to be an exorbitant overstatement. (The **I** seems to suggest John as the author of this verse though that is uncertain.) Yet the Gospels record only a small sample of Jesus' words and works. Someone has estimated that a person can read aloud Jesus' words recorded in the Gospels in only about three hours. But if all that the infinite Son of God said and did in His Incarnation were pondered, the resulting commentary would be endless.

APPENDIX

The Story of the Adulteress (7:53–8:11)

Five questions need to be considered before commenting on this story: (1) Is it

Scripture? (2) Was it written by John? (3) Is it ancient and true, that is, historical? (4) Is it canonical? (5) If it was not originally part of John's Gospel, why is the material placed before 8:12 in most English Bible versions? Questions 1 and 4 are closely related but are not identical. As to question 1, the consensus of New Testament textual scholars is that this section was not part of the original text. For Protestants who accept that judgment, this fact settles the issue of canonicity (question 4): the passage is not part of the biblical canon. However, for Roman Catholic scholars canonicity means that this passage is authoritative because it is in the Vulgate. So even though the passage may not have been part of John's original manuscript, Catholics nevertheless accept the passage as having God's authority because the Vulgate includes it. Question 2, on the passage's Johannine origin, is also tied to question 1. Not only do many Greek manuscripts lack these verses, but those that do include them often mark them with asterisks or obeli. In addition various ancient Greek manuscripts include the passage in five different locations (after John 7:36, after 7:44, after 7:52, after 21:25, and after Luke 21:38). Both the textual evidence and stylistic data in the passage indicate that this is non-Johannine material.

Most commentators answer question 3 (Is it historical?) by yes. If this judgment is correct, then this is a rare extrabiblical authentic tradition about Jesus. John alluded to other things Jesus did (John 21:25) so this story may be one of those events. The answer to the fifth question seems to be that the material was placed before 8:12 in most Bible versions because the contents of this section relate well to two statements of Jesus in chapter 8 ("I pass judgment on no one" [8:15], and "Can any of you prove Me guilty of sin?" [8:46]).

7:53. This verse shows that this story was a continuation of some other material. The original connection is now lost.

8:1-2. Since **Jesus** regularly taught **in the temple courts . . . the people** daily **gathered** to hear **Him.** As Luke wrote, "Each day Jesus was teaching at the temple, and each evening He went out to spend the night on the hill called the Mount of Olives, and all the people came early in the morning to hear Him at the temple" (Luke 21:37-38).

8:3-6a. Jesus' teaching was interrupted by some **teachers of the Law and . . . Pharisees.** They held a strict application of **the Law** to life. The **woman,** who may have been married, was **caught in adultery.** According to the Law there had to be two witnesses to confirm the guilt of a person accused of a crime (Deut. 19:15). Being **caught in the act** of intercourse normally seems unlikely, so the religious leaders may have deliberately planned to catch her in the act. The man should have been brought in with the woman, but perhaps he had escaped. The purpose of bringing this woman before **Jesus** was to discredit Him as a **Teacher.** If He condemned her, He would lose favor with the common people. If He did not, He would be disagreeing with **Moses.**

8:6b-8. Many have tried to guess what **Jesus** wrote **on the ground.** Some suggest He wrote the sins of the accusers. Others propose that He wrote the words of Exodus 23:1, "Do not [be] a malicious witness." Still others say He simply traced **His finger** in the dust while preparing to respond, but that seems unlikely. Since it is impossible to know, any conjecture is fruitless. His response—that only **one** who **is without sin** can judge—pointed to their own sinfulness and at the same time to Himself as the only competent Judge because of His sinlessness (cf. John 8:16). Then He **wrote on the ground** again.

8:9-10. While **Jesus** was still stooped down, His authoritative word (cf. Matt. 7:28-29) struck conviction of sin in their hearts. **The older ones** left **first,** perhaps because they had the wisdom to recognize the sin in their hearts and lives. Since the witnesses and the accusers left, the legal case against the woman was dropped.

8:11. Jesus' words again reveal Him as the Master Teacher. He rebuked **sin** but He gave the woman hope for a new **life.** Theologically Jesus could forgive her sin because He has that authority (cf. Mark 2:8-12) and because He is the Lamb of God who bore "the sin of the world" (John 1:29). Besides having the divine ability to forgive her sin, His manner of dealing with her was gracious. He was revealed to her as the One who is "full of grace" (1:14).

BIBLIOGRAPHY

Barrett, C.K. *The Gospel according to John.* 2d ed. Philadelphia: Westminster Press, 1978.

Bernard, J.H. *A Critical and Exegetical Commentary on the Gospel according to St. John.* The International Critical Commentary. 2 vols. Edinburgh: T. & T. Clark, 1928. Reprint. Naperville, Ill.: Allenson & Co., 1953.

Brown, Raymond E. *The Gospel according to John.* 2 vols. The Anchor Bible. Garden City, N.Y.: Doubleday & Co., 1966, 1970.

Gaebelein, Arno C. *The Gospel of John.* Rev. ed. Neptune, N.J.: Loizeaux Bros., 1965.

Godet, Frederic. *Commentary on the Gospel of John.* Reprint (2 vols. in 1). Grand Rapids: Kregel Publications, 1979.

Hendriksen, William. *Exposition of the Gospel according to John.* New Testament Commentary. 2 vols. in 1. Grand Rapids: Baker Book House, 1953, 1954.

Kent, Homer A., Jr. *Light in the Darkness: Studies in the Gospel of John.* Grand Rapids: Baker Book House, 1974.

Lightfoot, R.H. *St. John's Gospel: A Commentary.* Edited by C.F. Evans. London: Oxford University, Press, 1956.

Lindars, Barnabas. *The Gospel of John.* New Century Bible. London: Marshall, Morgan & Scott, 1972.

Morgan, G. Campbell. *The Gospel according to John.* New York: Fleming H. Revell Co., n.d.

Morris, Leon. *The Gospel according to John.* The New International Commentary on the New Testament. Grand Rapids: Wm. B. Eerdmans Publishing Co., 1971.

_____. *Studies in the Fourth Gospel.* Grand Rapids: Wm. B. Eerdmans Publishing Co., 1969.

Sanders, J.N., and Mastin, B.A. *A Commentary on the Gospel according to St. John.* Harper's New Testament Commentaries. New York: Harper & Row, Publishers, 1968.

Schnackenburg, Rudolf. *The Gospel according to St. John.* Vol. 1: *Introduction and Commentary on Chapters 1-4.* 1968. New York: Seabury Press, 1980. Vol. 2: *Commentary on Chapters 5-12.* 1979. New York: Crossroad Publishing Co. 1982.

Tasker, R.V.G. *The Gospel according to St. John: An Introduction and Commentary.* The Tyndale New Testament Commentaries. Grand

John

Rapids: Wm. B. Eerdmans Publishing Co., 1960.

Tenney, Merrill C. "John." In *The Expositor's Bible Commentary*, vol. 9. Grand Rapids: Zondervan Publishing House, 1981.

—————. *John: The Gospel of Belief.* Grand Rapids: Wm. B. Eerdmans Publishing Co., 1948.

Turner, George Allen, and Mantey, Julius R. *The Gospel according to St. John.* The Evangelical Commentary on the Bible. Grand Rapids: Wm. B. Eerdmans Publishing Co., n.d.

Westcott, B.F. *The Gospel according to St. John: The Greek Text with Introduction and Notes.* 2 vols. London: John Murray, 1903. Reprint (2 vols. in 1). Grand Rapids: Baker Book House, 1980.

Harvest Hills Alliance Church
199 Harvest Wood Dr. N.E.
Calgary, AB. T3K 3T7
Ph.226-0990 Fax.226-2019